Library of
Davidson College

HANDBOOK OF
APPLIED PSYCHOLINGUISTICS
Major Thrusts of
Research and Theory

HANDBOOK OF APPLIED PSYCHOLINGUISTICS
Major Thrusts of Research and Theory

Edited by

SHELDON ROSENBERG
Department of Psychology and
Institute for the Study of Developmental Disabilities
University of Illinois at Chicago Circle

LAWRENCE ERLBAUM ASSOCIATES PUBLISHERS
1982 Hillsdale, New Jersey

Copyright © 1982 by Lawrence Erlbaum Associates, Inc.
All rights reserved. No part of this book may be reproduced in
any form, by photostat, microform, retrieval system, or any other
means, without the prior written permission of the publisher.

Lawrence Erlbaum Associates, Inc., Publishers
365 Broadway
Hillsdale, New Jersey 07642

Library of Congress Cataloging in Publication Data
Main entry under title:

Handbook of applied psycholinguistics.

   Bibliography: p.
   Includes indexes.
   Contents: Applied psycholinguistics, introduction,
foundations, and overview/Sheldon Rosenberg—Theoret-
ical issues in the study of word recongition/Frank R.
Vellutino—Psycholinguistic processes in writing/
John B. Black—[etc.]
    1. Psycholinguistics—Handbooks, manuals, etc.
2. Applied linguistics—Handbooks, manuals, etc.
I. Rosenberg, Sheldon. [DNLM: 1. Psycholinguistics.
BF 455 H236]
P37.H3   401'.9   81-9891

ISBN 0-89859-173-2   AACR2

Printed in the United States of America

*THIS BOOK IS DEDICATED
TO MY FRIENDS AND TEACHERS*
*Eugene S. Gollin
and
James J. Jenkins*

Contents

Preface xi

List of Contributors xiii

INTRODUCTION

1. **Applied Psycholinguistics: Introduction, Foundations and Overview**
   Sheldon Rosenberg   1

READING, WRITING AND LANGUAGE LEARNING

2. **Theoretical Issues in the Study of Word Recognition: The Unit of Perception Controversy Reexamined**
   Frank R. Vellutino   33

   Introduction   33
   The Unit of Perception In Word Recognition:
       Contemporary Theories   40
   The Unit of Perception as Relative   79
   Synthesis   170

viii   CONTENTS

3. **Psycholinguistic Processes in Writing**
   John B. Black — 199

   Introduction   199
   Protocol Analysis of Writing   200
   Pauses During Writing   204
   Levels of Writing Ability   206
   Facilitating Writing   208
   Writing Stories By Computer   211
   Conclusions   213

4. **Second-Language Learning and Bilingualism in Children and Adults**
   Barry McLaughlin — 217

   Introduction   217
   Processes of Second-Language Learning   220
   The Development of a Second Language   224
   Intervention Programs   236
   Bilingual Competence   243
   Conclusion   248

DISCOURSE PROCESSES

5. **Prose Comprehension in Natural and Experimental Settings: The Theory and Its Practical Implications**
   Roy Freedle and Jonathan Fine — 257

   Basic Discourse Concepts and Experimental Studies   258
   Social Context and Communication   272
   Final Remarks   290

DISORDERS OF FIRST-LANGUAGE DEVELOPMENT

6. **The Nature of Specific Language Impairment in Children**
   Laurence B. Leonard — 295

   Introduction   295
   Etiology and Correlates in Language Impairment   297
   The Speech of Language-Impaired Children   306
   Language Impairment: Delay or Difference?   318
   Summary   321

7. The Language of the Mentally Retarded: Development Processes, and Intervention
Sheldon Rosenberg   329

Introduction   329
Multidimensional Studies of Language Behavior   331
Studies of Syntactic Behavior in the Mentally Retarded   341
Semantics   351
Phonology   358
Pragmatics   364
Linguistic Performance   368
The Linguistic Environment   377
Language Training   380
General Discussion   384

8. Language in Infantile Autism
David Fay and Rebecca Mermelstein   393

Introduction   393
The Autistic Language Disorder   396
Echolalia   405
Etiology   409
Treatment   412
Behavior Modification   414
Conclusions   422

9. The Language Development of Deaf Children and Youth
Stephen P. Quigley and Cynthia M. King   429

Introduction   429
Deafness and Language Development   429
Language Intervention Systems   434
Present Status of Language Performance   437
Language and Cognition   447
Communication Patterns and Language Development   452
Oral English and Language Development   452
Manual English and Language Development   456
ASL and Language Development   458
In Conclusion   468

x CONTENTS

ADULT LANGUAGE DISORDERS

10. A Psycholinguistic Assessment of Adult Aphasia
Alfonso Caramazza and Rita Sloan Berndt   477

Introduction   477
The Syndromes of Aphasia   483
A Theoretical Model of Language Organization   492
Phonological Factors In Aphasia   495
Syntactic Breakdown in Aphasia   501
Studies of the Lexicon in Aphasia   516
Semantic Operations in Aphasia   523
Conclusion: The Importance of Aphasia Research   525

11. Adult Schizophrenic Language
Sheldon Rosenberg and Leonard Abbeduto   537

Anticipatory Remarks   537
Introduction   538
Schizophrenic Speech Production   540
Schizophrenic Comprehension   560
Cortical Functioning and Language in Schizophrenia   569
Concluding Remarks   583

Author Index   591

Subject Index   611

Preface

The chapters of this handbook contain critical integrative reviews of research and theory in the major areas of the field of applied psycholinguistics, the field in which applied problems of language and communicative functioning and development are approached from the standpoint of basic research and theory in psycholinguistics and related areas of cognitive psychology. The book was designed to meet the needs of reseachers, practitioners and graduate students from such disciplines as education (including special education), language learning, linguistics, neurology, psychiatry, psychology, and speech and hearing for such reviews, although the state of research in an area and a desire to stress research and theory in substantive areas resulted in a decision not to include chapters on the measurement of linguistic maturity, language intervention, the language of the learning disabled child, language and environmental deprivation, language and mania, language and senile dementia, and the design of written and oral information and computer command language.

A chapter dealing exclusively with dialect and social class differences in language and communication had been planned but its prospective author withdrew from the project without warning at a time when it was impossible to replace him with another author. Language measurement and intervention are discussed briefly in Chapter 1 and there is a discussion of literature on language intervention in certain of the chapters. The reader is introduced to the field of applied psycholinguistics as a whole in Chapter 1, which also discusses its basic underpinnings and overviews the contents of the present volume.

The grouping of the various substantive chapters reflects my perception of the current organization of the field. Thus they appear under the headings Reading, Writing and Language Learning; Discourse Processes; Disorders of First-Language

Development; and Adult Language Disorders. The contributors, however, selected and organized the literature in their areas of expertise as they saw fit.

My experience with a graduate survey course in applied psycholinguistics gave birth to the idea for the present volume: there was available no single book that reflected the scope of the field (from problems of normal communicative development—e.g., reading and writing—to adult language disorders), its organization, and its deep commitment to basic research and theory. It is hoped that the present volume will serve as such a book and to bring professional researchers and practitioners in the many areas of applied psycholinguistics into contact with recent developments in and outside of their own immediate area. Also, contact with developments outside one's immediate concerns will, it is hoped, lead to the discovery of ways in which research and theory in one area of applied psycholinguistics (e.g., second-language learning) might suggest ways to advance the work in another area (e.g., language intervention). Finally, the perceptive reader will not miss noting in the pages of the present handbook, the many ways in which basic theoretical claims in psycholinguistics and related areas of cognitive psychology are put to the test in the arena of applied psycholinguistics.

Sheldon Rosenberg
Evanston, Illinois

List of Contributors

Leonard Abbeduto Department of Psychology, University of Illinois at Chicago Circle, Box 4348, Chicago, Illinois 60680

John B. Black Department of Psychology, Yale University, Box 11A Yale Station, New Haven, Connecticut 06520

Rita Sloan Berndt Department of Psychology, The Johns Hopkins University, Baltimore, Maryland 21218

Alfonso Caramazza Department of Psychology, The Johns Hopkins University, Baltimore, Maryland 21218

David Fay Room 6A—304A, Bell Laboratories, Naperville and Warrenville Roads, Naperville, Illinois 60540

Jonathan Fine Educational Testing Service, Princeton, New Jersey 08541

Roy Freedle Educational Testing Service, Princeton, New Jersey 08541

Cynthia M. King Department of Speech and Hearing Sciences, University of Illinois at Urbana—Champaign, 901 South Sixth St., Champaign, Illinois 61820

Laurence B. Leonard Department of Audiology and Speech Sciences, Purdue University, West Lafayette, Indiana 47907

Barry McLaughlin Studies in Psychology, Adlai E. Stevenson College, University of California, Santa Cruz, Santa Cruz, California 95064

Rebecca Mermelstein Department of Psychology, University of Illinois at Chicago Circle, Box 4348, Chicago, Illinois 60680

Stephen P. Quigley Department of Speech and Hearing Sciences, University of Illinois at Urbana—Champaign, 901 South Sixth St., Champaign, Illinois 61820

Sheldon Rosenberg Department of Psychology and Institute for the Study of Developmental Disabilities, University of Illinois at Chicago Circle, Box 4348, Chicago, Illinois 60680

Frank R. Vellutino Child Research and Study Center, The University of Albany, 1400 Washington Ave., Albany, New York 12222

INTRODUCTION

1 Applied Psycholinguistics: Introduction, Foundations and Overview

Sheldon Rosenberg
University of Illinois at Chicago Circle

Definitional Matters

The revolution in basic research and theory in psycholinguistics and related areas of cognitive psychology that began shortly after the publication of Chomsky's *Syntactic Structures* (1957)[1] has had a profound influence on conceptions of applied problems (e.g., language and communication disorders; the assessment of linguistic and communicative knowledge and performance capabilities; reading, writing, second-language learning, and learning from texts and lectures). As a result of this influence, we have witnessed changes in applied research and educational and clinical practices that reflect the view that applied problems should be approached from the standpoint of basic research and theory in psycholinguistics (developmental, experimental, and social) and related areas of cognitive psychology (perception, memory, problem solving, conceptual behavior; in other words, information processing generally).

For some years now, basic research and theory in psycholinguistics have been oriented mainly toward answering the following questions.

1. How are syntactic, semantic, phonological, lexical, and pragmatic linguistic units, structures, and operations represented and organized psychologically?

---

[1] As a result of Chomsky's influence, psycholinguists, both basic and applied, were for a number of years primarily interested in characterizing and accounting for general aspects of the form and content of utterances. In recent years, however, we have witnessed a sharp increase in work on the pragmatic aspects of utterances, that is, their *use* in communication, as well as the development of a serious interest in individual differences in all aspects of language and language behavior.

2. What are the psychological mechanisms by which speech is produced, comprehended, and memorized?

3. What is the course of development of linguistic knowledge and of linguistic performance capabilities?

4. How are linguistic knowledge and linguistic performance capabilities acquired, and what are the variables that influence their acquisition?

5. How are linguistic knowledge and linguistic performance capabilities represented and organized neurologically?

6. How does language interact with thought and other aspects of cognition?

7. Do linguistic knowledge and performance vary as a function of social variables?

Clearly, the major thrusts of basic research and theory in psycholinguistics are first-language acquistion and performance, and the variables that influence them, in normal individuals, whereas the field of applied psycholinguistics concerns itself with: (1) the acquisition, utilization, and impact of those communicative and other cognitive achievements in normal language users that are dependent on first-language acquisition and performance (i.e., reading, writing, textual and classroom learning, second-language learning, and bilingualism); (2) the application of basic principles of psycholinguistics and related areas of cognitive psychology to research and practice in the design of written and oral information (e.g., documents, instructions, advertisements) and computer language; (3) the study of the impact of dialect and social-class differences in first-language acquisition on linguistic and communicative performance and on reading, writing, and learning from texts and lectures; (4) the application of basic research and theory in psycholinguistics and related areas of cognitive psychology to the study and treatment of language and communicative disorders in children and adults, including delayed language development, autistic language, reading disorders, writing disorders, phonological disorders, adult aphasia, adult schizophrenic language, and linguistic and communicative disorders associated with senile dementia, deafness, blindness, motor impairment, environmental deprivation, learning disabilities, and mental retardation); and (5) the assessment of linguistic maturity and communicative competence in language-disordered children and adults from the vantage point of what we know about first-language development and performance in non-language-disordered individuals. (The reader will note, of course, that a number of the subareas of applied psycholinguistics are interrelated.)

Publications in Applied Psycholinguistics

The influence of the "Chomskian revolution" in basic psycholinguistics and related areas of cognitive psychology on the field of applied psycholinguistics was evident in some of the papers that appeared in a book that was edited by

Rosenberg and Koplin (1968) and in the many books (see Table 1.1) and journal articles that have appeared since then. Not until 1980, however, did we witness the creation of an interdisciplinary behavioral science journal (*Applied Psycholinguistics:* Cambridge University Press) devoted entirely to the publication of original articles in all the subareas and on all aspects of applied psycholinguistics (as herein defined) by workers in such fields as psychology, speech and hearing, linguistics, educational psychology, special education, English composition, sociology, language learning, artificial intelligence, psychiatry, and neurology.

Major Questions in Applied Psycholinguistics[2]

For the reader who is not familiar with the scope of applied psycholinguistics and the nature and extent of its dependence on basic research and theory in psycholinguistics and related areas of cognitive psychology, I have listed following a number of the major questions in applied psycholinguistics in the context of relevant basic research and theory. In addition, for most of these applied questions, I have supplied some references to the relevant basic literature. Some of the references are to literature reviews and texts and some to source articles and books.

1. What is the nature and organization of mature linguistic knowledge in language-disordered and normal adults? (Chomsky, 1965, 1975, 1977, 1979, 1980; Fillmore, 1968; Greenberg, 1977; Halle, Bresnan, & Miller, 1978; Halliday, 1970; Halliday & Hasan, 1976; Jacobs & Rosenbaum, 1968; Levin, 1977; Quirk & Greenbaum, 1973; Searle, 1969, 1976; Smith, 1979; Smith & Wilson, 1979.)

2. What is the course of first-language development in the domains of syntax, semantics, phonology, and pragmatics in each of the populations of language-disordered children, and how does it compare with what has been observed in the case of normal first-language development? (Abrahamsen, 1977; Anglin, 1977; Bates, 1976a, 1976b; Brown, 1973; Clark & Clark, 1977; Collins, 1979; Crystal, Fletcher, & Garman, 1976; Dale, 1976; de Villiers & de Villiers, 1978; Fletcher & Garman, 1979; Foss & Hakes, 1978; Huxley & Ingram, 1971; Lenneberg & Lenneberg, 1975a; Menyuk, 1977; Morehead & Morehead, 1976; Nelson, 1978; Palermo & Molfese, 1972; Schiefelbusch, 1978a; Sinclair, Jarvella, & Levelt, 1978.)

3. What are the variables that influence first-language development in the various populations of language-disordered children, and how do they compare

---

[2]A fact that will not escape the reader's attention is that applied psycholinguistic research is an important source of confirmation and disconfirmation for many of the claims of basic psycholinguistic and cognitive theory.

TABLE 1.1
A Selected List of Book-Length Works in Applied Psycholinguistics

Reading	
Gibson and Levin, 1975	Reber and Scarborough, 1977
Kavanagh and Mattingly, 1972	Smith, 1973
	Vellutino, 1979
Discourse learning	
Anderson, Spiro, and Montague, 1977	Freedle, 1977, 1979
Cazden, John, and Hymes, 1972	Freedle and Carroll, 1972
deBeaugrande, 1980	
Second-language learning	
Albert and Obler, 1978	Hatch, 1978
Andersen, 1980	Hornby, 1978
Burt, Dulay, and Finocchiaro, 1977	McLaughlin, 1978
Burt, Dulay, and Hernandez-Chavez, 1973	Richards, 1974, 1978
Diller, 1980	Ritchie, 1978
Language disorders	
Aaronson and Rieber, 1975	Lee, 1974
Berry, 1976	Lenneberg and Lenneberg, 1975b
Bloom and Lahey, 1978	Lesser, 1978
Blumstein, 1973	Morehead and Morehead, 1976
Caramazza and Zurif, 1978	O'Connor, 1975
Conrad, 1979	Quigley, Steinkamp, Power,
Curtiss, 1977	and Jones, 1978
Edwards, 1979	Rochester and Martin, 1979
Goodglass and Kaplan, 1972	Schiefelbusch, 1978a, 1978b
Ingram, 1976	Schiefelbusch and Lloyd, 1974
Kavanagh and Strange, 1978	Schlesinger and Namir, 1978
Klima and Bellugi, 1979	Wyke, 1978

with those that influence first-language development in normal children? (Brown, 1973; de Villiers & de Villiers, 1978; Moerk, 1980; Parisi & Giannelli, 1979.)

4. What are the strategies and processes by which the first language is acquired by members of the various populations of language-disordered children, and how do they compare with strategies and processes of first-language acquisition in normal children? (Block & Kessel, 1980; Clark & Clark, 1978; Clark & Sengul, 1978; Corrigan, 1980; Craig & Gallagher, 1979; Cromer, 1976b; Erreich, Valian, & Winzemer, 1980; MacWhinney, 1978; Moerk, 1977; Slobin, 1970, 1973; Snyder & McLean, 1976; Snyder-McLean & McLean, 1978; Stewart & Hamilton, 1976; Trembath, 1972; Whitehurst, 1977.)

5. What are the extent and nature of individual differences in first-language and communicative development, competence, and performance in language-disordered individuals, and how do such differences compare with those that are found in studies of individual differences in normal individuals? (Fillmore,

1. INTRODUCTION, FOUNDATIONS AND OVERVIEW   5

Kempler, & Wang, 1979; Leonard, Newhoff, & Mesalam, 1980; Nelson, 1973, 1974.)

6. Is there any evidence for an impairment of the innate biological language acquisition system that many observers feel is involved in normal first-language acquisition in language development in any of the populations of language-disordered children? (Aitchison, 1977; Caplan, 1980; Collins, 1979; Cooper, 1975; Dingwall, 1975; Eilers, Wilson, & Moore, 1979; Goldin-Meadow, 1979; Greenberg, 1978; Hécaen, 1976; Hegde, 1980; Krashen, 1975; Lenneberg, 1967; Lenneberg & Lenneberg, 1975a; Levelt, 1975; Miller & Lenneberg, 1978; Morton, 1970; Munsinger & Douglass, 1976; Piatelli-Palmarini, 1980; Rosemont, 1978; Snow & Hoefnagel-Höhle, 1977, 1978; Walker, 1978.)

7. Are there any differences between any of the populations of language-disordered children and normal children in the hemispheric lateralization of language functions? (Bever, 1975; Caplan, 1980; Dennis & Whitaker, 1976; Hécaen, 1976; Huxley & Ingram, 1971; Hiscock & Kinsbourne, 1978; Kinsbourne, 1975; Lenneberg & Lenneberg, 1975a; Mirabile, Porter, Hughes, & Berlin, 1978; Satz, Bakker, Teunssen, Goebel, & Van der Vlught, 1975; Tomlinson-Keasey, Kelly, & Burton, 1978; Van Duyne, Bakker, & de Jong, 1977.)

8. Are first-language performance processes (i.e., comprehension, production, memory for linguistic input) different in language-disordered children and adults from what they are in normal children and adults? (Benedict, 1979; Bonvillian, Raeburn, & Horan, 1979; Bridges, 1980; Chapman & Kohn, 1978; Chapman & Miller, 1975; Clark & Clark, 1977; Cole & Perfetti, 1980; de Villiers, Tager-Flusberg, Hakuta, & Cohen, 1979; Foss & Hakes, 1978; Huttenlocher, 1974; Jay, Routh, & Brantley, 1980; Keeton, 1977; Keil, 1980; Perry & Shwedel, 1979; Razel, 1978; Scholes, Rasbury, Scholes, & Dowling, 1976; Shatz, 1978; Starr, 1974; Tyler & Marslen-Wilson, 1978; Washington & Naremore, 1978; Wetstone & Friedlander, 1973.)

9. What is the impact of nonlinguistic cognitive development on first-language development in language-disordered children, and how does it compare with what we know concerning the relationship between nonlinguistic and linguistic cognitive development in normal children? (See Table 1.2.)

10. What is the impact of language on nonlinguistic cognitive development in the various populations of language-disordered children and in normal children? (Blank, 1974, 1975; Bowerman, 1978; Deutsch, 1979.)

11. What are the nature and role of the linguistic input to young language-learning language-disordered children, and how do they relate to what is known about the nature and role of the linguistic input to young language-learning normal children? (Blount & Padgug, 1977; DePaulo & Bonvillian, 1978; Fraser & Roberts, 1975; Furrow, Nelson, & Benedict, 1979; Messer, 1978, 1980; Snow, Arlman-Rupp, Hassing, Jobse, Joosten, & Vorster, 1976; Snow, 1977; Snow & Ferguson, 1977.)

TABLE 1.2
A Selection of References on the Relationship between Nonlinguistic
and Linguistic Cognitive Development in Normal Children

Beilin, 1975	Lenneberg and Lenneberg, 1975a
Bruner, 1975a, 1975b, 1978	Macnamara, 1972, 1977
Bullowa, 1979	Moerk, 1975
Cairns and Hsu, 1978	Ninio and Bruner, 1978
Corrigan, 1978	Piattelli-Palmarini, 1980
Cromer, 1976a	Prawat and Jones, 1977
Donaldson, 1978	Ratner and Bruner, 1978
Donaldson and McGarrigle, 1974	Rodgon, 1976
Dore, 1979	Siegel, McCabe, Brand, and Matthews, 1978
Folger and Leonard, 1978	
Golinkoff and Kerr, 1978	Sinclair, 1971, 1975
Gowie and Powers, 1979	Sinclair-deZwart, 1973
Greenfield and Westerman, 1978	Tanz, 1974
Huxley and Ingram, 1971	Wells, 1974
Inhelder, 1978	

12. Do the general-purpose information-processing capacities (e.g., short-term memory) and operations (e.g., rehearsal, monitoring, perceptual encoding, retrieval) of members of the various populations of language-disordered children and adults differ from those of normal children and adults as to their influence on language and communicative performance? (Chi, 1977; Clark & Clark, 1977; Cohen & Sandberg, 1977; Foss & Hakes, 1978; Huttenlocher & Burke, 1976.)

13. Does metalinguistic awareness develop in the same way in the various populations of language-disordered children that it does in normal children? (Carr, 1979; deVilliers & deVilliers, 1972; Kuczaj, 1978; Leonard, Bolders, & Curtis, 1977; Sinclair, Jarvella, & Levelt, 1978.)

14. How do individual and group differences in language and communicative competence and performance in normal individuals influence speech intelligibility and communication?

15. Are there individual differences in normal language competence and performance that relate in any way to the ease with which children learn to read and write or learn a second language?

16. What do basic research and theory in psycholinguistics and related areas of cognitive psychology tell us about how best to prepare texts, lectures, instructions, advertisements, and documents so as to facilitate comprehension and learning? (The appropriate source material here is the literature in experimental psycholinguistics and information processing. See Clark & Clark, 1977, and Foss & Hakes, 1978, for reviews of work in the first area, and Anderson, 1980, and Bransford, 1979, for reviews of the literature in the second area.)

17. What are the implications of basic research and theory in psycholinguistics and related areas of cognitive psychology for the problem of assessing linguistic and communicative maturity in the various populations of language and

communicatively disordered children and adults? (See the references for Questions 1, 2, 5, 8, 12, and 14.)

18. What are the implications of basic research and theory in psycholinguistics and related areas of cognitive psychology for the problem of language training in the various populations of language-disordered children and adults? (See the references for Questions 1, 2, 3, 4, 9, 11, 12, and 13.)

19. In what ways are learning to read and write influenced by aspects of native-language competence and performance in normal children?

20. Does the development of metalinguistic awareness in normal children influence in any way their development of reading, writing, or a second language? (Donaldson, 1978; Sinclair, Jarvella, & Levelt, 1978.)

21. In what ways, if any, are second- and first-language acquisition in normal individuals similar as regards order of mastery of linguistic structures and acquisition processes? (Appropriate here, of course, is the literature on first-language development.)

22. What, if anything, is the impact of the development of writing on subsequent language development and performance in normal individuals? (Ingram, 1975; Olson & Nickerson, 1978.)

23. Do reading, writing, and second-language learning influence in any way subsequent cognitive development and performance in normal individuals? (Donaldson, 1978.)

24. Are linguistic knowledge and performance organized differently in aphasic adults than they are in normal adults? (Clark & Clark, 1977; Foss & Hakes, 1978.)

25. In what way (or ways) does the language of adult schizophrenics differ from that of normal adults? (See Question 24.)

It should be clear by now that there are many different kinds of questions that confront the field of applied psycholinguistics. The previous list is not exhaustive, however; but even so, the reader may wish to keep it in mind as he or she proceeds through the substantive chapters of the present volume.

The Measurement of Linguistic Maturity

In view of the fact that no separate chapter was included in the present volume that deals with language assessment, some remarks on this topic follow.

There are many reasons why one might wish to assess formally linguistic maturity or competence (Dale, 1976), including such communicative capabilities as the mechanisms of conversational interaction, for example, to evaluate the effects of experimental variables in research, to ascertain an individual's mastery of a second language, to evaluate a language enrichment program for primary-school children, to identify children or adults who may be in need of speech and language therapy, or to identify specific aspects of language-disordered children's or adults' problems prior to initiating a therapeutic program. An examination of the literature on language assessment, however, suggests that the major concern of applied psycholinguists interested in the development of formal language assessment programs has been the diagnosis of disorders of first-language development. We limit our remarks in this section, therefore, to this concern. Our intent, however, is not to review all or some particular portion of the literature in this area or the tests that have been published but, rather, to attempt to identify certain of the implications of basis research and theory in psycholinguistics and related areas of cognitive psychology for the problem of assessing first-language capabilities.

Reviews of work on assessment are to be found in Bloom and Lahey (1978), Carrow (1972), Cicciarelli, Broen, and Siegel (1976), Crystal, Fletcher, and Garman (1976), Dale (1976), Irwin and Marge (1972), Miller, (1978), Muma (1978), and Yoder (1974). Examples of tests and other assessment procedures are those of Blank and Franklin (1980), Cantwell, Howlin, and Rutter (1977), Carrow (1968, 1973, 1974), Crystal, Fletcher, and Garman (1976), Fluharty (1974), Gaddes and Crocket (1975), Hedrick and Prather (1975), Ingram (1971), Lee (1971, 1974), Lee and Canter (1971), Muma (1973, 1978), Naor and Balthazar (1975), Quigley and King (1980), Rees and Shulman (1978), and Reynell and Huntley (1971)—see also the extensive list of tests in Appendix C of Bloom and Lahey (1978) and relevant items in the Buros (1972) *Yearbook*. Evaluations of specific assessment measures can be found in Crockett (1974), Kirk and Kirk (1978), Larson and Summers (1976), Longhurst and Schrandt (1973), Prutting, Gallagher, and Mulac (1975), Ratusnik and Koenigsknecht (1975), Scharf (1972), Shriner (1969), Sommers, Erdige, and Peterson (1978), Waryas and Ruder (1974), and Williams, Marks, and Bialer (1977). Some of the factors that influence assessment are identified in articles by Chapman and Kohn, (1978), Chapman and Miller (1975), Hart (1975), Huttenlocher (1974), Johnson (1974), Limber (1976), Perry and Shwedel (1979), Sattler (1970), Shatz (1978), Stick and Norris (1979), and Wetstone and Friedlander (1973). Some useful children's and developmental norms for assessment purposes can be found in Bloom and Lahey (1978), Craig and Gallagher (1979), Crystal, Fletcher, and Garman (1976), deVilliers and deVilliers (1978), Koenigsknecht and Friedman (1976), Miller (1978), Prutting (1979), Richardson, Calnan, Essen, and Lambert (1976), and Shriner and Miner (1968). (The reader should also consult the reference list for Question 17, p. 7.)

The achievements of basic research and theory in psycholinguistics and related areas of cognitive psychology have a variety of implications for the problem of assessing linguistic maturity. Two of the more obvious ones are listed in the following, for illustrative purposes.

1.0 A description of mature linguistic knowledge and its development is logically prior to any attempt to assess language maturity developmentally.

During the early years of the Chomskian revolution there was a total or nearly total dependence on transformational grammar for a description of mature lan-

1. INTRODUCTION, FOUNDATIONS AND OVERVIEW   9

guage. In recent years, however, changes that have taken place in linguistic theory (including semantics and the theory of speech acts) and in our knowledge of the psychological reality of linguistic structures in child and adult language users have led psycholinguists to adopt a more eclectic approach to the problem of representing linguistic knowledge. Thus, at present, in assessing language competence developmentally, we are likely to want to examine (against norms of normal language development, taking into account central tendencies and variability, evidence of differential mastery in the comprehension and production modes and dialect differences where appropriate) at least the following:

1.1 Intonation prior to the appearance of the first words and subsequently.

1.2 The form, content, and functions of one-word utterances prior to the appearance of productive combinatorial speech.

1.3 Phonological achievements and processes.

1.4 The use of multiword routines (i.e., multiword utterances that operate syntactically as if they were single words).

1.5 The form, content, and function (semantic relational and speech act) of "unmodulated" simple "sentence" structures, beginning with two-word utterances.

1.6 Pronominalization and deixis.

1.7 Word order.

1.8 Such "modulators" of the meaning of simple sentences as tense, number, possession, auxiliaries, negation, interrogatives, imperatives, and articles.

1.9 The elaboration of noun and verb phrases through the use of prepositional, adjectival, and adverbial structures.

1.10 The topic-comment, given-new relation as expressed through word order, contrastive stress and syntactic structure.

1.11 Sentence-combining operations, including relativization, complementation, nominalization, comparatives, and the use of coordinating and subordinating conjunctions.

1.12 The structures of discourse cohesion.

1.13 The mechanics of conversation (e.g., turn-taking, fulfillment of conversational obligations, conversational repairs).

1.14 Knowledge of indirect speech acts.

1.15 The form, content, and organization of the internal lexicon.

Because of the time involved, particularly in the case of children who are developing language at an abnormally slow rate, longitudinal assessment of individual children is impractical. However, the price one pays for not being able to assess linguistic maturity longitudinally may be high, inasmuch as most language structures, including lexical items, undergo gradual change that may include in the case, for example, of a syntactic structure, semantically inappropriate usage, ungrammatical usage (vis-à-vis the adult grammar), grammatical but inconsistent usage, and consistent (grammatically and semantically) appropriate usage. The price one pays, of course, is not being able to determine whether or not the course of language development in a child shows evidence of deviance. The fact that a given structure in the adult grammar is used or not tells us nothing about the course of mastery of that structure.

2.0 It is necessary to take into account in the development of measures of language competence the likelihood that language *performance* (i.e., speech production, speech comprehension, and memory for linguistic input) can be influenced by a variety of factors other than the language user's knowledge of the phonological (including the intonational), syntactic, lexical, semantic, and pragmatic structure of his or her native language, including the conventions of conversation. For example:

2.1 The language user's knowledge of the world, including his or her knowledge of stereotyped everyday routines, such as *going to the doctor, to school,* or *to a restaurant* (Schank & Abelson, 1977).

2.2 Cognitive strategies peculiar to language processing.

2.3 General-purpose information-processing capabilities (e.g., attention, perceptual encoding, short-term memory maintenance rehearsal, organization, serial processing, parallel processing, long-term memory search and retrieval, problem solving and conceptual capabilities, and self-monitoring).

2.4 Sensory status.

2.5 Motor proficiency.

2.6 Motivation and emotional maturity.

2.7 Social traits.

2.8 Redundancies created by context, linguistic, and nonlinguistic.

2.9 Idiosyncratic linguistic performance styles.

2.10 The language user's knowledge of and attitude toward characteristics of the speaker or hearer.

We need to take such factors into account, of course, in order to avoid, wherever possible, designing assessment procedures that confound the measurement of linguistic knowledge with the measurement of factors that influence an individual's ability to utilize his or her linguistic knowledge. However, inasmuch as many linguistic performance factors are organismic in nature, we are only able to validly assess (or approximate an assessment of) linguistic knowledge or competence in many language-disordered children if we also assess directly sensory status (hearing and vision) motor proficiency, emotional maturity, *fluid* and *crystallized* intelligence (Horn, 1976), short-term memory capacity, neurological status, and the like. Moreover, because it is likely that certain linguistic performance disorders may also retard or otherwise interfere with language acquisition itself, the assessment of these disorders is essential to the task of prescribing appropriate language intervention.

In view of the fact that some of the linguistic performance factors we have been discussing apply differentially to the comprehension, production, and memory performance modes (e.g., entries 2.2, 2.3, and 2.4), it should be possible to identify children who may be suffering from a linguistic performance disorder by administering language assessment procedures in all three performance modes. Conversely, we are not likely to consider that a child might be suffering from a competence disorder unless he or she fails to show mastery of linguistic structures in at least the comprehension and production modes.

It should be clear from this discussion that a thoroughgoing developmental assessment of linguistic and related capabilities should indicate, ideally: (1) the *presence* of disordered language; (2) the *nature* of the disorder, that is, whether it involves (with specifics) phonology, intonation, syntax (including grammatical morphology), lexicon, semantics, pragmatics, discourse cohesion, or some combination of these components of language; (3) the *origin* of the language disorder, that is, whether it involves a failure to acquire aspects of linguistic knowledge, the loss of linguistic knowledge, or a performance deficit, or a combination of these factors; and (4) the *course* of the language disorder—whether it has resulted in delayed language development, deviant language or language development, or a combination of delay and deviance.

The interested reader will find further discussions of the implications of relevant basic research and theory for the problem of assessing linguistic maturity in Crystal, Fletcher, and Garman (1976), Dale (1976), Miller (1978), and Muma (1978).

Language Intervention

No systematic attempt was made in the present volume to review in detail the available work on language intervention, although some authors (see chapters by Fay and Mermelstein, Rosenberg, and Quigley and King) did choose to discuss this topic. It would have been too large an undertaking to have attempted to include a detailed treatment of this topic; besides, there have appeared recently in the literature a number of volumes devoted exclusively or partially to language intervention (Bloom & Lahey, 1978; Muma, 1978; Schiefelbusch, 1978a, 1978b; Schiefelbusch & Lloyd, 1974), as well as a number of articles and chapters containing proposals regarding language intervention (Bowerman, 1976; Crystal, Fletcher, & Garman, 1976; Lahey & Bloom, 1977; MacDonald & Blott, 1974; Mahoney, 1975; Mahoney & Seely, 1976; L. Miller, 1978; Prutting & Connally, 1976; Rees, 1975; Snyder & McLean, 1977; Snyder-McLean & McLean, 1978; Waryas, 1973; Willbrand, 1977; Yule, Berger, & Howlin, 1975).

Other articles that are likely to be of interest to applied psycholinguists involved with language intervention are those of Brown, 1976; Clark and Clark, 1978; Corrigan, 1980; Elardo, 1971; Friedman and Friedman, 1980; Leonard,

1975; Moerk, 1977; Sachs, Bard, and Johnson, 1981; Stewart and Hamilton, 1976; Whitehurst, 1977; Whitehurst and Vasta, 1975; and Wilcox and Leonard, 1978.

Finally, the basic research and theory in psycholinguistics and related areas of cognitive psychology that has influenced language intervention research and program development is identified in Question 18 (p. 7). Of importance have been information on the representation of mature linguistic knowledge, the course of first-language development, the variables that influence first-language development, the strategies and processes by which the first language is acquired, the impact of nonlinguistic cognitive development on first-language development, the nature and role of the linguistic input to young language-learning children, general-purpose information-processing capacities and operations, and the development and significance of metalinguistic awareness.

Other Areas

Several areas of applied psycholinguistics, it was decided, were not sufficiently developed to warrant a chapter in the present volume. These areas are listed now, with one or more references.

Language and learning disability (Wiig, 1976).
Language and environmental deprivation (Curtiss, 1977, 1979, 1980; Curtiss, Fromkin, Krashen, Rigler, & Rigler, 1974; Edwards, 1979; Fromkin, 1975; Sachs, Bard, & Johnson, 1981).
Language and mania (Durbin & Martin, 1977).
Language and senile dementia (deAjuriaguerra & Tissot, 1975; Gustafson, Hogberg, & Ingnar, 1978; Obler & Albert, 1980).
The design of written and oral information—including, for example, documents, instructions, and advertisements—and computer language (Felker, 1980).

Overview

The linguistic knowledge and communicative competencies of normal individuals continue to grow during the elementary school years and beyond, as reflected in both comprehension and production. Applied psycholinguists, however, have a special interest in work in the domains of reading, writing, and second-language learning. It was important, therefore, that these three topics be represented in the present handbook. However, these topics are not only important in their own right but because of a growing belief that the development and achievements of reading, writing, and a second language may figure in the subsequent development of linguistic knowledge (in particular, complex lexical knowledge and complex sentential and discourse structures) and nonlinguistic capabilities (Donaldson, 1978; Genesee & Hamayan, 1980; Ingram, 1975; Kagan, 1980; Olson & Nickerson, 1978).

The reader will note that the extensive and critical review of research and theory in reading by Vellutino in the present volume encompasses three major aspects of this topic (i.e., reading processes, development, and disorders), each of which is frequently treated in a separate review. The advantage of Vellutino's broad coverage of the literature, however, is that it gave him an opportunity to formulate an integrated characterization and interpretation of the many issues and research findings in this massive area. Moreover, Vellutino makes clear throughout his chapter the extent to which work on reading has been influenced by basic research and theory in psycholinguistics and related areas of cognitive psychology and, in particular, normal first-language development. At the heart of his account, from a substantive standpoint, one finds emphasis placed upon the importance of understanding: (1) the unitization process in word recognition; (2) that the unit of perception in word recognition is relative; (3) the contribution of contextual cues to reading; (4) the contribution of the reader to the word recognition process (in particular, the linguistic and nonlinguistic knowledge and information-processing strategies he or she brings to the task of reading development and performance); and (5) how characteristics of word stimuli influence reading.

The first thing one notes, when he or she views the literature on writing for the first time, is that research and theory in this area are in their infancy. Clearly, serious psycholinguistic and other cognitive work on writing processes and their development represent a recent development in applied psycholinguistics. This is not surprising, however, inasmuch as related basic research and theory in speech production were neglected for years by experimental and developmental psycholinguists, as well as by cognitive information-processing theorists (Rosenberg, 1977). We were fortunate, therefore, when Black agreed to prepare a critical review of the literature on writing relevant to the objectives of applied psycholinguistics. The level of importance that writing has achieved in recent years in the schools (in elementary and secondary schools and in colleges), however, will most assuredly result in a rapid increase in the amount of attention that applied psycholinguists devote to this topic. Indeed, I am willing to hazard the prediction that writing will soon become as important an area as reading has been and that a major source of inspiration for this development will be the growing belief that the acquisition and maturation of writing skills will enhance an individual's already available linguistic and related nonlinguistic capabilities.

Before we can achieve any serious understanding of the impact of writing in other areas, however, we have to make progress in understanding writing per se, including how individuals make use of available first-language knowledge and speech production capabilities in writing development and performance and in understanding the relationship between writing and reading.

Some progress has been made in our understanding of basic speech planning and execution processes in mature language users in recent years (Clark & Clark, 1977; Cooper & Paccia-Cooper, 1980; Cooper & Walker, 1979; Foss & Hakes, 1978; Rosenberg, 1977; Siegman & Feldstein, 1979), but little is known about their development in children.

Like reading, second-language learning is a well-developed area of applied psycholinguistics and, therefore, one that reflects extensively the impact of basic research and theory. Additionally, however, second-language learning has become one of the battlegrounds on which certain of the claims of some of the theorists who propose that there is a strong innate biological component in first-language acquisition are being tested (Snow & Hoefnagel-Höhle, 1977, 1978). Moreover, the related area of bilingualism has figured in our understanding of basic first-language acquisition processes (Slobin, 1971).

A question concerning second-language learning that has evidently never been raised as regards reading or writing is whether learning another language interferes with one's first-language development and/or performance. This question, however, has been and continues to be an important one in the area of second-language learning and bilingualism, as McLaughlin's review indicates (this volume; also Gray & Cameron, 1980).

One of the highlights of McLaughlin's chapter is, for example, his discussion of the processes of second-language learning and, in particular, the similarities, differences, and interactions involving second- and first-language acquisition at different stages of development (i.e., childhood, adolescence, adulthood). Another highlight is his critical treatment of the literature on biological factors in second-language learning, which leads him to conclude that "the evidence for a biologically based critical period in second-language learning is not convincing."

Another highlight is of special interest in that it is part of the general question of the impact of reading, writing, and second-language learning on cognitive development. I refer here to his treatment of the question "Does a bilingual have more cognitive flexibility than a monolingual does?"

The final topic in the present volume that is not concerned with language disorders is discourse processes. Students of discourse processes have addressed such problems as learning from texts and lectures (Anderson, Spiro, & Montague, 1977; Carroll & Freedle, 1972), document design (Felker, 1980), advertising (Bruno & Harris, 1980), general aspects of prose comprehension (Freedle & Fine, this volume), and cross-cultural communication processes—in particular the problem of miscommunication (Freedle & Fine).

Freedle and Fine introduce the reader to basic concepts in the general domain of prose comprehension that are clearly applicable in a variety of areas, one of them being writing. Thus, to the extent that there are constraints on the creation of prose that relate to the requirement of listener or reader comprehension, there is a need to train writers to be sensitive to these constraints. The problem of miscommunication, therefore, arises not only in cross-cultural communication but in writing as well.

As Freedle and Fine point out, the problem of cross-cultural miscommunication arises in the area of bilingual education, which is an area that is also treated by McLaughlin (this volume).

As we saw earlier, in the section Major Questions in Applied Psycholinguistics, a number of issues relate to all the populations of children who suffer from disorders of first-language development (i.e., Questions 2, 3, 4, 5, 6, 7, 8, 9, 10, 11, 12, 13, 17, 18): (1) the course of first-language (including communicative) development; (2) the variables that influence first-language development; (3) the strategies and processes by which the first language is acquired; (4) individual differences in first-language development; (5) the innate biological language acquisition system; (6) the hemispheric organization of language functions; (7) first-language performance processes; (8) the relationship between nonlinguistic cognitive and first-language development; (9) the impact of language on nonlinguistic cognitive development; (10) the nature and role of adult linguistic input in first-language development; (11) general-purpose information-processing capacities and operations; (12) metalinguistic awareness; (13) language assessment; and (14) language intervention.

It was not possible to address all of these issues in the chapters on developmental language disorders in the present handbook, one of the reasons being the availability of relevant research and/or theory pertaining to the various issues.

Among the issues Leonard treats in his critical review of the literature on specific language impairment (or what some investigators call delayed language development) are those of individual differences in first-language development, adult linguistic input in first-language development, the relationship between nonlinguistic cognitive and first-language development, first-language performance processes, and the course of first-language development. Thus Leonard makes the reader aware at the start that language-impaired children do not constitute a homogeneous population but display individual differences in both production and comprehension. This has led some investigators to adopt rigorous criteria for subject selection, but, as Leonard points out, the fact of individual differences raises questions concerning the generality of the findings of particular studies sampling particular subgroups of language-impaired children.

When language interactions between adults and language-impaired children are compared with language interactions involving adults and normal children, some differences emerge that will require careful examination in future research.

Leonard's review of the available literature on nonlinguistic cognitive and first-language development in language-impaired children reveals instances in which difficulties were encountered on some Piagetian and nonverbal intelligence tasks that led him to conclude that "language impairment might best be described as a set of conditions where language ability is considerably more depressed than nonverbal intelligence, not as a set of conditions where language disability exists in the presence of normal nonverbal intelligence." Thus it is likely that there are factors other than nonlinguistic cognitive ones that are implicated in the language difficulties of language-impaired children. One possible factor is the difficulties some language-impaired children appear to encounter processing certain rapidly presented acoustic stimuli, thus suggesting that a performance factor may be involved in their language impairment.

As regards the question of the course of first-language development in language-impaired children, Leonard's review reveals a picture of developmental lag and/or arrest at an early age in the domains of syntax, semantics, pragmatics, and phonology rather than a picture of linguistic deviance. This picture is complicated, however, by language-impaired children's persistent use of linguistic structures that are more in evidence at earlier ages in normal children and by some differences between language-impaired and normal children in the relationship among linguistic structures.

It is clear from Leonard's review that although progress has been made in our understanding of language impairment in children, much work still remains to be done. In addition to the important question of the etiology or etiologies of language impairment in children, there is, among other things, a strong need for detailed extended longitudinal investigations of the course of first-language development in individual language-impaired children and detailed assessments of the final achievements in the language capabilities of adults who were language impaired as children.

On the basis of Rosenberg's review in the present volume, it appears that the mentally retarded present a picture of disordered language development associated with serious disordered nonlinguistic cognitive development and motivational and other linguistic performance problems as well. However, like language-impaired children, they too display a wide range of individual differences, both linguistically and nonlinguistically, and, moreover, differential rates of development of different aspects of language. Furthermore, like language-impaired children, the mentally retarded display a developmental lag and/or arrest in language development in the domains of syntax, semantics, and phonology. Their achievements in the domain of pragmatics (specifically in conversational interaction), however, may, to some extent, outdistance their achievements in the other domains of language competence (Rosenberg, this volume; Abbeduto & Rosenberg, 1980).

Three other conclusions arrived at in the course of Rosenberg's review of literature on the language of the mentally retarded that are of interest in light of Leonard's findings for language-impaired children are the conclusions that "No convincing case has been made for the frequent claim that certain nonlinguistic achievements necessarily antedate and/or pace language development in the mentally retarded"; that "Mothers' speech to young language learning mentally retarded children has not been shown to differ from mothers' speech to young language learning nonretarded children."; and that "Etiology *per se* does not appear to be implicated in language development and functioning in the mentally retarded."

Autistic children also present a picture of language delay and/or arrest (rather than deviance) but one that is complicated by the presence of severe emotional and interpersonal problems and, in many or most instances, mental retardation as well. Moreover, unlike language-impaired and nonautistic mentally retarded children, autistic children, most likely as a result of their severe emotional and interpersonal problems, tend to be especially vulnerable in the domain of language use (i.e., pragmatics; Fay & Mermelstein, this volume; Blank & Milewski, 1981). It is interesting to note, however, the existence of some evidence that autistic children may outdistance language-impaired children in the domain of phonological development.

As one would expect, there are proposals in the literature regarding an involvement of nonlinguistic cognitive deficits in the language disorders of autistic children, but, as Fay and Mermelstein point out, the claims that have been made thus far are not convincing.

The previous summary statement regarding the course of first-language development in autistic children, it should be pointed out, applies primarily to syntax and phonology, because little is known regarding semantic development in this population of language-disordered children.

A significant feature of both Rosenberg's and Fay and Mermelstein's chapters is their treatment of work on language intervention, although the treatment in Fay and Mermelstein is more extensive than that in Rosenberg's chapter.

Finally, it should be pointed out that Leonard, Rosenberg, and Fay and Mermelstein as well paint a picture of development of language competence or knowledge complicated by the presence of certain linguistic performance deficits.

Prelingual deafness, in particular, profound deafness, carries with it some problems of language development that are not faced by the other populations of language-disordered children that we have been discussing. Some linguistic contact of an interactive nature with an adult or older child appears to be required for normal auditory–vocal language development (Sachs, Bard, & Johnson, 1981). However, because the auditory–vocal channel is not the only means by which our capacity for language can be realized (there is also, for example, the visual–manual domain), the impact of prelingual deafness on language development will vary depending on the nature and extent of early compensatory intervention in cases of prelingual deafness, including that provided by parents.

However, a complicating factor in the study of language development in deaf children, as Quigley and King indicate in their present review, is the result of the fact that "Most deaf children are exposed in infancy and early childhood to a variety of systems, the relative merits and effectiveness of which are continually being debated." These may include signing, finger spelling, speech, lipreading, writing (and reading), gestures, or some combination of systems.

The development of reading and writing competence have become important goals of language training for the deaf, evidently not only because of their importance in school and in evaluating language training programs but because of the role they play in communication generally for the deaf. However, as Quigley and King's review indicates, the deaf are at an obvious disadvantage in these areas, even after years of formal education. (Not surprisingly, they also suffer at the same time from serious problems of speech intelligibility.)

The reader will recall at this point my earlier remarks concerning the possibility of a positive relationship between literacy and subsequent linguistic and nonlinguistic cognitive development in normal children. Should future research confirm this relationship, we would want to examine in the laboratory its implications for the continued development of language and other aspects of cognition in older deaf children and deaf adults.

Worthy of special note is Quigley and King's critical discussion of literature on language and cognition in deaf children. As Quigley and King indicate, according to the work of Furth and his associates, "the cognitive development of deaf people is similar to that of hearing people when language is not a factor in the cognitive task." They indicate further, however, that the presence of serious methodological problems in this research means that "their conclusions need to be tempered...."

The issues raised by Quigley and King in their section on language and cognition are crucial to the question of which first-language system (e.g., finger spelling versus American sign language) best meets the communicative and other (in particular, the reading education) needs of deaf individuals.

The course of language development in the deaf is examined by Quigley and King in the context of a variety of modes of exposure to English. The picture that emerges is not altogether clear in the case of exposure to oral English, at least as far as the course of language development is concerned. In the visual–manual channel, however, observations of manual counterparts of syntax, semantics, and phonology suggest that the course of language development in the deaf is similar to what it is in the auditory–vocal channel in normal hearing children.

The reader with a special interest in language development in deaf children will also want to read Quigley and King's (1980) recently published review of the research program of Quigley and his associates on the development of English syntax as assessed through writing (and to some extent reading) tasks. In the main, according to Quigley and King (1980), syntactic development in deaf and hearing individuals is similar although "greatly retarded" in the deaf. Moreover, deaf subjects appear to be particularly vulnerable in the domain of complex sentences, which suggests that language development may level off earlier in deaf than in normal individuals. Additionally, the kinds of errors deaf subjects make suggest that they acquire language in a manner similar to that of normal hearing individuals.

Thus, once again, we find, amid evidence of differences, fundamental similarities between a population of language-disordered children and normal children vis-a-vis aspects of language development. And, moreover, despite the differences the present discussion of disorders of first-language development have revealed among disorders associated with: (1) minimal nonlinguistic cognitive dysfunction; (2) mental retardation; (3) emotional, social, and nonlinguistic cognitive dysfunctions; and (4) auditory deprivation, there exist some fundamental similarities.

Needless to say, these findings suggest that there may be certain built-in (i.e., innate) biases in our capacity for first-language acquisition that to a significant extent serve to protect us from widely differing kinds of developmental insult.

Consistent with this notion of built-in biases, it should be noted, have been observations of the spontaneous development of communicative gestures in young prelingual deaf children (Goldin-Meadow & Feldman, 1977; Quigley & King, this volume).

There is one final point I would like to make here (see, also, the relevant discussion in Quigley & King, this volume). To the extent that there are differences between a manual language acquired early and a subsequent vocal language, the problems the deaf encounter with the second language can be examined in the context of what we already know about second-language learning and bilingualism in normal hearing children.

The impact basic research and theory in psycholinguistics and related areas of cognitive psychology has had on applied problems is nowhere better illustrated than it is in the area of adult aphasia, as the present review by Caramazza and Berndt indicates. In the main, the work in this area has been concerned with determining in adults who have suffered left hemispheric damage to critical language areas: (1) the structure (phonological, lexical, syntactic, semantic) of the language spoken and comprehended; (2) whether or not there has been a loss of linguistic competence or knowledge; (3) whether linguistic performance (e.g., speech planning, speech comprehension) and general-purpose information-processing factors (e.g., attention, memory) have been affected; (4) the impact of the language dysfunction on other areas of cognitive functioning; and (5) whether compensatory linguistic performance mechanisms and strategies have been developed by the aphasic patient.

The most striking finding in the applied psycholinguistic research in the area of aphasia, as the present review indicates, is that to a significant extent, when language functions break down in adults in the face of neurological insult, the breakdown is organized and consistent with what we know or can reasonably surmise concerning the organization of linguistic knowledge and the organization and operation of linguistic performance and related general-purpose information-processing capabilities in normal adults.

However, this finding is not just significant for our understanding of adult aphasia, for as Caramazza and Berndt point out, the results of contemporary psycholinguistic research in adult aphasia are helping basic researchers in psycholinguistics and neurolinguistics to evaluate the psychological reality and origin of proposed structures, components, and operations of normal language capabilities. The contribution of contemporary psycholinguistic research in adult aphasia to basic issues is exemplified in the following exerpt from Caramazza and Berndt's chapter.

> Our impression is that it is relatively easy to characterize syntactic impairments and that such impairments are closely associated with lesions in the anterior zones of the language area. In contrast, phonological and semantic deficits appear to take many different forms and can result from insult to widely varying sites. There are probably several explanations for this observed pattern, and the most interesting is that syntactic processing enjoys some special biological status that is not shared by the other components.

Caramazza and Berndt go on to cite some evidence in support of this view from, for example, studies of split-brain patients.

Of all the areas we have discussed in the present overview, adult schizophrenic language has been influenced least by developments in basic research and theory in psycholinguistics. Moreover, as Rosenberg and Abbeduto's review chapter has revealed, research in this area has been plagued by serious methodological and other problems. Therefore, what we have available to us from this research are working hypotheses rather than firm conclusions.

One of these is that the evidence suggests that the occasional disruptions one notes in the speech of some schizophrenics are more suggestive of the existence of a linguistic performance rather than a linguistic competence disorder and one, moreover, that is associated with high arousal (anxiety), attentional disturbances, and delusional thinking. These disruptions, furthermore, tend to occur at the level of discourse and may or may not produce speech that is incoherent to the listener. Incoherent speech, however, with the features of schizophrenic speech, is not unique to this population, because it has also been observed to occur sometimes in some manics, in some adult aphasics, and in some normals.

Some interesting proposals have appeared in the literature that have to do with the cortical organization of language and other cognitive functions in schizophrenics that will require careful further evaluation in the laboratory.

ACKNOWLEDGMENT

Preparation of this chapter was made possible in part by support from the Illinois Institute for Developmental Disabilities, Dr. Kenneth R. Swiatek, Director.

REFERENCES

Aaronson, D., & Rieber, R. (Eds.). Developmental psycholinguistics and communication disorders New York: New York Academy of Sciences, 1975.

Abbeduto, L., & Rosenberg, S. The communicative competence of mildly retarded adults. *Applied Psycholinguistics,* 1980, *1,* 405-426.
Abrahamsen, A. A. Child language: *An interdisciplinary guide to theory and research.* Baltimore: University Park Press, 1977.
Aitchison, J. *The articulate mammal.* New York: Universe Books, 1977.
Albert, M. L., & Obler, L. K. *The bilingual brain: Neuropsychological and neurolinguistic aspects of bilingualism.* New York: Academic Press, 1978.
Andersen, R. W. (Ed.). *New dimensions in research on the acquisition and use of a second language.* Rowley, Mass.: Newbury House, 1980.
Anderson, J. R. *Cognitive psychology and its implications.* San Francisco: Freeman, 1980.
Anderson, R. C., Spiro, R. T., & Montague, W. E. (Eds.). *Schooling and the acquisition of knowledge.* Hillsdale, N.J.: Lawrence Erlbaum Associates, 1977.
Anglin, J. M. *Word, object and conceptual development.* New York: Norton, 1977.
Bates, E. *Language and context: the acquisition of pragmatics.* New York: Academic Press, 1976. (a)
Bates, E. Pragmatics and sociolinguistics in child language. In D. M. Morehead & A. E. Morehead (Eds.), *Normal and deficient child language.* Baltimore: University Park Press, 1976. (b)
Beilin, H. *Studies in the cognitive basis of language development.* New York: Academic Press, 1975.
Benedict, H. Early lexical development. *Journal of Child Language.* 1979, *6,* 183-200.
Berry, P. (Ed.). *Language and communication in the mentally handicapped.* London: Edward Arnold, 1976.
Bever, T. G. Cerebral asymmetries in humans are due to the differentiation of two incompatible processes: Holistic and analytic. In D. Aaronson & R. W. Rieber (Eds.), *Developmental psycholinguistics and communication disorders.* New York: New York Academy of Sciences, 1975.
Blank, M. Cognitive functions of language in the preschool years. *Developmental Psychology,* 1974, *10,* 229-245.
Blank, M. Mastering the intangible through language. In D. Aaronson & R. W. Rieber (Eds.), *Developmental psycholinguistics and communication disorders.* New York: New York Academy of Sciences, 1975.
Blank, M., & Franklin, E. Dialogue with preschoolers: A cognitively-based system of assessment. *Applied Psycholinguistics,* 1980, *1,* 127-150.
Blank, M., & Milewski, J. Applying psycholinguistic concepts to the treatment of an autistic child. *Applied Psycholinguistics,* 1981, *2,* 65-84.
Block, E. M., & Kessel, F. S. Determinants of the acquisition order of grammatical morphemes: A reanalysis and reinterpretation. *Journal of Child Language,* 1980, *7,* 181-188.
Bloom, L., & Lahey, M. *Language development and language disorders.* New York: Wiley, 1978.
Blount, B. G., & Padgug, E. J. Prosodic, paralinguistic, and interactional features in parent-child speech: English and Spanish. *Journal of Child Language,* 1977, *4,* 67-86.
Blumstein, S. *A phonological investigation of aphasic speech.* The Hague: Mouton, 1973.
Bonvillian, J. D., Raeburn, V. P., & Horan, E. A. Talking to children: The effects of rate, intonation, and length on children's sentence imitation. *Journal of Child Language,* 1979, *6,* 459-467.
Bowerman, M. Semantic factors in the acquisition of rules for word use and sentence construction. In D. M. Morehead & A. E. Morehead (Eds.), *Normal and deficient child language.* Baltimore: University Park Press, 1976.
Bowerman, M. Semantic and syntactic development: A review of what, when, and how in language acquisition. In R. L. Schiefelbusch (Ed.), *Bases of language intervention.* Baltimore: University Park Press, 1978.
Bransford, J. D. *Human cognition.* Belmont, Calif.: Wadsworth, 1979.
Bridges, A. SVO comprehension strategies reconsidered: The evidence of individual patterns of response. *Journal of Child Language,* 1980, *7,* 89-104.
Brown, I., Jr. Role of referent concreteness in the acquisition of passive sentence comprehension through abstract modeling. *Journal of Experimental Child Psychology,* 1976, *22,* 185-199.

Brown, R. *A first language: The early stages.* Cambridge, Mass.: Harvard University Press, 1973.
Bruner, J. S. From communication to language: A psychological perspective. *Cognition,* 1975, *3,* 255-287. (a)
Bruner, J. S. The ontogenesis of speech acts. *Journal of Child Language,* 1975, *2,* 1-19. (b)
Bruner, J. S. The role of dialogue in language acquisition. In A. Sinclair, R. J. Jarvella, & W.J.M. Levelt (Eds.), *The child's conception of language.* Berlin: Springer-Verlag, 1978.
Bruno, K. J., & Harris, R. J. The effect of repetition on the discrimination of asserted and implied claims in advertising. *Applied Psycholinguistics,* 1980, *1,* 307-321.
Bullowa, M. (Ed.). *Before speech.* Cambridge: Cambridge University Press, 1979.
Buros, O. K. (Ed.). *The mental measurement yearbook* (Vol. 7). Highland Park, N.J.: Gryphan Press, 1972.
Burt, M., Dulay, H. C., & Hernandez-Chavez, E. *Bilingual syntax measure.* New York: Harcourt Brace Jovanovich, 1973.
Burt, M., Dulay, H., & Finocchiaro, M. (Eds.). *Viewpoints on English as a second language.* New York: Regents, 1977.
Cairns, H. S., & Hsu, J. R. *Who, why, when* and *how:* A developmental study. *Journal of Child Language,* 1978, *5,* 477-488.
Caplan, D. (Ed.). *Biological studies of mental processes.* Cambridge, Mass.: MIT Press, 1980.
Cantwell, D., Howlin, P., & Rutter, M. The analysis of language level and language function: A methodological study. *British Journal of Disorders of Communication,* 1977, *12,* 119-135.
Caramazza, A., & Zurif, E. B. (Eds.). *Language acquisition and language breakdown.* Baltimore: Johns Hopkins University Press, 1978.
Carr, D. B. The development of young children's capacity to judge anomalous sentences. *Journal of Child Language,* 1979, *6,* 227-241.
Carroll, J. B., & Freedle, R. O. (Eds.). *Language Comprehension and the acquisition of knowledge.* Washington: Winston, 1972.
Carrow, M. W. The development of auditory comprehension of language structure in children. *Journal of Speech and Hearing Disorders,* 1968, *33,* 99-111.
Carrow, E. Assessment of speech and language in children. In J. E. McLean, D. E. Yoder, & R. L. Schiefelbusch (Eds.), *Language intervention and the retarded.* Baltimore: University Park Press, 1972.
Carrow, E. *Test for auditory comprehension of language.* Austin, Texas: Learning Concepts, 1973.
Carrow, E. A test using elicited imitations in assessing grammatical structure in children. *Journal of Speech and Hearing Disorders,* 1974, *39,* 437-444.
Cazden, C. G., John, V. P., & Hymes, D. (Eds.). *Functions of language in the classroom.* New York: Teachers College Press, 1972.
Chapman, R. S., & Kohn, L. L. Comprehension strategies in two and three year olds: Animate agents or probable events? *Journal of Speech and Hearing Research,* 1978, *21,* 746-761.
Chapman, R. S., & Miller, J. F. Word order in early two and three word utterances: Does production precede comprehension? *Journal of Speech and Hearing Research,* 1975, *18,* 355-371.
Chi, M. T. H. Age differences in memory span. *Journal of Experimental Child Psychology,* 1977, *23,* 266-281.
Chomsky, N. *Syntactic structures.* The Hague: Mouton, 1957.
Chomsky, N. *Aspects of the theory of syntax.* Cambridge: MIT Press, 1965.
Chomsky, N. *Reflections on language.* New York: Pantheon, 1975.
Chomsky, N. *Essays on form and interpretation.* New York: North-Holland, 1977.
Chomsky, N. *Language and responsibility.* New York: Pantheon, 1979.
Chomsky, N. *Rules and representations.* New York: Columbia University Press, 1980.
Cicciarelli, A., Broen, P., & Siegel, G. Language assessment procedures. In L. L. Lloyd (Ed.), *Communication assessment and intervention strategies.* Baltimore: University Park Press, 1976.
Clark, E. V., & Clark, H. H. Universals, relativity and language processing. In J. H. Greenberg (Ed.), *Universals of human language* (Vol. 1). Stanford: Stanford University Press, 1978.

1. INTRODUCTION, FOUNDATIONS AND OVERVIEW 23

Clark, E. V., & Sengul, C. J. Strategies in the acquisition of deixis. *Journal of Child Language,* 1978, *5,* 457–475.
Clark, H. H., & Clark, E. V. *Psychology and language.* New York: Harcourt Brace Jovanovich, 1977.
Cohen, R. L., & Sandberg, T. Relation between intelligence and short-term memory. *Cognitive Psychology,* 1977, *9,* 534–554.
Cole, R. A., & Perfetti, C. A. Listening for mispronunciation in a children's story: The use of context by children and adults. *Journal of Verbal Learning and Verbal Behavior,* 1980, *19,* 297–327.
Collins, W. A. (Ed.). *Children's language and communication.* Hillsdale, N.J.: Lawrence Erlbaum Associates, 1979.
Conrad, R. *The deaf school child.* London: Harper & Row, 1979.
Cooper, D. E. *Knowledge of language.* New York: Humanities Press, 1975.
Cooper, W. E., & Paccia-Cooper, J. *Syntax and speech.* Cambridge, Mass.: Harvard University Press, 1980.
Cooper, W. E., & Walker, E. C. T. (Eds.). *Sentence processing: Psycholinguistic studies presented to Merrill Garrett.* Hillsdale, N.J.: Lawrence Erlbaum Associates, 1979.
Corrigan, R. Language development as related to stage 6 object permanence development. *Journal of Child Language,* 1978, *5,* 173–189.
Corrigan, R. Use of repetition to facilitate spontaneous language acquisition. *Journal of Psycholinguistic Research,* 1980, *9,* 231–241.
Craig, H. K., & Gallagher, T. M. The structural characteristics of monologues in the speech of normal children: Syntactic nonconversational aspects. *Journal of Speech and Hearing Research,* 1979, *22,* 46–62.
Crockett, D. J. Component analysis of within correlations of language-skill tests in normal children. *Journal of Special Education,* 1974, *8,* 361–375.
Cromer, R. F. The cognitive hypothesis of language acquisition and its implications for child language deficiency. In D. M. Morehead & A. E. Morehead (Eds.), *Normal and deficient child language.* Baltimore: University Park Press, 1976. (a)
Cromer, R. F. Developmental strategies for language. In V. Hamilton & M. D. Vernon (Eds.), *The development of cognitive processes.* London: Academic Press, 1976. (b)
Crystal, D., Fletcher, P., & Garman, M. *The grammatical analysis of language disability.* New York: Elsevier, 1976.
Curtiss, S. *Genie: A psycholinguistic study of a modern-day "Wild Child".* New York: Academic Press, 1977.
Curtiss, S. Genie: Language and cognition. *UCLA Working Papers in Cognitive Linguistics,* 1979, *1,* 15–62.
Curtiss, S. The critical period and feral children. *UCLA Working Papers in Cognitive Linguistics,* 1980, *2,* 21–36.
Curtiss, S., Fromkin, V., Krashen, S., Rigler, D., & Rigler, M. The linguistic development of Genie. *Language,* 1974, *50,* 528–554.
Dale, P. S. *Language development: Structure and function* (2nd ed.). New York: Holt, Rinehart & Winston, 1976.
deAjuriaguerra, J., & Tissot, R. Some aspects of language in various forms of senile dementia. In E. H. Lenneberg & E. Lenneberg (Eds.), *Foundations of language development* (Vol. 1). New York: Academic Press, 1975.
deBeaugrande, R. *Text, discourse and process: Toward a multidisciplinary science of texts.* Norwood, N.J.: Ablex, 1980.
Dennis, M., & Whitaker, H. A. Language acquisition following hemidecortication: Linguistic superiority of the left over the right hemisphere. *Brain and Language,* 1976, *3,* 404–433.
DePaulo, B. M., & Bonvillian, J. D. The effect on language development of the special characteristics of speech addressed to children. *Journal of Psycholinguistic Research,* 1978, *7,* 189–211.

Deutsch, W. The conceptual impact of linguistic input. A comparison of German family children's and orphans' acquisition of kinship terms. *Journal of Child Language,* 1979, *6,* 313-352.
deVilliers, J. G., & deVilliers, P. A. *Language acquisition.* Cambridge, Mass.: Harvard University Press, 1978.
deVilliers, J. G., Tager-Flusberg, H. B., Hakuta, K., & Cohen, M. Children's comprehension of relative clauses. *Journal of Psycholinguistic Research,* 1979, *8,* 499-518.
deVilliers, P. A., & deVilliers, J. G. Early judgments of semantic and syntactic acceptibility by children. *Journal of Psycholinguistic Research,* 1972, *1,* 299-310.
Diller, K. (Ed.). *Individual differences and universals in language learning aptitude.* Rowley, Mass.: Newbury House, 1980.
Dingwall, W. O. The species specificity of speech. In D. P. Dato (Ed.), *Developmental psycholinguistics: Theory and applications.* Washington, D.C.: Georgetown University Press, 1975.
Donaldson, M. *Children's minds.* Glasgow: Fontana/Collins, 1978.
Donaldson, M., & McGarrigle, J. Some clues to the nature of semantic development. *Journal of Child Language,* 1974, *1,* 185-194.
Dore, J. What's so conceptual about the acquisition of linguistic structures? *Journal of Child Language,* 1979, *6,* 129-137.
Durbin, M., & Martin, R. L. Speech in mania: Syntactic aspects. *Brain and Language,* 1977, *4,* 208-218.
Edwards, J. R. *Language and disadvantage.* New York: Elsevier, 1979.
Eilers, R. E., Wilson, W. R., & Moore, J. M. Speech discrimination in the language-innocent and the language-wise: A study in the perception of voice onset time. *Journal of Child Language,* 1979, *6,* 1-18.
Elardo, R. The experimental facilitation of children's comprehension and production of four syntactic structures. *Child Development,* 1971, *42,* 2101-2104.
Erreich, A., Valian, V., & Winzemer, J. Aspects of a theory of language acquisition. *Journal of Child Language,* 1980, *7,* 157-180.
Felker, D. B. (Ed.). *Document design: A review of the relevant research.* Washington, D.C.: American Institutes for Research, 1980.
Fillmore, C. J. The case for case. In E. Bach & R. T. Harms (Eds.), *Universals in linguistic theory.* New York: Holt, 1968.
Fillmore, C. J., Kempler, D., & Wang, W. S.-Y. (Eds.). *Individual differences in language ability and language behavior.* New York: Academic Press, 1979.
Fletcher, P., & Garman, M. (Eds.). *Language acquisition.* Cambridge: Cambridge University Press, 1979.
Fluharty, N. B. The design and standardization of a speech and language screening test for use with preschool children. *Journal of Speech and Hearing Disorders,* 1974, *39,* 75-88.
Folger, M. K., & Leonard, L. B. Language and sensorimotor development during the early period of referential speech. *Journal of Speech and Hearing Research,* 1978, *21,* 519-527.
Foss, D. J., & Hakes, D. T. *Psycholinguistics.* Englewood Cliffs, N.J.: Prentice-Hall, 1978.
Fraser, C., & Roberts, N. Mother's speech to children of four different ages. *Journal of Psycholinguistic Research,* 1975, *4,* 9-16.
Freedle, R. O. (Ed.). *Discourse production and comprehension.* Norwood, N.J.: Ablex, 1977.
Freedle, R. O. (Ed.). *New directions in discourse processing.* Norwood, N.J.: Ablex, 1979.
Freedle, R. O., & Carroll, J. B. (Eds.). *Language comprehension and the acquisition of knowledge.* Washington, D.C.: Winston, 1972.
Friedman, P., & Friedman, K. A. Accounting for individual differences when comparing the effectiveness of remedial language teaching methods. *Applied Psycholinguistics,* 1980, *1,* 151-170.
Fromkin, V. An update on the linguistic development of Genie. In D. P. Dato (Ed.), *Developmental psycholinguistics: Theory and applications.* Washington, D.C.: Georgetown University Press, 1975.

Furrow, D., Nelson, K., & Benedict, H. Mothers' speech to children and syntactic development: Some simple relationships. *Journal of Child Language,* 1979, *6,* 423-442.

Gaddes, W. H., & Crockett, D. J. The Spreen-Benton aphasia tests; normative data as a measure of normal language development. *Brain and Language,* 1975, *2,* 257-280.

Genesee, F., & Hamayan, E. Individual differences in second language learning. *Applied Psycholinguistics,* 1980, *1,* 95-110.

Gibson, E. J., & Levin, H. *The psychology of reading.* Cambridge, Mass.: MIT Press, 1975.

Goldin-Meadow, S. Structure in a manual communication system developed without a conventional language model: Language without a helping hand. In H. Whitaker & H. A. Whitaker (Eds.), *Studies in neurolinguistics* (Vol. 4). New York: Academic Press, 1979.

Goldin-Meadow, S., & Feldman, H. The development of language-like communication without a language model. *Science,* 1977, *197,* 401-403.

Golinkoff, R. M., & Kerr, J. L. Infants' perception of semantically defined action role changes in filmed events. *Merrill-Palmer Quarterly,* 1978, *24,* 53-61.

Goodglass, H., & Kaplan, E. *The assessment of aphasia and related disorders.* Philadelphia: Lea and Febiger, 1972.

Gowie, C. J., & Powers, J. E. Relations among cognitive, semantic, and syntactic variables in children's comprehension of the minimum distance principle: A 2-year developmental study. *Journal of Psycholinguistic Research,* 1979, *8,* 29-42.

Gray, V. A., & Cameron, A. C. Longitudinal development of English morphology in French immersion children. *Applied Psycholinguistics,* 1980, *1,* 171-181.

Greenberg, J. H. *A new invitation to linguistics.* New York: Anchor, 1977.

Greenberg, J. H. (Ed.). *Universals of human language* (Vol. 1). Stanford, Calif.: Stanford University Press, 1978.

Greenfield, P. M., & Westerman, M. A. Some psychological relations between action and language structure. *Journal of Psycholinguistic Research,* 1978, *7,* 453-475.

Gustafson, L., Hogberg, B., & Ingnar, D. H. Speech disturbances in presenile dementia related to local cerebral blood flow abnormalities in the dominant hemisphere. *Brain and Language,* 1978, *5,* 103-118.

Halle, M., Bresnan, J., & Miller, G. A. *Linguistic theory and psychological reality.* Cambridge, Mass.: MIT Press, 1978.

Halliday, M. A. K. Language structure and language function. In J. Lyons (Ed.), *New horizons in linguistics.* Great Britain: Penguin, 1970.

Halliday, M. A. K., & Hasan, R. *Cohesion in English.* London: Longman, 1976.

Hart, B. The use of adult cues to test the language competence of young children. *Journal of Child Language,* 1975, *2,* 105-124.

Hatch, E. (Ed.). *Second language acquisition.* Rowley, Mass.: Newbury House, 1978.

Hécaen, H. Acquired aphasia in children and the ontogenesis of hemispheric functional specialization. *Brain and Language,* 1976, *3,* 114-134.

Hedge, M. N. Issues in the study and explanation of language behavior. *Journal of Psycholinguistic Research,* 1980, *9,* 1-22.

Hedrick, D., & Prather, E. *Sequenced inventory of communication development.* Seattle: University of Washington Press, 1975.

Hiscock, M., & Kinsbourne, M. Ontogeny of cerebral dominance: Evidence from time-sharing asymmetry in children. *Developmental Psychology,* 1978, *14,* 321-329.

Horn, J. L. Human abilities: A review of research and theory in the early 1970s. *Annual Review of Psychology,* 1976, *27,* 437-486.

Hornby, P. A. (Ed.). *Bilingualism: Psychological, social and educational implications.* New York: Academic Press, 1978.

Huttenlocher, J. The origins of language comprehension. In R. L. Solso (Ed.), *Theories in cognitive psychology: The Loyola Symposium.* Hillsdale, N.J.: Lawrence Erlbaum Associates, 1974.

Huttenlocher, J., & Burke, D. Why does memory span increase with age? *Cognitive Psychology,* 1976, *8,* 1-31.
Huxley, R., & Ingram, E. (Eds.). *Language acquisition: Models and methods.* London: Academic Press, 1971.
Ingram, D. If and when transformations are acquired by children. In P. Dato (Ed.), *Developmental psycholinguistics: Theory and applications.* Washington, D.C.: Georgetown University Press, 1975.
Ingram, D. *Phonological disability in children.* New York: Elsevier, 1976.
Ingram, T. T. S. The Edinburgh articulation test. In R. Huxley & E. Ingram (Eds.), *Language acquisition: Models and methods.* New York: Academic Press, 1971.
Inhelder, B. Language and thought: Some remarks on Chomsky and Piaget. *Journal of Psycholinguistic Research,* 1978, *7,* 263-268.
Irwin, D., & Marge, M. (Eds.). *Principles of childhood language disabilities.* New York: Appleton-Century-Crofts, 1972.
Jacobs, R. A., & Rosenbaum, P. S. *English transformational grammar.* Waltham: Blaisdel, 1968.
Jay, S. M., Routh, D. K., & Brantley, J. C. Social class differences in children's comprehension of adult language. *Journal of Psycholinguistic Research,* 1980, *9,* 205-217.
Johnson, D. L. The influences of social class and race on language test performance and spontaneous speech of preschool children. *Child Development,* 1974, *45,* 517-521.
Kagan, D. M. Syntactic complexity and cognitive style. *Applied Psycholinguistics,* 1980, *1,* 111-122.
Kavanagh, J. F., & Mattingly, I. G. (Eds.). *Language by ear and by eye.* Cambridge, Mass.: MIT Press, 1972.
Kavanagh, J. F., & Strange, W. (Eds.). *Speech and language in the laboratory, school, and clinic.* Cambridge, Mass.: MIT Press, 1978.
Keeton, A. Children's cognitive integration and memory processes for comprehending written sentences. *Journal of Experimental Child Psychology,* 1977, *23,* 459-471.
Keil, F. Development of the ability to perceive ambiguities: Evidence for the task specificity of a linguistic skill. *Journal of Psycholinguistic Research,* 1980, *9,* 219-230.
Kinsbourne, M. The ontogeny of cerebral dominance. *Annals of the New York Academy of Sciences,* 1975, *263,* 244-250.
Kirk, S. A., & Kirk, W. D. Uses and abuses of the ITPA. *Journal of Speech and Hearing Disorders,* 1978, *43,* 58-75.
Klima, E., & Bellugi, U. *The signs of language.* Cambridge, Mass.: Harvard University Press, 1979.
Koenigsknecht, R. A., & Friedman, P. Syntax development in boys and girls. *Child Development,* 1976, *47,* 1109-1115.
Krashen, S. The development of cerebral dominance and language learning: More new evidence. In D. P. Dato (Ed.), *Developmental psycholinguistics: Theory and applications.* Washington, D.C.: Georgetown University Press, 1975.
Kuczaj, S. A., II. Children's judgments of grammatical and ungrammatical irregular past tense verbs. *Child Development,* 1978, *49,* 319-327.
Lahey, M., & Bloom, L. Planning a first lexicon: Which words to teach first. *Journal of Speech and Hearing Disorders,* 1977, *42,* 340-350.
Larson, G. W., & Summers, P. A. Response patterns of pre-school-age children to the Northwestern syntax screening test. *Journal of Speech & Hearing Disorders,* 1976, *41,* 486-497.
Lee, L. L. *Northwestern syntax screening test.* Evanston, Ill.: Northwestern University Press, 1971.
Lee, L. L. *Developmental sentence analysis.* Evanston, Ill.: Northwestern University Press, 1974.
Lee, L. L., & Canter, S. M. Developmental sentence scoring: A clinical procedure for estimating syntactic development in children's spontaneous speech. *Journal of Speech and Hearing Disorders,* 1971, *36,* 315-338.

Lenneberg, E. H. *Biological foundations of language.* New York: Wiley, 1967.
Lenneberg, E. H., & Lenneberg, E. *Foundations of language development* (Vol. 1). New York: Academic Press, 1975. (a)
Lenneberg, E. H., & Lenneberg, E. *Foundations of language development* (Vol. 2). New York: Academic Press, 1975. (b)
Leonard, L. B. The role of nonlinguistic stimuli and semantic relations in children's acquisition of grammatical utterances. *Journal of Experimental Child Psychology,* 1975, *19,* 346-357.
Leonard, L. B., Bolders, J. G., & Curtis, R. A. On the nature of children's judgments of linguistic features: Semantic relations and grammatical morphemes. *Journal of Psycholinguistic Research,* 1977, *6,* 233-245.
Leonard, L. B., Newhoff, M., & Mesalam, L. Individual differences in early child phonology. *Applied Psycholinguistics,* 1980, *1,* 1-6.
Lesser, R. *Linguistic investigations of aphasia.* New York: Elsevier, 1978.
Levelt, W. J. M. What became of LAD? *PDR Press Publications in Cognition,* 1975, No. 1.
Levin, S. R. *The semantics of metaphor.* Baltimore: Johns Hopkins University Press, 1977.
Limber, J. Unravelling competence, performance and pragmatics in the speech of young children. *Journal of Child Language,* 1976, *3,* 309-318.
Longhurst, T. M., & Schrandt, T. A. M. Linguistic analysis of children's speech: A comparison of four procedures. *Journal of Speech and Hearing Disorders,* 1973, *38,* 240-249.
MacDonald, J. D., & Blott, J. P. Environmental language intervention: The rationale for a diagnostic and training strategy through rules, context, and generalization. *Journal of Speech & Hearing Disorders,* 1974, *39,* 244-256.
Macnamara, J. Cognitive basis of language learning in infants. *Psychological Review,* 1972, *79,* 1-13.
Macnamara, J. (Ed.). *Language learning and thought.* New York: Academic Press, 1977.
MacWhinney, B. The acquisition of morphophonology. *Monographs of the Society for Child Development,* 1978, *43,* Serial No. 174.
Mahoney, G. J. Etiological approach to delayed language acquisition. *American Journal of Mental Deficiency,* 1975, *80,* 139-148.
Mahoney, G. J., & Seely, P. B. The role of the social agent in language acquisition: Implications for language intervention. In N. R. Ellis (Ed.), *International review of research in mental retardation* (Vol. 8). New York: Academic Press, 1976.
McLaughlin, B. *Second-language acquisition in childhood.* Hillsdale, N.J.: Lawrence Erlbaum Associates, 1978.
Menyuk, P. *Language and maturation.* Cambridge, Mass.: MIT Press, 1977.
Messer, D. J. The integration of mothers' referential speech with joint play. *Child Development,* 1978, *49,* 781-787.
Messer, D. J. The episodic structure of maternal speech to young children. *Journal of Child Language,* 1980, *7,* 29-40.
Miller, G. A., & Lenneberg, E. (Eds.). *Psychology and biology of language and thought.* New York: Academic Press, 1978.
Miller, J. F. Assessing children's language behavior: A developmental process approach. In R. L. Schiefelbusch (Ed.), *Bases of language intervention.* Baltimore, Md.: University Park Press, 1978.
Miller, L. Pragmatics and early childhood language disorders: Communicative interactions in a half-hour sample. *Journal of Speech and Hearing Disorders,* 1978, *43,* 419-436.
Mirabile, P. J., Porter, R. J., Jr., Hughes, L. F., & Berlin, C. I. Dichotic lag effect in children 7 to 15. *Developmental Psychology,* 1978, *14,* 277-285.
Moerk, E. L. Piaget's research as applied to the explanation of language development. *Merrill-Palmer Quarterly,* 1975, *21,* 151-169.

Moerk, E. L. Processes and products of imitation: Additional evidence that imitation is progressive. *Journal of Psycholinguistic Research*, 1977, *6*, 187-202.

Moerk, E. L. Relationships between parental input frequencies and children's language acquisition: A reanalysis of Brown's data. *Journal of Child Language*, 1980, *7*, 105-118.

Morehead, D. M., & Morehead, A. E. (Eds.). *Normal and deficient child language*. Baltimore: University Park Press, 1976.

Morton, J. (Ed.). *Biological and social factors in psycholinguistics*. Urbana, Ill.: University of Illinois Press, 1970.

Muma, J. R. Language assessment: The co-occurring and restricted structure procedure. *Acta Symbolica*, 1973, *4*, 12-29.

Muma, J. R. *Language handbook*. Englewood Cliffs, N.J.: Prentice-Hall, 1978.

Munsinger, H., & Douglass, A. The syntactic abilities of identical twins, fraternal twins, and their siblings. *Child Development*, 1976, *47*, 40-50.

Naor, E. M., & Balthazar, E. E. Provision of a language index for severely and profoundly retarded individuals. *American Journal on Mental Deficiency*, 1975, *79*, 717-725.

Nelson, K. Structure and strategy in learning to talk. *Monographs of the Society for Research in Child Development*, 1973, *38*(1-2, serial No. 149).

Nelson, K. Concept, word, and sentence: Inter-relations in acquisition and development. *Psychological Review*, 1974, *81*, 267-285.

Nelson, K. E. (Ed.). *Children's language* (Vol. 1). New York: Gardner Press, 1978.

Ninio, A., & Bruner, J. The achievement and antecedents of labelling. *Journal of Child Language*, 1978, *5*, 1-15.

Obler, L. K., & Albert, M. L. Language and aging: A neurobehavioral analysis. In D. Beasley & G. A. Davis (Eds.), *Speech, language, and hearing: The aging process*. New York: Grune & Stratton, 1980.

O'Connor, N. (Ed.). *Language, cognitive deficits and retardation*. London: Butterworths, 1975.

Olson, D. R., & Nickerson, N. Language development through the school years. In K. E. Nelson (Ed.), *Children's language* (Vol. 1). New York: Gardner Press, 1978.

Palermo, D. S., & Molfese, D. L. Language acquisition from age five onward. *Psychological Bulletin*, 1972, *78*, 409-428.

Parisi, D., & Giannelli, W. Language and social environment at 2 years. *Merrill-Palmer Quarterly*, 1979, *25*, 61-75.

Perry, F. L., Jr., & Shwedel, A. Interaction of visual information, verbal information, and linguistic competence in the preschool-aged child. *Journal of Psycholinguistic Research*, 1979, *8*, 559-566.

Piattelli-Palmarini, M. (Ed.). *Language and learning: The debate between Jean Piaget and Noam Chomsky*. Cambridge, Mass.: Harvard University Press, 1980.

Prawat, R. S., & Jones, H. A longitudinal study of language development at different levels of cognitive development. *Merrill-Palmer Quarterly*, 1977, *23*, 115-120.

Prutting, C. A. Process: The action of moving forward progressively from one point to another on the way to completion. *Journal of Speech and Hearing Disorders*, 1979, *44*, 3-30.

Prutting, C. A., & Connally, J. E. Imitation: A closer look. *Journal of Speech and Hearing Disorders*, 1976, *41*, 412-422.

Prutting, C. A., Gallagher, T. M., & Mulac, A. The expressive portion of the NSST compared to a spontaneous language sample. *Journal of Speech and Hearing Disorders*, 1975, *40*, 40-48.

Quigley, S. P., & King, C. M. Syntactic performance of hearing impaired and normal hearing individuals. *Applied Psycholinguistics*, 1980, *1*, 329-356.

Quigley, S., Steinkamp, M., Power, D., & Jones, B. *Test of syntactic abilities*. Beaverton Ore.: Dormac, 1978.

Quirk, R., & Greenbaum, S. *A concise grammar of contemporary English*. New York: Harcourt Brace Jovanovich, 1973.

Ratner, N., & Bruner, J. Games, social exchange and the acquisition of language. *Journal of Child Language,* 1978, *5,* 391-402.

Ratusnik, D. L., & Koenigsknecht, R. A. Internal consistency of the Northwestern syntax screening test. *Journal of Speech & Hearing Disorders,* 1975, *40,* 59-68.

Razel, M. A processing model for children's sentence comprehension: A discussion of two studies by Janellen Huttenlocher. *Journal of Psycholinguistic Research,* 1978, *7,* 17-23.

Reber, A. S., & Scarborough, D. L. (Eds.). *Toward a psychology of reading: The proceedings of the CUNY conference.* Hillsdale, N.J.: Lawrence Erlbaum Associates, 1977.

Rees, N. S. Imitation and language development: Issues and clinical implications. *Journal of Speech & Hearing Disorders,* 1975, *40,* 339-350.

Rees, N. S., & Shulman, M. I don't understand what you mean by comprehension. *Journal of Speech and Hearing Disorders,* 1978, *43,* 208-219.

Reynell, J., & Huntley, R. M. C. New scales for the assessment of language development in young children. *Journal of Learning Disabilities,* 1971, *4,* 10-18.

Richards, J. C. *Error analysis: Perspectives on second language learning.* New York: Longmans, Green, 1974.

Richards, J. C. (Ed.). *Understanding second and foreign language learning.* Rowley, Mass.: Newbury House, 1978.

Richardson, K., Calnan, M., Essen, J., & Lambert, L. The linguistic maturity of 11-year-olds: Some analysis of the written compositions of children in the national child development study. *Journal of Child Language,* 1976, *3,* 99-115.

Ritchie, W. C. (Ed.). *Second language acquisition research: Issues and implications.* New York: Academic Press, 1978.

Rochester, S., & Martin, J. R. *Crazy talk.* New York: Plenum, 1979.

Rodgon, M. M. *Single-word usage, cognitive development and the beginning of combinatorial speech.* Cambridge: Cambridge University Press, 1976.

Rosemont, H., Jr. Gathering evidence for linguistic innateness. *Synthese,* 1978, *38,* 127-148.

Rosenberg, S. (Ed.). *Sentence production.* Hillsdale, N.J.: Lawrence Erlbaum Associates, 1977.

Rosenberg, S., & Koplin, J. H. (Eds.). *Developments in applied psycholinguistics research.* New York: Macmillan, 1968.

Sachs, J., Bard, B., & Johnson, M. L. Language learning with restricted input: Case studies of two hearing children of deaf parents. *Applied Psycholinguistics,* 1981, *2,* 33-54.

Sattler, J. M. Racial experimenter effects in experimentation, testing, and psychotherapy. *Psychological Bulletin,* 1970, *73,* 137-160.

Satz, P., Bakker, D. J., Teunssen, J., Goebel, R., & Van der Vlugt, H. Developmental parameters of the ear asymmetry: A multivariate approach. *Brain and Language,* 1975, *2,* 171-185.

Schank, R. C., & Abelson, R. *Scripts, plans, goals, and understanding.* Hillsdale, N.J.: Lawrence Erlbaum Associates, 1977.

Scharf, D. J. Some relationships between measures of early language development. *Journal of Speech and Hearing Disorders,* 1972, *37,* 64-74.

Schiefelbusch, R. L. (Ed.). *Bases of language intervention.* Baltimore: University Park Press, 1978. (a)

Schiefelbusch, R. L. (Ed.). *Language intervention strategies.* Baltimore: University Park Press, 1978. (b)

Schiefelbusch, R. L., & Lloyd, L. L. *Language perspectives—Acquisition, retardation, and intervention.* Baltimore: University Park Press, 1974.

Schlesinger, I. M., & Namir, L. (Eds.). *Sign language of the deaf.* New York: Academic Press, 1978.

Scholes, R. J., Rasbury, W. C., Scholes, I. B., & Dowling, K. Sentence comprehension and short-term memory: Some developmental considerations. *Language & Speech,* 1976, *19,* 80-86.

Searle, J. R. *Speech acts.* Cambridge: Cambridge University Press, 1969.

Searle, J. R. A classification of illocutionary acts. *Language in Society,* 1976, *5,* 1–23.
Shatz, M. On the development of communicative understanding: An early strategy for interpreting and responding to messages. *Cognitive Psychology,* 1978, *10,* 271–301.
Shriner, T. H. A review of mean length of response as a measure of expressive language development in children. *Journal of Speech and Hearing Disorders,* 1969, *34,* 61–68.
Shriner, T. H., & Miner, L. Morphological structures in the language of disadvantaged and advantaged children. *Journal of Speech and Hearing Research,* 1968, *11,* 605–610.
Siegel, L. S., McCabe, A. E., Brand, J., & Matthews, J. Evidence for the understanding of class inclusion in preschool children: Linguistic factors and training effects. *Child Development,* 1978, *49,* 688–693.
Siegman, A. W., & Feldstein, S. *Of speech and times: Temporal speech patterns in interpersonal contexts.* Hillsdale, N.J.: Lawrence Erlbaum Associates, 1979.
Sinclair, A., Jarvella, R. J., & Levelt, W. J. M. (Eds.). *The child's conception of language.* Berlin: Springer-Verlage, 1978.
Sinclair, H. Sensorimotor action patterns as a condition for the acquisition of syntax. In R. Huxley & E. Ingram (Eds.), *Language acquisition: Models and methods.* New York: Academic Press, 1971.
Sinclair, H. Language and cognition in subnormals. In N. O'Connor (Ed.), *Language, cognitive deficits, and retardation.* London: Butterworths, 1975.
Sinclair-deZwart, H. Language acquisition and cognitive development. In T. E. Moore (Ed.), *Cognitive development and the acquisition of language.* New York: Academic Press, 1973.
Slobin, D. I. Universals of grammatical development in children. In G. B. Flores d'Arcais & W. J. M. Levelt (Eds.), *Advances in psycholinguistics. Amsterdam:* North-Holland, 1970.
Slobin, D. I. Developmental psycholinguistics. In W. O. Dingwall (Ed.), *A survey of linguistic science.* College Park, Md.: Linguistics Program, University of Maryland, 1971.
Slobin, D. I. Cognitive prerequisites for the development of grammar. In C. A. Ferguson & D. I. Slobin (Eds.), *Studies of child language development.* New York: Holt, Rinehart and Winston, 1973.
Smith, F. *Psycholinguistics and reading.* New York: Holt, Rinehart and Winston, 1973.
Smith, N. V. Syntax for psychologists. In J. Morton & J. C. Marshall (Eds.), *Psycholinguistics 2.* Cambridge, Mass.: MIT Press, 1979.
Smith, N., & Wilson, D. *Modern linguistics: The results of Chomsky's revolution.* Bloomington, Ind.: Indiana University Press, 1979.
Snow, C. E. The development of conversation between mothers and babies. *Journal of Child Language,* 1977, *4,* 1–22.
Snow, C. E., Arlman-Rupp, A., Hassing, Y., Jobse, J., Joosten, J., & Vorster, J. Mothers' speech in three social classes. *Journal of Psycholinguistic Research,* 1976, *5,* 1–20.
Snow, C. E., & Ferguson, C. A. *Talking to children.* Cambridge: Cambridge University Press, 1977.
Snow, C. E., & Hoefnagel-Höhle, M. Age differences in the pronunciation of foreign sounds. *Language & Speech,* 1977, *20,* 357–365.
Snow, C. E., & Hoefnagel-Höhle, M. The critical period for language acquisition: Evidence from second language learning. *Child Development,* 1978, *49,* 1114–1128.
Snyder, L. K., & McLean, J. E. *American Journal of Mental Deficiency,* 1976, *81,* 338–349.
Snyder, L. K., & McLean, J. E. Deficient acquisition strategies: A proposed conceptual framework for analyzing severe language deficiency. *American Journal of Mental Deficiency,* 1977, *81,* 338–349.
Snyder-McLean, L. K., & McLean, J. E. Verbal information gathering strategies: The child's use of language to acquire language. *Journal of Speech and Hearing Disorders,* 1978, *43,* 306–325.
Sommers, R. K., Erdige, S., & Peterson, M. K. How valid are children's language tests? *Journal of Special Education,* 1978, *12,* 393–407.

1. INTRODUCTION, FOUNDATIONS AND OVERVIEW

Starr, S. Discrimination of syntactical errors in children under two and one-half years. *Developmental Psychology,* 1974, *10,* 381-386.
Stewart, D. M., & Hamilton, M. L. Imitation as a learning strategy in the acquisition of vocabulary. *Journal of Experimental Child Psychology,* 1976, *21,* 380-392.
Stick, S. L., & Norris, J. A. Use of situational cues by preschool children. *Journal of Psycholinguistic Research,* 1979, *8,* 111-121.
Tanz, C. Cognitive principles underlying children's errors in pronominal case-marking. *Journal of Child Language,* 1974, *1,* 271-276.
Tomlinson-Keasy, C., Kelly, R. R., & Burton, J. K. Hemispheric changes in information processing during development. *Developmental Psychology,* 1978, *14,* 214-223.
Trembath, A. A. Comparison of sensitivity to the surface and deep structure of sentences in children. *Language & Speech,* 1972, *15,* 51-57.
Tyler, L. K., & Marslen-Wilson, W. Some developmental aspects of sentence processing and memory. *Journal of Child Language,* 1978, *5,* 113-129.
Van Duyne, J. J., Bakker, D., & deJong, W. Development of ear-asymmetry related to coding processes in memory in children. *Brain and Language,* 1977, *4,* 322-334.
Vellutino, F. R. *Dyslexia: Theory and research.* Cambridge, Mass.: MIT Press, 1979.
Walker, E. (Ed.). *Explorations in the biology of language.* Montgomery, Vt.: Bradford Books, 1978.
Waryas, C. L. Psycholinguistic research in language intervention programming: The pronoun system. *Journal of Psycholinguistic Research,* 1973, *2,* 221-237.
Waryas, C., & Ruder, K. On the limitations of language comprehension procedures and an alternative. *Journal of Speech and Hearing Disorders,* 1974, *39,* 44-52.
Washington, D. S., & Naremore, R. C. Children's use of spatial prepositions in two- and three-dimensional tasks. *Journal of Speech and Hearing Research,* 1978, *21,* 151-165.
Wells, G. Learning to code experience through language. *Journal of Child Language,* 1974, *1,* 243-269.
Wetstone, H. S., & Friedlander, B. Z. The effect of word order on young children's responses to simple questions and commands. *Child Development,* 1973, *44,* 334-340.
Whitehurst, G. J. Comprehension, selective imitation, and the CIP hypothesis. *Journal of Experimental Child Psychology,* 1977, *23,* 23-38.
Whitehurst, G. J., & Vasta, R. Is language acquired through imitation? *Journal of Psycholinguistic Research,* 1975, *4,* 37-59.
Wiig, E. H. Language disabilities of adolescents: Implications for diagnosis and remediation. *British Journal of Disorders of Communication,* 1976, *11,* 3-17.
Wilcox, M. J., & Leonard, L. B. Experimental acquisition of WH-questions in language-disordered children. *Journal of Speech and Hearing Research,* 1978, *21,* 220-239.
Willbrand, M. L. Psycholinguistic theory and therapy for initiating two-word utterances. *British Journal of Disorders of Communication,* 1977, *12,* 37-46.
Williams, A. M., Marks, C., & Bialer, I. Validity of the Peabody picture vocabulary test as a measure of hearing vocabulary in mentally retarded and normal children. *Journal of Speech & Hearing Research,* 1977, *20,* 205-211.
Wyke, M. A., (Ed.). *Developmental dysphasia.* London: Academic Press, 1978.
Yoder, D. E. Evaluation and assessment of children's language and speech behavior. In M. V. Wisland (Ed.), *Psychoeducational diagnosis of exceptional children.* Springfield, Ill.: Thomas, 1974.
Yule, W., Berger, M., & Howlin, P. Language deficit and behavior modification. In N. O'Connor (Ed.), *Language, cognitive deficits and retardation.* London: Butterworths, 1975.

READING, WRITING AND LANGUAGE LEARNING

2 Theoretical Issues in the Study of Word Recognition: The Unit of Perception Controversy Reexamined

Frank R. Vellutino
Child Research and Study Center
The University at Albany

INTRODUCTION

How does a skilled reader recognize a word? This question has generated an impressive body of literature over the years, and exploration of its parameters and dimensions has consumed the energies of researchers studying mental processes since before the turn of the century (Cattell, 1886a, 1886b; Erdmann & Dodge, 1898; Pillsbury, 1897). Understanding of the word recognition process is, of course, related to the more general question of how an individual extracts meaning from written language and is, in fact, propaedeutic to an understanding of the critical processes involved in learning to read. Historic and contemporary interest in reading is no accident because, to reiterate Huey's (1908) much quoted comment: To completely analyze what we do when we read would almost be the acme of a psychologist's achievements, for it would be to describe very many of the most intricate workings of the human mind [p. 6].

Ironically, the theoretical issues of central concern to investigators who were among the first to conduct laboratory study of the reading process continue to preoccupy present-day researchers, and many of these issues are yet unresolved. Reminiscent of the early inquiries of Cattell and others are the multitude of studies and theoretical expositions that seek to define the unit of perception in word recognition. And debated no less now than in years past are certain critically related issues—namely, the degree to which word recognition involves serial versus parallel or holistic processing of component letters, direct versus phonologically mediated access to lexical entries, and sequential/hierarchical (bottom–up) versus context driven (top–down) and/or interactive processing of letter and word features. The present chapter is primarily concerned with the first of those mentioned—the unit of perception issue. The controversy that surrounds this issue stems from vastly different theoretical views as to the level of analysis at which word recognition is most likely facilitated. The currently debated alternatives correspond to processing units at the level of word features, component letters, letter clusters, and whole words, but there is as yet no research evidence that unequivocally favors one over the other. At the same time, there is reason to believe that any one of these units might be critically involved in the recognition process, depending on the nature and purpose of the task set before the perceiver, the construction of the materials he or she encounters in that task, and the competencies he or she has available to engage it. A number of studies have recently shown, for example, that the level of visual analysis may vary in accord with task demands, implying perhaps that word recognition necessitates a variety of strategies that the skilled reader apparently has at his or her disposal. Such findings could also be taken as an indication that the unit of perception is relative rather than absolute, the latter being the explicit assumption adopted by most researchers studying the problem over the years. If so then the concept would require redefinition. Thus a major objective of this chapter is to reexamine the unit of perception issue in light of certain research findings and theoretical arguments that highlight the variable nature of the word recognition process as well as the flexibility that characterizes the human information processor in achieving veridical perception. This latter point, itself, underscores a factor that has been sorely neglected in the literature and that is the qualitative differences in word recognition that might be occasioned by individual differences in the skill of the reader.

A curious paradox exists in that almost all the research available in the study of word perception and the models that have been offered to characterize this process have been generated on the basis of work done with highly skilled adult readers—typically college students. Furthermore, very few of those who have attempted to formalize the structural and functional components of word recognition have made an effort to incorporate developmental and/or individual difference variables into their conceptualizations of the process. Yet consideration of these variables could conceivably alter or at least illuminate even critical dimensions of given models so as either to limit or to increase their explanatory power. At the same time, it is likely that qualifications issueing from pointed study of developmental and individual differences in the process variables involved in learning to read would eventuate in the construction of more comprehensive models of word perception that would not only increase our understanding of the process but could also account for differences that might be found between the skilled and less skilled reader. Thus, a second major objective of the present chapter is to analyze critically the unit of perception issue within a developmental framework, systematically relating alternative conceptualizations emanating from work done with mature readers to theoretical arguments and empirical findings emanating from the study of reading ability in young children. The assumption motivating this analysis is that a comprehensive understanding of the complex mechanisms employed by fluent readers in identifying a word cannot be achieved without a comprehensive understanding of the mechanisms employed by the developing reader in doing so. Although no claim is made that such understanding has been achieved, there is now enough suggestive evidence from comparative study of skilled and less skilled readers to qualify theoretical constructs that have emerged from the study of word recognition in fluent adult readers.

The exposition that follows is divided into *four* sections. The first presents a brief description of the major concepts and schematics that are employed in the word recognition models to be discussed and is designed to lend structure to the discussions of those models. The second section defines the unit of perception issue, presenting both a brief chronology of the opposing viewpoints as well as more detailed descriptions of contemporary theories that advocate respective units of processing (i.e., features, letters, letter clusters, and whole words). Although the bulk of the discussion in this and subsequent sections is concerned with the unit of perception controversy, certain related issues are, of necessity, touched upon, in particular, the question of whether the letters in a word are processed serially or in parallel, the importance of phonologic mediation in word recognition, and the role of context in the recognition process.

The third section constitutes documentation of the contention that the unit of perception is relative and is itself divided into three major subsections. The first of these subsections is concerned with the influence of contextual factors on word recognition and specifically discusses the methodological differences in the studies that have yielded conflicting results and highlights two significant observations: (1) that experimental procedures employed in these studies typically created perceptual biases in their subjects that favored particular theories being evaluated; and (2) that these subjects were quite able to vary their perceptual strategies in accord with the dictates of the task presented to them. The second subsection is focused upon the structural and functional differences among the words that may be encountered by the reader and presents evidence that such differences necessitate different processing strategies for recognition and identification. The arguments advanced in the latter sections are buttressed in the third subsection, which discusses the unit of perception issue within a developmental framework. The major theme that evolves in this section is that skilled reading represents the end product of a protracted developmental progression characterized by a gradual transition from constrained to flexible modes of visual analysis, some of which are unconscious and automatic and some of which are optional and deliberate. The converse of this theme is that unskilled reading implies inflexible and idiosyncratic modes of analysis, and research contrasting processing strategies in skilled and unskilled readers is presented.

Two Convenient Heuristics

A Three-Stage Model of Memory

Before proceeding to the substantive issues to be discussed, it would seem useful to characterize briefly the component systems theoretically involved in word recognition and the types of information processed by those systems. Figure 2.1 presents a three-stage model of memory taken from Atkinson, Herrmann, and Wescourt (1974). In simplified form, the model depicts the processing components that might be involved in recognizing and identifying a word, from initial pickup of its physical features to production of an identifying response. The first

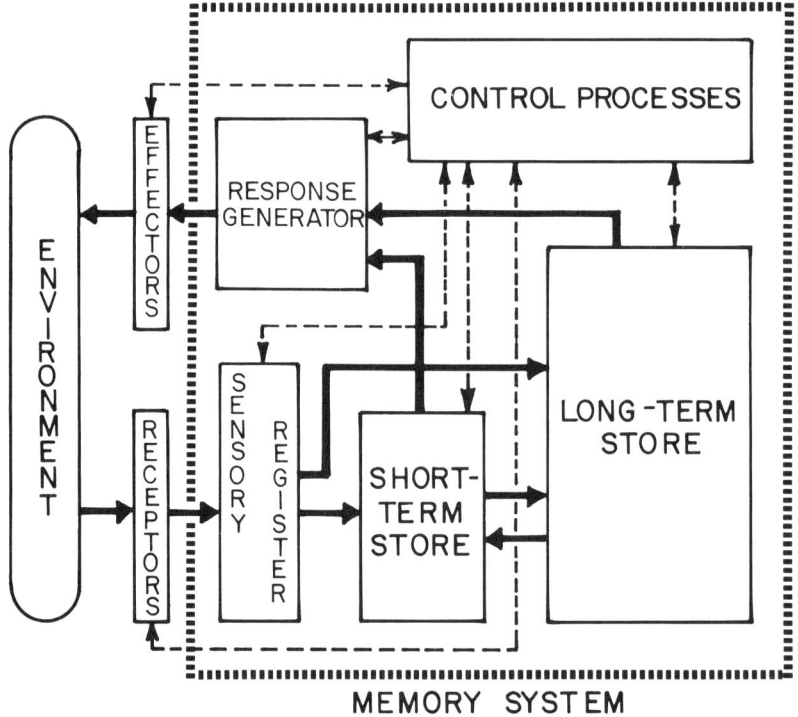

FIG. 2.1. Three-stage model of memory depicting stages of information processing (taken from Atkinson, Hermann, & Wescourt, 1974, with permission of the authors and publisher).

component—*sensory register*—encompasses processes that record physical stimuli in raw uncoded forms for very brief durations (e.g., 200–300 msec for visual stimuli, Sperling, 1963). It is during this stage of processing that the visual features of letters and words are believed to be analyzed and encoded.

The second major component depicted is *short-term store,* or working memory, as it is called by some. This is believed to be a limited capacity system, able to retain from five to nine "chunks" of information for short durations (approximately 30 sec, Glanzer & Cunitz, 1966), depending on one's ability to organize and rehearse the material to be retained. It seems reasonable to suppose that the type of lexical information processed by short-term memory would vary with the skill of the reader and the nature of the reading task. In the case of word analysis, an enterprise that often consumes the energies of beginning readers, letter and word features as well as letters and/or letter clusters might constitute respective processing units. The fluent reader, in contrast, more often utilizes short-term memory for temporary storage of words and phrases, while processing the constituents of sentences encountered in running text.

Long-term memory is an unlimited capacity system that retains information indefinitely, but retrieval of particular items is dependent on one's ability to set up a mental "filing system" that facilitates efficient search and location. With regard to word recognition and identification, long-term memory might be considered the repository of all the information contained within and about a written word, which obviously includes associations with its verbal counterpart in spoken language. Such information encompasses a word's *graphic* or visual features, its *orthographic* or structural components, its *phonologic* or auditory characteristics, and its *syntactic* and *semantic* properties, the latter two referring, respectively, to its functional use in sentences and its meaning (Gibson, 1971). That component of long-term memory that records and catalogs lexical information—that is, information about a word's featural characteristics—is often termed the *lexicon.*

The output component of the processing model presented in Fig. 2.1 is referred to as the *response generator.* The response generator is intended to refer to the complex of processes responsible for selecting the naming response and for programming the articulatory movements necessary for pronunciation.

Some models of the word recognition process incorporate an executive component that links memorial subsystems to one another, facilitates selective attention, determines coding and rehearsal strategies, and (by virtue of multiple feedback loops) generally performs a monitoring function that serves to validate accurate perceptions and correct misperceptions. This component is termed *control processes* in the model depicted in Fig. 2.1. Control processes are almost certainly involved in new learning (Calfee, 1975; Vellutino, 1979) and by some accounts (Rumelhart, 1977) play a dynamic role in identifying familiar words as well.

The final point to be made concerning the memory model presented in Fig. 2.1 is that the subsystems are interconnected, both by direct lines of transmission and by virtue of the links that two component systems commonly have with a third. This feature of the model will be especially useful in contrasting theories of word recognition that respectively advocate direct and mediated access to word meanings stored in long-term memory.

Types of Information Involved in Word Recognition

The information-processing model discussed in the preceding section provides a broad schematic that roughly corresponds with stages of memory that might be involved in word recognition and identification, but it does not detail particular mechanisms that characterize respective stages relative to the types of information processed by those mechanisms. Table 2.1 provides such detail. The information outlined is arrayed in rough correspondence with the sensory, perceptual, and cognitive components of word recognition and identification, but (as indicated by the asterisks) the so-called "unit of perception" varies with given theories. The processes listed in items 1, 2, and 3 constitute the sensory components of word recognition, the mechanisms responsible for these components encompassing the sensory register stage of information processing (Fig. 2.1). Item 1 refers to the light-wave pattern created by the word stimulus. Item 2—the icon—refers to an encoded representation of the physical energy given off by the stimulus, maintained in temporary storage for approximately 250 msec. This stage of visual processing is what Massaro (1975) terms preperceptual visual storage (see Fig. 2.2) and initiates feature detection, a process characterized by differential sensitivity to the graphic features of a word stimulus (lines, curves, angles, supraletter features such as the "roundness" of CO or the "squareness" quality of IN) and, by some accounts (Estes, 1977, Johnson, 1977), information as to the orientation and position of letters. Feature detection thereafter energizes the feature analysis process (item 3), during which the unique characteristics of letters (item 4), letter groups (item 5), and/or whole words (item 6) are analyzed and mapped onto corresponding codes in long-term memory that transform a word's graphic features into units of recognition. The output of feature analysis constitutes the input to the perceptual component of word recognition, as conceptualized in given models to be discussed. The perceptual component is not graphically depicted in the memory model presented in Fig. 2.1 but is characterized in most models as a processing stage intermediate to the sensory and short-term memory stages of information processing (see Fig. 2.2). Item 4 earmarks component letters as the units of perception, and items 5 and 6 earmark letter clusters and whole-word patterns as perceptual units.

Item 7 refers to the phonologic component of word recognition, which corresponds, respectively, to phonologic recoding and articulatory programming. Phonologic recoding is the process whereby letter strings are transformed into abstract representations of the sound sequences that comprise a printed word,

TABLE 2.1
Types of Information, Component Processes, and Output Responses Hypothesized
in Different Theories of Word Recognition

			Types of Theories			
Types of Information	Process	Responses	Feature Theories	Component Letter Theories	Letter Cluster Theories	Whole-Word Pattern Theories
1. Light energy	Stimulation of visual receptors		X	X	X	X
2. Icon	Brief visual storage	Feature detection	X	X	X	X
3. Letter and/or supraletter features	Analysis of letter features	Feature discrimination and encoding	X	X	X	X
4. Letter strings	Letter recognition	Letter encoding		X[a]	X	
5. Orthographic patterns (spelling clusters, vocalic center groups, etc.)	Letter parsing and grouping	Letter cluster and/or syllable encoding		X	X[a]	
6. Whole-word features and/or patterns	Whole-word pattern analysis	Whole-word pattern encoding	X[a]			X[a]
7. Phonologic	Phonologic recoding and/or articulatory programming	Pronunciation and/or naming		X	X	
8. Semantic and syntactic	Cognition and conceptualization	Comprehension of meaning	X	X	X	X

[a]Type of information constituting unit of perception.

considered by some to be prerequisite to its recognition (Gough, 1972; Spoehr & Smith, 1973). Articulatory programming accords roughly with response selection and pronunciation.

Finally, item 8 depicts what may be termed the *cognitive* or *conceptual component* of the word recognition process. The cognitive component stores information as to a word's meaning and its use in sentences, referring, respectively, to its semantic and syntactic characteristics. Atkinson et al. (1974) suggest that such knowledge depends in part on the storage of "conceptual codes" that define the "classes of conceptual relations that may be entered by the concept represented by a word [p. 104]." It is noted subsequently that although there is considerable agreement as to the type of information processed by the conceptual component of the memory system, by no means is there a consensus as to the role of such information in word recognition.

In sum, the schematics presented in Fig. 2.1 and Table 2.1 should make it clear that the word recognition process is exceedingly complex, involving the integration of five major classes of information: *graphic, orthographic, phonologic, semantic,* and *syntactic*. The use of such information in the word recognition process and the means by which it may be utilized has been the object of close scrutiny for over 80 years, and research in the area has generated certain controversial issues that are yet unresolved. It is those issues to which I now turn my attention.

THE UNIT OF PERCEPTION IN WORD RECOGNITION: CONTEMPORARY THEORIES

As already noted, one of the unresolved controversies in the study of word recognition is the processing level at which visual analysis of a letter string facilitates discrimination of a familiar word, otherwise termed the *unit of perception* (see Table 2.1). This question was originally raised by Cattell (1886a, 1886b), who found that subjects could identify two four-letter words better than three or four unrelated letters at brief tachistoscopic exposures. He also found that the time taken to perceive a whole word (measured in latencies) was no greater than the time taken to perceive a single letter. Cattell concluded from these results that words must be recognized as integrated wholes and that we do not therefore perceive their component letters separately. Thus for Cattell the word rather than the letter was the unit of perception. This idea was reinforced by research undertaken by Erdmann and Dodge (1898), who demonstrated that whole words could be identified at distances too great to permit identification of their letters.

Cattell's suggestion that the whole word is the unit of perception was the dominant theme in the scattered accounts that appeared during the first half of the twentieth century. This view was no doubt buttressed by the work of the Gestalt psychologists (Kohler, 1929; Wertheimer, 1923), whose influential theories eschewed atomistic explanations of perceptual phenomena and gave rise to the deceptively simple but rather encompassing characterization that the "whole is something other than the sum of its parts." The whole-word theory therefore went unchallenged until the middle of the fifth decade when Miller, Bruner, and Postman (1954) produced results that suggested that the word advantage observed on short-term memory tasks need not be attributed to the preeminence of the word as an integrated unit and may instead be associated with the sequential redundancy that characterizes English orthography. These authors found that briefly exposed pseudowords, having letter distributions that closely approximated the statistical structure of printed English (e.g., *vernalit* and *ricaning*), were identified much better than random letter strings presented under identical stimulus conditions. It was suggested, in explanation of these findings, that an implicit knowledge of orthographic structure facilitates interletter predictability, thereby compensating for short-term memory limits by increasing the size of the processing unit (or "chunk") while maintaining invariance in the total amount of information to be processed. Thus the word *CHUNK* contains three processing units rather than five, because the letters in the clusters *CH* and *NK* often appear in the same sequence in printed English and therefore constitute redundant information. The net affect is that *CHUNK* would be no more difficult to remember on a short-term memory task than the three unconnected letters, *ZTQ* and less difficult than the letter string *ZTQMR,* which contains five processing units rather than three.

Miller et al.'s (1954) study is significant in that it provided initial evidence that it is not necessary to postulate a perceptual unit as large as the word in order to account for the word advantage effect observed by Cattell (1886a, 1886b) and others, inasmuch as a similar effect was demonstrated in comparisons of pseudowords and randomly arrayed letters. It is also important because the research findings and the conclusions drawn constitute a sharp departure from traditional interpretations of perceptual phenomena (e.g., Gestalt theorizing) and are more in line with the information-processing theories of cognitive functioning that emerged at the time (Shannon, 1951). However, the results of this investigation did not permit specification as to whether the word advantage effect is a perceptual phenomenon or an interpretive phenomenon resulting from inferential or decision processes at the level of short-term memory (Broadbent, 1967; Neisser, 1967). The data also left unanswered the more basic question of just how a familiar word is recognized and at what level of processing. Thus, Gibson, Pick, Osser, and Hammond (1962) essentially replicated Miller et al.'s (1954) findings, systematically varying the "pronounceability" of letter strings presented to subjects, and concluded that the word advantage is a perceptual effect. They also concluded that the spelling cluster rather than the word or letter is the unit of perception. Both conclusions were based on the idea that words and pronounceable pseudowords are inherently more perceptible than random letter strings, because, unlike random letter strings, they can be analyzed in accord with spelling-sound correspondences, which were thought to be perceptual invariants that facilitate economy of processing and discrimination of distinctive features (Gibson, 1971). This interpretation was not widely accepted, in part because the beneficial effect of pronounceability was later observed with deaf subjects (Gibson, Shurcliff, & Yonas, 1970). And while a conceptualization of word perception that is quite similar to the spelling cluster hypothesis materialized a short time later (Spoehr & Smith, 1973), other investigators have provided support for the alternative possibilities that the letter (Massaro, 1973) and the letter feature (Rumelhart & Siple, 1974; Smith, 1971) constitute respective units of perception.

Complicating the picture still further is the fact that the whole-word theory proved to be more tenacious than might have been predicted earlier. Specifically, Reicher (1969), using a postcue (partial report) procedure that controlled for sequential redundancy and short-term memory factors, demonstrated that single letters could be recognized better when embedded in words than within the context of random letter strings. To be specific, on trials on which subjects were presented with brief exposures of real words (e.g., *WORD*) and asked to report a single letter from that word immediately after, the (forced choice) response alternatives were always the target letter and a foil that completed the spelling of another real word (e.g., *K* and *D*). Reicher also found that a letter could be recognized better within a word than when presented alone and concluded from these results that a word must be a higher-order unit that provides more information for component letter recognition than does a random letter string or a letter itself. He therefore suggested that previous interpretations attributing the "word superiority" effect to orthographic redundancy or guessing biases may be in error. Wheeler (1970) replicated Reicher's findings, controlling for sensory processing factors as well as attentional and response bias, and came to a similar conclusion. Although these findings did not go unchallenged (Massaro, 1973; Thompson & Massaro, 1973), the word as perceptual unit hypothesis was effectively revived and came to have a number of latter day advocates (Johnson, 1975, 1977; Johnston & McClelland, 1973) who have argued with refreshed vigor against word perception theories that postulate subword components as units of recognition.

It should be clear from this brief chronology that the theoretical arguments generated by psychologists' attempts to define the unit of perception in word recognition has gone full circle during the past 85 years. Indeed, there seems to be little more consensus than during the period directly following Cattell's initial paper on the topic. This is somewhat disconcerting, given the fact that the conflicting arguments issue from relatively well-articulated theories evaluated, for the most part, by well-designed and well-executed studies that have frequently yielded directly opposite findings. How can we account for this state of affairs? Is there any way that these disparate positions can be reconciled? One obvious possibility is that particular experimental procedures, employed in studies addressing the issue, may have differentially biased subjects toward processing word constituents at different levels of analysis. As evident in a later section, there is reason to believe that this explanation can account for much of the disparity in the research findings reported in the literature. However, a more encompassing explanation can be offered. I would like to suggest that ultimate resolution of the controversy surrounding the perceptual unit issue may well be occasioned by serious consideration of the possibility that the unit of perception in word recognition is relative rather than absolute and depends on three important factors: (1) the conditions under which a given word is encountered; (2) the structural characteristics of the word itself; and (3) the knowledge, experience, and skill of the reader.

The first of these is exemplified in the possibility that the level of processing required for word perception may vary in accord with whether or not a given word is encountered in isolation, as in most studies addressing the unit of perception issue, or within the context of meaningful sentences. It seems to me that a word presented in a meaningful context often necessitates only a global analysis of intraword components, inasmuch as the number of contextually appropriate alternatives having graphic and orthographic characteristics in common with the stimulus word is greatly reduced. In contrast, a word presented in isolation often requires a more fine-grained analysis before a discrimination can be made, because without meaningful context the number of possible alternatives having (graphic and orthographic) characteristics in common with the stimulus is greatly magnified. This, of course, underscores the second factor just mentioned, that the level of processing will be significantly influenced by the structural characteristics of the word itself.

In all likelihood, words that have a high degree of visual and structural similarity will necessitate a good deal more processing at subword levels than do words that have a minimal degree of similarity. Thus word pairs such as *was* and *saw* no doubt prompt visual analysis at the letter level, whereas the words *hippopotamus* and *Mississippi* are easily discriminated from most other words at the whole-word level.

However, the probability that a given processing strategy will be employed in discriminating one word from another would itself seem to be dependent on the skill of the reader such that the greater the skill, the more flexible and efficient the level of analysis. This presents the possibility of individual differences with respect to typical processing modes, the implication being that there is some degree of variability in the tendency to analyze words more often at one level than at another.

I discuss each of these factors in greater detail in a later section and attempt to document my arguments with recent research findings issuing from the study of processing differences in skilled as compared with less skilled readers. However, before doing so, it is instructive to review each of the competing theories of word recognition that advocate particular units as the basis for word perception, adding my own editorial comments as seems indicated. In each instance, the unit of perception is taken as the level of processing required to effect recognition and identification of a letter string as a familiar percept.

Feature Theories

Extraction-Type Theories

In an extensive review of the topic, Smith and Spoehr (1974) distinguish between "extraction"- and "interpretation"-type theories of word perception, both typically emphasizing word features as the basis for recognition (see Table 2.1). The earliest type of extraction theory that appeared in the literature is exemplified in Pillsbury's (1897) suggestion that the features that distinguish a word's shape (ascenders, descenders, etc.) constitute the primary basis for its recognition. This particular explanation, though once popular, no longer has much currency and would seem to be questioned by the fact that words can be recognized regardless of whether they are printed in lowercase letters, uppercase letters (E. Smith & Haviland, 1972), or alternating cases (F. Smith, Lott, & Cronnell, 1969). Thus extraction theories that emerged subsequently typically posit that the features that discriminate given words are, more often, the unique features of the individual letters that comprise those words and/or the supraletter features that characterize combinations of letters (e.g., the "squareness" quality of NI). For example, in attempting to account for the word superiority effect (i.e., that letters can be perceived better in words than in nonwords or when presented alone), Wheeler (1970) suggested that words contain "more features" with which to discriminate component letters, including overall shape and supraletter and letter characteristics. Implied here is an interactive process whereby familiarity with a word's multiple features directly influence one's ability to extract discriminating information as, for example, in distinguishing between the response alternative K and D after a brief exposure to the stimulus word, *WORK*.

An alternative suggestion made by Wheeler (1970) is that extraction of relevant features may occur more selectively, such that features extracted initially may direct subsequent processing so as to maximize the probability of detecting features that facilitate discrimination (Feigenbaum, 1963). The common factor in both of these suggestions is attentional limitations, compounded by short-term memory constraints that impede perception of letters in the whole word less than perception of letters presented singly or in random strings, inasmuch as the information contained in the word facilitates selective processing of relevant featural information.

Wheeler's second suggestion is compatible with Rumelhart's (1970) limited capacity theory of letter recognition, in that both make reference to attentional limitations in the extraction of featural information. However, this aspect of the two theories would seem to be questioned by Shiffrin and Gardner's (1972) finding that sequential presentations of letter stimuli occasion no better performance in letter recognition than simultaneous presentations, suggesting that feature extraction is an automatic process that is not influenced by selective attention and capacity limitations. Although it is not difficult to imagine ways in which selective attention might affect letter and word discrimination, it may be that attentional limitations reflect processes subsequent to feature extraction, as suggested by Herman and Kantowitz (1970). The question is yet open and depends on additional research for its resolution; however it is worth noting that it relates to the more general question of whether or not higher-order cognitive processes can directly influence feature extraction, which it will be seen is a critical issue in the study of word recognition.[1]

Interpretation or Feature Redundancy-Type Theories

F. Smith's Theory. To continue, the second variety of feature theory discussed by Smith and Spoehr (1974)—that is, the "interpretation" theory—has received somewhat greater accord in the literature. Interpretation theories assign much more responsibility to decision processes than do extraction theories and place particular emphasis on the reader's implicit knowledge of orthographic structure as a functional component of these processes. I first discuss the feature redundancy theory of F. Smith (1971).

Smith assumes that the features that uniquely define a word are the features of the component letters in that word, extracted simultaneously from all letter positions. However, in Smith's model, word recognition is mediated neither by prior recognition of a word's component letters nor by recognition of combinations of those letters. He suggests instead that a word's representation in long-term memory includes several functionally equivalent feature lists for each letter in that word, along with information as to the sequential dependencies, which can occur among given letters, as defined by English orthography. The feature lists for each letter are functionally equivalent in that each defines a different size or shaped character, corresponding to a particular letter category (e.g., A, a, α). This aspect of the model is in keeping with the observation that words can be recognized in a variety of different fonts and cases.

In an attempt to circumvent the obvious strain on memory that would seem to be occasioned by the acquisition and functional use of such detailed information (Massaro, 1975), Smith proposes that the sequential dependencies that characterize the letters in English orthography facilitate the development of what he terms "criterial sets" of features defining a given word. These constitute a limited

---

[1]Wheeler (1970) offered a third alternative, which in essence suggests that the feature extraction process may yield fragmented information that prompts "sophisticated guessing" (Neisser, 1967; Newbigging, 1961) as to a word's identity. Although sophisticated guessing cannot be ruled out as a partial explanation for performance under some circumstances (e.g., with highly degraded stimuli), it falls short as a general explanation for word recognition phenomena and for the word superiority effect in particular. This is illustrated by Reicher's (1969) finding that letters were recognized better in words than in nonwords, even when the letter alternatives were known beforehand. Similarly, E. Smith and Haviland (1972) equated words with nonwords for distributional and sequential redundancy and found that the word-nonword difference was maintained.

sampling of the features derived from respective letters in that word that allow recognition to take place economically, that is, on the basis of a select array of distinguishing features, the sum of which is smaller than the total number that might be required for recognition of the letters themselves. In other words, the total number of features required to recognize the word *HORSE* might be less than the number yielded by adding the respective totals required for recognition of each letter in that word.

Smith's characterization of the word recognition process is straightforward. Upon initial input, the feature discrimination process yields a candidate set of letter features that tentatively define a stored word category, and the reader's implicit knowledge of orthographic redundancy allows selective and efficient sampling of stimulus features until the correct match is made and the word's meaning is apprehended. The word's name or pronunciation is considered to be a "trivial" by-product of this process, access to meaning being direct and unfettered by phonologic or sound mediation. This course would be characterized in the memory model described earlier (Fig. 2.1), as initiating in the sensory register where feature discrimination and extraction take place, proceeding directly to long-term memory wherein the word is comprehended and culminating in a naming response if this component of the response generator is activated.

Supporting evidence for Smith's theory comes primarily from two sources. The first, issues from studies by Smith and his associates, demonstrating that words can be recognized in alternating cases (F. Smith, 1969; F. Smith et al. 1969). Smith concludes from these findings that functionally equivalent feature sets must be the basis for identifying words rather than particular letter shapes. Yet these results could as readily be taken as support for a letter-based theory of word recognition, inasmuch as Smith's studies provide no firm evidence that letter features rather than the letters themselves facilitate recognition of stimulus words presented in alternating cases.

The second source of evidence comes from F. Smith's (1969) demonstration that sequential dependencies between letters in English orthography facilitate word recognition. This finding is, of course, reliable (Gibson et al., 1962; Miller et al., 1954) and has been replicated several times over. However, it provides no more support for feature theories than it does for component letter- or cluster-type theories of word perception, because each incorporates constructs that lean heavily upon the structural regularities of printed English for their validation. Thus the support Smith has marshaled for his theory is not compelling.

Two final points might be made about Smith's theory. First, it is one of several direct access theories (Morton, 1969; Rumelhart & Siple, 1974), which make the assumption that a word's meaning is accessed directly without any intermediate stages of processing. Thus, according to Smith, apprehension of an orthographically constrained sequence of letter features that represent a given word immediately makes contact with stored representations of that word's semantic and syntactic characteristics, from which its phonologic characteristics (e.g., its name) are derived. The second point is that, in Smith's model, semantic and syntactic redundancy are assigned as much importance as orthographic redundancy, all three variables facilitating selective sampling of letter and word features as well as text processing at higher levels of integration. Thus, he allows for the possibility that such information can directly affect the feature extraction process. However, Smith has not attempted to formalize the interrelationships among these latter variables and, to my knowledge, has produced no research support for either the direct access or the contextual components of his model.

Rumelhart and Siple's Theory. A more elaborate formalization of the feature redundancy-type theory is the word recognition model described by Rumelhart and Siple (1974). This model is similar to Smith's in that both postulate that a select sampling of letter features constitutes the basis for word recognition rather than prior identification of the letters themselves. Both also incorporate the notion that orthographic redundancy facilitates feature selection. However, it differs from Smith's in that it incorporates a decision process that attempts to account for an individual's subjective expectations as to the probability that a particular stimulus will appear in a given context. This component of the model was designed to account for word frequency effects that had been demonstrated in previous research (Broadbent, 1967; Morton, 1969; Neisser, 1967), the implication from such studies being that high-frequency words are more "perceptible" than low-frequency words. Rumelhart and Siple's (1974) model also goes beyond Smith's in that it empirically defines a prototypical feature set consisting of straight-line segments of different lengths and orientations that permit explicit quantification of the "functional features" that might facilitate the recognition process.

The important parameters in Rumelhart and Siple's model are presumed to be interactive. As in similar models, feature extraction follows exponential decay of the iconic image and is thus probabilistic. If the extraction process yields a functional set of features that exactly match the (featural) description of a stored word category, the word is identified. If the extraction process is imperfect and yields only a candidate set of functional features, the decision process generates several alternatives having these features in common, determined to greater or lesser extent by subjective probabilities as to the occurrence of respective items in the candidate set. The probabilities themselves are influenced, in part, by contextual factors and by an individual's a priori expectations, operationally defined in the form of word frequencies and the like. The final response selected is characterized as conforming to a Bayesian response rule that, by definition, incorporates both sets of parameters in determining the probability that a particular word occur.

It should be evident that in the theory of word recognition advanced by Rumelhart and Siple the decision processes specified might roughly accord with the control process depicted in the memory model presented in Fig. 2.1. Control processes presumably facilitate a dynamic flow of information among the various components of memory and, according to the theory, could directly influence feature detection and extraction.

Rumelhart and Siple tested their theory by comparing computer-generated data with experimentally derived results obtained in their laboratory. Subjects (college students) were given brief presentations of three letter strings that could be words, nonsense syllables, or unconnected letters, each type of stimulus occurring with differing probabilities. The dependent measure was full report of each letter string in correct order, scored accordingly. Stimulus characteristics were orthogonally varied and included *string frequency, transitional probabilities of letters,* and *letter confusability,* the last being based on the prototypical feature set mentioned earlier. Subjective probabilities were estimated from subjects' error patterns and the objective frequencies of the three different types of letter strings.

The computer-generated data were in close accord with the experimentally derived data, and all three parameters were found to have significant effects on response selection. Particularly significant was the success of the model in predicting interactions between given parameters, performance generally increasing with high string frequency, high transitional probability, and low letter confusability.

The foregoing results, although impressive, do not provide unequivocal support for the feature redundancy model of Rumelhart and Siple. For one thing, the experimental procedure employed (i.e., reporting letter sequences) did not lend itself to whole-word encoding and there is no necessary reason to believe that subjects were processing units any larger than the letter. To be specific, the entire stimulus set consisted of only three letter items comprised of letters with a high degree of similarity (all were straight-line figures), which may have prompted subjects to be more fine-grained in their analysis of word stimuli. In addition, the letter strings consisted of both words and nonwords, and all stimuli were presented randomly, which meant that subjects did not know when they would encounter one or the other stimulus type. These contingencies almost guaranteed component (perhaps even serial) letter processing. Supporting this interpretation are the subjective probabilities estimated from the distribution of subjects' errors, respectively: $P(\text{word}) = .12$; $P(\text{syllable}) = .40$; and $P(\text{letter}) = .47$. Given the likelihood that specific letters of many of the "syllable" responses were inferentially derived from the transitional probabilities associated with particular letter sequences, it would seem that the evidence could be taken as favoring letter rather than syllable or whole-word processing.

E. Smith and Spoehr (1974) raise a related question in pointing out that the full report procedure used by Rumelhart and Siple does not adequately control for response bias, thus presenting the possibility that obtained as well as simulated results reflect interpretive rather than perceptual processes. In fact, as also pointed out by E. Smith and Spoehr (1974), the frequency effect disappears with a forced-choice response procedure (Baron & Thurston, 1973), which further undermines the model as articulated.

The previous contraindications notwithstanding, feature redundancy theories such as F. Smith's and Rumelhart and Siple's can nevertheless account for the word superiority effect along with word frequency and word familiarity effects quite adequately. The blanket assumption that encompasses these effects is that the individual's familiarity with the featural attributes of given words facilitates recognition of the letters within those words. Thus, letters are recognized better in words than in random letter strings, because the individual has stored efficient criterial sets that facilitate discrimination. Similarly, words that are frequently encountered in print are processed more rapidly and more efficiently, because the reader is intimately better acquainted with their distinguishing features than with words that appear less often. In this connection, one might ask how else can discrimination occur, if not by feature analysis, in the case of word pairs such as *dad* and *bad, pig* and *big,* and *buck* and *duck* that are identical except for one graphic feature? Feature theories would seem to be able to account for the skilled reader's ability to effect such fine-grained discriminations more parsimoniously than theories that suggest that word constituents are processed at higher levels. Feature theories would also seem to be viable in explaining the skilled reader's ability to adopt a "global features" mode of processing (i.e., use of word length, shape, unique letter combinations, and the like) for discrimination, both when presented with words that are readily discriminated in any context—for example, words such as *Mississippi, hippopotamus,* and *Albuquerque*—and when encountering words that, in particular contexts, are highly predictable, as in the case of words such as *orthographically, pseudoword,* and *unequivocal,* which appear in papers such as the present one quite frequently. It would therefore seem that printed words are often recognized by means of feature level processing, although this by itself does not constitute sufficient validation of feature theories as the exclusive explanation for all word recognition phenomena.

Indeed, aside from the formidable processing load necessitated by any theory that requires memory for functionally equivalent feature sets for every letter in every word in one's reading vocabulary,[2] feature theories run aground on their inability to account for the repeated finding that orthographically legal pseudowords can be "perceived" practically as well as real words and, by some accounts (Baron & Thurston, 1973), equally as well. Stored feature lists, which according to the theory constitute the primary means for identifying familiar

---

[2]Massaro (1975, p. 226) points out that F. Smith's model provides no mechanism for "normalizing" features with respect to the particular font in which a word is printed. Thus, in recognizing a single word, the reader is forced to analyze the output of 26 times the total number of criterial feature lists for each letter in that word instead of only 26 feature lists, the number of analyses required if letters rather than letter features were the units of perception.

words, cannot possibly be the means by which we perceive letter strings that we have never seen before.

F. Smith (1971) attempts to circumvent this problem by postulating a mediational process that is utilized only when unfamiliar words or pseudowords are encountered.[3] He suggests that, under such circumstances, the unfamiliar item is parsed into subword units of varying sizes that are perceived either directly, by virtue of the reader's acquaintenance with visual-semantic or visual-acoustic relationships, *or* by analogy, through one's acquaintance with a word constituent that is a "fragment" of a familiar word. Thus, in the case of a new word, for example, *VIDEOTAPE* (to use F. Smith's example), the individual might have integrated the visual-acoustic and semantic features of the component word *TAPE*, as well as the visual and acoustic features of *DEO*, as in *RODEO*, but may have no feature list for *VI*. In this instance, he draws upon his knowledge of the visual-acoustic features, which comprise this word fragment, as encountered in words such as *vim, vinegar,* and the like. F. Smith is careful to point out, however, that such analyses are not mediated by letter-sound relationships and, in each instance, concerns feature level rather than letter or cluster level processing involving phonologic mediation.

F. Smith's rejection of phonologic mediation in pseudoword analysis seems a bit extreme, considering the likelihood that one identifies such words partly through the use of spelling-to-sound correspondences (Spoehr & E. Smith, 1973). Nevertheless, his characterization of mediated versus immediate word identification *is* consonant with the suggestion that the skilled reader has a variety of processing strategies available to him or her that he or she uses flexibly and efficiently, in accord with the requirements of the material he or she is asked to read. However, there are several other theories, which offer alternative explanations of the word-pseudoword contrast, word frequency effects, and of course the unit of perception. It suits my purpose to turn my attention to these.

Component Letter Theories

Unlike direct access models, such as those just discussed, component letter theories of word recognition have in common the premise that word recognition is mediated by prior recognition of a word's constituent letters (see Table 2.1). Thus, it is assumed that the recognition process takes place in discrete stages, beginning with (1) feature detection and extraction, carried out by the sensory component of memory, followed by (2) featural synthesis, which results in letter recognition, followed by (3) an interpretive process, which facilitates word recognition, and culminating in (4) an identifying response (see Fig. 2.1 and description of stages of memory). However, the functional components of the recognition process differ significantly in the models that have been proposed,

---

[3]To my knowledge, Rumelhart and Siple have not explicitly addressed this problem.

which themselves can be classified into two general types: those that suggest that the letters in a word are processed serially (left to right) and those that suggest that they are processed simultaneously or in parallel. I briefly discuss the theories articulated by major proponents of each type of model.

Gough's Serial Processing Model

Perhaps the best known and most widely cited serial processing theory of word recognition is that of Gough (1972). This author's conceptualization constitutes a strict rendering of unidirectional-(bottom-up) type models of word recognition, the process being characterized roughly as follows. Upon presentation of a printed word, an iconic representation (see Fig. 2.1 and Table 2.2) of the letters in that word is formed, up to a maximum of some 15 to 20 characters with each visual fixation. Letters are "read out" of the icon serially and are recognized at a rate of approximately one every 10 to 20 msec. As each letter is recognized, it is coded into an abstract phonemic representation (rather than an implicit speech sound[4]) by means of grapheme-phoneme correspondence rules that could either be derived from the reader's implicit knowledge of phonologic transformations (i.e., "systematic phonemes" as hypothesized by Chomsky & Halle, 1968) or by virtue of acquired knowledge of such rules, as suggested by Venezky (1970). The phonologically transcribed string is thereafter employed to access the lexical meaning of the stimulus, which in the case of connected text is then deposited in short-term or primary memory until integrated with other words in the text by semantic and syntactic processes that facilitate comprehension. If oral reading is involved, a response programmer assigns an appropriate articulatory code for each word in the stimulus that allows overt execution of the naming response for each.

In support of his model, Gough cites research findings from two separate sources. The first is Sperling's (1963) observation that subjects could report one additional letter of a randomly arrayed string for approximately every 10-msec increase in display time prior to presentation of a masking stimulus. From this he concluded that letter recognition must take place at a rate of between 10 and 20 msec per letter. The second comes from two other studies conducted by Gough and his associates (Gough & Stewart, 1970; Stewart, James & Gough, 1969), in which it was found that the time taken to pronounce given words increases linearly with the number of letters in those words. These results were taken as evidence that the letters in a word are processed serially.

The serial processing component of Gough's theory has been criticized by several authors. Both Brewer (1972) and Massaro (1975) made note of the fact that Sperling's (1963) study confounded display time with icon duration, thereby

---

[4]Gough believes that speech recoding is an unlikely means for accessing the lexicon, because this mode of access would not be fast enough to account for the speed with which a written word can be comprehended, as estimated by comparisons of naming latencies (Stewart et al., 1969) with decision latencies for accessing categorical meanings (Rohrman & Gough, 1967).

leaving Gough's rate of processing estimate in doubt. And as also pointed out by these authors, neither Sperling's (1963) results nor the results from Gough's laboratory provide any necessary support for a serial letter processing model of word recognition and could as readily be interpreted as support for a parallel processing model. In fact, Sperling himself (1967, 1970) produced results that he considered to be consonant with a simultaneous rather than a serial readout of a word's component letters. Furthermore, the study of Stewart et al. (1969) did not control for response factors, and, as suggested by Massaro (1975, p. 262), the word length effect observed in this study could have been due to the fact that words of greater length take longer to pronounce.

Additional evidence against the serial processing component of Gough's model comes from the work of two other researchers, who evaluated this hypothesis independently. Briefly, Kolers (1970) reported that subjects found it very difficult to identify words when their component letters were presented serially at the same fixation point. Similarly, Travers (1973, 1974, 1975) found that subjects had much greater difficulty identifying words when their letters were presented serially and adjacent to one another than when they were presented simultaneously, and they had particular difficulty in doing so when each letter was individually masked following brief exposure. These data, taken together, seriously undermine the notion that words are recognized through serial processing of their component letters.

Another serious contraindication to Gough's model comes from studies, such as those of Reicher (1969) and Wheeler (1970), that demonstrate that letters can be recognized better in words than when presented singly. As pointed out by Gough himself, in a later publication (Gough & Cosky, 1977), no serial model can account for this finding, because such models predict that under limited exposure conditions the presence of more than one letter in a display should have a deleterious rather than a facilitative effect on letter recognition.

Equally problematic, in Gough's opinion, is Cosky's (1976) observation that words comprised of letters that are easily discriminated (as measured in recognition latencies) are recognized no more rapidly than words comprised of letters that are difficult to discriminate. If word recognition is mediated through letter recognition, then the time taken to perceive a word should be directly related to the time taken to perceive its component letters. Because this was not found to be the case, the serial processing model is effectively questioned.

Interestingly enough, these results question the validity of any model that advocates component letter processing as a prerequisite to word recognition and not just the serial processing models. I return to this point in a subsequent section but, at this juncture, defer further discussion of the issue.

Gough's suggestion that word recognition necessarily involves letter–sound mapping was criticized no less vigorously than the serial processing component of his model. Brewer (1972) initiated the attack by pointing out that phonologic mediation may not be the only means for accessing the lexicon, as illustrated in the skilled reader's ability to assign differential meanings to homophones such as "chute" and "shoot" that have identical pronunciations but different spellings. Massaro (1975, p. 263) offers a similar criticism and also points out that Gough's theory makes no provision for the role of context in disambiguating homophones, as is necessitated not only by homophonic words but also by phrases such as *the miner mined* and *the minor mind* that are phonologically identical but semantically different. Although Gough acknowledged that his model might have to be revised to accommodate homophones (Kavanagh & Mattingly, 1972, p. 367), he nevertheless held to the idea that phonologic recoding is necessarily involved in the recognition process. However, aside from passing mention of a study conducted by Rubenstein and his associates (Rubenstein, Lewis, & Rubenstein, 1971), which obtained results supporting the phonologic recoding hypothesis, Gough presented no evidence that the letters in a printed word are systematically mapped onto phonemic representations that, in turn, facilitate recognition.

The mandatory role of phonologic mediation in word perception is, of course, rejected by direct access theorists who subscribe to the view that a word's visual components are directly "wired" to its semantic/syntactic components—that is, its meaning—and have no necessary relationship with its phonologic characteristics. I have already discussed the theories of F. Smith and Rumelhart and Siple, each of which incorporates this view. In models such as these, a word's meaning is said to be accessed at the time of recognition, and information provided by surrounding context (orthographic, semantic, syntactic) is believed to facilitate the identification process, a possibility that is not considered in Gough's model.

Yet, logical and theoretical contraindications notwithstanding, there are others besides Gough who endorse the notion that phonological recoding is a necessary vehicle to word recognition and still others who question the idea. Foremost among the former group are Rubenstein et al. (1971). Employing the lexical decision procedure, wherein subjects are asked to judge the lexicality ("Is this a real word?") of words and nonwords (pronounceable pseudowords and random letter strings), these authors found that homophonic words yielded longer latencies than nonhomophonic words. They also found that latencies for "NO" responses to pseudohomophones (e.g., BRANE) were longer than latencies for "NO" responses to pseudowords that were not homophonic (e.g., SLINT). It was concluded from these results that lexical access occurs via a phonological code, which of course would be consistent with Gough's model.

However, the results of Rubenstein et al.'s (1971) study have been questioned on several counts. First, as pointed out by Coltheart, Davelaar, Jonasson, & Besner (1977), the homophonic and nonhomophonic words used in this study did not control for word frequency, part of speech, or number of letters, all of which were later found to affect lexical decision times (Frederiksen & Kroll, 1976). Second, there was no control for the possibility that the pseudohomophones employed were visually similar to their real-word counterparts, which has also been shown to be a factor affecting latency of response to pseudowords (Coltheart et al., 1977). In a follow-up investigation that attempted to control for these factors, Coltheart et al. (1977) *was* able to replicate Rubenstein et al.'s (1971) findings for homophonic and nonhomophonic pseudowords, even after equating these stimuli for visual similarity (BRANE/BRONE). In contrast, these authors found *no* differences between response latencies for homophonic and nonhomophonic words (e.g., SAIL and GAZE) matched for frequency and part of speech. It was therefore concluded that phonologic recoding is not necessarily involved in the recognition of real words, but is quite likely involved in processing pseudowords.

The results of several other studies have often been taken as support for the idea that phonologic mediation is a necessary component of word recognition. I mention briefly only a few (see Bradshaw, 1975 for a comprehensive review). Conrad (1964) found that visually presented letters, having acoustically similar names, prompted more intrusion errors than letters that were not acoustically similar. Acoustic similarity effects were also obtained by Krueger (1970) on a letter-search task. At the same time, Corcoran (1966) as well as Corcoran and Weening (1968) observed that "pronounced" letters were easier to detect in proofreading than unpronounced letters (e.g., "silent" e's). Although the relevance of these findings to word recognition and reading can be questioned, Hardyck and Petrinovich (1970) found evidence for implicit speech in the silent reading of difficult material. Similarly, Klapp (1971; Klapp, Anderson, & Berrian, 1973) found that latencies for same/different judgments were greater for picture–name pairs when the names had more syllables, suggesting that the number of syllables increased the difficulty level of the task. These studies lend support to the idea that phonologic recoding may be employed under some circumstances, for example, when lexical access is either unnecessary, as with pseudowords, or difficult to achieve, as in the case of words and sentences depicting less familiar concepts. However, they do not necessarily support the notion that such recoding is *always* involved in word recognition.

Finally, Meyer, Schvanevelt, and Ruddy (1974) presented subjects with word pairs, varying in graphic and phonologic similarity, and found that a lexical decision for a target word such as *TRIBE* was made more rapidly if it had been preceded by a graphically and phonologically similar word, such as *BRIBE,* than if it had been preceded by a word such as *FENCE*, which shared no features with the (target) word. Conversely, a target word, such as *TOUCH,* preceded by a word such as *COUCH,* that was graphically similar but phonologically dissimilar was responded to more slowly than a target word preceded either by a graphically and phonologically similar word or by a word that was totally dissimilar to the target. These findings provide some evidence for phonologic mediation on a short-term memory task but again do not prove that phonologic mediation is always involved in word recognition. Of greater significance is the fact that the results could not be replicated in a later study by Becker, Schvaneveldt, and Gomez (1973). They are therefore inconclusive.

On the negative side of the issue, Baron (1973) found that subjects took less time to decide that visually and phonologically congruent phrases (e.g., MY NEW CAR) sounded meaningful than to decide that phonologically congruent but visually anomalous phrases (e.g., MY KNEW CAR) sounded meaningful. He also found no differences in decision latencies for visually anomalus phrases (e.g., MY KNEW CAR versus OUR NO CAR) when subjects were asked to judge whether they "looked meaningful," although they did make more errors on such phrases when they were phonologically congruent (MY KNEW CAR). Thus, although in the latter instance there was evidence of *some* tendency toward phonologic coding, the results of this study are more compatible with the view that subjects can access word meanings without phonologic mediation.

Perhaps the most compelling evidence against the phonologic recoding views of Gough (1972) and Rubenstein et al. (1971) comes from a study by Forster and Chambers (1973). These authors reasoned that if grapheme–phoneme conversion is obligatory for lexical access and pronunciation, naming speed should be the same for words and pronounceable pseudowords. On the other hand, if naming speed involves a "dictionary search," with the naming response occurring after lexical access, words should be named faster than nonwords, and high-frequency words should be named faster than low-frequency words. The results favored a dictionary search rather than a grapheme–phoneme conversion model.

In an additional contrast, the experimenters compared naming times and lexical decision times for the same samples of words and pseudowords. A phonological recoding model predicts that naming and lexical decision times should be correlated for both words and pseudowords, because grapheme–phoneme conversion is presumably involved in both instances. The dictionary search model predicts, on the other hand, that naming and lexical decision latencies should be correlated in the case of words (because they both involve lexical access time), but the two processes should *not* be correlated in the case of pseudowords, because naming for these stimuli requires only the application of grapheme–phoneme correspondence rules and does not involve lexical access. The results again favored the dictionary search model.

It is worth noting that Frederiksen and Kroll (1976) obtained results similar to that of Forster and Chambers (1973), in that none of the factors shown to affect speed of naming (i.e., number of letters, size of initial consonant cluster, and complexity of vowel translations) had any affect on lexical decision latencies. However, as pointed out elsewhere (Davelaar, Coltheart, Besner, & Jonasson, 1978), both studies are based on the assumption that phonologic and articulatory encoding are equivalent and this may not be the case. Thus, although the two data sets admittedly provide compelling support for the view that phonological recoding is not a prerequisite to lexical access, it would be premature to dismiss this notion on the basis of these two studies alone.

It should be apparent from the foregoing that the role of phonologic mediation in word recognition is yet uncertain and the issue will no doubt be controversial for some time to come. It is interesting to note, in this connection, that several authors (Baron, 1977; Coltheart et al., 1977; Forster, 1979; LaBerge, 1979; LaBerge & Samuels, 1974) have suggested that there may be multiple access routes to lexical entries, a conceptualization that would not only account for many of the conflicting findings in the literature but would also be consistent with the idea that the skilled reader has a variety of alternative processing strategies available to him.

To summarize, Gough's theory has not fared very well in tests of its critical constructs. The serial processing component of his model has had particular difficulty surviving experimental analysis, and phonologic recoding, as an obligatory component of the recognition process, has had little more success in laboratory study. Yet, there must be some instances in which a left-right processing strategy would be useful, for example, in reliably encoding visually similar words that can be identified only by taking account of the order of their letters (*was, saw, top, pot, form, from*). Although the letters in these words may be processed in parallel by the highly skilled reader, I would not be surprised to find evidence for focal attention to letters that critically discriminate these words, such as the initial consonants in *was* and *saw,* perhaps as a remnant of a processing strategy acquired earlier to effect precision in matching word and name codes. Similarly, there is suggestive evidence that identification of words that are not highly familiar may to some extent involve phonologic mediation as pointed out in a previous section. As will be noted in a later section, the use of phonologic mediation is far more evident in developing readers than it is in fluent readers. Thus, the possibility remains that neither of these processing strategies can be completely dismissed as vehicles to word recognition, at least under some circumstances.

The more general notion that words are recognized by prior recognition of component letters has had much greater acceptance than either the serial processing or phonologic mediation components of Gough's model. The inherent assumption, in alternative models that have been proposed, is that the letters in a given word are processed simultaneously or in parallel rather than serially as suggested by Gough. The next section presents a prominent example of this type model.

Massaro's Parallel Processing Model

Unlike serial processing models such as Gough's, parallel processing models of word recognition incorporate the notion that featural information is extracted from a word's component letters simultaneously rather than letter by letter in strict sequential order. Of the parallel processing models that have been proposed, one that is very clearly articulated and well developed is that of Massaro (1975). This conceptualization, not unlike most information-processing models, characterizes word recognition as a sequence of hierarchically structured and discrete processing stages taking place in real time. It also emphasizes the influence of contextual as well as stimulus factors, these variables constituting independent sources of information that combine multiplicatively to effect recognition. However, Massaro's theory differs from others in the role assigned to context, the utility of orthographic structure in particular being conceptualized quite differently than in other models.

A schematic representation of the model is presented in Fig. 2.2. Its major components, in the functional sense, are the *feature detection, primary recognition,* and *secondary recognition* stages of the word recognition process, corresponding roughly to the sensory, perceptual, and cognitive aspects of memory, as depicted in Fig. 2.1 and Table 2.2. The perceptual and cognitive components of the model are directly linked to *generated abstract memory* and the *rehearsal/recoding function,* the latter two corresponding to the short-term memory and control components in Fig. 2.1, respectively. With the exception of feature detection and analysis, all the processes involved in word recognition are characterized as having access to information stored in long-term memory.

As in most information-processing models, a word stimulus impinging upon the visual receptors initiates feature detection, which is considered to be a "wired-in" process, characterized by a passive transduction of the individual features of a word's component letters. Featural information is analyzed and encoded from all letter positions simultaneously and is thereafter transmitted to *preperceptual visual storate,* which temporarily houses a synthesized representation of the physical properties of the stimulus. (Preperceptual visual storage appears to be essentially the same as iconic storage as described earlier; see Table 2.1).

The output of the feature analysis stage of word recognition constitutes the input to the primary recognition stage, which assembles the isolated features in preperceptual visual storage into a sequence of letters temporarily stored in *synthesized visual memory.* In effecting letter synthesis, the primary recognition process also draws upon information stored in long-term memory, which for the

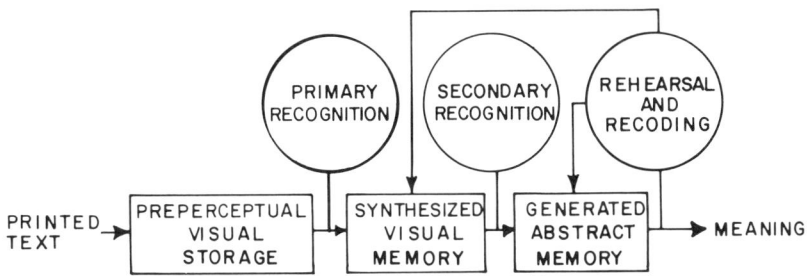

FIG. 2.2. Model of the reading process as conceptualized by Massaro (taken from Massaro, 1975, p. 242, with permission of the author and publisher).

skilled reader includes a feature list for each letter of the alphabet in addition to knowledge of English orthography. Features abstracted from each letter in the stimulus display are matched against prototypical (or "normalized") representations of prospective matches in long-term memory. Because the feature analysis for "candidate" letters takes place at different rates (depending on the nature of the stimulus, the presentation conditions, etc.), the primary recognition process typically operates with partial stimulus information, thereby necessitating the use of orthographic information to resolve uncertainty and ambiguity.

To cite an example used by Massaro (1979), if feature analysis has resolved an __ o i n in a four-letter string but has yielded a feature set for the remaining letter that would identify either c or e, the primary recognition process would synthesize c, without any further analysis, because e in that letter set would be orthographically illegal. In this instance, orthgraphic context is viewed as facilitating perception of the letter set which constitutes the word, but its contribution is considered to be independent of the contribution made by feature analysis.

As noted earlier, the output of the primary recognition process is recognition of a letter string, temporarily stored in synthesized visual memory. The secondary recognition process then searches for the best match in (long-term) lexical memory, in an attempt to transform this (letter) string into a "meaningful form." The end result is an identifying response and/or temporary storage in generated-abstract or short-term memory, the latter course being especially likely in reading connected text. The secondary recognition process, in this instance, makes use of both structural and contextual information, yielding either a precise match or the closest approximation, depending on the discriminability of a particular word as well as the probability of that word's occurrence in a particular context. It is important to note here that the term "meaningful form," as used by Massaro, has reference not only to higher-order abstract codes that are presumably lexical in the case of real words but also to phonologic or morphophonologic representations. This would seem to allow for the possibility of mediated identification (e.g., grapheme–phoneme correspondence or analogy) of connected letter strings, at least under some circumstances. However, the author has not been explicit on this point, except for the role he assigns to the rehearsal-recoding component of the model, which corresponds to short-term working memory common to both speech perception and reading. It is presumably in working memory that recoding takes place, but the conditions under which it occurs are ill-defined in Massaro's theory.

Finally, Massaro points out that semantic and syntactic information, like orthographic structure, may often facilitate word recognition by constraining the alternatives that may be appropriate in given contexts and, further, that such information may even facilitate recognition of a word whose letters have not all been identified. However, he is careful to point out that meaningful context constitutes an independent source of information that combines with the outputs of feature analysis and primary recognition to effect recognition and identification of a word but does not directly affect perception of the letters in that word.

Evidence in support of Massaro's theory has been derived from a number of studies directed largely toward demonstration of the role played by orthographic structure in the recognition process. At the same time, considerable evidence has been marshaled against unitization-type models, which advocate that word recognition is contingent upon perception of higher-order units such as letter clusters, syllables, or whole words. The first of these studies, not surprisingly, questioned the conclusion from the Reicher (1969) and Wheeler (1970) studies that perception of letters within words is mediated by the supraletter properties of words rather than the dynamic application of orthographic rules. It will be recalled that both these authors presented subjects with a choice between two response letters (e.g., K and D), after a brief exposure to a word (or nonword) containing one of these alternatives (e.g., WORD). The subject's task was to indicate which of the two appeared in that word, and it was found that target letters were identified better in words than nonwords (or when presented alone). Because each of the alternatives could have completed a real word, it was inferred that the observed advantage of words over nonwords could not be attributed to the synthesizing power of orthographic structure, as proposed earlier (Miller et al., 1954).

Massaro (1975) contends that the Reicher (1969) postcue procedure did not adequately control for orthographic structure, insofar as subjects could have been synthesizing the target letters prior to presentation of the alternatives. To use Massaro's example, on initial presentation of the stimulus, featural analysis may yield sufficient (featural) information to identify the letters W O R and the curve of the letter D, which in turn could generate the candidate set D, O, or Q. However, only D is orthographically legal in the letter string W O R. The subject can therefore use this information to synthesize the stimulus word prior to presentation of the response alternatives. This would facilitate an advantage of words over nonwords and single letters in choosing the correct letter alternatives. Massaro thus concludes that presentation of the response alternatives, after presentation of the word stimulus, probably did not eliminate the effects of redundancy.

In support of this conjecture, Thompson and Massaro (1973) found that visual similarity of letter alternatives did *not* have any observable effect when the postcue procedure was employed but did significantly affect performance with a fixed set of alternatives that the subjects knew beforehand (C, G, P, R. A<u>C</u>E, A<u>G</u>E, A<u>P</u>E, A<u>R</u>E). In this instance, a letter rather than a word advantage was observed. Massaro (1973) later replicated these findings and, in addition, found no difference between word and nonword trigrams (V<u>C</u>H, V<u>G</u>H, V<u>P</u>H, V<u>R</u>H) on the embedded letter tasks. These results are consistent with those of other studies, which have found that the word superiority effect disappears when the response alternatives are known in advance (Bjork & Estes, 1973; Estes, Bjork,

& Skaar, 1974). Massaro (1975) suggests that this procedure facilitates a letter advantage not only because orthographic redundancy is effectively controlled, but also because the detrimental effects of lateral masking are no longer offset by the "beneficial" effects of redundancy.

Massaro (1975) interprets these findings as support for a letter-based model of word recognition, contending that they demonstrate the importance of both orthographic structure and component letter processing in word perception. However, although these data could be taken to mean that orthographic structure is partially responsible for the word superiority effect, they do not necessarily support Massaro's contention that the single letter is invariably the unit of perception. In addition, there is nothing in the data obtained in these studies that precludes the possibility that the effect is, to some extent, attributable to the influence of processing units larger than the single letter (Baron, 1978). Furthermore, the observation of Thompson and Massaro (1973), Massaro (1973), and others that prior knowledge of letter alternatives can eliminate the word superiority effect need not necessarily be interpreted as support for Massaro's theory, because this finding may indicate nothing more than the fact that the skilled reader can accommodate to task demands, which, under the precue conditions of the studies in question, favor letter rather than word level processing (Estes, 1975a, 1975b, 1977).

In a number of studies conducted recently, Massaro has attempted to strengthen his model by more clearly defining the conditions under which stimulus characteristics and orthographic context are influential. In one such study (Massaro & Klitzke, 1977), letter, word, and nonword recognition were evaluated as a function of exposure duration and orthographic structure, employing a Reicher- (1969) type paradigm. The critical result, presumably supporting Massaro's theory, is that orthographic structure was found to be influential only in the case of brief exposure durations. Under these circumstances, word recognition was more accurate than letter recognition; but, under conditions of unlimited processing time (no masking stimulus), letter recognition was better than word recognition.

In a related study (Massaro, 1979), the identity assigned to an ambiguous letter—for example, c—was found to vary with orthographic context—for example, c*dit* versus c*oin*. However, this was not the case when the critical feature (length of the horizontal bar) more closely approximated either *e* or *c*. Massaro was able to simulate the results of these two studies with theoretically derived quantifications, which led him to conclude that stimulus and contextual variables make independent contributions to letter and word recognition.

A final study (Massaro, Venezky, & Taylor, 1979) employed a letter search paradigm and independently varied orthographic regularity, letter position frequency (Mayzner & Tresselt, 1965), and letter similarity to determine their relative importance in the recognition of letters embedded in nonword strings. Using college sophomores and sixth graders as subjects, it was found that the first two variables had a relatively small effect on letter recognition in the case of the predesignated targets, but a much larger effect when targets were presented after exposure of respective letter strings. In contrast, letter similarity was influential under the former condition but not under the latter. It was concluded that orthographic structure affects only the primary recognition stage of letter and word recognition, whereas letter similarity affects the feature extraction stage.

The uniform conclusion drawn from these studies is that stimulus and contextual factors influence different processing stages. A corollary assumption, critical to Massaro's theory, is that feature analysis at given letter locations is not affected by information extracted from other letter locations or by higher-order information, contrary to nonindependence type theories (Wheeler, 1970; F. Smith, 1971; Johnson, 1975) that suggest that context can directly influence the feature analytic process. Thus, according to the theory, component letters become the units of perception in word recognition.

However, here again, Massaro's interpretations of the research findings can be questioned. Although it seems reasonable to infer that one's implicit knowledge of orthographic regularity, letter position frequency, and the like may have functional utility for word recognition under certain conditions, it does not necessarily follow that single letters are always the units of (word) perception. There seems to be little doubt that there are many instances wherein single-letter discrimination is the primary basis for word discrimination, as with words such as *lend* and *send* that differ by only one letter, but Massaro's data provide us with no compelling reason to believe that all words are recognized in this manner. In fact, a letter processing strategy may be inferred to explain the results of two of the studies discussed earlier (Massaro, 1979; Massaro & Klitzke, 1977), because the word stimuli in these studies differed by only one letter. In contrast, a feature level strategy may be inferred in the case of the predesignated target procedure of Massaro et al. (1979), because orthographic regularity and letter position frequency were minimally effective under this condition. Although orthographic regularity and letter position frequency did affect performance under the postcue condition, this finding does not unequivocally support the notion that the component letters in a particular string are always processed individually. It is interesting to note in this connection that subjects rated letter strings that were characterized both by orthographic regularity and high letter position frequency to be most like real words, but the effect of positional frequency was due almost entirely to orthographic regularity. This suggests that the "wordlike" nature of a letter string is more directly related to the sequential dependencies of its component letters than to the location of individual letters, which in turn allows for the possibility that combinations of letters are often functional in word perception. It may be, for example, that the orthographically regular/high position frequency letter strings employed in the study of Massaro et al. (1979) often facilitated processing in larger units, which would give these stimuli an advantage over the other letter strings under the postcue condition. Unfortunately, the data provide no basis for assessing this possibility, but the authors' interpretation of their results is nonetheless equivocated.

It would seem in view of the foregoing that a more defensible generalization that may be abstracted from the studies conducted by Massaro and his associates is that the skilled reader typically adopts economical processing strategies that maximize the probability of letter and word discrimination. Consistent with this suggestion is the possibility that the recognition and identification of some words involves the processing of perceptual units larger than the letter but smaller than the whole word. Implied here is a parsing process whereby a word's component letters are grouped into clusters and/or syllables and matched against orthographic, phonological, and/or morphophonological representations in long-term memory. The utility of hypothesizing such a process is exemplified in the case of structurally ambiguous words such as *fathead, father, feather* that respectively yield legal or illegal lexical entries, depending on how the letters in these words are grouped. Derivatives that contain morphological units that alter syntactic properties also require parsing of letter groups into functionally separate units (e.g., *turn—turning; pump—pumped; judge—judgment*), as do many polysyllabic words containing structural redundancies (e.g., *discriminability, nationality, disability, recognition, conventional*). At the same time, there are many words that contain letter clusters that correspond invariantly with single phonemes (e.g., *s*hop) and that contain letters that correspond with different phonemes when they are adjacent to other letters (*s*oap and *h*op). It is conceivable that recognition and identification of these respective sets necessitate different processing strategies. Massaro's model makes no provision for these structural differences and, in particular, for capitalizing upon grapheme/phoneme or morphophonological redundancy when it occurs, which is quite often in the case of orthgraphies based on an alphabet.

I should also reiterate in connection with the latter that Massaro's model does not make explicit the means by which unfamiliar words or orthographically regular pseudowords are identified. A closely related problem inheres in the fact that it does not adequately account for the fact that high-frequency words seem to be processed more readily than low-frequency words and pseudowords (Forster & Chambers, 1973; Morton, 1969). If words are recognized solely by means of rule-based integration of their component letters, then there should be no substantial difference in the speed or accuracy with which real words and pseudowords are identified, but this does not appear to be the case. Thus, the model seems incomplete in this respect.

Letter Group Theories

Several theories of word perception are notable for their attempts to capitalize on the spelling–sound invariance that characterizes many letter strings appearing in printed English. These have in common the idea that a word's constituent letters may be grouped into functional units that mediate recognition and identification of that word. They also have in common the notion that grouping principles are derived from spelling-sound correspondence rules inherent in English orthography. They differ, however, in the ways in which they conceptualize the parsing and matching process. Two such theories are, respectively, Gibson's (1965) cluster theory and the Vocal Center Group theory of Spoehr and Smith (1973). I discuss Gibson's theory first.

Gibson's Cluster Theory

An alternative to the feature redundancy type theories of F. Smith (1971) and Rumelhart and Siple (1974) is Gibson's (1965) cluster theory. Both types of theory are similar in two respects: Each advocates that the letter feature is the unit of analysis and each incorporates the notion that featural redundancy is functional in word recognition. However, they differ in their conceptualizations of the matching units stored in long-term memory. Whereas the first two theories suggest that letter features are matched with stored representations of whole words, Gibson's theory suggests that letter features are matched with representations of letter clusters, termed *spelling patterns*. Two separate characterizations of such units were offered by Gibson, each derived from empirical research. In the conceptualization initially articulated (Gibson, 1965), the spelling pattern was described as a pronounceable letter cluster, unitized by virtue of its invariant relationship with phonetically legal sound sequences in spoken language. Gibson (1965, 1971) theorized that the detection and functional use of invariant relationships is an inherent characteristic of both the human information processor and the perceptual learning process, because it is an attitude that breeds efficiency and economy in the acquisition of any new skill. It would therefore be logical to assume that the developing reader would eventually become sensitized to spelling-sound correspondences, which exist in written English, and that these would in time have utility in word perception.

The foregoing version of letter cluster theory was provided initial support by a seminal study conducted by Gibson and her associates (Gibson et al., 1962), which found that pronounceable pseudowords, such as GLURCK, were more accurately perceived than were nonpronounceable pseudowords such as CKURGL. This was true when both written reproduction and matching were employed as respective response measures. Essentially the same results were obtained in a subsequent study employing first- and third-grade children as subjects (Gibson, Osser, & Pick, 1963). In a more fine-grained analysis of the results of the Gibson et al. (1962) study, it was found (Gibson, 1964) that summed bigram and trigram frequencies did not correlate with performance when pronounceability and word length were held constant. Gibson tentatively concluded from these findings that spelling patterns generated by grapheme-phoneme correspondence rules constitute units of perception in word recognition.

A subsequent study by Gibson and her associates (Gibson et al., 1970) led to a significant modification of the original version of the letter cluster theory, insofar as the performance patterns of deaf subjects on pronounceable and unpronounceable pseudowords were found to be similar to that of normal hearing subjects. As a result of this finding, it was suggested that it is the structural characteristics of English orthography—specifically its rule-based and predictable nature—that facilitates word perception rather than pronounceability per se. However, it was pointed out in this same paper (Gibson et al., 1970, p. 71) that because orthographic structure evolved in relation to speech, the invariant patterns embedded in written English may differentially affect normal hearing and deaf individuals learning to read. If so then the processing mechanisms that take account of orthographic structure may operate differently in these two groups, a question that remains unanswered to date.

In the most recently articulated version of her theory (Gibson, 1971, 1977; Gibson & Levin, 1975), Gibson broadens her conceptualization of the word recognition process and places less emphasis on the unit of perception issue. Unlike other theorists who have attempted to characterize the process, Gibson has not been explicit as to the inner workings of the systems involved in word recognition, at least not in the highly formalized sense in which the information-processing models available are typically described. Instead, she outlines some general principles of perceptual learning and several working hypotheses, which nonetheless provide a coherent account of important word recognition phenomena and are especially notable for their emphasis upon alternative processing modes and their consideration of developmental factors.

She points out that a word contains five different classes of information that the perceiver must account for: *graphic, orthographic, phonologic, semantic,* and *syntactic.* Such information is believed to be processed sequentially and hierarchically so that momentary attendance to one set of features precludes processing of the others. It is also suggested that the order of pickup of particular word features is determined by task utility and that the perceiver's focus will be self-regulating and economical. Thus, in the natural setting, reading for meaning implies a different perceptual attitude than does proofreading, and the fluent reader is able to shift his processing strategies in compliance with task demands. In the laboratory setting, partial report procedures such as letter search and like tasks would be characterized by different processing strategies than would full report procedures, such as naming or semantic categorizing.

Gibson suggests, further, that the feature analytic process and, more generally, skill in word recognition should be viewed as a developmental progression characterized by functional asymmetry in attention to the meaning and structural characteristics of printed words. Thus, during the initial stage, the reader is said to be maximally attentive to meaning, as demonstrated in controlled observations (Biemiller, 1970; Weber, 1970), which indicate that reading errors during this period are determined more often by the semantic and syntactic characteristics of given words than by their structural similarities. At an intermediate stage, when the individual is maximally involved in code acquisition, he becomes increasingly sensitive to both the structural regularities (orthographic and phonologic) and the distinguishing features of the words he encounters and is therefore less attuned to their semantic and syntactic characteristics. At a later stage, when fluency in word decoding is greater, a word's semantic and syntactic features are again in ascendence, in accord with the fluent reader's preoccupation with meaning, but he may shift focus implicitly or at will, depending on task demands.

It should be apparent that Gibson's later formulations are more in keeping with a level of processing approach to word perception than are her initial characterizations of the recognition process. Although her theory does not appear to be isomorphic with the notion that the unit of perception is relative rather than absolute, the general principles she has outlined are not inconsistent with this point of view. She is also one of the few theorists that have attempted to relate the word perception process to developmental changes. However, the status of Gibson's spelling cluster hypothesis is not clear from her later writings (Gibson, 1971, 1977; Gibson & Levin, 1975). Furthermore, the author has not, to date, addressed certain critical difficulties encountered by any feature redundancy theory that posits a matching unit that is larger than the letter but smaller than the word. For one thing, such theories have no way of accounting for the word superiority effect, at least not without additional assumptions. More damaging is the fact that Gibson's theory is logically inconsistent, as pointed out by Smith and Spoehr (1974), in that it provides no mechanism for parsing letter strings into spelling patterns before the letters in those strings are recognized.

On the other hand, a spelling pattern model that is able to overcome this problem could explain many of the capabilities of the fluent reader, most notably the ability to decode unfamiliar words and pseudowords; but again some modification of the current theory is required. This brings me to the second letter group theory I wish to discuss.

Spoehr and Smith's Vocalic Center Group Theory

Of the models discussed thus far, only Gough's (1972) suggests that phonologic recoding constitutes an intermediate processing stage in word recognition. Another such model is that of Spoehr and Smith (1973). Unlike Gough, who proposes that single letters are recoded into systematic phonemes, these authors suggest that letter groups, comprising syllable size units, are mapped onto phonologic representations in long-term memory. Such a theory immediately confronts one with the parsing problem noted in the previous section. However, Spoehr and Smith (1973) deal with this problem by suggesting that parsing begins after a word's component letters have been identified rather than before, thus circumventing the major objection to spelling pattern models.

The theory, in brief, is as follows. Upon presentation of a stimulus word, feature extraction takes place at each letter position simultaneously, and letter features are matched to individual letter categories stored in long-term memory. The encoded letter representations are then placed in sensory storage (see Fig.

2.1 and 2.2), while letter groups are systematically parsed or segmented into higher-order units called *vocalic center groups* (VCGs). Segmentation into VCGs is the critical process that mediates word recognition and, as conceptualized, is essentially a trial-and-error progression. As originally defined by Hansen and Rogers (1965), a VCG constitutes a letter string containing one vocalic element, which may either be a vowel or a diphthong, typically combined with from one to three consonants or, in some instances, no consonants. Derived from research in speech production (Liberman, Ingram, Fisher, Delattre, & Cooper, 1959), the VCG is considered to be the smallest pronunciational unit carrying a complete specification of its phonemic constraints and is therefore considered a most efficient unit for phonologic recoding (Rozin & Gleitman, 1977). Thus, according to the theory, the perceiver implicitly parses a word into one or more VCGs, in an effort to match these units with phonologic representations that will access the lexicon and effect recognition. The parsing process itself is conceptualized as rule generated, and Spoehr and Smith (1973) have outlined how such rules may be applied. To illustrate the process, I use the example provided by Smith and Spoehr (1974).

Table 2.2 presents the parsing rules developed by these authors. If, for example, the word PARSING were to be segmented, rule 1 would mark the position of the vowels. Rule 2 would group the initial P with the first vowel A and the final NG with the I. The medial cluster RS remains and because the pattern of internal vowels and consonants is VCCV, rule 3b is applied to arrive at the division PAR and SING constituting two VCGs that correspond with the familiar two-syllable word stored in lexical memory. However, the word itself is accessed by means of a recoding or "translation" process that matches the phonologic representations of these two VCGs with the lexical entry corresponding with

TABLE 2.2
Parsing Rules Generated by Spoehr and Smith for Partitioning Vocalic Center Groups (taken from Smith & Spoehr, 1974, with permission of the authors and publisher)

Rule 1. Mark Positions of Vowels

Rule 2. Unitize Initial Consonant(s) with Initial Vowel and Final Consonant(s) with Final Vowel

Rule 3. Parse Intermediate Consonant(s) According to Following:

    a. ... VCV ... ⟶ ... V + CV ...
    b. ... VCCV ... ⟶ ... VC + CV ...
    c. ... VCCCV ... ⟶ ... VC + CCV ...

Rule 4. If Previous Rules Yield an Inappropriate Result, Reparse Intermediate Consonant(s) According to the Following:

    a. ... VCV ... ⟶ ... VC + V ...
    b. ... VCCV ... ⟶ ... V + CCV ...
    c. ... VCCCV ... ⟶ ... V + CCCV ...

these items. Spoehr and Smith (1973) are careful to point out that the translation stage is conceived as a "true" perceptual stage (Smith & Haviland, 1972), unlike some models (Eriksen, Pollack, & Montague, 1970; Klapp, 1971) that place the recoding process on the response side of word recognition and identification.

Evidence for the VCG model was initially derived from three related studies conducted by Spoehr and Smith (1973). In one of these studies, it was found that tachistoscopic report accuracy for vocalized responses was greater for one-syllable words than for two-syllable words. Qualitative analyses of error patterns suggested that the probability of an error was greater across syllabic boundaries than within a syllable, but a subsequent analysis (with one- and two-syllable words matched for length, frequency, and initial letter) suggested that vocalic center groups rather than syllables function as perceptual units.

Although the results of the latter study could be attributed to response bias or guessing strategies rather than to perceptual factors, a subsequent study in this series obtained a VCG effect, employing a Reicher-type postcue procedure that used single letters embedded in words as the dependent measure. Because the response was not delayed, short-term memory as well as response factors were effectively controlled.

Yet another study in this series demonstrated that accuracy of tachistoscopic report was equivalent for monosyllabic and bisyllabic two-digit numerals, suggesting that the performance differences observed on these respective word types are not due to implicit speech or response execution (Eriksen et al., 1970; Klapp, 1971; Klapp et al., 1973). It was concluded from these experiments that the VCG effect is a perceptual rather than a response effect.

In a later paper, Spoehr and Smith (1975) extend the VCG model by more explicitly defining the means by which VCGs are converted into a speech code. Following a model of the speech production process proposed by MacKay (1972), it was suggested that words parsed into one or more VCGs are further decomposed into one or two letter units, which can be assigned phonetic representations isomorphically. Thus, as illustrated in Fig. 2.3, the pronounceable pseudoword FRASH (which contains a single VCG) would be initially partitioned into consonant and vowel consonant subgroupings, termed "nodes," and examined to see if the resulting units could be represented by single phonemes. If not then each is further subdivided until grapheme–phoneme correspondence is achieved, the number of subdivisions required being referred to as "depths." An additional assumption of the model is that syllabic recoding of unpronounceable strings such as FRSH and RSHF requires the application of a vowel insertion procedure (represented in Fig. 2.3 as the inclusion of the unstressed vowel /ə/) applied whenever a phonotactic rule[5] is violated. It therefore follows that (unpronounceable) letter strings that do *not* violate phonotactic rules

---

[5]A phontactic rule is a rule for generating a pronounceable letter string.

68 VELLUTINO

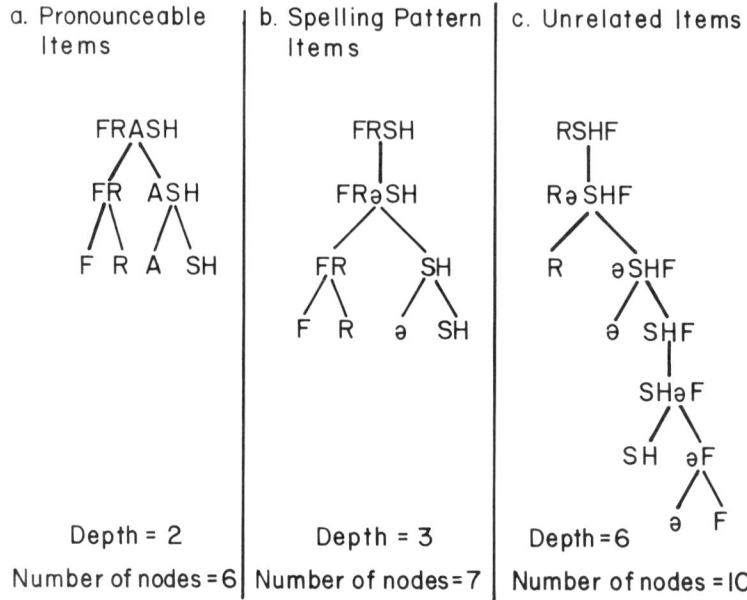

FIG. 2.3. Schematic diagram of syllabic recoding process proposed by Spoehr and Smith, illustrated with three different types of nonwords. The insertion of the unstressed vowel (/ə/) is illustrated in templates b and c (taken from Spoehr & Smith, 1975, with permission of the authors and publisher).

(e.g., FRSH) require fewer recoding operations than letter strings that do violate such rules (e.g., RSHF) and should be less perceptible.

The syllabic recoding modification of the VCG model was initially evaluated by Spoehr and Smith (1975) (using a Reicher-type paradigm), who found that although words and pronounceable pseudowords (BLAST, BLOST) were better perceived than were unpronounceable letter strings, unpronounceable strings comprised of phonotactically legal spelling patterns (BLST) were better perceived than those that were randomly arrayed (LSTB). These results were replicated in a subsequent investigation, which also found that VCG units violating phonotactic rules (e.g., RNOT), were perceived less accurately than those that did not (e.g., ROST). A third study provided evidence that vowel insertion rules generated by the model are actually employed in syllabic recoding. Spoehr and Smith interpret these findings as compatible with their revised VCG model, which they suggest can also account for the results obtained by Gibson et al. (1962) and others (Miller et al., 1954) with pronounceable and unpronounceable nonwords.

In the most recent study evaluating the revised VCG model, Spoehr (1978) provides additional evidence for syllabic recoding. Specifically, letters embedded within words containing letter clusters that can be assigned a single phoneme (e.g., SH A R K) were detected more accurately than letters embedded within words comprised exclusively of single-letter phonemes (S T A R K). These findings were replicated in a second experiment, which also demonstrated that syllabic and phoneme length effects are additive and represent independent sources of variance. An important point made by Spoehr in connection with these two investigations is that phoneme length effects constitute more direct evidence of a phonological recoding process in word recognition than either syllable length effects or spelling pattern contrasts (Gibson, 1965, 1970). As suggested by the author, the parsing of syllables and letter clusters could occur exclusively on the basis of the visual properties of a given word, but this is not true in the case of parsing at the phonemic level because the phoneme is a basic unit in verbal rather than visual processing.[6]

In the same investigation, Spoehr (1978) provides an important qualification of Spoehr and Smith's revised VCG model. Again using a Reicher-type paradigm, it was found that syllable and phoneme length effects were evident only under backward masking stimulus conditions. It was suggested in explanation of these findings that a verbal recoding strategy is employed when stimulus processing is interrupted (masking), but a visual matching strategy can be inferred with unlimited processing time (no mask). Spoehr suggests further that such differences may reflect the availability of versatile processing strategies for word recognition, with the parsing and recoding strategy being applied whenever stimulus conditions demand such recoding. Smith and Spoehr (1974) make a similar point. This idea is, of course, compatible with the central theme of this chapter and could serve to obviate at least some of the criticisms of the VCG model, certain of which might be usefully outlined at this point.

Analogous to a similar point made in our discussion of Gibson's letter cluster theory, the fact is that without additional assumptions the VCG model or any model that postulates subword units as the exclusive basis of word recognition has difficulty in accounting for the word superiority effect (Reicher, 1969; Wheeler, 1970) and similar word advantage phenomena such as the word fre-

---

[6]It might be asked at this point why Spoehr and Smith (1975) have postulated an elaborate mechanism for parsing and translating strings into VCGs and phonemes, if individual letters are fully analyzed prior to phonologic recoding. A related question is just how their model differs from that of Gough, who suggests that words are recognized by mapping individual letters onto systematic phonemes. An obvious answer to the first question is that many spelling-to-sound correspondences cannot be determined, except by reference to the environments in which they occur, and subsyllabic units often do not contain a sufficient amount of information to encode such patterns accurately, as exemplified in words containing ambiguous spelling clusters such as FATHER, FATHEAD. In answer to the second question, suffice it to point out that whereas, in Gough's model, grapheme-phoneme mapping occurs as each letter is identified in a serial (left-right) progression, in Spoehr and Smith's model, the recoding process occurs after all component letters are identified and after each of the VCGs contained within a word is located.

quency effect (Morton, 1969) and the "word priority" effect (Sloboda, 1977), which is discussed later. Although Smith and Spoehr (1974) suggest that such effects are not very robust, in a more recent review Baron (1978) concludes that they are robust indeed and, in fact, quite tenacious.[7]

A second criticism (Massaro, 1975, pp. 263-266) is that the VCG model does not explain how the parsing process can be successfully accomplished with partial letter information (typical of the stimulus conditions in most laboratory studies), without some mechanism for utilizing orthographic constraints to fill in missing letters. However, this criticism, although valid in reference to the model as initially articulated (Spoehr & Smith, 1973), would not appear to be applicable to the revised model (Spoehr, 1978; Spoehr & Smith, 1975), because the means by which orthographic and phontactic constraints influence the parsing process is specified.

Third, Spoehr and Smith's (1973, 1975) model inherits all the logical theoretical, and empirical contraindications that have been leveled at phonologic recoding models. As indicated earlier, phonologic mediation models make no provision for the role of context and cannot therefore account for the recognition and identification of homophonic and homographic words that rely on contextual information for disambiguation. Neither do they incorporate mechanisms that might account for variations in stress patterns (e.g., permit versus permit) in accessing a word's meaning. As pointed out elsewhere (Baron, 1977; Baron & Strawson, 1976), phonological recoding models do not readily explain the skilled reader's ability to recognize "exception" words that are not generated on the basis of grapheme-phoneme correspondence rules (e.g., TONGUE, EPOCH, ANSWER, WAS). Furthermore, a strict application of the logic behind phonologic recoding models runs aground on the results of lexical decision studies (Forster & Chambers, 1973; Frederiksen & Kroll, 1976) and those employing similar methodologies (Baron, 1973) demonstrating that word meanings can be accessed directly without phonologic mediation. At the same time, such models do not adequately account for the failure to find differences in decision latencies for homophonic and nonhomophonic words when these are matched for important contextual variables such as frequency and part of speech (Coltheart et al., 1977).

These contraindications would not be so damaging to models such as Spoehr and Smith's (1975), if an alternative strategies view of word recognition is adopted; in fact, these authors themselves suggest that word meanings may

---

[7]In fact, in one of the studies by Spoehr and Smith (1975), better performance was noted for real words (e.g., BLAST) as contrasted with pronounceable pseudowords (e.g., BLOST), but this was not found to be the case in a subsequent study. The authors gave no explanation for this disparity, but it is possible that the stimulus sets employed in the former study (because they included five-letter items) more often taxed short-term memory than did the stimuli employed in the latter study (which included only four-letter items). In such instances, familiar words might be provided some advantage.

sometimes be accessed on the basis of the visual properties of a word alone (Smith & Spoehr, 1974, p. 263). It would therefore seem that the Spoehr and Smith (1975) model has utility in explaining at least some word processing phenomena, in particular, the skilled reader's ability to identify unfamiliar words and pseudowords.

However, one additional question can be raised about the VCG model. Specifically, it might be asked just how the verbal recoding of a letter string influences the visual perception of that string. Some sort of interactive process seems implied, as when a given word is unsuccessfully parsed (e.g., FATHER → *FAT HER*), and the the meaningless translation that ensues (/FAT/ /HER/) precipitates visual reorganization on a second parse, such that one "perceives" different letter groups as units (e.g., FA THER). However, the authors have not been explicit as to the mechanisms involved, except to suggest that parsing and recoding increases the size of the processing unit and thereby enhances perceptibility (Spoehr, 1978; Spoehr & Smith, 1975). This lack of definition underscores an inherent ambiguity in virtually all the models discussed thus far, and that is their respective conceptualizations of the perceptual process itself. Some, such as Massaro (1975), conceive of word perception as the resolution of the feature analytic process and thereby place it closer to the sensory component of word recognition. Others conceptualize the phenomenon as an interpretive process and are thus closer to the identification and response components of recognition. I have more to say about this issue but now turn my attention to a representative example of the whole-word models that have emerged in recent years— Johnson's pattern unit model—which is no less ambiguous as to the definition of perception than any of the others presented.

A Whole-Word Model: Johnson's Pattern-Unit Theory

As noted earlier, whole-word theories of word recognition—afforded their initial credibility by the seminal studies of Cattell (1886a, 1886b)—were seriously challenged by latter-day theories of information processing, which suggested that unitization-type conceptualizations such as Cattell's may be oversimplified (Miller et al., 1954). However, work done later (Reicher, 1969; Wheeler, 1970) provided new impetus for such models and several studies conducted subsequently led to the formulation of a number of modified versions of Cattell's whole-word theory that are currently influential (Johnson, 1975; 1977; 1979; Kahneman & Henik, 1975; Theios & Muise, 1977). Of these, the most elaborate and highly formalized is the pattern-unit model articulated by Johnson (1975, 1977, 1979).

Figure 2.4 presents a schematic characterization of this model. Not unlike other contemporary theorists, Johnson (1977) conceives of the word recognition process as a series of discrete stages, with no interaction between stages up to the level of icon formation. The first stage of processing is carried out by what the

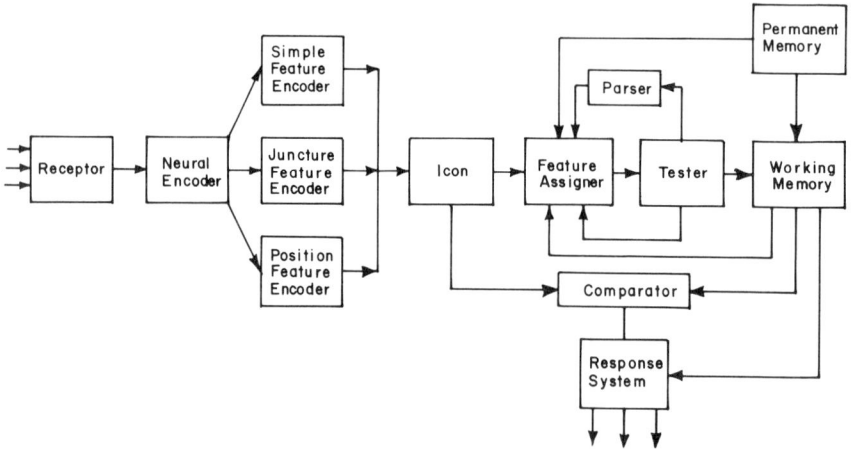

FIG. 2.4. Diagram of Johnson's pattern-unit model (taken from Johnson, 1977, with permission of the author and publisher).

author refers to as the *perceptual component,* described as an unlimited capacity system that facilitates successive encodings of the visual stimulus. Thus, sensory receptors "transduce" the physical properties of a word into "undifferentiated neural activity," thereafter acted upon by filter-like mechanisms that respond differentially to visual–spatial information (Anderson, 1973). These mechanisms are thought to be sensitive to three different kinds of information, independent of one another: *simple features* such as horizontal, diagonal, vertical, and curved lines; *juncture features,* such as intersections and angles; and *positional features* that represent the order of the items in a spatial layout.

The output of the perceptual component of the pattern-unit model is the *icon* that is described as an encoded representation of the visual properties of the stimulus. As in other models, the icon is viewed as an exponentially decaying image that has longevity beyond the point where stimulation is terminated. But, whereas in most other models the icon is conceived as an unintegrated complex of sensory features, in the pattern unit model, it is described as a "unitary encoding" that derives its cohesiveness from the higher-order juncture features and the unique spatial relationships characteristic of the component items in a particular display. In other words, the model suggests that the iconic image is a precognitive, strictly perceptual phenomenon that is encoded into a single unit by virtue of the physical contiguity of its component features.

The second stage of processing, in the pattern-unit model, is the "transfer" stage, which interfaces perception and memory and is carried out by the "transfer mechanism." The transfer mechanism (analogous to control processes in Fig. 2.1) receives the iconic representation from the perceptual component and, by means of a "feature assigner" (see Fig. 2.4), assigns a unitary encoding in the form of a fixed and limited number of features, drawn from long-term memory. Feature sets may be assigned either by orthographic rules or by grapheme–phoneme correspondence rules, resulting in lexical and phonologic representations, respectively. It is assumed that all inputs to the transfer mechanism from the perceptual component are themselves unitary encodings that transcend the featural characteristics and/or separate encodings of subunits in the display, for example, the letters in a word.

Following assignment of a tentative encoding to the icon, a "tester–parser" attempts to determine the adequacy of the initial encoding. If a unitary encoding is found to be inadequate (as in the case of unconnected letters such as SQXP), then the feature assigner is signaled and a second attempt is made to encode the icon. After a fixed (criterion based) number of attempted encodings, the display is fractionated into smaller units (e.g., letters, letter clusters, syllables, vocalic center groups) by the "parser" and unitary encodings are assigned to each subunit. Thus there could be as many encodings as there are subunits.

The penultimate stage of processing is the working memory and comparison stage. During this stage, encodings relayed by the transfer mechanisms are held in temporary storage to be matched, integrated with subsequent input, or compared with other encodings stored in long-term memory. Comparison and matching operations are carried out by the "comparator," which automatically matches items coded in the same form.

The final stage of processing is the response stage, which is not detailed in the pattern-unit model, except for the suggestion that the comparator signals the response system when a response is called for.

Johnson's (1977) conceptualization of the stages in word recognition is definitive in its emphasis on the unitary or holistic quality of both the perceptual and memorial components of the process. As regards the perceptual component, it is evident that although Johnson considers the feature to be the unit of analysis, some whole-word representation would seem to be the matching unit in long-term memory, and in fact the author is quite clear in his suggestion that perception of a given word does not entail perception of its component letters (Johnson, 1975, 1977). Memorial encodings are similarly characterized. However, Johnson leaves the nature of such encodings unspecified, except to suggest that they are limited in number and could be either lexical or phonological representations, which, for example, could be taken as having reference to a word's meaning and its name, respectively. Inherent in both characterizations are certain experimental predictions, namely that: (1) word perception, under adequate viewing conditions, should be unaffected by the number of letters in a word; and (2) word perception should be faster than perception of a letter embedded within a word but no more rapid than perception of single letters. A corollary assumption, common to both predictions, is that word perception is independent of letter perception or—put another way—that the visual code for a word is not derived from the visual codes for its component letters. Several studies, designed to evaluate these hypotheses, constitute Johnson's initial documentation of the pattern-unit model.

In the first of three separate experiments addressing this issue (Johnson, 1975), subjects (college students) were presented with target stimuli and several decks of highly dissimilar probe words, each for an unlimited amount of processing time (300 msec and no mask). Targets were either words varying in length (four to six letters) or single letters, and each was presented before administration of given decks of probe words. For word targets, subjects were asked to match target with probe words; for letter targets, each was asked to indicate whether a probe word contained the target letter. The dependent measure was latency of response. Consistent with the experimental prediction, word matching took less time than matching target letters with letters within words, even when the target letter was the first letter of a word. There was no effect of word length on latencies for the word targets, but there was a significant length effect for letter targets. In addition, *no* responses for words took longer than *yes* responses, contrary to component letter theories of word recognition. The results are interpreted as favoring the pattern-unit model, and the apparent word advantage in these experiments has come to be known as the "word priority effect" (Sloboda, 1977).

A second experiment in this series (Johnson, 1975) employed a procedure similar to that used in the first, except that targets and probes consisted of either one- and two-syllable, five-letter words or single letters. Targets and foils appeared with equal frequency to control for differential practice with the target. The critical finding is that single letters were matched as quickly as words, whereas no differences were found between yes and no responses nor between one- and two-syllable words.

In the third and final experiment in this series (Johnson, 1975), asymmetry in the frequency of target and foil probes was eliminated by changing the target for every display. Words and letters were again used as both targets and probes, but there were *two* letter-search conditions, one using only single letters as targets and probes and another using the first letter of a word as the probe letter. Words were again matched faster than (initial) letters in words, and the latencies for matching words and those for matching single letters were not significantly different. At the same time, single letters took less time than matching single letters with the initial letters of given words.

In several other experiments using the target-probe procedure (Johnson, 1977), word frequencies as well as word lengths were varied orthogonally, and there were no differences that could be attributed to these two variables, even when different targets were used for each item in a series (Johnson, 1977, p. 115). However, in yet another study employing this experimental procedure, word length effects *were* found for consonant letter strings and pronounceable pseudowords but, again, not for real words. Notable is the fact that in these studies, as well as in all the studies reported by Johnson, discriminations were made under optimal processing conditions; that is, the stimuli were not degraded, no masking procedures were employed, and stimulus exposures were for extended durations (at least 300 msec).

Johnson's (1975) interpretations of his results have been challenged by a number of authors. Henderson (1975), for example, questioned the absence of word length differences in Johnson's studies, pointing out that the word foils employed in these studies were highly dissimilar, thereby presenting the possibility that subjects utilized a selective search strategy that effectively diminished any word length differences that might have otherwise accrued.[8] Similarly, Massaro and Klitzke (1977) suggest that Johnson's (1975) finding of no differences between word matches and single-letter matches may have been due to the failure to control for the similarity of word foils, the inference in this instance being that the lateral masking effects normally produced by adjacent letters in a word string may have been offset by the advantage occasioned by the highly discriminable foils. Thus, an advantage of letters over words was observed by Massaro and Klitzke (1977) rather than no differences between these variables when similar and dissimilar foils were randomly interspersed. The authors concluded from these findings that a parallel processing model provides a more parsimonious explanation of Johnson's finding than does a pattern-unit model. Essentially, the same conclusion was drawn by Sloboda (1976), who obtained similar results.

Henderson (1975) also questioned Johnson's (1975) suggestion that the pattern-unit model is necessarily supported by the observation that respective word and letter matching took less time than matching target letters with letters embedded within words. Sloboda (1976) raises the same question, as do Massaro and Klitzke (1977). These authors uniformly suggest that word and single-letter matching involves less processing time than searching for a letter within a word, because subjects are forced to adopt a more stringent discrimination criterion for the embedded letter task than for the other two, particularly when the word- and letter-matching tasks employ highly dissimilar stimuli. Furthermore, each argues that a letter integration model could as readily account for Johnson's findings as the pattern-unit model, pointing out in addition that Johnson (1975) did not evaluate his hypothesis with target letters embedded in random letter strings. A letter integration model would predict that detection of target letters in words

---

[8]Johnson (1975) assumes that an exhaustive search strategy would be predicted by serial letter-processing models of word perception for *yes* responses but not *no* responses; with dissimilar word pairs, *no* responses could be made on the basis of the first different letter detected. Johnson (1975) also suggests that a parallel processing model of word perception would be precluded by the failure to find word length differences with dissimilar targets and probes, inasmuch as a parallel processing model would predict that larger letter sets (in the case of words of greater length) would increase the probability that a word pair would be discriminated on the basis of a single letter. However, Henderson (1975) questions this assumption, pointing out that increases in letter set size are apt to be negatively accelerated such that differences between four and six letters (Experiment 1, Johnson, 1975) would most likely go undetected.

would take as much or less time (because of orthographic constraints) than detection of target letters in random strings, whereas a pattern-unit model would predict that letter detection in words would be slower because of the additional time required for fractionating a unitary encoding.

Contrary to the pattern-unit model, Sloboda (1976) found that searching for letters in nonwords was no more rapid than searching for letters within words, and both took more time than matching single letters (Experiment I). Sloboda also found that the *less* a letter array looked like a word (e.g., when letters were arrayed in the shape of a diamond), the *more* time it took for letter detection (Experiment II), a finding that would not conform with the pattern-unit model. At the same time, Krueger (1970) and Novik and Katz (1971) both found that letter-search time was more rapid with words than with random letter strings, which is also at variance with the pattern-unit model.

On the other hand, Johnson (1977) reports that subjects were able to process a single letter (e.g., S) faster than that same letter embedded either in all different (SBJFQ) or all same letter strings (SSSSS), contrary to a letter integration model, which would predict that discrimination, in such instances, can be made on the basis of the first letter processed. Furthermore, Sloboda (1976, Experiment III) found that searching for a letter in a word was more time-consuming than matching words with other words, even when similarity of word foils was controlled. He also found that *no* responses were slower than *yes* responses when the foils were highly similar to target words. At the same time, word matching with dissimilar foils was, on the average, more rapid than word matching with similar foils, suggesting that the processing strategies employed by subjects were different under the respective stimulus conditions.

Clearly, the studies evaluating the pattern-unit model have yielded conflicting results, whereas the interpretations of reliable findings are ambiguous and theoretically biased. Yet it seems to me that such disparity can be reconciled if one adopts a multilevel processing view of word recognition and identification rather than *either* a holistic *or* a component letters view. A multilevel processing approach would account for Johnson's word length and word-matching results, if it is assumed that highly discriminable words can be perceived holistically with no letter parsing needed for recognition. In contrast, words that have a high degree of similarity may necessitate parsing at the letter, letter cluster, and/or feature levels and would therefore take more time to process than would dissimilar words. Even dissimilar words may to some extent be parsed at a lower level, if the subject cannot be certain as to whether a probe word will be similar or highly dissimilar to a target word, as in the case of the random presentation procedure employed by Massaro and Klitzke (1977). In contrast, detection of letters embedded within words and nonwords will typically be more time-consuming than word or letter matching, because parsing is always required on such tasks and discrimination is compounded by lateral masking effects.

How then can a multilevel processing view account for Sloboda's (1976, Experiment III) finding that searching for a letter in a word took longer than matching two words, even when word foils were highly similar to words containing the target letter? Sloboda's (1976) interpretation is similar to but not entirely consistent with the one offered here. He suggests that although the letter-search task entails comparisons of letter codes, the word-matching task entails comparisons of name codes, which takes less time overall than letter-by-letter matching, even though both tasks are presumably contingent upon the prior availability of component letters. This interpretation would, of course, be consistent with a multilevel processing approach, in that coding differences are inferred for the two different tasks. However, Sloboda's interpretation does not necessarily account for the shorter latencies he observed on word matching with dissimilar foils as compared with word matching with similar foils, which incidentally was observed by Massaro and Klitzke (1977) as well.[9] If name code matching was the only variable accounting for the differences between the word matching and letter within word-matching tasks in Sloboda's (1976) Experiment III, why were reaction times in the dissimilar foils condition faster than in the other two conditions? Sloboda would suggest that less processing was required under the dissimilar foils condition, because discrimination could be made on the basis of a single letter and this is, of course, a distinct possibility. However, it could also be true that recognition of probe words, under the dissimilar foils condition, was at the whole-word level with no parsing below that level. Indeed, this would seem to be a more efficient processing strategy if, as Sloboda suggests, comparisons of targets and probes utilized name codes as the matching variable. Thus Sloboda's findings do not rule out the possibility of whole-word processing under some circumstances and are quite consistent with a multilevel processing and flexible strategies approach to word recognition.

It should be noted, in connection with the foregoing, that the pattern-unit model is not incompatible with the multilevel processing view suggested here, insofar as it makes provision for the parsing of configurations that cannot be assigned a unitary coding. However, the model is inherently contradictory in its assumption that a word's component letters are *not* perceived (''seen'') prior to the recognition of the word itself, for if this were the case, there would be no way in which the perceiver would know that a unitary encoding could not be assigned to a particular letter string. Furthermore, this assumption is inconsistent with recent research findings, which suggest that the ''word priority'' effects that have been demonstrated in the collection of studies addressing the issue are

---

[9]It is interesting to note that reaction times to dissimilar word foils in Massaro and Klitzke's (1977) study (p. 295, Table 1) were, on the average, longer than reaction times to dissimlar word foils in Sloboda's (1976) study (Experiment III, p. 98, Table 3). Although direct comparisons are risky, it can at least be speculated that the differences may be due to the fact that Massaro and Klitzke employed randomized presentations of similar and dissimilar foils, whereas Sloboda employed blocked presentations of these stimulus sets. Thus, subjects encountering similar and dissimilar foils at random may have been processing more often at the letter level, whereas subjects encountering only dissimilar foils may have been processing for the most part at the whole-word level. If so, then we can be more confident in the interpretation of Sloboda's findings offered here.

located at a processing stage beyond what Johnson (1975, 1977) has termed the perceptual stage. Thus Sloboda (1977) found that stimulus conditions (high and low illuminance) did *not* differentially affect letter within word and word matching, respectively, but increasing the number of probe stimuli against which to match given targets enhanced the advantage of word matching over letter within word matching, thereby suggesting that the word priority effect accrues at the comparison rather than at the so-called perceptual stage of word recognition. In addition, Marmurek (1977) found that letter within word matching was faster than word matching when targets and probes were presented simultaneously, but the reverse pattern was observed when presentation of probes was delayed, leading Marmurek to draw a similar conclusion. These findings are, of course, contrary to the pattern-unit model as originally articulated, because the model would predict that word matching would take less time than letter within word matching under both presentation conditions. They are more in keeping with Sloboda's (1977) and Marmurek's (1977) suggestions that higher-order encoding is responsible for the word priority effect.

Interestingly enough, Johnson (1979) has recently revised his earlier position, acknowledging that the letters in a word must be "seen" to be assigned a unitary encoding. He also speculates that such encoding takes place at a higher "cognitive" level and provides some support for this position in demonstrating that words can be identified more rapidly in connected text than can letters within words, regardless of whether the subject is asked to search for a word after given only its meaning beforehand or given the word itself beforehand. This revision of the model effectively shifts Johnson's definition of the perceptual unit away from the sensory side of word recognition and closer to the cognitive or interpretative side of the process, underscoring once again the inherent ambiguity that characterizes this concept.

Finally, inasmuch as Johnson's model is in essence a whole-word model of word perception, it enjoys all the benefits that accrue to such models, for example, the ability to account for word superiority, frequency, and familiarity effects. Yet, unlike the other whole-word models discussed (Rumelhart & Siple, 1974; Smith, 1971), Johnson's model assigns no significant role to verbal context, at least none that I could discern. In fact, it is very definitely a multistage, "bottom-up"-type conceptualization and, in this respect, is more like the component letter theories discussed.

Summary

As I have attempted to indicate in my remarks thus far, each of the word recognition models discussed has both strengths and weaknesses, not only by virtue of their logical consistency and their ability to account for the research findings available but, most important, by virtue of their ecological validity. On the positive side, it seems clear that each can, in some measure, account for certain of the word recognition phenomena that have been studied over the years, as manifested at least in observations of the processing strategies employed by the skilled reader. On the negative side, it seems reasonable to suggest that none of the models reviewed reconcile to any compelling degree the disparate findings emerging from comparative tests of hypotheses generated by given conceptualizations, though some incorporate assumptions that allow for alternative explanations of such findings. But more significant is the fact that none, as presently formulated, has the means for dealing with the degree of complexity that characterizes written English or for accommodating the degree of flexibility in processing that such a complex symbol system demands, indeed, the type of flexibility that, in my estimation, characterizes the human information processor. None, for example, can at once account for the skilled reader's ability to process highly discriminable words (*zero, catalyst, gym*) holistically and yet shift to letter level or feature level processing with words less easily discriminated (*cat/cut, show/snow*), while explaining his or her ability to decode unfamiliar words and orthographically regular pseudowords (*glurck*), to identify orthographically irregular or exception words (*epoch*), to disambiguate homographs and homophones (*lead; yolk/yoke*), to distinguish between compounds and pseudocompounds (*fathead versus father and feather*), and in general to process running text selectively and in various size units. Furthermore, none of the models reviewed, save for Gibson's (1971), have included assumptions that allow for variations in mode of processing that may vary with the skill of the reader. As we shall see, there is reason to believe that such assumptions are a necessary component of any comprehensive model of word recognition. The remainder of this chapter more directly addresses these issues in an effort to document the multilevel processing view of word recognition articulated throughout this text.

THE UNIT OF PERCEPTION AS RELATIVE

Having discussed the most prominent single-unit models of word recognition available in the literature, it seems appropriate to turn my attention to the theoretical foundations and supporting evidence for the presumption that the unit of perception in word recognition is relative rather than absolute.

As I indicated earlier, it is my contention that the perceptual unit is determined by three interacting contingencies: (1) the context in which a word is encountered; (2) the characteristics of the word itself; and (3) the skill of the reader. Each of these significantly influences the strategies utilized to access the lexicon. Inherent in this contention is the assumption that such diverse influences necessitate selection of a processing strategy that maximizes the probability of encoding a letter string in a way that will effect recognition as economically as possible. Thus, in the next section, I discuss a conceptualization of the word recognition process that allows for different processing modes—Estes' (1975b, 1977) hierarchical filter model. Estes' is one of two such models that have appeared in the literature in recent years, the other being that of LaBerge and Samuels (1974). However, Estes' model is highlighted in this section, because this author has specifically addressed issues raised by the results of studies already discussed and also because his conceptualization of the recognition process lends greater cohesion to the disparate findings that characterize these studies than any of the models discussed thus far.

The more general concern, in this section, is the influence of context on the processing strategies utilized by the perceiver. For present purposes, context is defined broadly and should be taken to include such factors as the environment in which the perceiver encounters a letter or word target (i.e., in local context such as letters in words versus nonwords, among similar versus dissimilar letters and words, in isolation versus meaningful text); the material he encounters; the conditions under which he encounters such material (i.e., experimental conditions); the set of the perceiver, as induced by the nature of his task; and the instructions he is given. My purpose is to add substance to the argument that contextual factors influence the level at which a letter or word is processed and to this end I specifically focus upon laboratory studies demonstrating differential effects of context, depending on the methodologies employed.

The Role of Context in Letter and Word Recognition

Contextual Determinants of the Word Superiority Effect: Estes' Hierarchical Filter Model

It seems reasonable to suggest, relative to the study of cognitive processes, that from the time that Wundt and his progenitors set out to explore the inner workings of the human mind up to the present there has been neither a more ubiquitous nor a more extensively investigated phenomenon than the word advantage effect. Indeed, as pointed out earlier, we have come full circle during the past 85 years, and what was initially considered to be a rather striking example of the human perceiver's inherent disposition toward unity and cohesion in perception (Cattell, 1886a, 1886b) and later reinterpreted as a classic illustration of the human information processor's ability to synthesize a complex array by means of a rule generated program (Massaro, 1975; Miller et al., 1954) has again been interpreted as a unitary phenomenon (Johnson, 1975, 1977, 1979; Kahneman & Henik, 1975; Theios & Muise, 1977) and debate over the choice between these two interpretations continues (Henderson, in press).

The word advantage effect has taken two forms in laboratory investigations of word recognition, one of which has been called the *word superiority effect* (Reicher, 1969; Wheeler, 1970), and the other, the *word priority effect* (Sloboda, 1977). In studies demonstrating a word superiority effect, target stimuli are always single letters, whereas probe stimuli (letters, words, pseudowords) vary from trial to trial and are presented under stimulus conditions characterized by low signal-to-noise ratios. The word priority effect, in contrast, is demonstrated in studies varying the target stimuli (letters or words) while keeping the probe stimuli (words or groups of words) constant, and each is presented under stimulus conditions characterized by high signal-to-noise ratios. The results of both type studies have been offered as evidence for the preeminence of the word as an integrated unit, but as we have seen, the interpretations of these results and of word advantage effects in general are conflicting. Common to both, however, is the fact that word advantage effects are found to be present or absent, depending on the stimulus conditions and the nature of the stimuli presented to subjects. I have already suggested that a multilevel processing view of word recognition might account for these disparities more adequately than any of the theories discussed thus far, and Estes (1975b, 1977) and his associates have conducted a series of studies that specifically evaluated this possibility. The results of these studies not only lend credence to the levels of processing notion advocated here but also became the basis for construction of a word recognition model that is essentially compatible with this conceptualization. It is therefore instructive to describe Estes' model briefly.

Figure 2.5 presents a schematic characterization of Estes' (1977) hierarchical filter model of letter and word recognition. As seen, the model is depicted as a hierarchical arrangement of subsystems corresponding to memory traces or "engrams" from past experience, alternatively called "control elements" (Estes, 1972, 1975b) or "detectors" (Estes, 1977). Control elements with similar properties are organized in ascending order at the levels of *features, letters,* and *letter sequences,* such as clusters, syllables, and words. Control elements at given level are differentially sensitive to their counterparts in printed words. Feature detectors are sensitive to both the global features of a printed word and the features of its individual letters, whereas letter and letter sequence detectors are sensitive, respectively, to familiar patterns in one's experience, corresponding to letters of the alphabet (presumably in alternative fonts), and to frequently recurring sequences of letters, corresponding to letter groups and words. Feature analysis is assumed to take place on letter sets simultaneously, and it is contended that the letters in a word must be recognized before the word itself is recognized.

Following Anderson (1973), Estes proposes that this hierarchical arrangement of control elements functions as an ascending "filter" system, whereby detectors at given levels respond only to stimulus patterns that match those established in long-term memory. Detectors activated by stimulus input at one level in the hierarchy transmit "patterns of excitation" to control elements at the next level, which in turn respond only to input patterns from the lower level that can be matched with *their* counterparts in permanent memory, and so on. If at given levels no match is found, transmission to the next level is blocked. The system, therefore, "sifts" information from one level to the next and is said to be efficient, in that a small number of feature detectors can account for all the letters of the alphabet, which in turn account for a much larger number of words. Letter

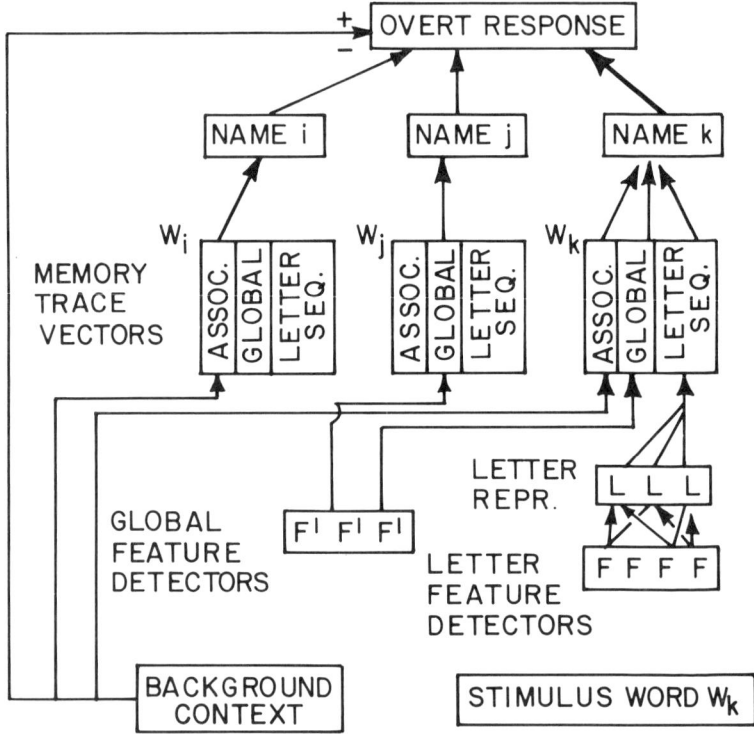

FIG. 2.5. Graphic depiction of Estes' hierarchical filter model for letter and word recognition (taken from Estes, 1977, with permission of the author and publisher).

detectors are presumed to be activated simultaneously, but patterns of excitation from given letter sequences are transmitted to subsets of word representations that have attributes in common. Thus, by extension, words with overlapping letters and featural characteristics become possible candidates for generalization error, but the probability of such error is minimized because of the fact that word representations in long-term memory incorporate other types of information to aid discrimination, for example, supraletter or global features, contexts in which given words have appeared (and are thus appropriate or inappropriate), meaningful associates with other words, and information as to the similarities and differences in letter sequences, which might facilitate critical discriminations.

Estes obviously considers the flow of sensory information to be unidirectional and independent of contextual information from trace vectors in long-term memory. However, after sensory processing has produced a candidate letter set, various types of contextual information begin to influence the recognition process. Such information includes background context, such as the environment in which a letter or word appears and the peculiarities of the perceiver's task, in addition to specific associates generated by the word itself or any of its constituents. Input from contextual information received prior to or simultaneous with the stimulus word will lead to partial activation of both the stimulus word and words having attributes in common with that word. Input from global feature detectors will have the same effect. In contrast, inputs from letter feature detectors and the letters themselves directly activate the representation of the stimulus word in memory.

The various inputs, independently generated from the several sources mentioned, converge upon the trace vectors for the stimulus word giving rise to an identifying response, such as naming or yes/no matching. Inputs from a single letter or an unpronounceable nonword are presumed to be processed in the same manner, but the output of letter level processing would find no match in long-term memory at the word level and would therefore process these stimuli solely at the level of letter names. The model does not explicate how pronounceable pseudowords would be identified, but I assume that this would be accomplished via grapheme–phoneme correspondence rules or by analogy with real words, because familiar letter sequences that comprise parts of words are said to be represented as units in long-term memory.

As noted earlier, Estes' model was formulated on the basis of a series of experiments evaluating the word superiority effect, which (it will be recalled) refers to the observation that subjects are able to match letter targets with letters embedded in words better than with letters embedded in nonwords and better than with those presented individually after only a brief tachistoscopic exposure. I have already made reference to the companion studies of Thompson and Massaro (1973) and Massaro (1973), demonstrating that this effect can be eliminated when response letters are known beforehand. Studies by Bjork and Estes (1973) and Estes et al., (1974) obtained similar results. But whereas Massaro (1975) infers from these results that the word superiority effect can be most parsimoniously attributed to the application of orthographic rules as an aid to letter recognition, Estes suggests that the effect is due to a variety of factors, depending on the conditions under which stimuli are presented.

As a first step in distinguishing between various alternatives, Estes (1975a, 1975b) employed a method he called the "postexposure probe technique." In one study employing this method (Experiment IIA), subjects were presented with single letters, words, and nonwords (anagrams of word stimuli), with target letters remaining constant for each triad: either *L* or *R*. This was essentially a modified Reicher paradigm, so that both target letters completed a real word. Furthermore, none of the letter targets were known in advance. Masking stimuli (dollar signs) were presented before and after presentations of target stimuli, all for very brief durations. Each letter target was presented in the same location, but for single letter targets noise characters were presented in the vacant letter positions to equate stimuli for lateral masking effects (# # L #, C O L D, O D L C).

Upon presentation of the postmask, a small arrow appeared under the position at which the letter target appeared, and the subjects' task was to indicate which letter appeared in that location.

The significant findings are as follows. First, the overall analysis produced the typical word superiority effect, with words having an advantage over nonwords and single letters. However, qualitative analyses of error patterns yielded results that do not conform to the orthographic redundancy hypothesis of Massaro (1975). For one thing, comparisons of errors on word and nonword trials yielded no differences between the two in proportion of $\underline{L}$ and $\underline{R}$ errors. If one were using orthographic rules to disambiguate target letters that were *not* fully processed, then the number of L-R errors should be greater on word than on nonword trials, but this was not the case. Indeed, the advantage of words over single letters was due, exclusively, to subjects' tendency to make more omission errors (no response) on single-letter trials than on word trials, suggesting that a more conservative response mode was adopted by subjects on single-letter trials. At the same time, comparisons of word and nonword trials indicated that only transposition or letter sequencing errors differentiated the two stimulus sets rather than L-R, intrusion, or omission errors. Furthermore, when subjects made either an L or R response to probe stimuli, the percentage of correct identifications among the three context conditions did not differ. These results suggest that a word context helps reduce uncertainty as to the location, rather than the identity of a target letter.[10] Thus, by extension, a word context does not narrow the range of response alternatives, as suggested by the orthographic redundancy hypothesis (Massaro, 1975), nor does it have any direct effect on target discriminability.

However, in several other experiments evaluating the effects of word context, Estes (1975a) was able to define the conditions under which redundancy *is* operative. In two related studies, employing slightly different postprobe proce-

---

[10]Estes (1972) theorizes that positional uncertainty of the letters in a string often arises because of an inherent limitation, characteristic of the visual system, in processing visual input stimulating peripheral locations on the retina. Specifically, it is suggested that the density of input channels from the retina to feature detectors decreases from the fovea to the periphery, so that feature information from items in the visual field that are sufficiently close together must often utilize the same channels, if input from these items stimulates receptors toward the periphery. Thus, Estes et al. (1976) found that report accuracy for the letters in a multielement string dropped off from foveal-to-peripheral locations and that: (1) accuracy was greatest at the endpoints of a letter string, thereby creating serial position effects; and (2) most of the errors were letter position rather than letter identity errors. These authors also found that positional errors were correlated with digram frequency (Underwood & Schultz, 1960) in that substitutions involving given letter pairs were often the higher-frequency digrams. For example, CH (a high-frequency digram) was more often substituted for HC (a low-frequency digram) than was HC substituted for CH. Estes et al. (1976) conclude from these findings that one benefit derived from knowledge of orthography is compensation for positional uncertainty when letter strings are presented under less than optimal stimulus conditions. Hence, the role of word contexts as a partial explanation of the word superiority effect.

dures, subjects were presented with letter targets (L or R) first and the three context conditions: noise characters ($ $ # $), words (F O # D), and nonwords (D F # O), either immediately following termination of the letter stimulus (Experiment IIB) or 200 msec after (Experiment IIC). Under the "immediately following" condition, a word advantage was again observed, but error analyses under this condition indicated that subjects were inclined to fill in perceptual gaps (i.e., when target letters were not clearly identified) by trying to complete a word. This tendency was reflected in a higher percentage of correct responses on single-letter trials than on word and nonword trials, in instances when the subject made either an L or R response to probe stimuli. However, there were *no* differences among these conditions when presentation of the word contexts was delayed, which of course reduces the utility of such stimuli. Estes points out that in these latter studies letter location effects were minimized, allowing the conclusion that orthographic redundancy may be influential in response selection when context is fully available (as in the "immediately following" condition) but not when context is available for very brief durations (as in the Reicher-Wheeler studies) or not available at all. This interpretation, of course, contrasts with Massaro's (1975) explanation of the word superiority effect.

Complimenting these findings are the results of one other study in this series (Estes, 1975a, Experiment I). Of specific interest was whether or not a word context actually influences detection of the features embedded within words ("perceptual" effect) or the tendency to respond with a bias for forming words when letters are perceived imperfectly ("inferential" or redundancy effect). The first alternative (perceptual effect) predicts a difference, favoring word contexts between trials on which both letter alternatives form words (WW) and those on which both form nonwords (NN), because redundancy effects are presumably controlled. The second alternative (inferential effect) predicts that differences, favoring word contexts, would appear in comparisons between trials on which incorrect letter alternatives change words to nonwords (WN) and those on which incorrect letter alternatives change nonwords to words (NW), and *only* on trials on which context letters are better perceived than target letters. In such instances, a word advantage will be manifested in better performance on WN trials than on NW trials.

Estes and his associates (Bjork & Estes, 1973; Estes et al., 1974) had already found no differences between WW and NN trials when target and context letters were presented simultaneously for brief exposures with target alternatives known beforehand. In contrast, a difference favoring WN over NW trials was observed: (1) when the target letter appeared briefly, followed by the context letters for a protracted exposure duration; and (2) when both target and context letters appeared simultaneously, with context letters available for a protracted duration, the effect being larger under the latter condition. Estes (1975b) concluded from these results that the benefits provided by word context accrue at the level of inference rather than at the level of feature analysis.

The major conclusion drawn by Estes (1977) from the results of the studies just discussed is as follows: When a discrimination can be made on the basis of a feature difference between familiar targets known beforehand, word contexts influence performance only by contributing redundant information and only when stimulus conditions allow context to be operative. However, he suggests that the same should *not* be true when full identification of target items is required. Under such circumstances, context may: (1) affect the individual's threshold for generating an identifying response; (2) facilitate positional accuracy; or (3) help identify the target as a member of a familiar letter group. Estes suggests that the first influence mentioned may be responsible for the advantage that has been observed in discriminating letters in words better than letters presented singly (Reicher, 1969; Wheeler, 1970). The second and third types of influence are illustrated in a later study reported by Estes (1977). In this study no differences in performance between WW and NN conditions were observed when target letters were presented beforehand, but differences favoring the WW condition were evident when target letters were cued after presentation of the WW and NN contexts. The same was true when the positions of target letters was the dependent measure. In the precue condition, it is likely that subjects were discriminating at the feature level, whereas both word and letter level processing were probable vehicles for discrimination under the postcue conditions, consistent with the hierarchical filter model.

Finally, in a study by Estes and Allmeyer (reported by Estes, 1977), subjects were presented with four letter words (W), pronounceable pseudowords (P), and nonword strings (N) under very brief exposure durations (25 to 200 msec) and asked to judge the lexicality of each stimulus as well as to indicate how many letters of each were identified thereafter. Consistent with the hierarchical (versus a globel features) model, it was found that accuracy of lexical decisions was above chance only when all four letters of a string were identified. Further, it was not until at least two letters of a given string had been identified that the W and P strings manifested an advantage over the N string in identification of the third letter; and it was not until three letters had been identified that the W string manifested an advantage over the P string in identification of the fourth letter. These results conform to Estes' model, insofar as both pronounceable trigrams and real words are assumed to have representations in long-term memory, whereas nonword strings are not so represented. They are also consistent with the idea that the letters in a word must be recognized in order to identify that word. However, this notion must be tempered somewhat by the fact that Estes' use of four-letter words biases one toward this conclusion, insofar as the identity of many four-letter words cannot be determined without knowledge of the fourth letter, and in such instances letter level processing is often required for disambiguation.

The results of the studies by Estes and his associates provide rather substantial support for this author's hierarchical filter explanation of word recognition and, by extension, for the notion that the unit of perception is relative rather than absolute. By postulating that a word (defined as a unique letter sequence) and its components constitute multiple representations in long-term memory, Estes' model allows for multilevel processing of letters and words, an inherent assumption of the model being that processing at given levels can be implicitly initiated or terminated, depending on task demands and contextual factors. According to the theory, such factors serve to preactivate control elements at particular levels while raising thresholds for those at other levels, thereby facilitating selective attention to critical discriminators. The experiments investigating the word superiority effect provide support for this notion and also demonstrate that the advantage provided by word context accrues at the cognitive rather than the perceptual level. But here again the definition of "perceptual level" is ambiguous. For example, Estes (1977, p. 23) suggests that the advantage of the hierarchical filter model is that it enables the perceiver to "see what is there," unencumbered by higher-order information. But "seeing" all the letters in a word is not the same as recognizing and identifying the word itself, inasmuch as words are defined by invariant letter sequences that must be encoded in ways that allow these processes to take place. As noted earlier, some words have identical sequences but must be dissected and grouped differently to be recognized, as in the case of compounds versus pseudocompounds. At the same time, many unfamiliar words and orthographically regular letter strings have no lexical representations in long-term memory and in spite of this can be identified. Estes' model does not explicitly account for such contingencies, although it does have the basic structural characteristics necessary for doing so, given some additional assumptions. I comment further upon Estes' model but for now turn to some additional findings in support of my position.

Some Additional Qualifications on the Word Superiority Effect

The results of several other studies evaluating the word superiority effect further illustrate the degree to which experimental manipulations of local context influence the processing strategies of the perceiver. The dependent measure in each of these studies is, of course, letter recognition in word versus nonword contexts, and the major question addressed, as in all other studies evaluating the issue, is whether the word superiority effect is a perceptual or cognitive phenomenon. Of particular interest in the experiments to be discussed is the interaction of stimulus factors, word contexts, and instructional variables in determining the levels at which discriminations are made. A brief summary of the salient findings of relevant studies will suffice to illustrate these influences.

Johnston and McClelland (1973) evaluated the reliability of the Reicher (1969) and Wheeler (1970) findings, employing: (1) blocked presentations of words and single letters, to evaluate a "set" to perceive words as a possible source of the word advantage effect; (2) viewing of response alternatives outside of the tachistoscope, to control for inadvertant masking of single letters; (3)

lateral masking and position cuing of single letters, to evaluate the influence of contour and positional uncertainty (location in space) on single-letter perception; and (4) patterned and white noise masks to assess the differential effects of the two. The experimental contrast was between the matching of words differing in one letter and single-letter matching. In spite of position cuing favoring single letters, the word superiority effect was again observed but only under the pattern mask condition. In fact, under the white noise condition, a single-letter advantage was observed, perhaps because of persisting after images, which allowed more complete processing of letter and word stimuli. Although these findings are consistent with Estes' suggestion that orthographic context facilitates performance at the inferential rather than the perceptual level, the authors leaned toward the latter interpretation.

One other finding of interest in this study is the absence of performance differences between single letters, with and without adjacent masks. This suggests that the contrast effects provided by word contexts cannot account for Reicher's (1969) and Wheeler's (1970) observation that, under brief exposure conditions, letters in words can be perceived better than letters presented singly.

A subsequent study by Johnston and McClelland (1974) provides evidence that the way in which subjects deploy their attention is a factor that influences letter and word discrimination. Briefly, it was found that subjects who were instructed to focus on a letter embedded in the center of a word were less accurate in identifying that letter than subjects who were told to focus upon the word as a whole. This finding was interpreted as support for the idea that whole-word perception influences letter feature extraction.

The complexity of the issues surrounding the explanation of the word superiority effect and the contradictory nature of the conceptualizations that have addressed these issues is further illustrated in the following series of arguments and counterarguments.

Smith and Haviland (1972) evaluated Thompson and Massaro's (1973) contention that redundancy is not controlled in the Reicher–Wheeler paradigm by giving subjects practice with highly redundant nonwords in addition to explicit knowledge of the rules for constructing those words, and *still* found a word superiority effect. Massaro (1973) countered that the word and nonword trials in Smith and Haviland's study were not blocked in such a way as to maximize the probability that the subjects became proficient in using redundancy to facilitate letter recognition. It will be recalled, in this connection, that in separate studies by Thompson and Massaro (1973), Massaro (1973), Bjork and Estes (1973), and Estes et al. (1974) a letter rather than a word advantage was observed when subjects were presented with restricted letter alternatives prior to experimental trials. This was interpreted by Massaro as support for the redundancy hypothesis rather than the Reicher–Wheeler interpretation.

But this conclusion is itself contraindicated by the results of studies conducted later, which *did* use restricted letter alternatives and yet obtained a word superiority effect. For example, unlike the experiments just mentioned, Carr, Lehmkuhle, Kottas, Astor-Stetson, and Arnold (1976) employed blocked rather than randomized presentations of stimulus sets and not only obtained a word superiority effect but also found that the effect is least likely to occur when the target letter occupies the middle position, which was the case in the Thompson and Massaro (1973) and Massaro (1973) studies. The authors suggest that the observed differences might be due to more effective deployment of attention to multiple-word features under the blocked presentation condition utilized in their study.

Similarly, Spector and Purcell (1977) presented subjects with restricted as well as unrestricted letter sets, and both conditions yielded a word superiority effect of about the same magnitude. This study differed from previous studies in that the stimulus sets (four-letter items) subtended a visual angle of 0.6°, which is much smaller than those employed in other investigations involving word and nonword comparisons (from 3.3° to 4.5°). Unlike the study of Carr et al. (1976), randomized rather than blocked presentations were employed and a word superiority effect was nevertheless observed. Of additional interest in this investigation is the fact that a serial position effect was evident for nonwords but not for real words and also that the restricted-letter alternatives condition yielded better performance for nonwords than did the unrestricted alternatives condition. These data suggest that the words were processed holistically, whereas the nonwords were processed letter by letter. Reinforcing these findings are the results of a subsequent study by Purcell, Stanovich, and Spector (1978), which employed restricted response letters, prior knowledge of alternatives, randomized presentations, and certainty as to position of critical letters. In spite of these constraints, a word superiority effect was obtained. Noteworthy is the fact that the stimulus sets were identical to those used by Massaro (1973) (AC̲E, AG̲E, AP̲E, AR̲E versus VC̲H, VG̲H, VP̲H, VR̲H). Even more important is the fact that a very small visual angle (0.5°) was subtended by each set, which seemed to be the critical differences accounting for the conflicting findings yielded by these studies.

But in a later investigation employing fixed-letter alternatives (Greenberg & Krueger, 1980), word and nonword stimulus sets (three-letter sets) subtended a larger visual angle (2.1°), and a word advantage was nevertheless observed. However, in this study, holistic processing of letter strings was fostered by: (1) having subjects make lexicality judgments for each stimulus, while discriminating target letters; and (2) presenting the two types of stimuli in blocks. Distinctiveness of letter stimuli and positional certainty were also systematically varied. Although no word superiority effect was found for a Massaro replication condition, the effect *was* observed in both the lexical judgment and blocked presentations conditions. The magnitude of the effect was greatest with blocked presentations, position certainty, and distinctive letters, especially when the target was in the first position. The authors suggest that both the set to process words as wholes *and* visual angle are important determinants of the word superiority effect.

To continue, Mezrich (1973) attributed the word superiority effect to the fact that words lend themselves to verbal coding more readily than letters and obtained an advantage for letters over words when subjects were forced to vocalize letter stimuli prior to probe matching. This finding, of course, implicates short-term memory as the critical factor, but Appleman (1976) obtained a *word* advantage when word and nonword matches were presented simultaneously, thus controlling for memory. Appleman interpreted this finding as support for Estes' (1975a, 1975b) positional uncertainty explanation of word effects.

Finally, Baron and Thurston (1973) found that single letters embedded in words and pronounceable nonwords were detected better than those embedded in unpronounceable nonwords, but there were no differences in performance observed in word and pronounceable nonword contrasts. This effect was thought to be attributable to orthographic regularity, whereas word frequency, meaning, phonologic coding, and memory limitations were ruled out as significant determinants. However, Manelis (1974) pointed out that Baron and Thurston employed only low-frequency words, did not equate the number of word and nonword stimuli presented to subjects, and may have attenuated any advantage for words that might be occasioned by meaning and familiarity by giving them repeated presentations of stimulus sets. Manelis controlled for these factors by: (1) using a large number of high-frequency words for the word sets; (2) equalizing the number of word and nonword stimuli; (3) presenting subjects with each stimulus only once; and (4) contrasting blocked and randomized presentations of stimulus sets. As in the Baron and Thurston (1973) study, the experimental task was detection of letters embedded in words and pronounceable nonwords. A word advantage was observed under both blocked and randomized presentations. However, the effect was more pronounced under blocked presentations, suggesting that subjects could alter their processing strategies so as to maximize the gains accrued with word stimuli. The author concluded that meaning and familiarity *are* important determinants of the word superiority effect and considered the possibility that either a phonologic encoding model or a modified version of Wheeler's (1970) feature selection model might account for the findings.[11]

The foregoing congerie of disparate research findings illustrates well the

---

[11]Manelis (1974), like Wheeler (1970), adopts the essential features of Feigenbaum's (1963) discrimination net model in proposing that word identification might involve a series of critical "tests" at given letter positions, such that the outcome of each test in turn determines the next one made. After a series of such tests, a word would be uniquely identified. For example, if the features for the letters ___ O S T had been identified, then the next test made would be directed toward a restricted letter set: C, H, L, M, or P. However, Manelis points out that his conceptualization differs from that of Wheeler's (1970) in that such tests would be made *after* the feature extraction process is complete and would thereby function as a retrieval mechanism rather than a feature selection device.

extent to which variations in experimental methodologies have shaped conflicting characterizations of the word recognition process and of the unit of perception issue in particular. It is also clear from these findings that under some circumstances word contexts *do* facilitate letter discrimination, but the locus of this effect remains in dispute. Yet if one considers the fact that a word contains a variety of types of information (Gibson, 1971) that may facilitate discrimination in qualitatively different ways, many of the disparate findings might be reconciled. This in itself does not resolve the unit of perception issue, but it is consistent with the idea that contextual factors can influence the processing strategies generated by the perceiver. In the aforementioned experiments, various types of orthographic context appeared to be influential in determining the level of processing at which letter discriminations were made. In the next section, I present evidence that a word's status in connected text as well as its lexical properties can affect the perceiver's mode of processing.

Verbal Context Effects in Word Recognition

A number of investigations have demonstrated that various types of verbal context can influence the word recognition process. Three such effects have been studied. One has been observed in studies demonstrating that appropriate and inappropriate sentence contexts differentially affect visual recognition thresholds. The second is reflected in apparent differences in the size of the processing unit when words are encountered in thematic material as opposed to unconnected text. The third has been manifested in studies showing that lexical relatedness can affect the recognition process. I briefly document each of these in turn.

Sentence Contexts. One of the first demonstrations that verbal context can positively influence the word recognition process was provided by Tulving and Gold (1963). These authors measured recognition thresholds for tachistoscopically presented words as a function of preexposure sentence contexts that varied on two dimensions: congruence of target words with sentence contexts, and amount of information provided by sentence contexts (the latter defined as the number of words comprising complete and incomplete sentences, respectively). The major findings of note in this study are that recognition threshold for target words decreased monotonically, with increases in the number of words completing sentences that were compatible with those words. In contrast, recognition thresholds for target words increased monotonically, with increases in the number of words completing sentences that were incompatible with those words. The authors concluded from these findings that contextual and stimulus factors are inversely related determinants of the word recognition process, such that less stimulus information is required for recognition of a target word when relevant context is available.

This conclusion was reinforced in a subsequent study by Tulving, Mandler, and Baumal (1964). In this study, exposure duration and amount of contextual information were systematically varied. There were eight exposure durations, ranging from 0 to 140 msec and four levels of sentence context, the number of words in each sentence having been *zero, two, four,* and *eight,* respectively. Of particular interest in this investigation was the question of how stimulus and contextual factors combine to facilitate tachistoscopic recognition. One possibility is that these influences are independent and additive, which essentially is the position adopted by the component letter theorists already discussed (Gough, 1972; Massaro, 1975; Estes, 1972, 1975a, 1975b, 1977). Tulving et al. (1964) equated this hypothesis with the statistical definition of independence, defined as

$$P_{d,c} = P_d + P_c - P_d P_c$$

where p_d is the probability of a correct response at a given level of exposure duration and p_c is the probability of a correct response with a given amount of context, defined as the number of words in a sentence.

A second possibility is that the two sources of information are redundant. Thus:

$$P_{d,c} = P_c, \quad \text{if } P_c > P_d$$
$$P_{d,c} = P_d, \quad \text{if } P_d > P_c$$

A third possibility is that the two sources of information are interactive (rather than independent and additive) and thereby facilitate recognition above the level predicted by the independent sources hypothesis:

$$P_{d,c} > P_d + P_c - P_d P_c$$

The results of the study support hypothesis 3. The stimulus and context conditions combined yielded higher proportions of correct responses at recognition thresholds that were lower than those that characterized either the stimulus-alone or context-alone conditions, the F ratio for this interaction being statistically significant. This effect was evident at all stratifications corresponding with these conditions and increased monotonically with increases in exposure durations and amount of context. Furthermore, the probabilities for expected proportion of correct responses at given levels of exposure durations and sentence length were consistently underestimated by the independence/additivity formula, suggesting that the interaction hypothesis might be seriously considered.

It is interesting to note that the sentence contexts in which target words were embedded facilitated between 4% and 43% improvement in word recognition accuracy, in comparison with words presented in isolation; this range encompassed all exposure durations and all levels of context (range for complete sentences between 24% and 43%). These data provide rather substantial support for the notion that contextual information facilitates word recognition. However, they once again raise the question of whether or not context exerts its effect at the level of perception or at a later stage of processing. A strict rendering of the interactionist view suggests that context affects perception, whereas an equally rigid account of the independent processes view suggests that context affects memory and/or inferential behavior. Tulving et al. (1964) are a bit circumspect on this issue, pointing out that the data do not provide much insight as to *how* stimulus and contextual information combine to facilitate word recognition and that the effect might be limited to the particular response measure employed (i.e., the probability of correct responding). They also point out that although the independence/additivity formula consistently underestimates obtained response probabilities, a different measure, based on logit transformations of these probabilities, yields a function that supports the independent processes hypothesis.

That the concerns expressed by Tulving et al. (1964) may be valid is suggested in a later study by Gough, Alford, and Holley-Wilcox (1978). These investigators reasoned that the experimental procedure employed by Tulving et al. (1964) may have underestimated stimulus parameters and thus response probabilities by virtue of the fact that subjects were limited to a single response for each target word. Gough et al (1978) modified this procedure by allowing subjects an unlimited number of responses to a given target word and thereafter based the estimates of the stimulus parameter on the proportion of subjects who included that word among their responses. The modification yielded (response) probability estimates that were in greater accord with obtained results than were those derived from the procedures used by Tulving et al, thus supporting the independent processes explanation of contextual effects.

Additional support for the facilitating role of context in word recognition comes from a study conducted by Morton (1964). Employing a procedure similar to that used by Tulving and Gold (1963), randomly assigned subject groups were presented brief exposures of the same list of words under three different conditions: (1) at the end of incomplete sentences in which occurrences of target words are highly probable; (2) at the end of incomplete sentences in which occurrences of target words are less probable; (3) at the end of a row of X's, a no-context condition. Transitional probabilities for the occurrence of given target words at the end of particular sentences were derived from an independent sample. Duration exposures were incremented through the method of ascending limits, and the dependent measure was response threshold.

As in the Tulving et al. studies, lower thresholds were associated with the high probability context condition, and performance in the low probability context condition was little better than performance in the no-context condition. Because a stringent criterion for accuracy was adopted (two successive correct responses) and because subjects were instructed *not* to guess, the results were not thought to be due to response bias. Furthermore, there were a large number of errors based on the stimulus properties of target words, suggesting that stimulus as well as contextual factors were involved in the recognition process.

Morton (1964) concludes from these findings that context lowers recognition thresholds, such that fewer visual cues are needed to discriminate and identify given words. He also suggests that the contextual influences observed can be characterized as "perceptual" effects, in that words were recognized at exposure durations that would normally be inadequate for recognition of those words without the aid of context. This interpretation accords with Estes' (1975b, 1977) suggestion that, under some circumstances, context may facilitate economy of processing in visual word recognition, by activating discriminating cues at given levels of processing. Yet, as discussed earlier, Estes does *not* believe that context *directly* influences perception. However, on close inspection, the differences between Morton's and Estes' interpretation of contextual effects appears to be a difference in semantics rather than substance, thus underscoring once again the confusion engendered by the way in which different researchers characterize and/or conceptualize the perceptual process. Indeed, Morton (1964) explicitly states that stimulus and contextual information are independently derived and that their (separate) effects are additive rather than interactive in the qualitative sense. In fact, in two subsequent papers (Morton, 1968, 1969), he generates a number of mathematical proofs, based on results reported in the relevant literature (which include data taken from Tulving et al., 1964) and rather convincingly demonstrates that stimulus and contextual factors constitute independent sources of information.[12] This, of course, accords with Estes' position.

Alternative interpretations of the effects of context notwithstanding, it is clear from the studies discussed in this section that words embedded in running text are processed differently than words presented in isolation, and the data are consistent with the notion that the processing levels at which words are discriminated might be significantly affected by contextual information. Whether such effects are truly "perceptual" or "cognitive," depends (it would seem) on one's respective definitions of perception and cognition, as I have attempted to indicate. It is, nevertheless, clear from the results that less visual information is required for word discrimination when relevant context is available than when it is not available, which is consonant with the levels of processing notion engendered here. Still more support for this idea comes from studies evaluating the effect of thematic material on the size of the processing unit, which I briefly discuss in the following section.

---

[12]It is worth noting that Morton's (1964) results constitute the seminal documentation of his "logogen" theory of word recognition, which has had a good deal of currency in the literature. According to this theory, each printed word is represented in long-term memory by a unique neural entity termed the *logogen*. The logogen is essentially a "counting device" that tallies the number of attributes defining a given word and that "fires" whenever the number of attributes rises above a certain threshold value. When this happens, a response corresponding with word recognition is made available. The logogen has a certain "resting" threshold that can be lowered by stimulation from the printed word it represents and from words with similar attributes (*visual, semantic, syntactic,* and *phonologic*). It can also be lowered by appropriate contexts and each source of stimulation increments the attribute count independent of the other. Because the effects of stimulus and contextual information are additive, their combined effects can lead to word recognition when either, by itself, does not raise the attribute count high enough for recognition to occur.

Thematic Material and the Unit of Processing. Drewnowski and Healy (1977) have characterized the reading process in a way that is quite compatible with the levels of processing conceptualizations of word recognition that have appeared in the literature (Estes, 1975b, 1977; Gibson, 1971; LaBerge & Samuels, 1974). These authors suggest that reading involves the processing of graphic, orthographic, lexical, and syntactic information, in rough correspondence with five different types of hierarchically arranged processing units: *letters, letter groups, words, phrases,* and *clauses* or *sentences*. In contrast to Gibson's (1971) suggestion that processing at respective levels is mutually exclusive, it is assumed that particular units are accessed in parallel and that processing at higher levels can be completed before processing at lower levels. It is further assumed that "identification" of a unit at one level results in continued processing at that level, without necessary completion of processing at lower levels. Thus, the reader may identify one word and move on to the next without processing all the letters or letter groups within that word.

A final assumption is that, in the course of normal reading, material at the "highest level" (phrases and sentences) is in primary focus, but material at lower levels is processed at the same time. The level at which the text is encoded is determined by the stimulus materials used and the nature of the task, but the ability to effectively engage in multilevel processing is dependent on the knowledge and skill of the reader, which can be taken to refer, respectively, to the processing units the reader has available as well as the degree to which he is able to utilize such information flexibly and efficiently in word recognition and identification.

It would be expected from Drewnowski and Healy's (1977) conceptualization that successful processing at the word level may often terminate processing at the letter or the letter group level before these word constituents are apprehended. Conversely, impaired processing at the word level would make it more likely that processing at the letter or letter group levels would proceed to completion. These expectations were evaluated in a study conducted by Healy (1976).

The primary purpose of this study was to determine whether or not words are identified in units larger than the letter. In a previous investigation, Corcoran (1966) observed that subjects asked to search for the letter *e* in words presented in running text missed this letter more often in silent *e* words (e.g., lake) than in words in which *e* was pronounced and most often when this letter was embedded in the word *the*. Three possible explanations were offered: (1) that silent *e*'s are not encoded phonologically and therefore missed; (2) that highly redundant words such as *the* (which contain *e*'s) are *not* processed; and (3) that silent *e*'s are in the terminal position and may go unnoticed. Healy (1976) offered a fourth possibility: that high-frequency words, such as *the,* will be processed as units or chunks, thus increasing the probability that component letters will not be registered and/or encoded. This was referred to as the "unitization" hypothesis.

Four related experiments were conducted. The first was essentially a replication of Corcoran's study, but in this instance subjects were asked to search for the letter *t* rather than the letter *e* in *the*'s encountered in running text. They were also presented with a "scrambled letter" condition in which *the*'s appeared in the same locations but in the midst of random letter strings derived from the words in the original passage. The major finding was that total errors, reading time, and the proportion of *t* errors in *the* locations were significantly greater in the prose condition than in the scrambled letter conditions. Because the conditional proportion of errors for detecting *t*'s in *the*'s was well above chance for the prose condition and well below chance for the scrambled letter condition, a speed/accuracy tradeoff was thought to be an unlikely explanation of the findings. Because Corcoran's results were, in essence, replicated with the *t* in *the* as the target letter rather than the *e,* the terminal location explanation offered by this author was ruled out.

However, inasmuch as the results of this study would be consistent with both the redundancy and the unitization hypotheses, and because *t*'s are not pronounced in the consonant digraph *th,* leaving the phonologic encoding hypothesis intact, two other experiments were conducted. The first of these was designed to evaluate the redundancy hypothesis further. Subjects were presented the same *t* detection task, but this time *the*'s were embedded in scrambled *word* passages rather than in prose or scrambled letter passages. Although the speed and accuracy measures for *t* detection errors fell midway between the prose and scrambled letter passages as might be expected, the proportion of *t* errors in *the* locations were *not* significantly different in the prose and scrambled word passages. This finding provides indirect support for the unitization hypothesis. Because *the*'s are less redundant in the scrambled word passage than in the prose passage, one might have expected significantly fewer errors in the former (suggesting that *the*'s were not processed in the prose passage), but this was not the case.

The intent of the third experiment was to distinguish between the unitization and the phonologic encoding explanation of the letter-search errors observed in the previous studies. Subjects were again presented with the *t* detection task, but this time the *t*'s appeared in the archaic and less familiar word *thy* as well as in the word *the,* each embedded in identical scrambled word passages. Accuracy in letter detection was significantly greater in the *thy* condition, which would be at variance with the phonologic encoding hypothesis, inasmuch as the *th* digraph is pronounced exactly the same way in both *thy* and *the.* It was suggested that lack of familiarity with *thy* may have caused subjects to attend more to this word than to *the,* the more familiar of the two.

A final experiment directly evaluated the possibility that familiar words are more likely to be processed as units than are unfamiliar words, familiarity in this instance being defined in terms of word frequency. Accordingly, high- and low-frequency words (equated for length and *t* locations) were presented in scrambled word passages and subjects were again asked to search for the letter *t.*

Consistent with expectations, high-frequency words engendered more detection errors than did low-frequency words. It was concluded from the results of these studies that the skilled reader often processes words in units larger than the letter, this strategy being especially probable in the case of high-frequency words. Healy (1976) cautioned, however, that her findings should not necessarily be taken as support for the size of the perceptual unit employed in reading, because the effects demonstrated in these studies may accrue at higher levels.

In a subsequent investigation, Drewnowski and Healy (1977) provide support for the idea that familiar word sequences may be read in units larger than the word. To summarize briefly, in five separate experiments, subjects were asked to read prose or scrambled word passages in which syntactically legal phrases were either present or absent. They were also asked to read prose passages either arrayed vertically in list format or presented in mixed-type cases. Subjects in each condition were asked to circle a letter (*t* or *n*), a letter cluster embedded in a word (ra*ther* or h*and*le) or a high-frequency word (*the* or *and*). Consistent with expectations, subjects made a large number (beyond chance) of detection errors on the high-frequency words *the* and *and* when these words appeared either in prose passages or in syntactically legal phrases embedded in scrambled word passages. Such errors were significantly reduced when they appeared in inappropriate syntactic contexts and in prose passages appearing in mixed-type cases, both conditions apparently disrupting phrase processing. In contrast, these effects were not observed for the control word *ant,* which has a lower frequency than the other two words. These results were taken as support for the notion that familiar word sequences may be read in units larger than the word, perhaps in short phrases or sentences.[13] Because there were fewer detection errors observed in both the mixed-type cases and the inappropriate syntax conditions, the possibility that the effects observed in these studies may take place at the "perceptual" level was *not* ruled out. In fact, the authors consider the possibility that subjects may scan either visual or auditory images of respective targets but could not decide between the two interpretations (Drewnowski & Healy, 1977, p. 647).

On the other hand, it is possible that both types of representations are activated whenever written text is processed and that subjects draw upon one or the other, depending on task demands. Thus, in processing prose material, phonologic codes may be preeminant owing to their utility in extracting meaning from running text (Kleiman, 1975); but, in processing syntactically inappropriate material or even prose material disrupted in some way, as in the mixed-type case

---

[13]It might be noted, in connection with this, that Healy's results and those of Drewnowski and Healy would appear to be at variance with Krueger's (1970) finding that target letters were detected more readily when they appeared in displays comprised of sentences and scrambled prose than when they appeared in displays comprised of nonwords. However, in Krueger's study, subjects were asked to *search* for target letters rather than to *read* paragraphs, and it is likely that the processing strategies employed by subjects under these two conditions are significantly different.

condition in the present study, there may be greater utility in relying more heavily upon visual representations of the text. This interpretation would account for Corcoran's (1966) silent *e* findings as well as for Healy's (1976) and Drewnowski and Healy's (1977) results. In any case, Drewnowski and Healy's uncertainty points up once again the inherent difficulty in distinguishing between perceptual processes on the one hand and interpretive and/or response processes on the other, and as noted earlier the distinction between these variables would ultimately seem to be determined by one's respective definitions of perception and cognition.

Nevertheless, the results of the foregoing studies provide considerable support for the idea that connected text can influence the level at which individual words are processed, which is to suggest that the semantic and syntactic components of language are influential.[14] This, of course, raises the question of whether similar effects would be observed in the case of words that are taxonomically related, in which case verbal context effects would issue from the semantic and/or structural properties shared by given words rather than from their function and/or meaning in discourse material. The following section briefly summarizes research that supports this possibility.

Lexical Priming Effects in Word Recognition. I discussed earlier a study by Meyer et al (1974) in which it was found that lexical judgments for given target words (e.g., *TRIBE*) were made more rapidly when they were preceded by words that were graphically and phonologically similar (e.g., BRIBE) than when they were preceded by words that either shared no features with the target words (e.g., FENCE) or were graphically but not phonologically similar to these words (COUCH/TOUCH). Although these findings were taken as evidence for phonologic mediation of the word recognition process, they

---

[14]Gough et al. (1978) have taken issue with the notion that context increases predictability of spoken or printed words, and they are especially disdainful of the view held by some authors (Goodman, 1970; Smith, 1971) that the reader actively generates hypotheses about words to be encountered in discourse material on the basis of verbal context. In several related studies designed to evaluate this characterization of the reading process, Gough et al. observed that verbal context facilitates prediction of only one in every four words encountered in running text. At the same time, they found that inaccurate predictions retard recognition. It was suggested from these findings that the positive effects that might accrue from the ability to predict approximately 25% of the words that might appear in connected text would be outweighed by the negative effects of inaccurate prediction of the remaining 75%. Gough et al. also adduced evidence that constraining the number of words that a subject could encounter on a given trial had no significant effect on word recognition latencies beyond two alternatives, thereby replicating previous findings (Pierce & Karlin, 1957). They conclude from both of these results that the role of verbal context in facilitating word recognition may be greatly exaggerated by some authors and that information about the stimulus is a more important determinant of success in recognition than is verbal context. Perfetti and Roth (in press) come to a similar conclusion (see discussion on pp. 200–201.)

(along with the results of other relevant studies) can be placed in a more general problem area concerned both with the nature of lexical memory (Collins & Loftus, 1975; Collins & Quillian, 1970) and the lexical properties of words as determinants of the word recognition process (Meyer et al., 1975). The latter area is, of course, of particular interest here and encompasses a series of studies by Meyer and his associates, demonstrating what appears to be a kind of "priming" effect of one word upon latency of a recognition response to a conceptually related word.

The primary intent of these studies was to evaluate the influence of semantic context upon word recognition within the framework of what Meyer et al. (1975) term, a "spreading-excitation" (p. 102) model of the recognition process (Collins & Loftus, 1975; Collins & Quillian, 1970). According to this theory, mental representations of words are stored at distinct "locations" in lexical memory in a hierarchical network of related concepts. Activation of a given concept node at one level will tend to spread to concept nodes for related words at other levels, the magnitude of the effect being correlated with the proximity of one word to another in the hierarchy. Thus, if a subject is presented with the word *doctor*, activation will "spread" to semantically related words, such as *nurse*, facilitating subsequent recognition of that word.

Meyer, Schvaneveldt, and Ruddy (1972) hypothesized that the context provided by semantically related words would be manifested in a way consistent with the spreading activation model, such that prior recognition of one word would lower the response latency for a related word. However, it was assumed that context would affect the retrieval rather than the "stimulus encoding" or perceptual stage of processing, the implication being that these stages are independent of one another. A lexical decision task was used to evaluate these possibilities. Subjects were presented with associated (NURSE–DOCTOR) and unassociated (BREAD–DOCTOR) word pairs along with nonword pairs under both degraded and intact stimulus conditions, and speed of lexical judgments were recorded. Decisions were faster for both associated and intact word targets, but the effect of context was especially evident under the degraded stimulus condition. Because the interaction for stimulus quality and semantic context was statistically significant, the possibility that stimulus and contextual information interact at the encoding stage was considered. However, the possibility that these two variables interact at a later stage was not ruled out.

The second study in the series is the one by Meyer, Schvaneveldt, and Ruddy (1974) discussed earlier. This study was designed to provide information as to the types of stimulus representations that may be employed in recognizing a printed word. However, graphic and phonologic similarity of words were varied instead of semantic context and stimulus quality. The major findings that emerged from this investigation have already been discussed, the most significant being that both the graphic and phonologic constitutents of a word appeared to be influential in lowering response thresholds for lexical decisions. As noted earlier, this finding was interpreted as support for a phonemic conversion stage in word recognition. It was also suggested that the phomemic transformation process could serve to "minimize" the effects of stimulus degradation on subsequent stages, although it was not made clear just how this would take place.

In a third study reported, the results from a replication of Experiment I were compared with results from a modification of this investigation. As in the first experiment, lexical judgments were made for word and nonword pairs presented under intact and degraded stimulus conditions, priming words being either related or unrelated to target words. In the second condition, this procedure was modified in that target words were pronounced, and lexical decisions were made for priming words. Consistent with previous findings, response times were faster for both the semantically related word pairs and those that were not degraded, and the magnitude of the context effect was greatest with degraded stimuli. This was true for both the pronunciation and lexical judgment conditions. As might be expected, response latencies on the pronunciation task were significantly lower than those on the lexical judgment task, but none of the three-way interactions was statistically significant. Meyer et al. (1975) suggest that the results from all three experiments are consistent with a phonologic mediation model of word recognition and speculate that the similarity of the performance patterns yielded by the lexical decision and pronunciation tasks support the idea that stimulus and contextual variables interact at the stimulus encoding stage of word recognition. These authors also suggest that "spreading excitation" may "increase the sensitivity of visual feature analyzers that form graphemic representations of associated words," thereby accounting for the advantage occasioned by such words.

On the other hand, Meyer et al.'s (1975) interpretation of their results is not obligatory. For one thing, they extrapolate beyond their data in suggesting that subjects were necessarily employing phonemic codes for word recognition in Experiments 1 and 3. This suggestion was based largely on the yoked assumptions that: (1) grapheme/phoneme conversion mediates word recognition, as suggested by the results on the lexical decision tasks employed in Experiment 2; (2) instructions to subjects in Experiment 3 to use the first pronunciation they could think of resulted in grapheme/phoneme conversion in word identification, thus avoiding lexical access; and (3) the performance patterns on the lexical decision (Experiment 1) and pronunciation (Experiment 3) tasks were similar. These assumptions are unwarranted. Although there is reason to believe that phonologic mediation may have been a determinant of performance in Experiment 2, owing to the nature of the tasks, there is no independent evidence that such mediation was always involved in either the lexical decision task of Experiment 1 or the pronunciation task in Experiment 3. Indeed, in spite of the fact that the pronunciation task was designed to promote grapheme-phoneme conversion (that is, by including pronounceable pseudowords and real words on the same stimulus set), it is possible that some or even all of the real words were named by means of direct access rather than mediated processing. Thus, the results of these studies provide us with no compelling reason to believe that stimulus and contextual information interact at the stimulus encoding stage of word processing, if by stimulus encoding Meyer et al. (1975) mean something akin to feature extraction. The authors themselves suggest that graphemic and phonemic representations could conceivably be processed in parallel rather than in serial fashion, which would mean that the observed interaction between stimulus and contextual information occurred at the retrieval stage of word recognition and identification rather than the stimulus encoding stage. Given that the influence of the associated words was particularly evident with degraded stimuli, one might reasonably infer that the context effects observed in these studies occurred at the inferential level rather than at the level of stimulus encoding. This inference would seem to be less applicable to the second experiment in this series (Meyer et al., 1974) because the procedures employed may have disposed subjects toward the use of phonologic mediation to aid in making lexical judgments. At any rate, the results are ambiguous, and there is reason to doubt the author's conclusions.[15]

By now the reader should have discerned that the evidence supporting the role of context in word recognition is rather diverse and compelling. The results of the Meyer et al. (1975) studies provide yet another illustration that contextual information can positively influence word recognition and identification. However, their unique contribution is in the demonstration of the fact that such effects can occur strictly by virtue of a word's lexical and structural properties and further that they are quite rapid and automatic. They therefore increase the generality of the phenomenon.

Insofar as lexical priming creates a state of increased "readiness" to perceive a constrained word set, it can be considered a special case of the more general category of events traditionally classified as "perceptual set" phenomena (Bruner, 1957; Neisser, 1967) and defined by the facilitative effects of expectancy upon perception. The final context effect I wish to discuss can also be placed under this rubric but differs from the other contextual effects discussed in that it is manifested in the visual organization of the letters in a word rather than the visual discrimination of those letters or of the word itself. The following section briefly summarizes two studies that have evaluated this phenomenon.

---

[15]Meyer et al's. (1975) suggestion that verbal context activates lexical entries having common semantic attributes is consonant with suggestions made by Morton (1969) and Estes (1977) that context lowers the recognition thresholds for words that are highly predictable in given environments. But whereas Meyer et al. hypothesize that context sensitizes visual feature analyzers and thereby hastens feature extraction, Morton and Estes are of the opinion that it serves only to lower the criterion of acceptance in matching stimulus attributes with stored representations of those attributes and has no direct effect on feature extraction.

Expectancy and Perceptual Organization

In evaluating Gibson et al.'s (1962) suggestion that the spelling cluster mediates the recognition process, Aderman and Smith (1971) raised the question of whether or not the functional unit in word perception is variable. These authors (1971) specifically took issue with the idea that pronounceability confers unity on particular letter groups, pointing out that a letter string must be recognized before it is pronounced. As a possible solution to this problem, they offered Neisser's (1967, p. 115) suggestion that one's expectancy for what he or she will perceive determines the way in which letters will be grouped and, thus, the size of the unit(s) of recognition.

In testing this hypothesis, subjects were presented with two types of nonword letter strings: one comprised of pronounceable spelling clusters (e.g., SWILG) and the other comprised of unconnected letters (LGISW). The dependent measure was memory for a probe letter, and the experimental procedure conformed essentially to that used by Reicher (1969). The major independent variable was expectancy for either spelling clusters (SP) or unconnected letter strings (UL), subjects being assigned randomly to experimental conditions conforming to these expectancies. Thus, on the first 15 trials, subjects in the SP group were presented only with spelling cluster strings and those in the UL group with unconnected strings. However, on trial 16, subjects in the SP group were presented with an unconnected letter string, whereas those in the UL group were presented with a spelling cluster string, thereby disconfirming their expectancies. Performance indices included proportion correct and latency of response, and the critical comparisons were between trials 15 and 16 for each group.

As predicted, subjects who expected a spelling cluster string and thereafter received such a string had the highest proportion of correct responses. Conversely, subjects who expected an UL string and received an UL string had the lowest proportion of correct responses and did not perform much better when presented with a SP string, that is, when their expectancies were disconfirmed. The authors suggest that the SP expectancy group was processing letter strings at the letter cluster level, whereas the UL expectancy group was processing these stimuli at the letter level. This interpretation would account for these and two other findings. The first is the observation of no between-group differences under the expect UL–receive UL and expect SP–receive UL conditions. The second is apparent in the latency data. Specifically, under the expect SP–receive UL condition, subjects manifested longer response latencies than under any of the other three conditions, suggesting that the latter handicapped them more than any of the others, perhaps because it was the only circumstance in which they were required to shift their processing strategies.

The results of this study provide rather convincing evidence that expectancy can significantly influence perceptual organization. More important, the data directly support the notion that spelling clusters as well as individual letters are represented in long-term memory and that orthographic context may be involved in the selection of given units for further processing.[16]

However, the more general question is just *how* contextual information facilitates selection of a given processing strategy. This question has been of central concern to LaBerge and his associates in recent years, and his work is relevant here. In expanding a model of the reading process originally articulated by LaBerge and Samuels (1974), LaBerge (1977, 1979), like Estes (1975b, 1977), postulates the existence of neural structures, termed "context nodes," that selectively activate multilevel representations corresponding with the visual constituents of a printed word. Consistent with Estes' model, there are postulated representations for *features, letters, spelling patterns,* and *words,* which in the course of perceptual learning become linked to the *phonologic, semantic,* and *syntactic* systems as well as to each other. The interconnections that are established among these word constituents comprise an elaborate network that allows for a variety of means by which a word may be identified or information embedded in that word may be accessed, depending on task demands. Activation of the context nodes themselves presumably occurs in a variety of ways, which include the perceiver's task, the nature of the material presented to him or her, and perceptual "sets" or attitudes that may be deliberately induced (e.g., through instructions).

In a seminal study evaluating the effects of context on perceptual organization, Petersen and LaBerge (1977) employed a procedure similar to that used by Aderman and Smith (1971). Termed the "list induction technique," this procedure was essentially a visual matching task wherein subjects were presented with *either* a list comprised primarily of familiar spelling clusters (e.g., *sh, tr, cl*) and a few unfamiliar clusters (e.g., *lc, hs*) *or* a list comprised primarily of unfamiliar spelling clusters and only a few familiar clusters. The intent was to create respective sets for processing either spelling clusters or individual letters. The measures of particular interest were response latencies when subjects' expectancies were confirmed, compared with those resulting from disruption of expectancies. This procedure was, of course, similar to that employed in the Aderman and Smith (1971) study.

Consistent with the experimental predictions, latencies for matching familiar clusters and those for matching unfamiliar clusters were *not* significantly different when the stimulus list was predominantly comprised of the unfamiliar clusters, suggesting that subjects were processing both types of stimuli as indi-

---

[16]It should be noted that the results of the Aderman and Smith (1971) study, although consonant with Neisser's expectancy theory, does not necessarily validate this conceptualization. As pointed out by E. Smith and Spoehr (1974), Neisser's theory constitutes a limited solution to the parsing problem inherent in models such as Gibson et al. (1962) that postulate perceptual units larger than the letter but smaller than the word. However, as noted earlier, other solutions to this problem have been offered.

vidual letters. In contrast, processing time for unfamiliar letter clusters was 100 msec longer than processing time for familiar clusters when the stimulus list was comprised primarily of the familiar clusters, suggesting that subjects were biased toward processing familiar letter pairs as units and were therefore disrupted by presentations of unfamiliar pairs. These data reinforce the results of the Aderman and Smith (1971) study and are in keeping with the notion that context can activate codes at different levels of processing (Estes, 1975b, 1977).

Of additional interest are two other studies employing the list induction technique, which evaluated the possibility that expectancies for particular syntactic and semantic constructions can influence visual processing. In the study evaluating syntactic processing, words that are typically paired as noun phrases (e.g., *adjective-nouns*) were processed more rapidly than those that are typically paired as subjects and predicates (e.g., *noun-verb*) when matching lists consisted mainly of noun-phrase pairs. However, in lists containing mostly subject-predicate pairs there were no differences in response times between the two types of constructions. It was suggested that these effects were induced primarily by expectancies presumably created by subjects' implicit knowledge of a syntactic rule—that is, that *adjective-noun* elements are typically combined as noun phrases, whereas *noun-verb* elements are typically combined as subjects and predicates.

In the study assessing the effects of semantic information on visual processing, results similar to those emerging from the lexical priming studies were obtained. Specifically, probe words from one taxonomic category elicited shorter latencies than those from a different taxonomic category when most of the words on a particular matching list came from the first category. These results are, of course, analogous to those obtained on the syntax study, and both complement those yielded by the study evaluating the processing of spelling clusters.

Summary

It should be clear from the research reported in this section that the facilitative effects of contextual information on letter and word recognition are well-documented. This was found to be true in the case of orthographic context and was observed in studies evaluating the word superiority effect. It was also true for verbal context, the effects of which were apparent in studies demonstrating that appropriate word and sentence contexts and thematic material can influence the recognition process. Contextual effects were evident on such diverse measures as visual recognition thresholds, speed and accuracy of letter and word detection, latency in making lexical decisions, and speed of word naming. Orthographic and verbal context effects were also observed in studies evaluating the influence of perceptual set on letter and word recognition, wherein it was demonstrated that a set to perceive one type of stimulus either facilitated or disrupted perception of another, depending on whether one's expectancies were confirmed or disconfirmed.

Of particular interest in the studies reviewed is the apparent effects of given types of contextual information upon the levels at which written text may be processed. Two major conclusions may be drawn from these studies: (1) that multilevel codes corresponding to given words and their constituents are represented in long-term memory; and (2) that the particular codes selected for processing are determined in part by contextual variables, thereby facilitating discrimination at a given level of processing.

However, it should also be clear from the foregoing review that the way in which context does interface with the stimulus—in particular, the locus of contextual effects—is very much in dispute. The existing evidence favors the notion of independent processing of stimulus and contextual information, but a number of studies have yielded results that suggest that context may directly influence visual processing. Particularly compelling examples are the studies by Aderman and Smith (1971) and Petersen and LaBerge (1977), which demonstrate that the expectations created by orthographic context may directly influence perceptual organization and thus stimulus encoding.

But here again we find ourselves in that interpretive "gray area" wherein one theorist's definition of perception is another's definition of inference and/or memorial comparison. If, for instance, one's definition of perception encompasses only resolution and apprehension of a word's component letters (i.e., "seeing" the letters), then results such as those obtained by Aderman and Smith (1971) and Petersen and LaBerge (1977) should not be interpreted as support for the notion that context may directly influence perception. Indeed, unidirectional models such as Massaro's (1975) could as readily account for the findings as contextually based models such as Smith's (1971) and Rumelhart and Siple's (1974) or, for that matter, whole-word models such as those of Johnson (1977) that are, in effect, interactive.

However, if one's definition of perception is meant to encompass the particular way in which letters in a word are grouped, then the results of the Aderman and Smith (1971) and Petersen and LaBerge (1977) studies as well as those yielding similar results (for example, many of the studies evaluating the word superiority effect) may be taken as support for the idea that, under some circumstances, context can influence perception directly. If so, then an interactive model might be more appropriately invoked to account for such findings.

Clearly, there is considerable ambiguity here, and there is little doubt that the issue will not easily be resolved without more lucid definitions of the concepts in question. It might be pointed out, in this connection, that models such as Estes' (1975b, 1977) and that of LaBerge and Samuels (1974) lend themselves to interpretative ambiguity in postulating the existence of multilevel representations for words and word constituents, while resting on the assumption of independent and unidirectional processing stages. In fact, it seems to be inherently inconsistent to suggest that word recognition phenomena in general imply complete independence of stimulus and contextual influences and at the same time contend that word processing entails the activation of representations at different levels that may work in concert to effect recognition. The latter construct would seem to account for one's ability to perceive the *th* as a unit in the word *feather,* thereby encoding the letters in that word in a way that increases the probability of correct identification. It does not seem unreasonable to suggest in such an instance that the surrounding context provided by the letters that comprise this word facilitates (unit) perception of the *th* cluster as the initial unit of the second syllable of the word rather than *t* and *h* as two separate units (corresponding, respectively, with the last and first letters of the familiar words *feat* and *her*). Thus, by extension, to postulate the existence of separate codes for the letter sequences *feat, th,* and *her* or even *eat* and *at,* all of which are contained within the larger unit *feather* (which is also presumed to be represented separately) is to suggest that stimulus and contextual factors may not always exert their influence independent of one another, contrary to the independence and unidirectional processing assumptions in the models in question, hence their inconsistency.

Nevertheless, models such as Estes' (1975b, 1977) and LaBerge and Samuels' (1974), in my estimation, account for the multiform knowledge utilized by the skilled reader in word recognition and identification better than single unit models, which by definition do not incorporate multilevel representations. On the other hand, it would seem that additional assumptions need to be incorporated in these models to explain one's ability to dissect and encode an ambiguous letter string so as to ensure recognition and identification. I return to this issue but turn now to consideration of the stimulus itself as an important influence in the recognition process.

The Characteristics of the Word Stimulus

In our review of the relevant studies investigating the issues of concern here, it became clear that one very important determinant of the processing units involved in word recognition is the particular characteristics of the word stimuli employed. Stimulus characteristics that differentially affected performance in these studies include visual similarity, word length, orthographic regularity, lexical membership, word frequency, pronounceability, number of syllables, consonant and vowel complexity, and part of speech. Others that may have been influential in any given case, though not specifically varied, include meaning and degree of abstractness. Obviously, the amount of information contained within a single word is vast, encompassing as it does the *graphic, orthographic, phonologic, semantic,* and *syntactic* components of written and spoken language (Gibson, 1971). A moment's reflection will reveal that a word is imbued with properties that are not only unique to that word but also characteristic of words in general. Baron (1978) has referred to this distinction as *word-specific* and *general knowledge,* the former referring to such qualities as a word's unique visual features, its meaning, use in sentences, and particular name and the latter having reference to the rule-generated properties of printed words, as, for example, the regularity of their spelling patterns and their pronounceability. When a word's relationship with other words is factored into one's attempt to understand word recognition and identification, it will become clear that these are complexly determined processes.

Accordingly, the sections that follow attempt to bring into sharper focus the complex nature of a single printed word. The intent here is to provide the reader with some appreciation of the categories of information that must be processed in order to identify a given word. It is also my purpose to provide him or her with a sense of the knowledge the individual must acquire in order to engage in multilevel and flexible processing. Thus, the developmental focus that characterizes this section will not escape notice.

For the sake of convenience, I discuss the topic under three general headings, corresponding with given classes of information contained within a word: *visual information, phonologic information,* and *semantic/syntactic information.* However, when indicated, I attempt to distinguish between word-specific and general knowledge in accord with the distinction made by Baron (1978).

Visual Information

A word's visual characteristics of course constitute the most obvious of the multiple determinants of the word recognition process, and it seems important to evaluate their contribution to this process. There is little doubt, for example, that the degree to which a word stimulus is similar to or different from others that the reader has encountered will have a significant effect on the strategies he or she employs in processing that stimulus. This fact is amply demonstrated in the studies reviewed in the foregoing sections. Thus, in experiments conducted by Thompson and Massaro (1973) and Massaro (1973), letter similarity apparently necessitated feature level processing; in studies conducted by Johnson (1975, 1977), Sloboda (1976), and Massaro and Klitzke (1977), letter or word level processing appeared to be dependent on whether the word stimuli presented to subjects were either similar or dissimilar.

That visual similarity among letters and words becomes the occasion for fine-grained discrimination is not surprising. But what is not so apparent is the extraordinary nature of such discrimination and the degree of perceptual learning that must take place before the processing strategies necessary for precision become firmly engrained (LaBerge & Samuels, 1974). This is true for letter recognition, which necessitates detection of the graphic featural differences among letters of the alphabet, as well as for word recognition, which requires discrimination of letter sequences, in addition to discrimination of the letters themselves. Each type of information serves a different purpose in effecting recognition and identification, and each may be utilized in different measure. Although the skilled reader can apprehend both types simultaneously and automatically, the fledgling or unskilled reader may not have such facility either because he or she does not have the necessary information available in a usable form or because he or she does not become disposed toward using it even when it is available.

It is therefore instructive to review research that documents certain critical properties of the graphic and orthographic characteristics of printed words, highlighting where indicated the developmental aspects of the acquisition process.

Graphic Characteristics. In making reference to the role of a word's graphic characteristics, I am mainly referring to the visual features of the letters in a word. In order for a word to be recognized, most if not all of its letters must be discriminated, and, as demonstrated by Estes (1977), recognition of some words requires that all of their respective letters be apprehended (e.g., lea__). Because combinations of letters contain the coded information that allows one to symbolize language, letter recognition is of critical importance in word recognition and identification and in learning to read in general.

It has long been known that young children take time to learn to discriminate and name letters of the alphabet and that individuals differ in the rate at which such skill is acquired. Thus, a number of investigators have been concerned with the discriminability of alphabetic characters as well as the developmental factors involved in learning to distinguish these items. Studies involving young children include that of Davidson (1935), which is notable in that it was one of the first to demonstrate that printed letters are to varying degrees confusing for beginning readers. It also provided initial documentation of the fact that such confusion is prolonged for poor readers. However, a more informative study, in the detail it provides as to letter discriminability per se, is that of Dunn-Rankin (1968). This author systematically paired 21 of the most commonly employed lowercase letters of the alphabet, utilizing a contrast procedure developed by Ross (1939). Subjects were presented with letters in pairs and asked to select the one that most resembles a target letter. Each of the 21 letters served as targets for 210 possible letter pairs, and similarity scales were generated using correlation techniques.

The analysis revealed that letters can be clustered in groups with similar properties based on such factors as size, form, axial rotation, and topological line-to-curve transformations. Not surprisingly, letter pairs with similar features were found to be most confusing (e.g., b/d, d/p, c/e). Of interest is the fact that certain letter pairs that were difficult to distinguish did not always bear a reciprocal relation to one another. For example, whereas l was seen as most like i, the reverse was not true.

A well-known study by Gibson, Gibson, Pick, and Osser (1962) was concerned with the developmental course of letter discrimination. Children, ages four to eight, were given visual-matching tasks, using several types of transformations of standard figures. Performance in general improved with age. As in the Dunn-Rankin (1968) study, figures that changed only in orientation occasioned all subjects considerable difficulty in discrimination and were especially confusing to children in the youngest age group. Topological transformations yielded the fewest errors, whereas changes in linear perspective were the most troublesome. Line-to-curve transformations also occasioned some difficulty, depending on the number of changes. Performance patterns observed with the letterlike forms were cross-validated against a sampling of uppercase common letters, using the same transformation principles, and the two data sets were found to be highly correlated. The authors conclude that improvement in letter discrimination is related to perceptual learning of the "features or dimensions of differences which are critical for differentiating letters [p. 904]."

A subsequent study by Gibson and her associates (Gibson, Osser, Schiff, & Smith, 1963) evaluated discriminability of uppercase letters, using a feature matrix generated for 26 letters of the alphabet (Gibson, 1969). Following work done in speech perception (Jakobsen, Fant, & Halle, 1961), the matrix was divided into four general featural categories (*straight, curve, redundancy,* and *discontinuity*), describing 12 different features. Children and adults served as subjects. In general, confusion errors were related to the number of features in common, errors and reaction times increasing as the number of features shared by two different letters increased.

The results of studies, such as those just mentioned, make it clear that letter discrimination is a formidable task, especially for young children and, further, that the processing strategies required to detect distinctive features in grapheme patterns are acquired over a protracted period. That letter discrimination is formidable, even for skilled readers, is demonstrated in a later study by Bouma (1971). In this investigation, confusion errors were deliberately fostered by presenting adult subjects lowercase letters, either at a relatively large distance or in peripheral vision. Bouma was able to partition the resulting confusion errors (see Table 2.3) into three categories: *small letters, ascenders,* and *descenders.* Small letters were confused only with other small letters and so on. The author suggests that height or height-to-width ratios may constitute distinguishing features and made reference to the "envelope" of a letter as a basic feature determining shape discrimination. The envelope is defined as the smallest enclosing polygon without indentations. Thus *a* and *z* have roughly rectangular envelopes, whereas *o* and *c* have circular envelopes, these respective pairs being more readily confused with one another. Noteworthy is the fact that Bouma's (1971) results conform closely to those of Dunn-Rankin (1968), in spite of the differences in their approaches in generating confusability matrices. This finding suggests that the

TABLE 2.3
Confusion Matrix Indicating Percentage of Occurrences of Given Responses to Particular Letter Stimuli (taken from Bouma, 1971, with permission of the author and publisher)

	Stimulus	a	s	z	x	e	o	c	n	m	u	r	v	w	d	h	k	b	t	i	l	f	g	p	j	y	q	
Small	a	62	3			7	1		6	5	1				5	2		3		3			2	3			2	a
	s	33	10	3		14	3		8	8	7	2	2		2								3	3			2	s
	z	19	6	12	2	14		2	4	1		11	2	1	1			5	2	4		4	8	4	2		1	z
	x	13	3	6	32	9	2		6	1	2	4	4	2						2		1	4	3			1	x
	e					19	3		34	5	2	7	10	7	2	1	2		2				2	3			2	e
	o					5			11	57	7	4	4	3	1	1			2				1	4				o
	c					8	2		29	19	19	2	1		4	2			2			1	6	3			2	c
	n					6			1	1		56	21	4					2	6		2		1	1			n
	m					9	2		1			4	79	1					1								2	m
	u					1				2		11	9	56					2	5			3	3	1	5	1	u
	r	1	1	1		5			1	1		55							12	4		13	4	3				r
	v					1			1			2	72	17												5		v
	w					1					3	1	22	70										2				w
Ascenders	d	4				1			2	2				2	83			2	1								5	d
	h	2					4		2	2						80	2	14	2	2	2							h
	k	2				2			2	1	2				2	17	51	14						2				k
	b						1									27	3	62										b
	t	2	2			2			2					3	2	2	5	4	59	11		5						t
	i								1						4	2	2		8	69	10	2			2			i
	l		2			2			1						4	4		1	3	50	26	2			9			l
	f											5			2				3	2		81	2				1	f
Descenders	g	3				6	2		2	1					4			2					25	9	3	3	31	g
	p								1	1		4	2					8					2	84			1	p
	j														5				1	3	5	3						j
	y																						2			82		y
	q	2				2	3			1	2				5	1							6	3	1		74	q
		a	s	z	x	e	o	c	n	m	u	r	v	w	d	h	k	b	t	i	l	f	g	p	j	y	q	

graphic features that may facilitate or impede letter discrimination are not idiosyncratic.

Most studies evaluating the structural characteristics of letters of the alphabet have attempted to define their common and distinguishing features in the elemental sense, but few have attempted to catalog the particular relations among given features that make letters more or less discriminable. That this may be an important, though somewhat neglected, line of inquiry is suggested by the results of a recent study by Lockhead and Crist (1980). In this study, evidence was provided that it is not the graphic features alone that facilitate letter discrimination but relations between features within letters as well as relations between letters. Thus, when subjects (young children and adults) were presented with letters sharing identical features, modified so as to change the relationships between these features (b p), discrimination was more accurate than when they were presented with the same letters printed in commonly used fonts.

It should be apparent from the previous remarks that letter recognition is a complex task in its own right. Facility in letter discrimination implies considerable perceptual learning and thus, the acquisition of increasingly more efficient processing strategies, which no doubt include selective and "automatic" attention to critical discriminators (LaBerge & Samuels, 1974). That letter discrimination is an important skill for word recognition has been well-documented over the years and would seem to be particularly important in distinguishing between visually similar words that differ in only a few letters or letter features (e.g., how/now). However, there is little doubt that it is only one of a collection of interrelated skills necessary to engage successfully in word decoding (Samuels,

1972). Recall, in this connection, Cosky's (1976) interesting finding that words comprised of letters that are very similar to one another occasioned skilled readers no more difficulty on recognition tasks than did words comprised of letters that are more easily discriminated. Although this finding could be taken as evidence that component letter processing is *not* important for word recognition (Gough & Cosky, 1977) as noted earlier, a more conservative inference is that the visual properties that uniquely define a word are derived not only from the letters that comprise that word but also from the relations between and among those letters. Thus the ability to take account of and remember other important attributes, such as the order in which a word's letters are arrayed and the structural regularities characteristic of words in general, are equally important determinants of the word recognition process, and the acquisition of such information also takes time to develop. I turn now to these particular aspects of the word stimulus.

Orthographic Characteristics. The orthographic information contained within a word essentially defines its structural attributes, as embodied in the unique spelling created by the particular order in which its letters are arrayed. A word's spelling contains two general types of orthographic information that mediate recognition and identification: combinations of letters that distinguish it from other words and combinations of letters that it has in common with other words and which occur with enough regularity to be derived by spelling rules. As noted earlier, Baron (1978) refers to the former as word-specific information and to the latter as general or rule-governed information. Both word-specific and rule-governed properties are used in recognizing and identifying a printed word, but the perceiver may rely more heavily on one or the other, depending on the structure of that word and the processing attitude he or she has acquired. It is instructive to characterize briefly each type of information, making reference to relevant research where indicated.

Word-Specific Information. There are two ways in which the visual attributes that define a particular word may be characterized. The first has reference to its most salient properties, namely, its letters, invariantly ordered, and its global features—specifically, its shape, length, and the unique visual effects created by its letters in combination. Such attributes render words more or less distinctive and may be emcompassed under the rubric *whole-word familiarity*.

The second way in which word-specific information may be characterized is defined by the degree of visual similarity that exists among and between various words. As I have indicated, word similarity significantly influences the individual's processing strategies and thus the information that he accesses to effect identification. Structurally dissimilar words may require processing only at the global or whole-word level, especially if they can be anticipated in given contexts. Structurally similar words, on the other hand, may necessitate fine-grained visual processing, in particular, component letter and feature analysis, which obviously implies attendance to subword units. I first discuss the notion of whole-word familiarity.

Whole-Word Familiarity. Whole-word familiarity results, of course, from varying degrees of exposure to different words and basically refers to one's ability to recognize a letter string as a familiar lexical entry. That the effect is real has been amply demonstrated over the years, most notably in lexical decision studies wherein latency differences have typically favored common words over uncommon words, pseudowords, and random letter strings. This is a reliable phenomenon that has been observed in a very large number of experiments, indeed in many of those discussed earlier (Forster & Chambers, 1973; Frederiksen & Kroll, 1976; Manelis, 1974; Meyer et al., 1975).

The results of these investigations make it clear that the word familiarity effect cannot be explained solely by orthographic regularity or even by "wordness" per se, because it is especially pronounced with common words, as just mentioned.

The performance patterns observed in the lexical decision studies seem to be closely related to a similar pattern observed in studies using a different format—one that may also be taken as support for whole-word familiarity—the word frequency effect. This too is a very reliable phenomenon and, in fact, one of the most extensively investigated (Neisser, 1967). The word frequency effect was originally studied by Howes and Solomon (1951) and Solomon and Howes (1951), who found that words that appear often in written text by some normative standard (Thorndike & Lorge, 1944) have lower recognition thresholds than words that appear less often. This phenomenon would seem to be due, in part, to visual familiarity, though its derivation is not clearly understood and has for years been in dispute. The central question addressed in this controversy is whether or not the differential thresholds observed for high- and low-frequency words reflect perceptual or response bias. This is an important distinction, for if the word frequency effect *were* due solely to response bias, then no claim could be made that it is a manifestation of whole-word familiarity. Indeed, taken to its extreme, the response bias explanation would exclude the stimulus as a significant determinant of the effect (Goldiamond & Hawkins, 1958).

In an attempt to elucidate this distinction, Broadbent (1967) evaluated several theories emphasizing response rather than perceptual processes as the locus of the word frequency effect and concluded that this phenomenon is due to a "criterion bias."[17] According to this hypothesis, high-frequency words require less

---

[17]Broadbent (1967) tested three other response bias models against empirically derived data. One was characterized as a "pure guessing" model, as described in a well-known study by Goldiamond and Hawkins (1958), who demonstrated that high-frequency words were more often emitted as responses to briefly exposed "stimuli," even when no stimuli were presented (i.e., when S's "perceived" a smudge as a real word). A second model was termed "sophisticated guessing." This

stimulus information for recognition than do low-frequency words, because the probability of encountering words that appear more often in print is significantly greater, thus creating a perceptual set that favors such words. Broadbent (1967) also suggested that the word frequency effect cannot be attributed exclusively to either stimulus or contextual factors but results, instead, from the interaction of both types of information, independently derived. Morton (1968, 1969) came to a similar conclusion, after testing several single-factor models against recognition threshold data obtained by Brown and Rubenstein (1961).

Word frequency effects have also been found with children. For example, Pearson and Studt (1975) presented first and third graders with high- and low-frequency words at the end of "rich," "medium," and "poor" context sentences and asked them to identify each on the basis of partial stimulus information (i.e., a word's letters presented piecemeal). Subjects required fewer letters for identification of the more common stimuli, especially when they appeared in rich sentence contexts. This pattern was particularly evident in the older, more experienced readers, both findings being consistent with the notion of whole-word familiarity.

However, a familiarity explanation of these results is attenuated somewhat by the fact that frequency and context interacted significantly, thereby making it difficult to determine their separate contributions. Yet a subsequent study by Perfetti and Hogaboam (1975) also evaluated word frequency effects in children and obtained essentially the same results. In this investigation, third- and fifth-grade skilled and unskilled readers were presented with high- and low-frequency words as well as pronounceable pseudowords and compared on speed of naming each type of stimulus. The critical finding is that subjects in all groups named high-frequency words more rapidly than either low-frequency words or pseudowords, the differences between these stimuli being greater in the unskilled than in the skilled reader groups. These results, in combination, reinforce the idea that word frequency effects are partly attributable to whole-word familiarity.

In spite of the controversy generated by competing explanations of the word frequency effect, it is likely that this phenomenon is due in part to the individual's recollection of the visual attributes that uniquely identify a particular word. Still more support for this interpretation is derived from several studies that specifically evaluated visual and verbal correlates of whole-word familiarity. To be specific, Eichelman (1970) found that reaction times for skilled readers on visual-matching tasks were shorter for word pairs than for nonword pairs, these differences being evident in the case of both *same* and *different* responses. He

---

model suggests that partial stimulus information limits the range of alternatives from which the response is selected, but within this range the individual will still be biased toward the most probable response. The third model was called an "observing response" model and is based on the assumption that an implicit bias toward perceiving high-frequency words creates a set toward inattention to information that would facilitate discrimination of low-frequency words.

also found that reaction times for *same* responses to words having the same name were greater for those that differed in letter case. These effects were attributed to word familiarity.

Because the results of Eichelman's study did not completely rule out the possibility that verbal coding may have been partly responsible for his findings, a follow-up study was conducted by Pollatsek, Well, and Schindler (1975). Subjects (college students) were asked to match word and random letter pairs that were either identical or different with respect to either letter case or a single letter. To distinguish between visual versus lexical and/or phonologic effects, some of the *different* word pairs were homophones and some were not. Certain of the homophonic words were semantically different (e.g., *FLEA-FLEE*) whereas others differed only in letter case (e.g., *FLEE-FLEe*). Response latency for same–different matching was the dependent measure, subjects being instructed to consider as *different* only those letter string pairs that were not physically identical.

The major finding of note is that response latencies were shorter for words than for nonwords, even for pairs of letter strings that differed only in case (e.g., *site-SITE*). Furthermore, the size of the word–nonword difference (i.e., the familiarity index) was comparable for both case and letter name differences, suggesting that judgments were made on the basis of visual rather than lexical or phonologic information. At the same time, there was no appreciable increase in the word–nonword difference in contrast of homophones differing in one letter (semantic effect) and those differing only in case (visual effect). Neither was there any apparent advantage for nonhomophones over homophones in matching words differing in one letter. These findings are consistent with the idea that a word's graphic and orthographic features are significant determinants of the word familiarity effect.

Reinforcing this suggestion is yet another finding from this study, and that is that the magnitude of the familiarity index decreased as the number of letter case differences increased, which is to say that words consisting of uniform fonts may have been more familiar than words consisting of different fonts. This is contrary to the suggestion made by Smith (1971), that a word comprised of letters in different cases can be recognized as readily as a word comprised of the same letter cases.

Pollatsek et al (1975) conclude from these findings that the visual characteristics of a printed word are partly responsible for word familiarity. However, they caution (p. 328) that their results do not allow a determination as to whether or not such effects are produced by any of a word's visual attributes other than orthographic legality, given that comparisons were between words and random letter strings.

Interestingly enough, Pollatsek et al. (1975) suggest that the word familiarity effects observed in their study are not likely due to an early encoding stage, such as feature extraction, but perhaps to processing either at an intermediate stage in which the visual stimulus undergoes additional encoding (e.g., forming of larger perceptual units, such as letter clusters) or at a comparison stage wherein verbal codes provide the visual system with feedback that facilitates attendance to critical differences that might effect recognition. These interpretations are consonant with the views of several authors (Johnson, 1979; Manelis, 1974; Smith & Spoehr, 1974), who suggest that letter recognition may not be the terminal stage in perceptual processing.[18]

Although it is true that the results of the Pollatsek et al., (1975) study would be consistent with the idea that orthographic structure alone can account for word familiarity effects, it should be noted that this interpretation would not account for the repeated finding in studies employing the lexical decision paradigm that response times to real words are significantly shorter than response times to pseudowords, the effect being especially pronounced in the case of high-frequency words. In my opinion, such results provide rather strong evidence that familiar words contain visual information in addition to orthographically redundant spelling patterns that contribute to their memorability. What is the nature of this information?

Most basic, of course, is the information provided by a word's component letters. Each of the letters in a word consists of an aggregate of specific features that not only define the shape of each letter but collectively define that word. A word's letters are ordered invariantly, which is another critical piece of information that distinguishes one word from another. And while the idea has had little currency in the literature, save for the work of Wheeler (1970), I am nonetheless inclined to believe that the supraletter characteristics created by given combinations of letters within a word may also contribute to its distinctiveness. Geminate letter clusters, to me, have always been salient word features (e.g., *book, aardvark, Mississippi*); but, to illustrate the point further, consider the following misspellings of the familiar word, *psychology: pyschology, pschyology, pyshcology, phycsloogy, pyhcsoloyg*. The reader will note that the first misspelling appears to be the closest approximation to the correct ordering because there is only one letter reversal, the first five letters of the word are yet in close

---

[18]Pollatsek et al. (1975) cited three pieces of evidence in support of this suggestion. First, that studies by Schindler, Well, and Pollatsek (1974) and Well, Pollatsek, and Schindler (1975) have, respectively, shown that neither 180° rotations of letter strings nor the introduction of gaps between letters in given strings reduced the size of word–nonword differences, but such manipulations *did* increase reaction times to both types of stimuli. This suggests that these respective effects take place at different stages, the physical manipulation variable probably affecting feature extraction and the word–nonword variable effecting stimulus encoding at a later stage.

The second piece of evidence cited by Pollatsek et al. was derived from the study by Aderman and Smith (1971), discussed earlier, which found that expectancy can disrupt the size of the differences between pseudoword and random letter strings. The third piece of evidence issues from studies that have demonstrated that the familiarity effect disappears when discriminations can be made on the basis of selective processing of word constituents (Baron, 1975; Barron & Pittenger, 1974; Well et al., 1975).

proximity, and the sequence of the remaining letters is intact. The second misspelling is not so much like the original but might be accepted by the less discerning eye because most of the letter combinations are intact. But no one would be fooled by the last three misspellings, because too many of the letter combinations that define the correct item have been disrupted. This is true, even though the letters in the first and last halves of the word remain in close proximity to one another.

It would seem, therefore, that particular letter combinations *do* create specific visual patterns that may contribute to word familiarity in the global sense. Reinforcing this suggestion is the Pollatsek et al. (1975) finding that the (word familiarity) effect is significantly reduced when words are presented in alternating cases, the contrary views of Smith and his associates notwishstanding (F. Smith, 1969, 1971; F. Smith et al., 1969). Indeed, even these authors found that speed of reading-connected text was considerably slower when words appeared in alternating cases. In view of these and similar findings (Brooks, 1977; Drewnowski & Healy, 1977), I submit that the supraletter features embedded in a word constitute one of several types of visual information utilized by the skilled reader in discriminating and recognizing that word. Two other types of information that are similarly employed are *word shape* and *length,* and I can be brief.

Word shape was at one time considered an important determinant of wholeword familiarity (Pillsbury, 1897), but there is no substantial research support for this idea, most likely because the fonts typically employed in printed English do not yield much variability on this dimension. On the other hand, word shape may be a useful discriminating feature for some word stimuli under certain circumstances. Consider, for example, the obvious shape differences between the words *cat* and *bug,* which could be helpful cues in initial learning or under the degraded stimulus conditions that characterize most laboratory studies.

However, word length would seem to be a more functional discriminator, in that a sizable number of words that one encounters regularly can be categorized quite readily by length. Many of the functor words are typically two and three letters in length, whereas English vulgates are typically four letters long and, I trust, highly familiar for reasons not extensively studied in the laboratory.

Word length as a factor contributing to the word recognition process has been studied extensively over the years, and there is ample reason to believe that this variable does significantly influence word processing. This was first noted by Cattell (reported in Huey, 1908), who observed that words of greater length require a longer exposure duration for correct report than do shorter words. This effect was later replicated by McGinnies, Comer, and Lacy (1952) and by Postman and Adis-Castro (1957), who used more sophisticated experimental techniques. Cattell (1886b) also found that naming latencies for longer length words were greater than those for short words, an effect replicated more recently by Cosky (Gough & Cosky, 1977) when number of phonemes and syllables were controlled (see footnote on p. 123). However, it is not yet clear whether word length exerts its primary influence on perceptual or response processes, as evident in our analysis of the word recognition theories presented earlier. For example, polysyllabic words tend also to be words of greater length, and as we have seen, some theorists (Spoehr & Smith, 1973) suggest that printed words must be parsed into lower level perceptual units before they can be identified. If so, then it follows that lengthy words require more parsing than words that are not very lengthy. It is also true that longer length words place a greater strain on memory, particularly for the beginning reader. The individual must, therefore, find ways of condensing this information, and it is likely that he gradually develops a variety of strategies for doing so, for example, searching for recursive units within a word (characteristics), searching for morpheme boundaries (identification), and the like. Thus, it may be that length affects both perceptual and response processes to some degree, though the extent to which this is true is an open question. Suffice it to reiterate at this juncture the suggestion that word length *is* an important determinant of word processing, its most ostensible effect being inherent in its status as a global feature under which certain words may be reliably categorized. Its heuristic value for settling the unit of perception issue is quite another matter, one that was discussed in detail earlier and need not be discussed any further.

The whole-word features just described are, of course, those that are most salient. They are functional in that they serve to constrain the comparison process to words that can be categorically defined by given combinations of these specific attributes. However, because of the redundant nature of English orthography, many words have several overlapping characteristics that necessarily call for fine-grained discrimination. This brings me to the second type of word-specific knowledge that the skilled reader must acquire in order to effect recognition and identification, specifically, letter and letter feature information to distinguish visually similar words.

Subword Units.   As noted throughout this text, discrimination of visually similar words requires more detailed processing of their constituent letters in order to detect the subtle difference between them. Indeed, it is in accounting for the perceiver's ability to take note of such differences, that the little made distinction between the terms *recognition* and *identification* becomes important. Researchers typically use these terms interchangeably, but they are *not* one and the same. The two processes are, of course, related and might best be conceived as two separate points on a continuum. Recognition may be described as an affirmative (though not necessarily accurate) response to a stimulus, having similar or identical featural characteristics to one stored in the lexicon. Identification may be viewed as an accurate, as well as affirmative response to a given stimulus, implying full knowledge of its visual and sound counterparts, as well as a functional acquaintance with its meaning.

To appreciate the fact that recognition and identification are not synonymous, consider the likelihood that a word mistaken for a visually similar word gives rise to bona fide recognition effects as exemplified perhaps in Pillsbury's (1897) well-known finding that subjects perceived misspelled words as familiar (e.g., FOYEVER as FOREVER) and had little awareness of the misspellings. More common illustrations are provided in observations of the errors made by beginning readers in misidentifying visually similar words, such as *bad* and *dad* and *was* and *saw,* which differ only with respect to the orientation and/or sequences of their component letters. Young children do not initially attend to such differences, and it takes time to acquire the knowledge and perceptual attitudes necessary to do so (Calfee, 1977; Gibson, et al., 1962).

However, the most persuasive evidence that recognition differs from identification is provided by semantic substitution errors, such as calling the printed word *cat,* /*kitty*/ or /*dog*/. It is clear that the individual who makes such an error, has internalized a representation of the stimulus word, since the response to that word is another word in the same taxonomic category, implying recognition of a familiar percept. It is also clear that he has not yet acquired the information necessary to distinguish the stimulus word from other linguistic referents in that category. Errors of this type are commonly observed in beginning readers, who have not yet learned the grapheme-phoneme associates that would assist them in identifying words accurately. Interestingly enough, they are also found in brain injured adults (Marshall and Newcombe, 1973), who have lost the ability to identify printed words through the application of grapheme-phoneme correspondences (see discussion in Skill of the Reader section). Thus, it would seem that recognition of a given word necessitates contact, only with its visual components, but identification of that word requires the cross-referencing and integration of its visual, phonologic and semantic-syntactic components.

To understand the distinction between recognition and identification, is to appreciate the fact that words having one or more features in common, necessitates processing strategies that differ from those that can be readily discriminated from one another. When the individual "perceives" a letter string as a familiar word, but misidentifies it, he has subjectively "recognized" that string as a unique item in the lexicon, and in most cases, can be credited with a near miss. Thus a child who calls *bad dad* or *was saw* on a random basis, has no doubt acquired mental representations of each pair as meaningful units, but he may not have acquired the perceptual attitudes necessary to discriminate between them, which is to suggest that he is processing each of these words wholistically, and has not yet encoded their subtle differences. However, with appropriate feedback, feature as well as letter level processing will be adopted to disambiguate the *bad-dad* pair, while serial letter processing will no doubt be utilized for reliable identification of *was* and *saw*. It seems reasonable to assume, that in learning to make such distinctions, the child might derive considerable assistance from other word attributes. For example, when one word in a pair is misidentified, knowledge of the meanings of each of the words, and of how they are used in sentences, might occasion the type of feedback that alerts him to the visual characteristics that differentiate the two. Similarly, knowledge of letter-sound associates or even letter names, may serve as useful mnemonics to assist in stabilizing the orientation and sequences of the letters in these words. In this event, the *bad dad* discrimination might be aided by deliberately "sounding out" these words, thereby encouraging focal attention to the graphic features which differentiate the letters *b* and *d*. *Was* and *saw* might be distinguished simply by using the sounds of their initial consonants as verbal mediators to aid, both in programming a left-right scan, and in retrieving their whole word labels.

The presumption here is that such operations, whether self-generated or externally prompted (e.g., by a teacher), will result in a shift from wholistic to component letter and feature level processing of respective words in each pair, as the vehicles to recognition and identification. With more experience, the subunits comprising each word will be re-integrated, and the words themselves will again be processed as wholes; but the reader's perceptual attitude will have been reorganized in that the recognition process will now incorporate focal attention to critical discriminators.

To illustrate further, the child who calls *loin lion,* may only have a stored representation of the printed word *lion* as a meaningful lexical entry, quite probably, because he has had no prior exposure to *loin*. In this instance, he retrieves the most readily available referent, the familiar word *lion*. This does not mean, however, that this same child did not accurately "perceive" each of the letters in the word *loin,* or even that he misperceived their sequence. What it most likely means, is that the sequence difference that distinguishes *loin* from *lion* was seen, but not registered and encoded, simply because the child's experience provided him with neither the information nor the motive for doing so.

But when he learns the meaning of the word *loin,* and it becomes a firmly entrenched word in his vocabulary, he must then acquire the coded information, and the processing strategies necessary for distinguishing between this word and its visually similar counterpart. Left-right scanning of individual letters, to take account of the sequence difference in the medial positions of these words, is one type of processing strategy that might be utilized in learning to distinguish between them. Note, however, that this strategy would be more effective for *lion* than it would for *loin,* if the child were employing grapheme-phoneme translation, to aid in the discrimination process, since a strict application of letter-sound correspondences would recover the correct lexical entry for *lion,* but produce the two syllable non-word /lō-/ĭn/ for *loin*. *Loin,* on the other hand, might be more readily identified, by processing the dipthong *oi* as a single unit. This would be an especially convenient strategy, if the individual had already learned to perceive this cluster as a unit, perhaps because of previous exposure to words such as *coin, oil, spoil,* and *boil*.

At any rate, it seems reasonable to speculate, that in learning to disambiguate *lion* and *loin,* the child might come to adopt *two* different processing strategies, a left-right scan for lion, encoding the letters *l i o n* as units, because of the letter-sound regularity which characterizes this word; and perhaps parallel processing for *loin*, encoding *l oi* and *n* as units, since this strategy avoids letter by letter sound translation, and thereby increases the probability of correct identification.

As the decoding of these words becomes highly practiced, it is likely that the more laborious left-right strategy for *lion* is abandoned, and wholistic processing is utilized for this word as well as for *loin*. However, it is probable that vestiges of early discriminating strategies remain, such as focal attention to the *i* in the second position of *lion* and unit perception of the *oi* in *loin*. It would also seem to be true, that these two words would necessitate only global features processing, when presented in running text, since they have different meanings, and would be likely to occur only in given contexts.

Avoiding semantic substitution errors of the type described above (*cat* → *kitty* or *dog*), represents a somewhat different discrimination problem in that the visual characteristics of the stimulus and response words are dissimilar. However, the remedy for the problem is essentially the same, insofar as visually and semantically similar words both require some degree of structural analysis and attendance to distinguishing features for accurate identification.

The intent of the foregoing illustrations, is to add substance to the basic theme of this paper, that the unit of perception is relative. It should be clear, from the examples given, that the development of differential approaches to perceptual analysis, is initiated by the beginning reader's early encounters with word stimuli that have many features in common. It should also be apparent, that, in such instances, and perhaps in learning to read in general, there is a developmental transition initiating with the processing of global and salient features, progressing to a more analytic mode and eventuating in reorganized and better integrated whole-word perception, with the means for making fine-grained discriminations when the necessity arises. I shall document these contentions further but turn now to the other type of orthographic information contained within a word— general or rule-governed information.

General Information. At several points throughout this chapter, reference is made to research documenting the utility of orthographic regularity as an aid to word recognition. Indeed, much of the discussion of the issues addressed is concerned with the role of structural redundancy in the recognition process, and it becomes clear that not all theorists are in agreement as to how a word's orthographic structure facilitates recognition of that word. Thus, Massaro (1975) asserts that one's implicit knowledge of orthographic rules synthesizes recognition of a word's component letters in the dynamic sense, whereas Estes (1975b, 1977) suggests that such information disambiguates letter position uncertainty, especially when a word stimulus cannot be fully processed. F. Smith (1971), on the other hand, is of the opinion that orthographic redundancy mediates word recognition by facilitating selective and economical sampling of letter features, and Gibson (1971) adopts a similar position. But, whereas F. Smith (1971) contends that letter features are encoded as whole words with no intermediate processing involved, Gibson (1971) suggests that letter features are encoded as orthographically regular spelling patterns, which mediate whole-word perception.

These disparate views notwithstanding, there is some consensus that orthographic redundancy facilitates word recognition and identification in two important ways. First, because of inherent constraints as to the letter sequences that are permissible in English orthography (*sh*-legal—*xq*-illegal), the perceiver is presumed to be able to utilize orthographic rules to: (1) distinguish between legal and illegal spelling patterns; and (2) generate and/or infer probable letter sequences in given word and subword contexts. Determination of orthographic legality appears to be basic in that it facilitates discrimination between words and unconnected letters. The ability to generate probable letter sequences is no less important insofar as it allows one to identify words and familiar letter clusters on the basis of partial or degraded stimulus information, a circumstance that characterizes word processing in the natural setting as well as in the laboratory (Estes, 1977).

That the skilled reader's ability to distinguish between words and nonwords is partly attributable to his implicit knowledge of orthographic structure seems amply documented in lexical decision studies (Forster & Chambers, 1973; Frederiksen & Kroll, 1976), which uniformly demonstrate that words and pronounceable pseudowords can be processed more rapidly than randomly arrayed letters. There is also substantial support for the idea that orthographic redundancy is able to compensate for partial stimulus information. Thus, using very brief exposures, Massaro and Klitzke (1977) found (see also Massaro, Venezky and Taylor, 1979) that letters can be identified more readily when they are embedded in words and orthographically regular pseudowords than when they are embedded in unconnected letter strings. At the same time, Estes and his associates (Estes, 1975a, 1975b, 1977, Estes, Allmeyer, & Reder, 1976) have adduced considerable evidence that knowledge of orthographic structure aids in discriminating letter sequences when stimulus conditions do not permit optimal resolution, as in peripheral vision.

There is also a good deal of agreement as to a second way in which orthographic redundancy might influence word recognition and identification. Insofar as given letter combinations occur recursively in written English (*qu, ing, tion, ed*), the skilled reader is able to: (1) utilize familiar patterns to reduce the amount of visual information he or she must process to effect letter and word discrimination; and (2) employ these patterns to aid in identifying new or less familiar letter strings. Support for these suggestions is derived from many of the studies discussed in this chapter, the most widely cited being those conducted by Miller et al. (1954) and by Gibson and her associates (Gibson, Gibson, Pick & Osser, 1962; Gibson, Osser and Pick, 1963; Gibson, Shurcliff & Yonas, 1970). Each of these investigations employed brief exposure as well as full report procedures and found that orthographically legal letter strings were reproduced more accurately than orthographically illegal strings.

Reinforcing these findings are the results of a study conducted by Johnson (1977, pp. 116-117), and three by Krueger and his associates (Krueger, 1970; Krueger, Keen, & Rublevich, 1974; Krueger & Weiss, 1976). The Johnson (1977) study is especially relevant, in that it constitutes a more direct test of the notion that structural invariance facilitates economy in visual processing. In brief, this author independently varied orthographic redundancy and length of letter strings on visual-matching tasks and found not only that words and orthographically legal pseudowords were processed more rapidly than consonant letter strings but also that greater string length significantly increased response times only on the consonant strings. It would appear from these results that orthographically illegal arrays are processed at the component letter level, whereas words and pseudowords are processed at higher levels.

To continue, in all three of the Krueger investigations, subjects were asked to detect target letters embedded either in words or among scrambled letters, and it was found that visual search for target letters in words was faster than visual search for target letters among scrambled letters. The study by Krueger et al. (1974) is especially notable, in that this same pattern was observed in fourth-grade children as well as in adults. Letter detection in these two groups was also more rapid with third-order pseudowords than with the scrambled letter sets, and the proportional differences among these three types of stimuli were approximately the same for both groups.

Of additional interest are two other results obtained in the most recent of these studies (Krueger & Weiss, 1976): (1) that visual search was more rapid for words than for nonwords, even when the subject's task was to search for the absence rather than the presence of target letters; and (2) that accuracy in detecting absent letters was greater for nonwords than for words that were deliberately "mutilated" (BAKFRY), reminiscent of "proofreading" errors. Such findings might best be explained by a multilevel processing model. The critical assumption here is that acquaintance with the spellings of familiar words had a beneficial effect on speed of processing, while impairing accuracy of detection, a reasonable inference being that an exhaustive search was not utilized with words but was utilized with the scrambled letters.

A clear implication from these and other studies addressing the issue (F. Smith, 1969; F. Smith et al., 1969) is that a functional acquaintance with orthographic structure can significantly influence the level(s) at which a letter string and/or any of its constituents is recognized and identified. Thus, implicit knowledge that *xrcgp* is an illegal array would incline the perceiver toward processing that array at the letter level, whereas familiarity with the redundant spelling clusters *gl ur ck* in the pronounceable pseudoword *glurck* would seem to promote processing at the cluster level. On the other hand, recognition of the familiar word, *church,* would likely occur at the whole-word level, especially if it were presented in a highly constrained semantic context. The familiar and frequently recurring clusters *ch ur ch* would also be encoded as separate units, simultaneous with encoding of the word as a whole if, as seems likely, each had been "unitized" at an earlier stage in mediated identification of *church* and other words containing one or another of these clusters (e.g., *chop, match, fur, hurt*).

It follows from the previous illustrations that the encoding of polysyllabic words and words of greater length would be a more complicated enterprise than would the encoding of monosyllabic and/or short words, inasmuch as the former typically contain several redundant clusters. It seems likely however that degree of reliance on redundant clusters in word processing would be determined in part by: (1) the number of these units embedded in a given word; (2) the degree of familiarity with and functional utility of each unit in the reader's experience; and (3) the knowledge and skill of the reader. Thus the words *discriminate, discrimination, discriminating,* and *discriminated* contain several high-frequency spelling clusters (e.g., *dis, cr, ed, tion, ing*) that may be utilized in identifying them, either through the use of grapheme–phoneme correspondence rules or by analogy with other words containing the same units. The minimally skilled reader who has come to perceive these clusters as units would no doubt utilize them to facilitate precise discrimination of words in this set, implying synthesis of component clusters encoded separately (e.g., *dis cr im in a tion*). Yet, as already noted, separate (though simultaneous) encoding of recursive units would no doubt be characteristic of the skilled reader as well, particularly in the case of words such as these that contain both free (*criminate*) and bound morphemes (*dis, ed, ing, tion*). It seems likely that these latter units are encoded apart from their respective word roots, not only because they have occurred in a variety of word contexts but more importantly because they have meanings that transcend the meanings of their roots.

Support for the notion that polysyllabic words would often entail more complex encoding is derived from the work of Spoehr and Smith discussed earlier (Spoehr, 1978; Spoehr & Smith, 1973, 1975; Smith & Spoehr, 1974). It will be recalled that these authors found that words containing more than one vocalic center group took longer to process than did words that contained only one such unit, suggesting that polysyllabic words require more parsing than do monosyllabic words.[19] Similarly, a number of investigators have adduced evi-

---

[19]Gough and Cosky (1977) report results that run counter to the idea that speed of processing is significantly influenced by syllabic structure, contrary to the findings of Spoehr and Smith (1973, 1975), discussed earlier. Briefly, Cosky (unpublished manuscript) compared recognition latencies for tachistoscopically presented words, systematically varying word length, number of phonemes, and number of syllables, and found that only word length reliably affected the latency measures. However, as pointed out by Cosky himself, the results are equivocated by the fact that he did not adequately control for visual angle, which has been shown to be a significant determinant of recognition thresholds in studies utilizing the brief exposure technique (Spector & Purcell, 1977; Purcell, Stanovich & Spector, 1978). Furthermore, over half of the subjects in the sample employed in

dence that suggests that free and bound morphemes are encoded separately (Murrell & Morton, 1974; Taft & Forster, 1975; van der Molen & Morton, 1979; see following discussion). It would seem from such findings that polysyllabic words do involve more complex encoding than do monosyllabic words, and it may be that such differences arise not only because polysyllabic words typically contain a larger number of processing units but also because the linguistic structure of particular units in the functional sense is more complexly determined.

The foregoing analysis is consistent with the assertion that a word's visual constituents are encoded in different size units, many of which are comprised of invariant letter sequences that have a high degree of redundancy in English orthography. As should be evident from the discussion, the benefits that can be derived from a working knowledge of orthographic structure are employed, not only by the highly skilled reader but by the developing reader as well. Yet, it is also true that such benefits accrue only after extensive experience in reading, which is to say that the young child is not immediately attuned to the structural invariance embedded in the words he or she may encounter in first learning to read, and it takes some time before he becomes so attuned. Indeed, a number of studies have shown that there are sizable individual differences in the beginning reader's understanding of the relationship between print and sound, let alone sensitivity to orthographic structure (Lundberg & Torneus, 1978; Rozin, Bressman, & Taft, 1974).

Similarly, there is reason to believe that normally the child does not acquire a functional knowledge of orthographic redundancy until sometime between second and fourth grade and that such knowledge is not firmly entrenched and automatized until later. To be specific, Gibson, Osser and Pick (1963) presented first and third graders with brief exposures of three-, four-, and five-letter words, orthographically legal (pronounceable) pseudowords, and random letter strings and found that only the third graders identified the orthographically legal pseudowords substantially better than the random letter strings, whereas all subjects performed best on the word sets. At the same time, Rosinski and Wheeler (1972) found that first graders performed at the level of ''chance'' when asked to categorize pronounceable and unpronounceable letter strings on the basis of which ''was more like a real word.'' In contrast, accuracy for second and third graders, on the same task, ranged between 70% and 80%. Golinkoff (1974) obtained similar results in a modification of this experiment.

Cosky's study ($N = 15$) *did* appear to be affected by syllabic structure, suggesting that individual differences may have been influential in this study. Thus, the possibility that syllabic structure affects word recognition cannot be rejected solely on the basis of the data reported by Cosky and, in fact, would be more in keeping with the notion that the skill of the perceiver and the nature of the stimulus are important determinants of the processing strategies utilized on tasks such as those employed in his study.

In a very comprehensive study involving children from kindergarten through eleventh grade, Doehring (1976) presented subjects with matching (visual–visual and auditory–visual), visual scanning, and oral reading tests and found that latencies favoring legal over illegal letter arrays decreased steadily from third grade on. Of additional interest in this study is the observation that matching of real words was more accurate and more rapid than matching of pseudowords, especially at the upper-grade levels. This finding is consistent with the suggestion made earlier that the word familiarity effects observed in previous research (Pollatsek et al., 1975) transcend orthographic structure, inasmuch as speed of processing was greater for real words not only in comparison with orthographically illegal strings but in comparison with orthographically legal pseudowords as well.

The results of these investigations are important insofar as they indicate that the strategies employed by children in processing letter strings change significantly along the age/grade continuum, especially as they become more sensitive to orthographic redundancy. Indeed, it is in their initial encounters with the visual similarities inherent in recursive letter strings that children begin to dissect the orthography analytically, at first to effect precise discrimination (as in distinguishing *snow* and *show*) but later to apprehend structural redundancies that may be useful in word identification (e.g., *ch* in *church* and *chop*). Such redundancies are discovered at an increasingly rapid pace, and in learning to use them efficiently the child acquires a variety of perceptual attitudes that will come to facilitate word discrimination flexibly and economically.

This characterization is, of course, in line with Gibson's (1971) suggestion that children become more attuned to the structural invariants embedded in English orthography as they acquire skill in "breaking the code." It is also consistent with the notion that a word's constituents may eventually be coded in units that are functional at different levels of processing. It is no doubt during the period encompassing code acquisition that the fledgling reader shifts from a global and superficial processing mode to the more analytic approach that will allow him or her to acquire the comprehensive repertoire of visual codes that the skilled reader employs in identifying both familiar and new words. Additional support for this hypothesized transition is provided by separate studies conducted by Biemiller (1970) and Weber (1970), both of which yielded evidence that decoding errors at the beginning stages of reading were generalizations derived from a word's meaning, whereas decoding errors at a later stage issued from a word's visual structure. Such findings suggest that with experience children begin to internalize coded representations of a word's visual characteristics (Ehri, 1980) along with coded representations of other word features, and it is in learning to "cross-reference" these multiple codes that the child learns to diversify his or her processing strategies and thus enhance his or her skill in word recognition and identification. This brings me to the third major type of featural information that may influence perceptual organization of a particular letter string—its phonologic attributes.

Phonologic Information

The phonologic information contained within a printed word encompasses the sound sequence comprising its name as well as the phonemic counterparts of its constituent letters. As discussed in a previous section, the degree to which a printed word's phonologic attributes enter into the recognition process is an issue that has generated considerable controversy over the years and yet continues to do so. At one extreme are theorists, such as Morton (1969), F. Smith (1971) and Rumelhart and Siple (1974), who suggest that access to a lexical entry is direct in that a word's visual attributes can activate the meaning it represents without any recourse to its auditory components. At the other extreme are those such as Gough (1972) and Spoehr and Smith (1973) who contend that lexical access necessarily involves the phonologic recoding of subword units through the use of grapheme–phoneme correspondence rules. In discussing the arguments for and against these disparate positions, I suggested that although the findings to date must be considered inconclusive, the weight of the evidence favors the idea that phonologic mediation is not an obligatory component of the recognition process in skilled readers.

On the other hand, there is ample reason to believe that phonologic mediation *is* essential to the identification (as contrasted with recognition) of unfamiliar words and pseudowords, support for this notion being derived mainly from the fact that skilled readers can pronounce (orthographically legal) letter strings they have never seen before. At the same time, some of the findings discussed suggest that, under certain circumstances, phonologic recoding *may* be involved in the processing of familiar words. Recall, for example, Corcoran's observation (Corcoran, 1966; Corcoran & Weening, 1968) that pronounced letters are easier to detect in proofreading than are unpronounced letters (e.g., "silent" e's). Consider also the results of Meyer et al. (1974), who found that congruence between the graphic and phonologic characteristics of priming words and target words (BRIBE/TRIBE) enhanced speed of lexical decisions, whereas incongruence in these attributes (COUCH/TOUCH) significantly impaired decision speed. Such findings would seem to indicate that a word's auditory components are available and readily accessible to the skilled reader and may in some measure be utilized in word recognition. A similar interpretation might be applied to Hardyck and Petrinovich's (1970) finding that implicit speech is used in the silent reading of difficult material and to Spoehr's (1978) observation that variability in the number of syllables and/or phonemes contained in given words affects letter detection only when stimulus processing is interrupted (e.g., with backward masking). Although the point was not made before, other investigators have presented evidence that short-term memory for connected text may rely heavily upon phonologic coding (Kleiman, 1975; Levy, 1975; Perfetti & Goldman, 1976; Perfetti & Lesgold, 1978). Thus it appears that a word's auditory components may indeed be functional in the processing of written material, although the role of phonologic recoding in word recognition per se remains in dispute.

I suggested earlier that resolution of the controversy surrounding the phonologic recoding issue may inhere in the contention of some researchers, that word recognition and identification can occur either by direct or indirect access routes (Baron, 1977; Coltheart et al., 1977; Forster, 1979; LaBerge, 1979; LaBerge & Samuels, 1974). According to this point of view, the visual properties of a printed word simultaneously activate representations of a word's meaning and its phonologic attributes. In the first instance (direct access), verification of lexical status (recognition) is direct, and identification (naming) occurs after the word's meaning is apprehended. In the second instance (indirect access), verification of lexical status occurs by means of spelling–sound translation and meaning is apprehended after the word has been identified. Put another way, it is assumed that the direct route entails the activation of specific associations between the visual and semantic/syntactic features that uniquely define a word, whereas the indirect route entails the activation of the sound counterparts of redundant spelling patterns not unique to that word. It is further assumed that, in the skilled reader, each of these processes is automatic as a result of extensive practice in using both access routes, and component mechanisms operate in parallel, independent of one another.

However, there is *not* uniform agreement as to how alternative pathways facilitate word recognition and identification. Thus LaBerge and Samuels (1974) suggest that lexical verification is a discrete event and the means for accessing the lexicon is optional, depending on the task at hand. Similarly, Forster (1979) and others (Meyer & Ruddy, 1973) propose a multilevel "race" model, wherein recognition and/or identification are dependent on the computational equipment characteristic of each processing system and the mental operations necessary to complete processing. On the other hand, Coltheart et al. (1977) are of the opinion that word recognition is the end result of a continuous incremental process whereby the visual and phonologic systems provide independent inputs to the lexicon, which are "summed" by a "counter" (termed a "logogen" following Morton, 1969) that produces a recognition response after a certain threshold value has been reached. Similarly, Baron (1977) suggests that both access routes convey information that will facilitate and/or enhance word recognition and identification, though the direct route is presumed to be faster under ordinary circumstances and may be more often utilized by the skilled reader.

It should be clear that, in spite of these conflicting characterizations of lexical processing, dual access theories are more in keeping with the multilevel processing view of word recognition adopted here than are single access theories. Furthermore, they would seem to have greater ecological validity than these latter theories in that they more accurately reflect the complex and variable nature of the word stimulus, the information and skills that must be acquired before the individual becomes a fluent reader, and the complexity of word processing in general. And, relative to the topic under consideration, variability in the phonologic structure of printed words not only contributes significantly to this complexity but is an important determinant of the skilled reader's processing strategies as well.

In order to document this contention, let me extend the point made earlier that word recognition and identification necessarily involve the processing of word-specific and rule-based information (Baron, 1977, 1978). As I indicate in the previous section, both types of information must be apprehended in discriminating among printed words, and the utility of each in doing so depends in part on the degree to which a word's orthographic characteristics are similar to those of other words the individual has encountered. A high degree of similarity calls for fine-grained discrimination and, by definition, involves the processing of sub-word units for accurate identification. A low degree of similarity necessitates only global or holistic processing strategies, characterized by attendance to salient word discriminators, such as length, shape, supraletter features, and the more informative letters and letter combinations like those at the terminal positions (Marchbanks & Levin, 1965). As pointed out earlier, some words are intrinsically discriminable (e.g., *zero, xylophone, Mississippi*), and the names and meanings of these words are no doubt connected with their visual properties quite readily through rote learning. Yet many words initially learned by rote (e.g., *saw, lion*) may later be confused with similar appearing words (e.g., *was, loin*), and the individual must therefore acquire knowledge that will allow him to disambiguate. In such instances, rule-based knowledge can effectively supplement word-specific knowledge, and discrimination will necessarily involve the cross-referencing of whole-word and subword units.

But the distinction between rule-based and word-specific information is important, not only in learning to discriminate the visual attributes of orthographically similar words but in discriminating their phonologic attributes as well, because this information is often utilized for precise identification. Thus, in this context, rule-based information encompasses both words that can be pronounced through the use of grapheme–phoneme correspondences rules (*cat–fat*) *and* those that can be pronounced, either through analogy with other words (*late, mate*) or through the use of morphophonologic rules of a more complex nature (*ed, ing, nation* → nationality; Chomsky, 1970; Baron, 1977) Many words encountered in English orthography are of this type. Although initially confusing, they are eventually mastered by those who detect their phonologic redundancy, which ultimately affords a good deal of economy in visual processing (Gibson, 1971, 1977; Gibson, Osser & Pick, 1963).

Rule-based information may also facilitate word-specific learning, as in the case of words such as *was* and *saw,* wherein discrimination might be effected by using initial consonant sounds as convenient mnemonics to stabilize correct ordering of component letters. Conversely, word-specific associations would seem to be involved in learning to discriminate exceptions to the rules, such as *dough, cough,* and *bough,* that have highly similar spellings but very different pronunciations. It is likely that initial identification of such words relies heavily upon rote association of their spellings and their names and meanings, in which case some edifying mnemonic to remind the individual of their exceptionality might also be learned by rote (e.g., *dough* sounds like *doe,* which sounds like *toe,* which sounds like *no*).

At all events, it would seem that the phonologic characteristics of a particular letter string can significantly influence the way in which that string is processed and may be especially influential in determining the size of the processing unit(s) in skilled as well as less skilled readers. Words characterized by a high degree of orthographic redundancy are often characterized by spelling–sound invariance as well. Thus the invariant letter combinations that comprise such words, by virtue of their functional utility in initially discriminating between and among them as well as their utility in identifying new words, will come to be perceived as units even when they appear in familiar whole-word contexts.

On the other hand, words that are *not* highly redundant are not, by definition, comprised of many spelling–sound invariants. The individual learning to identify such words will therefore tend to rely more heavily upon specific associations between the orthographic characteristics that uniquely define them as wholes on the one hand and their respective names and meanings on the other. Focal attention to subword units would be involved in such learning only when fine-grained discriminations are required (e.g., *are* versus *arc*). Similar strategies will quite likely be employed when one is learning to identify exception words but, as noted earlier, identification of such words will no doubt necessitate acquisition of more elaborate mnemonics to facilitate precision.

The proposed distinction between word-specific and rule-based learning is, of course, consistent with Baron's (1977, 1978) conceptualization of the word identification process and essentially defines two qualitatively different though complementary strategies for lexical access and retrieval, utilizing two general classes of information: representations that uniquely define whole words and representations that define subword units characterized by spelling–sound correspondence. It seems likely that fluent reading necessitates the acquisition and active interchange of both types of information. But aside from naturalistic observation that instructional and/or individual difference variables may result in differential use of whole-word and part-whole learning strategies (Chall, 1967), there has been little controlled laboratory study evaluating the idea that these two approaches can be differentiated *or* that individuals may vary in their inclination to favor one (strategy) over the other. However, a few investigators have evaluated these possibilities and their findings are notable.

In one such experiment, Brooks and Baron (cited in Brooks, 1977) specifically compared whole-word and rule-based learning employing novel alphabetic characters comprising five-letter words. Odd- and even-numbered subjects (college students) were presented with two lists of English words to be associated with words written in the novel alphabet, one represented by characters that were grapheme–phoneme invariants and another represented by characters that were not invariant on these two dimensions, as in paired-associates learning (see Fig. 2.6). Each subject received the same words, but each was presented with given words in either the graphophonemic or paired-associates condition, in accord with group membership. Lists were equated for information content, and subjects were given extensive practice on each type of list. The dependent measure was time taken to read each list evaluated on successive blocks of trials.

It was found that although initial learning was more rapid under the paired-associates condition, learning under the rule-based condition eventually surpassed paired-associates learning. Apparently, subjects exposed to the rule-based condition began to "discover" and make functional use of the spelling-sound

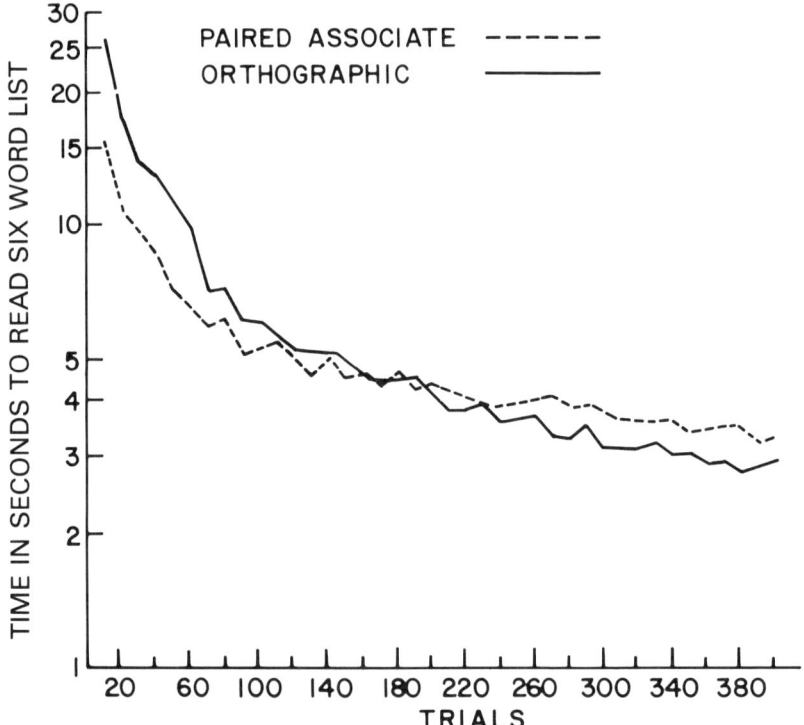

FIG. 2.6. Graph depicting time taken in seconds (log scale) to identify each of two sets of six words over 400 trials of practice in study by Brooks and Baron (cited in Brooks, 1977; figure also taken from this reference with permission of the author and publisher).

invariants contained in the redundant stimulus set after a sufficient amount of practice with these stimuli. These findings support the idea that a word's phonologic attributes are important determinants of the processing units employed in recognition and identification and are entirely consistent with the notion that word-specific and rule-based learning represent distinctly different processing strategies, partly determined by the nature of the stimulus.

Although the Brooks and Baron study was conducted with adults, Hartley (1970) obtained similar results with kindergarten children. Briefly, this author evaluated the differential utility of teaching whole words: (1) in isolation; (2) with pictorial aids; and (3) within sentence contexts, using two different-type word lists. One was characterized by a high degree of spelling–sound correspondence among stimulus words (*hen, ten, pen, men*) and another was characterized by very low correspondence among these words (*men, swing, how, care*). Subjects were randomly assigned to one of the six treatments (presentation × list type) and presented with four sets of stimulus words, in blocks of four, over a period of 5 days. All subjects were then given a transfer test consisting of four real words and four nonsense words, using phonemic elements from the stimulus sets to which they were exposed (*sing, Ken, make, row, ren, kow, ling,* and *hake*). On the tenth day after initial training, each was administered a posttest of all 16 words originally learned. The important finding for present purposes is that, on all contrasts made (initial learning, transfer, and posttesting), performance on the spelling–sound correspondence list was best when words were presented without the aid of sentence contexts. However, the reverse pattern was observed in the case of the low correspondence words, and pictorial cues were equally effective with both list types. Apparently, context impaired the use of redundancy in identifying words on the high similarity list but facilitated identification of words on the low similarity list, suggesting that two different strategies were employed for learning respective lists. These findings are consistent with Brook's and Baron's results, thereby reinforcing the notion that word-specific and rule-based learning constitute different perceptual attitudes, determined in part by qualitatively different (not mutually exclusive) types of stimulus information. A similar conclusion was drawn by Ehri and Roberts (1979) and by Ehri and Wilce (1980) after obtaining results that conform closely to those obtained by Hartley (1970).

Additional support for the word-specific, rule-based distinction is derived from a study conducted by Baron and Strawson (1976). These authors asked subjects (college students) to pronounce a list of orthographically "regular" words, which conform to spelling–sound rules (e.g., *chart, twig, loan*), along with a list of "exception" words, which violate such rules (e.g., *epoch, cough, should*). Each also pronouned a list of (pronounceable) nonwords that are homophonic with other English words, and the real-word lists were matched for frequency of occurrence. It was found that pronunciation of exception words took longer and was less accurate than pronunciation of regular words, and the exception words were almost as difficult to pronounce in terms of these performance criteria as the nonwords. It would thus seem that spelling–sound associations are more important for identifying orthographically regular words than are word-specific associations, whereas word-specific associations are more important for identifying exception words than are spelling–sound associations.

That there may be individual differences in the use of these strategies, even among adult readers, is suggested by the results of two other studies conducted by Baron. In the first of these investigations (Baron, 1977; Baron & Strawson, 1976), subjects (*college students*) were grouped in accord with a hypothesized preference for using word-specific or rule-based information for word identification. Word-specific processors (*called "Chinese"*) were those who could visually recognize misspellings of difficult words (*e.g., argueable versus arguable*) better than they could apply graphonophonic rules to identify homophonic pseudowords (*caik*). Rule-based or orthographic processors (*called "Phonecians"*) were those who showed the reverse pattern. These groups were then given lists of regular and exception words to read in *mixed, upper,* and *lower* typecase print. In order to offset an expected advantage for reading the regular words, low-frequency words were selected for the regular list and high-frequency words for the exception list. Time taken to read each list was the dependent measure.

Two findings are important here. First, although the overall difference between the two lists was not significant (validating the word frequency procedure), the mixed typecase condition hampered speed of processing the exception words, more so than the regular words. This finding reinforces the idea that identification of exception words relies more heavily upon word-specific associations than does identification of regular words, which would seem to depend more on rule-based associations. Second, the word-specific processors performed better on the exception words than they did on the regular words, whereas the opposite pattern was manifested in the rule-based learners. Thus, it seems reasonable to suggest that even relatively skilled readers differ in the extent to which they rely on one strategy or the other for word identification, though it must also be true that they utilize both for this purpose in some measure.

Baron (1979) extended these results in a later study with children in second and fourth grade, characterized by different levels of achievement in reading. In brief, it was found that impaired readers could be separated in accord with differential tendencies to use word-specific and rule-based information for word learning. Thus, in rule-based learners, ability to read nonsense words (e.g., *lut*), applying graphophonemic rules, was correlated more highly with the ability to read regular words (e.g., *cut*) than with the ability to read exception words. Furthermore, rule-based learners made more sound generalization errors on exception words (/tauf/ for *tough*) than did word-specific learners, who made more meaning generalization errors (*sit* for *seat*). A similar pattern was also evident among normally developing readers, in that children who rely heavily on rules were also found to be confused more by reading words (presented in succession) that had similar spellings but different sounds (*maid, said*) than were children who rely on word-specific associations. Of additional interest is the finding that ability to read exception words was correlated more highly with ability to read regular words than with ability to read nonsense words, suggesting that both specific associations and rules are used to read regular words, that rule-based learners use both grapheme–phoneme invariance (*cat–fat*) and analogy (*maid–raid*) in identifying new words, and that instruction can facilitate the differential use of these processing strategies.

The foregoing results suggest that phonologic information does, indeed, influence the size of the perceptual units that may be employed in word recognition and identification. To the extent that the developing reader utilizes spelling–sound correspondences in learning to decode unfamiliar or unreliably identified words, he or she will come to perceive, as units, spelling patterns contained within those words that were instrumental in stabilizing their identification. Thus, whereas the word *church* will be processed holistically by the individual who can rapidly identify it, familiar clusters that comprise this word will nevertheless be perceived as units (e.g., *ch ur ch; chur ch*) as in other words in which they appear (e.g., *ch*ick, hat*ch,* f*ur,* h*ur*t, *chur*n), especially if they were employed in learning to identify these words.

Because the discovery and functional use of spelling–sound correspondences takes place over a protracted period, sound-mediated identification frequently entails the reorganization of earlier percepts. For example, global processing of *lion* will no longer be effective when the child initially encounters the word *loin,* and discrimination will thereafter necessitate fine-grained processing, perhaps facilitated through the application of grapheme–phoneme correspondence rules. If this strategy is employed, then *lion* might for a time be perceived as a four-unit word, whereas *loin* is perceived as a three-unit word, inasmuch as the *oi* in *loin* is assigned one rather than two phonemes. Similarly, in learning to disambiguate the pseudocompound *father,* the inexperienced reader might erroneously apprehend the familiar words *fat* and *her* but, with appropriate feedback, utilize prior knowledge of the sound counterparts of alternative letter groupings (e.g., *th, ther*) to aid in recovering the correct pronunciation. In doing so, he or she no doubt alters his processing strategies so as to perceive these letter combinations as units whenever the word is encountered.

This is not to suggest, however, that words that can be identified by spelling–sound rules are perceived piecemeal by the skilled reader, because fluent reading involves holistic processing of familiar words, characterized by simultaneous access of rule-based and word-specific properties. Indeed, it is the cross-referencing and integration of these two categories of information that ultimately provides the basis for alternative access routes and thus development of flexible and efficient strategies for word recognition and identification. The contention, therefore, is that spelling-to-sound redundancies that are available to the developing reader will often be used in learning to identify a given word because of the economy inherent in rule-based learning. Such redundancies will thereafter be integrated with whole-word or word-specific features, and both will be permanently represented as qualitatively different components that define the word as a unique lexical entry. Accordingly, *church* is *not* perceived by the skilled reader as six invariantly ordered letters to which a name and a meaning are attached but as a familiar and meaningful unit comprised of redundant letter clusters (*ch ur, chur*) that are accessed along with the word as a whole. *Father* must also be perceived as a meaningful whole by the skilled reader, but its letters will be processed in combinations that avoid apprehension of anomalous components while effectively recovering its pronunciation (*fa ther*).

It should be apparent that the foregoing analysis is consistent not only with the dual access theories of word processing mentioned earlier but also with the conceptualization of Gibson and her associates (Gibson, Osser, & Pick, 1963) and that of Spoehr (Spoehr, 1978; Spoehr & Smith, 1973, 1975) at least insofar as these theories suggest that spelling–sound correspondences are significant determinants of the size of the perceptual units that may be employed in word identification. The present conceptualization differs from both, however, in advocating that there is *no* single unit of perception in skilled reading and that facility in word recognition and identification is dependent on availability of word-specific as well as rule-based representations that complement one another in the identification process. Furthermore, implied in the present analysis is the notion that any parsing of word constituents into syllable and/or phoneme size units, as advocated in Spoehr's theory: (1) is limited by the extent of one's knowledge of spelling–sound correspondences; (2) may vary from word to word; and (3) may not be obligatory, contrary to the theory as originally articulated (see the earlier discussion for Spoehr's qualification of this position on p. 69).

At any rate, it should be clear from the arguments advanced herein that the processing units that may be employed in word recognition and identification are complexly determined and rely upon a functional acquaintance with a word's multiple features. Thus far, I have discussed the means by which a word's graphic, orthographic, and phonologic characteristics may be influential in word processing, and I now consider the possible influence of its semantic and syntactic features.

Semantic–Syntactic Information

A word's semantic properties have reference to the particular concept or entity symbolized by that word, and its syntactic properties refer to its use in sentences, which is constrained by grammatical principles inherent in the language. Thus, semantic information is word specific, whereas syntactic information is rule-based, and the two taken together define a word's meaning.

The meaning signified by a printed word would seem to be yet another determinant of the processing unit in word perception. Indeed, Gibson (1977) suggests that meaning "contributes to the unity and coherence" (p. 167) of a letter string and has adduced evidence in support of this idea. I have already made reference to the findings of Gibson, Osser, and Pick (1963), who observed that first and third graders identified simple three-letter words (e.g., *PUT*) more accurately than pronounceable and unpronounceable anagrams of these words: *TUP, TPU*). Analogously, Gibson et al. (1964) found that meaningful initials (e.g., *RKO, IBM*) were recognized and recalled better by college students than were pronounceable and unpronounceable strings that were also anagrams of the meaningful sets (*KOR, KRO*). These results are consistent with the view adopted by other researchers (Barron & Pittenger, 1974; Manelis, 1974), who suggest that meaning is a special property of printed words that contribute to their memorability in ways that transcend their surface characteristics.

However, this idea is by no means uniformly accepted, a fact that became especially evident in the discussion of the word superiority effect. Recall, in this connection, that Baron and Thurston (1973) found no significant advantage for real words over pronounceable pseudowords on a Reicher-type letter detection task, whereas Manelis (1974) *did* find such an advantage when high-frequency words were employed and stimuli were presented only once. Manelis (1974) concludes from these findings that meaning and familiarity both contribute to the word superiority effect, but Baron (1978) points out that these two variables are confounded in Manelis' (1974) study. He also suggests that familiarity is a more likely determinant of the word superiority effect, inasmuch as repeated presentations of both word and pseudoword stimuli yielded no performance differences between the two stimulus sets (Baron & Thurston, 1973). In fact, this finding is inconsistent with the idea that meaning engenders any significant advantage for words over pseudowords in perceptual processing; that is, subjects would no doubt become more familiar with nonsense words as a result of repeated exposures of these stimuli, but nonsense words remain meaningless in spite of repeated exposures.

However, Barron and Pittenger (1974) also presented subjects with repetitions of stimulus sets, in this case on same/different matching tasks, and *did* find an advantage for words over pseudowords and random strings even when these stimuli were equated for bigram and trigram frequency. These results were interpreted as support for the view that meaning significantly influences word perception. Conversely, Pollatsek et al. (1975) controlled for meaning by changing only the letter case of standard and matching stimuli (FLEA, FLEa) and found what may be interpreted as a familiarity effect.

At the same time, there is, as we have seen, considerable evidence that meaningful context can have a measurable effect on related phenomena, such as the *recognition threshold* (Morton, 1968, 1969; Tulving et al., 1963, 1964), *latency of a recognition response* (Meyer et al., 1974), and the *size of the processing unit* in connected text (Drewnowski & Healy, 1977; Healy, 1976), implying some sort of interaction between a word's semantic–syntactic and its orthographic characteristics in effecting recognition. These findings coupled with those from the Baron and Pittenger (1974) and Pollatsek et al. (1975) studies would seem to indicate that meaning and whole-word familiarity *do* make separate (though not entirely independent) contributions to the word recognition process, allowing us to speculate at least about the possible ways in which the semantic–syntactic attributes of a given word might shape the perceiver's processing strategies.

Perhaps the most useful course in delineating various possibilities would be to again adopt a developmental perspective, because this type of analysis tells us something about the derivation of the strategies that may be employed by the skilled reader in processing printed words. Thus, of immediate interest is the question of how a word's semantic–syntactic features might affect the processing strategies adopted by the beginning reader in learning to identify words he or she initially encounters. I am in accord with Gibson's (1971, 1977) suggestion that meaning plays the dominant role at this level of experience, given the individual's natural inclination to assimilate new information to knowledge already acquired. It would therefore be expected that in his or her attempts to discriminate the first words he or she sees in print, the child would rely more heavily on the meanings of those words than on their structural characteristics and as a result would be inclined to attend to and incorporate only their salient orthographic features as the basis for recognition. Thus the perceptual attitude that would most likely typify the neophyte would essentially involve global processing, in which case distinguishing attributes at the whole-word level (e.g., *cat* versus *elephant*) would be readily associated with verbal labels representing objects that are meaningful to the child.

That this mode of processing is characteristic of beginning readers is suggested in the results of the studies by Biemiller (1970) and Weber (1970) cited earlier in which it was found that the most common word substitution errors made by such children in processing connected text were semantically and syntactically derived. It was not until they acquired more experience in reading that their errors were based upon the structural similarities between stimulus and response words. These findings are consistent with Gibson's (1971, 1977) suggestion that meaning confers unity on a printed word, which makes it a very handy vehicle for initial word identification.

However, undue reliance on meaning and on a word's most salient visual attributes soon occasions the child some difficulty in this enterprise, because there are many words in English orthography that have a high degree of graphic and orthographic similarity, for example, minimally contrasted words such as *was-saw, lion* and *loin*. It is in encountering words of this type that the child begins to diversify his or her processing strategies, underscoring a second way in which a word's semantic–syntactic properties can influence the processing unit. The reference here is to the inherent feedback provided by running text when the child misidentifies a word and substitutes a grammatically incongruous word. Under such circumstances the individual who is well-acquainted with the meaning and syntax of both the presented word and its erroneous substitute will quite likely make note of features that distinguish these words and attempt to encode information that will thereafter facilitate discrimination. Such encoding will, of course, necessitate significant alteration in the perceptual attitude that occasioned the generalization error, as when left-right processing is substituted for holistic processing, to distinguish *was* from *saw,* perhaps with the aid of spelling-sound mnemonics to stabilize accuracy in name retrieval. As suggested earlier, strategies that initially facilitated stable discrimination will be retained in some measure by the skilled reader, selective attention to the initial consonants in *was* and *saw* being one such example.

A third way in which a word's semantic and syntactic characteristics can significantly influence one's processing strategies in beginning reading becomes evident in contrasting words that differ with respect to their substantive qualities, because variability on this dimension differentially affects a word's memorability. As any competent first-grade teacher will testify, content words, such as concrete nouns and adjectives used in conjunction with concrete nouns, are learned as "sight" words more readily than less substantive words, such as abstract nouns (e.g., truth) and functor words (i.e., verbs, prepositions, conjunctions, and pronouns), because concrete words are more easily associated with meaningful objects and experience. Abstract nouns and functor words on the other hand have no concrete referents to aid identification, and they are linguistically more complex, given that the meanings they convey are in part determined by syntactic rules that relate them to other words (Begg & Clark, 1975; Begg, Upfold, & Wilton, 1978). Thus, high meaning contentives will readily be organized at the whole-word level by the beginning reader and will be processed at that level, unless and until he or she begins to discover the structural redundancies inherent in the orthography. If and when this occurs, redundancies contained within words originally learned as wholes will be explicated, facilitating more diverse and flexible processing of those words.

However, because their semantic-syntactic features are more complex, initial learning of the more abstract words will involve greater reliance upon structural information, such as spelling-sound correspondences, invariant letter positions and the like, especially to aid identification of those that prove to be more troublesome. Note in this connection that many functor words are also characterized by a high degree of orthographic similarity (e.g., *them, they; when, where*), making exclusive reliance upon rote association of their names and whole-word features a hazardous enterprise. The child learning to discriminate such words will therefore need to develop more meticulous and flexible processing strategies, perhaps utilizing both rule-based and word-specific information to effect stable identification.

An assumption, common to the foregoing illustrations, is that the linguistic properties of printed words—specifically, the way in which their verbal counterparts represent meaning—will significantly influence the visual processing strategies employed in learning to identify them. Such learning will in turn shape the processing modes employed in fluent reading. Still another example of this relationship can be observed in the case of derived words having common roots.

To illustrate, words such as *bombard, bombardier, bombing, bombed* derive their meanings from the root word *bomb,* but each has a slightly different meaning, which can be employed only in particular contexts. Each also has a specified pronunciation, which cannot be reliably derived from the application of surface phonological rules that yield spelling–sound correspondences. Chomsky (1970) points out that the pronunciations of such words are derived from deep phonological rules that limit the phoneme sequences possible in spoken English. Thus the sound associated with the letter *b* in the terminal position of *bomb* is eliminated by a consonant deletion rule in the words *bomb, bombing,* and *bombed,* because pronunciation of these words would otherwise be anomalous. The *b* sound *is,* however, heard in the words *bombard* and *bombardier,* because its use yields legitimate pronunciations in both instances. Yet in all of these words, the spelling pattern conforming to the root word is intact, because the semantic component of this word remains constant in all the derivatives. At the same time, the semantic components of the form class determinants vary, as exemplified in *bombed* and *bombing,* wherein *ed* places the verb in the past tense and *ing* places it in the progressive tense. These words are, in fact, comprised of two morphemes, a free morpheme signifying the meaning of the root word and a bound morpheme signifying the meaning associated with a particular syntactic construction. It would therefore seem reasonable to expect that visual processing of derivative words would entail unit perception of the free and bound morphemes contained within those words.

Evidence to support this conjecture is derived from research conducted by several investigators. Briefly, Gibson and Guinet (1971) presented third and fifth graders as well as college students with brief exposures of inflected and uninflected words and pseudowords (*start, started; trast, trasted; rtsta, rtstaed*) and found that these subjects produced more correct endings on inflected items than on uninflected items, the proportional number increasing with age. They also found that inflected words prompted morphological substitutes (e.g., *starting* for *started*) more often than uninflected words, both findings suggesting that bound morphemes are perceived as units.

Similar results were obtained by Murrell and Morton (1974). These authors had college students learn a word list consisting of: (1) root words (e.g., *hang*); (2) inflected words containing the same root morpheme (*hanging*); and (3) words having visual and acoustic similarity to the root word (*hangar*). Subjects were then given a tachistoscopic recognition task, and it was found that pretraining on a derivative word facilitated tachistoscopic recognition to a greater extent than pretraining on a visually and acoustically similar word. In addition, analysis of error responses suggested that root and suffix morphemes are recognized independently, in that substitution errors often contained the same root morphemes but different suffixes. It was also found that suffixes were recognized better than roots. The results combined were thought to be consistent with the view that the morpheme is the unit of processing in adult readers.

In another such experiment, Taft and Forster (1975) found that nonwords that are stems of prefixed words (e.g., *juvenate*) took longer to classify on lexical decision tasks than nonwords that are not stems (e.g., *pertoire*). Prefixed nonwords containing real stems (e.g., *dejuvenate*) took longer to classify than those that did not contain real stems (e.g., *depertoire*). Furthermore, words that can occur both as free and bound morphemes (e.g., *vent*) took longer to classify when the bound morpheme (e.g., *prevent*) was more frequent. The authors conclude from these findings that prefixed words are decomposed into constituent morphemes prior to lexical access, consistent with the notion that free and bound morphemes are processed separately.

In yet another study addressing the question, van der Molen and Morton (1979) asked adult subjects to remember plural nouns presented visually and found that they made a significant number of errors wherein the plural morpheme was detached from its root. This finding was taken as evidence for a morpheme-based as opposed to a unitary word code, reinforcing the idea that free and bound morphemes are perceived as units in word recognition.

The results of the foregoing studies support the contention that a word's semantic–syntactic properties can influence the unit of perception. One final way in which this might occur is in the processing of running narrative. There is, of course, abundant evidence that words embedded in meaningful text require less detailed processing for accurate identification than words presented in isolation. This is true for both skilled and less skilled readers and is due largely to the predictability of particular words in given contexts, as well as to the reader's familiarity with the meanings and structural characteristics of those words. The theoretical explanations offered to account for this phenomenon were outlined earlier and need not be discussed further.

Summary

In the foregoing sections, I have tried to substantiate the contention that the unit of perception—that is, the level at which a word must be processed to distinguish it from other words—is partly determined by the stimulus properties of the word itself. A word's most ostensible attributes are embodied in the graphic features that comprise its letters. These are important to discriminate not only because it is a word's letters that define it but also because some words are differentiated only on the basis of a single letter or letter feature and thus require detailed analysis at these levels to effect accurate identification. Other words are more distinctive and can be identified on the basis of global features, such as length, shape, and salient letter combinations. They do not therefore require the degree of processing necessary to identify visually similar words, depending of course on the context in which they appear.

But a word's distinctiveness is determined not only by its graphic features but also by its semantic and syntactic features, which together define its meaning. Because meaning is inherently useful in acquiring new information, the beginning reader will be naturally inclined to rely more upon a word's semantic and syntactic characteristics than upon its structural characteristics in learning to identify that word. His processing strategies will therefore be quite global, inasmuch as the dominant learning mode will typically involve rote association of a word's salient visual features with its name and meaning, this process often referred to as whole-word learning.

However, because of the high degree of visual similarity that characterizes English orthography and because not all words can be readily learned by rote (particularly those that are more abstract and complex), exclusive reliance upon meaning and whole-word association will, in the normally developing reader, be preempted by more diverse processing modes as the child discovers the orthographic and phonologic redundancies embedded in the words he or she encounters. These include invariant letter clusters, letter position frequencies, spelling–sound correspondences, and letter strings defining free and bound morphemes appearing in different combinations. Such information will come to be utilized in a rule-generated way, both in fine-graining discrimination of words originally learned holistically (e.g., *lion* versus *loin*) and in acquiring new words with increasingly greater facility. Because of the economy in processing provided by structural redundancy, the child begins to dissect the orthogrpahy more meticulously and more comprehensively, a course that eventuates in the acquisition of detailed information about a word's multiple features, as well as more diverse and flexible means for identifying that word and words in general.

Having acquired such information, the mature reader is again inclined to process words holistically, with maximum attendance to their meanings. However, word perception at this level of experience is qualitatively different from that at an earlier stage; it is more highly differentiated, accesses more information at a glance (both word-specific and rule-generated), and entails selective attention to intraword units at critical levels of processing, so as to facilitate discrimination and identification economically and efficiently in accord with task demands.

It therefore follows that the individual who has not acquired such detailed information will not have developed the diverse and flexible processing strategies that would allow him or her to identify words in the most efficient and economical manner, which brings me to the third and final determinant of the unit(s) of perception I wish to discuss.

The Skill of the Reader

Word-Processing Differences in Young Readers: Definition of Subgroups

I have suggested repeatedly that children who are developing normally in reading and who eventually acquire fluency in this skill come to utilize both word-specific and rule-generated information in identifying printed words and have differentiated a word's multiple features to a level that allows maximum flexibil-

2. WORD RECOGNITION AND THE UNIT OF PERCEPTION

ity and efficiency in the identification process. Normal readers typically acquire an age-appropriate corpus of whole words that they can rapidly identify on sight, are increasingly able to employ spelling–sound correspondences (i.e., grapheme–phoneme invariants, analogies, etc.) in identifying new words, and have age-appropriate language development that allows them to make effective use of contextual information in doing so. It seems reasonable to suggest that in such individuals the processing units will gradually diversify, in accord with their growing ability to differentiate the structural characteristics of the words they encounter. Features that broadly and uniquely define whole words will be incorporated along with those that distinguish between low contrast words, such as subtle differences in letter sequences and the presence or absence of certain letters and letter features, so also will spelling–sound units that have facilitated economy and stability in new learning. Of no small importance in nurturing such diversification is the child's growing competence in oral and written spelling. Indeed, word decoding and spelling soon become complementary and mutually reinforcing processes, and the information acquired in these two enterprises is cross-referenced and gradually integrated into an elaborate and hierarchically embedded network of functionally distinct codes or processing units that are readily available, not only for making critical discriminations, but also for accessing the lexicon via alternative routes and for identifying letter strings that have never been encountered.

Impaired readers on the other hand are not as facile as normal readers in word processing, because they lack information about one or more word features. The perceptual strategies acquired by such individuals are characterized by distinct tendencies to process a word's visual components either superficially or over-analytically, oftentimes accompanied by the failure to utilize knowledge that they may have available to assist in word decoding (e.g., word meanings, part-whole relationships, etc.). Some children from this group are only mildly or moderately impaired in reading, whereas others are more severely impaired. The less impaired readers can be separated into two groups, defined by differences in word learning, which conform to the dichotomy suggested by Baron (1977, 1979). Thus, one group consists of children who are inclined to process words holistically through rote association of salient visual characteristics, with word names and meanings. At the same time, they do not systematically incorporate detailed information as to a word's internal structure, and therefore fail to make sufficient use of the redundant and rule-generated information embedded in the orthography. In effect, they do not readily acquire the code and learn new words idiographically. As a result, they: (1) typically place an undue burden on memory, as the number of words they encounter proliferates; (2) have few alternative means for discriminating visually similar words; (3) do not ultimately acquire as large a corpus of sight words as skilled readers, and do not have a comparable rate of acquisition, except in the early stages of learning (Chall, 1967); (4) cannot readily identify new words (or pseudowords), because they do not have a sufficient repertoire of spelling sound correspondences to do so; and (5) as is true of all impaired readers are poor in spelling and written expression. Such children do not appear to have any significant language deficits, have essentially normal intelligence, and generally rely heavily upon verbal context to aid recall. The primary processing unit for this group would seem to be an undifferentiated whole word, owing to the limited information they incorporate as to the structural redundancies embedded in the orthography.

In contrast to whole-word learners are those children whose approach to word identification is characterized by undue investment in structural analysis, as well as inordinate reliance upon spelling–sound correspondences in both reading and spelling. Such children are less inclined than whole-word learners to make extensive use of meaning and contextual information in learning to identify words. They therefore do not store an adequate number of words they can rapidly identify on sight and often misapply spelling–sound correspondences, for example, in identifying exception words (*maid* versus *said*). The identification process for these youngsters is typically plodding and laborious, and they have a great deal of difficulty in negotiating connected text. They too have significant impairments in spelling and written expression. However, they sustain no ostensible deficiencies in language and also have normal intelligence. For such children the processing units most readily available are letters and letter clusters, owing to their failure to incorporate reliably features that broadly define whole words, as well as information that allows them to identify words that do not conform to spelling–sound rules. It should be apparent that individuals from this group conform to Baron's description of rule-based learners.

Severely impaired readers are distinguished from those in the other two groups in that they have extreme difficulty in both whole-word and rule-based learning and do not readily acquire either a substantial number of sight words or a functional knowledge of spelling–sound correspondences. As a consequence, they are grossly deficient in all aspects of reading, spelling, and written expression. In spite of normal intelligence, adequate instruction, and the absence of other extenuating attributes (e.g., severe emotional disorder), such children make painfully slow progress in reading, and their processing strategies tend to be superficial and unstable. Because they have particular difficulty in using the alphabetic code to acquire spelling–sound correspondences, the words they *can* identify are typically learned by rote. Although they have little recourse but to rely on word meanings to aid recall, they are not as effective as normal readers in utilizing verbal context to assist in identifying words in running text. It would seem from their unreliable performance patterns that the processing units for such children are typically fragmented and idiosyncratic and the whole-word representations they do internalize often occasion them generalization errors, because they are not highly differentiated.

The foregoing characterizations are based, in part, upon the author's observations of children studied in the laboratory as well as in the natural setting but also derive support from work done elsewhere. Certainly Baron's (1979) account of the processing differences he observed in his poor reader samples accords with the present descriptions of the two less impaired reader groups outlined above. However, additional support comes from other sources as well. Clinicians and educators have often made reference to the fact that poor readers do not constitute a homogeneous group (Boder, 1971, 1973; Johnson & Myklebust, 1967; Kinsbourne & Warrington, 1966) and have typically suggested that different processing strategies that define particular subgroups are associated with qualitatively different types of neurological disorder. Although this interpretation seems unwarranted, especially when applied to mildly or moderately impaired readers, one such conceptualization is notable not only because of its similarity to the subgroups characterized previously but also because the procedures used to identify these groups are quite similar to those employed by Baron. The reference here is to the work of Boder (1971, 1973), who distinguishes three different types of impaired readers, or "dyslexics," to use her terminology. One type, the "dysphonetic dyslexic," is similar to Baron's word-specific learner and is said to rely primarily upon a whole-word strategy for word identification because of difficulty in learning spelling-sound relationships. Such difficulty is presumed to be also apparent in an inability to spell phonetically and is attributed to central auditory disorder. A second type, the "dyseidetic dyslexic," is similar to Baron's rule-based learner and is described as unduly reliant on spelling-sound correspondences because of basic difficulty in visual perception and visual memory. Spelling in such individuals tends to be phonetic. A third type, the "dysphonetic-dyseidetic dyslexic," is the most severely impaired of the three and is described as having extreme difficulty learning both spelling-sound correspondences and whole words, which of course is a pattern that we have observed in the severely impaired subtype outlined previously.

Boder's classification procedure in brief contrasts these groups on reading and spelling of the same words. Word lists, graded for difficulty level, are first presented for rapid identification, and those not readily identified are presented for further analysis. The proportion of words named with dispatch is compared with those that are either unknown or "sounded out," and individuals who have the highest proportion of words in these respective categories are tentatively identified as dysphonetic and dyseidetic. Children are then asked to spell both the rapidly named and unknown words, and the types of spelling errors made on each list are contrasted. A limited ability to sound out words, the inability to spell phonetically, and a sizable number of whole words rapidly named defines the dysphonetic dyslexic. Conversely, a comparatively small number of whole words rapidly named, a larger number that are sounded out correctly, and a preponderance of phonetic spelling errors defines the dyseidetic dyslexic. By extension, very poor performance in all these areas defines the mixed type, or dysphonetic-dyseidetic dyslexic. Noteworthy is the author's description of dysphonetics as more inclined toward semantic substitution errors in oral reading than toward phonetic substitutions, whereas the reverse pattern is said to be observed in the dyseidetic group. The most severely impaired readers, by Boder's account, tend to make many errors of both types, and their oral reading is generally characterized by many ommissions and long pauses. Also noteworthy is her observation that the majority of poor readers encountered have more difficulty acquiring spelling–sound correspondences than in learning whole-word meaning associations.

Boder's (1971, 1973) classification schema is based on clinical observation and the instruments she employed for "differential diagnosis" were not standardized. However, Camp and Dolcourt (1977) have attempted to formalize Boder's procedures and obtained results that lend additional credence to the broad categories she has outlined.

The previous descriptions refer, of course, to the perceptual attitudes adopted by abnormally developing readers, but there is reason to believe that even some normally developing readers may adopt certain limiting processing strategies in identifying printed words. Support for this idea is derived from a study recently reported by Frith (1978, 1980). This author observed that the spelling errors of children (12-year-olds) who were good readers but poor spellers (GRPS) were similar to those of children who were good in both reading and spelling (GRGS), in that both types of errors were more often phonetic than orthographic. This was in contrast to the spelling errors of children poor in both reading and spelling, which included an approximately equal number of errors of each type. These findings might be an indication that GRPS children process printed words globally and therefore do not become sensitive to the subtle differences in orthographic structure that facilitate precision in spelling, for example, awareness of inconsistencies in phoneme–grapheme translation (e.g., *bread* versus *bred*). If so, then similar error patterns should be evident in reading as well as in spelling and this was indeed the case. In comparisons of the reading strategies employed by GRPS and GRGS subjects, it was observed that children in the former group were inclined to identify words on the basis of partial cues, whereas word identification among children in the latter group was characterized by more detailed processing. For example, when real words that were read correctly by both groups were altered slightly, so as to convert them into pronounceable nonsense words (*saucer, laucer*), the GRPS group made more pronunciation errors than the GRGS group, suggesting that GRPS subjects used the more superficial "look-say" method for identifying the corresponding real words rather than grapheme–phoneme translation, which by definition requires component letter processing. The GRPS subjects were also less accurate than the GRGS subjects in detecting misspellings in words and were generally less proficient whenever a given task necessitated fine-grained discrimination.

Of particular interest is the finding that children in the GRPS group had more difficulty in reading connected text containing misspelled words (e.g., Boocks hellp us . . .) than in reading the same passage containing words with inverted triangles substituted for missing letters (Boo▽s he▽p us . . .). Indeed, the GRPS subjects performed as well as those in the GRGS group on the missing letter passage but not so well on the misspelled words passage. Apparently, the misspelled words created visual effects that were more confusing to the GRPS subjects than to the GRGS subjects, perhaps because children in the latter group were better able to shift to a component letter strategy. The missing letter condition, on the other hand, forced both groups to identify words on the basis of partial cues, which is the type of stimulus information that was typically utilized by the GRPS group in word processing, hence the failure to find differences between the two groups on the inverted triangle task.

These findings are entirely consistent with those of Baron (1977, 1979), Boder (1971, 1973), and others (Camp & Dolcourt, 1977), all of whom have observed individual differences in mode of processing printed words. Combined, they provide persuasive if not conclusive evidence that developing readers may differ in the strategies they employ in word recognition and identification and that such differences will have a significant effect upon related skills, such as spelling. If so, then one might reasonably infer that the use of different processing strategies eventuates in the storage and functional use of qualitatively different types of mental representations and also that the failure to diversify one's perceptual attitude in word processing will lead to difficulty in mastering the mechanics of reading and/or spelling because of the inability to internalize the varieties and types of information necessary for precision. Conversely, impaired ability to acquire such information will constrain the development of diverse and flexible processing strategies, and the two circumstances, in time, become mutually impeding.

A reasonable question to ask at this juncture, assuming the validity of the foregoing conceptualization, is just how individual differences in word processing strategies arise. I underscored earlier the suggestion made by Boder and others (Johnson & Myklebust, 1967; Kinsbourne & Warrington, 1966) that such differences are a consequence of neurological disorder affecting visual and auditory functioning, but I expressed in passing the opinion that this interpretation may not be warranted, especially when applied to mild and moderately impaired readers. It seems more likely that these children have experientially derived gaps in their knowledge, either because of instructional biases to which they have been exposed or because of idiosyncratic tendencies to construe word identification as either a holistic or an analytic enterprise during the initial stages of reading. Indeed, Chall (1967) reported individual differences in the tendency to learn words either as wholes or through structural analysis depending on whether children had been exposed to "meaning emphasis" or "code emphasis" instructional programs, respectively. This account presents a more parsimonious explanation of processing differences in less impaired readers and spellers, than do neurologically based accounts that have appeared in the literature.

On the other hand, constitutional deficits of one sort or another might well lie at the root of processing differences in the more severely impaired reader, but even this is debatable. These are important distinctions to make, inasmuch as the vehicles for acquiring the information and thus the processing units employed for word identification might be different in the constitutionally as opposed to the experientially impaired reader and speller. For example, Boder's theory impliies that the units of processing available to the dyseidetic dyslexic would necessarily be the letter and letter cluster, because this individual is presumed to be neurologically deficient in the storage and/or retrieval of whole-word representations. Conversely, letter and letter clusters would not be available as processing units for the dysphonetic dyslexic, theoretically because of basic difficulty in phonologic processing. The point is that if etiological theories such as Boder's are correct, then one might frame his or her theory of word identification a bit differently than if they do not accurately account for the origin of individual differences in word processing. It is therefore instructive to review selected findings from studies evaluating hypothesized causes and correlates of disordered reading.

Basic Process Differences in Poor and Normal Readers

Visual Processing. By far the most frequently cited cause of reading disability in young children is disorder in visual perception and visual memory. There are two forms of this hypothesis: the *strong* version and the *weak* version. The strong version was originally articulated by Orton (1925), who suggested that disabled readers suffer from a basic disorder in visual form perception, characterized by optical reversibility in letter and word perception. This curious deficit was believed to be manifested in the mislabeling of visually similar configurations—as when a poor reader calls *b d* or *was saw*—and was thought to be associated with the failure to establish hemispheric dominance. The weak version of this theory was advanced by Hermann (1959) and states simply that the poor reader is hampered by an inherited disposition toward spatial confusion but *not* by deficient form perception (i.e., literally "seeing" *b* as *d* or *was* as *saw*). Implied in these and like theories (Bender, 1957; Boder, 1971, 1973) is the notion that reading disability is caused by a breakdown, either at the feature analytic or comparison stages of visual processing, though none of the theories is explicit as to these possibilities being largely clinically based.

Vellutino and his colleagues tested the perceptual deficit hypothesis in a series of related studies evaluating the etiology of reading disorder in severely impaired readers (see Vellutino, 1979 for a comprehensive review) and found no evidence to support either the strong or the weak versions of this conceptualization. In the first two of these studies (Vellutino, Smith, Steger, & Kaman, 1975; Vellutino, Steger, & Kandel, 1972), poor and normal readers (ages 7–14) were presented with brief exposures (500–600 msec) of three-, four-, and five-letter words; scrambled letters; Arabic numerals; and geometric designs and asked to copy them from memory. These subjects were then presented a second time, with all but the geometric designs (again for brief exposures), but on this presentation they were asked to name each stimulus. The instructions made it clear to subjects that they were to pronounce each word and then to spell out its letters immediately after pronunciation. They were also told that scrambled letter sets and numerals should be spelled out in correct order and that they might see "different things" each time.

It was found that poor readers performed much better on the copying tasks than on the naming tasks and performed as well as normal readers on the copying tasks, except for the five-letter words, which (for the youngest age group) taxed the upper limit of visual short-term memory. Thus, the poor readers often copied *was* correctly but called it *saw* and manifested a similar disparity on other letter and word stimuli. Interestingly enough, on the stimulus word *loin,* the majority of subjects up to sixth grade—normal readers as well as poor readers—did exactly the same thing: copied the word correctly but named it *lion.* Most also spelled the letters out correctly, immediately after misnaming the word. Because none of these subjects could define the word *loin,* we assumed that they retrieved the only semantic referent available to them and did not take note of their error.

In studies using essentially the same presentation format (Vellutino, Pruzek, Steger, & Meshoulam, 1973; Vellutino, Steger, Kaman, & DeSetto, 1975), poor readers performed as well as normal readers on tasks involving immediate visual recall of the letters in varying length words printed in Hebrew, which for these subjects was a novel orthography. However, none performed as well as children learning to read and write Hebrew. Noteworthy in these studies is the fact that subjects were required to remember a word's letters in order, and the absence of group differences obviously indicates that poor readers are able to apprehend order information as well as normal readers. Also noteworthy is the finding that poor and normal readers, unfamiliar with Hebrew, manifested identical (left-right) scanning tendencies, as measured by the location of letters omitted in their reproductions of the stimulus words. Directional scanning in these groups was, of course, opposite to the (right–left) pattern manifested by the children familiar with Hebrew.

The foregoing results, taken together, seriously undermine perceptual deficit explanations of reading disability, such as Orton's (1925) and Hermann's (1959). Specifically, they suggest that the naming and pronunciation errors, often observed in severely impaired readers, are *not* due to a basic deficit in visual feature analysis or letter recognition and are most likely the result of dysfunction in verbal mediation, for example, name retrieval and/or spelling–sound translation. These findings are, of course, at variance with Boder's (1971, 1973) suggestion that "dysdeidetic dyslexics" (who are apparently less impaired than the poor readers evaluated in our studies) suffer a basic defect in visual processing that impedes them in whole-word learning. However, the results would not be inconsistent with the possibility that such children are impeded by overanalytic processing strategies that they have acquired as a result of instructional biases and the like. I am therefore inclined to adopt the latter view to explain strategy differences in poor readers of this sort.

As regards our discussion of the unit of perception issue, the results obtained in these studies are important for two reasons. First, they underscore once again the distinction between recognition and identification in word processing. When subjects were presented with stimulus words that are visually similar to words with which they were more familiar, there were a large number who produced the names of the more familiar words on the verbal labeling portion of the test (*saw* for *was, lion* for *loin, from* for *form, clam* for *calm*) but spelled out the letters of the stimulus words correctly immediately after misnaming each. This pattern was observed more often in poor readers but was evident in the normal readers as well, even some at the upper age levels (sixth grade). Clearly, these children subjectively "recognized" these stimulus words but did not always have the means for identifying them precisely, in spite of the fact that they could identify the letters in each word and order them correctly after only a brief tachistoscopic exposure.

This disparity relates to the second reason these findings are important to the unit of perception issue: They point to the fact that the word recognition theories currently available do not adequately distinguish between the recognition and identification processes, which is to suggest that they do not adequately address the issue of how a letter string is encoded so as to effect precise identification. Neither do they provide much insight as to the information that must be acquired nor the processing strategies that must be developed in order to effect such precision. I discuss this issue further but, for now, continue with my discussion of reader group differences in basic process functioning.

In spite of the absence of convincing evidence that poor readers sustain any significant deficits in visual processing, in the basic sense, there is reason to believe that such children do not acquire a functional knowledge of orthographic redundancy. They are therefore denied all the benefits that accrue to those who have acquired such knowledge. As we have seen, an intimate acquaintance with structural redundancy facilitates considerable economy, both in fine-grained discrimination of familiar words and in identification of new words, and the normal reader soon learns to capitalize upon such redundancy. However, the poor reader, because of more basic difficulty in associating visual and verbal symbols, does not readily detect the invariances and regularities embedded in English orthography and therefore does not have the means for synthesizing the enormous amount of visual information he or she will necessarily encounter in learning to identify printed words. This results in the tendency to process either too little or too much information in word identification and less than optimal success in this enterprise.

That poor readers apprehend and generalize structural redundancies less proficiently than normal readers is amply demonstrated in a series of studies conducted by Venezky, Calfee, and their associates. Using synthetic words such as *cipe* and *cabe,* Calfee, Venezky, and Chapman (1969) found that good and poor readers could be differentiated on their knowledge of spelling-sound correspondence rules (e.g., final *e* pattern, initial *c* pattern) from third grade through high school and college, suggesting that mastery of phonic generalizations and alphabetic coding is imperfect in some individuals even at these more advanced levels. Reader group differences in the acquisition of orthographic redundancies were also noted in two other studies conducted by these investigators (Venezky, Chapman, & Calfee, 1972; Venezky & Johnson, 1972).

Additional evidence that impaired readers have less sensitivity to structural regularity than do normal readers is provided in a study conducted by Mason (1975). This author hypothesized that the poor reader does not "directly perceive" the redundancy characteristic of the spatial locations of letters, defined as the frequency with which given letters occur in particular positions in words (Mayzner & Tresselt, 1965). Thus she distinguishes between direct perception and inferential knowledge of letter locations and conceives of insensitivity to such information as a basic process disorder stemming from central nervous system dysfunction. Although this interpretation is not necessary, given that insensitivity to spatial location could be experientially derived, Mason's results are of interest.

Four related experiments were conducted to evaluate the aforementioned hypothesis. Each compared good and poor readers (grade 6) on visual search tasks involving detection of target letters embedded in real words and nonwords that varied with respect to letter position frequency. In all four experiments, poor readers took more time than normal readers to detect letter targets in redundant visual displays, indicating that they are indeed less attuned than the normals to spatial redundancy. One finding that emerged in this study is of particular interest and that is the disparity in the shapes of error curves for good and poor readers, yielded by an analysis of serial position effects. Briefly, for the good reader, the distribution was bow-shaped, indicating that speed of processing was greater for letters located at the terminal positions of letter sets. However, the distribution for poor readers was linear, indicating that processing speed was greater for items in the first few letter positions. These findings suggest that the poor readers were processing letters serially (left to right), whereas the normal readers were processing letters simultaneously or in parallel. One may also infer from the results, that parallel or holistic processing is the preferred strategy of the skilled reader, whereas serial processing may be used more often by the less skilled reader, an inference that receives additional support from research findings that are discussed in a subsequent section.

It may be reasonably concluded from this brief review that the poor reader, although not perceptually deficient in the strict sense, is "perceptually inefficient" (Vellutino, 1980) in that his or her strategies in word processing are either global and superficial or overanalytic, slow, and plodding. The question therefore arises as to how the learner comes to strike the proper balance between processing too little and too much information in acquiring skill in word identification and in reading in general. The obvious answer is that he or she acquires detailed knowledge of the structural redundancies inherent in English orthography to assist him or her in discriminating words efficiently. The less obvious answer is that the acquisition of such information is itself related to the child's language ability, in both the broad and fine sense. Because reading is primarily a language-based skill, it is reasonable to suppose that one's efficiency in processing written text would be in direct proportion to his or her ability to use linguistic information to assist in forming the associative bonds necessary to incorporate both the rule-generated and word-specific knowledge he or she must acquire in learning to read. I refer, of course, to the child's "growing ability to selectively attend to distinctive features of letters and words by virtue of his or her expanding knowledge of their phonologic, semantic and syntactic attributes" (Vellutino, 1979, p. 253). We have already seen how such information may influence the ways in which the individual dissects the orthography, and it therefore becomes important to ask whether deficiencies in linguistic functioning might be associated with impaired reading ability. I turn now to consideration of this possibility, focusing initially on reader group differences in the phonologic components of spoken and written language.

Phonologic Processing. A number of investigators have suggested that some children with reading problems sustain basic and/or experiential deficits in phonologic processing, which lead to significant difficulties in abstracting and generalizing the sound counterparts of written language. Two different conceptualizations of such difficulty have emerged over the years. One that has been popular among practitioners is that of Wepman (1960, 1961), who suggests that some poor readers are impaired in their ability to discriminate speech sounds, as a result of neurological "maturational lag." This notion emerged from studies evaluating auditory discrimination in elementary school children (Wepman, 1960, 1961) in which it was found that a significant number of deficient readers in first and second grade could not always indicate reliably whether minimally contrasted words (e.g., *pin* and *pen*) were either "same" or "different." However, Wepman's findings are confounded by the fact that a young child's conceptualization of *same* and *different* may not be equivalent to that of older children (or adult examiners) and reader group differences may have been due to response bias (Vellutino, DeSetto, & Steger, 1972) rather than to basic deficiencies in auditory discrimination. More important is the possibility that poor performance on such a task may not be due to acoustic difficulties but to the inability to explicate phonemic differences in words that one can implicitly discriminate. Thus Shankweiler and Liberman (1972) demonstrated that poor readers could accurately vocalize minimally contrasted words presented to them singly but were unable to segment these same words at the level of the phoneme. This brings me to the second major conceptualization of phonologic deficiency in poor readers that has appeared in the literature, one that has gained increased currency in recent years.

The reference here is to the work of Liberman, Shankweiler, and their associates. These authors suggest that code acquisition requires an explicit knowledge of the phonetic structure of both the spoken and printed word. Specifically, the beginning reader must become aware that a word can be segmented into component phonemes and that alphabetic characters represent phonemes rather than syllables or some other unit of speech. Thus the child must not only be able to discriminate between words such as *pin* and *pen* but he or she must also make explicit the three different phonemes contained within each of these words, if he or she is to develop facility in associating them with their graphic counterparts. According to the theory articulated by these investigators, the poor reader is deficient in phonemic segmentation, either because he or she has difficulty in encoding information phonologically or because he or she is not implicitly disposed toward doing so. This, in turn, impedes him or her in code acquisition as well as in performance on other tasks that depend on phonologic encoding, such as short-term memory for linguistic information.

Support for this theory is provided in a number of studies designed by Liberman and Shankweiler. In one of the first of these studies conducted, Liberman, Shankweiler, Fischer, and Carter (1974) evaluated nursery-school, kindergarten, and first-grade children and found that phonemic segmentation is very difficult for youngsters at these age levels and develops very gradually. They also found that segmentation ability in beginning readers in first grade was significantly and positively correlated with reading ability, both in this grade and one year later. Similar findings were obtained in separate studies conducted by Helfgott (1976), Zifcak (1976), and Treiman (1976).

However, more direct evidence that poor readers sustain basic difficulty in phonologic coding is provided by the results of several other studies conducted by these investigators. Briefly, Liberman, Shankweiler, Liberman, Fowler, and Fischer (1977) found that poor readers did not perform as well as normal readers on a measure involving short-term memory for rhyming and nonrhyming letters presented visually, but the disparity in performance on these two types of stimuli was greater for normal readers than for poor readers. Similar results were obtained in a second study using auditory presentations of these materials rather than visual presentations (Shankweiler & Liberman, (1976). The authors conclude from these results that normal readers are more inclined than poor readers to code information phonologically, thus accounting for their tendency to be confused more than the poor readers by the rhyming letters.

Reinforcing the aforementioned findings are the results of a study recently completed by Vellutino and Scanlon (1979). These authors contrasted poor and normal readers (second and sixth graders) on a test of phonemic segmentation ability as well as on tests of phonologic memory, verbal labeling, and code acquisition. The segmentation test required that subjects analyze the phonemic structure of stimuli presented auditorily and involved analysis of both familiar words and phonetically pronounceable pseudowords. The phonologic memory test involved free recall of auditorily presented nonsense words having phonemes in common (*zab, vab, goz, gov*). After extensive practice in remembering these stimuli, each subject was administered the verbal labeling test. This was an association learning task, which paired the same nonsense words presented for free recall with novel cartoonlike drawings. The code acquisition test was administered thereafter and paired the nonsense words presented on the free recall and verbal labeling tests with novel alphabetic characters that corresponded invariantly with each of the phonemes in respective (nonsense) words. The free recall task was designed to: (1) contrast poor and normal readers on memory for linguistic units that, by definition, do not allow the use of meaning or concrete referents to aid recall; and (2) to give both groups extensive practice in learning the responses that were to be used on the paired-associates tasks subsequently administered. The paired-associates tasks were intended to be analogous, respectively, to object naming and to whole-word learning of real words containing grapheme–phoneme invariants (e.g., *cat, can, rat, ran*), thereby simulating alphabetic coding.

Poor readers did not perform as well as normal readers on the test of segmentation ability. They were also less proficient than the normals on the test of free recall and on the verbal labeling and code acquisition measures. The results suggest that poor readers sustain a basic deficit in phonologic memory, which appears to be associated with dysfunction both in object naming and in alphabetic coding consistent with the theory advanced by Liberman and Shankweiler.

Finally, Snowling (1980) compared "dyslexic" and normal readers, equated for reading age (7 to 10 years), on intermodal and intramodal matching of pronounceable nonsense words and found differences between these groups favoring the normal reader only on visual–auditory matching. Furthermore, the normal readers improved with age, whereas the poor readers did not show such improvement. It was concluded that dyslexics are significantly impaired in grapheme-to-phoneme conversion but have no apparent difficulty in visual and auditory discrimination. This conclusion is consistent with Vellutino's (1979) observation that severely impaired readers (from grades 1 through 8 inclusive) were much less able than normal readers to decode pronounceable nonsense syllables, indicating that they find it extremely difficult to acquire spelling–sound invariants.

The foregoing results afford considerable support for the contention that poor readers sustain significant impairment in phonologic processing that hampers their progress in code acquisition and in reading in general. It should be apparent that such disorder would adversely affect the individual's ability to acquire a comprehensive and functional knowledge of orthographic redundancy and thereby limit his or her flexibility in word processing. However, a disorder of this type may constitute only one of several types of linguistic anomaly that eventuate in reading difficulty. It will therefore be useful to review selected findings from studies that have addressed the possibility that poor readers may also be impaired in the broader aspects of language.

Semantic and Syntactic Processing. I discussed earlier the possible ways in which the semantic and syntactic components of language can influence word learning, as well as the strategies one generally employs in processing printed words. It should be clear from that discussion that deficient knowledge as to a word's meaning or limited information about the many contexts in which it may appear diminishes the probability that it will become part of an associative network that will facilitate reliable identification of that word. At the same time, significant impairment in one's grasp of the syntactic properties of given words or in comprehension of particular syntactic constructions will make it difficult to employ sentential context to assist in word identification. It is therefore important to evaluate the degree to which poor readers are characterized by impairments in semantic and syntactic processing.

Such an evaluation was undertaken in a comprehensive review by the present author (Vellutino, 1979), and it was generally concluded that poor readers do *not* sustain any foundational deficits in semantic processing, when such disorder is defined as a:

> basic malfunction in abstracting the common meanings of individual words, inability to organize thematic material globally, and in sensitivity to meaning bearing units in phrases or sentences. On the other hand, there is reason to believe that access to specific word meanings or meanings coded contextually is not always efficient in such children, owing to more subtle malfunction in word encoding or retrieval, which, in turn, results in inefficient processing in short-term memory [pp. 263-264].

To illustrate, Waller (1976) presented poor and normal readers in fifth grade with a sentence recognition task to ascertain the degree to which these subjects would encode the *meaning* or *structural* components of the text. Distractors changed: (1) the meaning of a given sentence; (2) the content and retained meaning; or (3) both content and meaning.

The important finding for present purposes is that poor readers made more recognition errors than normal readers, only on distractor sentences that changed the content, but not the meanings of sentences initially presented. The author concluded that memory for details (specific words, phrases, tense markers, etc.) is faulty in such children, but probably not semantic memory, in the global sense.

In a similar study, employing third and fifth graders, Golinkoff and Rosinski (1976) compared poor and normal readers on speed of naming pictures and found that these groups were equally encumbered by semantically interfering words printed on those pictures, suggesting that poor readers could abstract meanings directly from the visual properties of printed words. However, poor readers *did* take longer than normal readers to decode common words and pronounceable pseudowords, implying again that although such children have no basic impairments in abstracting meaning, they do have difficulty in code acquisition.

That the decoding and comprehension problems observed in poor readers may both be the result of phonetic coding difficulties is suggested in a series of studies conducted by Perfetti and his associates (see Vellutino, 1979, for a review). In the first of these investigations, Perfetti and Goldman (1976) evaluated third- and fifth-grade reader groups and found that poor readers performed as well as normal readers on a task that did not tax verbal coding ability (auditory memory for probed digits). However, they *did* find differences favoring the normal readers when words in sentences were the targets rather than digits. Similarly, Perfetti, Bell, and Goldman (reported in Perfetti & Lesgold, 1978) found that poor and normal readers (third and fourth graders) remembered target words better within than across clause boundaries, suggesting that both groups employed the structural characteristics of sentences in much the same way. In contrast, poor readers' memory for specific target words was generally below that of normal readers.

Finally, Perfetti, Hogaboam, and Bell (reported in Perfetti and Lesgold, 1978, 1979) found that poor readers could match pictures and spoken words (semantic access) as rapidly as normal readers, but took longer than the normals to match printed and spoken words (phonologic access), although the difference was not statistically significant. More important is the observation that matching speed was slower among poor readers on both picture and printed word matching, when category words, spoken by the examiner (e.g., "animals"), were matched with items subsumed under those categories. These findings suggest that, although semantic processing is basically intact in poor readers, access to higher order meanings may, under some circumstances, be labored in such children, presumably because linguistic representations of semantic categories and category members are not well integrated.

It may be concluded, from the foregoing results, that poor readers have no more difficulty than normal readers in comprehending semantic information in the general sense. Yet they do appear to be less able on tasks involving the use of verbal codes in short-term memory. This, in turn, leads to inefficiency in encoding semantic information, which becomes apparent on measures of listening as well as reading comprehension. One possible reason that poor readers have less ability than normal readers in verbal encoding is that they may be significantly impaired in word retrieval. Thus, it is noteworthy that a number of studies have found substantial differences between these two groups on rapid decoding and object naming tasks.

Perfetti and Hogaboam (1975) presented moderately impaired and normal readers (third and fifth grade) with high- and low-frequency words, as well as

2. WORD RECOGNITION AND THE UNIT OF PERCEPTION   155

pronounceable pseudowords and found that naming speed in the impaired readers was significantly below that of the normal readers on all measures, although the magnitude of the differences between these groups was less on high frequency words. Similarly, Denckla and Rudel (1976a) found that severely impaired readers (ages 8 to 11) did not perform as well as normal readers on rapid naming of common objects presented pictorially. Denckla and Rudel (1976b) obtained similar results, in contrasts of comparably selected reader groups (ages 7 to 12), on rapid naming of colors, lowercase letters, numerals, and common objects. More recently, Wolf (in press) verified Denckla and Rudel's findings, using procedures similar to those used by these authors. Thus the evidence that disabled readers may be characterized by basic difficulties in name retrieval, whereas seminal, is highly suggestive and merits further study.

Still more support for the possibility that poor readers suffer verbal encoding deficits is provided in a study recently conducted by Vellutino and Scanlon (1980). These investigators compared poor and normal readers in second and sixth grades on free recall of concrete and abstract words and found that the normal readers performed significantly better than the poor readers on recall of both types of stimuli. However, the disparity between these groups was greater on the abstract words and was especially evident at the younger age levels. It is possible that the poor readers had more difficulty on the abstract words not only because such words have no concrete referents but also because they are linguistically more complex. That this may be the case is suggested in a gratuitous finding, which emerged from post hoc analyses of substitution errors made by these two groups. Whereas the largest proportion of such errors made by poor readers was semantically similar intrusions (e.g., remembering *prince* for *queen*), for normal readers the majority of substitution errors were either phonologic (*fought* for *thought*) or syntactic (*choose* for *choice*) intrusions. These results suggest that poor readers rely more heavily upon the semantic than upon the phonologic and syntactic components of language to aid recall. Normal readers, on the other hand, apparently make use of all three of these attributes for this purpose, implying that normal readers are linguistically more sophisticated than poor readers and thus have greater facility in verbal encoding.

Finally, it would seem to be intuitively sound to infer that a child with a well-developed vocabulary will have acquired one of the important skills necessary to learn to read and, conversely, that a child whose knowledge and functional use of words is deficient will be hampered in acquiring skill in reading. There is in fact correlational evidence in the literature that poor readers do, by and large, have deficient vocabularies (Monroe, 1932; Raulin, 1962; Ravenette, 1961), but the most convincing evidence that the relationship may be causal comes from the few studies available that have evaluated very young children. Specifically, de Hirsch, Jansky, and Langford (1966) as well as Jansky and de Hirsch (1972) both found significant correlations between measures of vocabulary in kindergarten and reading achievement in second grade. Similarly,

Fry, Johnson, & Muehl (1970) compared poor and normal readers in second grade and found that the poor readers' knowledge of words was less substantial than that of normal readers. Vellutino (1979, p. 262) reports similar findings. Thus, existing evidence suggests that many beginning readers do indeed have poorly developed vocabularies, which may well hamper their efforts in acquiring skill in reading. Interestingly enough, there is evidence that this relationship obtains even in adult readers, as we shall see below (Butler & Hains, 1979).

As regards syntactic competence, the literature provides suggestive evidence that poor readers do not perform as well as normal readers on various measures of linguistic functioning, which include understanding of specific syntactic constructions, facility with grammatical inflections, use of sentential context to assist in word identification, and expressive language in general.

To be specific, Fry et al., (1970) contrasted poor and normal readers in second grade on the content and structural aspects of their spoken language and found that poor readers generally employ less complex and less sophisticated language than do normal readers. These patterns were manifested in more limited speaking vocabularies; less fluency in terms of linguistic output; less frequent use of complete sentences, subordinate clauses, and embedding; less subject–verb agreement (suggesting difficulty in morphological usage); and limited use of verbal abstractions. These findings were reinforced in subsequent studies by Brittain (1970), Wiig, Semel, and Crouse (1973), and Vogel (1974), all of whom reported similar patterns in poor and normal reader contrasts involving children in the early elementary grades.

Indirect support that poor readers may be characterized by syntactic deficiencies is provided by the results of several studies that indicate that these children do not utilize verbal context as efficiently as normal readers either in sentence comprehension or in word identification. Briefly, both Cromer and Wiener (1966) and Guthrie (1973) used the cloze procedure, and found that poor readers (grades 2 through 5) did not perform as well as normal readers in producing lexical alternatives that would make sentences grammatically correct, suggesting some insensitivity to syntax. Similarly, Steiner, Wiener, and Cromer (1971) found that training in text organization had little effect upon poor readers' ability to identify words presented in discourse material but prompted more superficial processing (and thus more errors) in normal readers (see Vellutino, 1979 for a more comprehensive review).

It seems reasonable to infer from the research available that poor readers do indeed have some degree of difficulty in the processing of semantic and syntactic information that impedes their efforts in learning to read. The weight of the evidence suggests that such difficulty may be caused by more basic deficits in related linguistic skills, such as phonologic encoding, word retrieval, and verbal memory, which results in a good deal of inefficiency in processing connected text because of short-term memory problems. This apparently impairs their ability to make effective use of verbal context to aid the word identification process, which further compounds the difficulties they encounter in using contextual information effectively.

Given the reader group disparities in the basic process and informational content areas discussed previously, it would be logical to expect that word processing strategies in poor and normal readers might be qualitatively different at given points along the age/grade continuum. In the next section, evidence is presented that confirms this expectation in work done with both children and adults. However, before proceeding it should be noted that etiological theories, other than the ones discussed here, have been offered in explanation of specific reading disability in young children. Most notable are the intersensory deficit theory of Birch (1962) and the serial processing deficit theory of Bakker (1972) and others (Corkin, 1974). Both conceptualizations have elsewhere been carefully analyzed and found to be lacking (Vellutino, 1977, 1979), but discussion of either is beyond the scope of this chapter.

Word-Processing Strategies in Skilled and Less Skilled Readers: Some Manifestations in Children and Adults

One prediction issuing from the assumption that processing strategies might differ in skilled and less skilled readers is that the developmental course will be disparate in these two groups and that processing modes will vary in accord with the individual's expanding facility in word identification. Indeed, the reader is reminded of Gibson's (1971) suggestion that children are differentially sensitive to the meaning (semantic/syntactic) and structural (graphic, orthographic, phonologic) attributes of printed words during the course of learning to read. Thus, beginning readers are maximally attentive to word meanings but become much more attuned to their structural characteristics while learning to "break the code." With increased facility in word decoding, they again become maximally attentive to meaning except for extraordinary circumstances such as proofreading. This generates the specific hypothesis that normal readers at intermediate stages of development of skill in reading (roughly between grades 1 and 6) would manifest greater variability in their use of meaning and structural principles of categorization than they would in later grades when their attention to word structure should be minimal and their attention to meaning should be maximal. Poor readers, on the other hand, because of basic decoding problems, do not become attuned to orthographic regularity at the same rate as normal readers and should therefore manifest a different developmental pattern, perhaps being more often sensitive to the meanings of words they can identify than to their structural regularities.

In order to test this hypothesis, (Vellutino, Scanlon, De Setto and Pruzek, 1981) poor and normal readers in grades 1 through 6, randomly selected ninth graders, and college students were presented with 16 sets of words (six in a set) that could be categorized either on the basis of their structural or meaning characteristics (e.g., *duck, truck; moose, caboose; boat, goat—structure; duck, moose, goat; truck, caboose, boat—meaning*). Words in each set were randomly disarrayed, and subjects were simply asked to put those "that belong together in separate piles." Scoring to determine classification strategies was based only on those words that could be identified by a particular subject. In general, it was found that normal readers were more variable in their use of structural and meaning categories between grades 1 and 6 than they were beyond this level (ninth grade and college level) when most subjects categorized word sets primarily on the basis of their meanings. These trends are depicted in Fig. 2.7, where the semantic/syntactic classifications of normal readers in grades 1 through 6 are presented. It can be seen that most normal readers (though not all) within this range did *not* consistently place the words they could identify into semantic/syntactic categories, often employing structural categories instead. This was

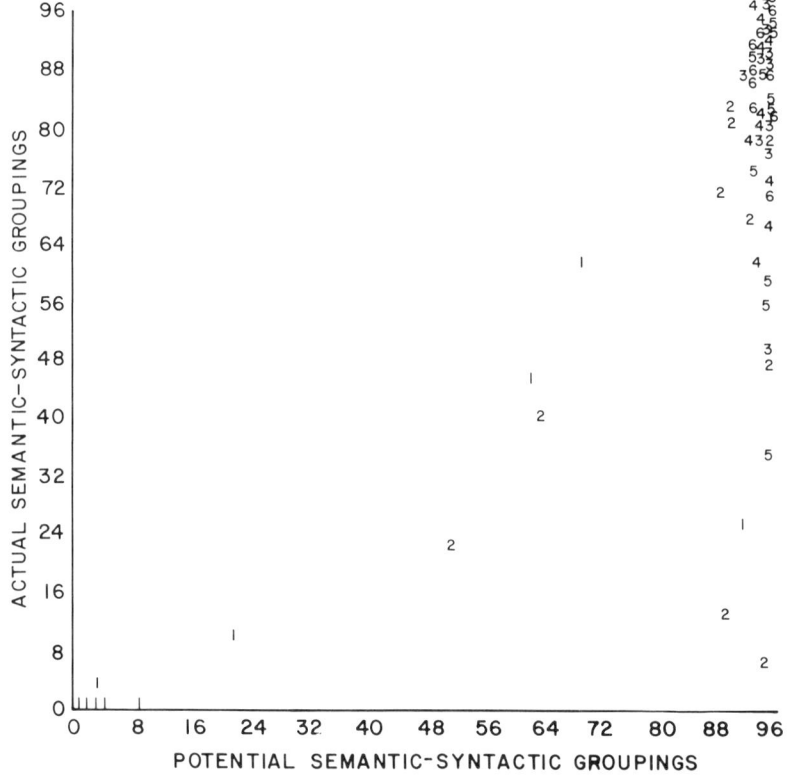

FIG. 2.7. Scatter diagram depicting the relationship between number of sight words potentially available for placement in semantic-syntactic categories and number of words actually placed in semantic-syntactic categories for normal readers in grades 1 through 6 (taken from Vellutino, Scanlon, DeSetto, & Pruzek, in press, 1981).

particularly true of subjects in the lower grades (first and second), some of whom classified on the basis of structural principles almost exclusively. In contrast, sixth graders more consistently grouped the stimulus words on the basis of meaning, as did ninth graders and college students, although these latter groups are not shown on the graph.

Poor readers on the other hand manifested a slightly different pattern. As noted in Fig. 2.8, the distribution is decidedly linear, indicating that these subjects more often placed the words they could identify in meaning rather than in structural categories. This finding suggests that the poor readers were less sensitive to the orthographic patterns embedded in the word stimuli than were the normal readers. Additional support for this possibility is provided by one other

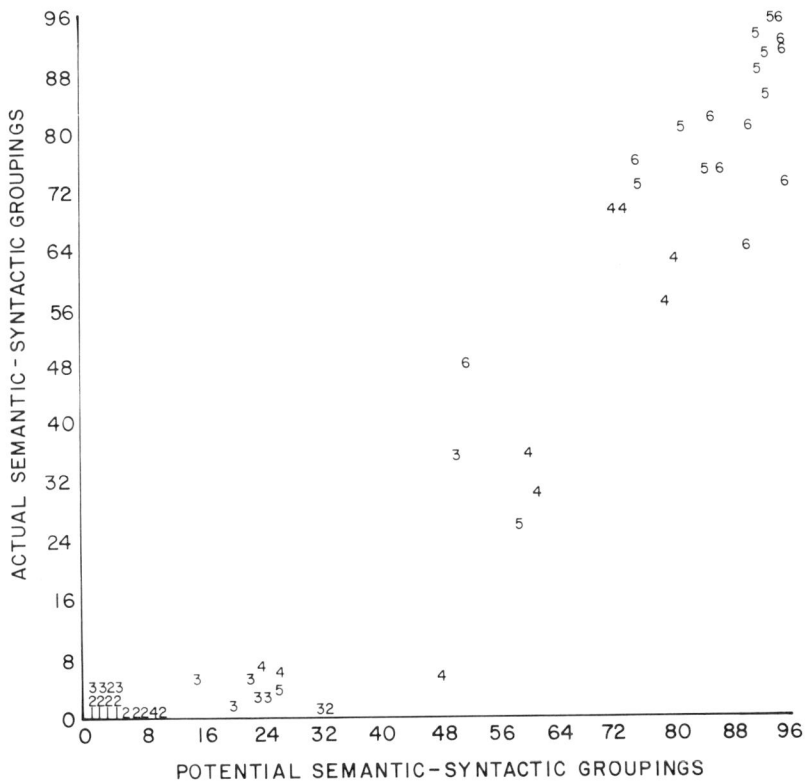

FIG. 2.8. Scatter diagram depicting the relationship between number of sight words potentially available for placement in semantic–syntactic categories and number of words actually placed in semantic–syntactic categories for poor readers in grades 1 through 6. All first grade poor readers would be located at the (0,0) coordinates of the graph had space permitted. (Taken from Vellutino, Scanlon, DeSetto, & Pruzek, in press, 1981.)

observation. In post hoc analyses, it was found that when words *were* classified on the basis of structure, poor readers employed idiosyncratic principles rather than redundancy principles for classification more often than normal readers. For example, poor readers often grouped words together containing the same letter, regardless of the spatial locations of that letter in those particular words. Both data sets, of course, suggest that these two groups employ qualitatively different processing strategies at different points along the age/grade continuum.

The child's growing awareness of orthographic structure implies not only greater differentiation of invariant letter sequences and like redundancies but also a measurable transition from less efficient coding strategies, such as serial processing or random sampling of letter and word features, to more efficient strategies that allow one to process word constituents simultaneously and holistically. Such a developmental pattern was observed in several studies conducted by Samuels and his associates. Briefly, Samuels, LaBerge, and Bremer (1977) presented subjects (grades 2, 4, 6, and college) with words varying in length (three to six letters) and asked them simply to press a response button if the word presented was from an animal category. The dependent measure was latency of response. It was found that response times for children in the lower grades increased sharply with an increase in letter length, implying either left–right serial processing in these subjects or random letter by letter processing.

However, in the older, more experienced readers, response times did *not* vary as a function of letter length, suggesting that these subjects were processing words as wholes with letter and word features being apprehended simultaneously and, no doubt, more efficiently. Noteworthy in this study is the finding that older less skilled readers as well as younger normal readers were inclined toward inefficient letter-by-letter processing. Similar results were obtained in a subsequent study conducted by McCormick and Samuels (1978). At the same time, Terry, Samuels, and LaBerge (1976) found that skilled readers at the college level employed a comparable strategy with words presented as mirror-image transforms. Thus, it would seem that left–right serial or (random) letter-by-letter processing is often the natural course with material that is not well-integrated although, as we have seen, some poor readers are not inclined to be analytic, and Samuels' studies may not have included such individuals.

To continue, a number of investigations have evaluated the degree to which verbal context and reading ability interact in word identification, and their results provide additional insight into the differential processing strategies employed by poor and normal readers. I have already mentioned the study by Steiner et al. (1971) in which it was found that poor readers in fifth grade did not make effective use of prior organization of information presented in paragraphs to assist in identifying words in sentences comprising those paragraphs. In this investigation, subjects were presented with a synopsis of main ideas before reading a particular passage. This procedure did not significantly reduce word identification errors in poor readers from which it can be concluded that context may not always compensate for decoding problems. On the other hand, the procedure *increased* the incidence of errors in normal readers, suggesting that these subjects adopted a more economical processing strategy characterized by less attention to visual detail.

In a later study, Samuels, Begy, and Chen (1975-1976) employed a semantic priming technique similar to the one used by Meyer et al. (1974) in comparisons of elementary-school reader groups in the use of verbal context in word identification. Of particular interest was the degree to which context would reduce latency of response to words *all* subjects could identify. Target stimuli (e.g., *cat*) were presented briefly (for variable durations) just after presentation of context words (e.g., *black*). It was found that poor readers had longer latencies than normal readers and did not profit as much as normal readers from prior exposure to the context words. In addition, the poor readers did not perform as well as the normals in guessing at target words from partial letter cues (*black* c __ __). These data are consonant with the findings obtained in the study by Steiner et al. (1971). Both suggest that poor readers do not have as much ability as normal readers to utilize verbal context to assist in word identification. It is likely that this disparity is partly due to the fact that poor readers have less structural information available to them, but it also seems likely, given the results discussed earlier, that lexical information is organized differently in these groups.

The study just reported evaluated the influence of verbal context on word identification when visual cues that are normally used in word processing are disrupted. Two other studies employing cue disruption procedures also found processing differences in poor and normal readers. Specifically, Kolers (1975) presented both groups (seventh graders) with normal and transformed text printed in reversed typology and found that poor readers had more difficulty analyzing the transformed passages than did normal readers. An obvious inference here is that normal readers had incorporated more highly differentiated representations of the words presented in normal typology, thereby allowing them greater flexibility than the poor readers in generating processing strategies that would assist in analyzing the reversed typology.

Using a different format, Rayner and Kaiser (1975) found differences favoring normal readers in speed as well as identification of multilated target words, again demonstrating the normal readers' superiority in making effective use of partial letter information.

That word-processing strategies vary in accord with reading ability and context is further documented in a series of studies reported by Perfctti and Roth (in press), contrasting (elementary grade) skilled and less skilled readers on speed of word processing with and without meaningful context. In one experiment reported by these authors (Perfetti, Goldman, & Hogaboam, 1979), target words were embedded in story contexts, presented piecemeal on separate cards. After completing a portion of the text, subjects were presented with the next word on a screen for rapid identification. Predictability of each target word was independently determined, and vocalization latencies were plotted against a predictability index determined by the percentage of subjects who accurately anticipated words presented on a sentence completion task. The major finding was that less skilled readers were more context-dependent than skilled readers, although both groups profited significantly from context. For poor readers, the effect of context was especially evident on longer length and less familiar words, whereas, for normal readers, there was only a modest difference in performance on different word types as a result of context. Thus, for skilled readers, word processing was rapid and efficient, and context had less time to execute. However, for less skilled readers, processing was slow and laborious and context had more time to become operative.

Also of interest in this study are results obtained when subjects were asked to predict target words from stories and identify each immediately after each prediction. Although all subjects identified a word they had accurately predicted more rapidly than those that were not accurately predicted, latencies for skilled readers' responses to *unpredicted* words were as short or shorter than the latencies for less skilled readers' responses to *predicted* words, indicating that skilled readers are at once better at using context and less dependent on it.

This finding is reinforced in the results of yet another study reported by Perfetti and Roth (in press). Skilled and less skilled readers were presented with high, moderate, and low constraining sentences and asked, on a given presentation, to generate as many acceptable responses as they could think of in 15 secs. The result of interest is that although less skilled readers produced more responses, skilled readers generally produced more appropriate responses, suggesting that they were better able to use context in generating grammatically acceptable alternatives.

One other finding reported by Perfetti and Roth (in press) is notable. In a series of related studies, wherein reading skill, context, and stimulus degradation were orthogonally varied, the uniform finding was that skilled readers were better able than less skilled readers to tolerate significant amounts of stimulus degradation (up to 42% missing letters), the difference between the two groups being approximately 21%. Although both groups were able to use contextual constraints to compensate for degraded stimuli, skilled readers were more facile in trading off one type of information with another.

It may be inferred from the results reported thus far that the (comparatively) skilled reader is a more informed processor of printed material than the less skilled reader and is much better able to shift from one level of processing to another in availing himself of a given type of information contained in written text when a task requires the apprehension of such information. An especially lucid illustration of this capability, from a developmental standpoint, is provided in a study conducted by Drewnowski (1978). This investigation is similar to that reported by Drewnowski and Healy (1977), which I discussed earlier, except that children as well as adults were used as subjects, and those in the younger sample were stratified in accord with grade level and reading ability. The purpose of the study was to evaluate the processing strategies employed by individuals at different levels of ability and experience in reading as a function of text structure. As in the previous study, subjects were asked to search for the letter *t* in the word *the,* embedded in connected and unconnected text. Changes in the pattern of detection errors were expected to "reflect the highest level of processing that is attained by subjects at a given stage of reading acquisition" (Drewnowski, 1978, p. 403).

The rationale for this study followed closely that of Drewnowski and Healy (1977), the central thesis being that reading entails the simultaneous processing of multilevel codes that are available on a selective basis. The codes that become available first are those to which the reader is primarily attendent, in accord with task demands. Processing at higher levels may therefore be completed prior to completion of processing at lower levels, inasmuch as higher level information (e.g., meaning) may become available before lower level units (e.g., words and letters) are fully processed. Thus detection of a letter in a high-frequency word, such as *the*—in this case the letter *t*—would be more successful when the word is embedded in unconnected text than when it is embedded in connected text, because it may not always be fully processed when reading for meaning. This pattern was observed in adults (Drewnowski & Healy, 1977), and the intent was to assess the degree to which it would be observed in children at given levels of experience and achievement in reading. Accordingly, children from grades 1 through 5 were separated into good and poor reader groups, and these subjects along with college students were presented with: (1) prose passages containing instances of *the,* either alone or embedded in other words (e.g., mo*the*r); (2) scrambled word sets, comprised of words taken from the passage; (3) scrambled letters containing *t*'s and other letters; and (4) words from the passage presented in list format. The task was to circle all instances of the letter *t*. The expectation was that letter level processing would be characteristic of children who are relatively insensitive to passage structure and would be manifested in conditional error percentages at or near chance in all passages. Thus, it was predicted that letter level processing would occur more often among younger children and poor readers. Whole-word or phrase level processing was expected to be characteristic of more experienced and more able readers, as manifested in a higher percentage of detection errors for the prose passages, scrambled word passage, and word list than for the scrambled letter passage.

The results, in brief, are as follows. The percentage of detection errors made by first-grade children on all passages was no better than chance as predicted. Chance level performance was also observed for all subjects above that level on the scrambled letter passage and word list. Percentage of detection errors for these subjects on scrambled word and prose passages were significantly above chance level and also varied with grade and reading ability. There were significant differences between first graders versus second and third graders on these measures, but it was not until fourth grade that detection errors on the prose passage rose significantly above detection errors on the scrambled word passage. Beyond this level—that is, in fifth graders and adults—performance on the scrambled word passage declined steadily, whereas performance on the prose passage remained at a relatively high level, dropping off somewhat in the adult subjects.

In order to evaluate the effects of reading ability, independent of grade level, the performance of good and poor readers in first and fifth grade was compared. At the first-grade level, good readers made more detection errors than poor readers on the prose and scrambled word passages as well as on the scrambled letter passage. However, the good readers made fewer detection errors than did the poor readers on the word lists. At the fifth-grade level, good readers made more detection errors than did poor readers on the prose and scrambled word passages, but the reverse was true on the scrambled letter passage and word list.

It is clear from these findings that both the units of processing that were available to subjects and the preferred mode of processing changed significantly with experience in reading and varied with the skill of the reader. It is also clear that stimulus and contextual effects were operative, inasmuch as the processing strategies employed by subjects were determined, in part, by the target word and the condition under which it appeared. These results constitute impressive evidence for the contention that the unit of perception is relative, in that they rather handily demonstrate that the level at which a critical discrimination is made in word processing is determined by the joint effects of *context*, the *characteristics of the word stimulus*, and the *skill of the reader*.

The study just discussed provides a convenient developmental contrast between adults and children, and the results are illuminating. It raises the question, however, of whether there would yet be individual differences among adult readers in preferred modes of processing printed words and, if so, whether they might correlate with individual differences in reading ability. Unfortunately, the literature addressing these questions is scant, quite likely because the possibility of significant variation among skilled readers in mode of word processing has not been seriously considered. Yet, as we have seen, Baron and Strawson (1976) have provided suggestive evidence that adult skilled readers might, indeed, vary as to their differential reliance on whole-word (Chinese) as opposed to spelling-sound (Phonecians) representations in word identification, which would not be entirely surprising if one takes note of the fact that such differences can be found in children as well, both among skilled and less skilled readers (Baron, 1979; Boder, 1971; Camp & Dolcourt, 1977; Frith, 1980). Thus, of interest are the results of two other studies that specifically evaluated word processing in adult readers as a function of individual differences in reading ability.

The first of these studies was conducted by Mason (1978). This author acknowledged Baron and Strawson's (1976) suggestion that a word may be identified either by direct "visual" access using word specific associates or indirectly through the use of spelling–sound correspondences. However, Mason hypothesized that highly skilled readers would tend to use the former route, because it is presumably more efficient, whereas less skilled readers would be inclined to use the latter, though it was not made explicit why this might be so. In order to test these hypotheses, four separate experiments were conducted, using college students dichotomized on the basis of reading comprehension scores. The skilled readers ranged between the 90th and 99th percentiles on the comprehension measure, and the less skilled readers ranged between the 14th and 40th percentiles. The first experiment used a procedure identical to that employed by Baron and Strawson (1976), except that stimuli were presented one at a time instead of in lists of 10. Word stimuli were those used by Baron and Strawson and consisted of 40 regular and 40 exception words, each presented twice, once in mixed case and once in lowercase. The dependent measures were mean error and mean vocalization latency.

The skilled readers made fewer errors and had shorter latencies than the less skilled readers on both the regular and exception words. Both groups made more errors on exception words than on the regular words, but neither group manifested significant differences between these stimuli on the latency measure. As regards letter case, less skilled readers made more errors under the mixed case condition than under the lowercase condition, but this difference was not observed in the skilled readers. However, both groups had longer vocalization latencies on the mixed case condition. Mason interpreted these findings to mean that words are not recognized as wholes (i.e., because skilled readers made no more errors on mixed case than on lowercase words) and that lexical access does not involve phonologic recoding in either skilled or less skilled adult readers.

However, a more encompassing explanation is that the skilled readers were not only more proficient at word identification than the less skilled readers but were also better able to alter their processing strategies to overcome the disruptive effects of the mixed case condition. It is likely that the skilled readers used a letter level strategy under the latter circumstances and that the less skilled reader continued using a whole-word strategy. This would explain one other finding, and that is that less skilled readers had an unusually high incidence of errors on the mixed case version of the word *toll* (tOIL), which they were inclined to identify as *toil*.

The second experiment was designed to evaluate whether the reader group differences observed in Experiment 1 were due to the articulatory or to the visual and/or name retrieval components of word processing. The same stimuli used in Experiment 1 were employed with independent samples of comparably selected reader groups, and vocalization latencies and errors were again employed as dependent measures. The procedure was modified, however, in that half the subjects were required to delay their responses for 2 sec. The group differences observed in the first experiment were replicated, using the procedure employed in that experiment. However, the differences were negligible under the delayed naming condition, suggesting that it is the perceptual and cognitive components of word processing that distinguishes the two groups rather than the speech-motor components.

Experiment 3 evaluated the effects of lexicality, spatial redundancy, and word length by presenting subjects with high-frequency words and pronounceable pseudowords varying in length (four and six letters) and degree of spatial redundancy, that is, letter position frequency (Mayzner & Tresselt, 1965). The reader groups were independently selected, and vocalization latency was the dependent measure. Skilled and less skilled readers differed on the naming variable only on the six-letter pseudowords. However, whereas length was a factor for the skilled readers only on the nonwords, the two additional letters on the six-letter sets increased the naming latencies of the less skilled readers on both the words and pseudowords. Spatial redundancy was not found to affect the real words, but on pseudowords high redundancy words were named faster than low redundancy words. On the other hand, redundancy was used differentially by the two groups. Skilled readers profited from redundancy on both four- and six-letter words (thus compensating for length differences), but this effect was apparent in less skilled readers only on the four-letter items.

Experiment 4 used the same materials as in Experiment 3 but added a 2-sec delay condition. Subjects were again independently selected. Under this condition, the reader group differences disappeared, again suggesting that the differences observed in the previous experiment were due to word processing variables rather than speech-motor functioning.

Mason makes special note of the fact that substantial individual differences in word identification ability can yet be observed in college level adults who might otherwise be taken as varying minimally in this ability. Yet she concludes that both skilled and less skilled readers access the lexicon directly from print, most likely because it is more efficient than the indirect route, which involves phonologic recoding. However, she points out that the highly skilled readers must have made full use of the alphabetic principle in learning to read, because differences favoring this group in the decoding of nonsense words were yet apparent. Mason (1978) also underscores the fact that the skilled readers could make better use of orthographic redundancy in forming visual representations of letter strings to aid in word identification, which is to suggest that less skilled readers "may go from print to sound using a visual access, not because the visual route is fast, but because the phonological route is too slow [p. 580]."

Mason's (1978) results are significant, because they demonstrate clear-cut disparities between college level readers not only in comprehension and word identification ability but also in the fund of structural information available for decoding letter strings and in the efficiency with which the two groups engaged this enterprise. Complementing these findings are the results of a subsequent study by Butler and Hains (1979). These authors tested college students on naming latency (Experiment 1) and speed of lexical decision (Experiment 2), using unrestricted word sets (selected at random from Kucera & Francis, 1967), which varied in *length* (1-14 letters), *number of syllables* (1-5), *word frequency* (40-84.2), *Scientific Frequency Index* (Carroll & White, 1973), and *age of acquisition* of each stimulus word (6-16 years, Carroll & White, 1973). The individual difference variable was knowledge of vocabulary. These measures were subjected to systematic regression analyses, using reaction time as the criterion measure.

The important findings are: (1) reaction time for word naming was affected by word length, word frequency, and age at which a word was first acquired; (2) subjects with high vocabulary scores named words more rapidly than subjects with low vocabulary scores but took longer than the latter subjects to make lexical decisions; (3) high vocabulary subjects were less affected by word length than low vocabulary subjects on both the naming and lexical decision tasks, suggesting that those in the high vocabulary group processed words more holistically than those in the low vocabulary group.

These results permit no inferences as to causal relationship, but they do provide suggestive evidence that individual differences in knowledge and skill of the reader may correlate reliably with group and individual differences in word processing, even in adult readers. Furthermore, the data are consistent with the results of studies, such as those conducted by Samuels et al. (1977) McCormick & Samuels (1978) and Terry et al. (1976), in suggesting that less experienced or less able readers process words less efficiently than those with more experience and greater skill in reading.

Finally, two other findings that have appeared in the literature are worth mentioning here. First, Jackson and McClelland (1975) found that neither foveal nor peripheral letter identification differentiated fast and slow readers, but amount of information encoded on each fixation *did* separate the two groups. The latter variable was measured with unrelated letter strings and a Reicher-type forced-choice task, using word alternatives (*plain/plaid*) embedded in short sentences. The authors suggest that fast readers process letter and word information more rapidly than slow readers, not because of sensory processing differences or guessing strategies (Goodman, 1970) but because they pick up more information at a glance, which I suspect is due to the fact that fast readers have more information about letters and words to begin with.

The second finding comes from work done by neuropsychologists studying acquired language and reading disorders in adults. One such anomaly is of interest here, in that it provides compelling evidence that one stores multilevel representations of printed words that are utilized differentially in word processing. I refer to a syndrome observed in left-hemisphere damaged patients, alternately termed "deep" (Marshall & Newcombe, 1973) and "phonemic" (Shallice & Warrington, 1975) dyslexia. Two such patients have been studied extensively, and the most striking aspect of the linguistic impairments incurred by these individuals is the selective loss of the ability to translate letters and letter groups into their phonemic counterparts. At the same time, they demonstrate intact ability to associate printed words with semantic referents, as manifested in a significant incidence of *semantic substitution* errors in oral reading (*edition—journal*) along with *derivational (danger—dangerous), visual (origin—organ)*, and *paraphasic*-type errors (*disaster—"like danger, airplane, crashed"*). In addition, they have virtually no ability to decode pronounceable pseudowords and, when presented with real words, have particular difficulty identifying those that are more abstract, especially functor words (*the—and*). Concrete words, on the other hand, are more easily identified, presumably because of their association with imageable referents.

In one illustrative study evaluating word processing in these two patients, Patterson and Marcel (1977) verified that neither of them could decode pronounceable pseudowords correctly. In contrast, they performed quite normally on a lexical decision task employing real words and pronounceable pseudowords as compared with a normal control group. There was one exception, however, and that is that they took no longer to respond to homophonic pseudowords (brane) than to nonhomophonic pseudowords, unlike subjects in the control group, who *did* manifest longer latencies to the former stimuli. This result was taken as yet another manifestation that these patients are unable to encode printed words phonologically.

These findings are impressive. The patterns manifested by phonemic dyslexics are roughly analogous to those observed in milder forms in young children (e.g., Boder's "dysphonetic dyslexic" and Baron's word-specific learner) who read imperfectly and in some cases very poorly. The common thread in both instances is the unavailability of necessary information by means of which to effect precision in word identification. In this case, the information lacking is the phonologic counterpart of a given letter string, which for children appears to be necessary for acquiring the code. Such information must also be functional for adults, in a way that precludes the type of anomalous encoding observed in the phonemic dyslexic. Indeed, it would seem from these findings that the phonologic component of printed words may well have something akin to a monitoring function in word processing and may, therefore, have somewhat greater utility in adult readers than that allowed in some models of word recognition (F. Smith, 1971). At any rate, it is difficult to imagine how the response patterns observed in phonemic dyslexics could occur if one did not store multilevel representations of the information contained in a printed word, and it is significant that the knowledge acquired from the studies conducted with these patients is consistent with the view of the word identification process presented herein.

Summary

In this section, I have attempted to document the contention that the experience and skill of the reader is a significant variable contributing to the processing strategies and thus the perceptual units that may be employed in identifying printed words. The central theme throughout is that the highly skilled reader has stored a richly elaborated fund of information about a word's multiform features and has coded functional information at each respective level of processing. He or she thereby has a variety of means by which to differentiate and encode distinguishing word features so as to allow ready access to the lexicon. The skilled reader has acquired associations between a word's global and most salient visual properties on the one hand and its semantic and syntactic counterparts on the other, which obviously include the unique visual patterns created by the particular ordering of its letters along with its length, shape, name, and meaning. He or she has also become intimately acquainted with a word's structural redundancies—which implies a firm knowledge of orthographic invariants as well as spelling-sound consistencies and inconsistencies—and can utilize this knowledge for efficient discrimination among familiar words as well as for identification of new words. The skilled reader has available a large corpus of words he or she can identify on sight not only because he or she can readily retrieve names and meanings associated with a word's most salient visual features but also because he or she can dissect that word with dispatch and attend to the lower level attributes (letters and letter features) that differentiate it from orthographically similar words whenever fine graining is necessitated. Because of sophisticated linguistic ability, he or she has a rich fund of contextual information that allows him or her to process words in running text efficiently and economically, most often accessing higher level representations, such as words and phrases, that allow him or her to extract meanings embedded in broader contexts. In short, highly skilled readers have encoded multiple representations of the information contained within printed words, and for them the unit of perception is relative and variable inasmuch as they are able to adjust their processing strategies to conform with task demands.

Less skilled or impaired readers, on the other hand, have not acquired functional codes at each respective level at which a word's constituents may be processed. Those who are developing normally are hampered only by lack of experience, but those who are impaired to any significant degree may be hampered either by instructional biases or constitutional deficits that prevent them from integrating the visual and linguistic relationships that facilitate code acquisition. Individuals who sustain mild or moderate impairments in visual-linguistic integration are often observed to be primarily inclined either toward global features processing, wherein the characteristic processing unit is the undifferentiated whole word, or toward overanalytic processing, wherein letters and letter clusters are the characteristic processing units. The unit of perception in such individuals is, therefore, less variable than in highly skilled readers and conforms typically to their characteristic perceptual attitude in organizing and encoding a word's visual components. Such difficulties can also be observed in related skills, such as spelling, wherein their products again reflect the internalized representations of word constituents upon which they rely most heavily.

Severely impaired readers have difficulty in acquiring both whole-word and component letter representations, and for them the units of perception are more often idiosyncratic, constituting a diverse collection of unreliable encodings that typically include undifferentiated whole words as well as a large number of word fragments to which they frequently generate incorrect name and meaning associates. Because they have particular difficulty in acquiring spelling–sound relationships, their acquaintance with orthographic redundancies is more defective than the mildly or moderately impaired readers, and the coded representations of printed words that they incorporate are even less elaborated than those of children in these latter groups.

Inasmuch as less skilled and poor readers do not have the degree of facility in word identification characteristic of the highly skilled reader, they are forced to rely more heavily upon contextual information than the skilled reader. But, for the very same reason, they are not able to utilize context as efficiently. Obviously, less skilled and poor readers do not have the flexibility in processing characteristic of highly skilled readers and, for these individuals, the unit of perception is less relative. Such differences can be found even among adults.

SYNTHESIS

In discussing the relative merits of the word recognition models reviewed, I pointed out that although each provides plausible explanations for a variety of word processing phenomena, none in its present form is able to account for the full range of effects reported in the literature.

The feature theories discussed, insofar as they advocate that letter and/or word features are matched against stored representations of whole words, can be classified as whole-word theories. They would therefore seem to be able to account reasonably well for the various word advantage effects observed in studies evaluating the diverse manifestations of this phenomenon (i.e., word superiority, word priority, word frequency, word familiarity). Feature theories also provide plausible explanations for one's ability to adopt economical processing strategies in discriminating words that differ on many featural dimensions, particularly when they appear in meaningful contexts. In addition, such theories would seem to be well-equipped to explain one's ability to identify words on the basis of partial stimulus information, a circumstance that obtains in free reading situations as well as under the more artificial stimulus conditions characteristic of laboratory study.

Feature level processing might also be inferred as a partial explanation of how one discriminates words that are identical, save for a single-letter feature (*snow/show; bad/dad*), and it has been offered as the logical means by which one identifies words that are presented in mixed cases and/or fonts.

However, the feature theories discussed run into difficulty on several counts. For one thing, most of these theories assume that local and/or global context can directly influence the extraction of featural information, but this assumption is incompatible with evidence that indicates that feature extraction is an automatically executing process that is carried out exclusively by the sensory system, uninfluenced by attentional mechanisms or capacity limitations (Estes, 1975b, 1977; Massaro, 1979; Shiffrin & Gardner, 1972). Although there would seem to be little doubt that attentional factors and capacity limitations can and do influence word discrimination and identification, particularly in less skilled readers (LaBerge & Samuels, 1974), it is likely that such influences operate at a stage of processing subsequent to feature extraction (Herman & Kantowitz, 1970).

I mentioned previously that feature level processing would seem to be involved in the case of words that can be discriminated on the basis of only a single feature, but paradoxically feature theories have not been explicit as to how such fine graining is accomplished. In fact, the basic logic behind feature theories appears to be at variance with the common observation that skilled readers typically identify words with precision. Indeed, it is because of the enormous processing load occasioned by the need to sort through functionally equivalent feature lists (in matching the letters in stimulus words with stored representations of those words) that feature redundancy theorists are forced to rely so heavily upon the idea that words are discriminated by contextually guided sampling of word features. Yet feature sampling does not adequately explain how the skilled reader discriminates words that have a large number of features in common, particularly when they are encountered out of context or in uncertain or misleading contexts (Morton, 1964; Perfetti & Roth, in press; Tulving et al., 1963, 1964), nor would it explain how the less skilled reader learns to be precise in discriminating such words.

The third and most general problem encountered by feature theories is their rejection of the idea that whole-word perception ever entails perception of subword units. It seems pointless to hypothesize that word recognition precludes recognition of letters or letter clusters; not only because the available evidence suggests otherwise (Estes, 1977; Massaro, 1979; Massaro & Klitzke, 1977; Vellutino, Steges, & Kandel, 1972; Vellutino, Smith, Steges, & Kaman, 1975) but also because it is illogical to do so. Words are comprised of letters, and letters are comprised of graphic features, and one is embedded in the other, hierarchically ordered. Whenever a word is presented, information at each level of processing, although perhaps not in focal attention at the same time, is apprehended at the same time (Drewnowski, 1978; Drewnowski & Healy, 1977; Healy, 1976). It therefore seems reasonable to expect that recognition would normally take place at the highest level at which a word's constituents are integrated, that is, at the whole word level. To suggest that a word may be processed as a whole is to suggest that it is perceived as a unit, but this does not mean that its letters are not seen and recognized, because letters make up words, and a sufficient number of letters must be apprehended before a word can be apprehended (Estes, 1977). Conversely, recognition of a word's letters does not ensure recognition and identification of that word, which is to suggest that its letters must be encoded in a way that achieves these ends. But, in order to be so encoded, they must be perceived. Indeed, I cannot see how it could be otherwise.

Still another contraindication to contemporary feature theories is that feature level processing is *not* necessarily implied, as some have suggested (F. Smith, 1969; F. Smith et al., 1969) in the observation that words presented in mixed cases and/or fonts can be identified. Suffice it to say, on this point, that component letter theory provides a more parsimonious explanation of one's ability to accomplish this feat than does feature theory, not only because it would be more economical to process such stimuli at the letter level but also, I believe, because one tends to process written material at the highest level of integration possible, which (in the mixed cases and fonts conditions) is typically the letter level. Serial processing would be especially useful in identifying words comprised of different letter shapes, in that one could put his or her knowledge of word spellings to good advantage in compensating for the disruptive effects of this material. This explanation would account for the uniform finding that presentation of words in mixed cases and/or fonts leads to increased response latencies among skilled as well as less skilled readers (Baron & Strawson, 1976; Brooks, 1977; Manelis, 1974; Mason, 1978; Pollatsek et al., 1975; F. Smith, 1969; F. Smith et al., 1969).

Finally, the feature theories available do not provide an adequate explanation of how the skilled reader can identify pseudowords. F. Smith (1971) suggests that this is accomplished through analogy with parts of familiar words rather than by means of grapheme–phoneme translation and insists that identification by analogy takes place at the feature level rather than at the level of letters or letter clusters. Although there is good reason to believe that both unfamiliar words and pseudowords are often identified partly through analogy (Baron, 1977; Glushko, 1979),[20] such evidence does not rule out the possibility that grapheme–phoneme

---

[20]Glushko (1979) has obtained results that suggest that the skilled reader identifies both real words and pseudowords resembling real words by analogy. Specifically, he found that "exception" words like *HAVE* take longer to read aloud than "regular" words like *HAZE,* and a similar finding was obtained with "exception pseudowords" like *TAVE,* which resemble irregular real words. On the other hand, "regular pseudowords" like *TAZE* took less time to read aloud than did the irregular pseudowords. Glushko concludes from these results that words and pseudowords are pronounced through analogy with familiar words rather than through the use of abstract grapheme–phoneme correspondence rules. He also infers that letter strings sharing features with a presented letter string are activated along with the presented string and may occasion generalization error. He, therefore, suggests that the presented string is pronounced by "using procedures for determining how to modify the activated information in order to synthesize the desired articulatory program [p. 678]." However, two questions are left unanswered by Glushko. First, what *are* the procedures that modify the

associations are also used for identifying these stimuli. Indeed, if analogy were the only means by which children learned to identify new words, then those who rely primarily on whole-word processing strategies to do so would suffer no significant impairments in learning to read, and (as I have demonstrated) this is not the case.

The other whole-word theory evaluated is Johnson's pattern-unit model (Johnson, 1975, 1977). This conceptualization incorporates the assumption that letter and word features are directly assigned a unitary encoding at the "perceptual" stage of processing, which in effect precludes letter recognition. Words are therefore identified as wholes and letter strings are parsed only if they cannot be matched with a coded representation in long-term memory.

Much of what I have said about the feature theories discussed previously applies to Johnson's model as well. Obviously the remarks made about the ability of whole-word theories to account for word advantage effects are applicable, as are the arguments questioning the view that letter recognition is not necessary for word recognition. However, as noted earlier, a later statement made by Johnson (1979) acknowledges the possibility that a word's letters must be "seen" in order for that word to be recognized and further that the (unitary) encoding of letter strings takes place after the letters in a given string become available. Here Johnson seems to be aligning himself with others, who have suggested that letter recognition is not the terminal stage in perceptual processing (Manelis, 1974; Marmurek, 1977; Pollatsek et al., 1975; Sloboda, 1977). However, he does not make clear either in the earlier version of his theory or in the later version what is meant by a unitary encoding. The latter presumably refers to some means by which the information contained within a printed word is integrated, but this is left unspecified. Thus the concept remains amorphous.

Finally, Johnson's model would seem to be lacking in that it makes no apparent provision for the role of verbal context in facilitating word recognition and identification. On the other hand, it is not incompatible with the multilevel processing view adopted here, in that it provides for the parsing of letter strings that cannot be identified as familiar words, which implies multiple encoding of word constituents. Thus the theory holds promise in this regard.

As with the other formulations reviewed, component letter theories of word perception have both strengths and weaknesses. I indicated earlier that some words can only be identified by taking account of all of their letters (e.g., *mean, meat, lean*), whereas others have so many overlapping features that all of their letters must be fully processed and subtle differences noted before they can be

---

activated information to achieve correct pronunciation of the presented stimulus? Second, if grapheme–phoneme correspondence rules are never utilized in pronouncing real words or pseudowords, how does the reader manage to pronounce the *H* in *HAVE* and *HAZE* as well as the *T* in *TAVE* and *TAZE*?

discriminated from one another (*bad, dad; now, how; casual, causal*). Both letter and feature level processing are necessary for identifying such words unless, of course, they appear in such highly constrained contexts that salient features processing would suffice.

I have already suggested that letter level processing is the logical explanation for one's ability to identify words presented in mixed letter cases and/or fonts, and the arguments advanced to support this suggestion need not be reiterated. I might add, however, that component letter processing is inferred in such instances, not because letters are the sole units of perception as some suggest but because the visual patterns one normally uses for word recognition are disrupted. Thus, it would be logical to expect that a word's constituents would be processed at the highest level of integration permitted, which for words presented in mixed cases and fonts is the letter level, as I indicated previously.

The point just made alludes to one of several limiting aspects of component letter theories: they, by definition, assume that a word's letters are the exclusive processing units effecting recognition and identification. As I have stressed throughout this chapter, the likelihood is that the highly skilled reader acquires multilevel representations of word constituents that are integrated and utilized in complementary fashion in word processing. Yet neither of the component letter models discussed allows for this possibility.

One of these models—Gough's (1972)—incorporates the assumption that a word's letters are processed serially and systematically mapped onto abstract phonemic representations, resulting in identification of that word without the aid of context. In addition to its failure to consider the possibility of whole-word processing as a viable means for accessing the lexicon, this characterization is questioned by evidence that suggests that serial processing and phonologic mediation, although probably used extensively by beginning readers, are not the primary or exclusive mechanisms used by skilled readers for identifying printed words. Gough's model also seems lacking, in that it makes no provision either for the synthesizing power of orthographic structure or for the facilitating role of verbal context, the utility of both variables having been well-documented in the literature. Yet, it does explain how the skilled reader can identify unfamiliar words and pseudowords.

The other model discussed—Massaro's (1975)—advocates that letters are processed in parallel and identified as a word through the application of orthographic rules and higher level interpretive processes that may utilize information provided by verbal context. However, stimulus and contextual factors are believed to make independent contributions to word recognition, and context is said to have no direct effect upon letter perception.

As noted earlier, this model is vulnerable, both because it does not consider the possibility of whole-word processing in word recognition and because of its narrow definition of orthographic structure. As regards the premise that words are not processed as wholes, it can be stated in contention that although a word is comprised of letters, which must be seen in order for that word to be recognized, the word itself is a separate entity, defined not only by its letters but also by the interrelations among these letters. Furthermore, for the skilled reader, a word contains a large amount of diverse, highly differentiated, and well-integrated information embodied in its meaning as well as its structural characteristics, and the associations stimulated by that word are qualitatively different than the associations stimulated by each of its letters. Thus, to suggest, as does Massaro (1975), that a word is simply a collection of invariantly ordered letters, integrated by orthographic rules, does not seem to me to capture either the complexity or the essence of a word. Indeed, if this were the case, then we could not distinguish words from pseudowords.

I must also contend with Massaro's definition of orthographic structure. It seems to me that when the developing reader becomes sensitized to the structural regularities and redundancies embedded in English orthography, his or her sensitivity is reflected not only in the ability to generate orthographically legal letter sequences on the basis of abstract rules (as in identifying words from partial stimulus information) but also in the tendency to perceive directly recursively grouped letters as units (e.g., *sh*op, pu*sh,* ac*tion,* na*tion*). The failure to consider this possibility seems incongruous, for if recursive letter sequences were not actually perceived as units, much of the synthesizing power of orthographic redundancy would be lost.

One can also fault Massaro's model in that it fails to explicate the means by which unfamiliar words or pseudowords are identified. The author ascribes no role to phonologic mediation in identifying familiar words, and it is not clear what role he ascribes to this mechanism in the identification of these other stimuli. Thus the model seems incomplete in this respect.

Finally, neither Gough nor Massaro adequately addresses the word frequency issue, which is not surprising because word frequency effects afford support for whole-word theories and both theorists reject the notion of whole-word processing.

Both of the letter cluster theories considered advocate that word perception necessarily involves the partitioning of a word stimulus into subword units, but they differ in their conceptualizations of how this is accomplished. In Gibson's (1965) theory, letter features are extracted in parallel and are directly matched against stored representations of orthographically regular letter clusters, thus precluding letter recognition. However, in Spoehr and Smith's theory, letters are first recognized (also in parallel) and then parsed into vocalic center groups (VCGs), and these become the matching units in long-term memory rather than redundant clusters that do not necessarily include vocalic elements. Unlike Gibson, Spoehr and Smith advocate phonemic recoding of letters in the VCGs that comprise a word as the vehicle for recognizing that word. Neither theory is explicit as to the role of context, although both allow for the possibility of alternative processing modes, which implicates contextual variables as potentially influential in the word identification process.

Both of the cluster theories outlined can, of course, account for the synthesizing power of orthographic redundancy, but only Spoehr and Smith's can explain one's ability to identify unfamiliar words and pseudowords, because it advocates the use of phonologic recoding as a processing mechanism. However, neither of these theories can account for word advantage effects, nor do they have any means of accounting for the facilitating effects of verbal context. On the other hand, more recent statements made by these authors (Gibson, 1977; Spoehr, 1978; Smith & Spoehr, 1974) allow for the possibility that words may be identified by means of direct visual access, and a revision of Gibson's original cluster theory (Gibson, 1971) is notable for its emphasis upon the use of different processing modes associated with experience in reading. Thus both of these conceptualizations can be broadened in ways that would give them more explanatory power.

The final word recognition paradigm reviewed is Estes' hierarchical filter model (1975b, 1977). This model is unlike any of the others discussed, in that it assumes the existence of multilevel codes (termed "control elements"), which facilitate detection of word constituents at each level of processing. Thus, there are separate codes for letter and salient word features, letters, letter clusters, and letter sequences representing whole words, and each is said to be differentially sensitive to its respective counterpart in word stimuli. Because they are hierarchically ordered, they function as an "ascending filter" system, and detectors at a given level respond only to stimulus patterns that can be matched with representations stored in long-term memory. When a match is found, the detectors corresponding to that pattern are activated and transmit a pattern of excitation to the next highest level and so on. Failure to find a match at a given level terminates the flow upward, and recognition is precluded, as when random letter strings are perceived as nonwords.

The model also incorporates the notion that letter and word features are activated simultaneously and that this information, along with "background" information form verbal and orthographic context, are processed independently and combine to effect word recognition. A particularly useful characteristic of the model is that it provides for selective processing at given levels, depending on the nature of the task set before the perceiver, verbal context, and like factors. Such information is said to preactivate control elements at a particular level and elevate thresholds at others, thereby facilitating attention to critical discriminators. Estes has also garnered evidence that the visual system operates imperfectly in registering order information in the peripheral regions, and the model makes provision for the use of orthographic context in compensating for such errors.

In my estimation, Estes' model is more encompassing than any of those reviewed. By postulating that a word and its components constitute multilevel representations in long-term memory, it is potentially able to explain the major word processing phenomena reported in the literature, which obviously include the various word advantage effects, the ability to identify words presented in different letter cases and fonts, economy and selectivity in processing, the ability to identify words on the basis of partial stimulus information, and the ability to make effective use of orthographic and verbal context. The model's structural characteristics would also accommodate the diverse types of information and the flexibility in processing necessary to effect precision in word identification and, ultimately, to become a skilled reader. Thus, it potentially accommodates individual differences in reading ability.

However, the model falls short of achieving this degree of generality on several counts. First, Estes is not always explicit as to how certain important word perception phenomena might be explained, for example, the apparent role of phonologic information in word processing, the way in which one identifies unfamiliar words and pseudowords, and the means by which precision in word identification is effected. Second, the model presumably allows only direct visual access to the lexicon, which is contrary to accumulating evidence that there are alternative vehicles for lexical entry. Third, it appears to be weakened by the inconsistency inherent in postulating the existence of multilevel representations for words and word constituents, while resting on the assumption of independent and unidirectional processing stages characterized by complete independence of stimulus and contextual information.

Suffice it to point out in relation to the first two of these problems that all theories that advocate only one mechanism for identifying printed words can be questioned by research findings that suggest that: (1) there may be at least two lexical access routes for printed words, one involving direct visual access and the other involving phonologic mediation; (2) there may be individual differences in the relative use of both routes; (3) those who tend to utilize one or the other exclusively may be significantly impaired in reading. I have, of course, cited extensive research evidence to support each of these possibilities and provided documentation that phonologic translation may have functional utility for skilled as well as less skilled readers. For example, there is reason to believe that phonologic information and linguistic information in general significantly influence the ways in which beginning readers dissect the orthography and thus the degree to which they acquire the multilevel codes that Estes highlights in his model. Indeed, there is now a great deal of evidence that individuals who have difficulty in one or more aspects of language, particularly in the use of the phonologic components of printed and spoken words, have difficulty in learning to read. It has also been suggested on the basis of empirical findings derived from work done with adults that spelling–sound associates may supplement visual-meaning associates in the word identification process (Baron, 1977; Coltheart et al., 1977; Forster, 1979). Similarly, Marshall (1976, pp. 109-131) speculates that "the phonologic route to meaning provides an independent check upon the accuracy of the semantic representation obtained by direct addressing from visual analysis [p. 116-117]." Thus, in skilled readers, phonologic information might be important both in enhancing and in monitoring direct access operations, functions that may go unnoticed until they are disrupted in some way. This possibility is suggested in the remarkable reading behaviors of the phonemic dyslexic patients discussed earlier, who apparently lost the use of the phonologic code in word identification. Estes' model would therefore seem to be lacking in its failure to incorporate assumptions that reflect the apparent utility of phonologic information in word processing.

The third shortcoming noted in Estes' model of word recognition is, in my judgment, the most basic of all. As pointed out previously, the model seems to be somewhat inconsistent in postulating the existence of multilevel representations of words and word constituents, while it suggests that stimulus encoding proceeds unidirectionally, independent of the influence of local and/or global context. Such inconsistency is exemplified in the fact that it does not adequately account for the differential encoding of pseudocompounds, such as *feather*, and true compounds, such as *fathead*, as pointed out in earlier sections of this chapter. It is apparent that orthographic context is important for defining morpheme boundaries in such words, and it would seem that the activation of codes at respective levels of processing (e.g., *feat eat th her*), which is assumed in Estes' model, would have to be monitored in a way that would suppress activation of anomalous associates. Implied here is some sort of interaction between the critical letters in these words (i.e., *t* and *h*) and the orthographic context provided by surrounding letters that would disambiguate perception of the words as wholes. However, such an interaction is rejected in Estes' model, hence the inconsistency.

In addition to the specific problems noted in the respective word recognition models reviewed, yet another defect that is characteristic of most of these models is that few consider either the variable nature of the word stimulus or individual differences in reading ability as factors that might differentially affect word processing. As regards the first of these two factors, I have provided strong documentation, I think, for my contention that a word's structural and meaning attributes significantly influence the mechanisms and strategies that may be employed in first learning to identify that word and in identifying it thereafter. Yet, of the word recognition models discussed, only Gibson's (1971) model and that of Spoehr and Smith (1973) have been explicit in defining how different word features might influence word processing, and both authors have adduced research evidence to support this possibility.

On the other hand, a number of other researchers have provided considerable documentation in studies of both children and adults that word attributes both directly and indirectly affect the processing strategies employed in identifying printed words and that there are individual differences in the use of such strategies (Baron, 1979; Baron & Strawson, 1976; Brooks, 1977). Such results, along with the theoretical arguments presented earlier, would seem to provide ample reason to consider the role of the stimulus in framing one's model of word perception.

As for the ability of the reader, I indicated earlier that this variable has theoretical significance in that it underscores the possibility that individuals differ significantly in the degree to which they have incorporated the amount and types of information necessary for accuracy and fluency in word identification and in the strategies they are able to employ in identifying printed words. This is most clearly demonstrated in comparing the acquired knowledge and the processing strategies characteristic of skilled and less skilled readers. Skilled readers have much more coded information available to them and can cross-reference word features with a degree of facility that allows them maximum flexibility in word processing. For them the processing units and thus the vehicles for word discrimination are highly relative and vary with task demands. This is not true of less skilled and poor readers, who have a limited amount of information available to them, as is evident in their word processing strategies and in the nature of their errors in word identification.

The latter point, once again, touches upon an important issue underscored earlier. I suggested that none of the word perception models presently available adequately distinguishes between word recognition and word identification and that the failure to do so reflects the failure to address the issue of how the reader learns to discriminate words having similar visual characteristics. This distinction has theoretical significance in that it necessitates careful analysis of the mechanisms one ultimately employs to identify words accurately, as well as the information and the perceptual attitudes he or she acquires in doing so. To appreciate this fact, consider once again the substitution errors made by normal and poor readers in the studies conducted by Vellutino et al. (1972, 1975) described earlier. Recall that when the children were given tachistoscopic presentations of words such as *loin* and *calm,* they often named them incorrectly, using names of more familiar words (i.e., *lion* and *clam*). However, these same children were asked to spell out the letters of these words directly after their attempts to name them and most did so correctly. Feature theorists might suggest that the observed disparity in naming and spelling is due to the fact that the children had not yet acquired the position information needed to disambiguate the two stimulus words, because these words were not prominent in their speaking vocabularies and may not have been encountered in print. Although this is likely, the explanation by itself says nothing about how the developing reader acquires information that would allow him or her to discriminate between visually similar words such as these or about the processing strategies he or she employs to effect precision in discrimination. Neither does it account for the fact that the letters in the stimulus words in question were perceived and identified correctly, contrary to a major premise of feature theory that word recognition precludes letter recognition. This finding would be contrary to Johnson's pattern-unit model for the same reason. Thus the basic logic behind both theories is effectively questioned.

Gough's theory could not explain why the substitution errors made by most of the children were semantically and visually derived rather than phonologically derived, and Spoehr and Smith's model would fail on similar grounds. A few children produced the two-syllable nonword *lo in* in attempting to pronounce the stimulus word *loin,* suggesting that they *did* employ a phonologic recoding strategy, but this was not characteristic of the group as a whole. If anything, this finding is more in keeping with a variable encoding than with a unitary encoding model of word identification and is thus contrary to both Gough's theory and Spoehr and Smith's theory as originally articulated.

Both Massaro's and Estes' models would explain the children's ability to reproduce the letters in the stimulus words in correct order, and both might suggest that "interpretive" processes did not have sufficient information to effect precision. It could nevertheless be argued that these stimuli were encoded as familiar whole words after the letters in respective words became available. If so, then both models would be at a loss, because neither provides an adequate explanation of how such errors occur and how they are ultimately avoided. In addition, neither can account for the fact that some children apparently employed a phonologic recoding strategy to identify the stimulus words, because these models make no provision for phonologically mediated identification of printed words.

Finally, Gibson's (1965, 1971) model would hold that the children's substitution errors were partly based on their familiarity with the more meaningful words and occurred because they had limited experience with structural analysis. Although this may be true of children in the lower grades (e.g., second and third), it is not true of children in the upper grades. Furthermore, Gibson's theory could not explain why the letters in these words were identified and ordered correctly, given that it advocates that the letter feature rather than the letter is the unit of perception.

Clearly, none of the models reviewed adequately and/or completely explains the performance patterns manifested by the children in these studies, and the findings contradict some of the major premises adopted by certain of these models relative to the unit of perception. I would venture to guess that most of the children in the sample apparently encoded the stimulus words as familiar whole words, but this did not preclude accurate perception of their component letters even to the point of taking account of their order. At the same time, accurate perception of the words' component letters did not ensure accuracy in identifying them. The children obviously utilized the stimulus information available to them but lacked higher-order information that would have allowed precise identification. They also employed different encoding strategies, though most relied on direct visual access rather than phonologic mediation in processing the stimulus words. The important point to underscore here is that one or another of these manifestations would be left unexplained by respective word recognition models. The recognition-identification distinction thus underscores the need for more precise definition of the encoding and comparison processes and calls for significant alteration of current conceptualizations of the unit of perception. The skill of the reader variable relates directly to each of these modifications, because it raises the question of how one learns to adjust for the asynchrony between what he or she sees in print and how he or she interprets what is seen.

Closely related to the recognition-identification issue discussed previously is another issue I addressed earlier, and that is the interpretive ambiguity that characterizes the ways in which the concept of perception is defined in the models analyzed in this chapter. Some theorists' definition of perception seems to be closer to the sensory component of word recognition (i.e., "seeing" the letters in a word), whereas that of other theorists appears to be closer to the interpretive component of this process (i.e., grouping and/or interpreting letters). A good example of this distinction is provided by a technique used by Massaro (1979) in a study in which ambiguous letters were presented in different orthographic contexts: c*ent* versus c*dit*. Massaro would insist that the orthographic context provided by the letters adjacent to the ambiguous letter and the stimulus characteristics of this letter make independent contributions to the identification of these two words and that context does not affect the extraction of features from any of the letters in these words, including the ambiguous letter. Rumelhart (1977), on the other hand, would suggest that the information provided by orthographic context interacts with the stimulus information provided by the ambiguous letter and directly influences interpretation of this letter, which he seems to equate with feature extraction. Yet both would agree that the critical letter *is* ambiguous and that these two words can be identified as real words, in spite of the ambiguity of the critical letter. Thus, for Massaro, perception of the ambiguous letter constitutes resolution of sensory processing, whereas, for Rumelhart, perception of this letter is a matter of interpreting the stimulus.

This problem, of course, relates to the more general question of how contextual and stimulus information are combined and is important here, because it underscores, once again, the incongruity of multilevel and unidirectional processing in word identification, as postulated in theories such as Estes' (1977) and LaBerge and Samuels' (1974) that incorporate both features. These authors would be courting inconsistency if they suggested that orthographic context has no effect on letter encoding in the case of the examples given, because they would no doubt agree with Rumelhart that the (orthographic) environments in which critical letters are placed (c*d*it, fa*t*her, fa*t*head) does affect the way in which they are perceived. There must therefore be some sort of interaction between stimulus and contextual variables to account for such interpretive differences, but this does not mean that sensory processing is in any way affected by context (Shiffrin & Gardner, 1972), contrary to the position taken by Rumelhart.

A partial resolution of the problem would be to assume, along with other authors (Manelis, 1974; Pollatsek et al., 1975), that interactive processes are operative after featural extraction is completed. Thus sensory processing would take place, uninfluenced by orthographic and/or verbal context, but such variables would interact with stimulus information beyond this level, affecting both perceptual organization of a word's letters and higher level identification. Perceptual operations would include unit perception of recursive letter groups (*ch ur ch*), definition of morpheme boundaries in words containing root and bound morphemes (*walk ed*), definition of morpheme boundaries in ambiguous words (*feather* versus *fathead*), synthesis of polysyllabic words and/or words of great length (*re present a tion*), and fine-grained discrimination of words with many overlapping features (*was saw; loin lion; show snow*). Identification operations would include apprehension of meaning, name retrieval, phonologic recoding, and pronunciation. The degree to which any one of these operations is utilized would, of course, depend on the context in which these words appeared, the nature of the stimulus, and the perceptual units available to the reader at given levels of processing, which brings me back to Estes' model.

As I have said, the most attractive feature of this model is that it has the structural components that would facilitate the flexibility in processing characteristic of the highly skilled reader, but such flexibility seems to me to be obviated by the "bottom-up" feature of the model. Indeed, the major advantage of a multilevel processing model is that it allows selection of the level(s) of processing that would facilitate critical discriminations in the most efficient manner possible, and this implies some means by which stimulus and contextual information can be cross-referenced on a running basis. It is not clear to me, for example, how the hierarchical filter system would prevent activation of the words *feat eat at* and *her* in the word *feather,* without some mechanism that suppresses such activation after the letters in this word become available. More specifically, in proceeding upward from the letter to the letter sequence level (see Fig. 2.5), how does the filter mechanism group the letters in this word, say as opposed to the letters in true compounds, such as *fathead*? Estes suggests that supplementary information provided by global feature detectors, orthographic and verbal context, and like variables serves to lower thresholds for certain units (e.g., the *th* in fea*th*er) and raise thresholds for others, but I do not see how such selective processing could transpire, if the flow of information is unidirectional.

Even if it ultimately proves to be the case that perceptual processing of word stimuli does proceed unidirectionally, as Estes and others suggest, there might still be the need for some sort of interactive mechanism that would be functional at the interpretive stage of processing to effect successful integration of a word's multiple constituents (*visual, semantic, syntactic,* and *phonologic*), so as to allow precision in identifying that word.

The utility of such a mechanism is illustrated in the error patterns often observed in developing readers, as well as in the adult dyslexic patients discussed earlier. A child who sees the word *cat* and calls it *kitty* has obviously made contact with the semantic and syntactic components of each of these words, but in order to learn to read and spell both precisely he or she will have to acquire more information about their graphic, orthographic, and phonologic characteristics, and learn to cross-reference these stimulus features in ways that avoid generalization errors of the types exemplified. The dyslexic patients, on the other hand, have lost the ability to cross-reference these word features and consequently have extraordinary difficulty in avoiding such errors.

What therefore seems lacking in Estes' model, and most others, is a control mechanism (see Fig. 2.1) that would facilitate the type of cross-referencing of word features that appears to be necessary to achieve precision in word identification. Rumelhart (1977) has provided a more elaborate version of Rumelhart and Siple's (1974) interactive model in which he outlines such a mechanism. In brief, he describes a central processor called a "message center," which maintains a running list of "hypotheses" accepted from several "knowledge sources" (stimulus characteristics, word meaning, context), along with a subjective estimate of the probability of a given item occurring in a particular context. The message center coordinates the information coming in from the various knowledge sources and provides feedback that leads to acceptance or rejection of hypotheses concerning presence or absence of a particular word attribute. The interactions among these knowledge sources (coordinated by the message center) eventually facilitates a "decision" as to the word's identity.

A similar conceptualization is provided by Forster (1976, pp. 257–287). This author likens the word identification process to the workings of a reference library. The "books" in the library are analogous to the entries in the "lexicon" or "master file," and an "access file" describes a word's orthographic, phonologic, and semantic/syntactic characteristics, corresponding, respectively, to *direct access, phonologically mediated access,* and *access through meaning.* When a printed word is presented, initial entry may be via one or another of these routes (independent of one another), and processing at this stage results in selection of a tentative "match" with the stimulus, pending a "postlexical cross-checking" of the word's featural characteristics to effect precise identification. Such cross-checking is made possible by the fact that lexical entries contain complete descriptions of word attributes, and those entries that tentatively match the stimulus word can be checked against that word as well as against each other. Forster's model apparently differs from Rumelhart's in that interactive processes occur after rather than before lexical access.

In my opinion, both of these conceptualizations have some appeal, inasmuch as they afford a means by which feedback from and to the various information sources can effect the type and level of stimulus processing that results in accurate and efficient word identification. Such feedback would seem to be important to avoid generalization errors as well as to develop the means for correcting such errors when they do occur. Interactive processing to achieve the former effect would seem to be characteristic of the skilled reader. Interactive processing to achieve the latter would seem to be more often evident in the less skilled and developing reader. Although it is not abundantly clear whether or not such processing affects perception as well as identification, I am inclined to believe that it influences both functions in the various ways described earlier.

It would therefore seem that Estes' model and others that advocate multilevel encoding (LaBerge & Samuels, 1974) would be greatly enhanced by control mechanisms, such as those outlined in Rumelhart's and Forster's models, that would allow them greater flexibility than they now possess. On the other hand, models such as Rumelhart's and Forster's would be greatly enhanced by incorporation of the structural components of Estes' model, and both Estes and Rumelhart might seriously consider a role for the phonologic component of printed words, because this attribute may well have functional utility in skilled as well as in less skilled readers. In connection with the latter point, the models of each of these theorists as well as most others reviewed must ultimately address the issue of individual differences in reading ability, in view of accumulating evidence that even so-called skilled readers may not identify words in exactly the same way or with the same degree of facility.

It should be apparent from the arguments advanced herein that in advocating that the perceptual unit is relative I have essentially redefined the concept in a way that I believe is more in keeping with the complex nature of word processing and the flexibility of the human information processor. Rather than suggest that words are recognized and identified through the processing of single units against which stored representations are matched, it would seem to be more accurate to suggest that units at the respective levels of processing, which define word constituents, are apprehended simultaneously and that the level at which a perceiver discriminates a given word from other words in the lexicon might reasonably be considered the unit of perception for that particular word. This conceptualization implies that *all* the visual information contained within a printed word is apprehended by the perceiver but that the unit that is in focal attention at the time at which a critical discrimination is made—that is, the unit that finalizes identification—is variable, depending of course on the context in which the word is presented, the nature of the stimulus, and the information available to and typically utilized by the perceiver. It also implies that an accurate discrimination might be made at one level before processing of lower level constituents is completed, which again depends on the three contingencies just mentioned.

Thus a word that is easily discriminated from other words (*Mississippi*) or one that appears in a highly constrained context may be identified at the level of salient word features. However, a word that is less easily discriminated from other words must be processed more fully, particularly when it appears in an ambiguous or uncertain context or when presented in isolation. In such instances, discrimination may ultimately take place at the letter level (*mean–meal; casual–causal*), letter feature level (*bad–dad*), or letter cluster level (*batter–bather*) but might well involve detailed processing at all of these levels, which becomes especially probable with polysyllabic words.

The level at which a word is processed also depends on the nature of the perceiver's task, a point initially emphasized by Gibson (1971) and later reemphasized by Drewnowski and Healy (1977). Thus when reading for meaning, words and phrases are in focal attention; when proofreading, a deliberate attempt is made to process at the letter and letter feature levels. I am, of course, congenial to Drewnowski and Healy's suggestion that processing at all levels is initiated simultaneously and that processing of higher level units may be completed before processing of lower level units. This is in contrast to Gibson's (1971) suggestion that processing at one level precludes processing at another level. One reason that the former conceptualization is more appealing is that it is consonant with the dual access theories of word identification, a formulation that has a good deal of currency in the literature and one that I believe more accurately reflects the complexity and variability of the word identification process than do the single access theories currently available.

We have, at last, come to the end of this long discourse. My major purpose was to question the long-held notion that there is a single unit of perception in word identification. The dynamic interaction of contextual factors, stimulus characteristics, and individual difference variables were found to be important determinants of the processing units utilized by the perceiver in identifying printed words, and it became evident that the effect of each on the identification process is in need of greater exploration, though some have had much more extensive treatment in the literature than others. The skill of the reader has been the most neglected, but the results from recent work done in this area of inquiry provide highly suggestive evidence that individuals differ significantly in the strategies they employ in word processing and thus in the mental representations of word constituents that they ultimately incorporate. Indeed, the observation of such differences is perhaps the most compelling evidence garnered in this review for the concept of multilevel coding and thus the relativity of the unit of perception.

Finally, the need for a model of word identification with greater ecological validity should be evident, and I have attempted to suggest ways in which this might be accomplished. Certain of the models currently available have considerable promise in this regard, but, as I have indicated, they are limited in a variety of respects, the most general being their failure to consider the variable and dynamic nature of word processing as well as the individual differences that may influence this enterprise. This chapter was written to highlight the importance of considering these variables in theory building, and I hope it has accomplished its intended purpose.

ACKNOWLEDGMENTS

The author is indebted to Cynthia Parry, whose helpful comments assisted greatly in the preparation of this chapter. Thanks are due also to Veronica Carney and Melinda Taylor, who typed and helped to edit far too many revisions of the chapter. I wish to acknowledge also the fact that a good deal of the research conducted by the author, and reported herein, was supported by a research grant (5R01HDO965803) from the National Institute of Child Health and Human Development. The chapter itself was also supported, in part, by this same grant.

REFERENCES

Aderman, D., & Smith, E. E. Expectancy as a determinant of functional units in perceptual recognition. *Cognitive Psychology*, 1971, *2*, 117-129.

Anderson, J. A. A theory for the recognition of items from short memorized lists. *Psychological Review*, 1973, *80*, 417-438.

Appelman, I. B. The word superiority effect: Dependence on short-term memory factors. *Memory and Cognition*, 1976, *4*, 156-161.

Atkinson, R. C., Herrmann, D. J., & Wescourt, K. T. Search processes in recognition memory. In R. L. Solso (Ed.), *Theories in cognitive psychology*. Hillsdale, N.J.: Lawrence Erlbaum Associates, 1974.

Bakker, D. J. *Temporal order in disturbed reading—Developmental and neuropsychological aspects in normal and reading-retarded children*. Rotterdam: Rotterdam University Press, 1972.

Baron, J. Phonemic stage is not necessary for reading. *Quarterly Journal of Experimental Psychology*, 1973, *25*, 241-246.

Baron, J. Mechanisms for pronouncing printed words: Use and acquisition. In D. LaBerge & S. J. Samuels (Eds.), *Basic processes in reading: Perception and comprehension*. Hillsdale, N.J.: Lawrence Erlbaum Associates, 1977.

Baron, J. The word-superiority effect. In W. K. Estes (Ed.), *Handbook of learning and cognitive processes* (Vol. 6). Hillsdale, N.J.: Lawrence Erlbaum Associates, 1978.

Baron, J. Orthographic and word specific mechanisms in children's reading of words. *Child Development*, 1979, *50*, 60-72.

Baron, J., & Strawson, C. Orthographic and word-specific mechanisms in reading words aloud. *Journal of Experimental Psychology: Human Perception and Performance*, 1976, *2*, 386-393.

Baron, J., & Thurston, I. An analysis of the word-superiority effect. *Cognitive Psychology*, 1973, *4*, 207-228.

Barron, R. W., & Pittenger, J. B. The effect of orthographic structure and lexical meaning on same-different judgments. *Quarterly Journal of Experimental Psychology*, 1974, *26*, 566-581.

Becker, C. A., Schvaneveldt, R. W., & Gomez, L. M. *Semantic, graphemic and phonetic factors in word recognition*. Paper presented at the Psychonomic Society Meeting, St. Louis, 1973.

Begg, I., & Clark, J. M. Contextual imagery in meaning and memory. *Memory and Cognition*, 1975, *3*, 117-122.

Begg, I., Upfold, D., & Wilton, T. D. Imagery in verbal communication. *Journal of Mental Imagery*, 1978, *2*, 165-186.

Bender, L. A. Specific reading disability as a maturational lag. *Bulletin of the Orton Society*, 1957, *7*, 9-18.

Biemiller, A. The development of the use of graphic and contextual information as children learn to read. *Reading Research Quarterly*, 1970, *6*, 75-96.

Birch, H. Dyslexia and maturation of visual function. In J. Money (Ed.), *Reading disability: Progress and research needs in dyslexia*. Baltimore: Johns Hopkins Press, 1962.

Bjork, E. L., & Estes, W. K. Letter identification in relation to linguistic context and masking conditions. *Memory and Cognition*, 1973, *1*, 217-223.

Boder, E. Developmental dyslexia: A diagnostic screening procedure based on three characteristic patterns of reading and spelling. In B. Bateman (Ed.), *Learning disorders*. Seattle: Special Child Pub., 1971.

Boder, E. Developmental dyslexia: A diagnostic approach based on three atypical reading-spelling patterns. *Developmental Medicine and Child Neurology*, 1973, *15*, 663-687.

Bouma, H. Visual recognition of isolated lower-case letters. *Vision Research*, 1971, *11*, 459-474.

Bradshaw, J. L. Three interrelated problems in reading: A review. *Memory and Cognition*, 1975, *3*, 123-134.

Brewer, W. F. Is reading a letter-by-letter process? In J. F. Kavanagh & I. G. Mattingly (Eds.), *Language by ear and by eye: The relationships between speech and reading*. Cambridge, Mass.: MIT Press, 1972.

Brittain, M. M. Inflectional performance and early reading achievement. *Reading Research Quarterly*, 1970, *6*, 34-48.

Broadbent, D. E. The word frequency effect and response bias. *Psychological Review*, 1967, *74*, 1-15.

Brooks, L. Visual pattern in fluent word identification. In A. S. Reber & D. L. Scarborough (Eds.), *Toward a psychology of reading*. Hillsdale, N.J.: Lawrence Erlbaum Associates, 1977.

Brown, C. R., & Rubenstein, H. Test of response bias explanation of word-frequency effect. *Science*, 1961, *133*, 280-281.

Bruner, J. S. On perceptual readiness. *Psychological Review*, 1957, *64*, 123-152.

Butler, B., & Hains, S. Individual differences in word recognition latency. *Memory and Cognition*, 1979, *7*, 68-76.

Calfee, R. C. Memory and cognitive skills in reading acquisition. In D. D. Duane & M. B. Rawson (Eds.), *Reading, perception and language*. Baltimore: York Press, 1975.

Calfee, R. C. Assessment of independent reading skills: Basic research and practical applications. In A. S. Reber & D. L. Scarborough (Eds.), *Toward a psychology of reading*. Hillsdale, N.J.: Lawrence Erlbaum Associates, 1977.

Calfee, R. C., Venezky, R. L., & Chapman, R. S. *Pronunciation of synthetic words with predictable and unpredictable letter-sound correspondences* (Technical Report No. 71). Wisconsin Research and Development Center for Cognitive Learning, 1969.

Camp, B. W., & Dolcourt, J. L. Reading and spelling in good and poor readers. *Journal of Learning Disabilities*, 1977, *10*, 300-307.

Carr, T. C., Lehmkuhle, S. W., Kottas, B., Astor-Stetson, E. C., & Arnold, D. Target position and practice in the identification of letters in varying contexts: A word superiority effect. *Perception and Psychophysics*, 1976, *19*, 412-416.

Carroll, J. B., & White, M. N. Word frequency and age of acquisition as determiners of picture-naming latency. *Quarterly Journal of Experimental Psychology*, 1973, *24*, 85-95.

Cattell, J. McK. The time it takes to see and name objects. *Mind*, 1886, *11*, 63-65. (a)

Cattell, J. McK. The time taken up by cerebral operations. *Mind*, 1886, *11*, 377-392. (b)

Chall, J. *Learning to read—The great debate*. New York: McGraw-Hill, 1967.

Chomsky, C. Reading, writing, and phonology. *Harvard Educational Review*, 1970, *40*, 287-309.

Chomsky, N., & Halle, M. *The sound pattern of English.* New York: Harper and Row, 1968.
Collins, A., & Loftus, E. A spreading activation theory of semantic processing. *Psychological Review,* 1975, *82,* 407-428.
Collins, A. M., & Quillian, M. R. Does category size affect categorization time? *Journal of Verbal Learning and Verbal Behavior,* 1970, *9,* 432-438.
Coltheart, M., Davelaar, E., Jonasson, J., & Besner, D. Access to the internal lexicon. In S. Dornic (Ed.), *Attention and performance VI.* New York: Academic Press, 1977.
Conrad, R. Acoustic confusions in immediate memory. *British Journal of Psychology,* 1964, *55,* 75-84.
Corcoran, D. W. J. An acoustic factor in letter cancellation. *Nature,* 1966, *210,* 658.
Corcoran, D. W., & Weening, D. L. Acoustic factors in visual speech. *Quarterly Journal of Experimental Psychology,* 1968, *20,* 83-85.
Corkin, S. Serial-ordering deficits in inferior readers. *Neuropsychologia,* 1974, *12,* 347-354.
Cosky, M. J. The role of letter recognition in word recognition. *Memory and Cognition,* 1976, *4,* 207-209.
Cosky, M. J. Word length effects in word recognition: Evidence from word naming latency data. Unpublished manuscript, St. Olaf College, 1977.
Cromer, W., & Wiener, M. Idiosyncratic response patterns among good and poor readers. *Journal of Consulting Psychology,* 1966, *30,* 1-10.
Davelaar, E., Coltheart, M., Besner, D., & Jonasson, J. Phonological recoding and lexical access. *Memory and Cognition,* 1978, *6,* 391-402.
Davidson, H. P. A study of the confusing letters B, D, P, and Q. *Journal of Genetic Psychology,* 1935, *47,* 458-468.
de Hirsch, K., Jansky, J., & Langford, W. *Predicting reading failure.* New York: Harper and Row, 1966.
Denckla, M. B., & Rudel, R. Naming of pictured objects by dyslexic and other learning disabled children. *Brain and Language,* 1976, *39,* 1-15. (a)
Denckla, M. B., & Rudel, R. Rapid 'automatized' naming (R.A.N.): Dyslexia differentiated from other learning disabilities. *Neuropsychologia,* 1976, *14,* 471-479. (b)
Doehring, D. G. Acquisition of rapid reading responses. *Monographs of the Society for Research in Child Development,* 1976, *41,* 1-54.
Drewnowski, A. Detection errors on the word *the*: Evidence for the acquisition of reading levels. *Memory and Cognition,* 1978, *6,* 403-409.
Drewnowski, A., & Healy, A. F. Detection errors on *the* and *and*: Evidence for reading units larger than the word. *Memory and Cognition,* 1977, *5,* 636-647.
Dunn-Rankin, P. The similarity of lower-case letters of the English alphabet. *Journal of Verbal Learning and Verbal Behavior,* 1968, *7,* 990-995.
Ehri, L. The role of orthographic images in learning printed words. In J. F. Kavanagh & R. L. Venezky (Eds.), *Orthography, reading, and dyslexia.* Baltimore: University Park Press, 1980.
Ehri, L. C., & Roberts, K. T. Do beginners learn printed words better in context or in isolation? *Child Development,* 1979, *50,* 675-685.
Ehri, L. C., & Wilce, L. S. Do beginners learn to read function words better in sentences or in lists? *Reading Research Quarterly,* 1980, *15,* 451-476.
Eichelman, W. H. Familiarity effects in the simultaneous matching task. *Journal of Experimental Psychology,* 1970, *86,* 275-282.
Erdmann, B., & Dodge, R. *Psychologische Untersuchungen uber das Lesen.* Halle: M. Niemeyer, 1898.
Eriksen, C. W., Pollack, M. D., & Montague, W. E. Implicit speech: Mechanism in perceptual coding. *Journal of Experimental Psychology,* 1970, *84,* 502-507.
Estes, W. K. An associative basis for coding and organization in memory. In A. W. Melton & E. Martin (Eds.), *Coding processes in human memory.* Washington, D.C.: Wintons, 1972.

Estes, W. K. The locus of inferential and perceptual processes in letter identification. *Journal of Experimental Psychology: General*, 1975, *104*, 122-145. (a)

Estes, W. K. Memory, perception, and decision in letter identification. In R. L. Solso (Ed.), *Information processing and cognition: The Loyola Symposium*. Hillsdale, N.J.: Lawrence Erlbaum Associates, 1975. (b)

Estes, W. K. On the interaction of perception and memory in reading. In D. LaBerge & S. J. Samuels (Eds.), *Basic processes in reading*. Hillsdale, N.J.: Lawrence Erlbaum Associates, 1977.

Estes, W. K., Allmeyer, D. H., & Reder, S. Serial position functions for letter identification at brief and extended exposure durations. *Perception and Psychophysics*, 1976, *19*, 1-15.

Estes, W. K., Bjork, E. L., & Skaar, E. Detection of single letter and letters in words with changing versus unchanging mask characters. *Bulletin of the Psychonomic Society*, 1974, *3*, 201-203.

Feigenbaum, E. A. The simulation of verbal learning behavior. In E. A. Feigenbaum & J. Feldman (Eds.), *Computers and thought*. New York: McGraw-Hill, 1963.

Forster, K. I. Accessing the mental lexicon. In R. J. Wales & E. Walker (Eds.), *New approaches to language mechanisms*. Amsterdam: North-Holland Pub., 1976.

Forster, K. I. Levels of processing and the structure of the language processor. In W. E. Cooper & E. C. Walker (Eds.), *Sentence processing: Psycholinguistic studies presented to Merrill Garrett*. Hillsdale, N.J.: Lawrence Erlbaum Associates, 1979.

Forster, K. I., & Chambers, S. M. Lexical access and naming time. *Journal of Verbal Learning and Verbal Behavior*, 1973, *12*, 627-635.

Frederiksen, J. F., & Kroll, J. F. Spelling and sound: Approaches to the internal lexicon. *Journal of Experimental Psychology: Human Perception and Performance*, 1976, *2*, 361-379.

Frith, U. From print to meaning and from print to sound or how to read without knowing how to spell. *Visible Language*, 1978, *12*, 43-54.

Frith, U. *Cognitive processes in spelling*. New York: Academic Press, 1980.

Fry, M. A., Johnson, C. S., & Muehl, S. Oral language production in relation to reading achievement among select second graders. In D. J. Bakker & P. Satz (Eds.), *Specific reading disability: Advances in theory and method*. Rotterdam: Rotterdam University Press, 1970.

Gibson, E. J. On the perception of words. *American Journal of Psychology*, 1964, *77*, 667-669.

Gibson, E. J. Learning to read. *Science*, 1965, *148*, 1066-1072.

Gibson, E. J. *Principles of perceptual learning and development*. New York: Appleton-Century-Crofts, 1969.

Gibson, E. J. The ontogeny of reading. *American Psychologist*, 1970, *25*, 136-143.

Gibson, E. J. Perceptual learning and the theory of word perception. *Cognitive Psychology*, 1971, *2*, 351-368.

Gibson, E. J. How perception really develops: A view from outside the network. In D. LaBerge & S. J. Samuels (Eds.), *Basic processes in reading: Perception and comprehension*. Hillsdale, N.J.: Lawrence Erlbaum Associates, 1977.

Gibson, E. J., Bishop, C. H., Schiff, W., & Smith, J. Comparison of meaningfulness and pronounceability as grouping principles in the perception and retention of verbal material. *Journal of Experimental Psychology*, 1964, *67*, 173-182.

Gibson, E. J., Gibson, J. J., Pick, A. D., & Osser, H. A developmental study of the discrimination of letter-like forms. *Journal of Comparative and Physiological Psychology*, 1962, *55*, 897-906.

Gibson, E. J., & Guinet, L. Perception of inflections of brief visual presentations of words. *Journal of Verbal Learning and Verbal Behavior*, 1971, *10*, 182-189.

Gibson, E. J., & Levin, H. *The psychology of reading*. Cambridge, Mass.: MIT Press, 1975.

Gibson, E. J., Osser, H., & Pick, A. D. A study of the development of grapheme-phoneme correspondences. *Journal of Verbal Learning and Verbal Behavior*, 1963, *2*, 142-146.

Gibson, E. J., Osser, H., Schiff, W., & Smith, J. An analysis of critical features of letters, tested by a confusion matrix. In a basic research program on reading. Cooperative Research Project No. 639. Washington, D.C.: U.S. Office of Education, 1963.

Gibson, E. J., Pick, A., Osser, H., & Hammond, M. The role of grapheme-phoneme correspondence in the perception of words. *American Journal of Psychology,* 1962, *75,* 554-570.

Gibson, E. J., Shurcliff, A., & Yonas, A. Utilization of spelling patterns by deaf and hearing subjects. In H. Levin & J. P. Williams (Eds.), *Basic studies in reading.* New York: Basic Books, 1970.

Glanzer, M., & Cunitz, A. R. Two storage mechanisms in free recall. *Journal of Verbal Learning and Verbal Behavior,* 1966, *5,* 351-360.

Glushko, R. J. The organization and activation of orthographic knowledge in reading aloud. *Journal of Experimental Psychology: Human Perception and Performance,* 1979, *5,* 674-691.

Goldiamond, I., & Hawkins, W. F. Vexlerversuch: The log relationship between word-frequency and recognition obtained in the absence of stimulus words. *Journal of Experimental Psychology,* 1958, *56,* 457-463.

Golinkoff, R. *Children's discrimination of English spelling patterns with redundant auditory information.* Paper presented to American Education Research Association, New Orleans, February 1974.

Golinkoff, R. M., & Rosinski, R. R. Decoding, semantic processing, and reading comprehension skill. *Child Development,* 1976, *47,* 252-258.

Goodman, K. S. Psycholinguistic universals in the reading process. *Journal of Typographic Research,* 1970, *4,* 103-110.

Gough, P. B. One second of reading. In J. F. Kavanagh & I. G. Mattingly (Eds.), *Language by ear and by eye: The relationships between speech and reading.* Cambridge, Mass.: MIT Press, 1972.

Gough, P. B., Alford, J. A., & Holley-Wilcox, P. *Words and contexts.* Paper presented at the National Reading Conference, St. Petersburg Beach, November 1978.

Gough, P. B., & Cosky, M. J. One second of reading again. In N. J. Castellan, D. B. Pisoni, & G. R. Potts (Eds.), *Cognitive theory* (Vol. 2). Hillsdale, N.J.: Lawrence Erlbaum Associates, 1977.

Gough, P. B., & Stewart, W. *Word vs. nonword discrimination latency.* Paper presented at the Midwestern Psychological Association, 1970.

Greenberg, S. N., & Krueger, L. E. Limitations on the word superiority effect with a fixed target set. *Bulletin of the Psychonomic Society,* 1980, *15,* 25-28.

Guthrie, J. T. Reading comprehension and syntactic responses in good and poor readers. *Journal of Educational Psychology,* 1973, *65,* 294-299.

Hansen, D., & Rogers, T. S. An exploration of psycholinguistic units in initial reading. In *Proceedings of the symposium on the psycholinguistic nature of the reading process.* Detroit: Wayne State University, 1965.

Hardyck, C. D., & Petrinovich, L. F. Subvocal speech and comprehension as a function of the difficulty level of reading material. *Journal of Verbal Learning and Verbal Behavior,* 1970, *9,* 642-647.

Hartley, R. N. Effects of list types and cues on the learning of word lists. *Reading Research Quarterly,* 1970, *6,* 97-121.

Healy, A. F. Detection errors on the word *the*: Evidence for reading units larger than letters. *Journal of Experimental Psychology: Human Perception and Performance,* 1976, *2,* 235-242.

Helfgott, J. Phonemic segmentation and blending skills of kindergarten children: Implications for beginning reading acquisition. *Contemporary Educational Psychology,* 1976, *1,* 157-169.

Henderson, L. Do words conceal their component letters? A critique of Johnson (1975) on the visual perception of words. *Journal of Verbal Learning and Verbal Behavior,* 1975, *14,* 648-650.

Henderson, L. *Orthography and word recognition.* London: Academic Press, in press. [Cited in R. W. Barron, Development of visual word recognition: A review. To appear in T. G. Waller & G. E. MacKinnon (Eds.), *Reading research: Advances in theory and practice* (Vol. 2). New York: Academic Press, 1981].

Herman, L. M., & Kantowitz, B. H. The psychological refractory period effect: Only half the double stimulation story? *Psychological Bulletin,* 1970, *73,* 74-88.

Hermann, K. *Reading disability.* Copenhagen: Munksgaard, 1959.
Howes, D. H., & Solomon, R. L. Visual duration threshold as a function of word-probability. *Journal of Experimental Psychology,* 1951, *41,* 401-410.
Huey, E. B. *The psychology and pedogogy of reading.* New York: Macmillan, 1908. (Reprinted, Cambridge, Mass.: MIT Press, 1968.)
Jackson, M. D., & McClelland, J. L. Sensory and cognitive determinants of reading speed. *Journal of Verbal Learning and Verbal Behavior,* 1975, *14,* 565-574.
Jakobson, R., Fant, C. G. M., & Halle, M. *Preliminaries to speech analysis: The distinctive features and their correlates.* Cambridge, Mass.: MIT Press, 1961.
Jansky, J., & de Hirsch, K. *Preventing reading failure—Prediction, diagnosis, intervention.* New York: Harper and Row, 1972.
Johnson, D., & Myklebust, H. *Learning disabilities: Educational principles and practices.* New York: Grune and Stratton, 1967.
Johnson, N. F. On the function of letters in word identification: Some data and a preliminary model. *Journal of Verbal Learning and Verbal Behavior,* 1975, *14,* 17-29.
Johnson, N. F. A pattern-unit model of word identification. In D. LaBerge & S. J. Samuels (Eds.), *Basic processes in reading: Perception and comprehension.* Hillsdale, N.J.: Lawrence Erlbaum Associates, 1977.
Johnson, N. F. The role of letters in word identification: A test of the pattern-unit model. *Memory and Cognition,* 1979, *7,* 496-504.
Johnston, J. C., & McClelland, J. L. Visual factors in word perception. *Perception and Psychophysics,* 1973, *14,* 365-370.
Johnston, J. C., & McClelland, J. L. Perception of letters in words: Seek not and ye shall find. *Science,* 1974, *184,* 1192-1194.
Kahneman, D., & Henik, A. *Effects of visual grouping on immediate recall and selective attention.* Paper presented at Attention and Performance VI, Stockholm, July 1975.
Kavanagh, J. F., & Mattingly, I. G. *Language by ear and by eye.* Cambridge, Mass.: MIT Press, 1972.
Kinsbourne, M., & Warrington, E. K. Developmental factors in reading and writing backwardness. In J. Money (Ed.), *The disabled reader: Education of the dyslexic child.* Baltimore: Johns Hopkins Press, 1966.
Klapp, S. T. Implicit speech inferred from response latencies in same-different decisions. *Journal of Experimental Psychology,* 1971, *91,* 262-267.
Klapp, S. T., Anderson, W. G., & Berrian, R. W. Implicit speech in reading reconsidered. *Journal of Experimental Psychology,* 1973, *100,* 368-374.
Kleiman, G. M. Speech recoding in reading. *Journal of Verbal Learning and Verbal Behavior,* 1975, *14,* 323-340.
Kohler, W. *Gestalt psychology.* New York: Horace Liveright, 1929.
Kolers, P. A. Three stages of reading. In H. Levin & J. P. Williams (Eds.), *Basic studies on reading.* New York: Basic Books, 1970.
Kolers, P. A. Pattern-analyzing disability in poor readers. *Developmental Psychology,* 1975, *11,* 282-290.
Krueger, L. E. Search time in a redundant visual display. *Journal of Experimental Psychology,* 1970, *83,* 391-399.
Krueger, L. E., Keen, R. H., & Rublevich, B. Letter search through words and nonwords by adults and fourth-grade children. *Journal of Experimental Psychology,* 1974, *102,* 845-849.
Krueger, L. E., & Weiss, M. E. Letter search through words and nonwords: The effect of fixed, absent, or mutilated targets. *Memory and Cognition,* 1976, *4,* 200-206.
Kucera, H., & Francis, W. N. *Computational analysis of present-day American English.* Providence, R.I.: Brown University Press, 1967.
LaBerge, D. *Unitizing and automaticity in reading.* Invited address to the American Psychological Association Convention, San Francisco, August 1977.

LaBerge, D. The perception of units in beginning reading. In L. B. Resnick & P. A. Weaver (Eds.), *Theory and practice of beginning reading instruction*. Hillsdale, N.J.: Lawrence Erlbaum Associates, 1979.
LaBerge, D., & Samuels, S. J. Toward a theory of automatic information processing in reading. *Cognitive Psychology*, 1974, *6*, 293-323.
Levy, B. A. Vocalization and suppression effects in sentence memory. *Journal of Verbal Learning and Verbal Behavior*, 1975, *14*, 304-316.
Liberman, A. M., Ingram, F., Fisher, L., Delattre, P. C., & Cooper, F. S. Minimal rules for synthesizing speech. *Journal of the Acoustical Society of America*, 1959, *31*, 1490-1499.
Liberman, I. Y., Shankweiler, D., Fischer, F. W., & Carter, B. Explicit syllable and phoneme segmentation in the young child. *Journal of Experimental Child Psychology*, 1974, *18*, 201-212.
Liberman, I. Y., Shankweiler, D., Liberman, A. M., Fowler, C., & Fischer, F. W. Phonetic segmentation and recoding in the beginning reader. In A. S. Reber & D. L. Scarborough (Eds.), *Toward a psychology of reading—The proceedings of the CUNY conferences*. Hillsdale, N.J.: Lawrence Erlbaum Associates, 1977.
Lockhead, G. R., & Crist, W. B. Making letters distinctive. *Journal of Educational Psychology*, 1980, *72*, 483-493.
Lundberg, J., & Torneus, M. Nonreaders' awareness of the basic relationship between spoken and written words. *Journal of Experimental Child Psychology*, 1978, *25*, 404-412.
MacKay, D. G. The structure of words and syllables: Evidence from errors in speech. *Cognitive Psychology*, 1972, *3*, 210-227.
Manelis, L. The effect of meaningfulness on tachistoscopic word perception. *Perception and Psychophysics*, 1974, *16*, 182-192.
Marchbanks, G., & Levin, H. Cues by which children recognize words. *Journal of Educational Psychology*, 1965, *56*, 57-61.
Marmurek, H. H. C. Processing letters in words at different levels. *Memory and Cognition*, 1977, *5*, 67-72.
Marshall, J. C. Neurophychological aspects of orthographic representation. In R. J. Wales & E. Walker (Eds.), *New approaches to language mechanisms*. Amsterdam: North-Holland Pub., 1976, 109-131.
Marshall, J. C., & Newcombe, F. Patterns of paralexia: A psycholinguistic approach. *Journal of Psycholinguistic Research*, 1973, *2*, 175-199.
Mason, M. Reading ability and letter search time: Effects of orthographic structure defined by single-letter positional frequency. *Journal of Experimental Psychology: General*, 1975, *104*, 146-166.
Mason, M. From print to sound in mature readers as a function of reading ability and two forms of orthographic regularity. *Memory and Cognition*, 1978, *6*, 568-581.
Massaro, D. W. Perception of letters, words, and nonwords. *Journal of Experimental Psychology*, 1973, *100*, 349-353.
Massaro, D. W. *Understanding language: An information-processing analysis of speech, perception, reading, and psycholinguistics*. New York: Academic Press, 1975.
Massaro, D. W. Letter information and orthographic context in word perception. *Journal of Experimental Psychology: Human Perception and Performance*, 1979, *5*, 595-609.
Massaro, D. W., & Klitzke, D. Letters are functional in word identification. *Memory and Cognition*, 1977, *5*, 292-298.
Massaro, D. W., Venezky, R. L., & Taylor, G. A. Orthographic regularity, positional frequency, and visual processing of letter strings. *Journal of Experimental Psychology: General*, 1979, *108*, 107-124.
Mayzner, M. S., & Tresselt, M. E. Tables of single-letter and digram frequency counts for various word-length and letter-position combinations. *Psychonomic Science Monograph Supplements*, 1965, *1*, 13-32.

McCormick, C., & Samuels, S. J. Word recognition by second graders: The unit of perception and interrelationships among accuracy, latency, and comprehension. Unpublished manuscript, University of Minnesota, 1978.

McGinnies, E., Comer, P., & Lacy, O. L. Visual-recognition thresholds as a function of word length and word frequency. *Journal of Experimental Psychology*, 1952, *44*, 65-69.

Meyer, D. E., & Ruddy, M. G. *Lexical-memory retrieval based on graphemic and phonemic representations of printed words.* Paper presented at the meeting of the Psychonomic Society, St. Louis, November 1973.

Meyer, D. E., Schvaneveldt, R. W., & Ruddy, M. G. *Activation of lexical memory.* Paper presented at the meeting of the Psychonomic Society, St. Louis, 1972.

Meyer, D. E., Schvaneveldt, R. W., & Ruddy, M. G. Functions of graphemic and phonemic codes in visual word-recognition. *Memory and Cognition*, 1974, *2*, 309-321.

Meyer, D. E., Schvaneveldt, R. W., & Ruddy, M. G. Loci of contextual effects on visual word-recognition. In P. M. A. Rabbitt & S. Dornic (Eds.), *Attention and performance V*. New York: Academic Press, 1975.

Mezrich, J. J. The word superiority effect in brief visual displays: Elimination by vocalization. *Perception and Psychophysics*, 1973, *13*, 45-48.

Miller, G. A., Bruner, J., & Postman, L. Familiarity of letter sequences and tachistoscopic identification. *Journal of Genetic Psychology*, 1954, *50*, 129-139.

Monroe, M. *Children who cannot read.* Chicago: University of Chicago Press, 1932.

Morton, J. The effects of context on the visual duration thresholds for words. *British Journal of Psychology*, 1964, *55*, 165-180.

Morton, J. A retest of the response-bias explanation of the word-frequency effect. *British Journal of Mathematical and Statistical Psychology*, 1968, *21*, 21-33.

Morton, J. Interaction of information in word recognition. *Psychological Review*, 1969, *76*, 165-178.

Murrell, G. A., & Morton, J. Word recognition and morphemic structure. *Journal of Experimental Psychology*, 1974, *102*, 963-968.

Neisser, A. *Cognitive psychology.* New York: Appleton-Century-Crofts, 1967.

Newbigging, P. L. The perceptual reintegration of frequent and infrequent words. *Canadian Journal of Psychology*, 1961, *15*, 123-132.

Novik, N., & Katz, L. High-speed visual scanning of words and non-words. *Journal of Experimental Psychology*, 1971, *91*, 350-353.

Orton, S. T. "Word-blindness" in school children. *Archives of Neurology and Psychiatry*, 1925, *14*, 581-615.

Patterson, K., & Marcel, A. J. Aphasia, dyslexia, and the phonological coding of written words. *Quarterly Journal of Experimental Psychology*, 1977, *29*, 307-318.

Pearson, P. D., & Studt, A. Effects of word frequency and contextual richness on children's word identification abilities. *Journal of Educational Psychology*, 1975, *67*, 89-95.

Perfetti, C. A., & Goldman, S. R. Discourse memory and reading comprehension skill. *Journal of Verbal Learning and Verbal Behavior*, 1976, *14*, 33-42.

Perfetti, C. A., Goldman, S. R., & Hogaboam, T. W. Reading skill and the identification of words in discourse context. *Memory and Cognition*, 1979, *7*, 273-282.

Perfetti, C. A., & Hogaboam, T. W. The relationship between single word decoding and reading comprehension skill. *Journal of Educational Psychology*, 1975, *67*, 461-469.

Perfetti, C. A., & Lesgold, A. M. Discourse comprehension and sources of individual differences. In M. A. Just & P. A. Carpenter (Eds.), *Cognitive processes in comprehension*. Hillsdale, N.J.: Lawrence Erlbaum Associates, 1978.

Perfetti, C. A., & Lesgold, A. M. Coding and comprehension in skilled reading and implication for reading instruction. In L. B. Resnick & P. A. Weaver (Eds.), *Theory and practice of early reading*, Vol. 1. Hillsdale, N.J.: Lawrence Erlbaum Associates, 1979.

Perfetti, C. A., & Roth, S. Some of the interactive processes in reading and their role in reading skill. In A. M. Lesgold & C. A. Perfetti (Eds.), *Interactive process in reading*. Hillsdale, N.J.: Lawrence Erlbaum Associates, in press.

Petersen, R. J., & LaBerge, D. Contextual control of letter perception. *Memory and Cognition*, 1977, *5*, 205-213.

Pierce, J. R., & Karlin, J. E. Reading rates and the information rate of a human channel. *Bell System Technical Journal*, 1957, *36*, 497-516.

Pillsbury, W. B. A study in apperception. *American Journal of Psychology*, 1897, *8*, 315-393.

Pollatsek, A., Well, A. D., & Schindler, R. M. Familiarity affects visual processing of words. *Journal of Experimental Psychology: Human Perception and Performance*, 1975, *1*, 328-338.

Postman, L., & Adis-Castro, G. Psychophysical methods in the study of word recognition. *Science*, 1957, *125*, 193-194.

Purcell, D. G., Stanovich, K. E., & Spector, A. Visual angle and the word superiority effect. *Memory and Cognition*, 1978, *6*, 3-8.

Raulin, A. E. *Study of the relationship between silent reading and oral vocabulary of elementary school children*. Unpublished doctoral dissertation, New York University, 1962.

Ravenette, A. T. Vocabulary level and reading attainment. *British Journal of Educational Psychology*, 1961, *31*, 96.

Rayner, K., & Kaiser, J. S. Reading mutilated text. *Journal of Educational Psychology*, 1975, *67*, 301-306.

Reicher, G. Perceptual recognition as a function of meaningfulness of stimulus material. *Journal of Experimental Psychology*, 1969, *81*, 275-280.

Rohrman, N. L., & Gough, P. B. Forewarning, meaning, and semantic decision latency. *Psychonomic Science*, 1967, *9*, 217-218.

Rosinski, R. R., & Wheeler, K. E. Children's use of orthographic structure in word discrimination. *Psychonomic Science*, 1972, *26*, 97-98.

Ross, R. T. Optimal orders in the method of paired comparisons. *Journal of Experimental Psychology*, 1939, *25*, 414-424.

Rozin, P., Bressman, B., & Taft, M. Do children understand the basic relationship between speech and writing? The Mow-Motorcycle test. *Journal of Reading Behavior*, 1974, *6*, 327-334.

Rozin, P., & Gleitman, L. R. The structure and acquisition of reading 11: The reading process and the acquisition of the alphabetic principle. In A. S. Reber and D. L. Scarborough (Eds.), *Toward a psychology of reading—The proceedings of the CUNY conference*. Hillsdale, N.J.: Lawrence Erlbaum Associates, 1977.

Rubenstein, H., Lewis, S. S., & Rubenstein, M. A. Evidence for phonemic recoding in visual word recognition. *Journal of Verbal Learning and Verbal Behavior*, 1971, *10*, 645-657.

Rumelhart, D. E. A multicomponent theory of the perception of briefly exposed visual displays. *Journal of Mathematical Psychology*, 1970, *7*, 191-218.

Rumelhart, D. E. Toward an interactive model of reading. In S. Dornic (Ed.), *Attention and performance VI*. Hillsdale, N.J.: Lawrence Erlbaum Associates, 1977.

Rumelhart, D. E., & Siple, P. Process of recognizing tachistoscopically presented words. *Psychological Review*, 1974, *81*, 99-118.

Samuels, S. J. The effect of letter-names knowledge on learning to read. *American Educational Research Journal*, 1972, *1*, 65-74.

Samuels, S. J., Begy, G., & Chen, C. C. Comparison of word recognition speed and strategies of less skilled and more highly skilled readers. *Reading Research Quarterly*, 1975-1976, *1*, 73-86.

Samuels, S. J., LaBerge, D., & Bremer, C. *A developmental study of the unit of perceptual processing in word recognition*. Unpublished manuscript, University of Minnesota, 1977.

Schindler, R. M., Well, A. D., & Pollatsek, A. Effects of segmentation and expectancy on matching time for words and nonwords. *Journal of Experimental Psychology*, 1974, *103*, 107-111.

Shallice, T., & Warrington, E. K. Word recognition in a phonemic dyslexic patient. *Quarterly Journal of Experimental Psychology*, 1975, *27*, 187-199.

Shankweiler, D., & Liberman, A. M. Misreading: A search for causes. In J. F. Kavanagh & I. G. Mattingly (Eds.), *Language by ear and by eye: The relationships between speech and reading.* Cambridge, Mass.: MIT Press, 1972.

Shankweiler, D., & Liberman, I. Y. Exploring the relations between reading and speech. In R. M. Knights & D. J. Bakker (Eds.), *Neuropsychology of learning disorders: Theoretical approaches.* Baltimore: University Park Press, 1976.

Shannon, C. E. Prediction and entropy of printed English. *Bell Systems Technical Journal,* 1951, *30,* 50-64.

Shiffrin, R. M., & Gardner, G. T. Visual processing capacity and attentional control. *Journal of Experimental Psychology,* 1972, *93,* 72-82.

Sloboda, J. A. Decision times for word and letter search: A holistic word identification model examined. *Journal of Verbal Learning and Verbal Behavior,* 1976, *15,* 93-101.

Sloboda, J. A. The locus of the word-priority effect in a target-detection task. *Memory and Cognition,* 1977, *5,* 371-376.

Smith, E. E., & Haviland, S. E. Why words are perceived more accurately than nonwords: Interference vs. unitization. *Journal of Experimental Psychology,* 1972, *92,* 59-64.

Smith, E. E., & Spoehr, K. T. The perception of printed English: A theoretical perspective. In B. H. Kantowitz (Ed.), *Human information processing: Tutorials in performance and cognition.* Hillsdale, N.J.: Lawrence Erlbaum Associates, 1974.

Smith, F. The use of featural dependencies across letters in the visual identification of words. *Journal of Verbal Learning and Verbal Behavior,* 1969, *8,* 215-218.

Smith, F. *Understanding reading: A psycholinguistic analysis of reading and learning to read.* New York: Holt, Rinehart and Winston, 1971.

Smith, F., Lott, D., & Cronnell, B. The effect of type size and case alternation on word identification. *American Journal of Psychology,* 1969, *82,* 248-253.

Snowling, M. J. The development of grapheme-phoneme correspondence in normal and dyslexic readers. *Journal of Experimental Child Psychology,* 1980, *29,* 294-305.

Solomon, R. L., & Howes, D. H. Word frequency, personal values and visual duration threshold. *Psychological Review,* 1951, *58,* 256-270.

Spector, A., & Purcell, D. G. The word superiority effect: A comparison between restricted and unrestricted alternative set. *Perception and Psychophysics,* 1977, *21,* 323-328.

Sperling, G. A. Model for visual memory tasks. *Human Factors,* 1963, *5,* 19-31.

Sperling, G. A. Successive approximations to a model for short-term memory. *Acta Psychologica,* 1967, *27,* 285-292.

Sperling, G. A. Short-term memory, long-term memory, and scanning in the processing of visual information. In F. A. Young & D. B. Lindsley (Eds.), *The influence of early experience on visual information processing.* Washington, D.C.: National Academy of Sciences, 1970.

Spoehr, K. T. Phonological encoding in visual word recognition. *Journal of Verbal Learning and Verbal Behavior,* 1978, *17,* 127-141.

Spoehr, K. T., & Smith, E. E. The role of syllables in perceptual processing. *Cognitive Psychology,* 1973, *5,* 71-89.

Spoehr, K. T., & Smith, E. E. The role of orthographic and phonotactic rules in perceiving letter patterns. *Journal of Experimental Psychology: Human Perception and Performance,* 1975, *104,* 21-34.

Steiner, R., Wiener, M., & Cromer, W. Comprehension training and identification for poor and good readers. *Journal of Educational Psychology,* 1971, *62,* 506-513.

Stewart, M., James, C., & Gough, P. B. *Word recognition latency as a function of word length.* Paper presented at Midwestern Psychological Association, 1969.

Taft, M., & Forster, K. I. Lexical storage and retrieval of prefixed words. *Journal of Verbal Learning and Verbal Behavior,* 1975, *14,* 638-647.

Terry, P., Samuels, S. J., & LaBerge, D. The effects of letter degradation and letter spacing on word recognition. *Journal of Verbal Learning and Verbal Behavior,* 1976, *15,* 577-585.

Theios, J., & Muise, J. G. The word identification process in reading. In N. J. Castellan, D. B. Pisoni, & G. R. Potts (Eds.), *Cognitive theory* (Vol. 2). Hillsdale, N.J.: Lawrence Erlbaum Associates, 1977.

Thompson, M. C., & Massaro, D. W. The role of visual information and redundancy in reading. *Journal of Experimental Psychology,* 1973, *98,* 49–54.

Thorndike, E. L., & Lorge, I. *The teacher's word book of 30,000 words.* New York: Teacher's College, Columbia University, 1944.

Travers, J. R. The effects of forced serial processing on identification of words and random letter strings. *Cognitive Psychology,* 1973, *5,* 109–137.

Travers, J. R. Word recognition with forced serial processing: Effects of segment size and temporal order variation. *Perception and Psychophysics,* 1974, *16,* 35–42.

Travers, J. R. Forced serial processing of words and letter strings: A reexamination. *Perception and Psychophysics,* 1975, *18,* 447–452.

Treiman, R. A. *Children's ability to segment speech into syllables and phonemes as related to their reading ability.* Unpublished manuscript, Department of Psychology, Yale University, 1976.

Tulving, E., & Gold, C. Stimulus information and contextual information as determinants of tachistoscopic recognition of words. *Journal of Experimental Psychology,* 1963, *66,* 319–327.

Tulving, E., Mandler, G., & Baumal, R. Interaction of two sources of information in tachistoscopic word recognition. *Canadian Journal of Psychology,* 1964, *18,* 62–71.

Underwood, B. J., & Schultz, R. W. *Meaningfulness and verbal learning.* Philadelphia: Lippincott, 1960.

van der Molen, H., & Morton, J. Remembering plurals: Unit of coding and forms of coding during serial recall. *Cognition,* 1979, *7,* 35–47.

Vellutino, F. R. Alternative conceptualizations of dyslexia: Evidence in support of a verbal deficit hypothesis. *Harvard Educational Review,* 1977, *47,* 334–354.

Vellutino, F. R. *Dyslexia: Theory and research.* Cambridge, Mass.: MIT Press, 1979.

Vellutino, F. R. Dyslexia—Perceptual deficiency or perceptual inefficiency. In J. F. Kavanagh & R. L. Venezky (Eds.), *Orthography, reading, and dyslexia.* Baltimore: University Park Press, 1980.

Vellutino, F. R., DeSetto, L., & Steger, J. A. Categorical judgment and the Wepman test of auditory discrimination. *Journal of Speech and Hearing Disorders,* 1972, *37,* 252–257.

Vellutino, F. R., Pruzek, R. M., Steger, J. A., & Meshoulam, U. Immediate visual recall in poor and normal readers as a function of orthographic-linguistic familiarity. *Cortex,* 1973, *9,* 368–384.

Vellutino, F. R., & Scanlon, D. M. *The effect of phonemic segmentation training and response acquisition on coding ability in poor and normal readers.* Paper presented at the American Educational Research Association annual meeting, San Francisco, April 1979.

Vellutino, F. R., & Scanlon, D. M. *Free recall of concrete and abstract words in poor and normal readers.* Paper presented at the conference of Cognitive Processes in Reading, sponsored by the British Psychological Society, Exeter, England, March 1980.

Vellutino, F. R., Scanlon, D. M., DeSetto, L., & Pruzek, R. M. Developmental trends in the salience of meaning versus structural attributes of written words. *Psychological Research,* 1981, *43,* 1, Special Issue, edited by Uta Frith.

Vellutino, F. R., Smith, H., Steger, J. A., & Kaman, M. Reading disability: Age differences and the perceptual deficit hypothesis. *Child Development,* 1975, *46,* 487–493.

Vellutino, F. R., Steger, J. A., Kaman, M., & DeSetto, L. Visual form perception in deficient and normal readers as a function of age and orthographic linguistic familiarity. *Cortex,* 1975, *11,* 22–30.

Vellutino, F. R., Steger, J. A., & Kandel, G. Reading disability: An investigation of the perceptual deficit hypothesis. *Cortex,* 1972, *8,* 106–118.

Venezky, R. L. *The structure of English orthography.* The Hague: Mouton, 1970.

Venezky, R. L., Chapman, R. S., & Calfee, R. C. *The development of letter-sound generalizations from second through sixth grade* (Technical Report No. 231). Wisconsin Research and Development Center for Cognitive Learning, 1972.

Venezky, R. L., & Johnson, D. *The development of two letter-sound patterns in grades 1-3* (Technical Report No. 189). Wisconsin Research and Development Center for Cognitive Learning, 1972.

Vogel, S. A. Syntactic abilities in normal and dyslexic children. *Journal of Learning Disabilities,* 1974, *7,* 103-109.

Waller, T. G. Children's recognition memory for written sentences: A comparison of good and poor readers. *Child Development,* 1976, *47,* 90-95.

Weber, R. M. First graders' use of grammatical context in reading. In H. Levin & J. P. Williams (Eds.), *Basic studies in reading.* New York: Basic Books, 1970.

Well, A. D., Pollatsek, A., & Schindler, R. M. *Same* and *different* judgments of words and nonwords. *Perception and Psychophysics,* 1975, *17,* 511-520.

Wepman, J. M. Auditory discrimination, speech, and reading. *The Elementary School Journal,* 1960, *9,* 325-333.

Wepman, J. M. The interrelationships of hearing, speech, and reading. *The Reading Teacher,* 1961, *14,* 245-247.

Wertheimer, M. Principles of perceptual organization. *Psychologische Forschung,* 1923, *4,* 321-350. Translated and abridged in D. D. Beardslee & M. Wertheimer (Eds.), *Readings in perception.* New York: Van Nostrand, 1958.

Wheeler, D. D. Processes in word recognition. *Cognitive Psychology,* 1970, *1,* 59-85.

Wiig, E. H., Semel, M. S., & Crouse, M. B. The use of English morphology by high-risk and learning disabled children. *Journal of Learning Disabilities,* 1973, *6,* 457-465.

Wolf, M. The word-retrieval process and reading in children and aphasics. In K. Nelson (Ed.), *Children language* (Vol. III). New York: Gardner Press, in press.

Zifcak, M. *Phonological awareness and reading acquisition in first grade children.* Unpublished doctoral dissertation, University of Connecticut, 1976.

3 Psycholinguistic Processes in Writing

John B. Black
Yale University

INTRODUCTION

Recently there has been a surge of interest in studying the basic psychological processes involved in composing written discourse. In part, this new interest is motivated by a "writing crisis" that the news media declared after a National Assessment of Educational Progress (1975) study reported a decline in the writing performance of 13- and 17-year-old students. There was research on written composition prior to this time, but its emphasis was different from current writing research. Specifically, the earlier research focused on how best to teach writing (Steinberg, 1963, is typical), whereas the new research investigates the nature of the writing process itself. Three recent collections of papers personify this new orientation: the papers in Cooper and Odell (1978) pose a large number of important research questions, and the papers in Gregg and Steinberg (1980) and Frederiksen, Whiteman, and Dominic (in press) report initial studies that use new research methods to investigate writing. Much of what I describe in the following is drawn from the last two collections.

Is it true that students cannot write well? A careful study of the Fall 1979 entering class at the State University of New York at Buffalo (Cooper, Cherry, Gerber, Fleisher, Copley, & Sartisky, 1979) indicated that students do indeed have major writing problems. This study also pinpoints the locus of the problems. Specifically, the conclusions are that

> At the word and sentence level their [the students'] writing is nearly flawless. They have mastered standard usage and punctuation [p. 81]

but the students

— have great difficulty creating written text which has adequate connections and relationships from sentence to sentence.
— are unable to generate examples, anecdotes, and details to support generalizations [p. 83].

In short, the students "are careful editors but poor composers."

Thus the need is not for more drill in the mechanics of writing but for better teaching of the written composition process especially at the intersentence level. Prerequisite for a widespread improvement in the teaching of writing is a better understanding of the psychological processes used by writers. The lines of research described in the following promise to provide this basic knowledge. Because the study of the basic psychological processes involved in written composition is just beginning, the findings do not form a coherent picture as yet; so I have chosen to organize this chapter around the research methodologies that have been used rather than the research findings. Thus the following sections discuss the research that has been done using protocol analysis, writing pause times, analysis of writing ability levels, writing facilitation procedures, and computer modeling.

PROTOCOL ANALYSIS OF WRITING

The written composition process is a kind of problem solving. In particular, the writer has to solve the problem of how to evoke a certain state of mind in the reader; that is, writers have to determine what they can write that will communicate what they want to the readers. The research methodology of protocol analysis has proved to be valuable for studying how people solve problems (Newell & Simon, 1972), so it is natural to use it also to investigate writing. Flower and Hayes (1979) have taken this approach.

According to Hayes and Flower (1980), "a protocol is a description of the activities, ordered in time, which a subject engages in while performing a task." They use verbal, or "think aloud", protocols to investigate writing. Here writers not only compose texts but also verbally report everything they think while they are performing this task. These verbal reports are recorded and a transcript of that recording is the data to be explained.

Hayes and Flower also proposed a model of the writing process. This model divides writing into three major interacting processes—planning, translating, and reviewing. The planning process sets goals and creates a writing plan for composing a text that will meet those goals. The planning process has three subprocesses. Specifically, it is composed of generating relevant information by retrieving it from long-term memory, organizing the retrieved information, and setting goals for the text being composed. The translating process uses the writing plan to translate information in the writer's memory into written text. The reviewing process consists of reading and editing the text produced by the translating process. A closely related model was proposed by Bruce, Collins, Rubin, and Gentner (in press). This other model divides the writing process into idea production (with subprocesses of idea discovery and manipulation), text production, and text editing. When testing their model with the protocol data, Hayes and Flower only use the writing processes of generating, organizing, translating, and editing; these are exactly the same processes proposed by Bruce et al.

Hayes and Flower validated their model by showing that it could be "fit" to a writing protocol they collected. Specifically, they used the "metacomments" in the protocol as an independent variable to predict the dependent variables of protocol statement content, statement form, the number of ideas produced in the sections of the protocol, and the length of the related-idea chains in the protocol sections. Metacomments are comments that the writer makes about the writing process itself, and they indicate which of the four writing processes (i.e., generating, organizing, translating, and editing) is active at the time they are made. For example, comments like

And what I'll do now is simply jot down random thoughts.

and

Other things to think about in this random search are

indicate the generating process; comments like

Now I think its time to go back and read over the material and elaborate on its organization.

and

This is just the organization of a subpart

indicate the organizing process; and comments like

Let's try and write something

and

But let's build on this plan and see what happens with it

indicate the translating process.

When examining the metacomments for the writing protocol, Hayes and Flower found that it divided into three sections, with the first-section metacomments indicating generation; the second, organization; and the third, translation. Hence they predicted a similar breakdown when the "content" protocol items were classified. Two judges (the authors) classified each of the content items in the three protocol sections as produced by one of the four writing processes and the results conformed to the predictions. Specifically, on the average, 83% of the section 1 items were generation items; 65% of the section 2 items were organization items; and 75% of the section 3 items were translation items. There was also good interjudge agreement. Editing occurred about 10% of the time and was spread evenly over all three sections. Gould (1980) also found that editing was spread throughout composing sessions and that most editing changes were local instead of global. Thus Hayes and Flower successfully used the metacomments interpreted in terms of their model to predict the writing processes indicated by content classification of the protocol items.

This process breakdown of the protocol sections also has implications for the form of the protocol items in each section. In particular, during generation (section 1) and especially during translation (section 3) the protocol items should tend to be well-formed—that is, a grammatical construct; but during organization (section 2) the items should tend to be indented, numbered, and alphabetized— that is, structures indicating something like an outline. The data generally confirmed these expectations: 39% of the section 1 and 67% of the section 3 items were well-formed, whereas 92% of the section 2 items were outlinelike. Also 42% of the section 3 items were interrogative statements that seemed to indicate the writer was searching for ways to complete a sentence. This searching is also what one would expect during the translation process in section 3. Hence Hayes and Flower also successfully predicted the form of the protocol items in the three sections of the protocol.

A final prediction was that most of the ideas in the protocols would be produced during the generation process (section 1) and that these generation-process items would occur in chains of related items rather than in isolation. Once again the protocol data confirmed the expectation. Section 1 of the protocol introduced 32 ideas in chains with an average length of 6.4, whereas sections 2 and 3 introduced only 16 ideas and they occurred in short bursts with an average length of 2.

Thus Hayes and Flower (1980) have made a promising beginning, but much remains to be done. The most immediate tasks for Hayes and Flower are to analyze more than one protocol to see how general their results are across people and to test more aspects of their complex model using these protocol data. The need for gathering data from a number of people is highlighted by Kagan's (1980) finding of systematic individual differences in writing style. Specifically, Kagan found that such cognitive style variables as field independence correlated with writing style sophistication. Thus before drawing any firm conclusions about the writing process, we need to gather observations from enough writers to be reasonably certain that our conclusions are not based on the idiosyncracies of particular writers. In addition, protocol data cannot stand alone in verifying theories: Other kinds of evidence are needed. Relying only on the verbal reports of people is dangerous because we never know whether they are reporting what they are doing, what they are deluded in thinking they are doing, or what they think they ought to be doing (Nisbett & Wilson, 1977). For example, Cooper and Odell (1976) questioned published writers about how they write and found that the writers almost never reported using the "sound" of statements when composing. Yet when these writers were asked to evaluate potential changes in texts, they would often use statements like "it doesn't sound right" in rejecting the changes. For another example, Gould and Boies (1978a) found that people reported composing better letters when they were writing than when they were dictating, but later evaluations of these letters showed them to be of equal quality.

These studies warn us to be wary of taking verbal reports totally at face value. However, as Ericsson and Simon (1979) have shown, not all verbal report methods are the same. In particular, Ericsson and Simon made a major distinction between retrospective and concurrent verbal reports. Retrospective verbal reporting is retrieving and verbalizing memories of mental processes from long-term memory, that is, reporting on one's thinking some time after the thoughts occurred. Concurrent verbal reporting, on the other hand, is reporting one's thoughts as they occur, that is, verbalizing what is in short-term memory. As Ericsson and Simon argued, retrospective verbal reports are likely to be the most distorted; and concurrent verbal reports, the most veridical. To their credit, Hayes and Flower (1980) used concurrent reporting so their results are probably not so distorted as the retrospective verbal reports discussed by Cooper and Odell (1976) and Gould and Boies (1978a).

Ericsson and Simon (1979) also pointed out that sometimes instructions to concurrently report thought processes changed the way subjects solved problems. Thus it is important to ask whether the concurrent verbal reporting methods used by Hayes and Flower significantly changed the writing process they observed. Specifically, an experiment is needed that examines whether the manipulation of asking for concurrent verbal reporting of mental processes interacts with the other variables of interest. Finding an effect of reporting instructions would not be bothersome, but finding an interaction between reporting instructions and other variables of interest would provide evidence for the verbal reports distorting the writing process. For example, if we conducted such an experiment and found that asking for verbal reports increased the overall writing time (which we would almost certainly find), we would not be concerned unless there was also a change in the allocation of the time among the various subprocesses of writing (i.e., an interaction). Conducting such an experiment would also be valuable to discover whether asking for verbal reports improves writing. If so, then it might be a useful method for writing instruction (see "Facilitating Writing" on p. 208).

Although protocol analyses are valuable for explorations of the writing process, the conclusions reached need to be supported by data obtained using other research methods. What other research methods are available? Spontaneous speech errors (Fromkin, 1973) and pauses (Goldman-Eisler, 1968) have been employed to investigate the psychological processes used in speech. Errors and pauses during written composition could be similarly employed to investigate writing. In fact, some research has already been done on pauses during writing.

PAUSES DURING WRITING

Gould and Boies (Gould & Boies, 1978a, 1978b; Gould, 1978a, 1978b, 1979, 1980) and Matsuhashi and Cooper (1978) have examined the pause times of writers composing texts. Specifically, they had people write a series of compositions while they videotaped them. The videotapes were then analyzed frame by frame to yield a sensitive measure of how long the writers spent on each part of their compositions. Gould and Boies focused on the "macro" aspects of writing times for people writing letters. They found that planning pauses filled two-thirds of the composing time, whereas generating (actual writing) and reviewing together comprised the other one-third. Matsuhashi and Cooper reported a more "micro" analysis of these planning pause times. Each subject in their study wrote two expressing, two reporting, two persuading, and two generalizing compositions. These discourse types follow the classification schemes of Moffett (1968), Kinneavy (1971), and Britton, Burgess, Martin, Mcleod, and Rosen (1975).

Matsuhashi and Cooper were only able to analyze one writer's data for this first report, but their results are encouraging. In particular, they found that overall pause times for this writer were shortest for reporting, intermediate for expressing and persuading, and longest for generalizing. These differences provide some evidence that writers think and plan in different ways for these different discourse types. However, more interesting is the more detailed analysis of the pause times for reporting and generalizing. The longest pauses during reporting occurred before noun clauses that related an action in the chronology being reported, whereas the longest pauses during generalizing occurred before adverb clauses that specified a condition or reason for the assertion in the main clause. Although the analyses are tentative, these pause-time differences do seem to correspond to the different kinds of planning that the writer should be demonstrating for these different kinds of discourse.

The overall pause-time trends also indicated different composing rhythms for generalizing and reporting. In particular, when writing a generalizing composition, the writer alternated between long pauses before producing general statements and short pauses before illustrations of these general themes. When writing a reporting composition, on the other hand, the writer paused the longest in the beginning; then the pauses were shorter for the rest of the composition. Hence the writer worked at setting the stage for his report in the beginning and then quickly output the rest of it.

Although Matsuhashi and Cooper's results are very tentative, they do indicate that observing pauses is a workable research methodology for studying the detailed processes involved in writing. Of particular interest would be using this methodology together with protocol analysis to test the implications of the Hayes and Flower (1980) and Bruce et al. (in press) models. For example, are the pause-time differences between reporting and generalizing due to heavier use of organizing processes in generalizing than in reporting (with the other processes being the same)? Such questions could be answered by comparing some subjects' protocols while composing various discourse types with other subjects pause times while composing these types.

The writing pause-time research of Gould and Boies and Matsuhashi and Cooper are basically observational. The only experimental manipulations are at the very general level of observing pause times during reporting versus generalizing or during writing versus dictating and speaking. As Rosenberg (1977) argued for speech-pause research, observation of pause times can only indicate whether pause time covaries with some other factor; it cannot determine whether the variation in the other factor caused the variation in the pause time. Drawing detailed causal conclusions about pause times entails performing experiments in which some factors are explicitly manipulated and the consequent variation in "micro" pause times observed. Rosenberg performed such experiments with speech pauses. Specifically he gave subjects two nouns and they formed a sentence using these nouns. The data of interest were the pause times between when the subjects received the nouns and when they started saying the sentences. He found that these pause times were much shorter for related nouns than for unrelated ones. These results were consistent with the hypothesis that a major determinant of pauses in speech is the ease with which the semantic content of the utterance can be retrieved from long-term memory.

The primary importance of the Rosenberg experiments for writing research, however, is that they illustrate an experimental research methodology for studying pauses during composition. In corresponding writing experiments we would systematically vary the nature of the task given a writer and then observe how these variations affected his or her writing pause times. For example, we could vary the audience for which a sentence is written. We might tell one group of college undergraduate subjects that they were writing for a child, another group that they were writing for their peers, and a final group that they were writing for their professors. We would then cue each of the subjects with two nouns (as Rosenberg did) and measure how long it took them to start writing a sentence. One possible pattern of results would be the peer audience being faster than the professor audience with the child audience being even slower. This ordering would then indicate the relative amounts of effort that goes into writing for each of these audiences. Independent variation of the nature of the noun cues and the nature of the audience in the same experiment would allow us to determine how these two variables interact.

It would also be interesting to compare writing initiation times for cuing with two nouns versus a noun and a verb. Here verb-based linguistic theories (Fillmore, 1968; Schank, 1975) would expect the noun-verb cue to lead to faster initiation times than noun–noun cues. Two other candidate variables for investigating in experiments of this sort are the nature of the topic (e.g., level of abstraction of the topic) and the type of written discourse (using either the traditional classifications of Brooks & Warren, 1972, or the newer classifications of Moffet, 1968, and Britton et al., 1975).

Thus the preliminary results of Matsuhashi and Cooper (1978) observing "micro" pause times during writing promise that this research method will prove to be a profitable one for investigating written composition. However, this observational method should be supplemented with pause-time experiments similar to the ones Rosenberg (1977) reported for speech pauses.

LEVELS OF WRITING ABILITY

Composing a written text is a very strenuous task. Flower and Hayes (1979, 1980) dramatized this fact using a compelling metaphor for the writing process:

> A writer caught in the act looks much more like a very busy switchboard operator trying to juggle a number of demands on her attention and constraints on what she can do:
> —She has two important calls on hold. (Don't forget that idea.)
> —Four lights just started flashing. (They demand immediate attention or they'll be forgotten.)
> —A party of five wants to be hooked together. (They need to be connected somehow.)
> —A party of two thinks they've been incorrectly connected. (Where do they go?)
> —And throughout this complicated process of remembering, retrieving, and connecting, the operator's voice must project calmness, confidence, and complete control [p. 52].

As this metaphor emphasizes, writers have to juggle a number of different considerations simultaneously, so a major limit on how well people can write is how many ideas they can process at one time. Thus one natural method for classifying people's writing abilities is in terms of how may writing-related ideas they can handle simultaneously. Scardamalia (in press) has proposed a series of writing ability levels determined by the amount of information coordinated by writers.

Scardamalia presented children with information in the form of a matrix like the one shown in Table 3.1 and asked them to write a paragraph containing the information given in the matrix. Then she scored their written compositions according to how well they integrated the information in the matrix. In Level 1 (the lowest level) writing, there is no integration; each idea is presented separately. The following is an example of Level 1 writing for the matrix given in Table 3.1:

In the state of Michigan the climate is cool. In the state of Michigan the fruit crop is apples. In the state of California the climate is warm. In the state of California the fruit crop is oranges.

Level 2 writing integrates two ideas at a time. For example, a Level 2 writer might group the ideas in the matrix by state:

In Michigan the climate is cool and the fruit crop is apples. In California the climate is warm and the fruit crop is oranges.

Similarly, Level 3 writing integrates three ideas. For example, a Level 3 writer might notice the probable cause-effect relation between climate and crop in addition to grouping the ideas by state:

In Michigan the climate is cool so their fruit crop is apples. In California the climate is warm so their fruit crop is oranges.

Finally, a Level 4 writer would integrate all four of the ideas (i.e., state, climate, crop, and cause-effect relation):

In Michigan's cool climate they harvest apples but with California's warm climate oranges may be grown.

Scardamalia found these Level 4 compositions in some seventh graders but never in fifth graders.

Although these levels of writing are descriptive rather than explanatory, they are derivable from the more basic psychological model of text comprehension and production proposed by Kintsch and van Dijk (1978). Kintsch and van Dijk concentrated on text comprehension, but their model is also applicable to text production. This model has a working memory that is limited in the number of elementary ideas (simple propositions) that it can hold. During text comprehension the ideas are placed in the working memory where they are linked into a "coherence graph" reflecting their interrelations. These interconnected ideas are

TABLE 3.1
Matrix for Scardamalia (in press)
Writing Experiments

| | | *State* | |
		Michigan	California
At harvest	Climate	Cool	Warm
	Fruit Crop	Apples	Oranges

then stored in long-term memory. When matching this model to story-memory data, Kintsch and van Dijk obtained the best fit between the model's predictions and the data when they used a working memory size of four ideas.

To apply this model to Scardamalia's writing task, we need only alter the last step. Instead of storing the "coherence graph" in long-term memory, these integrated networks of ideas would be output as a written text. Thus Scardamalia's levels of writing ability can be simulated with the Kintsch and van Dijk model by varying the working memory capacity from one to four ideas. It is interesting to note that Level 4 writing corresponds to the working memory capacity of four that Kintsch and van Dijk obtained when applying their model to text recall by college students.

It would be informative to compare writing-based estimates of working memory capacity with reading-based ones for children of various ages to see if they always correspond. If they correspond in general, then observing a discrepancy in some people would mean that these people were weaker in one area than the other. Thus if testing a person's reading ability yielded a working memory capacity of three, whereas testing the person's writing ability yielded a capacity of only one, then we would know that this person was underachieving in writing.

This working memory explanation of the writing level results is not the only credible one. For example, another possible explanation is that effective working memory capacity remains constant but that writers at different levels are distinguished by the sentence-combining procedures they can use. Determining specifically what mental limitations are responsible for the writing levels found by Scardamalia is an important task for future research.

Thus one way of classifying writing ability is by how many ideas a writer is capable of integrating simultaneously. Writing levels determined in this manner reflect basic psychological processes because they measure how much working memory capacity or the kinds of sentence-combining procedures writers can effectively use during written composition.

FACILITATING WRITING

Because writing strains people's mental resources, it is important to devise methods for decreasing this strain in those who do not write well. Bereiter and Scardamalia (in press) proposed a number of procedures that facilitate writing by reducing the mental resources demanded at any particular time. However, reduction of working memory load is not a sufficient criterion for determining what will be a useful facilitation procedure. Bereiter and Scardamalia argued that the choice of facilitation procedures should be guided by an analysis of what is involved in learning to write. In particular, learning to write requires people to learn how to change and augment appropriately the communication skills learned in the context of oral conversation, so that they will apply to the new communication task of writing. Thus we would expect facilitation procedures that aid this conversation-to-written-text transition to be particularly useful. For example, during conversations people are prompted for the next part of the discourse by the person they are talking to, whereas in a written composition people have to generate these prompts themselves. Thus, from this perspective, we would expect that prompting writers with potential discourse elements would facilitate writing and the following research confirms this expectation.

In one facilitation procedure, the writers simply made a list of the content words representing the ideas they might use in their compositions. Anderson, Bereiter, and Smart (1979) found that this procedure dramatically increased the amount and variety of content in children's written compositions. Another facilitation method is providing the writers with a list of prompts that indicate the kinds of discourse elements they might want to use. Writers could refer to this list as they began each sentence and be reminded of the variety of sentence types available. Bereiter Scardamalia, Anderson, and Smart (1979) supplied children with a list of prompts like "give a reason for an opinion" and "tell more about the reason." The children wrote their composition by choosing one of these directives, writing a sentence obeying it, then choosing another directive, writing a sentence obeying it, etc. This procedure increased both the total number of sentence types and the number of different types used by the children.

Similarly, Bereiter and Scardamalia (in press) reported that giving children a list of sentence opener prompts like "I think," "For example" and "Even though" also facilitated children's writing. Another prompting technique that facilitates writing is cuing the writers with syntactic transformations for combining simple sentences into complex ones (Mellon, 1969; O'Hare, 1973).

However, not all procedures that might seem facilitating actually improve writing. For example, Atlas (1980) found that giving novice writers an outline as an "aid" actually reduced the quality of the compositions they produced. The problem was that the novices were not focusing on the concerns of their audience, and providing an outline that also did not mention the audience encouraged this bad habit. We can understand this result by taking the learning–facilitation perspective proposed by Bereiter and Scardamalia. Specifically, when communicating by conversation, the audience (i.e., the other person) is a salient part of the explicit conversational situation. When writing, on the other hand, the audience is not part of the explicit situation but has to be imagined by the writer. Thus if people are trying to write in the same way that they converse, they will slight the audience. Hence they need a facilitation procedure that will encourage them to think about the audience and not one that focuses them solely on the idea to be conveyed as the outline did. After finding this negative effect of providing an outline, Atlas used the audience-focusing facilitation procedure of having the audience for the composition respond to the composition in writing. This procedure was successful in improving the novice writers' compositions because it forced them to take account of the audience's concerns.

Scardamalia, Bereiter, and McDonald (1978) found that showing children a videotape that was inept at teaching the rules of a game led to their composing better written instructions for the game than they would have otherwise. Illustrating poor game instructions seemed to have made the children more sensitive to the task facing the audience that would read the instructions they wrote. Another possible facilitation procedure (untested at this time) is to use the cloze technique to provide feedback to writers. Nystrand (in press) has proposed using the cloze technique to evaluate writers. In this technique, readers are given written compositions with words periodically deleted. The readers must then guess what the omitted words were. According to Nystrand, the worse the writing, the more trouble readers will have "filling in the blanks." Showing writers what difficulties readers have in filling in missing words under certain circumstances might also serve an audience sensitizing function similar to the videotapes described previously.

Another writing facilitation procedure that might be suggested is using dictation. Gould and Boies (Gould & Boies, 1978a, 1978b; Gould 1978a, 1978b, 1979, 1980) have compared writing and dictation. Counter to what one might expect intuitively, Gould and Boies have found very little difference between writing and dictating. Specifically, subjects took approximately the same time to compose letters using dictation and writing, and the method used made no difference in the quality of their compositions. The reason for this no-difference result appears to be that writers spend most of their composition time (two-thirds according to Gould and Boies) planning what they are going to say rather than saying and reviewing it. Because this planning process is the same whether one is writing or dictating, which of these output methods is used makes little difference in the composition time. We might expect that written composition would be of higher quality than dictated composition because the written text could be edited more easily. However, Gould and Boies found that subjects did not engage in the "global" editing that would be facilitated by a written text but only in the "local" editing that could also be easily done while dictating. Thus whether one writes or dictates a composition makes little difference, so dictation does not appear to facilitate writing.

In addition to being useful for teaching writing, facilitation procedures may also provide methods for experimentally validating models of written composition like the Hayes and Flower (1980) model described earlier. One way of validating the division of writing processes into the subprocesses of generating, organizing, translating, and editing is to find variables that differentially affect these different processes. For example, having subjects list ideas before composing a text might only affect measures of idea generation (e.g., total number of propositions in the final text) and not measures of organizing, translating, and editing. Or it might affect measures of organization (e.g., propositional argument repetition as described by Kintsch, 1974) in addition to generation but not measures of translating and editing. On the other hand, the audience sensitization techniques described previously might affect measures of editing (e.g., number of changes made in the original composition) but not the others; and the transformational sentence-combining procedures might affect measures of translation (e.g., T-unit length as described by Hunt, 1965) but not the others.

Thus there are a number of useful procedures for facilitating writing by reducing the working memory load demanded by the composition process at any given moment and by aiding writers to augment the communication skills they have learned in the context of oral conversation. Expanding the available repertory of writing facilitation procedures and determining precisely when they are facilitory are important tasks for future research. These facilitation procedures are also promising candidates for factors to be manipulated in experiments that attempt to provide empirical validation for models of the written composition process.

WRITING STORIES BY COMPUTER

When studying any kind of human cognitive behavior, it is easy to inadvertently overlook many of the mundane pieces of tacit knowledge needed for the behavior. A valuable research methodology for discovering this tacit knowledge is to try designing a computer program that will exhibit the behavior. Schank and Abelson (1977) have used this method to discover several kinds of knowledge used in text understanding, and some of their conclusions have been further validated by experiments investigating human text understanding (Black & Bower, 1980; Bower, Black, & Turner, 1979). Meehan (1976) used the Schank and Abelson ideas to design a program that writes simple stories.

A striking aspect of Meehan's research is that he repeatedly built all the knowledge about the world and storytelling that he thought was needed into his program only to be surprised by the results when the program was executed by a computer. For example, at one point he had built many specialized rules about goals and plans to attain them into the program only to have the following story generated:

> One day Henry Crow sat in his tree, holding a piece of cheese in his mouth, when up came Bill Fox. Bill saw the cheese and was hungry. He said, "Henry, I like your singing very much. Won't you please sing for me?" Henry, flattered by his compliment, began to sing. The cheese fell to the ground. Bill Fox saw the cheese on the ground and was very hungry. He became ill [p. 130].

The program composed this story by utilizing the following pieces of knowledge (among others):

1. If a story character sees a piece of food, then that character becomes hungry (i.e., the goal of hunger is placed on the character's goal stack).

2. A character cannot hold something in his mouth and sing at the same time.
3. If one character wants to get another to do something, then he must bargain with him.
4. An initial type of bargaining to try is flattery.
5. If a story character is too hungry, then that character becomes ill.

Thus Bill Fox sees the cheese that Henry Crow possesses and so Bill becomes hungry. Because Bill now has the goal of alleviating his hunger, he adopts the plan of obtaining the cheese by using flattery to get Henry to sing and therefore drop the cheese. Henry sings and drops the cheese because holding the cheese is incompatible with singing. But then the story goes awry because Bill sees the cheese on the ground, which causes more hunger to be added to his goal stack, so now Bill is too hungry and becomes ill. Therefore the program needed to be adjusted to distinguish between stimulus and body state induced hunger. This story continued and ran into even more trouble:

> Henry Crow saw the cheese on the ground, and he became hungry, but he knew that he owned the cheese. He felt pretty honest with himself, so he decided not to trick himself into giving up the cheese. He wasn't trying to deceive himself either, nor did he feel competitive with himself. But he did dominate himself and was very familiar with himself, so he asked himself for the cheese. He trusted himself, but he remembered that he was also in a position of dominance over himself, so he refused to give himself the cheese. He couldn't think of a good reason why he should give himself the cheese, so he offered to bring himself a worm if he'd give himself the cheese. That sounded okay, but he didn't know where any worms were. So he said to himself, "Henry, do you know where any worms are?" But of course, he didn't, so he... [p. 131]

Here Henry has also seen the cheese so he becomes hungry and hence develops the goal of eliminating that hunger. He notes that a character in the story happens to possess the piece of food he wants, so he bargains with that character to obtain the food. He considers what kind of bargaining to use and settles on exchanging another object (a worm) for the desired food. All this seems correct, but the story took a wrong turn because two picayune details were omitted from the store of knowledge that the program used. One detail is that if a character drops something, then he no longer physically possesses it; the second is that if the other character that possesses an object is yourself, then you do not have to bargain for the object because you already possess it. Similar details are needed at the end of the previous story excerpt to keep Henry from bargaining with himself to discover the location of a worm.

Meehan (1976) gives an entire chapter full of these humorous "mis-spun tales," but the important point here is that it is hard to imagine any other research methodology that would have discovered that these subtle pieces of knowledge were needed to write reasonable stories. It would be instructive to construct a model of the written composition process that combined the Meehan and Kintsch and van Dijk models. In particular, this combination model would use the knowledge structures identified by Meehan but would integrate them in a limited working memory like the one used by Kintsch and van Dijk. Writers do not compose arbitrarily complex plans for story characters trying to attain goals, so a limited working memory is needed in the model to eliminate this possibility.

CONCLUSIONS

These preliminary studies of the psychological processes involved in written composition provide grounds for optimism about the future of this research area. Already a promising theoretical framework for investigating the composition process has begun to emerge. I think that the eventual theory will combine the writing processes observed in the Hayes and Flower (1980) protocol analyses with the working memory model of Kintsch and van Dijk (1978) and the real-world knowledge structures of Meehan (1976). However, there is a pressing need for controlled experimental studies that demonstrate the validity of this framework. Specifically, the desired experiments would show what factors affect what parts of the written composition process. The work of Gould (1980), Matsuhashi and Cooper (1978), Bereiter and Scardamalia (in press), Scardamalia (in press), and Atlas (1980) illustrate some of the experimental factors that can be manipulated and some of the measurements that can be made of human writing behavior.

A full account of the psychology of writing requires a theory of how writing is learned in addition to a theory of the writing process. Bereiter and Scardamalia (in press) have taken a fruitful approach to investigating how people develop writing skills. Specifically, they started with an analysis of the difference between producing oral and written discourse and then investigated what procedures facilitate better writing by adapting and augmenting existing oral communication skills.

Fortunately, practical application of research results to improve the teaching of writing does not have to wait until fully adequate theories of writing are developed. Already the results of Bereiter and Scardamalia (in press) and Atlas (1980) are amenable to direct application in the classroom. In addition, the experimental methods being developed to test writing process models and the facilitation procedures being developed to test learning models should provide many results of pragmatic importance while the theoretical models are still being refined. Thus I believe that the lines of research I have described are leading to major theoretical and practical insights into the written composition process.

ACKNOWLEDGMENTS

I thank the following people for providing valuable comments on an earlier version of this chapter: Sheldon Rosenberg, Marlene Scardamalia, Carl Bereiter, John Hayes, Martin Nystrand, and Erwin Steinberg. The writing of this chapter was supported by a grant from the Alfred P. Sloan Foundation. Reprints may be obtained from John B. Black, Yale University, Department of Psychology, Box 11A Yale Station, New Haven, Conn. 06520.

REFERENCES

Atlas, M. *Addressing an audience: A study of expert-novice differences in writing.* Unpublished manuscript, Carnegie-Mellon University, 1980.

Anderson, V., Bereiter, C., & Smart, B. *Activation of semantic networks in writing: Teaching students how to do it themselves.* Unpublished manuscript. The Ontario Institute for Studies in Education, 1979.

Bereiter, C., & Scardamalia, M. From conversation to composition: The role of instruction in a developmental process. In R. Glaser (Ed.) *Advances in instructional psychology* (Vol. 2). Hillsdale, N.J.: Lawrence Erlbaum Associates, in press.

Bereiter, C., Scardamalia, M., Anderson, V., & Smart, D. *An experiment in teaching abstract planning in writing.* Unpublished manuscript. The Ontario Institute for Studies in Education, 1979.

Black, J. B., & Bower, G. H. Story understanding as problem-solving. *Poetics,* 1980, 9, 223-250.

Bower, G. H., Black, J. B., & Turner, T. J. Scripts in memory for text. *Cognitive Psychology,* 1979, 11, 177-220.

Britton, J. L., Burgess, T., Martin, N., Mcleod, A., & Rosen, H. *The development of writing abilities (11-18).* London: Macmillan Education, 1975.

Brooks, C., & Warren, R. P. *Modern rhetoric.* New York: Harcourt Brace Jovanovich, 1972.

Bruce, B., Collins, A., Rubin, A. D., & Gentner, D. A cognitive science approach to writing. In C. H. Frederiksen, M. F. Whiteman, & J. D. Dominic (Eds.), *Writing: The nature, development, and teaching of written communication.* Hillsdale, N.J.: Lawrence Erlbaum Associates, in press.

Cooper, C., Cherry, R., Gerber, R., Fleisher, S., Copley, B., & Sartisky, M. *Writing abilities of regularly-admitted freshmen at SUNY/Buffalo.* Unpublished manuscript, University Learning Center, State University of New York, Buffalo, 1979.

Cooper, C., & Odell, L. Considerations of sound in the composing process of published writers. *Research in the Teaching of English.* 1976, 10, 103-115.

Cooper, C., & Odell, L. (Eds.). *Research on composing: Points of departure.* Urbana, Ill.: National Council of Teachers of English, 1978.

Ericsson, K. A., & Simon, H. *Verbal reports as data.* C.I.P. Working Paper No. 402, 1979.

Fillmore, C. J. The case for case. In E. Bach & R. T. Harms (Eds.), *Universals of linguistic theory.* New York: Holt, Rinehart, & Winston, 1968.

Flower, L. S., & Hayes, J. R. *A process model of composition.* Technical Report No. 1, Document Design Project, Carnegie-Mellon University, Pittsburgh, Pa., 1979.

Flower, L. S., & Hayes, J. R. The dynamics of composing: Making plans and juggling constraints. In L. Gregg & E. R. Steinberg (Eds.), *Cognitive processes in writing.* Hillsdale, N.J.: Lawrence Erlbaum Associates, 1980.

Frederiksen, C. H., Whiteman, M. F., & Dominic, J. F. (Eds.). *Writing: The nature, development, and teaching of written communication.* Hillsdale, N.J.: Lawrence Erlbaum Associates, in press.

Fromkin, V. A. (Ed.). *Speech errors as linguistic evidence*. The Hague: Mouton, 1973.
Goldman-Eisler, F. *Psycholinguistics: Experiments in spontaneous speech*. New York: Academic Press, 1968.
Gould, J. D. An experimental study of writing, dictating, and speaking. In J. Requin (Ed.), *Attention and performance VII*. Hillsdale, N.J.: Lawrence Erlbaum Associates, 1978. (a)
Gould, J. D. How experts dictate. *Journal of Experimental Psychology: Human Perception and Performance*, 1978, *4*, 648-661. (b)
Gould, J. D. *Writing and speaking letters and messages*. IBM Research Report, RC-7528, 1979.
Gould, J. D. Experiments on composing letters: Some facts, some myths, and some observations. In L. Gregg & E. R. Steinberg (Eds.), *Cognitive processes in writing*. Hillsdale, N.J.: Lawrence Erlbaum Associates, 1980.
Gould, J. D., & Boies, S. J. How authors think about their writing, dictating, and speaking. *Human Factors*, 1978, *20*, 495-505. (a)
Gould, J. D., & Boies, S. J. Writing, dictating, and speaking letters. *Science*, 1978, *201*, 1145-1147. (b)
Gregg, L., & Steinberg, E. R. (Eds.). *Cognitive processes in writing*. Hillsdale, N.J.: Lawrence Erlbaum Associates, 1980.
Hayes, J. R., & Flower, L. S. Identifying the organization of writing processes. In L. Gregg & E. R. Steinberg (Eds.), *Cognitive processes in writing*. Hillsdale, N.J.: Lawrence Erlbaum Associates, 1980.
Hunt, K. W. *Grammatical structures written at three grade levels*. Urbana, Ill.: National Council of Teachers of English, 1965.
Kagan, D. M. Syntactic complexity and cognitive style. *Applied Psycholinguistics*, 1980, *1*, 111-122.
Kinneavy, J. *A theory of discourse*. Englewood Cliffs, N.J.: Prentice-Hall, 1971.
Kintsch, W. *The representation of meaning in memory*. Hillsdale, N.J.: Lawrence Erlbaum Associates, 1974.
Kintsch, W., & van Dijk, T. A. Toward a model of text comprehension and production. *Psychological Review*, 1978, *85*, 363-394.
Matsuhashi, A., & Cooper, C. *A video time-monitored observational study: The transcribing behavior and composing processes of a competent high school writer*. Paper presented at the American Education Research Association Annual Meeting, Toronto, Ontario, Canada, 1978.
Meehan, J. R. *The metanovel: Writing stories by computer*. Research Report No. 74, Computer Science Department, Yale University, New Haven, Conn., 1976.
Mellon, J. C. *Transformational sentence-combining: A method for enhancing the development of syntactic fluency in English composition*. Research Report No. 10. Urbana, Ill.: National Council of Teachers of English, 1969.
Moffett, J. *Teaching the universe of discourse*. Boston: Houghton Mifflin, 1968.
National Assessment of Educational Progress. *Writing mechanics, 1969-1974: A capsule description of changes in writing mechanics*. Report No. 05-W-01. Denver, Colo.: National Assessment of Educational Progress, 1975.
Newell, A., & Simon, H. A. *Human problem solving*. Englewood Cliffs, N.J.: Prentice-Hall, 1972.
Nisbett, R. E., & Wilson, T. D. Telling more than we can know: Verbal reports on mental processes. *Psychological Review*, 1977, *84*, 231-259.
Nystrand, M. Using readability research to investigate writing. *Research in the Teaching of English*. in press.
O'Hare, F. *Sentence combining: Improving student writing without formal grammar instruction*. NCTE Report No. 15. Urbana, Ill.: NCTE, 1973.
Rosenberg, S. Semantic constraints on sentence production: An experimental approach. In S. Rosenberg (Ed.), *Sentence production*. Hillsdale, N.J.: Lawrence Erlbaum Associates, 1977.
Scardamalia, M. How children cope with the cognitive demands of writing. In C. H. Frederiksen,

M. F. Whiteman, & J. F. Dominic (Eds.), *Writing: The nature, development, and teaching of written communication*. Hillsdale, N.J.: Lawrence Erlbaum Associates, in press.

Scardamalia, M., Bereiter, C., & McDonald, J. D. Role-taking in written communication investigated by manipulating anticipatory knowledge. *Resources in Education,* August, 1978.

Schank, R. C. *Conceptual information processing*. Amsterdam: North-Holland Pub., 1975.

Schank, R. C., & Abelson, R. P. *Scripts, plans, goals, and understanding*. Hillsdale, N.J.: Lawrence Erlbaum Associates, 1977.

Steinberg, E. R. *Needed research in the teaching of English*. Washington, D.C.: U.S. Government Printing Office, 1963.

4 Second-Language Learning and Bilingualism in Children and Adults

Barry McLaughlin
*University of California
Santa Cruz*

In recent years interest in the area of second-language learning and bilingualism has increased remarkably. A major impetus was the so-called "Bilingual Education Act," Title VII of the Elementary and Secondary Education Act of 1967. Another factor has been developments in the field of first-language acquisition, with attendant spin-offs to second-language acquisition research. As more investigators have become interested in second-language learning, new journals have appeared (e.g., *Studies in Second Language Acquisition, Bilingual Review, Interlanguage Studies Bulletin*), and collections of readings have proliferated (e.g., Andersen, 1981; Burt, Dulay, & Finocchiaro, 1977; Diller, 1981; Hatch, 1978b; Larsen-Freeman, 1980; Richards, 1978; Ritchie, 1978).

These collections usually contain survey articles on various aspects of research on second-language learning and bilingualism. In addition, comprehensive reviews are available elsewhere (Cook, 1978; Hakuta & Cancino, 1977; McLaughlin, 1977, 1978b). I would like to be more selective here and focus on problem areas where research has been particularly active in recent years. A central theme of this chapter is that although a great deal of progress has been made in research on second-language learning and bilingualism, there is still a long way to go.

INTRODUCTION

It is customary to begin discussions of second-language learning with a review of definitional issues. Although such discussions have been generally unproductive, there are some recent developments that may eventually clear the muddy waters.

After touching on these issues, I want to say a few words about the politics of research on second-language learning and bilingualism.

The discussion of definitional issues can be tedious and I shall be mercifully brief here. The interested reader is referred to McLaughlin (1978b) and Hornby (1977) for recent treatments. Suffice it to say that there is no agreement as to what it means to be bilingual: Definitions run from rigorous to lax. Nor is there general agreement as to whether a speaker who speaks a nonstandard and the standard dialect should be thought of as a bilingual. An oft-cited distinction, that between compound and coordinate bilingualism, has been generally abandoned as empirically questionable.

Also problematic is the distinction between simultaneous and successive second-language acquisition. Is a 4-year-old child, when exposed to a new language, acquiring that language simultaneously with the first language? Suppose the child is 2 years old. I have argued (McLaughlin, 1978b) that the introduction of a new language in the case of a 2-year-old leads to simultaneous acquisition and that by 3 years acquisition is successive, with the first language (to some degree) established. Some support for this view comes from the finding that children raised from birth with two languages do not differentiate them at 2 years, though they do at 3 (Imedadze, 1960; Volterra & Taeschner, 1975). Nonetheless, determination that a language is acquired should ideally be made on the basis of linguistic, not chronological, criteria (Vihman & McLaughlin, in press).

A somewhat different approach has been taken by Lamendella (1977) in his distinction between primary-language acquisition, secondary-language acquisition, and foreign-language learning. *Primary-language acquisition* refers to the normal language learning process occurring between the ages of 2 and 5 years regardless of the number of languages involved and whether they are introduced simultaneously or successively. *Secondary-language acquisition* occurs in the "naturalistic" setting after the period of primary-language acquisition and may encompass two, three, or more languages learned simultaneously or in succession. *Foreign-language learning* occurs in the formal classroom situation and is cognitively quite different from secondary-language acquisition. Whereas secondary-language acquisition is directed at communicative competence, foreign-language learning is not. But secondary-language acquisition can occur in the classroom when either the learner or the method of instruction focus on communication (Lamendella, 1977). Similarly, one can learn formal aspects of a language in the "naturalistic" setting by using native speakers as informants (McLaughlin, 1978b).

What is important in this discussion is the recognition that the phenomenon of "second-language learning" can involve several different settings, goals, and cognitive processes. Some conventional terminology is needed to separate these differences and Lamendella's distinction between secondary-language acquisition and foreign-language learning is as good as any we have available. At least in a global sense, this distinction helps us to avoid the tendency of earlier researchers to ignore different types of second-language learning. Whether Lamendella is correct in restricting primary-language acquisition to the period between 2 and 5 years is more controversial. Perhaps primary-language acquisition occurs between 2 and 13 years or only up to 3 years. This is a complex issue that relates to one's view of the critical period hypothesis. As we shall see, there is considerable disagreement on this topic (Krashen, 1973; Molfese, Freeman, & Palermo, 1975; Seliger, 1978).

ESL and Bilingual Education

Most research on second-language learning (which I use here as a generic term to refer to both foreign-language learning and secondary-language acquisition) has been conducted by researchers in university settings. At least in the United States, researchers are generally connected with ESL (English as a Second Language) programs, often based in English or linguistics departments. Occasionally, investigators are trained in education departments and, in some rare cases, in psychology departments. For the most part, research centers on the learning of English as a second language—either in children or, more often, in adult ESL students. Because many researchers are connected with ESL programs, it is not surprising that foreign ESL students have been the objects of research concern. Nor is it surprising that much research is directed at applied issues relating to teaching English.

In contrast, research on bilingualism generally has been directed at students in bilingual education programs. The setting is the elementary and secondary classroom. Many people working in this area are bilingual; many, like the children they are studying, are from disadvantaged ethnic backgrounds. The researchers have generally been trained in education departments, often in programs focusing on bilingual/bicultural education. Although they are concerned with issues relating to instruction in English, their primary concern is with the bilingual/bicultural experience.

Researchers interested in second-language learning are generally members of TESOL (Teachers of English to Speakers of Other Languages), a national organization of ESL educators. The comparable organization for bilingual educators is NABE (National Association for Bilingual Education). There is some but not a significant amount of overlap in the membership of the two organizations. This is unfortunate and reflects, on the one hand, the reluctance of bilingual educators to become identified as teachers of English and, on the other hand, the failure of individuals trained in ESL programs to apply their expertise to bilingual education.

Although there are exceptions to these tendencies, the overall pattern has been counterproductive. What could be a fruitful cooperative enterprise is undermined by suspicion and entrenched interests. One would hope that in the future there will be a more concerted effort on the part of ESL and bilingual educators. This will require, more than anything else, the acknowledgment by both groups that students can learn English without giving up their traditional language and culture.

PROCESSES OF SECOND-LANGUAGE LEARNING

Two of the principal questions asked by researchers about second-language learning are (1) what are the processes involved and (2) how do they differ from the processes involved in first-language acquisition. Some researchers see the processes as essentially identical; other researchers see them as essentially different. The debate has been a lively one, but the dust is beginning to settle. This is an outcome of research in two empirical areas—error analysis and the so-called morpheme studies.

Error Analysis

In the 1950s and into the 1960s researchers believed that a combination of structural linguistics and behavioristic psychology would lead to insight into the nature of second-language learning. Structural linguistics was thought to provide a scientific description of the native language of the speaker and of the target language to be learned. Learning, according to behavioristic psychology, involved the formation of habits and the overcoming of interference. Hence to learn the target language it was necessary to know what first-language habits would interfere with the acquisition of the habits of the new language. The analysis of the structural elements of two languages (contrastive analysis) was thought to provide information as to what habits would produce most interference and therefore most difficulty for the learner.

The discovery that a large proportion of a second-language learner's errors were not predictable on the basis of contrastive analysis (Dulay & Burt, 1972; George, 1972; Lance, 1969; Richards, 1971) led researchers to an examination of the nature of errors in second-language learning. Many researchers were struck by the similarities between errors reported in the first-language acquisition literature for English and errors they were finding in the speech of second-language learners of English (Corder, 1967; Dulay & Burt, 1972; Natalicio & Natalicio, 1971). It seemed that the presence of the same errors in the two cases provided strong evidence that essentially the same processes are involved.

Unfortunately, the evidence is not unequivocal. As Hakuta and Cancino (1977) have pointed out, error analysis rests on the questionable assumption that an error is an appropriate unit of analysis. Research that indicates that a predominance of errors in a second-language learner's corpus are *intralingual* (reflecting developmental mistakes found in monolingual speakers) and not *interlingual* (reflecting the influence of the learner's first language) usually involves coding the omission of high-frequency morphemes—such as nouns and verb inflections and the verb *to be*—as intralingual errors. Because interlingual errors often involve large constituents or changes in word order, the relative opportunity of occurrence of the two types of errors is not equivalent. Furthermore, it may well be that second-language learners simply avoid certain linguistic structures on which they would be likely to make errors (Schachter, 1974). Conceivably such avoidance tendencies reflect structural differences between their first language and the target language.

Schachter and Celce-Murcia (1977) have pointed out some additional problems with the error-analysis approach. Among other things, they noted that it is difficult to be certain precisely what error a second-language learner is making or why the learner makes it. One and the same error can frequently be attributed to interlingual and intralingual causes. Indeed, this may not be an either–or proposition: There is evidence that some errors are the result of the interaction of both factors (Andersen, 1978).

Another problem with the error-analysis studies is that they typically are based on cross-sectional samples. There are relatively few studies that examine whether specific types of errors are prevalent at specific points in time or whether certain errors persist longer than others. There is some evidence that interlingual errors appear primarily at the early stages of development (Taylor, 1975a) and that they occur when learners are faced with particularly intransigent problems (Wode, 1976). There is also some evidence that their correction is quite gradual and the use of correct forms is variable (Hakuta & Cancino, 1977). The conclusion one comes to, I believe, is that both interlingual and intralingual errors occur in the speech of a second-language learner and that what is important is the determination of when and to what extent the different types of errors occur (McLaughlin, 1978b).

Morpheme "Acquisition" Studies

The so-called "morpheme acquisition" studies appeared to lend support to the notion that second-language learning involves essentially the same processes as first-language learning. The findings of Dulay and Burt (1974) that Chinese and Spanish children showed the same order of acquisition of 11 English morphemes suggested that there was a common sequence according to which children with different linguistic backgrounds learned certain structures in English. This sequence was also observed in adults learning English as a second language (Bailey, Madden, & Krashen, 1974). The sequence was not, however, the same as that observed in children acquiring English as a first language (Brown, 1973), but this was attributed to differences in cognitive abilities at different stages of development. Because older children and adults are more sophisticated than younger children in their cognitive and conceptual development, it was not surprising that their pattern of morpheme acquisition is different. What was seen to be important was the communality in the developmental sequence observed in the second-language studies. Researchers argued that the morpheme data provided convincing evidence that second-language learners do not use their own first language as a basis for approaching the target language. Rather there seem to be common, universal strategies employed by all learners, regardless of their first language.

The morpheme studies have come under attack from a number of directions. The findings may be instrument-specific. The instrument used in most studies was the Bilingual Syntax Measure (BSM) (Burt, Dulay, & Hernandez-Chavez, 1973). When children learning English as their first language were administered the BSM, they were found to display the acquisition order more resembling the order found in second-language learners than the order Brown (1973) found in first-language learners of English (Porter, 1977).

Furthermore, the findings of the morpheme studies are not, strictly speaking, related to *acquisition sequence* but rather *accuracy of use,* because the studies are cross-sectional in nature and measure the percentage of times subjects supply morphemes correctly in obligatory contexts. Several longitudinal studies have yielded orders of acquisition that did not correlate with the orders of accuracy of use obtained in cross-sectional research (Hakuta, 1974, 1976; Huebner, 1979; Rosansky, 1976).

There is also the possibility that interlingual factors are involved in determining the order in which second-language learners acquire English morphemes. Hakuta and Cancino (1977) have argued that the semantic complexity of the morphemes may vary depending on the learner's native language. They cited research that indicated that where a second-language learner's first language does not make the same semantic discriminations as the target language, more difficulty in learning to use these morphemes occurs than is the case for learners whose first language makes the semantic discriminations.

At the same time, there is in all likelihood a tendency for second-language learners to learn morphemes in a certain order because of the relative frequency of occurrence or perceptual salience of the morphemes in the linguistic input to which they are exposed. There is evidence that the order observed in adult subjects correlates highly with the frequency of the morphemes in the speech of ESL teachers (Larsen-Freeman, 1976). This suggests that the frequency of the forms in input influences what the second-language learner produces (Wagner-Gough & Hatch, 1975). Hence input factors predict a certain order in accuracy of use across learners from different linguistic backgrounds, whereas transfer from the first language may lead to exceptions to this universality.

L1 = L2: Strong versus Weak Positions

Where does this discussion leave us with respect to the question of the identity or difference between first- (L1) and second- (L2) language learning? It is my conviction that a great deal of fur has flown about because researchers have not made an important distinction. This is the distinction between the "strong" position that L2 is *identical* with L1 (L1 = L2) and the "weak" position that L2 is *similar* to L1 (L1 ≈ L2).

Whereas the early error-analysis research and the morpheme studies seemed to point to an identity of process between first- and second-language learning, much recent research of a longitudinal nature has, as we have seen, indicated some difficulties in making this assumption. There seem to be two factors operating and interacting in second-language learning: transfer from the first language and overgeneralization of the second.

Yet the presence of transfer factors in second-language learning does not mean that first- and second-language learning involve essentially different cognitive strategies. In both cases the learner uses what is available to crack the code of what is unknown. In acquiring their first language, children overextend rules, saying *I runned* or *two foots*. In such cases the child is applying a rule that works well sometimes but is not permitted in other situations. This does not differ from what an individual does in misapplying a rule from a first language to a second: One is doing what one can with what is available.

The weak position that second-language learning is basically similar though not identical with first-language acquisition is predicated on the notion that both processes involve essentially the same (perhaps universal) cognitive strategies. By this I mean that learners approach both tasks in essentially the same manner. They look for word-order regularities; they proceed from the simple to the more complex in syntactic development; they use context as a cue to meaning in semantic development; they overgeneralize lexical and morphological forms; they interpret what is unknown in terms of what is known.

This is not to deny the importance of neurological or maturational processes. There are obviously vast differences between the 3-year-old child and the 30-year-old adult. Adults possess superior memory heuristics and can thus retain longer input and discover meaning more easily. They have the lexicon of their first language to fall back on in attempting to decipher the lexicon of the second language. The adult can also process information more quickly and has more experiential knowledge than the child.

Even older children acquiring a second language can process that language differently than younger children acquiring a first language. For example, Felix (1978) reported that English-speaking children aged 4 to 7 years acquiring German naturalistically produced fewer different structures than native monolingual children. Initially the second-language learners he studied produced primarily copular sentences and isolated noun phrases, whereas the monolingual children produce a greater diversity of grammatical relations. This suggests that second-language learners operate syntactically, combining words according to a limited number of syntactic principles. The child acquiring a first language does not do this but operates presyntactically, combining words to express cognitive rather than syntactic relations. Because the older child has had linguistic experience, there is no need to go through the presyntactic stage. Other differences between the processes of first- and second-language learning have been described by Wode (1979).

In spite of these differences there is enough similarity between the strategies involved in first- and second-language learning to warrant capitalizing on what is known about first-language acquisition when confronted with pedagogical problems in second-language learning. This means, I believe, that Macnamara (1976), Cook (1969), and other authors, who have stressed the need for making the process of learning a second language resemble as much as possible the learning of a first language, are essentially correct in their orientation—not because of an identity of process between first- and second-language learning but because the focus of first-language acquisition is on communication and the same should be true of learning a second language. This is a topic to which I shall return shortly.

THE DEVELOPMENT OF A SECOND LANGUAGE

What can one say about developmental stages in the acquisition of a second language? To what extent do they mirror developmental stages one observes in first-language acquisition? These are questions that have stimulated a great deal of research attention. There are several different research paradigms possible, and one can look at developmental stages in children or in adult learners.

Research Methodology

One way of examining developmental stages in the acquisition of a second language is to follow a given subject longitudinally. This is called the *case-study* method and has several obvious limitations. For one thing, there is little guarantee that any single subject or small number of subjects is representative of a larger population. Often case studies have been conducted by linguists using their own children as subjects—a somewhat unique sample. There is also the problem of objectivity (especially when one is observing one's own children). The child's ill-formed utterances may be transformed into well-formed sentences. Mistakes may be overlooked or surpressed. The investigator may see what supports hypotheses of the study and may ignore other data.

A less obvious source of difficulty with the case study is that, unless the researcher is constantly observing the subject, large-scale changes may have occurred. Often researchers studying first-language development in children make their observations at biweekly or monthly intervals. These intervals are much too large for individuals learning a second language, because in many cases development can be quite swift. Often progress occurs in spurts and these changes will be masked unless observations are made at intervals close in time.

Nonetheless, very fine and careful case studies do exist. The classic, of course, is Leopold's four-volume study of his daughter Hildegard (Leopold, 1939, 1947, 1949a, 1949b). There are also some recent studies of high quality (Hatch, 1978b). These studies are a valuable source of data and, taken in conjunction with findings from research involving larger samples, begin to point the way to some specific generalizations about second-language learning.

Case studies can be contrasted to *cross-sectional* research in which groups of subjects at different ages (or different amounts of exposure to the target language) are compared at one point in time. Repeated measures are not taken on the same subject, but different groups of subjects serve as the basis for comparison. For example, an investigator may examine use of the English negative by groups of subjects with different amounts of exposure to English to determine the developmental progression of this grammatical form.

A weakness of this type of research, as Rosansky (1976) has noted, is that there is no assurance that group data accurately reflect the developmental progression of any one individual. Rosansky found that a cross-sectional analysis of morpheme accuracy data from a single subject did not correlate with longitudinal data from the same subject. Although Rosansky's analysis has been criticized (Hakuta & Cancino, 1977), she does raise an important issue. It may be that group data obscure important individual differences. Slower learners, for example, may show a very different developmental pattern than faster learners do, and these differences would be lost sight of in the averaging process involved in most cross-sectional research.

This problem has been confronted by Andersen (1978), who argued that cross-sectional methodology can be modified to take individual variation into account. He proposed that implicational analysis, a method often used in sociolinguistic research, be applied to second-language research data. Essentially, this method involves the analysis of attributes of language use such that the presence of a particular attribute in the speech of individuals being studied implies the presence of other attributes in their speech. The presence or absence of attributes in individual speakers or groups of speakers is displayed by an implicational table from which one can derive a "coefficient of reproducibility" (Guttman, 1944). This procedure provides information about the validity of the scale and allows one to single out individuals or groups whose performance does not conform to the implicational order.

Thus implicational analysis has the advantage of allowing simultaneous examination of systematicity and individual variation. Although this was not true of Andersen's data, it is possible to find not one but many implicational orders. It may be the case, for example, that the implicational model for certain attributes is different for slow and fast learners. Normal techniques of analysis would obscure these differences between subtypes of learners.

Neither Rosansky, who stressed the usefulness of longitudinal case studies, nor Andersen, who pointed out how much information can be gained from cross-sectional studies, would deny that both methods of data collection are necessary in second-language research. In the discussion that follows I draw from both methods in an attempt to determine what we know (and do not know) about developmental stages in second-language learning. First, I look at studies with children where the second language is typically acquired in a naturalistic setting. Then I look at research on adult second-language learning in the classroom.

Research with Children

Primary-Language Acquisition. In the bilingual case, when the young child learns two languages, acquisition of both languages appears to follow the developmental pattern characteristic of monolingual children. There is some evidence—phonetically, syntactically, and semantically—that the child, initially at least, prefers a single system: A single phoneme will be applied to both languages (Murrell, 1966; Rūke-Dravina, 1965); syntactically simpler structures will be learned before the more difficult equivalents in a second language (Imedadze, 1960; Kessler, 1972; Mikeš, 1967); a single word will be used to express a single meaning, with the word chosen sometimes from one language, sometimes from the other (Leopold, 1939; Volterra & Taeschner, 1975). There is a brief initial stage of language mixing, with subsequent differentiation (Vihman & McLaughlin, in press), though if one language predominates, the sound features, syntactic structures, and lexicon of the dominant language may be substituted for those of the subordinate language (Burling, 1959; Leopold, 1949a).

The perceptual salience or difficulty of the linguistic features of one language may dictate that the realization of certain semantic relations be delayed relative to their occurrence in the other language. For example, Imedadze (1960) found that her Georgian–Russian bilingual child first formed subject-to-object relations in Georgian on analogy with the more simple Russian form (adding an accusative ending to the object). Only later did the more complicated Georgian form appear, which demands the dative case ending for the psychological subject and the nominative case for the psychological object. Within each of the two languages, however, syntactic structures followed the same developmental sequence as they did for monolingual children. This finding has been generally supported by research on bilingual children (Carrow, 1971; Kessler, 1972).

Secondary-Language Acquisition. The issue is more complicated with children who have acquired one language prior to the acquisition of a second. Research in the early 1970s strongly suggested that the developmental sequence for children who are acquiring a second language is essentially the same as it is for monolingual children. That is, children acquiring a second language were thought to pass through essentially the same stages as a child acquiring that language as a first language. More recent research, however, has questioned this conclusion.

Case studies by Milon (1974) on the English negative, Ravem (1968, 1974) on the English question, and Dato (1971) on the Spanish verb phrase all supported the notion that second-language development in children progresses through stages similar to those observed in first-language speakers of the target language. In a cross-sectional study, Natalicio and Natalicio (1971) found that Spanish speakers acquired the English plural in a way that paralleled English rather than Spanish first-language structures. Dulay and Burt (1973, 1974), in their cross-sectional research on morpheme accuracy, also reported that the second-language system rather than the child's first language guides the acquisition process.

In contrast, studies by Wode (1976), Cancino, Rosansky, and Schumann (1974, 1975), and Hakuta (1976) indicate that the sequences Milon and Ravem found for the English negative and question are not obtained in all children learning English as a second language. There are several reasons for these discrepancies. Hakuta and Cancino (1977) pointed out that certain features of English are easier for children whose first language also possesses those features than for children whose first language lacks those features. For example, the English articles *a* and *the* require sophisticated semantic distinctions for their proper use—as in *a dog* and *the dog*. Consequently children whose first language makes this contrast—as French and Spanish do—will have less difficulty with the definite/indefinite article discrimination than will a child whose first language does not make this distinction (e.g., Japanese and Korean). This is supported by the research of Hakuta (1976), Cancino, Rosansky, and Schumann (1975), and Fathman (1975a).

Another reason for not finding the same developmental patterns in a second-language acquirer as in a monolingual child is that the child acquiring a second language may have recourse to first-language structures when confronted with particularly recalcitrant problems in the second language. There is some evidence for this from Wode's (1976) research on German-speaking children learning English as a second language. Some constructions appeared to reflect German word order and were not similar to any found in the speech of English-speaking children. Wode maintained that what superficially looks like a step backward is actually a strategy of reverting to the first language when trying to solve the riddle of the second.

It seems safe to conclude that the developmental sequence obtained in the speech of a second-language learner reflects the structure of that language. But it also seems, at this point in our knowledge, that the learner's first language may enter in, especially when features of the target language are new or markedly different from (or similar to) the first language. It should be pointed out, however, that almost all this research has focused on syntactic development. There has been much less research on phonological aspects of second-language acquisition and almost no research on semantic or pragmatic aspects. It is quite conceivable that in these areas the influence of the learner's first language, even in young children, will be more pronounced (Hakuta, 1981).

Interlanguage. The complex relationship between the speaker's first language and the target language is evidenced by a phenomenon known as "interlanguage" (Selinker, 1972). Selinker proposed that the interlanguage is a separate linguistic system that underlies second-language performance and that results from the learner's attempted production of the target language norm. Although the speaker's first language and the target language affects the interlanguage, the interlanguage differs from both the first language and the target language in systematic ways.

Initially the interlanguage hypothesis was applied only to adult second-language performance. But Selinker, Swain, and Dumas (1975) extended the hypothesis to children as well. They argued that under certain circumstances—when the second language was acquired successively and when it occurs in the absence of native-speaking peers of the target language—an interlanguage will develop in the speech of children. These conditions were realized in the subjects studied by Selinker and his associates—7-year-old children in a French "immersion program" in an English-language elementary school in Canada.

The children were 10 boys and 10 girls who had been instructed entirely in French by a native speaker during both kindergarten and the first grade. When studied at the end of the first grade, the children consistently used French to talk to their teacher and among themselves in the classroom setting. They had no trouble understanding French and could express in French what they wanted to say. They did not, however, speak French outside of class hours and had little contact with native French speakers of their own age.

Selinker, Swain, and Dumas (1975) argued that an analysis of the children's speech revealed a definite *systematicity* in the interlanguage. This systematicity was not seen to be predictable by grammatical rules but to be evidenced by recognizable strategies. By "strategy" was meant a cognitive activity at the conscious or unconscious level that involved the processing of second-language data in the attempt to express meaning. They focused on three such strategies: language transfer, overgeneralization of target language rules, and simplification.

The first of these strategies, language transfer, refers to the apparent application of first-language rules to target language forms. Such errors were earlier referred to as interlingual or transfer errors. Overgeneralization of target language norms involves the application of rules derived from the target language to forms where their application is not appropriate. This corresponds to intralingual errors discussed earlier. Simplification strategies were thought to be related to the transfer strategy and/or to overgeneralization of target language norms. Simplification could therefore involve the interaction of transfer and generalization strategies observed by Andersen (1978). Selinker and his associates, however, also suggested that simplification is a "superordinate strategy," with overgeneralization and language transfer types of simplification.

At this point I would like to defer, until the next section, discussion of the "strategies" involved in second-language acquisition. It appears that a number of different researchers with different perspectives are zeroing in on the same processes. It is not easy, however, to determine in any given instance that a learner is using a definite strategy. (This certainly is the lesson to be drawn from error-analysis research.) Furthermore, as Selinker, Swain, and Dumas pointed out, it is a mistake to base description of the learner's interlanguage solely on linguistic forms judged to be errors in terms of the target language. A full analysis of the systematicity of the interlanguage requires an explanation for why the learner gets certain forms correct and others wrong.

In contrast to Selinker and his associates, who opted for an analysis of the interlanguage based on learning strategies, Adjemian (1976) argued that the systematicity of the interlanguage should be analyzed linguistically as rule-governed behavior. In this view, the internal organization of the interlanguage can be idealized linguistically, just as any natural language. We may not be able to generate the interlanguage—or any language—through linguistic constructs, but we can learn something about the second-language learner's speech by making a series of descriptions of the learner's interlanguage. Adjemian cited Corder's (1973) suggestion that research be directed at the learner's "transitional competence"—that is, the set of grammatical intuitions about an interlanguage that a learner possesses at a given point in time. Once knowledge is obtained about transitional competence, Adjemian saw the researcher to be in a much better position to infer the psychological mechanisms at play. For this reason Adjemian argued that analysis of the systematicity of the interlanguage should begin with the regularities observed in a large body of data and should be directed at determination of the properties of the learner's grammar(s).

Whereas Selinker's term "interlanguage" stresses the structurally intermediate nature of the learner's language system between the first and the target language, Corder's (1973) notion of "transitional competence" and Nemser's (1971) term "approximative systems" emphasize the transitional and dynamic nature of the system. Adjemian (1976) also stressed the dynamic character of interlanguage systems, their *permeability*. Interlanguage systems are by their nature incomplete and in the state of flux. In this view the individual's first-language system is seen to be relatively stable, but the interlanguage is not. When placed in a situation that cannot be avoided, the second-language learner may use rules or items from the first language or may stretch, distort, or overgeneralize a rule from the target language in an effort to produce the intended meaning. This Adjemian sees to reflect the basic permeability of the interlanguage.

This brings us to another characteristic of the interlanguage that has attracted considerable attention recently—the notion of *fossilization*. Although this applies to children's language (Selinker, Swain, & Dumas, 1975), most discussions of fossilization have concerned adult second-language performers. Consequently, I shall turn now to research on factors affecting the development of second languages in adult learners.

Research on Adults

Fossilization. The process of fossilization was identified by Selinker (1972). This is the state of affairs that exists when the learner ceases to elaborate the interlanguage in some respect, no matter how long there is exposure, new data, or new teaching. Selinker maintained that such fossilization results especially from language transfer (French speakers who retain the uvulur /R/ in their English interlanguage, English speakers who use English word order in German sentences, etc.), but fossilization may also be the result of other processes. For example, strategies of communication may dictate to some individuals that they stop learning the language once they have learned enough to communicate (Vigil & Oller, 1976).

In spite of recent interest in the fossilization notion (Adjemian, 1976; Schumann, 1976; Selinker & Lamendella, 1978; Virgil & Oller, 1976), there are a large number of questions that need to be answered before we begin to understand why it is that individuals cease to elaborate the interlanguage. Obviously, the concept of fossilization needs to be more clearly operationalized. We do not know, for example, whether fossilization is a process that occurs suddenly at a given point in time or whether it is a slow and gradual process occurring over a span of weeks or even years. We do not know whether fossilization is a permanent state or a temporary plateau that a learner reaches before moving on to another temporary plateau.

It seems that fossilization is more likely in some language systems than in others. Fossilization in the phonological domain is a common occurrence, but what does it mean to speak of fossilization in the semantic or lexical domain? We know little about the sequence in which particular syntactic forms fossilize or whether they are language- or learner-specific. Nor do we know whether certain syntactic forms are more susceptible to premature stabilization than are others.

It seems likely that the topic of fossilization will occupy researchers concerned with second-language learning for years to come. If we can come to understand what factors—cognitive, motivational, social, neurological—affect when fossilization occurs, how long it persists, and how it can be surmounted, we have important information for intervention programs.

Attitude and Motivation. Schumann (1976) has argued that the point at which the interlanguage system fossilizes is directly controlled by the degree of acculturation of the learner to the target society. He called this variable "social distance." The greater the social distance, the less likely the learner is to approximate target-language norms.

Other researchers have isolated other attitudinal and motivational variables. The two main types of motivational variables that have been described are the "integrative," whereby it is the learner's intent to communicate actively with speakers of the target language, and the "instrumental," whereby the purpose of learning the language is more utilitarian (Gardner & Lambert, 1972; Gardner, Smythe, Clement, & Glicksman, 1976).

Attitudinal variables, in addition to Schumann's social distance factor, include "ego permeability" (Guiora, Beit-Hallahmi, Brannon, Dull, & Scovel, 1972), "alienation" (Larsen & Smalley, 1972), "empathy" (Guiora, Brannon, & Dull, 1972), and "ethnocentrism" (Gardner, 1978). Clarke (1976) saw the degree of "culture shock" and clash between levels of "modernity" to be an important factor in second-language learning. Lambert (1977) distinguished between "additive" bilingualism, in which the learner loses nothing by learning a second language, and "subtractive" bilingualism, in which the learner is forced to give up something.

Unfortunately, research on attitudinal and motivational factors has not provided simple answers. The research of Gardner and Lambert (1972) on integrative and instrumental motives indicated that there were cases where higher performance in second-language learning was associated with higher scores on integrative motivation; in other cases higher performance was associated with higher scores on instrumental motivation; in other cases neither variable correlated with better performance scores. It appears that personality factors, the learning situation, and feedback from achievement all play a role in moderating the effects of integrative and instrumental motivation.

Research on attitudinal variables reveals some, relatively weak, relationships. Few researchers have been concerned with issues of reliability and validity, so that even when fairly promising results are obtained, one is uncertain as to how to interpret them. Oller (1981) has argued that the relationship between affect and learning is dynamic, probably bidirectional, and unstable. Certainly the causal network is complex. If one is to assess the extent to which attitudes, motivation, and other variables affect achievement in learning a second language, a path analysis procedure—with recursive models—would seem to be more appropriate than the simple correlation studies we now have.

Tucker (1981) has pointed out that it may well be that contact is more important than motivational or attitudinal variables. Indeed, amount of contact may predict motivational and attitudinal factors, which in turn may affect achievement. Or it may be the other way around. In any event, path analytic procedures provide a methodology for testing these models, given reliable and valid measuring instruments.

Of course the attempt to uncover causal relationships between variables involved in second-language learning is formidable because of the large number of factors to be taken into consideration. Swain (1977) has attempted to delimit the relevant variables in a heuristic model that distinguishes among the input situation, the learner variables, the learning process, and what is learned (Fig. 4.1). The first set of variables—those relating to input—includes interaction in the natural environment and in instructional situations. As we shall see, there is increasing research interest in input, especially in such variables as "foreigner talk" and "teacher talk." In the learner variables Swain includes, besides attitudes and motivation, personality characteristics, cognitive style, aptitude, age, and past language experience. Under learning she includes "unconscious" and "conscious" strategies and processes, as described in Krashen's (1976a, 1976b, 1977, 1981) Monitor Model. Finally, there are the various dependent variables, including pragmatic aspects of language and discourse functioning.

The Monitor Model. Krashen's work on the Monitor Model is easily the most ambitious attempt to account for the processes involved in adult second-language performance. Krashen has presented a theory that has considerable intuitive appeal and that purports to integrate a great deal of research on various aspects of second-language performance. Central to the theory is the distinction between *acquisition* and *learning*. According to Krashen, acquisition is similar (if not identical) to the process by which children acquire a first language. It occurs through meaningful interaction in the natural communication setting. In acquiring a language, the speaker is not concerned with form but with meaning, nor is there explicit concern with error detection and correction. This contrasts with language learning where error detection and correction are central. Learning typically occurs in the classroom where formal rules and feedback provide the basis for language instruction.

Whereas the acquisition process is governed by universal strategies and leads to the acquisition of structures of the language in a fairly stable order, learning relies on the use of the monitor, whereby one's own performance is consciously altered so that it corresponds to what has been learned. The central claim of the Monitor Model is that conscious learning is available to the performer only as a monitor. Utterances are initiated by the acquisition system with conscious learning used to alter the output of the acquired system, sometimes before and sometimes after the utterance is produced. In other words, production is based on what is "picked up" through communication, with the monitor altering production to improve accuracy toward target-language norms.

Elsewhere (McLaughlin, 1978a) I have reviewed the claims of the Monitor Model in detail. I have argued that the model fails because the empirical underpinnings are weak. Ultimately the learning-acquisition distinction is not falsifiable because it rests on whether the processes involved are conscious or subconscious. Other approaches can equally well account for the phenomena in question; in fact, they do so more parsimoniously.

At this point it might be helpful to review an alternative account of the processes involved in second-language learning (McLaughlin, 1978a)—the third box in Swain's model (Fig. 4.1). In Table 4.1, I have outlined a set of

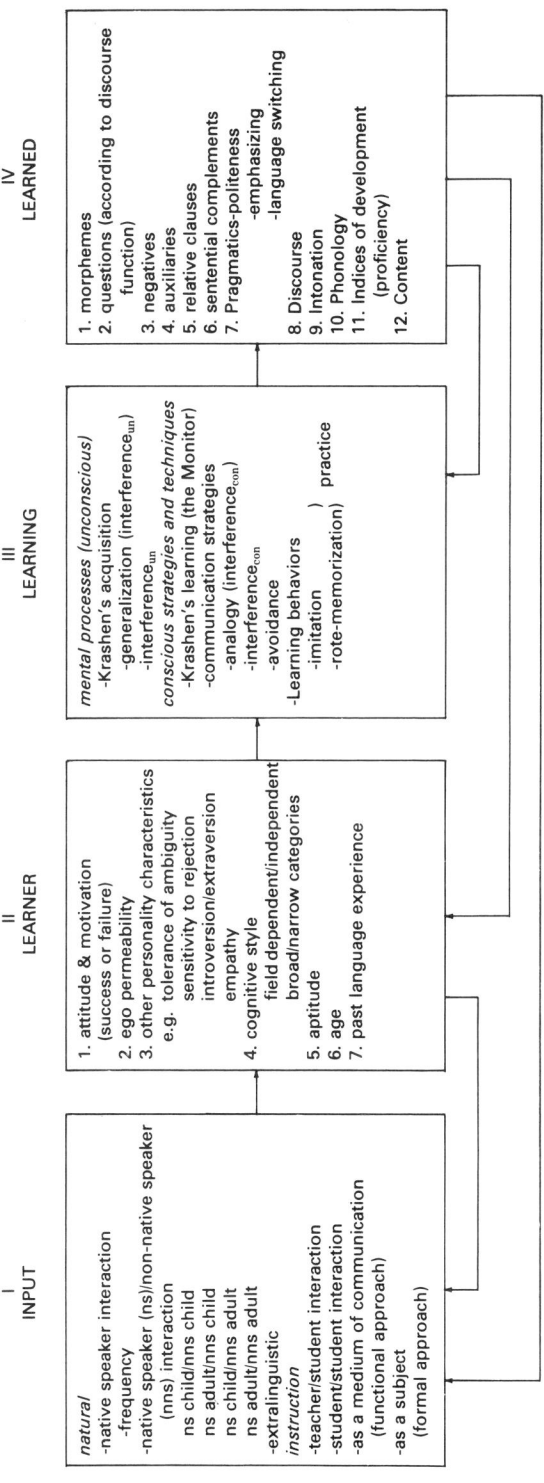

FIG. 4.1. A model of the second-language learner and second-language learning (from Swain, 1977; by permission of author).

"schemata." These schemata refer to infrastructures on all levels of linguistic functioning—syntactic, semantic, phonological, and pragmatic. They are built up sequentially over time through "the continual interaction of external impressions with internal systems" (Stern & Stern, 1907). Internal systems—whether they be thought of in terms of a generatively preprogrammed language acquisition device, a universal supergrammar, or the product of the cognitive abilities of the child—work on external input and produce this series of schemata, or "approximative systems" (Nemser, 1971), or "interlanguages" (Selinker, 1972) that for the most part "fossilize" at some distance from target-language norms.

Discovery Procedures. There are two kinds of discovery procedures that work on input to generate schemata. The first of these, "acquisition heuristics," is thought to be universal to all language learners and to affect learning. The second, "operating procedures," is thought to be variable in usage and to affect performance.

The first of the *acquisition heuristics* listed in Table 4.1 is simplification. This may be a misnomer, because, strictly speaking, the child or second-language learner cannot be said to simplify what they do not possess (Corder, 1971). At least in the psychological sense, simplification may be the wrong term. However, the schemata produced by first- and second-language learners are linguistically simpler, syntactically and morphologically, than target-language norms. Presumably, learners operate on some least-effort principle, transforming more complex input into more "simple" output.

Generalization refers to the tactic of using what is known to resolve the riddle of what is unknown. The backsliding of first-language learners (going from *went* to *goed* or *feet* to *foots*) is an instance of how learners use generalization to cope with the overload caused by too many new irregular forms. The second-language learner will use generalization to solve problems posed by the new language on analogy with the old one. Such transfer from the first language is more likely to occur in the early stages of the learning process (Taylor, 1975b) or when the

TABLE 4.1
Discovery Procedures in Second-Language Learning

I. Acquisition heuristics (universal and affect learning)
    Simplification
    Generalization
    Imitation
    Avoidance
    Slobin's "Operating Principles"
II. Operating procedures (variable and affect performance)
    Use of formal rules
    Use of repair requests
    Rote memory
    Talk/listen variation
    Fillmore's "Social and Cognitive Strategies"

learner is faced with a particularly difficult problem (Wode, 1976). It is also more likely to occur in classroom than in naturalistic learning situations (Selinker, Swain, & Dumas, 1975).

Imitation is postulated to be a universal discovery procedure for first- and second-language learning. There seems to be considerable variation on this score with some first-language learners showing little tendency to imitate utterances (Bloom, Lightbown, & Hood, 1975). In second-language research, however, children in naturalistic settings have been repeatedly observed to imitate whole utterances before having mastered the parts (Fillmore, 1976; Hakuta, 1974; Huang, 1971). This imitative use of "prefabricated constructions" or "formulaic expressions" that are gradually analyzed has not received much attention in research with adult second-language learners but is probably used by both adults and children in naturalistic settings where the input is complex and where learners are required to communicate (Krashen & Scarcella, 1978).

Avoidance has been studied in bilingual children, who have been observed not to use constructions they possess in one of their primary languages in a second language where the linguistic structures are more complex (Imedadze, 1967; Mikeš, 1967). The phenomenon of avoidance seems quite common in second-language learning (Schachter, 1974) and poses serious methodological problems for any analysis of errors in the second-language learning process (Schachter & Celce-Murcia, 1977).

The final acquisition heuristic I list refers to what Slobin (1971) called "operating principles." These are seen to be relatively specific universals in the ontogenesis of grammar. They include such tactics as "Pay attention to the ends of words," "Pay attention to the order of words and morphemes," "Avoid interruption or rearrangement of linguistic units," and "The use of grammatical markers should make semantic sense." Hatch (1976) has noted that some second-language learners show behavior that contradicts these operating principles, but these discrepancies seem to be the result of generalizing from the first language or early fossilization in the second.

Note that "operating principles," which are thought to be universal and affect learning, are distinct from what I refer to as *operating procedures*, which are subject to considerable individual variation in use and affect performance. I suspect that operating procedures are more important in second-language learning than in first—performance being more variable in second-language learning, both in terms of the rate of improvement and level of achievement attained. Presumably all first-language learners pass through the same developmental stages and achieve target-language norms. This is not necessarily the case in second-language learning.

The first operating procedure I list is the retrieval of rules that have been formally learned. In first-language use, for example, we may have recourse to formal rules learned in grammar school in editing such sentences as *The boy in the car was seen by her and me,* or *Whomever I gave the book to, returned it.* In a second language, recourse to formal rules is much more common, especially if the individual has learned the language primarily through error correction and rule isolation in the classroom.

By the use of repair requests I mean employing certain formulaic constructions to elicit help from native speakers, getting them to repeat or "repair" what they have said. The successful use of repair-soliciting tactics is especially important in adult second-language learning, since such techniques are quite useful as elicitation devices to obtain topic clarification (Hatch, 1978a). By saying *huh,* or echoing sentences to get them recycled, or using *pardon me* or *I don't understand,* second-language learners signal to native speakers that they need help. If they recycle the same topic with different native speakers, second-language learners build up vocabulary and can concentrate on morphology and syntax.

Rote memorization refers to the deliberate rehearsal of vocabulary on the part of the second-language learner without situational support. Whereas children usually are able to converse about objects in the immediate here and now, adults are often required to talk about abstract topics and themes. Consequently, vocabulary development becomes the prime task of adult learners.

By talk/listen variation I mean the tendency of individual second-language learners to take either a more active or more passive stance toward the target language. Some learners—especially, but not necessarily, children—plunge right in and start talking without concern about the errors they make. Other learners prefer to listen and develop their ability to comprehend what is being said before they attempt to do much communicating. No doubt such variation relates to personality factors—anxiety, attitude and motivation, ego permeability, social distance, inhibition and self-consciousness, and so forth (Schumann, 1975).

Finally, there are the "social and cognitive strategies" observed by Fillmore (1976) in the child second-language learners she studied. The social strategies the children seemed to follow led them to join the group and act as if they understood what was being said, to say something with a few well-chosen words, and to count on their friends. Cognitive strategies were to assume that what people were saying was directly related to the situation at hand, to use formulaic expressions as a means of decoding the target language, and to work on the big things first, saving the details until later. These strategies may be specific to children learning a second language in interacting with their peers. Adults may rely more on such operating procedures as the use of rules, rote memory, and listening.

INTERVENTION PROGRAMS

To this point I have been discussing the processes of second-language learning and the major areas of current research concern for investigators looking at the way in which children and adults learn a second language. I would now like to turn to some practical issues. When should one begin to introduce people to a second language? How is one to do this optimally? What are the best ways to structure a second-language program or a bilingual education program? Needless to say, these are questions that will be with us for some time, and one can only attempt to provide a sense of some current thinking.

Second-Language Learning

Three topics with practical implications for intervention programs have attracted a great deal of recent interest among second-language researchers: the learner's age, input and conversational interaction, and the communication model of language training. I would like to look briefly at each of these topics and then turn to a particular type of intervention program—that concerned with bilingual/ bicultural education.

The Learner's Age. Elsewhere I have reviewed the evidence on this subject (McLaughlin, 1978b). Whereas it has generally been assumed that children are superior to adults in all aspects of second-language learning, the evidence for their superiority is meager. In fact, under naturalistic conditions the presumed superiority of young children does not obtain: Older children were found to learn French morphology and syntax faster than younger children (Ervin-Tripp, 1974); teenagers were better at learning Dutch grammar than younger children (Snow & Hoefnagel-Höhle, 1978a); and older children were better at learning English grammar than younger children (Fathman, 1975b). Krashen, Long, and Scarcella (1979), in reviewing this literature, argued that the evidence supported the notion that older children and adults learn faster than younger children but that the younger the better as far as ultimate language proficiency is concerned. The second part of this generalization is not supported by research, however. The studies Krashen et al. cited deal chiefly (with one exception) with pronunciation, so that any conclusions about general language proficiency are unwarranted. Second, what evidence there is on syntactic acquisition shows older children (11-15) to retain their superiority over younger children (6-10) up to 1 year (Snow & Hoefnagel-Höhle, 1978b) and even up to 3 years (Fathman, 1975b). Finally, research with FLES (Foreign Languages in the Elementary School) programs indicates that children who begin to learn second languages later, especially in high school, catch up with children beginning earlier and reach the same criterion in a shorter period of time. Thus in terms of ultimate language proficiency, the-younger-the-better hypothesis is not supported. The evidence available at this point suggests that early adolescence is the best time to learn a second language, both in terms of rate of learning and eventual language proficiency.

One of the arguments for the purported superiority of young children in learning a second language is the critical period notion. Lenneberg (1967), an early advocate of this position, argued that the reason for the critical period was lateralization of brain functions—a process he thought was completed at puberty. Recently there has been a great deal of debate on this point. Some authors have argued that hemispheric specialization for language is achieved very early in life, perhaps at birth, whereas other authors place it later (Krashen, 1975). Other authors contend that there is a great deal of individual variation, with some individuals lateralized at about 8 years of age and others as late as 14 years, with variability within a large population assuming a normal distribution (Scovel, 1981). Seliger (1978) has proposed a multiple critical period hypothesis, arguing that variability in second-language learning in adults may be attributable to varying degrees of lateralization, the level of success being inversely proportional to the degree of interhemispheric specialization for language. Unfortunately, what data exist do not support this hypothesis (Scovel, 1981).

At this point the evidence for a biologically based critical period for second-language learning is not convincing. We do not even have criterion measures for such language domains as syntax, semantics, or pragmatics. What are the target language norms for these domains? Even in the area of pronunciation there is considerable difference of opinion as to what standard is to be used.

If differences in second-language learning ability can be shown to exist between adults and children, they can probably be explained without recourse to the critical period—or "frozen brain"—hypothesis. When people attribute superior language-learning ability to children, they frequently ignore the fact that the criterion for language proficiency differs for children and adults. Children talk about a restricted domain—usually concrete objects present in the here and now. Adults are expected to speak about a great deal more. Furthermore there are attitudinal and motivational factors that often favor children. Children are highly motivated to be like other children, whereas adults, though perhaps motivated by economic incentives, often have a spouse or a group of countrymen with whom they can interact. Adults may also be less willing than children to surrender the part of their identity associated with their native language; they may have less time to learn a second language than children; and usually adults tend to be more inhibited. All these factors favor children and yet, in spite of these advantages, the naturalistic studies cited earlier indicate that second-language learning is usually not inversely related to age. Certainly there are some adult immigrants who never learn to speak their new language well, but this may be explained on the basis of nonbiological factors. At least until we know more about the biology of language, to speak of a biologically based critical period for second-language learning seems premature (first-language learning is another issue). There may be a "sensitive period" for second-language learning, but the determinants are more psychological and social than biological.

Input and Conversational Interactions. The relevance of first-language research on input or "caretaker speech" to second-language learning has been pointed out by a number of authors (Krashen, 1978; McLaughlin, 1980).

Mothers and other caretakers develop a special and restricted lexicon when talking to young children; they usually limit their speech to refer to objects in the immediate here and now; they modify their speech patterns, using a higher overall pitch, often with a rising intonation at the end of sentences. Their speech is slower and more precise; there are more instances of emphatic stress; they repeat utterances and expand and elaborate what the child has said. There are also grammatical modifications—fewer verbs, modifiers, conjunctions, and prepositions; there is less use of third-person constructions, passive voice, and other more complicated constructions in speech addressed to younger children when compared to speech addressed to older children and adults (Snow, 1972; Snow & Ferguson, 1977).

This style of speaking to young children seems to have an important function in first-language acquisition. Sentences are kept short because of the need of gaining and holding a child's attention. Stress and repetition make words identifiable. Speech is slow and articulate so that the boundaries between words and sentences can be identified. Reference to the immediate context makes some hunches as to meaning possible. Speech to the young child is usually well-formed and intelligible and not beyond the child's comprehensive capacities. In other words, there is a rough tuning of the caretaker's speech to the child's communicative abilities with the caretaker providing the child with input that facilitates language acquisition. It is not so much that parents provide lessons in grammar—they modify their speech naturally to the child's abilities in order to communicate.

Some modifications are at the level of discourse. Bloom and her associates (Bloom, Lightbown, & Hood, 1975; Bloom, Rocissano, & Hood, 1976) have reported that their analyses of conversational interactions between parents and children reveal that children learning a first language use several strategies. Initially, children tend to imitate those lexical and structural features in adult speech that they are in the process of learning (not those they know well or that are entirely novel). Later, children begin to expand prior utterances, repeating the verb and adding something new. These changes in the child's speech were found to be accompanied by changes in parental speech, with the parents questioning more as children became increasingly capable of expanding utterances. Similarly, as the children imitated less, repetitions in parental speech decreased.

Presently research on first-language development is moving from the descriptive stage to attempting to determine how caretaker speech affects language acquisition. Although it is generally assumed that caretaker speech assists the child to learn the first language, it is not known how and to what extent it does so. We do not know, for example, whether increasing certain aspects of caretaker speech—such as expansions, repetitions, or various simplifications—will speed up language acquisition in children or whether it is simply a question of a threshold level—that is, whether certain features of caretaker speech must be present in some minimal amount for the child to develop first language normally.

Second-language research on input is still in the descriptive stage. Researchers are concerned with describing the characteristics of "foreigner talk" (the speech code people use to speak to a nonproficient speaker of their language) and "teacher talk" (the speech code used by foreign-language teachers in the classroom). Freed (1978), for example, has found that foreigner talk differs from caretaker talk along a number of dimensions, especially when the functional aspects of language are considered. Wagner-Gough and Hatch (1975) noted that the foreigner talk addressed to an older child differs markedly from that addressed to a younger child, in that there was more embedding, more idioms, a wider range of vocabulary, and more focus on activities displaced in time in the speech addressed to the older child. One suspects that this makes the task of the older learner more difficult.

The Communication Model. If this is indeed the case, if the nature of the input does affect language learning, then there are definite implications for the classroom. There seems to be a growing recognition that language instruction should be directed at assuring communicative competence (Jakobovits, 1970; Rivers, 1973). A number of authors have argued that language instruction should focus on communication, both in the teacher-student and the student-student relationship (Cook, 1969; Krashen, 1976a; Macnamara, 1976; McLaughlin, 1980).

In spite of the fact that classroom instruction is essentially the manipulation of input variables, we know almost nothing of how teachers talk in the foreign-language classroom. There is some evidence that, like foreigner talk, teacher talk differs from caretaker talk along a number of dimensions (Hatch, Shapira, & Gough, 1978; Henzl, 1979). Yet foreigner talk and teacher talk appear to be quite different. For example, Hatch and her associates (Hatch, 1978a) have found that people talking to adult second-language learners sometimes "shift up" rather than down in reselecting vocabulary.

> What do people in your country do for fun?
> For fun?
> For a good time.
> For fun?
> For entertainment.
> For fun?

Foreign-language teachers are less likely to do this, and they also simplify their grammar to a greater extent than the average person does when talking to a foreigner (Hatch, 1978a).

I have argued elsewhere that teachers should do this even more self-consciously (McLaughlin, 1980). If the language classroom is viewed as a communication setting, focus should be on topics of mutual concern that are concrete and immediate. Teachers should deliberately simplify syntax; limit vocabulary; keep utterances short; expand, prompt, repeat, and ask simple questions—just as caretakers do for children learning a first language. In other words, the conversational interaction should mimic as much as possible those interactions that occur in first-language acquisition.

These suggestions are tentative and may have to be modified as we come to know more about what in caretaker talk relates to language acquisition and more about the features of foreigner and teacher talk. There is, however, increasing acceptance of the notion that second-language learners, like children acquiring a first language, need not speak grammatically from the start and that errors, like those children make, are sources of feedback about false hypotheses. There is also increasing acceptance of the communication model, of the notion that the teacher's best strategy is one that gets students involved in meaningful communication. What is needed is more information about input variables—which ones affect language acquisition and why—so that a more deliberate manipulation of input variables would become feasible.

Bilingual Education Programs

Turning now to bilingual education programs, one is struck by how little impact developments in second-language research have had. There are a number of reasons for this, the most important one being that there has been so much confusion about precisely what a bilingual program should be. There are also serious practical problems—obtaining funding for the programs, training personnel, developing curriculum materials, and devising appropriate evaluation procedures.

Definitional Problems. A bilingual program refers to some configuration of instruction through the medium of two languages. Although the federal government has provided definitions of bilingual programs for legislative purposes, attempts to put the definitions into practice have resulted in a wide variety of programs. At least four types can be distinguished: (1) compensatory bilingual programs, in which the focus is on teaching English to those who do not know it to "compensate for" their "linguistic deficiencies" so that they will be able to participate effectively in the predominant culture; (2) enrichment bilingual programs, where the focus is on teaching students who speak English a second language to give them fluency in and appreciation of another language and culture; (3) transitional bilingual programs, where the goal is to use the students' native language as a medium of instruction only until they can function effectively in English; (4) maintenance bilingual programs, where the goal is not only to teach skills in English to students from a linguistic minority group but also to maintain language skills and literacy in the students' home language (Parker, 1978).

Whatever the type of bilingual program, the objectives of the program usually include teaching the second language (usually English) so that children acquire skills in understanding, speaking, reading, and writing. Depending on the type of program, the children may also receive help in reading and writing in their native language. There are a number of variations possible. In some cases one language is used one day and the other language on a second day. Sometimes the native language is used for part of the day and English for the rest of the day. Sometimes subjects are repeated in both languages. When there are too few limited English speakers for the school to provide a full bilingual program, a bilingual support program may be set up with resource material and personnel hired to tutor the children in their native language, while the child participates in regular English-medium instruction.

Evaluation of Bilingual Programs. Given this diversity, it is not surprising that evaluation of bilingual education programs presents a mixed picture. Although there is some evidence that bilingual education programs can significantly improve the educational achievement of minority children, weak programs can retard achievement and may produce children who are semiliterate or illiterate in both of their languages (Troike & Perez, 1978).

Recent evaluative studies are discouraging. Studies by the General Accounting Office, by the American Institute for Research, and by the National Institute for Education have drawn a bleak picture. There is little evidence from these studies that bilingual programs have been effective in spite of the millions of dollars that have been spent on them. For example, Cervantes (1977) reported on the results of 5 years of research done in a bilingual school district in Texas at the cost of 8 million dollars. Comparison of experimental bilingual schools and a monolingual control school revealed that there were no differences in academic achievement and little effect on such variables as self-concept, attitude toward school, and mobility aspirations. Experimental teachers' attitudes and behavior—even the use of Spanish in the classroom (!)—differed very little from the control group. The use of resource persons failed to have any effect.

Cervantes concluded that, even when funding is available, new methodology and new curriculum materials cannot in themselves produce greater academic achievement. What is critical is the readiness of parents, students, teachers, and administrators to accept a commitment to a bilingual program. The community must understand and support the program beforehand if it is to have any chance of success. In short, social factors may be the preeminent variables determining the outcome of a bilingual program.

The Future of Bilingual Education Programs. Nationwide evaluations, such as that conducted by the American Institute for Research, have been severely criticized by proponents of bilingual education on the grounds that such evaluations mix together good and bad programs and use faulty criteria for success. Certainly more attention needs to be given to determining what variables are relevant and important in evaluating bilingual education programs. Ethnographic methods have been proposed as a means of providing data upon which to base definitions of success or effective classroom participation (Mehan, 1977). This would presumably involve observational studies of teacher-student and student-student interactions, language use, how children learn, and how they display what they have learned. One would also like to see the development of evaluation procedures that provide teachers and administrators with feedback to assist them in modifying the program. Finally, because social factors seem to play a central role in determining the success of bilingual programs, parents, students, and other community members should be included in the planning and implementation of the evaluation design. The community's characteristics and the concerns and expectations of its members are central to any evaluation program.

In view of the unfortunate publicity resulting from negative evaluation studies, the survival of bilingual education programs depends on efforts to improve the quality of the programs. This means, above all, a greater research effort is needed. Contents of curricula, program objectives, teaching methodology, and teacher training all depend on research. Basic research is needed on the nature of bilingualism, on the relationship between linguistic development and school achievement, on the second-language learning process, on the transferability of reading skills from a native language to English, and on the long-term effects of specific teaching techniques.

Some of this research is being carried out in the field of second-language learning. For example, research in this field suggests that younger children are not necessarily better than older children in learning a second language, that social variables and individual differences play an important role in how well children learn a second language, that contact and language use are crucial determinants of language learning, and that formal language instruction is not necessarily the best way for all learners to learn a second language—rather communication in meaningful contexts optimizes learning for many learners. All of these research findings have application in the bilingual classroom. The problem is that there is a tendency for bilingual education to remain a self-contained field, resisting input from the outside and emphasizing ideological commitment (Troike & Perez, 1978). This is unfortunate if it means failure to draw on research findings that would improve the quality of bilingual education programs. If bilingual education is not to become merely another passing fad—similar to the FLES programs (Foreign Languages in the Elementary School) programs of the 1960s—there must be a commitment to research, especially cross-disciplinary research involving psycholinguists, sociolinguists, and researchers concerned with first- and second-language learning.

BILINGUAL COMPETENCE

One of the practical problems for bilingual education programs is that of determining language competence in each of the bilingual child's languages. I would like to comment briefly on this problem and then move on to discuss research on the effects of bilingualism on cognitive development and functioning. The goal of this section is to determine what can be said about what it means to be bilingual.

Assessment of Bilingualism

School districts with bilingual students must find some test instruments to determine students' language proficiency in order to comply with federal regulations. A number of instruments exist, but none is adequate. Furthermore the concept of language "dominance," used to identify the language in which the student is most proficient, is vague and imprecise. A student may use one language skillfully in one situation (e.g., school) but may be unable to use that language in another situation (e.g., home). Language proficiency is not a unitary concept but ranges across a large number of domains and roles. Students who score well on tests of grammatical knowledge are often unable to communicate effectively in a real-life setting. Similarly, the ability to speak a language fluently does not imply knowledge of how to read or write in that language.

Nonetheless most school systems test students for their "dominant" language and make placements accordingly. Researchers, however, have abandoned the concept of language dominance as scientifically worthless and have gone on to develop instruments that test knowledge of the functional uses of language in various situations. Unfortunately, these tests are long and complex and the school systems need something short and simple. As a result we have a situation in which the state of the art of language testing has not kept up with legal mandates (Shuy, 1978).

The best that can be hoped for, until better tests are devised, is the use of multimethod indicators—that is, the traditional tests should be used in conjunction with peer ratings, teacher ratings, self-reports, and parental reports. Although each of these methods is weak in itself, the composite picture is probably the best estimate of the child's language skills that we will be able to obtain under the circumstances.

A major issue that bilingual education programs face is deciding what is to be done with students who attain "bilingual competence." For example, once a native Spanish-speaking student attains a level of competence in English sufficiently high to function well in classes where English is the medium of instruction, is that student to be disqualified from participating in the bilingual program? This, of course, is the question of whether the program is to be a transitional or maintenance bilingual program. Those advocating maintenance programs argue that such programs offer a genuine opportunity for students to realize the full benefits of bilingual/bicultural education. A critical problem facing bilingual educators is convincing native English-speaking students of the value of such a bilingual/bicultural experience; otherwise such programs run the risk of ghettoizing or "tracking" ethnically segregated groups (Troike & Perez, 1978).

Bilingualism and Cognition

Elsewhere I have reviewed research on the effects of bilingualism on intelligence, language skills, educational attainment, emotional adjustment, and cognitive functioning (McLaughlin, 1978b). Although research is fraught with methodological pitfalls and few studies have been adequately controlled, it seems safe to say that bilingualism has little or no effect on intelligence. In those cases where a negative effect was found, this was due to verbal factors that put bilingual speakers at a disadvantage relative to monolinguals. Bilingual children have been found to do more poorly in academic subjects where verbal ability is a factor (depending on the bilingual's amount of exposure to and skill in the language). This suggests that bilingual children may need some special help with language in the early grades so that their initial disadvantage in command of the language does not prevent them from developing competence in areas with a large verbal component. The effect of bilingualism on emotional adjustment and attitudes toward other ethnic groups appears to depend on a large number of possibly uncontrollable environmental factors, especially the political climate and amount of contact.

One of the best controlled studies is the St. Lambert project (Lambert & Tucker, 1972). In this study, English-speaking children in Canada who were undergoing a bilingual experience were compared to a matched control group of their peers who did not undergo the bilingual experience. Tests of the two groups were made each year from kindergarten to the end of elementary school. The results of this research show the obvious positive effect of providing the children with knowledge of a second language and no negative effects on cognitive development or educational attainment. Of course, this may not always be the result of bilingual education and similarly designed studies are needed of various types of bilingual education with children of various linguistic and socioeconomic backgrounds.

Recently investigators have been less concerned with what effects bilingualism has on intelligence and school performance and have looked more closely at what bilingualism can tell us about the nature of intellectual development. There have been essentially two lines of research: The first is concerned mainly with the correlates between bilingualism and specific aspects of cognitive functioning; the second line of research is concerned with what can be learned about human cognitive processing through the study of bilingualism.

The Cognitive Correlates of Bilingualism. Does being bilingual affect the individual's way of thinking? Does a bilingual have more cognitive flexibility than monolinguals do? There is in fact some evidence that this is the case, both from studies conducted in this country (Feldman & Shen, 1971; Landry, 1974) and abroad (Balkan, 1970; Ianco-Worral, 1972; Peal & Lambert, 1962).

Landry (1974) argued that bilingual children have learned to overcome the negative transfer from their first language in learning their second, and this experience makes them less susceptible to negative transfer generally. As a result, bilinguals acquire a "flexibility set," which is beneficial in divergent thinking tasks that require inventiveness and originality. The child supposedly has developed an adaptability in learning a second language that can be used profitably on other cognitive tasks.

Not all the data are in on this particular question, however. For example, although experimental children in the well-designed St. Lambert project scored higher than control children on divergent thinking tasks at the lower grade levels, these differences were not found at the higher grade levels (Bruck, Lambert, & Tucker, 1974). Equally well-controlled longitudinal studies with children are needed, as well as research with adults—we know little about how bilingualism affects cognitive functioning in adults.

Lambert (1977) has noted that, although the bulk of the evidence favors the view that the bilingual experience has a positive effect on cognitive development, almost all studies dealt with bilinguals for whom the two languages involved had social value and respect. The learning of the second language did not involve its gradually replacing the individual's first language. This is often the case, however, for Spanish-speaking Americans who develop proficiency in English. Rather than being an "additive" form of bilingualism, their experience is with a "subtractive" form of bilingualism in which individuals often lose their ethnic language in acquiring a national language. Conceivably the effects of bilingualism on cognitive development are quite different in the "additive" and "subtractive" cases.

Bilingualism and Cognitive Processing. To what extent does bilingualism affect cognitive functioning? Do bilinguals have better means of storing linguistic information than monolinguals do? Does the contrast between linguistic systems aid the bilingual in the development of general conceptual thought? Are bilinguals more skilled at overcoming negative transfer effects? We cannot answer these questions at the present time, but there is increasing interest in the cognitive processes of bilingual individuals.

One attempt to specify the mechanisms whereby bilingualism affects cognitive processes was made by Ben-Zeev (1977) who cited evidence that: (1) bilinguals analyze language more intensely than monolinguals; (2) bilinguals are more sensitive to social and linguistic cues; (3) they become more aware of their languages as internally consistent systems than do monolinguals; and (4) bilinguals learn to simplify or "neutralize" the structures within a language. The first two of these processes are thought to have a potentially positive effect on symbolic processing. The last two may, but almost no research has been done on these mechanisms.

As evidence that bilinguals analyze language more intensively than monolinguals, Ben-Zeev (1977) cited her own research with Hebrew-English and Spanish-English bilingual children. Both groups were significantly lower than monolingual controls on the Peabody Picture Vocabulary Test but were significantly superior to monolingual children on symbol substitution. This was seen to reflect the bilingual's ability to analyze language as an abstract system, to grasp the basic idea that the structure of a language is different from the phonological representation of words.

As evidence that bilinguals were more sensitive than monolinguals to social and linguistic cues, Ben-Zeev cited results from her research that indicated that bilinguals scored higher than monolinguals in tasks requiring them to integrate details in telling a story to match a sequence of pictures and in classification tasks where cues would prompt subjects to restructure appropriately. Ben-Zeev argued that bilinguals have to learn to switch languages and this process requires sensitivity to external cues indicating the need to reorganize linguistic responses.

A great deal of experimental evidence is now available that indicates that bilinguals are able to keep their languages functionally separate when they speak. Nonetheless, concepts are not segregated in the bilingual brain according to the language of the words to which they are associated but are organized into one semantic system that underlies all the languages available to the individual (Albert & Obler, 1978; McLaughlin, 1978b; Segalowitz, 1977).

At the level of comprehension, however, bilinguals cannot selectively "tune out" one language or the other. Treisman (1964) reported that bilingual subjects experienced a great deal of interference when they had to say (shadow) immediately tape-recorded messages delivered to one ear while ignoring a message delivered to the other ear in a second language known to them. If the language delivered to the other ear was unknown, there was relatively less disruption.

In contrast, there is fairly strong evidence for a language switch mechanism to keep the languages separate in the production of speech. In chain-association tasks, when subjects are free to alternate between their two languages, they will tend to produce clusters in each language (Taylor, 1971). Similarly, there is a measured time increment in reading aloud from mixed lists, suggesting that it takes some effort on the subject's part to shift back and forth between languages (Macnamara & Kushnir, 1971).

The most convincing instance of the bilingual's linguistic sensitivity is simultaneous translation. To perform this task, bilinguals must switch codes in input and output. What is decoded in input in one language system must be encoded in output in the other. The semantic representation of the message in one language must be matched with the equivalent in the other. As one would expect, there is a relationship between skill at performing this task and degree of bilingualism (Treisman, 1965).

This suggests an important variable often ignored in research of this nature. There may be quite different consequences on cognitive functioning with different degrees of bilingualism. Perhaps some threshold must be passed before the beneficial effects of bilingualism appear (Cummins, 1979). Similarly, a bilingual who has little need for one language in daily life may not develop the linguistic sensitivity of bilinguals who use both languages daily. In any event, although we are beginning to accumulate some information, this is another area where the questions outnumber the answers.

CONCLUSION

In 1948 Werner Leopold called on linguists to follow his example and to investigate seriously the phenomenon of childhood bilingualism:

> America offers countless opportunities for observing infant bilingualism in the making. Children in immigrant families and in the Spanish-speaking Southwest often grow up with two languages.... I appeal to the few who are capable of carrying out such an investigation to add sorely needed case histories of infant bilingualism and infant language to the available material, as indispensable spade work for the higher purposes of linguistics [p. 11].

As Hatch (1977) has pointed out, it was many years before Leopold's plea was heeded. Only in the early 1970s was concerted research on childhood bilingualism and second-language learning begun. Before that there had been a great deal of speculative thinking, but case histories and empirical studies were few (McLaughlin, 1978b). In the past decade all this has changed drastically. Now we have a great number of studies on various aspects of second-language learning and bilingualism. In fact, as the research proliferates, it becomes increasingly difficult to see the forest for the trees.

I would like to provide an outline of the forest by summarizing those areas currently receiving most attention from researchers.

1. The question of the relationship between first- and second-language learning continues to be debated, although most investigators today would probably adopt what I have called the "weak position," that there is a similarity but not an identity between first- and second-language learning. Error analysis and the morpheme studies have shown that the influence of the first language was much less than was traditionally thought and that the structures of the second language and possibly universal acquisition strategies play an important role in second-language learning. But the learner *is* influenced by having learned a first language. Especially in the initial stages, it seems that second-language learning involves relying on first-language structures. Also, because the second-language learner is older, different memory heuristics and cognitive processes are involved in the learning process. But certain strategies—looking for word-order regularities, proceeding from the simple to the complex, using context as a cue for meaning, overgeneralizing lexical and morphological forms—seem to be used in

both first- and second-language learning. The challenge for researchers in the future is to ascertain the extent to which this is true. Conceivably, at certain points in the learning process and in certain situations, universal cognitive strategies for processing language are applied, whereas at other points and in other situations the learner tends to fall back on first-language structures.

2. The concept of "interlanguage" has received a great deal of attention recently. There have been a number of attempts to define the characteristics of the interlanguage and the ways in which it is modified. This task is far from complete, however, and represents perhaps the most challenging theoretical enterprise for the future. This means, among other things, that more needs to be known about the dynamic aspect of the interlanguage, what factors affect its permeability, and how it changes. At the same time, more needs to be known about the static and structural aspects of the interlanguage and about the "fossilization" process whereby the learner ceases to elaborate the interlanguage in some respect.

3. Related to this are questions concerning attitudinal and motivational factors. Although there has been a good deal of research on these topics, the results have been disappointing. It seems obvious that attitudinal and motivational factors play an important role in second-language learning. But attempts to get at these variables have suffered because of the difficulty in designing reliable and valid test instruments. The causal network also seems more complex than was supposed. Contact appears to be a powerful variable interacting with attitudinal and motivational factors. Here, in particular, more powerful analytic and statistical techniques are called for.

4. The field needs a good theory of the learning process. Krashen's Monitor Model is the most ambitious and exciting attempt in this direction. Nonetheless, I have argued here and elsewhere (McLaughlin, 1978a) that the model is neither empirically falsifiable nor parsimonious. We need a more adequate model along the lines—I would argue—of those suggested in "Discovery Procedures." Of course, the test of the pudding is in the eating, and more research and theory are needed before an adequate understanding of the second-language learning process will be possible.

5. We need to know more about the neuropsychology of language learning. There is a great deal of interesting work going on in this area presently, much of it upsetting the simpler models of the past. We now speak of "multiple critical periods," of "sensitive periods," of "degrees of hemispheric specialization." It appears that different language functions lateralize at different points in time; some may not lateralize at all. One of the most important challenges in this area is defining what it means to have phonological, syntactic, semantic, or pragmatic competence in a language. If conclusions are to be made about ways in which brain physiology affects language performance, the criterion measures of performance must be adequately defined. We will never know, for example, whether phonological development in a second-language is limited by physiolog-

ical factors unless we know what the target-language norms are for phonological development.

7. In discussing intervention strategies I have focused on the communication model and on research on input variables in first- and second-language learning. Language learning in the classroom involves essentially the manipulation of input variables and it may be that a great deal can be learned from research on caretaker speech to children learning the first language and from the ways in which people naturally alter their speech to foreigners. This obviously is not the whole story and a wide variety of teaching techniques should be explored. I would argue, however, that the most effective methods are those that focus on communication rather than on the eliminating of errors and that getting students to talk is more important than correcting their grammar.

7. Finally, there is the question of the cognitive correlates of bilingualism. Research directed at ascertaining the extent to which becoming bilingual affects cognitive functioning has been primarily with children, and little is known about the effects of becoming bilingual as an adult. Even with children, there is enough negative evidence to make one cautious about generalizing from findings suggesting that bilingualism has a positive effect on cognitive development. It may be that cognitive and linguistic variables, as well as sociocultural factors, have an effect upon the extent to which bilingualism influences cognitive development.

In general, there is a great need to look beyond main effects to interactions. What is true for most people may not be true for everyone or in every circumstance. This is the case both in assessing the effects of bilingualism and in making decisions about teaching methods and intervention strategies. Two methods of teaching or two bilingual education programs that are equally effective on the average may be quite different in effectiveness for two different groups.

Recently Cronbach and Snow (1977) have called for research directed at "aptitude × treatment interactions." By aptitude they mean dispositions, attitudinal variables, motivation, and aptitude per se. By treatment they mean instructional techniques and educational programs. They urged researchers to use designs specifically aimed at determining which person variables interact with which treatment variables.

To do so means using more powerful statistical procedures than we have been accustomed to. Experimental researchers often throw variance due to individual differences into the error term and so lose information. Those researchers dealing with correlations often fail to look at situational differences affecting their correlations. Cronbach and Snow advocated the use of regression analysis and path analytic procedures. These techniques, as well as scaling procedures such as implicational analysis (Andersen, 1978) and "quasi-experimental" techniques (Campbell & Stanley, 1963), will probably be receiving much more attention in the future.

Research on second-language learning and bilingualism has come far in the last 10 years, but the field is young and not all research has been of high quality. If the past tells us anything about the future, second-language researchers will follow first-language researchers in exploring the semantic and pragmatic as well as syntactic features of language development. Indeed, in the bilingual child, researchers in the second-language field have an ideal subject for studying the way in which the acquisition of formal devices for specific semantic content varies, because the complexity of the formal devices (e.g., word order, affixation) varies for the two languages (Slobin, 1971).

As an applied discipline, much research on second-language learning has at least an indirect bearing on intervention programs. There is need for research more directly relevant to those working in ESL and bilingual education programs, especially research exploring aptitude × treatment interactions. But above all, there is need for more communication between all the parties interested in second-language learning and bilingualism—linguists and psycholinguists, theorists and statisticians, researchers and practitioners—regardless of persuasion or constituency.

REFERENCES

Adjemian, C. On the nature of interlanguage systems. *Language Learning,* 1976, *26,* 297-320.

Albert, M. L., & Obler, L. K. *The bilingual brain: Neuropsychological and neurolinguistic aspects of bilingualism.* New York: Academic Press, 1978.

Andersen, R. An implicational model for second language research. *Language Learning,* 1978, *28,* 221-228.

Andersen, R. W. *The relationship between first-language transfer and second-language overgeneralization: Data from the English of Spanish-Speaking learners.* Paper presented at TESOL convention, Mexico City, April 1978.

Andersen, R. W. (Ed.). *New dimensions in research on the acquisition and use of a second language.* Rowley, Mass.: Newbury House, 1981.

Bailey, N., Madden, C., & Krashen, S. D. Is there a "natural sequence" in adult second language learning? *Language Learning,* 1974, *24,* 235-243.

Balkan, L. *Les effets du bilinguisme francais—Anglais sur les aptitudes intellectuelles.* Brussels: AIMAV, 1970.

Ben-Zeev, S. Mechanisms by which childhood bilingualism affects understanding of language and cognitive structures. In P. A. Hornby (Ed.), *Bilingualism: Psychological, social and educational implications.* New York: Academic Press, 1977.

Bloom, L., Lightbown, P., & Hood, L. Structure and variation in child language. *Monograph of the Society for Research on Child Development.* No. 2, 1975.

Bloom, L., Rocissano, L., & Hood, L. Adult-child discourse: Developmental interaction between information processing and linguistic knowledge. *Cognitive Psychology,* 1976, *8,* 521-552.

Brown, R. *A first language: The early stages.* Cambridge, Mass.: Harvard University Press, 1973.

Bruck, M., Lambert, W. E., & Tucker, G. R. Bilingual schooling through the elementary grades: The St. Lambert project at grade seven. *Language Learning,* 1974, *24,* 183-204.

Burling, R. Language development of a Garo and English speaking child. *Word,* 1959, *15,* 45-68.

Burt, M., Dulay, H., & Finocchiaro, M. (Eds.). *Viewpoints on English as a second language.* New York: Regents, 1977.

Burt, M. K., Dulay, H. C., & Hernandez-Chavez, E. *Bilingual syntax measure.* New York: Harcourt Brace Jovanovitch, 1973.
Campbell, D. T., & Stanley, J. C. Experimental and quasi-experimental designs for research on teaching. In N. L. Gage (Ed.), *Handbook of research on teaching.* Chicago: Rand-McNally, 1963.
Cancino, H., Rosansky, E. J., & Schumann, J. H. Testing hypotheses about second language acquisition: The copula and the negative in three subjects. *Working Papers in Bilingualism,* 1974, *3,* 80-96.
Cancino, H., Rosansky, E. J., & Schumann, J. H. The acquisition of the English auxiliary by native Spanish speakers. *TESOL Quarterly,* 1975, *9,* 421-430.
Carrow, E. Comprehension of English and Spanish by preschool Mexican-American children. *Modern Language Journal,* 1971, *55,* 299-307.
Cervantes, R. Report for conference on *Bilingual bicultural education comes of age.* Paper presented at convention of National Elementary Education Association, San Francisco, 1977.
Clarke, M. A. Second language acquisition as a clash of consciousness. *Language Learning,* 1976, *26,* 377-390.
Cook, V. J. The analogy between first- and second-language learning. *International Review of Applied Linguistics in Language Teaching,* 1969, *7,* 207-216.
Cook, V. J. Second language learning: A psycholinguistic perspective. *Language Teaching and Linguistics: Abstracts,* 1978, *11,* 73-89.
Corder, S. P. The significance of learners' errors. *International Review of Applied Linguistics in Language Teaching,* 1967, *5,* 161-170.
Corder, S. P. Idiosyncratic dialects and error analysis. *International Review of Applied Linguistics,* 1971, *9,* 147-160.
Corder, S. P. The elicitation of interlanguage. In J. Svartik (Ed.), *Errata: Papers on error analysis.* Lund: EWK Gleerup, 1973.
Cronbach, L. J., & Snow, R. E. *Aptitudes and instructional methods.* New York: Irvington, 1977.
Cummins, J. Linguistic interdependence and the educational development of bilingual children. *Review of Educational Research,* 1979, *49,* 222-251.
Dato, D. P. The development of the Spanish verb phrase in children's second-language learning. In P. Pimslear & T. Quinn (Eds.), *The psychology of second language learning.* Cambridge: Cambridge University Press, 1971.
Diller, K. (Ed.). *Individual differences and universals in language learning aptitude.* Rowley, Mass.: Newbury House, 1981.
Dulay, H. C., & Burt, M. K. Goofing: An indication of children's second language learning strategies. *Language Learning,* 1972, *22,* 235-252.
Dulay, H. C., & Burt, M. K. Should we teach children syntax? *Language Learning,* 1973, *23,* 245-258.
Dulay, H. C., & Burt, M. K. Natural sequences in child second language acquisition. *Language Learning,* 1974, *24,* 37-53.
Ervin-Tripp, S. Is second language learning like the first? *TESOL Quarterly,* 1974, *8,* 111-127.
Fathman, A. *Language background, age, and the order of English structures.* Paper presented at the TESOL convention, Los Angeles, 1975. (a)
Fathman, A. The relationship between age and second language productive ability. *Language Learning,* 1975, *25,* 245-253. (b)
Feldman, C., & Shen, M. Some language-related cognitive advantages of bilingual 5-year-olds. *Journal of Genetic Psychology,* 1971, *118,* 235-244.
Felix, S. W. Some differences between first and second language acquisition. In N. Waterson & C. Snow (Eds.), *The development of communication.* New York: Wiley, 1978.
Fillmore, L. W. *The second time around: Cognitive and social strategies in second language acquisition.* Doctoral dissertation, Stanford University, 1976.

Freed, B. *Speech adjustments: Talking to foreigners versus talking to children.* Paper presented at Los Angeles Second Language Research Forum, 1978.

Gardner, R. C. Social psychological aspects of second language acquisition. In H. Giles & R. St. Clair (Eds.), *Language and social psychology.* Oxford: Basil Blackwell, 1978.

Gardner, R., & Lambert, W. *Attitude and motivation in second-language learning.* Rowley, Mass.: Newbury House, 1972.

Gardner, R. C., Smythe, P. C., Clement, R., & Glicksman, L. Second-language learning: A social psychological perspective. *Canadian Modern Language Review,* 1976, *32,* 198-213.

George, H. V. *Common errors in language learning.* Rowley, Mass.: Newbury House, 1972.

Guiora, A. Z., Beit-Hallahmi, B., Brannon, R. C. L., Dull, C. Y., & Scovel, T. The effects of experimentally induced changes in ego states on pronunciation ability in a second language: An exploratory study. *Comprehensive Psychiatry,* 1972, *13,* 421-428.

Guiora, A. Z., Brannon, R. C. L., & Dull, C. Y. Empathy and second language learning. *Language Learning,* 1972, *22,* 111-130.

Guttman, L. A basis for scaling qualitative data. *American Sociological Review,* 1944, *9,* 139-150.

Hakuta, K. A preliminary report on the development of grammatical morphemes in a Japanese girl learning English as a second language. *Working Papers in Bilingualism,* 1974, *3,* 18-38.

Hakuta, K. Becoming bilingual: A case study of a Japanese child learning English. *Language Learning,* 1976, *26,* 321-351.

Hakuta, K. Some common goals for second and first language acquisition research. In R. W. Andersen (Ed.), *New dimensions in research on the acquisition and use of a second language.* Rowley, Mass.: Newbury House, 1981.

Hakuta, K., & Cancino, H. Trends in second-language acquisition research. *Harvard Educational Review,* 1977, *47,* 294-316.

Hatch, E. Language teaching and language learning. In E. C. Carterette & M. P. Friedman (Eds.), *Handbook of perception* (Vol. VII), *Language and speech.* New York: Academic Press, 1976.

Hatch, E. An historical overview of second language acquisition research. In C. A. Henning (Ed.), *Proceedings of the Los Angeles Second Language Research Forum.* Los Angeles: UCLA English Department, 1977.

Hatch, E. Discourse analysis and second language acquisition. In E. Hatch (Ed.), *Second language acquisition.* Rowley, Mass.: Newbury House, 1978. (a).

Hatch, E. (Ed.). *Second language acquisition.* Rowley, Mass.: Newbury House, 1978. (b)

Hatch, E., Shapira, R., & Gough, J. "Foreigner-talk" discourse. *ITL Review of Applied Linguistics,* 1978, 39-60.

Henzl, V. W. Foreign talk in the classroom. *IRAL,* 1979, *17,* 159-167.

Hornby, P. A. (Ed.). *Bilingualism: Psychological, social, and educational implications.* New York: Academic Press, 1977.

Huang, J. *A Chinese child's acquisition of English syntax.* Unpublished Master's thesis, University of California, Los Angeles, 1971.

Huebner, T. Order of acquisition vs. dynamic paradigm: A comparison of method in interlanguage research. *TESOL Quarterly,* 1979, *13,* 21-28.

Ianco-Worral, A. D. Bilingualism and cognitive development. *Child Development,* 1972, *43,* 1390-1400.

Imedadze, N. V. K psckhologicheskoy prirode rannego dvuyazychiya. *Voprosy Psikhologii,* 1960, *6,* 60-68.

Imedadze, N. V. On the psychological nature of child speech formation under conditions of exposure to two languages. *International Journal of Psychology,* 1967, *2,* 129-132.

Jakobovits, L. A. *Foreign language learning: A psycholinguistic analysis of the issues.* Rowley, Mass.: Newbury House, 1970.

Kessler, C. Syntactic contrasts in child bilingualism. *Language Learning,* 1972, *22,* 221-233.

Krashen, S. D. Lateralization, language learning, and the critical period: Some new evidence. *Language Learning,* 1973, *23,* 63-74.

Krashen, S. D. The development of cerebral dominance and language learning: More new evidence. In D. P. Dato (Ed.), *Georgetown University round table on languages and linguistics.* Washington, D.C.: Georgetown University Press, 1975.

Krashen, S. D. Formal and informal linguistic environments in language acquisition and language learning. *TESOL Quarterly,* 1976, *10,* 157-169. (a)

Krashen, S. Second language acquisition. In W. Dingwall (Ed.), *Survey of linguistic science.* Stamford, Conn.: Greylock, 1976. (b)

Krashen, S. The monitor model for second language performance. In M. Burt, H. Dulay, & M. Finocchiaro (Eds.), *Viewpoints on English as a second langauge.* New York: Regents, 1977.

Krashen, S. *The theoretical and practical relevance of simple codes in second language acquisition.* Paper presented at the Los Angeles Second Language Research Forum, 1978.

Krashen, S. Aptitude and attitude in relation to second language acquisition and learning. In K. Diller (Ed.), *Individual differences and universals in language learning aptitude.* Rowley, Mass.: Newbury House, 1981.

Krashen, S. D., Long, M., & Scarcella, R. C. Age, rate, and eventual attainment in second language acquisition. *TESOL Quarterly,* 1979, *13,* 573-582.

Krashen, S., & Scarcella, R. On routines and patterns in language acquisition and performance. *Language Learning,* 1978, *28,* 283-300.

Lambert, W. E. The effects of bilingualism on the individual: Cognitive and sociocultural consequences. In P. A. Hornby (Ed.), *Bilingualism: Psychological, social, and educational implications.* New York: Academic Press, 1977.

Lambert, W. E., & Tucker, G. R. *Bilingual education of children: The St. Lambert experiment.* Rowley, Mass.: Newbury House, 1972.

Lamendella, J. General principles of neurofunctional organization and their manifestation in primary and non-primary language acquisition. *Language Learning,* 1977, *27,* 155-196.

Lance, D. *A brief study of Spanish-English bilingualism: Final report.* Research Project Orr-Liberal Arts—15504. College Station, Texas, Texas A & M, 1969.

Landry, R. G. A comparison of second language learners and monolinguals on divergent thinking tasks at the elementary school level. *Modern Language Journal,* 1974, *58,* 10-15.

Larsen, D. N., & Smalley, W. A. *Becoming bilingual: A guide to language learning.* New Canaan, Conn.: Practical Anthropology, 1972.

Larsen-Freeman, D. An explanation for the morpheme acquisition order of second language learners. *Language Learning,* 1976, *26,* 125-134.

Larsen-Freeman, D. (Ed.). *Discourse analysis and second language research.* Rowley, Mass.: Newbury House, 1980.

Lenneberg, E. H. *Biological foundations of language.* New York: Wiley, 1967.

Leopold, W. F. *Speech development of a bilingual child: A linguist's record.* Vol. 1. *Vocabulary growth in the first two years.* Vol. 2. *Sound learning in the first two years.* Vol. 3. *Grammar and general problems in the first two years.* Vol. 4. *Diary from age two.* Evanston, Ill.: Northwestern University Press, 1939, 1947, 1949a, 1949b.

Leopold, W. F. The study of child language and infant bilingualism. *Word,* 1948, *4,* 1-15.

Macnamara, J. Comparison between first and second language learning. *Die Neueren Sprachen,* 1976, *25,* 175-187.

Macnamara, J., & Kushnir, S. L. Linguistic independence of bilinguals: The input switch. *Journal of Verbal Learning and Verbal Behavior,* 1971, *10,* 480-487.

McLaughlin, B. Second-language learning in children. *Psychological Bulletin,* 1977, *84,* 438-459.

McLaughlin, B. The monitor model: Some methodological considerations. *Language Learning,* 1978, *26,* 309-332. (a)

McLaughlin, B. *Second-language acquisition in childhood.* Hillsdale, N.J.: Lawrence Erlbaum Associates, 1978. (b)

McLaughlin, B. Linguistic input and conversational strategies in L1 and L2. *Studies in Second Language Acquisition,* 1980, *2,* 1-17.

Mehan, H. Viewpoint: Ethnography. In *Bilingual education: Current perspectives*. Vol. 1. *Social Science*. Arlington, Va.: Center for Applied Linguistics, 1977.

Mikès, M. Acquisition des categoires grammaticales dans le langage de l'enfant. *Enfance*, 1967, *20*, 289-298.

Milon, J. P. The development of negation in English by a second language learner. *TESOL Quarterly*, 1974, *8*, 137-143.

Molfese, D. L., Freeman, R. B., & Palermo, D. S. The ontogeny of brain specialization for speech and non-speech stimuli. *Brain and Language*, 1975, *2*, 356-358.

Murrel, M. Language acquisition in a trilingual environment: Notes from a case study. *Studia Linguistica*, 1966, *20*, 9-35.

Natalicio, D. S., & Natalicio, L. F. S. A comparative study of English pluralization by native and non-native speakers. *Child Development*, 1971, *42*, 1302-1306.

Nemser, W. Approximative systems of foreign language learners. *International Review of Applied Linguistics*, 1971, *9*, 115-123.

Oller, J. Research on the measurement of affective variables: Some remaining questions. In R. W. Andersen (Ed.), *New dimensions in research on the acquisition and use of a second language*. Rowley, Mass.: Newbury House, 1981.

Parker, L. L. Current perspectives. In *Bilingual Education: Current perspectives*. Vol. 5. *Synthesis*. Arlington, Va.: Center for Applied Linguistics, 1978.

Peal, E., & Lambert, W. E. The relation of bilingualism to intelligence. *Psychological Monographs*, 1962, *76*, 1-23 (No. 546).

Porter, J. A cross-sectional study of morpheme acquisition in first-language learners. *Language Learning*, 1977, *27*, 47-62.

Ravem, R. Language acquisition in a second language environment. *International Review of Applied Linguistics in Language Teaching*, 1968, *6*, 175-185.

Ravem, R. The development of Wh-questions in first and second language learners. In J. C. Richards (Ed.), *Error analysis: Perspectives on second language acquisition*. London: Longman, 1974.

Richards, J. Error analysis and second language strategies. *Language Sciences*, 1971, *17*, 12-22.

Richards, J. C. (Ed.). *Understanding second and foreign language learning*. Rowley, Mass.: Newbury House, 1978.

Ritchie, W. C. (Ed.). *Second language acquisition research: Issues and implications*. New York: Academic Press, 1978.

Rivers, W. From linguistic competence to communicative competence. *TESOL Quarterly*, 1973, *7*, 25-34.

Rosansky, E. J. Methods and morphemes in second language acquisition research. *Language Learning*, 1976, *26*, 409-425.

Rūke-Dravina, V. The process of acquisition of apical /r/ and uvular /R/ in the speech of children. *Linguistics*, 1965, *17*, 56-68.

Schachter, J. An error in error analysis. *Language Learning*, 1974, *24*, 205-214.

Schachter, J., & Celce-Murcia, M. Some reservations concerning error analysis. *TESOL Quarterly*, 1977, *11*, 441-451.

Schumann, J. H. Affective factors and the problem of age in second language acquisition. *Language Learning*, 1975, *25*, 209-235.

Schumann, J. H. Social distance as a factor in second language acquisition. *Language Learning*, 1976, *26*, 135-143.

Scovel, T. The effects of neurological age on non-primary language acquisition. In R. W. Andersen (Ed.), *New dimensions in research on the acquisition and use of a second language*. Rowley, Mass.: Newbury House, 1981.

Segalowitz, N. Psychological perspectives on bilingual education. In B. Spolsky & R. J. Cooper (Eds.), *Frontiers of bilingual education*. Rowley, Mass.: Newbury, 1977.

Seliger, H. W. Implications of a multiple critical period hypothesis for second language learning. In W. C. Richie (Ed.), *Second language acquisition research*. New York: Academic Press, 1978.
Selinker, L. Interlanguage. *International Review of Applied Linguistics*, 1972, *10*, 209-231.
Selinker, L., & Lamendella, J. Two perspectives on fossilization in language learning. *Interlanguage Studies Bulletin*, 1978, *3*, 143-191.
Selinker, L., Swain, M., & Dumas, G. The interlanguage hypothesis extended to children. *Language Learning*, 1975, *25*, 139-152.
Shuy, R. W. Toward a cross-disciplinary view. In *Bilingual education: Current perspectives*. Vol. 5. *Synthesis*. Arlington, Va.: Center for Applied Linguistics, 1978.
Slobin, D. I. Developmental psycholinguistics. In W. O. Dingwall (Ed.), *A survey of linguistic science*. College Park, Md.: University of Maryland Linguistics Program, 1971.
Snow, C. E. Mothers' speech to children learning language. *Child Development*, 1972, *43*, 549-565.
Snow, C. E., & Ferguson, C. A. (Eds.). *Talking to children: Language input and acquisition*. Cambridge: Cambridge University Press, 1977.
Snow, C., & Hoefnagel-Höhle, M. Age differences in second language acquisition. In E. M. Hatch (Ed.), *Second language acquisition*, Rowley, Mass.: Newbury House, 1978. (a)
Snow, C., & Hoefnagel-Höhle, M. The critical period for language acquisition: Evidence from second language acquisition. *Child Development*, 1978, *49*, 1114-1128. (b)
Stern, C., & Stern, W. *Die Kindersprache: Eine psychologische und sprachtheoretische Untersuchung*. Leipzig: Barth, 1907.
Swain, M. Future directions in second language research. In C. A. Henning (Ed.), *Proceedings of the Los Angeles second language research forum*. Los Angeles: UCLA English Department, 1977.
Taylor, B. P. Adult language learning strategies and their pedagogical implications. *TESOL Quarterly*, 1975, *9*, 391-399. (a)
Taylor, B. P. The use of overgeneralization and transfer learning strategies by elementary and intermediate students of ESL. *Language Learning*, 1975, *25*, 73-108. (b)
Taylor, I. How are words from two languages organized in bilinguals' memory? *Canadian Journal of Psychology*, 1971, *25*, 288-240.
Treisman, A. M. Verbal cues, language, and meaning in selective attention. *American Journal of Psychology*, 1964, *77*, 206-219.
Treisman, A. M. The effect of redundancy and familiarity on translating and repeating back a foreign and native language. *British Journal of Psychology*, 1965, *56*, 369-379.
Troike, R. C., & Perez, E. At the crossroads. In *Bilingual education: Current perspectives*. Vol. 5. *Synthesis*. Arlington, Va.: Center for Applied Linguistics, 1978.
Tucker, R. Comments on "Research on the measurement of affective variables: Some remaining questions" by John Oller. In R. W. Andersen (Ed.), *New dimensions in research on the acquisition and use of a second language*. Rowley, Mass.: Newbury House, 1981.
Vigil, N. A., & Oller, J. W. Rule fossilization: A tentative model. *Language Learning*, 1976, *26*, 281-295.
Vihman, M. M., & McLaughlin, B. Bilingualism and second language acquisition in preschool children. In C. J. Brainerd (Ed.), *Progress in cognitive development*. Vol. 1. New York: Springer Verlag, in press.
Wagner-Gough, J., & Hatch, E. The importance of input data in second language acquisition studies. *Language Learning*, 1975, *25*, 297-308.
Volterra, V., & Taeschner, T. *The acquisition and development of language by bilingual children*. Institute of Psychology, National Council of Research, Rome, 1975.
Wode, H. Developmental principles in naturalistic L1 acquisition. *Arbeitspapiere zum Spracherwerb*. No. 16. Department of English, Kiel University, 1976.
Wode, H. Operating principles and "universals" in L1, L2, and FLT. *IRAL*, 1979, *17*, 217-231.

DISCOURSE PROCESSES

5 Prose Comprehension in Natural and Experimental Settings: The Theory and Its Practical Implications

Roy Freedle and Jonathan Fine
*Educational Testing Service
Princeton, N.J.*

Discourse theory is in its infancy. Many of the problems we shall address illustrate problems at the very first stage of a science—the categorization phase. In this review we summarize some key concepts that have been proposed in the last decade for studying prose processing and its applications.

Several of the topics to be covered in the initial sections are staging, structures at different levels of a text, and rhetorical predicates. We then present an example illustrating some intrinsic problems with these categories in order to set the stage for demonstrating how knowledge is transformed as a function of exposure to texts. Thus part of the review emphasizes dynamic information-processing approaches to understanding text comprehension and text recall.

The early sections of this review deal with traditional laboratory and occasionally naturalistic approaches to prose comprehension from the perspective of Western culture. Then we present evidence that a wider perspective is necessary for gaining useful information of a practical and theoretical nature about communication using a cross-cultural approach. This latter section summarizes many naturalistic studies from the fields of ethnography and sociolinguistics.[1]

We suggest at several points where new research is needed and what the practical issues are.

---

[1]Parts of the second section of this chapter benefited from discussions with Dr. D. Tannen. Her review of sociolinguistics (Tannen, unpublished manuscript, 1978) proved helpful in locating several important studies.

BASIC DISCOURSE CONCEPTS AND EXPERIMENTAL STUDIES

Schema Theory and Its Applications

There are a number of ways to look at the structure of texts. Texts differ in terms of their purpose. Hence you find some texts that tell stories to *entertain* listeners; other texts may be written to *inform* readers about a scientific topic; other texts are written to *persuade* people about a point of view as in voting for a certain candidate; and so on. None of the texts represent what can be called pure types—every text is usually some mixture of these several functions. The differences in purpose often reveal themselves in structural features and also shifts in semantic content. Texts also differ in terms of what's critical for understanding a topic and what's less critical. Hence the internal structure of texts reflect a hierarchy of *importance* levels.

For a given type of purpose, the exact way one structures a text also depends on who the listener is and what the context is. For example, a story told to an adult will differ in detail from the "same" story told to a youngster. Also a story told in a classroom is likely to differ from the "same" story told at home—the context can make a difference. A good deal of research has been conducted on several of these issues: memory of different text types across different age groups, memory for important and less important assertions in a text across age groups, and memory for texts as a function of whether the setting (context) is naturalistic or a more formal experimental setting.

Schema theory has had a profound effect on recent work in discourse theory (Anderson, Spiro, & Montague, 1977; Chafe, 1977; Freedle, Naus & Schwartz, 1977; Kintsch, 1977; Mandler, 1978; Mandler & Johnson, 1977; Rumelhart, 1975; Schank & Abelson, 1977; Stein & Glenn, 1979). A good deal of this recent work has centered on the structure and recall of stories. It has been proposed that a grammar for narrative (story) discourse structure helps to clarify and define the internal representation of the information contained in a story *schema*. Such information provides a kind of template that aids the language user in both comprehending and recalling stories. By implication, if the language user fails to have a schema for a certain type of discourse, he/she should do poorly in both comprehending and recalling the information in this discourse. The growth in the details of this schema for stories has been the focus of work on studying students of different ages.

A brief sketch of the semantic categories (or nodes) that have proved useful in analyzing the story schema is helpful in clarifying the notion of a schema as a theoretical construct in discourse research. The following is adapted from Mandler and Johnson (1977).

A *setting* usually consists of stative information about one or more characters (e.g., "Mary lives in Kansas City.") The setting is followed by at least one episode. An *episode* consists of three basic parts—a *beginning,* a *development,* and an *ending* or *outcome.*

A beginning may be any sort of event. The listener's clue that setting information is complete and that the beginning node has been entered is usually signaled by a shift from a state description to an event description. "Mary lives in Kansas City. One day she went for a walk in the park and saw a robin. . . ." A development represents a shift to a reaction of a story character (e.g., "She was overjoyed at seeing the robin. . ."). The shift is from an external to an internal event with some implicit connection to a causal relation. For example, seeing the robin and being in the park made her joyous. The reaction makes the character the central "protagonist" in the episode. The reaction typically consists of two parts—a simple reaction that specifies an emotional response (joyous) or the thoughts of the protagonist and a goal. For the goal, the protagonist formulates a plan to deal with events as they unfold. A pathway to reach the goal completes the development section. A goal pathway consists of an attempt to reach the goal and the outcome of that attempt. The attempt may consist of a series of actions that the protagonist engages in to reach the goal. The outcome category indicates whether the attempt was successful or not. Other complications in goal path are also described in Mandler and Johnson (1977).

Several options are available for the ending category. The ending may have an "emphatic" character that resolves or wraps up a series of events (e.g., "finally after all her troubles of the day, Mary returned home to a warm bed.") An ending may also refer back to one or more nodes in the episode and may include a reaction on the part of another character.

In their study Mandler and Johnson found that the underlying grammar or schema of a story helped account for how children and adults comprehended and recalled each of several stories. Some of the story categories were found to be very *important* (necessary to make a well-formed story) and these were very often well-recalled; other story categories were found to be less critical (optional categories in terms of defining a well-formed story) and these tended to be less well-recalled by both children and adults. Brown and Murphy (1975) showed that children even as young as 4 years of age were better at recalling pictures that depicted a story or "logical" sequences than they recalled random or scrambled pictures. They were also better at maintaining the correct order when recalling the narrative and logical sequences. It was interesting also to find that when children were given the scrambled sequences, they tended to put them back into a narrative or logical order upon recalling the sequence. This latter finding strongly suggests the operation of an internal schema guiding recall.

In a related vein, Thorndyke (1977) showed superior recall for narratives when the content was organized into the typical canonical story grammar. Distorting the top-level (most important) structural relationships among the events (e.g., by removing the theme of a passage from its normal initial position and inserting it near the end) resulted in poorer comprehensibility ratings and poorer recall. Also Thorndyke found an interaction between amount of structure in the passage and presentation order of the sentences in the passage. For normal presentation order, the mean recall increased as passage structure increased, but for randomly ordered passages recall was not affected by the structure variable (Also see Kintsch, Mandel, & Kaminsky, 1977; Stein & Glenn, 1979).

Bower, Black, and Turner (1979) found that with script activities—narrative-type organizations that refer to stereotyped activities such as a restaurant script that includes entering the restaurant, going to a table (or stool), looking at the menu, ordering the food, receiving it, eating it, paying the cashier, and leaving—people tend to recall script actions in normal order even when they were presented in scrambled order. This again is strong evidence for the existence of such stereotyped scripts in memory; these structures become activated during the comprehension process and once activated are used to store and recall the information. One of the studies reported by Bower, Black, and Turner (1979) indicates that some interruptions of (or exceptions to) stereotyped scripts that have a clear temporal structure are very well-remembered. The reason that the exceptions are well-remembered (rather than erased in favor of a return to canonical order) is that the temporal scripts considered were 100% redundant and only new information was deviant. In contrast, the story schemata just described represented something less than 100% redundancy and hence there was a tendency for a choice to take place: Either see the whole schema as the information of primary importance or see the deviant information as more important.

McClure, Mason, and Barnitz (1979) studied another aspect of story comprehension from a canonical perspective using children from grades 3, 6, and 9. Three well-formed stories were constructed, but of the three only one was considered the canonical form. For example, in canonical form we have the following Lost Dog story: "Joan took a seven day trip with her family. Her little dog got lost on the trip. A month passed. Then one day a scratching noise was heard at the door. There was the dog. He had walked 700 miles to return home." Another well-formed story can be written in the following way: "Joan's little dog walked 700 miles to return home. He had gotten lost on a seven day trip. Poor Joan could not forget about him, even when she came home. A month passed. Then one day a scratching noise was heard at the door. There was the dog." This latter version places the conclusion of the canonical version as the first statement in the story. Notice that this story reads well in spite of the deviation from canonical order. McClure, Mason, and Barnitz (1979) found that children find the noncanonical structures harder to reorder than the canonical ones, thereby showing that it is not a question of whether a deviant story is simply ill-structured when it is scrambled and hence is hard to remember for that reason, but rather it is the deviance from canonical order even when well-formedness is preserved that accounts for the relative difficulty of the task. Age effects were also reported, indicating that the youngest students found the task harder than the older (see Baker, 1978, for further effects of canonical order on performance). We return to the concept of the narrative later in this chapter when we examine some complex issues concerning contextual and cultural effects on narrative processing.

Early Evidence Concerning Expository Processing

The easiest way to see that a shift in discourse genre need not represent a shift in the types of problems and issues that can be discussed is to consider the following example (taken from Freedle & Hale, 1979, p. 122):

Expository farmer passage	*Narrative farmer passage*
Here's how a farmer can get his stubborn horse into the barn.	Once there was a farmer who wanted to get his stubborn horse into the barn.
The farmer can go into the barn and hold out some sugar to get the horse to come and eat.	The farmer went into the barn and held out some sugar to get the horse to come and eat.
But if the horse does not like sugar, he will not come.	But the horse did not like sugar and he did not come.
Here's another thing he can do.	The farmer tried something else.
Suppose the farmer has a dog.	The farmer had a dog.
He can get the dog to bark at the horse.	He got the dog to bark at the horse.
This may frighten the horse and make him run into the barn.	This frightened the horse and made him run into the barn.

Although not every expository passage can be easily rewritten as a narrative passage (and vice versa), nevertheless the materials presented in Freedle and Hale show that one aspect of the different genres probably has much to do with the choice of verb tense structures. Hypothetical events are used throughout the expository passage, whereas real-time events (presented in present or past tense) are referred to in the narrative structure. Although this is not the place for an extended discussion of this problem, one can say that many expositions (like recipes) are of this hypothetical event type: It lists things you must or can do in order to obtain a certain result (like baking a chocolate cake for serving at a dinner). Other expositions as found in science texts may include long descriptive passages of the substances that go into producing a chemical reaction along with the procedures that must be followed to produce this reaction—in many ways this is like a recipe of ingredients and actions that can or should be performed in order to obtain a desired outcome. Detailed grammars of expositions, descriptions, and exhortations have as yet not been fully worked out.

Freedle and Hale (1979) and Freedle (1980) found that kindergartners responded more poorly on a recall task to both narratives and expositions than fourth graders. Also there was considerable evidence that kindergartners do not have good control of the hypothetical verb frames of expositions but have very good control of the simple past and present verb forms characteristic of many narratives.

In terms of applications of discourse theory, Freedle and Hale's work is interesting. They reasoned that much of early school work uses the story form for instruction purposes. Later grades tend to use an expository form for instruction. Freedle and Hale asked whether it was possible to increase kindergartners' comprehension and use of the unfamiliar expository form rapidly, and if so whether this could be the basis for introducing more of the expository-type materials to children in the very early grade-school years. Their results suggest that comprehension and control of the expository form can indeed be rapidly acquired, thereby setting the stage for further studies in how best to introduce this finding in the early grades.

Meyer and Freedle (1979) studied the ability of adults to recall expositions. What is unusual about their study is that they controlled the content of four expository texts but varied the top-level structure that introduced the material. For example, four top-level rhetorical structures were studied: *adversative* (which compares a favored view to an opposing view), *covariance* (which relates an antecedent to a consequent, somewhat like a cause–effect type ordering), *response* (which relates a problem to a solution), and *attribution* (which relates attributes to an event or idea). They found that the ability of adults to recall these four types of expositions differed significantly, both at the time of immediate recall and upon retesting 1 week later. The adversative and covariance passages were the easiest to recall, intermediate in difficulty was the response- (problem-solution) type exposition, with the attribution (list-type) structure the hardest to recall for both time periods.

The Meyer and Freedle study suggests another interesting application of discourse theory. If one has studied which structures are most easily understood by a particular population, then it should be possible to write materials for these populations in such a way as to increase the level of comprehension of the texts. For example, Meyer (1979) presented the results of some studies that suggested that older adults who have a similar educational background as the college students tested by Meyer and Freedle still comprehended the attributive or list-type structure better than other structures. Although this result needs further studies to affirm it, the idea that it suggests for applications is clear enough—rewrite the materials to fit the needs and capabilities of the population for whom the materials are intended.

Although some work on grammars of exposition has only recently begun (see appendix of Freedle and Hale chapter, 1979), it is interesting to note that a method for obtaining subjective grammatical structures for expositions (as well as stories) has been illustrated in work by Pollard-Gott, McCloskey, and Todres (1979).

Some Basic Structures in Prose

Crosscutting the classification of prose by its function (e.g., exposition, entertainment, persuasion) is a classification scheme that illustrates different levels by which any prose passage is structured. For example, in any well-formed passage some ideas are recognized as thematic and hence of primary importance to the overall passage; other statements are hence viewed or recognized as less important. What we review here are various methods by which to identify these aspects of prose and to study the effects that these various structures have on a subject's ability to comprehend and recall passages.

Meyer (1979) identifies nine variables that affect prose processing; of these we describe four variables that are explicitly or implicitly present in a text. Meyer indicates that some *contents* are easier to process than others (e.g., content that is conducive to imagery are more memorable) (Montague & Carter, 1973; Yuille & Paivio, 1969). As already suggested, the *structure* of prose also affects processing. Various techniques are now available for identifying prose structures; they are found in deBeaugrande and Dressler, 1979; deBeaugrande, 1980; Crothers, 1972; Frederiksen, 1972, 1975; Kintsch, 1974; Meyer, 1975; Grimes, 1975; Rumelhart, 1975; Clements, 1979.

A third factor is *emphasis,* which is a way of indicating that some parts of a text are more important than other parts. Studies dealing with this variable include Meyer (1975) who studied the effect of signaling on text recall (where signaling can be regarded as use of summarizing statements at the beginning of a text indicating what is to come) and found no clear effect of signals but did find a strong effect when information that was important in the text proper did facilitate recall. Clements (1979) presents a different definition of signaling importance (via staging), which is related to Meyer's (1975) idea of high-level versus low-level propositions. Clements' algorithm depends on three notions: explicit markers of importance in the text (e.g., saying "this is a crucial issue"), topic–comment structure to deduce importance, and old versus new distinctions of information in text, where new information is staged lower (less important) in the hierarchy than old information. His empirical results support the viability of these techniques for assigning importance levels within text.

Meyer discusses another variable called *perspective,* which reflects an interaction between the characters in a text (usually a story) and which character a reader/listener identifies with. The psychological consequences of identification reveal themselves in how a recall is organized and with how actions are rationalized. Anderson and Pichert (1978) had subjects recall a passage first from one perspective and then requested a switch in persepctive. They found that subjects recalled additional information that was relevant to the second perspective although they failed to include this information in their first recall; that is, some information was tagged to the particular character and this information was primed as one switched from one perspective (one character) to another perspective. Bower (1978) also has reported that causality is differentially assigned depending on who the subject identifies with in the narrative. The character that the subject originally identified with was seen to be controlled by external circumstances when things went wrong, whereas the mistakes of the other character in the story were attributed to their innate incompetence rather than external circumstances.

The Levels within a Text

Typically most prose texts consist of several levels. Meyer (1979) has identified the following organizers based in part upon earlier work by Grimes (1975):

1. Antecedent/consequent
2. Comparison
3. Collection
4. Description
5. Response

An *antecedent/consequent* relationship imputes a causal relationship between topics in a text. "Because of . . . x, y happened." where x and y can be strings of sentences in some text.

A *comparison* points out similarities and differences between two or more topics: There are three subtypes of comparisons identified by Meyer (1979): analogy, alternative, and adversative. Meyer gives the following examples: for analogy "You should be as careful choosing a puppy food as you are choosing a baby food"; her example for an alternative structure is "Heavy Duty Reynolds Wrap gives you two juicy options (for baking turkey): juicy and wrapped or juicy and tented." An adversative top-level structure is: "Consider . . . x, on the other hand consider . . . y" where x and y are both strings of sentences.

Meyer cites *collection* as a top-level structure that illustrates how ideas or events are related on the basis of some common property such as events that happen in a certain sequence (but are not causally related) or events that are ordered spatially, such as events at a carnival.

Meyer indicates that a *description* top-level structure presents a topic and attributes about this idea concerning who, what, where, when, and why.

Finally, Meyer defines a *response* top-level structure as a remark-and-reply or a question-and-answer or a problem-and-solution format. For example, one ad cited by Meyer indicates "Problem: After you've waxed the car, dried residue lingers around the grill . . . SOLUTION: A flagged-tip nylon paintbrush will remove the polish from crevices without scratching the paint."

Occurrence of Rhetorical Labels at Each of Several Levels of a Text

Although many of the rhetorical labels can occur at just the top-level of a text, it is also quite possible for these labels to occur simultaneously at lower levels in the same text. Also there is a potential problem with regard to assigning just one top-level label for any particular text. We illustrate both issues in the example given in Table 5.1 below.

We have analyzed the preceding text in terms of the labels that Meyer suggests for prose analysis. However, where we have noted an A and B for a given level in the text, *at least two* of the labels appear to apply equally well to the same portion of the text. For example, the opening four lines may relate to lines 5 to 19 as either parts of a time *collection* or units being linked in a *comparison* of temporal differences. Many text theorists fail to point out the inherent ambiguity and overlapping character in many of their labels and also fail to point out that even when the labels are not overlapping, it still is possible for a text segment to have several possible interpretations as in our example.

To substantiate our first claim, a *comparison* is said to point out similarities *and* differences between two or more topics; yet one subtype of comparison is strictly a comparison of differences (i.e., adversative) whereas another subtype is strictly similarities (i.e., analogy). Clearly these subtypes (e.g., analogy) dealing with similarities appear to be indistinguishable from the *collection* category that was defined as a structure relating ideas or events on the basis of *some common property*. Surely, a "common property" is identical to "similarities." Although we have less difficulty with some of the remaining labels, there is one other that we wish to point to as ambiguous: The *response* category includes remark and reply as a subtype. This label would appear to apply to the antecedent/consequent example of Meyer: "I switched from clay litter to Litter Green when my husband said 'get rid of the odors, or get rid of the cat.'" The husband utterance is the remark, and the decision to change is the "reply." This either calls into question whether the categories are distinct or raises the possibility that both categories apply to the same text string.

Our second claim was that many portions of text may truly have *multiple* labels that apply to them, not just one label. Our last example of remark/reply is a possible case in point. Poetry is a clear example of intentional semantic ambiguity where multiple labels are explicitly invited on the part of the reader; Gregory (1965) and Handscombe (1969) analyzed texts from this point of view. We claim that portions of ordinary prose anaiysis also can benefit from this approach. Work by Benson and Greaves (1973) also touches on some inherent ambiguity of natural language. A theory for multiple-category membership has been developed by Zadeh & King-Sun Fu (1975). There is some experimental

TABLE 5.1[a]
Illustration of Problems in Classifying Different Text Levels

Text	Line Number	Label(s)[b]	Level that Label(s) Applies to
"During the preceding centuries,	1	A: Collection; time early	Level 1
		B: Comparison; time difference	Level 1
there had been little reason	2		
to distinguish Flemish art proper	3		
from that of the rest of the Netherlands.	4		
But the 17th century,	5	A: Collection; time later	Level 1
		B: Comparison; time difference	Level 1
by separating the political destinies	6		
of the provinces,	7	A: cause (antecedent)	Level 2
had a profound effect	8	A: effect (consequent)	Level 2
on their spiritual evolution.	9	A: Comparison (adversative first part)	Level 2
The north,	10		
by freeing itself from Spanish dominion	11	B: Collection (space 1)	Level 2
was able to shake off Catholicism	12		
and take over the new Protestant discipline;	13		
while the south,	14	A: Comparison (adversative second part)	Level 2
on the contrary,	15	B: Collection (space 2) (especially if one removes the phrase "on the contrary")	Level 2
was still under Spain	16		
and remained one of the last	17		
[mighty and durable]	18	A: Collection (attribute string)	Level 3
strongholds	19		
of Catholicism in northern Europe...."			

[a] Adapted from R. Cogniat, *17th Century Painting*. New York: The Viking Press & Compass Books, 1964.
[b] Note: The same label (e.g., "collection") can apply at any level of a text. In this example, the label "collection" occurs at all three levels. The notation A and B for a label indicates that a particular portion of a text may actually have multiple labels attached to it. There are at least two reasons for this—see text for discussion of this problem.

evidence that bears on this issue of multiple labels. Freedle (1972) found that, for a given text string, it is not possible to assign a unique label to this in terms of identifying which subject matter label applied to it. Strings that had been randomly sampled from eight different subject matters (e.g., botany, physics, psychology, anthropology, geology, history, linguistics, physiology) were not perfectly identifiable in terms of which source they came from. Hence strings of text are ambiguous in terms of semantic labels that can be attached to them. A further aspect to this finding was that the difficulty in correctly identifying the "correct" source (the correct label) was shown to be a function of how many subject matters the person had to choose from.

Other Variables Affecting Text Processing: Organism and Situational Effects

An intuitive way to consider what is learned from texts—whether one reads it, listens to someone else read it aloud, or hears a teacher expound upon a topic in a classroom lecture—is to consider how information in the text becomes *transformed* as a result of being processed by the student or experimental subject. There are several ways of thinking about transformations: If a text consists of parts WXYZ (in that order), the X might be *primed* as more important than W. Or the *order* in which the text is recalled might be changed to YZWX. Or the information from X might be substituted by information that is: (a) a close paraphrase of the original; or (b) a related issue but not really that similar to the one in the original. So the recall might look like WaYZ, or WbYZ. Also a text can be modified by *adding to* what the original text says by including additional text (call the addition V, so that the recalled text might be WXYZV), or, where the material that is added, is only implicitly present in the original text. A final transformation that occurs quite often is deletion of critical (obligatory) parts of a text or deletion of nonobligatory parts of a text (simplification of text yielding still a well-formed text).

Briefly the transformations of knowledge from input to output (at the recall phase) are priming, reordering, substituting, adding, and simplifying or deleting.

After describing studies related to these transformations, we then deal with the more difficult and subtle problems concerning how knowledge is acquired in the first place; that is, although it is somewhat easy to discuss what variables distort (transform) knowledge once it is assumed to be represented in some form in memory, it is much more difficult to describe in general theoretical terms how any information gets into memory initially.

Priming Effects. Priming is a term that indicates how influences from inside and outside the organism affect what is remembered. Inside the organism (the language processor) refers to factors such as individual preferences for topics, individual preferences for style, and prior knowledge of a topic, which facilitate the processing of some portions of an input text over others. Factors outside the organism that prime text segments include: (a) experimenter effects such as requests for paying attention to particular ideas or requests to organize the information in a given way or requests to write versus orally recall the material, (b) situation effects outside the organism such as a formal social setting as evoked by a classroom or a university laboratory or an informal social setting as found at home.

Prior knowledge that a student brings to the learning task certainly affects the organization of new information that is received. Several studies have examined this. Gagne, Yarbrough, and Bell (1980) measured degree of prior knowledge for a passage in the following way. The subjects were asked to generate as many sentences as possible that connected something they already knew to something from each sentence in the text passage. The greater the number of generated sentences, the higher was their prior knowledge score.

After every person learned the passage to the same criterion of knowledge, it was found that subjects with greater assessed prior knowledge recalled the passage better after a 1-month delay than did students with lower prior knowledge. Schustack and Anderson (1979) studied the effect of subjects' knowledge of famous people in identifying fictional characters in a text with similar biographies. They found that the benefit of prior knowledge derives from the more elaborate encodings that this similarity of characters promotes. In particular they found that there must be obvious parallels between the new knowledge and the old knowledge in order for the beneficial effects of prior knowledge to operate in improving memory for the new information; also the benefit of this similarity also requires some cue to the old knowledge that becomes effective at the time of retrieval. This cue may either be generated by the learner or provided by the task.

Spilich, Vesonder, Chiesi, and Voss (1979) found that individuals with high knowledge in the topic of baseball needed less information to make correct recognition judgments, anticipated a greater percentage of high-level outcomes (goal states mentioned in the text), and were more superior at recalling event sequences than individuals with low knowledge scores.

Meyer and McConkie (1973) divided a text into three levels of topical importance—high, medium, and low importance. They then examined the rate at which new information was learned at each of these three levels as a function of repeated presentations of the text. Interestingly, the rate of acquiring new information was the same for each of the three levels for every presentation of the text.

Meyer and Freedle (1979) found an experimenter effect in priming. College students did best in recalling information that was primed by an adversative top-level structure (e.g., "There is . . . x but in contrast there is y," where x and y are both strings of sentences) as compared with the same information being presented by a response (problem/solution), antecedent/consequent (cause/effect), or attribution (list-type) structure.

In another study that examined experimenter-induced priming, Pichert and Anderson (1977) studied how information in a single text was differentially highlighted as a function of two ways to interpret the passage. The passage concerned a fairly wealthy family and their home along with its contents (and the surrounds), including such items as bicycles, a TV set, and a rare coin collection. One way to sort through the facts of the text was from the point of view of a burglar—the removable and valuable contents of the house became of prime importance. Another point of view was that of a prospective home buyer—now the details of house construction and the surrounding lands became of prime importance. Clearly priming can dramatically affect what is important in the very same text. Later Anderson and Pichert (1978) examined what effect these two points of view would have on the ability of experimental subjects to retrieve the information once they were asked to switch perspectives—that is, first the subject expected to retrieve information only from one point of view but was then also asked for another recall after pointing out that the material was amenable to another point of view. Interestingly the subject was able to retrieve new information not presented in the earlier recall, thereby clearly showing that there is an important distinction to be made concerning the encoding (input of information) phase and the decoding (output or recall) phase.

Reordering of Text Information. Again it is possible to examine the reordering transformation of the input text from the point of view of organism variables (subject's prior knowledge and preferences...), experimenter-induced variables, or context variables.

Mandler (1978) examined the ability of elementary school and adult subjects to recall stories that were interwoven within a single text. For example,

> Once there were twins, Tom and Jennifer, who had so much trouble their parents called them the unlucky twins. One day, Jennifer's parents gave her a dollar bill to buy the turtle she wanted, but on the way to the pet store she lost it. The same day, Tom fell off a swing and broke his leg. Jennifer was worried that her parents would be angry with her, so she decided to search every bit of the sidewalk where she had walked. Tom wanted to run and play with the other kids. . . .

An unembedded version of this story would be:

> Once there were twins, Tom and Jennifer, who had so much trouble their parents called them the unlucky twins. One day, Jennifer's parents gave her a dollar bill to buy the turtle she wanted, but on the way to the pet store she lost it. Jennifer was worried that her parents would be angry with her so she decided to search every bit of the sidewalk where she had walked . . . (plus all the rest of the statements dealing

with Jennifer only).... The same day, Tom fell off a swing and broke his leg. He wanted to run and play with the other kids... (plus all the remaining statements dealing with Tom only)...."

Both children and adults tended to recall the interleaved version of the story in standard form; that is, they reordered the input information in order to correspond to the more canonical story format. Clearly this can be attributed to the prior story knowledge that subjects brought to the experimental setting. We have already mentioned in an earlier section that scrambled passages tend to be recalled in standard canonical form (McClure et al., 1979; Thorndyke, 1977). This is another example of reordering due to a subject's prior knowledge being invoked.

Substitutions Made for Portions of Text. Not many studies explore the concept of substitutions, except indirectly. The problem of dealing directly with the notion of substitution is that what is substituted may be semantically different from what the original text asserted. Given that it is different, by what criteria could one possibly determine that the information stands in place of the original text? The only criterion would appear to be a purely structural one—that is, where in some sequence is the information put?

Addition: Elaborations that Go Beyond the Original Text. Mandler and Johnson (1977) found that first and fourth graders, as well as adults, elaborate semantic structures about equally often. This applied to a category that they called "reasonable elaboration" that was not directly stated information in the text but that was plausibly tied to some parts of it. Another category called "irrelevant or structural fillers" is more clearly a pure type of addition. Surprisingly, they found that adults are more prone to this type of addition than were the two younger groups.

Frederiksen (1975) presents results that also bear extensively on subjects' tendency to produce errors of commission. Three groups of subjects were studied. In one, pure memory for the passage was the goal. In a second, pure solutions to problems implicitly posed in the text was the goal. In the third, subjects had to be responsible for both memory for the text and suggested solutions to the problems posed in the text. Thus all reported differences were induced by experimenter instructions that affected the subject's goals. Significantly different results obtained across these three groups were found for "elaborative relations" (which are errors of intrusions that are neither directly stated nor implied in the text). The solution group showed the most elaborations. Also a small but significant effect across the three groups was found for semantic relationships. Finally, inferences that were implied by the text and explicitly added at the time of recall were significantly different across the three groups, with the memory-only group showing the fewest inferences.

Simplification and/or Destruction of Portions of a Text. Although there is some reason for separately listing simplification as different from destruction, we combine these categories because of the general similarity of the concepts. Basically by simplification we mean that a concept *can* be identified in a recall that matches the original text, but yet it does not exactly contain the richness of the original; by destruction we usually mean that an entire idea or structure has been deleted from the recall.[2] In the Frederiksen (1975) study, those subjects who had two basic tasks to contend with (both memory and solutions) also produced the greatest number of simplifications. This suggests that task load is the underlying variable that forces a subject to process information in a text quickly and somewhat shallowly.

Generally speaking, many studies show that total loss of parts of a text are related to the age of the subjects (Freedle & Hale, 1979; Mandler & Johnson, 1977; Stein & Glenn, 1979). Kintsch and Greene (1978) have presented a very interesting study that shows that the familiarity of the underlying story grammar is a critical variable that influences how much information is lost during recall. Kintsch and Greene point out that the particular story schemata are often culture-specific. The stories found in Western culture differ from those found for native Americans. They took an Apache folktale and contrasted it with a tale from the Grimm brothers. Entire episodes were found to be deleted from the Apache tale as one student told the story back to another student, who in turn told it to yet others. Most episodes remained intact however when the Grimm fairy tale was retold by the same process. Hence culture-specific schemata play a significant role in determining what will be preserved during recall; these schemata are part of the knowledge that subjects bring to the experimental laboratory and must be dealt with in explicit fashion when one studies various bilingual populations.

Graesser, Higginbotham, Robertson, and Smith (1978) reported an important study that compared prose processing in a naturalistic setting with processing in an experimental setting. Thus any differences in remembering will be attributable to situational or contextual setting. In the naturalistic setting, the students selected familiar topics from a newspaper available in the waiting room. They did not expect to be tested. What they remembered tended to be more active, narrative information than static descriptive information. In contrast, under the experimental setting, the topic was of course not guided by familiarity and there was no "narrative bias." Thus experimental contexts can differentially determine what is acquired from text.

---

[2] Actually the terms *simplify* and *destroy* only become clear when one specifies the "level" or maximum *unit* that is under consideration. Thus if the whole text (e.g., story) is the unit, then destroying a whole episode might be said to have "simplified" the whole text.

Some Other Essential Operators that Influence Text Comprehension

In all the several transformations that we have just discussed, there is a very difficult problem that lies buried—how is text information learned at all? What are the fundamental means by which people comprehend and learn information in text? This could be called the problem of information transformation at the *identity* level that leaves the original text information (i.e., its underlying meaning) *intact* in the memory of the language processor. (All the earlier transformations represented distortions of the original text.)

Most theories dealing with language processing employ a hierarchical structuring of knowledge with nodes of the hierarchy representing primitive units in the theory, whereas the connections among the nodes represent relations on pairs of the nodes. Such notions are needed to characterize *what* is internalized. There are two basic directions within the hierarchy that are believed to characterize the comprehension process: Either the direction is *top-down*, that is, from the most abstract level of the hierarchy to the lower regions, or it is *bottom-up*. Schemata that govern the upward or downward flow are an integral part of this process. Any particular comprehension process is probably some mixture of these two operations. Important limitations on how a particular comprehension process is realized is partly a reflection of such concepts as *data-limited* versus *resource-limited* systems. (See Adams & Collins, 1979, for a thorough discussion of these topics.) Unfortunately a detailed discussion of these important concepts is beyond the scope of the current review. Briefly, resource-limited means that if there are simultaneous demands for processing, the system's capacity to deal with all this information may be exceeded; thus, the system would be resource-limited. Two types of data-limited problems are pointed out. The first, called *signal data limits* suggests a poor quality input as when a handwritten postcard is virtually illegible. No amount of processing can improve or do away with the problem. A second type, called *memory data limits,* implies that the processor itself may not have the requisite knowledge for interpreting the signal; this would occur, for example, if one were attempting to comprehend a Japanese newspaper without having a full knowledge of the Japanese language (Bobrow & Norman, 1975).

Social Context and Communication—The Impact of Culture and Comprehension

Although most of the experimental studies have developed explicit theories and experimentally controlled evaluations of these theories, the sociolinguistic and anthropologically oriented communication studies have tended to be naturalistic and nonexperimental.[3] Thus although concepts (such as top-level structures and rhetorical predicates) have been explicitly developed and tested in the cognitive science and psycholinguistic literature, similar concepts and evaluations are missing from the naturalistic work, even though the same top-level structures may occur in the naturalistic texts. The failure to apply the same labels and concepts across these disciplines leads to an apparent disjuncture when we review the interesting literature on sociolinguistics and anthropological linguistics. Nevertheless the ideas that have emerged from this latter field are extremely important and pertinent to our review of how the learning process (the knowledge acquisition process in such applied settings as classrooms) is affected by variables other than text variables. These other variables involve use of dialogue as the means of imparting knowledge, use of social settings to inhibit or encourage knowledge acquisition, use of settings to make some discourse genres appropriate or inappropriate, use of certain topics in certain settings as appropriate or not to a particular culture, etc.

It is impossible to represent with any language all the nuances that can potentially be noted. Language is, in this sense, necessarily incomplete and ambiguous. We tend not to notice the ambiguity of language as long as we operate within the well-rehearsed norms of a particular language community; that is, by virtue of being in a language community for many years, a large repertoire of complex linguistic and paralinguistic schemata can be learned and come to function in an almost automatic way. These linguistic and paralinguistic norms (intonation cues, eye-gaze patterns, junctures for discourse groupings, etc.) are further smoothly merged with social conventions and values that must be honored in communication within a community—the notion of communicative competence (Gumperz & Hymes, 1972) is applicable here. Because communities differ in how sociolinguistic competence is realized in speech and because language is necessarily an incomplete representation of reality, the inevitable consequence is that error in communication is bound to occur. Hence miscommunications across cultures should be more prevalent than within cultures. Let's consider some of these examples.

Communication Breakdown: The Stresses of Cultures in Contact

One might naively suppose that serious breakdown in communication occurs only when complicated topics are being discussed. The communications of interest below though are typically not of that type. In fact, the failures in communi-

---

[3]The ethnographic material described in the second part of this review have also appeared in Freedle's chapter, in a book edited by John Harvey entitled *Cognition, Social Behavior, and the Environment*, to be published by Lawrence Erlbaum Associates, Hillsdale, N.J.; used with permission. This material was also presented in an invited APA address (see Freedle, 1979).

cation especially between people who come from different cultural backgrounds (but all of whom know English) often involve some of the most mundane of topics—asking a question, trying to provide helpful information, and the like. It is also worth noting that the individuals who are involved in the communication failure are often puzzled and cannot explain what went wrong—this signals the largely automatic processes by which communication is effected. As we shall see, researchers have isolated some of the largely unconscious and subtle cues by which full-fledged language community members carry out their largely successful communications. Hence when participants from outside this knowledge system bring a slightly different pattern of subconscious cues to bear for purposes of language comprehension, mismatches occur more frequently. The outcome of these mismatches unfortunately can often be unpleasant shouting, anger, wild accusations and so on. Mutual avoidance is also a likely outcome.

Some Simple Examples of Miscommunication

An Indian bus driver newly arrived on the job in London wishes to be polite and efficient. His customer steps into the bus. He says, "Exact change, please." The customer apparently didn't hear and asks for a repetition. The driver responds with "Exact change (pause), PLEASE." The traditional British customer takes offense for what is regarded as an attempt to act superior or to be cheeky, even though there is nothing in the situation that would make such an interpretation plausible. In reserved British culture, emphasis is avoided unless especially necessary. In the Indian language, emphasis that is here achieved by pausing and giving emphasis to the word "please" is customary in achieving clarification. A mismatch has occurred. The driver's job is now in jeopardy. Notice that the outcome of the mismatch, although not prescribed, is typically negative as it was here. This appears to be especially so when two strangers from different cultural backgrounds are involved. The example is from Gumperz (1977).

Another example of interest comes from Gumperz (1978). It involves an error in interpreting a "flat" intonation pattern used in pronouncing the word "gravy," again with negative consequences. An Indian woman has been hired to serve gravy in a cafeteria line serving British workmen. The British worker probably expects some pleasant chitchat possibly conveyed through use of dramatic intonation of words. The worker moves in place and approaches the woman serving gravy. Decorum in Indian society dictates that a woman remain reserved or "distant" in interacting with strangers. To accomplish conflicting demands, she merely inquires about whether the workman wishes gravy by uttering a flatly intoned "gravy." However, this puzzles the workman who cannot decipher the intonation pattern according to the language norms of his community. He decides she is trying to insult him; again mismatch in communication patterns has led to a negative outcome although other options could have been invoked to avoid a confrontation.

Nix and Schwarz (1979) have presented some interesting examples of how individuals from the Black subculture in the city of New York differ from White mainstream individuals in their interpretation of simple passages. They presented the following passage to individually tested Black students in their New York classrooms (students had to complete the passage by choosing which word makes the most sense to them at the end of the passage: "Sally loved animals. She brought home every stray animal that she could find, no matter what it looked like. Her mother declared that she adopted any animal as long as it was: A. lively; B. alive; C. large; D. lame.")

Most members of the majority culture pick option B (alive); members of the minority subculture tended to choose option A (lively). To investigate why this happened, an extensive interview was carried out by Nix and Schwarz to see how each person justified his or her choice.

It is difficult in a review piece to do full justice to the novel analysis that they bring to bear on their data, but the gist of their findings is that when option B (alive) was chosen, the passage subjectively organized into a topic-comment discourse frame; but when option A (lively) was chosen, it was internally represented as an action-reaction discourse frame. More particularly, choosing the option *lively* rather than *alive* as correct was justified because *alive* represents a truism and should be rejected on that basis. But the majority mainstream choice of *alive* in contrast was justified by indicating that this represented a stance of hyperbole and exaggeration. Thus both groups evoked reasonable criteria for justifying their choices, but the frames that helped guide their original selection were clearly different. To illustrate further these differences in interpretive frames, the students were asked whether the option "lame" would be correct. Those minority individuals who originally chose *lively* rejected *lame* because it is not a reasonable behavior for sensible people to waste money bringing home lame animals, whereas the group that originally chose *alive* accepted the possibility of choosing *lame* because "bringing home disabled animals is humane behavior sanctioned by the community." Thus the underlying frames differentiating the two groups was a pervasive sense of scarcity or abundance of money. It is more difficult to pinpoint the frame which led to the topic-comment versus the action-reaction differentiation. But it seems reasonable to expect to point to the cultural experiences as underlying the observed divergence in choices for purportedly the "same" surface utterances. This illustrates very clearly that language per se is ambiguous and that to comprehend a passage we must necessarily initiate interpretive frames to fill in the information that is unstated. Clearly, the two groups have filled in the missing information in different ways; hence, they must have used different interpretive frames in order to arrive at different justifications for their choices.

Not every interpretive difference is necessarily discovered by contrasting different culturally based groups. Even within a culture, deviations from normative use can be appropriate. For example, Frake (1975) suggests that on some occasions violation of a carefully prescribed ritual is used to communicate social messages such as solidarity and humor. Because members of the same community share the details of the proper ritual (i.e., have internalized a full schema of what it means to carry out the ritual in correct form), this shared knowledge (shared schemata) forms the background against which special meanings such as affection or humor or hostility can be marked or called attention to. Yet even within a culture, such deviations from the norm may be misinterpreted. This is just another way of demonstrating that language forms and context are *necessarily incomplete* in specifying the full intentions of the actors and speakers. Miscommunication can therefore occur, albeit less frequently, within a language community as well as across culturally different communities which are attempting to speak the "same" language. An extreme case could therefore be made for claiming that no two people speak exactly the "same" language simply because the interpretive competenceies of any two individuals, even members of the same language community, are in some details different. This extreme case can be justified by pointing out that instruction in becoming a member of a language community is never complete because we lack the conceptual tools for removing all sources of ambiguity from our attempts at instruction in the home and elsewhere.

The difference among individuals can be illustrated by reference to the concept of personal "themes" (Agar, 1979). Themes are similar to the notion of frame or schema, but Agar restricts the idea in his paper presumably to represent individual differences in world view; it is the personal philosophy and prevailing tendencies that an individual has of making sense of (interpreting) the situations he/she encounters. Prolonged informal interviews with three individuals reveals striking differences in the details of their respective themes. The subthemes used by Person 1 highlighted three concepts: (1) social control and interaction is a problem; (2) admiration and respect if the social-other demonstrates knowledge; the third theme represented the coordination of the first two themes as in (3) social control is a problem *unless* there is a demonstration of knowledge. Thus all three subthemes are interrelated for this person. A second person studied highlighted social independence. Yet another theme highlighted a lack of social independence. No third theme at the same "level" had yet emerged to bridge these two contradictory themes successfully. However, a third theme at an unspecified "level" did emerge: It involved the ability to "talk." To this person, talking need not imply social commitment, it is merely a way to have social contact without commitment. For the third person studied, the overwhelming theme in most aspects of the interaction involved his Chicano identity. This dominated the characteristics of subordinate themes such as family life, friends, religion, occupation. Thus this third person had evolved a hierarchic system of main theme and subthemes different in structure from the first two individuals. Undoubtedly a study of all individuals in a particular community would reveal some striking differences in the organization of their personal themes that are habitually invoked to interpret and make sense of the world about them and their interactions with the world. Such ideosyncratic differences are also potential sources of miscommunication.

Erickson (1976) has written an important paper concerning the subtle ways in which nonverbal cues of eye gaze can create the source of miscommunication across ethnic groups. Typically, when a Black teacher speaks to a Black student, he/she maintains eye contact while speaking; while listening each maintains only sporadic contact. Just the opposite holds for White teachers and students; that is, White speakers tend to allow their eyes to dart about while speaking, but when listening they maintain constant eye contact. This nonverbal communication habit would seem naively to be unimportant to *what* is being communicated and *how* it is being interpreted; but the naive view is wrong. When White teacher and Black student were combined, their "conflicting" gaze patterns led to the following miscommunications. The Black student appeared to be not listening or not understanding. This happened because the gaze mismatches led to a poor detection of the speaker's LRRM (listener-response-relevant-moment, which is a signal that some response from the listener, the Black student, is expected to indicate, for example, clear understanding) and a similar signal from the Black student was missed by the White teacher. The ultimate outcome of the miscommunication was, as before, a negative interpretation; the White teacher began to use one of two forms of hyperexplanation. Either he talked down to the student or he gave repeated reasons for his assertions. The student interpreted this to mean that the teacher thought he was stupid. Again miscommunication has led to negative evaluation.

The "raw" material out of which a culture fashions nonverbal rapport-type communication signals is suggested by some reviews of Kempton (manuscripts undated). Synchrony at the microlevel is demonstrated in the following wide range of behaviors: When someone speaks, the person exhibits self-synchrony, which means that the parts of their body move in synchrony with each other and with the speech. Also there is interpersonal synchrony so that a speaker's movements are in synchrony with the listener's. Although different parts of the body move at different speeds and in different directions, yet they change direction at the same time. Condon and Sander (1974) have found self-synchrony even in newborns. Kempton also reports synchrony in primates. Dyssynchrony also has been reported in pathological behaviors such as schizophrenia, aphasia, epilepsy, autism, and stuttering. Most importantly for its cross-cultural implications in miscommunication there is more synchrony observed between members of the *same* subculture including mothers and their infants and men and women of the same culture. Once culture superimposes obligatory patterns on some of these movements (e.g., to cue an intended interruption or the like), these subconsciously processed contextualization cues become part of the interpretative apparatus that can lead to successful communicative interactions or to puzzling unsuccessful miscommunications, as between members from different subcultures.

With respect to educational settings one may detect an example of how different patterns of synchrony may alter the quality of teacher–student interactions. Byers and Byers (1972) studied the nonverbal interactions between a White teacher and two Black and two White 4-year-old girls in a nursery school setting. The teacher appeared willing to interact equally with all students. But of the two most active students (one White, one Black) only one was more successful at catching the attention of the teacher, the White student. Eight out of 14 attempts were successful in catching her attention; but for the Black child only 4 out of 35 attempts to attract the teacher's eye were successful. Is this an example of mismatched patterns of synchrony? It seems likely for the following reasons. The White child timed her glances during those moments when the teacher was most likely to notice her; but the glances of the Black child were timed when the teacher's attention was focused elsewhere so that she did not realize the child was attempting to interact. These researchers also report what can be labeled here as an example of affective asynchrony. The White student approached the teacher at times that "naturally" led to the teacher's touching or hugging the child or having her sit on teacher's lap. But the Black student made "inappropriate" (asynchronous) moves at crucial moments. This resulted in fewer nonverbal expressions of affection.

Although Agar's (1979) study reveals persistent themes (schemata) at the level of individuals, a related study by Tannen (1979) reveals that there tend to be persistent themes for many members of a particular culture. These prevailing themes affect what significance is attached to everyday events, such as taking a bike ride past an orchard, encountering other individuals along the way, and the particular import of transfering food items. Of Tannen's many findings, the most relevant here in contrasting Greek and American groups are: (1) Americans comment on the film that they have seen by explicit reference to the film as a frame for guiding many aspects of their interpretations; the Greeks however seldom referred to the film per se in their comments; 2) there is a strong moral framework invoked in commenting on the film's actions by the Greeks, but this is infrequent among the Americans' comments; (3) Americans overtly remembered more details than the Greeks in one "falling" sequence; Tannen suggests that this omission may be tied to the Greeks' tendency to interpret events and ignore details that did not lend themselves to this interpretation.

Here we see that frames exist at many levels that filter the "raw" data of the film into a prevailing way of organizing and making sense of sequences of actions. Such different orientations can lead to miscommunication possibly when first-generation Greeks come to America, learn English, but persist in using these older interpretive frames to decide what is important to talk about and how one should realize this in speech. Tannen is currently engaged in analyzing data relevant to this last point.

Chafe (1976) suggests that there are wide differences in how cultures choose to structure details about a topic and how they make summarizing statements about the same topic. In conversation, he suggests that in Anglo culture we tend to begin by summarizing an event and then giving details. The Japanese, though, typically build up the details and then present the summary at the end. Such differences across speakers may contribute to disorientation or possibly impatience (e.g., "Get to the point, will you?").

Grimes (personal communication) has indicated that a difference in style exists even in Anglo culture among the various scientific disciplines in how they report their findings. He suggests that the rhetorical structure of articles in sociology and anthropology are oftentimes different from that of linguistics. A linguist tends to put his conclusions first and then gives details, much like a mathematician who presents his theorem first and then proceeds to prove it, whereas anthropologists discuss their methods and reasoning near the end of their papers. Such differences can create problems in smooth communication across disciplines.

Some Patterns of Communication among Native Americans

Additional evidence concerning cultural frames that create communication problems across members of different language-culture groups comes from an early paper by Cazden and John (1971). Teachers often regarded Indian children as "shy" and "reluctant to talk." In the Anglo culture this might be interpreted negatively as possible evidence of retarded language development or psychological problems. The same behavior in Indian children though probably has another explanation. Apache Indians consider it foolish to talk a great deal. Cazden and John indicate in the Sunrise Dance representing the coming-of-age of young girls that the girl's grandmother places her hand over the girl's mouth to indicate that silence is a virtue. In their literature review (also see Cazden, John, & Hymes [1972, pp. 331-394]) they indicate that Navajos freeze up when looked at directly. Teachers might respond to the Indian child's bowed head (avoiding gaze) with such inquiries as "What's the matter? Can't you talk? Don't you even know your own name?" In addition it has been reported that Navajos do not prefer to comment on a topic unless they regard themselves as highly proficient in it; to speak prematurely on a topic not fully mastered is considered a breach of intelligent behavior. Anglos, of course, have a different orientation because they regard practice as a prerequisite to obtaining full mastery. In other words a mismatch in rules concerning when it is proper to talk exists across several Indian cultures in comparison with Anglo culture. Furthermore, a mismatch in presuppositions concerning the role of practice as a necessary step to attaining full mastery of a topic also exists. Both of these mismatches typically creates negative assessments on the part of the ill-informed teacher when faced with Indian children in their classrooms, even though a close examination of the sources of the miscommunication reveals that a negative evaluation is probably unwarranted.

Philips (1972) studied the speech behavior of Indian children inside and outside the classroom. In their community, interactions among participants do not recognize the Anglo distinction between a performer and an audience. Furthermore, there is no clear sense of "leader" of an activity (as is assumed for the role of "teacher" in an Anglo community). Instead each person decides the degree to which they will participate in the activity at hand. All who are present are free to participate if they so choose. In the Anglo classroom studied by Phillips (1972), however, there are four types of social-participant structures, some of which merge with the sociocultural rules of the Indian children and some of which violate these norms. The four structures are as follows. (1) The teacher interacts with all the students, and it always is the teacher who decides whether to talk to just one person or all. Also a response from the student is obligatory, not a matter of individual choice. This clearly violates Indian norms. When the Anglo norms are violated, the child is probably labeled as "hostile" or "uncooperative." (2) A second structure used in the classroom involves the teacher interacting with just a subset of the class, such as in holding special reading sessions. Participation is mandatory, individuals are expected to perform verbally and singly rather than in chorus; the main purpose of this structure is to provide the teacher with an assessment of how much the student already knows of a certain skill; hence it presupposes incomplete mastery of a field, and it presupposes that individual responses will reflect incomplete mastery. This clearly violates Indian norms. Violation of Anglo norms here probably results in a student being labeled as incompetent with respect to the knowledge domain being assessed. (3) The third classroom structure consists of all students working independently. The teacher is explicitly available for teacher help; this help is forthcoming if the student requests or initiates the interaction. The other students do not witness the details of the student–teacher interaction. This pattern does not contradict Indian norms for interaction. (4) The fourth interaction structure (which occurs infrequently in upper primary grades and very seldom in the lower grades) is also consistent with Indian interaction norms. It involves the students being divided into small groups, run by the members of the group for purpose of special "group projects." The teacher is still available for supervision if requested.

In sum it is clear that detailed ethnographic studies of the actual nature of structured interaction in these "naturalistic" settings within and outside the classroom clearly places Indian children at a disadvantage in terms of maximally benefiting from classroom activities that are structured in such a way as to violate norms instilled in the children from birth on. Not only does it fail to provide them with an optimal means for instruction, but it also alienates them with frequent negative evaluations given them by nonunderstanding but well-meaning teachers.

Weeks (1976) has presented a wealth of information concerning different patterns of language use among Yakima Indians that helps to clarify additional sources of miscommunication.

The native language of Yakima children is English. Yet school personnel complained that these children seemed to have "language problems" of a largely unspecified nature. Data analyzed by Weeks contrasted Indian children's use of language with non-Indian children who lived on the Yakima Reservation and also contrasted both with non-Indian children from Palo Alto, California.

Among the important findings are the following. Answers to questions are not obligatory as it appears to be in Anglo culture. A question may be answered, perhaps at a later time. The typical pattern of question, answer, confirmation (as in "What time are we to leave?" "At 6." "OK.") is therefore atypical in conversations with these Indian children. Furthermore, when they do answer questions, it is often in the form of a question.

There is strong resistance to admitting to partial or no knowledge; hence these children typically will not say "I don't know." (It also helps to explain why they tend to answer a question with a question.) Yet this phrase is very common among Anglo children. This appears to be related to our earlier comments concerning the inappropriateness of speaking when one hasn't fully mastered some topic.

Indian children also are not inclined to guess. They would lose face if their guessed-at answer proved to be wrong. This again is related to community norms that governs when one should speak on a topic. Guessing however is a frequent occurrence among Anglo students, and Anglo teachers appear to encourage it.

Weeks reports that for the language tasks that she used to explore differences in language use between Indian and non-Indian children the following emerges. The Indian children depart from the stimulus pictures more and speak about related personal experiences. In presenting these experiences they often quote previous conversations in what appears to be verbatim form, thus giving a narrative register form to their comments: for example, "Grandma said, 'Tommy's going to get that boat and take us a ride on there. Waaaaay out there.'" "Where?" "Waaaaay out there." (All produced by the same student.)

The Yakima children often appeared to take control of the conversation by asking questions of the teacher. Anglo children rarely do this because it is assumed to be the role of the teacher to ask questions. Many of the questions asked by the Indian children were of a personal nature; Anglo children seldom asked personal questions. The Yakima children interpreted the interview as a friendly visit whereas the Anglo children assumed that there was a special purpose behind the interview ("What am I *supposed* to say?"). Anglo children regularly corrected the teacher if the teacher appeared to not understand something they said. Indian children did not correct the teacher. Also Indian children did not interrupt; in contrast the Anglo children and the non-Indian children at Yakima often interrupted the teacher.

In terms of distribution of summary comments versus details, none of the children studied in the interview summarized as an adult might. Yet the non-Indian children listed details in the pictures and began without any prompting by the teacher. The Indian children studied here picked up a picture and waited for the teacher to say something. When speaking, the Indian children often projected what might happen whereas the Anglo children spoke of what was directly in the picture.

It is clear that there are complex presuppositions behind these conversations. If one cannot specify what they are, an Anglo teacher is likely to misinterpret the motivations and significance of the Indian children's statements. Such a teacher is likely to feel ignored (they don't acknowledge questions) or feel their authority has been usurped (they begin asking the teacher questions) or feel that they don't stick to the point (they project what might happen and they use a narrative storytelling mode rather than just list facts). Yet all these misjudgments represent a failure to appreciate how cultures differently frame events and differently frame when it is proper to speak and how one must present the information.

Selected Aspects of Bilingual Classroom Interaction

The interesting reports and studies authored by Laosa (Laosa, 1975, 1977) on classroom interaction, especially for Latino populations in various regions of the United States, also reveals subtle patterns of discrimination. Many of the studies cited (see footnote 1, p. 257) appear to show more obvious evidence of overt discrimination based on ethnic differences. Racial prejudice functions as a characteristic of the individual, in this case classroom teachers, and so is related to Agar's (1979) idea of personal theme. Prejudice functions as a selective filter affecting how the external social world is perceived and how it is to be responded to.

Rubovits and Maehr (1973) studied teachers' interactions with White and Black students in seventh- and eighth-grade classes. Black students were treated less positively than Whites. In one experimental variable (the random labeling of students as gifted or nongifted) the surprising finding was that Black students who received the random label of gifted were subjected to more discrimination by teachers than Black students who were randomly labeled as nongifted. These researchers also found that teachers who were rated high on dogmatism (a rating reflecting an authoritarian outlook on life and intolerance toward those with different beliefs) tended to encourage their White students but ignored the Black students.

Jackson and Cosca (1974) examined classroom interactions involving Mexican American and Anglo students. Elementary as well as secondary schools were studied. The results in general showed that teachers praised and encouraged Anglo students more than Mexican American students. Teachers responded more positively to and used more of the ideas suggested by their Anglo students than those suggested by the Mexican Americans. Combining all three positive teacher behavior ratings (teacher accepts student's feelings; teacher praises student; teacher accepts student's ideas), it was found that the Anglo students received

40% more positive feedback than the Mexican American students. Teachers asked Anglo students 21% more questions and spent 23% more time talking to their Anglo students.

In addition to ethnic background, socioeconomic level interacts with teacher behaviors. Higher SES (socioeconomic status) children tend to receive most of the teacher's praise, whereas lower SES children receive more criticism (Davis & Dollard, 1940). Academic achievement interacts also with teacher behavior. High-achieving students receive more favorable comments from teachers (Heller & White, 1975). Brophy and Good (1970) found that high-achieving students initiated more interactions with the teacher, most teacher criticism was addressed to boys in a low-achievement group, and teachers demanded and praised quality performance more from the high-achieving than low-achieving students. Also, teachers provided less feedback to the low-achieving students.

Laosa (1977) has pointed out that Mexican Americans are at a distinct disadvantage in the average classroom situation because they embody all the characteristics that previous reserach has shown leads to poor interactions of teacher and student. Among these characteristics are: (1) difference in ethnic background; (2) likelihood of speaking a nonstandard English dialect; (3) low achievement; and (4) lower socioeconomic status. Because of this, it comes as no surprise when he indicates that 40% of all Mexican American students in the Southwest never complete high school whereas this is true for only 14% of the Anglo population. Laosa's research on teacher–student interactions for minority student populations documents the exact nature of unfavorable teacher–student interactions. Some of his most interesting findings are that a student's language dominance (Spanish or English) rather than the student's ethnic group membership per se was the primary source for eliciting a teacher's disapproving behaviors. This interacted with age in the following way. For non-English dominant students, there was an *increase* from kindergarten to second grade in the number of disapprovals given by teachers. However, just the opposite was true (a decrease) for students (both Anglo and Mexican American) who had English as their dominant language. Laosa sketches the long-term consequences for non-English dominant students. Increasing rate of discouragement by teachers coupled with a decreased rate of nonevaluative information feedback by teachers is likely to lead to disruptive attempts at capturing the teacher's attention (e.g., by playing pranks or speaking "out of turn") and/or developing a deep indifference for academic skills (e.g., indifference to arithmetic and reading) with an ultimate dropping out of the school system entirely. Laosa further points out the irony of bilingual–bicultural education as it was implemented in the classrooms that he studied—it is definitely no assurance of educational quality nor assurance of equality of opportunity for ethnic minority and limited-English-speaking students.

Ordinarily one might assume that just because the teacher has low expectancy concerning a particular student's performance that this in itself need not have any affect on how well the student learns the materials at hand. However, an ingenious study by W. B. Seaver (1973) indicates that even in an all-Anglo classroom low teacher expectancy does depress actual student accomplishments as assessed by eight measures of academic achievement: two grade-point averages from winter and spring terms, scores on word meaning, paragraph meaning, vocabulary, spelling, word-study skills, and arithmetic (subscales of Stanford Achievement Test). Neither students nor teachers knew they were involved in a study. Experimental and control groups were determined in the following way. If an older sibling was rated as "high" or "low" with respect to the previous eight measures, their younger sibling was placed in the *experimental* group if they both had the same teacher. The younger sibling was placed in the *control* group if they had different teachers. Thus if teacher expectancy influences the younger child's performance due to the teacher's earlier experiences with the older sibling, this design should reveal this. Note that the fact that siblings may in fact share similar abilities (a "smart" older child may have a "smart" younger sibling) is controlled for here by the way in which the control group has been defined. The significant effect of teacher expectations on performance was evident. High-scoring older siblings tended to have higher-scoring younger siblings in the experimental groups for all eight scores. For the low-scoring older siblings, their younger siblings scored lower in all but one of the eight scores, word-study skills. Significance in the expected directions across control and experimental groups, however, occurred on word meaning, paragraph meaning, and math. Thus even when variables concerning ethnicity and social class are *not* a concern, one can still detect differential teacher behaviors that prejudice how they respond to students based upon the "sins" of their older brothers and sisters.

It is clear that culture molds and defines inevitable aspects of behavior to signify more than one would believe is literally possible; that is, eye glances, body angle, eye blinks, head nodding, time intervals between these movements (rate and frequency), vocal emphasis, variation in voice pitch (intonation patterns), and so on. These inevitable behaviors, however, are segmented and grouped differently by different cultures to signify and clarify more than words alone can convey. This is the crux of the difficulty in understanding miscommunication.

The redundancy of context that pervades most discourse among members of the same culture is a protective agent against miscommunication. Repetitions of highly familiar events encourage casual cognitive monitoring of the significance of these events, but between cultures verbal interactions tend to be brief and infrequent. Thus the protective aspect of redundancy in prolonged pursuit of a topic or in frequent interaction is typically absent in cross-cultural encounters. Hence suspicions that make these encounters brief in the first place also contribute to a negative interpretation of intentions when contextual cues fail to provide *sufficient* cues to guide correct interpretations.

Difficulties and Implications for Revised Educational Practice

To reduce these sources of miscues one cannot suggest that people consciously try to stop all these behaviors. In normal unplanned conversation it seems likely that these extralinguistic behaviors are crucial for successful communication. It also seems unlikely that an adult (e.g., a teacher) is capable and willing to adopt these unconscious and highly patterned cues from *all* minority subcultures so as to assist communication for all members of a mixed ethnic classroom. A teacher, of course, who is knowledgeable that such pattern-specific behaviors *exist* and vary across subcultures and are crucial to understanding, is in a better position to avoid premature judgments concerning a student's thinking skills (stupid), motivation level (sluggish), personality characteristics (hostile, willful). Instead this more knowledgeable teacher could be taught to *pause and rethink* the cause of each clear failure to interact smoothly with a student. Not every failure may be reflected upon, but some significant proportion may be. Students might also be interested in *learning* these communication skills.

Linguistic Differences in Speech: Some Cognitive Speculations

A second area of importance concerns the language code itself—the lexicon, syntax, and semantics of a given dialect. The problems here can be as difficult and subtle as those we found for isolating nonlexical contextual cues in comprehension. Both are necessary to appreciate a wide range of miscommunications that regularly occur.

The Lexicon. Although the topic of the lexicon may appear unrelated to discourse issues, we include it here because it illustrated that all levels of communication are open to question in terms of isolating the sources of miscommunication. One of the few studies that tries directly to examine how words differ across subcultures is that of Dawis, Soriano, Siojo, and Haynes (1974). They studied words that are common to the dialects of the several groups studied, including Blacks, Mexican Americans, Native Americans, Oriental Americans, and Anglo-Americans. They obtained clear though indirect evidence that the words probably are different in what they signify across the different populations. Hall and Freedle (1975) have discussed some of the particulars of their findings. Additional evidence of lexical differences even among individuals of the *same* language community can be inferred from Freedle's (1970) word-sorting task where semantic nodes were combined by each individual into a hierarchic tree; the results showed that no two individual tree structures were identical.

Although differences can be found, there is strong evidence of a few lexical universals across cultures and languages. Thus there are two extreme views possible: Individual differences do exist; language community differences do exist; *but* there is a common core of ideas and terms that suggest that the underlying *processes* leading to semantic characterizations are probably identical even though the particular surface realizations may be different. Witkowski and Brown (1978) suggest universals exist for color terms (Berlin & Kay, 1969), lexical connotations (Osgood, May, & Miron, 1975), and affective responses (White, 1977). Other invariances have been reported for such broadly based categories as folk botany terms (Berlin, 1974) and folk zoological terms (Brown, 1977). Witkowski and Brown (1978) then suggest four principles of naming behavior: (1) conjunctivity (including binary opposition); (2) criteria clustering; (3) marking, and (4) dimension salience. For example, under binary opposition many languages contrast such dimensional polarities as wide/narrow and deep/shallow. They are similar with respect to isolating the same kinds of underlying dimensionality. Similarly, some dimensions count as more salient or important than other dimensions: For example, size is a very potent dimension. Many languages tend to cluster certain defining features (e.g., Bruner, Goodnow, & Austin [1956] indicate that the concept "bird" is associated with such criteria clusters as wings–feathers–bill). Environmentally the co-occurrence of wings–feathers–bill may be so regular that together they generate the necessary conditions for language community members to invent a lexical concept—bird—to reflect this environmental regularity, providing the concept is useful in their cultural activities. "Marking" also tends to have a regular process underlying it across languages. For example, in the adjective contrasts reported earlier (e.g., deep/shallow) it is frequently the case that one member of the pair functions as the unmarked "name" for the dimension, whereas the other functions as the marked end. That is, in asking about the dimension of "depth" of a lake the natural way to ask it is "how *deep* is it?" but it is not correct to ask "How shallow is it?" unless one wants to indicate a prior expectation that the lake is of small depth. The notion of conjunctivity (including binary opposition) is harder to grasp. Witkowski and Brown indicate that although one might think it possible to devise terms to reflect small, middle-sized, and large items along a size dimension (e.g., "wug" to refer to small animals and "mammal" to refer to large animals, and a third term to refer to medium-sized animals) but the principle of conjunctivity doesn't allow this. It also doesn't allow the combining of the extremes of a dimension into a category leaving out the middle-sized elements; this would make the dimension "circular" and probably would tend to destroy the linear dimension that perceptual comparisons have isolated in the environment. However there are rare instances where this does occur. Binary contrasts do preserve the principle of conjunctivity and so are found in many languages. To actually *name* a dimension by its middle region apparently never occurs; this also is implicated as conjunctivity by Witkowski and Brown (1978, p. 443). A mathematician would say that a linear dimension has a true zero point and an unbounded upper limit; that is, it is bounded at one end and unbounded at the other end. But a middle region of this dimension is unbounded at its "lower" end and similarly unbounded at its "upper" end; hence it is a very slippery beast to name and no language family names dimension in that way.

In short, there are perceptual aspects of exploring an environment that lead cognitively to the isolation of a few guiding principles out of which a language community constructs and selects its lexicon. The particular things that become named though and the exact way the environment is sectioned can differ across languages and cultures. What is invariant is the underlying *process*. Similarly, for other aspects of language, we develop expectations about normal routines that a culture engages in; these routines may have a name but they need not—the perceiving human still internalizes the regularities of sequences and co-occurrences in the routines and stores some type of cognitive *schema* for this routine. The *process* that leads to the internalized routine is probably the same for all cultures, but the contents and forms of those routines will differ across cultures. When humans from different cultures try to communicate; they will assume that they share similar content-based *schemata* for processing and organizing the world, whereas actually we only share similar *processes* for organizing the world. That is one source of miscommunication. Some of the work of Cole and Scribner (1974) indicates that one attempts to reflect the differences in the content-based groupings of objects in the culture, that psychological processes that are studied for the culture-appropriate grouping are found to be similar.

Interaction of Language Code (Dialect) Differences with Cognition. Hall, Cole, Reder, and Dowley (1977) found an interesting interaction between the dialect in which a story was read to a child and the ability of the child to retrieve information in a free recall of the story. Black children who spoke predominantly Black English were better able to recall the details of a story if that story had been presented in Black English as opposed to "standard" English. Exactly the opposite occurred for the White students—better recall if the story was presented in standard dialect as opposed to Black dialect. The two groups recalled the *same* amount of information correctly when the story had been presented to them in their primary dialect. The recall of White students was especially depressed when the story had been presented in Black dialect. These facts suggest that the ability to "frame" a recall (to use a story schema in the recall) definitely interacts with the language code that the story is presented in. Thus the ability to keep track of *where* one is with respect to the underlying story schema (Mandler, 1978) is interfered with if the language code is relatively unfamiliar; this in turn affects the ability to store and retrieve the information when it comes time to recall the material.

Hall and Freedle (1973) presented similar results at the level of recalling individual sentences presented either in black or standard dialect. Williams and Rivers (1972) also found that the apparent size of a student's vocabulary is dependent on what language code the words are presented in; for Black dialect speakers, if the test is administered in Black dialect, this significantly increases the estimate of vocabulary knowledge in contrast with scores obtained when the test is administered in standard dialect.

Hall and Freedle (1973) examined the implications of how the dialects are stored and accessed psychologically. In their sentence-recall task they reasoned that if *positive* correlations are obtained in retrieving the syntactic forms (correlations computed across forms within a dialect and similar forms across dialects were also computed) that such a pattern implies that these syntactic forms form a coherent system. Also zero or very small correlations across systems imply separate storage of the two dialects.

What they actually found was rather complex. For the older children tested (eight- and ten-year-olds) there was strong evidence that Black and standard dialects formed two distinct systems; but there was evidence of complex interconnections across the two dialects (some correlations across dialects were consistently negative implying some form of cognitive interference). In general though, the cross-dialect correlations tended to approach zero as expected if the two dialects were stored as separate knowledge systems. The younger preschool children (five-year-olds) showed evidence that both dialects were still cognitively represented as a single knowledge system; this was deduced from the generally large positive correlations both within and across the two language dialects that they were tested in. It appears that exposure to the school system may have been a significant contributor to the cognitive separation of the two language codes.

Other studies suggest that some form of performance interference exists when the nonpreferred language code is the basis for evaluation. With respect to reading comprehension, Stewart (1969) presented the following example. In standard English "His eye's open" may be misinterpreted by a Black dialect speaker to mean that both eyes are open because it resembles the Black dialect sentence "His eyes open" more than it does "His eye open"—this latter sentence though *is* the equivalent of the standard dialect sentence "His eye's open." Stewart also suggests that "He will be busy" may, to a Black-dialect speaker, be misinterpreted as implying habitual action because of the use of "be" in Black dialect to signal habitual action.

If Stewart's conclusions seem unlikely, just consider the results obtained by Ruddell (1963) and Tatham (1970). They found that standard English-speaking White children better comprehended material written in sentence patterns that more closely approximated their *oral* language patterns. This is true probably because these patterns were more familiar to them. Familiarity with the language code and ease in using it as a frame to aid in comprehension and recall is then very subtle because habitual ways of organizing a sentence provide a better schema to follow than grammatically equivalent patterns that are less frequently used. In like manner Stewart's ideas would suggest a similar conclusion.

Anderson (1977) engaged Anglo children (upper middle class) of different ages in semicontrolled settings (family versus classroom versus playing doctor) and varied the kinds of roles played in each setting in order to study the variety of speech styles that each child has in its repertoire at a given age group; this included studying different registers (e.g., using a "baby-talk" register for some situations versus using a more formal "grown-up" style for other situations). Increased flexibility in role playing with age was noted; increased range of controlling different speech registers was also noted. Three situations studied varied greatly in their difficulty for the young children; playing the teacher's role properly through register and grammatical choices and playing a "foreigner" role in other settings proved to be somewhat beyond the skills of the young children; hence the *schema* for appropriate role playing of these "types" had not yet been internalized to yield adequate speech productions. Studies of this type using bilingual language users of varying degrees of proficiency and varying ages would be very interesting. Are registers that are known and used in one language easily transferred to a less familiar language? Or must all the stages be moved through *de novo* in the new language?

Straker (1978) studied the use of formal and informal speech styles in semicontrolled settings. The interaction of role, setting, and topic was carefully controlled by the experimenter in order to test predictions stemming from the theoretical work of Fishman (1972). Straker examined eight situations to determine which language code (black English, standard English, or a mixture of the two) would be used to advance new information on a topic for each social situation. The "intimate" situations typically elicited black English throughout, and topical additions were often made by spontaneous turn taking (a new speaker would introduce new additions). But in the "formal" social settings, less black English was used and new information was obtained by asking questions. Straker also reports that of the three variables studied—topic, interlocutor, and setting—only the first two were significant factors in eliciting the use of standard or mixed dialects. But all three factors were significant in eliciting use of Black English. It seems probable that one can consider the results of this study to demonstrate that subjects were unconsciously using a guiding "schema" concerning appropriateness of use of language code and social turn-taking rules to unfold their conversational interactions smoothly. These schemata are probably a reflection of co-occurrence regularities within the language community and this co-occurrence favors the gestalt learning of a schema that serves to monitor decisions about what rule to use next, whether a new topic elaboration is legitimate, and so on. Without the schema as an overall guide, the thousands of decisions that would have to be made *de novo* would quickly overwhelm the limited human capabilities to handle the information. Thus schemata serve as a shortcut solution to information overload. One need only monitor *which* schema is appropriate at a given moment in order to determine whether one is using the "right" code (etc.) or not.

FINAL REMARKS

In our review of the literature we have tried to select topics that seem to be represented amply by the experimental literature. There are some areas of theory that have just begun to be investigated experimentally that we have not included in this review. However, we must stress their potential import for both experimental and theoretical advances. The work on cohesion by Halliday and Hasan (1976), Rochester and Martin (1979), and Fine (1978) represents an interesting beginning in this topic. In addition, the work on semantic relevance by T. van Dijk (1979) represents a new development that may prove valuable in future research. A large amount of work by people in the artificial intelligence field, although certainly related to our topic, was judged to be out of the scope of our review.

REFERENCES

Adams, M. J., & Collins, A. A schema-theoretic view of reading. In R. Freedle (Ed.), *New directions in discourse processing*. Norwood, N.J.: Ablex, 1979.

Agar, M. Themes revisited: Some problems in cognitive anthropology. *Discourse Processes*, 1979, *2*, 11-31.

Anderson, E. *Learning to speak with style: A study of the sociolinguistic skills of children*. Unpublished doctoral dissertation, Stanford University, Dec. 1977.

Anderson, R. C., & Pichert, J. W. Recall of previously unrecallable information following a shift in perspective. *Journal of Verbal Learning and Verbal Behavior*, 1978, *17*, 1-12.

Anderson, R. C., Spiro, R. T., & Montague, W. E. (Eds.). *Schooling and the acquisition of knowledge*. Hillsdale, N.J.: Lawrence Erlbaum Associates, 1977.

Baker, L. Processing temporal relationships in simple stories: Effects of input sequence. *Journal of Verbal Learning and Verbal Behavior*, 1978, *17*, 559-572.

Benson, J. D., & Greaves, W. S. *The language people really use*. Agincourt, Ontario: Book Society of Canada, 1973.

Berlin, B. Folk systematics in relation to biological classification and nomenclature. *Annual Review of Ecological Systems*, 1974, *4*, 259.-271.

Berlin, B., & Kay, P. *Basic color terms: Their universality and evolution*. Berkeley, Calif: University of California Press, 1969.

Bobrow, D. B., & Norman, D. A. Some principles of memory schemata. In D. G. Bobrow, & A. M. Collins (Eds.), *Representation and understanding: Studies in cognitive science*. New York: Academic Press, 1975.

Bower, G. Experiments on story comprehension and recall. *Discourse Processes*, 1978, *1*, 211-231.

Bower, G. H., Black, J. B., & Turner, T. J. Scripts in memory for text. *Cognitive Psychology*, 1979, *11*, 177-220.

Brophy, J. E., & Good, T. L. Teacher's communications of differential expectations for children's classroom performance: Some behavioral data. *Journal of Educational Psychology*, 1970, *61*, 365-374.

Brown, A. C., & Murphy, M. D. Reconstruction of arbitrary versus logical sequences by preschool children. *Journal of Experimental Child Psychology*, 1975, *20*, 307-326.

Brown, C. H. Folk botanical life-forms: Their universality and growth. *American Anthropologist,* 1977, *79,* 317–342.
Bruner, J. S., Goodnow, J. J., & Austin, G. A. *A study of thinking.* New York: Wiley, 1956.
Byers, P., & Byers, H. Nonverbal communication and the education of children. In C. B. Cazden, V. P. Johns, & D. Hymes (Eds.), *Functions of language in the classroom.* New York: Teachers College Press, 1972.
Cazden, C. B., & John, V. P. Learning in American Indian children. In M. Wax, S. Diamond, & F. Goring (Eds.), *Anthropological perspectives on education.* New York: Basic Books, 1971.
Cazden, C. B., John, V. P., & Hymes, D. (Eds.). *Functions of language in the classroom.* New York: Teachers College Press, 1972.
Chafe, W. L. *Preliminaries to a model of discourse.* Paper presented at the American Educational Research Assoc., San Francisco, April 21, 1976.
Chafe, W. Creativity in verbalization and its implications for the nature of stored knowledge. In R. Freedle (Ed.), *Discourse production and comprehension.* Norwood, N.J.: Ablex, 1977.
Clements, P. The effects of staging on recall from prose. In R. O. Freedle (Ed.), *New directions in discourse processing.* Norwood, N.J.: Albex, 1979.
Cogniat, R. *Seventeenth century painting.* New York: Viking Press, 1964.
Cole, M., & Scribner, S. *Culture and thought: A psychological introduction.* New York: Wiley, 1974.
Condon, W. S., & Sander, L. W. Synchrony demonstrated between movements of the neonate and adult speech. *Child Development,* 1974, *43,* 456–462.
Crothers, E. J. Memory structure and the recall of discourse. In R. O. Freedle & J. B. Carroll (Eds.), *Language comprehension and the acquisition of knowledge.* Washington, D.C.: Winston/Halstead/Wiley, 1972.
Davis, A., & Dollard, J. *Children of bondage.* Washington, D.C.: American Council on Education, 1940.
Dawis, R. V., Soriano, L. V., Siojo, L. R., & Haynes, J. *Demographic factors in the education of relations in analogy word pairs.* Tech. Report 3. Minneapolis: University of Minnesota, Dept. of Psychology, 1974.
deBeaugrande, R. *Text, discourse and process: Toward a multidisciplinary science of texts.* Norwood, N.J.: Ablex, 1980.
deBeaugrande, R., & Dressler, W. *Introduction to text linguistics.* London: Longman, 1979.
Erikson, F. *Talking down and giving reasons: Hyper-explanation and listening behavior in interracial interviews.* Paper presented at the International Conference on Non-Verbal Behavior, Ontario Institute for Studies in Education, Toronto, May 11, 1976.
Fine, J. Conversation, cohesive and thematic patterning in children's dialogues. *Discourse Processes,* 1978, *1,* 247–266.
Fishman, J. Domains and the relationship between micro- and macro-sociolinguistics. In J. Gumperz & D. Hymes (Eds.), *Directions in sociolinguistics: The ethnography of communication.* New York: Holt, Rinehart & Winston, 1972.
Frake, C. O. How to enter a Yakan house. In M. Sanches & B. Blount (Eds.), *Sociocultural dimensions of language use.* New York: Academic Press, 1975.
Frederiksen, C. H. Effects of task-induced cognitive operations in comprehension and memory processes. In R. O. Freedle & J. B. Carroll (Eds.), *Language comprehension and the acquisition of knowledge.* Washington, D.C.: Winston/Halstead/Wiley, 1972.
Frederiksen, C. H. Representing logical and semantic structure of knowledge acquired from discourse. *Cognitive Psychology,* 1975, *7,* 371–458.
Freedle, R. Some relations among nouns: The pursuit of semantic markers. *Proceedings of the 78th Annual Convention of the American Psychological Assoc.,* 1970, 63–64.
Freedle, R. Language users as fallible information processors. In R. O. Freedle & J. B. Carroll

(Eds.), *Language comprehension and the acquisition of knowledge.* Washington, D.C.: Winston/Halstead/Wiley, 1972.

Freedle, R. O. *Discourse theory, culture, and cognition: Current trends and applications.* Invited address. American Psychological Assoc., Sept. 4, 1979, New York.

Freedle, R. O. *Children's recall of narrative and expository prose: The acquisition of new discourse schemata.* Invited address. American Educational Research Assoc., April 9, 1980, Boston, Mass.

Freedle, R. O. Interaction of language use with ethnography and cognition. In J. Harvey (Ed.), *Cognition, social behavior, and the environment.* Hillsdale, N.J.: Lawrence Erlbaum & Associates, in press.

Freedle, R. O., & Hale, G. Acquisition of new comprehension schemata for expository prose by transfer of a narrative schema. In R. Freedle (Ed.), *New directions in discourse processing.* Norwood N.J.: Ablex, 1979.

Freedle, R. O., Naus, M., & Schwartz, L. Prose processing from a psychosocial perspective. In R. Freedle (Ed.), *Discourse production and comprehension.* Norwood, N.J.: Ablex, 1977.

Gagne, E. D., Yarbrough, D. B., & Bell, M. S. *Prior knowledge and the long-term recall of information.* Paper presented to the American Educational Research Assoc., Boston, Mass., April 1980.

Graesser, A. C., Higginbotham, M. W., Robertson, S. P., & Smith, W. R. A natural inquiry into the National Enquirer: Self-induced versus task-induced reading comprehension. *Discourse Processes,* 1978, *1,* 355-372.

Gregory, M. J. Old Bailey speech in *A tale of Two Cities. A Review of English Literature,* 1965, *6,* 42-55.

Grimes, J. E. *The thread of discourse.* The Hague, Holland: Mouton, 1975.

Grimes, J. E. Personal communication, 1979.

Gumperz, J. Sociocultural knowledge in conversational inference. In M. Saville-Troike, *28th annual roundtable, Monograph series on languages and linguistics.* Georgetown: Georgetown University Press, 1977.

Gumperz, J. The conversational analyses of interethnic communication. In E. Lamar Ross (Ed.), *Interethnic communication.* Southern anthropological society. Athens, Ga.: University of Georgia Press, 1978.

Gumperz, J., & Hymes, D. (Eds.). *Directions in sociolinguistics: The ethnography of communication.* New York: Holt, Rinehart & Winston, 1972.

Hall, W. S., Cole, M., Reder, S., & Dowley, G. Variations in young children's use of language: Some effects of setting and dialect. In R. Freedle (Ed.), *Discourse production and comprehension.* Norwood, N.J.: Ablex, 1977.

Hall, W. S., & Freedle, R. A developmental investigation of standard and nonstandard English among black and white children. *Human Development,* 1973, *16,* 440-464.

Hall, W. S., & Freedle, R. *Culture and language: The black American experience.* Washington, D.C.: Halstead/Wiley/Hemisphere, 1975.

Halliday, M. A. K., & Hasan, R. *Cohesion in English.* London: Longman, 1976.

Handscombe, R. J. George Herbert's "The Collar": A study in frustration. *Language and Style,* 1969, *3,* 29-37.

Heller, M. S., & White, M. A. Rates of teacher verbal approval and disapproval to higher and lower ability classes. *Journal of Educational Psychology,* 1975, *67,* 796-800.

Jackson, G., & Cosca, C. The inequality of educational opportunity in the Southwest: An observational study of ethnically mixed classrooms. *American Educational Research Journal,* 1974, *11,* 219-229.

Kempton, W. *The rhythmic basis of interactional micro-synchrony.* Unpublished manuscript (undated). Also Kempton's *Speech rhythm and social interaction: A review of microkinesic research.* Unpublished manuscript (undated).

Kintsch, W. *The representation of meaning in memory.* Hillsdale, N.J.: Lawrence Erlbaum Associates, 1974.
Kintsch, W. On comprehending stories. In M. Just & P. A. Carpenter (Eds.), *Cognitive processes in comprehension.* Hillsdale, N.J.: Lawrence Erlbaum Associates, 1977.
Kintsch, W., & Greene, E. The role of culture specific schemata in the comprehension and recall of stories. *Discourse Processes,* 1978, *1,* 1–13.
Kintsch, W., Mandel, T. S., & Kazminsky, E. Summarizing scrambled stories. *Memory and Cognition,* 1977, *5,* 547–552.
Laosa, L. Bilingualism in three Hispanic groups: Contextual use of language by children and adults in their families. *Journal of Educational Psychology,* 1975, *67,* 617–627.
Laosa, L. Inequality in the classroom: Observational research on teacher-student interactions. *Aztlan International Journal of Chicano Studies Research,* 1977, *8,* 51–67.
Mandler, J. A code in the node: The use of a story schema in retrieval. *Discourse Processes,* 1978, *1,* 14–35.
Mandler, J., & Johnson, N. S. Remembrance of things parsed: Story structure and recall. *Cognitive Psychology,* 1977, *9,* 111–151.
McClure, E., Mason, J., & Barnitz, J. An exploratory study of story structure and age effects on children's ability to sequence stories. *Discourse Processes,* 1979, *2,* 213–249.
Meyer, B. J. F. *The organization of prose and its effects on memory.* Amsterdam: North-Holland Pub., 1975.
Meyer, B. J. F. *A selected review and discussion of basic research on prose comprehension.* Research Report No. 4, Prose Learning Series, Dept. of Educational Psychology, Arizona State University, Tempe, Ariz., 1979.
Meyer, B. J. F., & Freedle, R. O. *Effects of discourse types on recall.* Research Report No. 6, Prose Learning Series, Dept. of Educational Psychology, Arizona State University, Tempe, Ariz., 1979.
Meyer, B. J. F., & McConkie, G. What is recalled after hearing a passage? *Journal of Educational Psychology,* 1973, *65,* 109–117.
Montague, W. E., & Carter, J. F. Vividness of imagery in recalling connected discourse. *Journal of Educational Psychology,* 1973, *64,* 72–75.
Nix, D., & Schwarz, M. Toward a phenomenology of reading comprehension. In R. Freedle (Ed.), *New directions in discourse processing.* Norwood, N.J.: Ablex, 1979.
Osgood, C., May, W. H., & Miron, M. S. *Cross-cultural universals of affective meaning* Urbana: University of Illinois Press, 1975.
Philips, S. U. Participant structures and communicative competence: Warm Springs children in community and classroom. In C. B. Cazden, V. P. John, & D. Hymes (Eds.), *Functions of language in the classroom.* New York: Teachers College Press, 1972.
Pichert, J. W., & Anderson, R. C. Taking different perspectives on a story. *Journal of Educational Psychology,* 1977, *69,* 309–315.
Pollard-Gott, L., McCloskey, M., & Todres, A. K. Subjective story structure. *Discourse Processes,* 1979, *2,* 251–281.
Rochester, S., & Martin, J. R. *Crazy talk: A study of the discourse of schizophrenic speakers.* New York: Plenum Press, 1979.
Rubovits, P., & Maehr, M. Pygmalion black and white. *Journal of Personality and Social Psychology,* 1973, *25,* 210–218.
Ruddell, R. B. *An investigation of the effect of the similarity of oral and written patterns of language structure on reading comprehension.* Unpublished doctoral dissertation, Indiana University, 1963.
Rumelhart, D. E. Notes on a schema for stories. In D. G. Bobrow & A. M. Collins (Eds), *Representation and understanding.* New York: Academic Press, 1975.

Schank, R. C., & Abelson, R. P. *Scripts, plans, goals, and understanding: An inquiry into human knowledge structures.* Hillsdale, N.J.: Lawrence Erlbaum Associates, 1977.

Schustack, M. W., & Anderson, J. Effects of analogy to prior knowledge in memory for new information. *Journal of Verbal Learning and Verbal Behavior,* 1979, *18,* 565-583.

Seaver, W. B. Effects of naturally induced teacher expectancies. *Journal of Personality and Social Psychology,* 1973, *28,* 333-342.

Spilich, G. J., Vesonder, G. T., Chiesi, H. L., & Voss, J. F. Text processing of domain-related information for individuals with high and low domain knowledge. *Journal of Verbal Learning and Verbal Behavior,* 1979, *18,* 275-290.

Stein, N. L., & Glenn, C. G. An analysis of story comprehension in elementary school children. In R. Freedle (Ed.), *New directions in discourse processing.* Norwood, N.J.: Ablex, 1979.

Stewart, W. A. On the use of Negro dialect in the teaching of reading. In. J. C. Baratz & R. Shuy (Eds.), *Teaching black children to read.* Washington, D.C.: Center for Applied Linguistics, 1969.

Straker, D. *Situational variables in language use.* Unpublished doctoral dissertation. Yeshiva University, New York, 1978.

Tannen, D. *Sociolinguistic bibliography (annotated).* Unpublished manuscript, University of California at Berkeley, April 1978.

Tannen, D. What's in a frame? In R. Freedle (Ed.), *New directions in discourse processing.* Norwood, N.J.: Ablex, 1979.

Tatham, S. M. Reading comprehension of materials written with select oral language patterns: A study at grades two and four. *Reading Research Quarterly,* 1970, *5,* 402-426.

Thorndyke, P. Cognitive structures in comprehension and memory of narrative discourse. *Cognitive Psychology,* 1977, *9,* 77-110.

van Dijk, T. A. Relevance assignment in discourse comprehension. *Discourse Processes,* 1979, *2,* 113-126.

Weeks, T. E. *Discourse, culture, and instruction.* Paper presented at the meeting of the American Educational Research Assoc., San Francisco, April 21, 1976.

White, G. *Conceptual universals in personality description.* Unpublished manuscript, Dept. of Anthropology, University of Calif. at San Diego, 1977.

Williams, R., & Rivers, W. *Mismatches in testing from black English.* Paper presented at the meeting of the American Psychological Assoc., Honolulu, Sept. 1972.

Witkowski, S. R., & Brown, C. H. Lexical universals. *Annual Review of Anthropology.* 1978, *7,* 427-452.

Yuille, J. C., & Paivio, A. Abstractness and the recall of connected discourse. *Journal of Experimental Psychology,* 1969, *82,* 467-471.

Zadeh, L. A., & King-Sun Fu (Eds.). *Fuzzy sets and their applications to cognitive and decision processes.* New York: Academic Press, 1975.

DISORDERS OF FIRST-LANGUAGE DEVELOPMENT

6 The Nature of Specific Language Impairment in Children

Laurence B. Leonard
Purdue University

INTRODUCTION

This chapter deals with a group of conditions collectively termed *specific language impairment*. These conditions, seen in approximately 1 in every 1000 children (Stevenson and Richman, 1976), are characterized by the late onset and slow development of language in children whose general intellectual abilities are not significantly below those expected for their chronological age. Longitudinal and follow-up studies of language impairment suggest that across time children with language impairments continue to have linguistic difficulties at least through childhood (Aram & Nation, 1978; deAjuriaguerra, Jaeggi, Guignard, Kocher, Maquard, Roth, & Schmid, 1965; Scott & MacVean, 1978; Weiner, 1972; Wolpaw & Nation, 1977) and adolescence (Morley, 1973; Weiner, 1974) and into early adulthood (Kerschensteiner & Huber, 1975). However, the long-term effects of language impairment may clearly vary with factors such as the nature and severity of the linguistic deficit, where, for example, children with less severe limitations may show the greatest development across time (Petrie, 1975).

Children exhibiting specific language impairment constitute a heterogeneous population. These children often seem similar only in that their intellectual abilities, as reflected on nonverbal tasks, exceed their linguistic abilities. Children may vary from slightly below normal to above normal in their intellectual abilities. For some children, language comprehension may present as much difficulty as language production, whereas for others difficulties may center principally on production. Children may vary too in the severity of their comprehension and/or production difficulties. Rapin and Wilson (1978) offer a good illustration of the heterogeneity in the language-impaired population. These investigators described four children with language impairment who differed from one another in their linguistic, perceptual, and intellectual characteristics. One child produced well-constructed and articulated utterances that were often unrelated to the situation at hand. This child performed poorly on tasks of short-term auditory memory. Another child spoke in unintelligible jargon and yet showed superior intelligence. A third child performed well on language comprehension and auditory memory tasks and demonstrated excellent performance on nonverbal intelligence measures. However, this child had extreme expressive syntactic and lexical limitations. The fourth child showed highly restricted syntactic, lexical, and phonological abilities, accompanied by limitations in language comprehension as well as in perception and memory of acoustic and visual stimuli.

The heterogeneity of the language-impaired population has prompted several investigators to include as subjects only those children meeting a stringent set of criteria. For example, the children serving as subjects in the study of Tallal and Stark (in press) exhibited: (1) a performance intelligence quotient of 85 or above; (2) a language comprehension age at least 6 months behind their performance mental age; (3) a language production age of at least 1 year behind their performance mental age; and (4) a composite language age (based on averaging the comprehension and production ages) at least 1 year behind both their performance mental age and their chronological age.

Criteria such as these have the advantage of maximizing replicability through a careful description of the children under investigation. Too few studies of language impairment, in fact, have presented adequate subject descriptions. As might be suspected from the illustrations provided by Rapin and Wilson (1978), however, there are a number of language-impaired children who may not meet all of these criteria. For example, T. Ingram (1972) proposed that language impairment in children may reflect a continuum from "mild" to "very severe." Children with mild difficulties show problems acquiring the speech sound (phonological) system of the language, although their use of semantic, syntactic, and pragmatic aspects of language seems within normal limits. Those children with moderate problems exhibit more severe phonological difficulties. In addition, their production of other features of language reflects a delay. Language comprehension in these children, however, seems normal. Children characterized as severe or very severe have comprehension as well as production difficulties, with the latter showing little tendency to ascribe any communicative significance to speech sounds. More recently, Aram and Nation (1975) have identified other patterns of linguistic difficulty seen in the language-impaired population. Given such a range and combination of linguistic difficulties that may be involved in language impairment, it would clearly be unsafe to conclude that findings based on the performance of one subgroup of children with language impairment holds for language-impaired children in general.

From an examination of the literature, it might appear that a number of distinct conditions within the language impaired population have been identified.

This impression has been created in part by the use of a number of terms to describe language impairment. These terms have included "congenital aphasia" (Vaisse, 1866), "retarded speech" (Hinckley, 1915), "infantile speech" (Menyuk, 1964), "developmental aphasia" (Benton, 1964), "delayed speech" (Lovell, Hoyle, & Siddall, 1968), "childhood aphasia" (Eisenson, 1972), "deviant language" (Leonard, 1972), "language disorder" (Rees, 1973), as well as "language impairment" (Menyuk, 1975). Although the investigators adopting these different terms have varied in their theoretical views on language impairment, the particular term used has been based more on the clinical label most prevalent at the time rather than on any intended distinction between groups of children with language impairment.

ETIOLOGY AND CORRELATES IN LANGUAGE IMPAIRMENT

The causes of language impairment in children remain as much in doubt today as they were in the nineteenth century when these conditions were first reported (Gall, 1835; Vaisse, 1866; Wilde, 1853). It seems quite possible that language impairment may be due to one of several factors, operating singly or in combination (Menyuk, 1978). Perhaps the most prevalent suspicion through the years has been that language-impaired children suffer from some minimal degree of cerebral damage (Benton, 1964). Such damage is often postulated to be bilateral, because the language development of these children is much slower than that of children suffering from unilateral damage as a consequence of cerebral insult to or surgical removal of the language-dominant hemisphere (Basser, 1962; Goodglass & Geschwind, 1976). In what seems to be the only case of language impairment that has been subjected to postmortem examination, damage was found to the auditory radiations to the temporal lobes bilaterally (Landau, Goldstein, & Kleffner, 1960). However, not all findings accord with this picture of language impairment. For example, Dalby (1975, cited in Rapin & Wilson, 1978) noted that of 87 pneumoencephalograms of children with language impairment 26 showed enlargement of the left temporal horn, 14 of both temporal horns, and 6 of the right. It is hoped that recent developments in neurological assessment procedures will shed additional light on this matter.

The literature on factors implicated in language impairment suggests a number of correlates to (and, some would argue, causes of) these conditions. These factors have included impairment in rhythmic ability (Kracke, 1975), sequencing ability (Stark, Poppen, & May, 1967), and difficulties in habituation following orienting responses to novel stimuli (Mackworth, Grandstaff, & Pribram, 1973). More recently Cromer (1978) has proposed that language-impaired children may exhibit a hierarchical structuring deficit. Cromer suggested, for example, that these children may have difficulty analyzing a complex behavior into its component parts in which the performance of some parts is postponed and performance of other parts takes priority. This seemed to have been reflected in the samples of writing Cromer obtained from language-impaired children. These children tended not to make use of devices that allow interruptions in the sentence, such as relative clauses or conjunctions joining two verbs with the same subject. Given recent evidence suggesting that the production of rhythmic sequences may also involve hierarchically structured units (Martin, 1972), Cromer suggested that a hierarchical disability may also account for language-impaired children's apparent deficits in sequencing and rhythmic ability. This proposal seems worthy of further exploration. However, it seems that a deficit in hierarchical structuring is not likely to account for a number of the limitations shown by language-impaired children. For example, these children are also slow in their acquisition of linguistic features such as words, simple grammatical constructions, grammatical morphemes (e.g., -s, -ed), and semantic notions (e.g., location, possession). It is difficult to see how such limitations can be due to problems in handling hierarchical structure.

Although the previous factors may prove to have some bearing on language impairment in children, the majority of recent studies devoted to variables implicated in language impairment have fallen into one of three areas. These are the environment of language-impaired children, the mental representational abilities of language-impaired children, and the auditory and speech perception abilities of these children.

Environmental Factors

There seem to be two principal reasons for exploring the role of the environment in language impairment. First, evidence is available suggesting that the relative stimulus deprivation experienced by children in orphanages is linked to depressed linguistic development (Weiner, in press). Given that language-impaired children's difficulties often cannot be attributed to biological or psychological factors, it has been reasoned that these children, too, may be environmentally deprived, albeit in the home. The second reason is that language-impaired children present a potential conflict to those with whom they interact (Cramblitt & Siegel, 1977). In terms of linguistic abilities they may project the impression that they should be spoken to in a manner consistent with the way one would address younger normal children. However, in terms of age and physical development they may present cues that ordinarily elicit more complex speech from the co-conversationalist.

Wulbert, Inglis, Kriegsmann, and Mills (1975) have offered evidence that the environment of language-impaired children is more restrictive and punitive and less responsive than that of normal children of the same age. However, the direction of influence was not clear. Although mothers of language-impaired children engaged in fewer play and language activities with their children than did the mothers of the normal children, they also reported that their efforts in this direction had been consistently rebuffed by the children. The direct observations of the language-impaired children's communicative behaviors made by Wulbert et al. seemed consistent with the reports of the mothers. Thus, the reluctance to interact seemed reciprocal, and it could not be assumed that the mothers of language-impaired children were different from mothers in general.

An investigation by Siegel, Cunningham, and van der Spuy (1979) seems to reinforce the findings of Wulbert et al. (1975). Mothers of language-impaired children were more controlling and directive than mothers of normal children of the same age. As in the Wulbert et al. study, the language-impaired children were less likely to initiate interactions and were less responsive and assertive than the normal children. Siegel et al. suggested, in fact, that the behaviors of the mothers of the language-impaired children may have been in response to their children's interaction characteristics; that is, they may have made greater use of prompting and directiveness to increase performance and responsiveness in their children.

Patti (1978) examined the interactions between language-impaired children and their mothers in terms of nonverbal measures such as eye gaze in addition to measures of a linguistic nature. These interactions were compared with interactions between age-matched normal children and their mothers. The normal children were found to look more often at their mothers and to combine gazing with speaking more often than the children with language impairment. Compared to the mothers of the language-impaired children, the mothers of the normal children looked more frequently both while speaking to their children and while listening to them speak. A higher frequency of mutual gaze while the child was speaking was also seen for the interaction between the normal children and their mothers. These findings suggest that interactions between language-impaired children and their mothers may differ from interactions between similar-aged normal children and their mothers. Patti stressed, however, that these differences rested with the dyads and cannot be clearly attributed to either the mothers or the children, independent of the other.

Although the communication patterns exhibited by mothers and their language-impaired children influence each other, there is evidence that a calculated and systematic change in one such pattern may lead to a corresponding change in the other. Whitehurst, Novak, and Zorn (1972) trained a mother of a language-impaired child to alter her verbal behavior on two parameters, level of conversation and level of imitative prompts, when interacting with her child at home. The influence of changes in these verbal behaviors was examined through the use of a baseline reversal design. The results indicated that the acquisition of new words by the child could be controlled by relatively small increases in the level of conversation and imitative prompts provided by the mother.

Cramblitt and Siegel (1977) examined the speech addressed to a language-impaired child and that addressed to his same-age, normal-speaking cousin by the language-impaired child's mother, father, and baby-sitter. The speech directed to the language-impaired child was more fluent, shorter in length, and simpler in syntax than the speech directed to the normally developing child. These findings are consistent with those of studies examining the speech addressed to younger versus older normal children, suggesting that the adults' speech may have been influenced by the language-impaired child's linguistic limitations.

Van Kleeck and Carpenter (1978) examined the speech directed to language-impaired children from a different perspective. In this investigation adults were brought into interaction with language-impaired children showing equivalent utterance length but varying degrees of language comprehension ability. The adults were unfamiliar with the children prior to the study. The findings indicated that the lower the children's comprehension abilities, the more likely the adults were to accompany their utterance with nonverbal cuing and to restrict the lexical diversity of their utterances. However, given the fact that no differences were seen on a number of other measures, Van Kleeck and Carpenter suggested that language comprehension may not be the primary variable influencing the speech adults direct toward language-impaired children in particular and, perhaps, children in general.

In summary, the interactions between adults (usually mothers) and language-impaired children are different in certain respects from interactions between adults and normal children of equivalent age. As noted by a number of investigators, it is not clear whether these differences are attributable to the adults, the children, or the adult-child dyads themselves. An additional point is that the designs of these studies have not permitted a determination of whether interactions between adults and language-impaired children are unusual or whether they simply resemble those taking place between adults and younger normal children. Had these studies used adult-child dyads using normal children equivalent to the language-impaired children in linguistic abilities (necessitating, of course, the use of normal children considerably younger than the language-impaired children) as well as adult-child dyads using age-matched normal children, this question may have been answered. It is hoped that future inquiry will be directed along these lines.

Mental Representation

Language impairment in children presents an interesting perspective from which to view theories concerning the relationship between cognitive and linguistic development. In particular, language impairment has implications for the theoretical framework of Piaget (1962). Central to the Piagetian position has been the view that language represents just one of several symbolic activities and that the acquisition of any linguistic feature can be traced to some more general cognitive attainment. It has been reasoned that if children experience difficulties with language, such children might also be expected to manifest a deficit in other forms of representation, such as symbolic play or imagery.

Inhelder (1963) seems to have been the first to explore this issue. Upon examining the representational abilities of one language-impaired child age 9;6, Inhelder found that the child could perform adequately only on Piagetian tasks requiring a minimum of symbolic representation. The child had particular difficulty on tasks requiring the use of representational imagery. For example, when asked to describe the direction of the level of water in a tilted glass container, the child was unable to disassociate the horizontal direction of the water from the inclined position of the container. Similar findings were obtained in a study by deAjuriaguerra et al. (1965) involving a number of language-impaired children ranging in age from 4;3 to 10;0. These children, too, had particular problems with tasks of representational imagery, as when they were asked to anlayze the movement of a projected shadow. Johnston and Ramstad (1977) reported similar findings in their study of language-impaired children's performance on representational imagery tasks. For example, the children had difficulty on a task where they were required to draw lines dividing circles or squares into equal sections.

In a study by Kamhi and Johnston (1979), the Piagetian task performance of language-impaired children was compared with the performance of a group of normal children matched for mental age (MA) and the performance of a group of normal children matched for mean utterance length (MLU). Kamhi and Johnston found that the language-impaired children performed at a lower level than the MA-matched normal children on the task requiring the greatest degree of representational imagery. In this task, the children had to feel geometric forms blindly and select the visual shapes that corresponded.

The symbolic play of language-impaired children has also been the focus of several investigations. Lovell et al. (1968) compared the level of symbolic play exhibited by 3- and 4-year-old language-impaired children and normal children matched according to age. No differences in symbolic play were noted for the younger ages. However, the younger normal children spent more time than the younger language-impaired children engaged in play representing a transitional level between mere practice play and symbolic play. The older normal children were found to spend more time in symbolic play than the older children with language impairment. In addition, a relationship was seen between the children's mean utterance lengths and the amount of time they spent in symbolic play.

The symbolic play behavior of language-impaired children has been examined from a somewhat different standpoint by other investigators. Brown, Redmond, Bass, Liebergott, and Swope (1975) examined the symbolic play of normal and language-impaired children matched for age in terms of the developmental level of symbolic play exhibited by the children. These investigators noted that the language-impaired children showed less adaptiveness in the use of objects and less integration of play behaviors around a theme. Williams (1978) examined symbolic play in terms of the number of symbolic play acts performed. She observed that fewer of these acts were performed by language-impaired children than by normal children of equivalent age.

The representational skills evolving during the sixth stage of sensorimotor development were explored in a study by Snyder (1976). Normal and language-impaired children operating at the single-word utterance level were compared in terms of their performance on the Uzgiris and Hunt (1975) scales of psychological development. The two groups performed similarly on five of the scales. However, the language-impaired children performed more poorly than the normal children on the scale assessing means–end schemes. The normal children generally displayed means–end schemes at the stage-six level whereas the language-impaired children were often limited to fifth stage means–end schemes.

In an investigation by Folger and Leonard (1978), comparisons of performance on the Uzgiris and Hunt (1975) scales were made between normal and language-impaired children producing only single-word utterances and between normal and language-impaired children producing two-word as well as single-word utterances. Thus the performance of the language-disordered children in this study was compared to that of younger children who were developing normally. No differences were seen between the groups at each of the two levels of utterance usage.

The investigations of language-impaired children's representational abilities are striking in their consistency. Without exception, these studies have found language-impaired children to be less developed than normal peers in several areas of mental representation. This evidence suggests that these children's difficulties may not be strictly linguistic in nature. As pointed out in Leonard (1979), the structural similarities between a number of representational and linguistic behaviors are notable. For example, a child's ability to use word forms to have an adult perform some act or reach an object otherwise unavailable to him/her shares certain structural properties with the ability to use alternate means to achieve some end, such as using a stick to reach some object. The ability to use a word to represent some absent object resembles the ability to use another object to stand for that object in play. To cite another example, the ability to use passive sentences shares certain features with the ability to perform reversible operations in conservation tasks. Structural parallels of this sort raise the possibility that more general representational deficits are responsible for language-impaired children's linguistic difficulties. However, a few recent papers offer data that cast doubt on the view that the relationship between linguistic and representational abilities is a causal one. Ingram (1977) and Dihoff and Chapman (1977) have noted individual children who, for example, used multiword utterances prior to the attainment of comparable representational abilities in nonlinguistic domains. Folger and Leonard (1978) have made similar observations in a study employing language-impaired as well as normal children. The fact that on occasion language-impaired children's linguistic abilities may exceed their abilities on nonlinguistic tasks of representational ability suggests that for these children, too, a "weak form" of the cognitive hypothesis may be most appropriate (Cromer, 1974, 1976); that is, it may be the case that for language-impaired children, as for normal children, underlying cognitive structures may be important but not sufficient to explain the acquisition of language.

Until recently the very issue of whether cognitive ability was important in the consideration of language impairment was in question. Historically, language impairment had been viewed as a linguistic deficit independent of the factor of intelligence. How, then, can findings indicating representational deficits in language-impaired children obtain? It seems to be the case that nonverbal intelligence may vary considerably, depending on the particular ability examined. Even on a battery of tasks based on the same theoretical framework, children may differ in their performance from task to task. For example, on the Uzgiris and Hunt (1975) scales of psychological development, a test battery based on Piagetian theory, language-impaired children tend to perform better on certain tasks, such as that assessing object relations in space, than on others, such as that assessing means–end relations (Folger & Leonard, 1978; Snyder, 1976). Therefore, it would seem likely that these children might also perform differently on tasks differing in their theoretical orientations, as when de Ajuriaguerra et al. (1965) noted for one 12-year-old language-impaired child an average performance score on the WISC and yet deficient performance on a Piagetian task of representational imagery. Similar findings have been reported by Johnston and Ramstad (1977). This seems to suggest that many language-impaired children perform at expected age levels only on certain nonverbal intelligence measures. Johnston (in press) has proposed that language-impaired children may perform relatively well on tasks involving visual perception of static figures, shapes, and designs, as seen on many items of the Leiter and WISC Performance scales. Thus, the traditional view that language impairment is free of factors of nonverbal intelligence seems in need of alteration.

The notion that children with language impairment necessarily perform within the normal range on at least some intelligence measure can also be questioned. Many investigators have selected as subjects only those language-impaired children who perform within the normal range on nonverbal intelligence measures (Stark, 1967; Tallal & Stark, 1980; Weiner, 1969). It is worth noting that such decisions may have been based on an overly strict interpretation of traditional definitions, such as that advanced by Benton (1964), that language-impaired children display linguistic deficits that are lower than those predicted by their intellectual abilities. Benton (1978) himself has pointed out that not all language-impaired children fall so clearly in the normal range of intelligence. Thus, language impairment might best be described as a set of conditions where language ability is considerably more depressed than nonverbal intelligence and not as a set of conditions where language disability exists in the presence of normal nonverbal intelligence.

Auditory and Speech Perception

For a number of years, a dominant theme in the literature on language impairment has been that language-impaired children exhibit difficulties in auditory processing. A substantial number of investigations have been directed toward examining these children's general auditory and specific speech discrimination, sequencing, and memory span abilities (Chalfant & Scheffelin, 1969). The findings from the large majority of these studies have been equivocal at best (Bloom & Lahey, 1978; Rees, 1973). More recently, however, evidence has emerged suggesting that language-impaired children may have particular difficulties processing acoustic stimuli presented at rapid rates.

Lowe and Campbell (1965) found differences in normal and language-impaired children's ability to judge which of two pure tones presented in succession occurred last. The language-impaired subjects required greater temporal separation between tones before they could accurately judge the order in which the tones were presented. Because the temporal separation required by the language-impaired children was over four times greater than the average duration of each phoneme during typical speech, Lowe and Campbell suggested that these children's linguistic difficulties may have been related to difficulties in sequencing rapidly presented acoustic signals. Unfortunately, the task used by Lowe and Campbell (1965) required children to make judgments using linguistic terms such as *high, low,* and *last.* It was not clear that steps were taken to ensure that the children comprehended these terms. This is particularly important because the normal and language-impaired children were matched according to age, creating a state of affairs where the group performing more poorly on the experimental task was also the group with more limited linguistic abilities.

Tallal and Piercy (1973a, 1973b) provided considerably more insight into language-impaired children's auditory perceptual abilities through a series of studies using a single group of language-impaired subjects. Using a task requiring no verbal response, Tallal and Piercy found that the language-impaired children were not significantly different than normal children matched for age in their ability to discriminate or sequence tones that were presented relatively slowly. However, when these same stimuli were presented more rapidly, the language-impaired children were significantly impaired in their performance. The language-impaired children required considerably more time than the normal children to even discriminate between the tones. Because tones must be discriminated before they can be sequenced, Tallal and Piercy reasoned that the findings of Lowe and Campbell (1965) may have been due to language-impaired children's difficulty with discrimination at rapid rates rather than with sequencing.

As a first step in examining whether language-impaired children's difficulty with rapidly presented acoustic signals may relate to their problems in acquiring language, Tallal and Piercy (1974) examined language-impaired children's ability to discriminate speech stimuli requiring rapid acoustic changes and speech stimuli involving no rapid changes. Relative to normal children of the same age, the language-impaired children had considerable difficulty discriminating speech stimuli involving rapid changes. Their performance on the stimuli involving no changes did not show the same deficiencies. In a subsequent study, Tallal and Piercy (1975) provided evidence that the language-impaired children's difficulty with the former type of stimuli was in fact due to the rapid acoustic changes in the stimuli rather than to formant transitions.

A further step in exploring the relationship between the children's difficulty with rapid acoustic changes and their language problems was taken in Tallal, Stark, and Curtis (1976). These investigators examined the language-impaired children's ability to discriminate between stop consonants in consonant-vowel syllables (/ba/ versus /da/) and between steady-state vowels (/ɛ/ versus /æ/). The consonant-vowel syllables were presented with 43-msec formant transition periods as well as with 95-msec formant transition periods. The children's performance on the discrimination task was compared to their performance on a production task, where they produced isolated vowels and diphthongs and nonsense syllables and words containing stop consonants and stop consonant clusters. As expected, the children performed most poorly on those stimuli in the discrimination task involving consonant-vowel syllables with short transition periods. Given the difficulty the children had with such stimuli, Tallal et al. predicted that they would have greater difficulty on those items on the production task involving the most rapid acoustic changes, the stops and stop clusters. This prediction was borne out by the results.

More recent investigations performed by Tallal and Stark (in press) using other groups of language-impaired children have substantiated, for the most part, the earlier work of Tallal and her colleagues. In addition, the Tallal and Stark findings have provided a further specification of language-impaired children's auditory discrimination difficulties. These children may not have difficulty with all types of rapid temporal cues but rather with those that are preceded or followed immediately by other acoustic cues, as within a syllable context. Interestingly, Tallal and Stark also found evidence for a deficit in visual processing, although the deficit was not as dramatic as seen for these children's auditory processing. Tallal and Piercy (1973b) had found no deficits in language-impaired children's performance on visual tasks. It can be noted, however, that Tallal and Piercy did not employ intervals between the visual stimuli of less than 30 msec, whereas the intervals for the auditory stimuli included those of 8 msec and 15 msec as well as intervals longer in duration. If the language-impaired children had moderate difficulties with visual discrimination in addition to their major auditory discrimination difficulties, the Tallal and Piercy stimuli may not have been sufficiently sensitive to detect them. In any case, the Tallal and Stark findings are similar to those of an earlier study by Poppen, Stark, Eisenson, Forrest, and Wertheim (1969) that language-impaired children may exhibit difficulties on visual processing tasks in addition to the more notable deficits in their auditory processing task performance.

The findings reported here suggest that a number of language-impaired children may display certain auditory processing deficits. At this point it is important to consider whether or not such deficits may be responsible for difficulties in acquiring language. Leonard (1979) has argued that the characteristics of language-impaired children's speech is not adequately predicted by their performance on auditory processing tasks. For example, sequencing difficulties might give rise to frequent use of metathesis (e.g. *pish* for *ship, deks* for *desk*); yet this phonological process is infrequent in occurrence. Difficulties in distinguishing rapid acoustic changes predicts the observed difficulties language-impaired children have with stop consonant–vowel and vowel–stop consonant productions relative to vowel productions, but they do not predict the fact that fricative–vowel and vowel–fricative productions give these children the greatest difficulty. It is interesting to note that Tallal et al. (1976) did not employ fricatives in their study of the perception–production relationship in language-impaired children. Even if difficulties with fricatives can be argued in terms of their perceptual characteristics (e.g., they have greater concentration of energy in the higher frequencies of the spectrum), left unexplained is the fact that the same fricative will be applied at different points in development as a function of its grammatical role. For example, *-s* is used as a plural before it is used as a contractible copula and as a contractible copula before it is used as a contractible auxiliary (Johnston & Schery, 1976).

If auditory processing deficits *do* play a causal role in language impairment, their influence on language-impaired children's speech would have to be characterized in a different manner. Instead of leading to specific error patterns, such deficits would have to have the more general effect of distorting these children's linguistic input, necessitating a greater period of time to "sort out" the relevant features of the input to acquire. The result might be a less-developed rather than a distinct use of language. The characteristics of language-impaired children's speech, reviewed in the following, are not out of line with such a possibility.

THE SPEECH OF LANGUAGE-IMPAIRED CHILDREN

Until the mid-1960s there were few systematic attempts to describe the linguistic abilities of children with language impairment. Descriptions of these abilities were limited to case studies of single children. However, since that time a number of group studies devoted to describing language-impaired children's linguistic abilities have appeared. Given the heterogeneity of the language-impaired population, the assumption that language-impaired children can be studied as a group is quite risky and no doubt most studies have been subject to wide intersubject variability. Nonetheless, general impressions of the linguistic abilities of language-impaired children have often emerged from these studies.

An inspection of the literature reveals a preponderance of studies dealing with language production, and relatively few aimed at exploring the language comprehension of language-impaired children. Although comprehension studies involving language-impaired children seem to have been increasing in number in recent years (Liles, Shulman, & Bartlett, 1977; Shatz, Bernstein, & Shulman, 1980; the comparison group in Tager-Flusberg, 1979), a clear picture of these children's comprehension skills has not yet emerged. Consequently, only those studies examining the production of language by these children is discussed here. These investigations seem best organized according to the major dimensions of language with which they deal: syntax, semantics, pragmatics, and phonology.

Syntax

Perhaps the first systematic attempt to compare the syntax of normal and language-impaired children was made by Menyuk (1964). In what proved to be the prototype for future studies, Menyuk collected spontaneous speech samples from normal and language-impaired children matched for age. The samples were then analyzed in terms of Chomsky's (1957) original theory of transformational grammar. Restricted forms were also noted in terms of whether they represented a substitution, redundancy, or omission of the adult form. The results indicated that a greater number of the normal children showed use of transformations, whereas a greater number of the language-impaired children showed use of restricted forms. In the same study, Menyuk reported longitudinal data from a normal child for the ages 2;0 and 3;0 and compared these data with those from a language-impaired child age 3;0. It appeared that more dissimilarities than similarities existed in the speech of the two children. Menyuk interpreted her findings as support for the position that the speech of normal and language-impaired children was qualitatively different.

Conclusions similar to those of Menyuk (1964) were drawn by Lee (1966), who compared the spontaneous speech of a normal child and a somewhat older language-impaired child according to their use of phrase structure sentence types. The language-impaired child did not show use of some of the sentence types evidenced in the speech of the normal child. Lee interpreted her findings as support for the view that a qualitative difference held between the syntax of the normal and language-impaired child.

A different tack was taken in an investigation by Leonard (1972). Instead of comparing the number of children in each group using a particular syntactic structure, Leonard's comparative measure was the frequency with which the children in each group used the structure. The children's use of syntactic structures was analyzed in the same manner as in Menyuk (1964). In addition, Leonard made use of the Developmental Sentence Scoring system of Lee and Canter (1971), a system that provides for the analysis of morphemes in grammatical classes such as personal pronouns, indefinite pronouns, and conjunctions. When the frequency of use of these structures and morphemes was examined, a number of differences between the normal and language-impaired children were noted. Those structures and morphemes seen in the adult linguistic system were more frequent in the speech of the normal children, whereas those representing restricted forms were more frequent in the speech of the children with language impairment. The morpheme scoring system used by Leonard also allowed for the computation of a score for each grammatical class that represented the level of development of the morphemes used in the class, independent of their frequency of usage. Although morphemes in five of the eight classes were used less frequently by the language-impaired children, Leonard observed that the developmental level of the morphemes used was as high as those used by the normal children. Similar findings have been reported in a more recent investigation by Johnston and Kamhi (1980).

With the appearance of Morehead and Ingram's (1970) study of language-impaired children's syntax, a new means of comparing the speech of normal and language-impaired children came into being. These investigators compared the syntax of language-impaired children with that of normal children matched for MLU, not chronological age. The strategy of matching according to MLU represented an important methodological refinement. MLU has been considered to be an acceptable general index of linguistic development. Thus, if differences are found between MLU-matched normal and language-impaired children, the conclusion could be drawn that the language-impaired children were doing something atypical for that period of linguistic development. Morehead and Ingram found the phrase structure and transformational rules reflected in the speech of the two groups to be very similar. The major difference that was observed was that the normal children used a greater number of lexical categories per sentence construction type.

Ingram (1972a) applied additional analyses to the Morehead and Ingram (1970) data. He noted that the normal and language-impaired children were highly similar in terms of the MLU levels at which copula and auxiliary forms appeared. The ranking of these forms in terms of frequency was also the same in the two groups. At the upper MLU levels, however, the language-impaired children used copula and auxiliary forms less frequently than did their matched normals. In a further examination of the Morehead and Ingram data, Ingram (1972b) ranked the children according to their MLU and determined which questions were used at each level of MLU. The resulting orders of question acquisition were highly similar for the normal children and the children with language impairment. However, the language-impaired children used questions less frequently.

Kessler (1975) examined the grammatical morphemes (e.g., plural, past tense markers) used in the speech of language-impaired children. She observed that a rank order of the grammatical morphemes based on the percentage of correct usage in obligatory contexts by these children was highly similar to the order reported by Brown (1973) for three normal children.

In another study of grammatical morpheme usage, Johnston and Schery (1976) analyzed spontaneous speech samples obtained from language-impaired children according to the lowest MLU level at which each grammatical morpheme was used in 90% of its obligatory contexts. The resulting sequence of grammatical morphemes was in good agreement with that seen in studies of normal children. Johnston and Schery also noted that the language-impaired children acquired the grammatical morphemes at higher MLU levels than was true for the normal children studied by other investigators. Similar findings were obtained in Trantham and Pedersen's (1976) report of one language-impaired child (Leonard, 1979) and in the studies of Steckol and Leonard (1979) and Albertini (1980) in which direct comparisons were made between normal and language-impaired children.

Perhaps the most detailed examination of grammatical morpheme usage by a language-impaired child was performed by Cousins (1979). Cousins followed the grammatical morpheme usage of one child for a period of 8 months, beginning at age 5;5. Consistent with previous studies, the child's use of grammatical morphemes emerged at a higher MLU level than is seen in normal children. When the grammatical morphemes studied by Brown (1973) were considered collectively, the order in which the morphemes emerged in the speech of the child was similar to that seen in normal children. However, when the grammatical morphemes were divided according to whether they occurred with noun-phrase constituents (e.g., plurals, articles) or verb-phrase constituents (e.g., past tense, auxiliaries), only the former showed a similar order of emergence to that of normally developing children. A close examination of her data led Cousins to the conclusion that factors such as sentence context and acoustic salience may have influenced the child's use of particular grammatical morphemes.

These investigations suggest that syntactic features provide language impaired children with considerable difficulty. The manner in which these difficulties manifest themselves is not altogether clear. Initial impressions were that the syntactic features evidenced in these children's speech were unique to this group. However, subsequent studies suggest that these features are essentially the same as those used by younger normal children. A syntactic feature may often be used with less frequency by language-impaired children than by their normal peers. In a number of instances, this difference parallels findings for younger versus older normal children; that is, children's early use of a feature is limited to certain contexts and relatively infrequent in occurrence. As the children develop, their increased proficiency with this feature enables them to make more frequent use of it. However, several investigators have observed frequency differences between normal and language-impaired children whose speech was matched on the basis of MLU, a general index of linguistic development. Thus, in certain cases the relationship between language-impaired children's use of syntax and their MLU may be different from that noted in normally developing children.

Semantics

Syntactic structure serves as the means by which semantic relations are coded in speech. For example, a young child may intend to express some semantic relation concerning possession and may code this notion through a noun + noun construction (e.g., *Daddy hat*). Alternatively, the relation of an action being performed on some object may be expressed via a verb + noun construction (e.g., *roll ball*). Given the difficulties language-impaired children exhibit with syntax, investigators have attempted to examine whether the semantic relations reflected in these children's speech differ from those evidenced in the speech of normal children.

Employing a modification of Fillmore's (1968, 1971) case grammar as a method of analysis, Leonard, Bolders, and Miller (1976) compared the speech of normal and language-impaired children matched for age as well as the speech of normal and language-impaired children matched for MLU. The children matched according to chronological age differed in their use of only two semantic relations. Both of these relations, representing early emerging relations, were used with greater frequency by the language-impaired children. Leonard et al. interpreted their findings as being consistent with the view that much of the language-impaired children's speech was still limited to fairly elementary relational meanings, quantitatively speaking. No differences were seen in the comparison between the speech of the normal and language-impaired children matched for MLU.

Other investigations exploring the semantic relations reflected in the speech of normal and language-impaired children were performed by Freedman and Carpenter (1976) and Leonard, Steckol, and Schwartz (1978). In both studies normal and language-impaired children were matched for MLU. Few differences were noted in the semantic relations reflected in the speech of the two groups of children. However, when differences occurred, the semantic relation was evidenced more frequently in the speech of the language-impaired children if the semantic relation represented an early-emerging one and more frequently in the speech of the normal children if it was a later-emerging relation.

Semantic relations were examined in a somewhat different manner by Johnston and Kamhi (1980). Using an analysis based on Antinucci and Parisi (1973), these investigators compared the speech of normal and language-impaired children matched for MLU. The language-impaired children were found to express fewer propositions per utterance than the normally developing children.

Surprisingly few studies have been directed at language-impaired children's lexical acquisition. Most of the studies that have appeared in the literature have been limited to case studies. Such studies have documented what might be expected; language-impaired children acquire their first words later than normal children, they acquire subsequent words more slowly than normal children, and on occasion these children make lexical errors. With regard to the late emergence of words, Bender (1940) observed a child who did not begin using words until after the age of 4;0. Werner (1945) studied a child who had not yet begun using words at age 5;0. A child studied by Hinckley (1915) did not begin using words until she reached the age of 6;0. In one of the few studies examining more than a single child, Morley, Court, Miller, and Garside (1955) noted ages of first-word acquisition ranging from 1;6 to 5;0 in 15 language-impaired children.

Nice (1925) performed one of the first studies documenting the fact that subsequent lexical development is slow in language-impaired children. The child studied by Nice had acquired only five words at age 2;0 and still had not acquired 50 words at age 3;0. Weeks (1974) came to somewhat similar conclusions in a longitudinal study of one child's slow speech development. This child did not acquire a 50-word vocabulary until she reached the age of 2;4.

A few early case studies of the words used by language-impaired children report instances of "unusual" word usage. For example, Nice (1925) observed a child using *fu* for *blow, ha* for *there, ah* for *mine,* and *cuggan* for *sister.* A number of other words, referring to vehicles and animals, were derived from imitations of the sounds made by their referents. Stumpf (1901) observed his son using *aja* as an expression of joy, and *ä* as an expression of disgust. Neither of these investigators viewed such words as intentional creations on the children's part. Stumpf could trace his child's words back to vocal patterns observed in the child's babbling or to words the child had heard. Nice suggested that the child's babbling may have acquired word status through their adoption by adults when speaking to the child. Greenfield (1973) has provided evidence of just such an occurrence in a normal child.

Weeks (1975) had an opportunity to observe the lexical characteristics of a child at a higher level of linguistic development. The child used two forms in her utterances that did not appear to have a referent. One form, *ee,* seemed to be used where a function word might be expected. The other form, *geekine,* was seemingly used in sentence slots appropriate for content words. Guillaume (1927) has observed the use of a phonological element in the form of a vowel for a variety of forms in the speech of a normal child at a comparable level of linguistic development. The child's form *geekine* appeared to be derived from *this kind* and was seemingly used when the child was unfamiliar with the lexical item it replaced (e.g., *ee geekine on*?, for *is tape recorder on*?).

Weeks (1975) observed some interesting lexical errors later in the development of the same child. For example, the child used *brooming* to describe the act of sweeping with a broom. This error may have been founded on the knowledge that a number of verbs (e.g., *combing, hammering*) are derived from instrumental nouns. Another error was the child's use of *barefeeting,* related perhaps to verbs such as *elbowing.* Such principled verb errors are not uncommon in the speech of normal children (Bowerman, 1974).

The investigations reviewed in this section suggest that language-impaired children display difficulties with semantic aspects of language. These children's semantic relations and lexical characteristics resemble those of younger normal children. In some instances, however, it appears that the semantic relation development of language-impaired children may lag further behind their MLU than seems to be the case for children who experience no language learning difficulties.

Pragmatics

During the last few years a number of investigators have begun to explore language-impaired children's use of speech in its social context. This has necessitated a change in focus from the structure or meaning of utterances to how effective the utterances are in communicating something to the listener. Perhaps the first study dealing with such pragmatic functions in language-impaired children's speech was that of Snyder (1976). Snyder's subjects consisted of normal and language-impaired children operating at the single-word utterance level of speech. The lexicons of the two groups of children were comparable. Snyder observed that the normal children more frequently used linguistic means to communicate with declarative and imperative intent. The language-impaired children more frequently used nonlinguistic means (e.g., gesturing) to communicate imperatives. The children's ability to communicate informative (nonredundant) situational elements was also analyzed. The normal children showed the ability to encode the informative contextual element with either linguistic or nonlinguistic means. However, the language-impaired children were primarily limited to signaling the informative element through nonlinguistic means.

Skarakis and Greenfield (1979) examined the treatment of redundant situational elements in the speech of normal and language-impaired children matched for MLU. The children were shown paired sets of pictures, each depicting a different continuous event over a series of three pictures. Within a pair, sets contrasted on which element was presented as constant (redundant) and which as changing in the final picture of each series. For each series, the first two pictures were described by the experimenter and the child was asked to describe the final picture. The normal and language-impaired children were found to perform in a similar manner on this task. At the lower MLU levels, the children showed a tendency to delete redundant information from their utterances, and those at higher MLU levels tended to refer to such information using pronominal forms.

Language-impaired children's use of politeness in making requests was the subject of an investigation by Prinz (1977). Politeness devices, such as the use of indirect forms (e.g., *Can you pass the butter?*) and the use of *please,* were used by the language-impaired children as well as the younger normal children with whom they were compared. However, these politeness devices were used less frequently by the children with language impairment.

Ball and Cross (1980) focused on the communicative functions served by the utterances produced by normal and language-impaired children matched for language comprehension ability. The two groups were similar in the frequency with which they produced utterances serving such functions as informing, interrogating, and commenting. However, the language-impaired children showed greater use of utterances serving a regulating function.

The operations used in discourse by language-impaired children were studied by Van Kleeck and Frankel (1981). Of particular interest was the children's use of focus operations, which represent mere repetitions of prior adult utterances, and substitution operations, which involve a repetition of part of the prior adult utterance but also alter the original utterance in some way. In keeping with findings from normally developing children, the language-impaired children at lower MLU levels relied principally on focus operations, and the child with the highest MLU showed considerable use of substitution operations.

Watson (1977) also examined language-impaired children's ability to participate in conversations. Parent–child interactions were studied using language-impaired children as well as normal children approximately matched according to age. The conversational responses of the language-impaired children showed a greater tendency relative to the normal children to continue the topic contained in the prior parent utterance. Further, these topic continuations were most frequently affirmations or denials of the preceding parent utterance. Relative to the normal children, the language-impaired children asked for clarifications infrequently and showed less use of information bearing comments on the topic raised in the utterance of the parent.

Whereas Watson's (1977) study examined language-impaired children's conversational abilities when interacting with adults, Fey, Leonard, Fey, and O'Connor (1978) examined these abilities when the language-impaired child's co-conversationalist was another child. Specifically, Fey et al. compared the speech of language-impaired children when interacting with normal children of the same chronological age with these same children's speech when interacting with normal children with comparable MLUs. Fey et al. observed that when interacting with the MLU-matched normals, the language-impaired children showed more reduced preverb length in sentence usage, were more conversationally assertive (Watson, 1977), and used a greater number of internal state questions (e.g., *Do you want to play?*) than when interacting with age-matched normals. These differences were quite similar to those seen in studies dealing with normal children's speech style modifications as a function of listener age and linguistic ability (Sachs & Devin, 1976; Shatz & Gelman, 1973).

Meline (1978) examined language-impaired children's performance on a referential communication task. In this task, the child was seated across the table from an adult listener, with a screen separating them. The child was required to provide the listener with sufficient information to enable him to stack a set of blocks with novel figures on them in the same order as the set of blocks in front of the child. The performance of the language-impaired children on this task was compared with that of a group of normal children with approximately equal MLU. Interestingly, Meline's findings differed from most studies examining language-impaired children's pragmatic abilities. The language-impaired children's communications resulted in greater listener ability to choose the correct referent blocks than the communications of the normal children. However, the language-impaired children were no more efficient in their communications than the normal children, as defined by the number of words required in producing an effective communication.

Gallagher and Darnton (1977) explored another conversationally related skill in language-impaired children. These investigators examined the characteristics of language-impaired children's revisions when the experimenter pretended that she did not understand what the child had said. Each language-impaired subject fell into one of Brown's (1973) language stages I, II, and III. These children's revisions were compared with those of normal children of equivalent MLU studied by Gallagher (1977). The language-impaired children were similar to the normal children in terms of the percentage of their responses constituting revisions of their prior response. In addition, the two groups were similar in the percentages reflecting repetitions of their prior response and failures to provide any response. However, differences became apparent when the proportional distribution of the types of revisions in the two groups was compared. For the normal children, the proportional distribution of the revision types changed with increasing MLU. Yet no such changes were seen in the language-impaired children. From lowest to highest MLU, the normal children initially showed a relatively high proportion of phonetic changes, then began showing an increase in constituent reductions, and finally displayed an increase in constituent substitutions. On the other hand, the language-impaired children were consistent in showing a relatively high proportion of phonetic changes and constituent reductions and a low proportion of constituent substitutions.

The paraphrase capabilities of language-impaired children were the focus of an investigation by Hoar (1977). Normal and language-impaired children matched for age were asked to produce paraphrases for stimulus sentences. The younger language-impaired children showed a greater number of failures to respond and repetitions than the younger normal children. For the younger children in both groups, paraphrase attempts tended to take the form of lexical substitutions. This tendency was particularly strong in the younger language impaired children. For the normal children of intermediate age, the predominant means of paraphrasing constituted syntactic rearrangements of the stimulus sentence. Such a tendency was seen only in the language-impaired children at the oldest age level studied.

The findings pertaining to pragmatic functions seem to suggest the following conclusions. Language-impaired children have difficulties with the use of most of the pragmatic features of language studied. The pragmatic features observed in the speech of normal children are also used by children with language impairment. However, language-impaired children use these features less frequently and seem to acquire them at a later age. In certain cases, these children fail to use the pragmatic features used by normal children operating at the same level of MLU.

Phonology

The phonology studies reviewed here are those that have included evidence that the phonological difficulties observed in the children involved were due to delays or differences in their organizational abilities rather than in their articulatory production abilities. Unfortunately, most investigations of this type have been limited to case studies of one or a few children with language impairment. In addition, few have included normal children for purposes of comparison. Thus, a review of these studies necessitates comparing their results with those obtained in studies of normal child phonology conducted by other investigators.

Applegate (1961) was one of the first investigators to attempt to characterize the phonological patterns in language-impaired children's speech. He observed two notable phonological processes in the speech of his two subjects, glottal stop replacement and stopping. Glottal stops were used only when the stops that they replaced were the same as a stop in a previous position in the word. For instance, *take* was produced in the adult manner, but *cake* was produced as *ca?* Applegate also noted that these processes operated in a fixed order. Glottal replacement of a duplicated stop was always applied prior to the stopping process that converted fricatives to stops. Thus, *toot* was produced as *too?* and *suit* was produced as *tuit*.

Another early study of the phonological characteristics of a language-impaired child's speech was performed by Haas (1963). The principal difficulties exhibited by this child involved phonological processes seen in very young normal children. These processes included unstressed syllable deletion (e.g., *nana* for *banana*), stopping (e.g., producing *p* for *f*), and fronting (e.g., *dood* for *good*).

Two language-impaired children served as subjects in an investigation by Compton (1970). The more general phonological processes seemingly involved in these children's speech were fronting, stopping, velar assimilation (e.g. *kake* for *take*), deaspiration of stop consonants, nasalization of vowels preceding nasal consonants, devoicing of final consonants, and denasalization of nasal consonants. All of these processes have been observed in younger normal children.

Weber (1970) examined the phonological characteristics of 18 language-impaired children. The children differed from one another in the particular processes operative in their speech. However, the processes were highly typical of those noted in the speech of younger normal children. The processes observed included fronting, devoicing, stopping, final consonant deletion, affrication (e.g., *chop* for *shop*), and the use of glides for liquids (e.g., *yee* for *Lee*).

Farwell (1972) was one of only a few investigators who studied both normal and language-impaired children. The phonological characteristics of two language-impaired children, ages 6;5 and 7;1, were compared with those of one normal child, age 2;9. Farwell did not provide an indication of whether the normal child was operating at the same general level of linguistic development as the language-impaired children. Only data pertaining to the use of fricatives were dealt with in her paper. Both the normal and language-impaired children showed instances of stopping and consonant cluster simplification (e.g., *snow* produced as *no*). Only the language-impaired children showed evidence of final consonant deletion; however, this process has often been noted in the normal children studied by other investigators. The language-impaired children in Farwell's study exhibited syntactic difficulties as well as phonological difficulties. Because the phonological processes seen in these children's speech were not distinguishable from those in previous investigators' data, this study provided evidence that the syntactic level of language-impaired children may vary widely without a significant difference in the level of the children's phonological development.

Another investigation of the phonological difficulties of a language-impaired child was conducted by Pollack and Rees (1972). The processes seen in this child's speech were fronting, the use of fricatives for affricates (e.g., *shew* for *chew*), and final consonant deletion. A child studied by Lorentz (1972) revealed evidence of the processes of consonant cluster simplification, deletion of final consonants, and metathesis in consonant clusters (e.g., *psot* for *spot*). Although metathesis is quite infrequent in occurrence, this process has been reported to occur on occasion in the speech of normal children as well (Compton & Streeter, 1977).

One of the most detailed reports on language-impaired children is a study by Oller, Anderson, Augustine, Groher, Hedrick, Holder, Levinson, Marquardt, Peterson, Prather, Schubert, Winstead, & Woodle (1972), appearing in abbreviated form in Oller (1973). The common processes observed by Oller et al. included consonant cluster simplification, the production of glides for liquids, stopping, fronting, and final consonant deletion. One of the children studied by Oller et al. demonstrated the less frequent tendency of metathesizing fricatives to the final position in words (e.g., *ash* for *sock*).

Edwards and Bernhardt (1973) also presented a detailed account of phonology in language-impaired children's speech. The large majority of processes observed in these children's speech were similar to those reported in the literature for normal child phonology. However, two children showed an unusual tendency to produce liquids and glides as a bilabial nasal. For one of these children this tendency seemed due to the common process of bilabial assimilation (e.g., *mabbit* for *rabbit*). However, for the other child such usage could not be easily attributed to assimilation processes (e.g., *mee* for *leash*). To my knowledge, such a process has not been reported for normal children. Another atypical process in a language-impaired child's speech was reported in a second paper by Lorentz (1974). He observed one child producing fricatives as liquids (e.g., *ling* for *sing*). However, this child also showed evidence of several more common processes, such as fronting and final fricative deletion. In a second paper by Compton (1975), the speech of a language-impaired child was described. No clearly atypical processes seemed evident in this child's speech.

Data originally reported by Hinckley (1915) have been subjected to a phonological analysis by Ingram (1976). According to this analysis, the child studied by Hinckley made use of a number of normal phonological processes. In addition, two processes not characteristic of normal children were observed. One was the occasional use of the bilabial nasal at the beginning of words (e.g., *book* produced as *mboo*). The other was the optional use of the linguadental for a variety of sounds, as seen in examples such as *tha* for *chair, watho* for *wagon,* and *peth* for *pencil.*

In the most recent work of Compton (1976), a summary of phonological analyses of 20 language-impaired children was presented. Compton concerned himself only with phonological rules applied to consonants in initial word position, initial consonant clusters, and consonants in final word position. An inspection of these rules reveals a number of phonological processes, all of which have been seen in normal child phonology.

A second study making use of a group of normal as well as language-impaired children was conducted by Schwartz, Leonard, Folger, and Wilcox (1980). The three language-impaired children were also exhibiting difficulties in acquiring syntax. Their speech was compared with that of three normal children, matched according to mean utterance length. Schwartz et al. found a number of similarities in the phonological processes used by the children in the two groups. An important aspect of this study was that it identified two phonological processes used by both the normal and language-impaired children that had been previously presumed to be used by only one of the two groups. These processes were the use of glottal stops in place of final consonants and reduplication (e.g., *baba* for *basket*).

Leonard, Miller, and Brown (1980) attempted to determine whether phonological processes observed in the speech of normal and language-impaired children actually function in the same way for both groups. These investigators focused on two processes, consonant assimilation and reduplication. In normally developing children, assimilation seems to serve the function of providing a source of substitution for a difficult consonant. Reduplication allows the child to produce a multisyllabic word at a point when such words cannot be pronounced in a nonreduplicated manner. Leonard et al. observed the same functions served by these processes in the speech of a group of language-impaired children.

It is clear from the available evidence that language-impaired children present difficulties in phonology. For the most part, the phonological processes operative in language-impaired children's speech are the same as those adopted by younger normal children. There are a very few exceptions, where a process not reported in the literature in normal child phonology has been noted in the speech of a language-impaired child.

Phonology studies employing a comparison group of normal children are uncommon, making it difficult to determine whether the phonological processes evident in language-impaired children's speech occur at the same MLU levels as they do in normal children. However, a close comparison between these studies and those reported in the literature on normal child phonology reveals some notable discrepancies. The phonological processes discussed here are most prevalent in normal children's speech during the two- and three-word utterance levels of development (Ingram, 1976). Although these processes can be seen in language-impaired children at comparable MLU levels (Schwartz et al., 1980), they may also be present in the speech of language-impaired children producing five- and six-word utterances (Haas, 1963). This suggests that language-impaired children may begin with normal phonological processes, but these processes may persist in these children's speech (Compton, 1976; Ingram, 1976; Leonard, 1979).

LANGUAGE IMPAIRMENT: DELAY OR DIFFERENCE?

Considerable attention has been paid to the issue of whether language-impaired children's linguistic development is delayed relative to that of normal children or altogether different. Unfortunately, this issue has been blurred both by limitations in methodology and by imprecise characterizations of "language delay" and "language difference."

One interpretation of "language difference" is that some linguistic feature evidenced in the speech of either language-impaired or normal children is not evidenced in the speech of the other group. The studies of Menyuk (1964) and Lee (1966) have been interpreted as showing evidence of this sort. However, the evidence from these studies is not compelling from this standpoint. An examination of Menyuk's group data reveals that only 2 of the 33 structures compared were used by one group and not the other. Menyuk also reported longitudinal data from a normal child for the ages 2;0 to 3;0. These data were compared to those from a language-impaired child, age 3;0. Menyuk concluded that more dissimilarities than similarities existed in the speech of the two children. A close inspection of these data reveals that those phrase structure and transformational forms acquired by the normal child by 2;6 were used by the language-impaired child. It appeared that only those phrase structure and transformational forms acquired by the normal child after 2;6 were absent from the speech of the language-impaired child. This raises the possibility that the findings may have been due to the fact that the language-impaired child was at least 6 months behind in the use of a number of syntactic structures.

Lee's (1966) study involved a comparison between the speech of a language-impaired child, age 4;7, and that of a normal child, age 2;1. Only the normal child was observed to use multiword utterances involving predicative and designative constructions. Although this finding gives the appearance of a language difference, it seems to be a product of using only two subjects. Language-impaired children studied by a number of other investigators (Freedman & Carpenter, 1976; Leonard et al., 1976) have shown use of the constructions absent from the speech of the language-impaired child studied by Lee.

Thus, with the exception of a few isolated phonological phenomena (Edwards & Bernhardt, 1973; Lorentz, 1974), a good case can be made for the view that language-impaired children make use of the same linguistic features seen in the speech of younger normal children. However, this does not necessarily imply that language-impaired children are merely delayed in their linguistic development. Two other factors must be considered. First, language-impaired children may be "different" from normal children because they use a particular structure with a frequency not seen in the speech of normal children at any point in development. Second, they may be "different," not in the particular linguistic structures they use but in the relationship among these structures relative to that seen in the speech of normal children. These factors are discussed in turn.

A difference in the frequency with which a structure is used by normal and language-impaired children does not always constitute a delay on the part of the latter group of children. To illustrate this point, select data obtained from children studied by Leonard et al. (1976) are presented in Table 6.1. The structures of interest involve object case pronouns in subject position (e.g., *Them go home*), constituting a restricted form, and the use of the copula (e.g., *Chris is here*), a form appearing in adult usage. It can be seen from this table that both the normal and language-impaired children used object case pronouns in subject position. Such usage was not seen in the oldest group of normal children. Although it is possible that normal children may show a higher degree of this type of usage at younger ages than those reported in Table 6.1, the trend across the age ranges studied seems to suggest otherwise. For the language-impaired children, the pattern of object case pronoun usage was quite different. These children showed a higher degree of such usage throughout the age range and a more prolonged increase in this usage with increasing age than seen in the data for the normal children. From these results, it seems reasonable to conclude that pronoun usage in subject position by the language-impaired children was different from, not simply more delayed than, that of the normal children. Although object case usage was seen in the normal children's speech at the younger ages, the degree to which they showed such usage never reached the level seen in the

TABLE 6.1
Percentage of Object Case Pronoun Usage in Subject Position and Copula Usage by Normal and Language-Impaired Children Studied by Leonard et al. (1976)

Age	Object Case in Subject Position		Copula	
	Normal	Language Impaired	Normal	Language Impaired
2;11–3;4	3	15	27	0
3;8 –4;2	11	21	40	15
4;8 –5;2	4	30	67	24
5;5 –5;8	0	32	94	50

speech of the language-impaired children. Thus, although a quantitative difference was seen between the two groups, the degree to which object case pronoun usage was seen in the language-impaired children was unlike that seen at any point in the span of normal development.

The copula usage reflected in Table 6.1 represents a different state of affairs. Both groups of children showed increasing use of this form with increasing age. Relative to the normal children, of course, the language-impaired children lagged behind in the development of the copula. These data reflect a quantitative difference representing a delay on the part of the language-impaired children. It should be noted that this interpretation is strengthened because data were obtained at several age levels. Quite a different impression might be formed if only one or two age levels were studied. For example, a comparison between the copula usage of the normal and language-impaired children at the youngest age level might suggest a qualitative difference between the groups, for at this age only the normal children were using this form. It would appear that this is the type of circumstance that has led previous investigators to report differences in the linguistic structures used by normal and language-impaired children.

Another impression that might be formed if data were obtained only at one or two age levels is that language-impaired children's development in the use of a linguistic structure ceases before mastery is attained. Such an impression could be the result of a comparison between the normal and language-impaired children's copula usage at the oldest age level. Although some language-impaired children may never achieve adult usage of a structure, evidence for such a view is not present in the copula usage reported in Table 6.1. The language-impaired children showed an increase in copula usage at each successive age level. A plateau in copula usage, where, for example, degree of copula usage failed to increase from 4;8–5;2 to 5;5–5;8, was not observed. Therefore, it would be premature to assume that copula usage would not show a further increase if data had been obtained from higher age levels.

Another factor involved in the delay versus difference issue is the relationship among the linguistic features in normal and language-impaired children's speech. Too often, linguistic features have been studied singly, without an examination of how the features relate to one another in the children's speech. Yet, as seen in the previous review, it is the nature of the relationship among linguistic features, next to their slower linguistic development, that most sets language-impaired children apart from normal children. The most illustrative examples involve phonology. A number of studies suggest that many of the simplification processes seen in the speech of children with language impairment are the same as those seen in the speech of younger normal children. This might ordinarily suggest that language-impaired children show a delay in phonological development. However, a close inspection of the literature reveals that a number of language-impaired children have made use of these simplification processes while producing utterances considerably longer and with greater syntactic complexity (Haas, 1963) than any produced by normal children during the point in development when they make use of these simplification processes. Similarly, the relationships between structures such as auxiliary emergence and auxiliary frequency of usage (Ingram, 1972a), developmental level of indefinite pronouns and indefinite pronoun frequency of usage (Leonard, 1972), and semantic relation frequency and mean utterance length (Leonard et al., 1978) have not been the same in normal and language-impaired children. Thus, although language-impaired children seem to show most of the same structures seen in normal children's speech, the relationships among these structures in language-impaired children seem to constitute a language difference. It is these relationships, as much as the use or nonuse of particular linguistic features, that seem responsible for the claims of some investigators (Haber, 1977) that language-impaired children's speech is different rather than delayed.

SUMMARY

Language impairment in children constitutes a group of conditions whose etiology seems unclear. Quite possibly, several factors operating in combination lead to linguistic difficulties in children. There are, however, several factors that at least serve as correlates of language impairment. The interactions between language-impaired children and the adults around them seem different in certain respects from the interactions between same-age normal children and adults. However, there is not yet grounds for assuming that the parents of language-impaired children have different interaction patterns than parents of normally developing children. It seems just as likely that their behaviors are influenced in turn by those of the children with whom they are interacting. Representational ability seems to be a factor implicated in language impairment. The available evidence suggests that even when language-impaired children perform within normal limits on performance intelligence tests, they may exhibit deficits in areas such as representational imagery or symbolic play. Although there seem to be some structural parallels between the representational and linguistic behaviors of these children, the few discrepancies reported suggest that language impairment is not caused by a representational deficit.

There is growing evidence that many language-impaired children have difficulties processing acoustic stimuli presented at rapid rates. If these difficulties contribute to these children's linguistic deficits, they do not do so in a clearly prescribed way. Language-impaired children's speech does not characteristically show the kinds of errors that might be expected if there was a precise correspondence between auditory processing and linguistic ability. Instead these auditory processing deficits would have to have the more general effect of delaying these children's linguistic development.

Despite clear individual differences among the speech patterns seen in language-impaired children, some general impressions can be gleaned from the literature. Both the linguistic features used and the linguistic errors committed by language-impaired children are reminiscent of those reflected in the speech of younger normal children. In this respect, it seems fair to conclude that most language-impaired children are delayed in their linguistic development. In another important respect, however, they seem to be different from normally developing children. Language-impaired children often make use of a less mature feature of language or fail to use some feature of language at a time when other linguistic features in their speech are more developed. Thus, the relationships among different linguistic features in language-impaired children's speech are often not the same as they are in the speech of normal children.

The proliferation of studies on language impairment in recent years has allowed for a fuller understanding of these children's abilities in language and related areas. It is hoped that this greater understanding will lead to the development of more promising hypotheses concerning possible determinants of language impairment. For on this matter, we still remain very much in the dark.

REFERENCES

Albertini, J. *The acquisition of five grammatical morphemes: Deviance or delay?* Paper presented at Symposium on Research in Child Language Disorders, Madison, 1980.

Antinucci, F., & Parisi, D. Early language acquisition: A model and some data. In C. Ferguson & D. Slobin (Eds.), *Studies of child language development.* New York: Holt, Rinehart & Winston, 1973.

Applegate, J. Phonological rules of a subdialect of English. *Word,* 1961, *17,* 186-193.

Aram, D., & Nation, J. Patterns of language behavior in children with developmental language disorders. *Journal of Speech and Hearing Research,* 1975, *18,* 229-241.

Aram, D., & Nation, J. *Preschool language disorders and subsequent school problems.* Paper presented to American Speech and Hearing Association, San Francisco, 1978.

Ball, J., & Cross, T. *Formal and pragmatic factors in childhood autism and aphasia.* Paper presented at Symposium on Research in Child Language Disorders, Madison, 1980.

Basser, L. Hemiplegia of early onset and the faculty of speech with special reference to the effects of hemispherectomy. *Brain,* 1962, *85,* 427-460.

Bender, J. A case of delayed speech. *Journal of Speech Disorders,* 1940, *5,* 363.

Benton, A. Developmental aphasia and brain damage. *Cortex,* 1964, *1,* 40-52.

Benton, A. The cognitive functioning of children with developmental dysphasia. In M. Wyke (Ed.), *Developmental dysphasia.* New York: Academic Press, 1978.

Bloom, L., & Lahey, M. *Language development and language disorders.* New York: Wiley, 1978.

Bowerman, M. Learning the structure of causative verbs: A study in the relationship of cognitive, semantic, and syntactic development. *Papers and Reports on Child Language Development,* 1974, *8,* 142-178.

Brown, R. *A first language: The early stages.* Cambridge, Mass.: Harvard University Press, 1973.

Brown, J., Redmond, A., Bass, K., Liebergott, J., & Swope, S. Symbolic play in normal and language-impaired children. Paper presented to the American Speech and Hearing Association, Washington, D.C., 1975.

Chalfant, J., & Scheffelin, M. *Central processing dysfunctions in children: A review of research.* Bethesda, Md.: National Institute of Neurological Diseases and Stroke, 1969.

Chomsky, N. *Syntactic structures.* The Hague: Mouton, 1957.

Compton, A. Generative studies of children's phonological disorders. *Journal of Speech and Hearing Disorders,* 1970, *35,* 315-339.

Compton, A. Generative studies of children's phonological disorders: A strategy for therapy. In S. Singh (Ed.), *Measurements in hearing, speech and language.* Baltimore: University Park Press, 1975.

Compton, A. Generative studies of children's phonological disorders: Clinical ramifications. In D. Morehead & A. Morehead (Eds.), *Normal and deficient child language.* Baltimore: University Park Press, 1976.

Compton, A., & Streeter, M. *Studies of early child phonology: Data collection and preliminary analyses.* Paper presented at Stanford Child Language Research Forum, Stanford, 1977.

Cousins, A. *Grammatical morpheme development in an aphasic child: Some problems with the normative model.* Paper presented at the Boston University Conference on Language Development, Boston, 1979.

Cramblitt, N., & Siegel, G. The verbal environment of a language-impaired child. *Journal of Speech and Hearing Disorders,* 1977, *42,* 474-482.

Cromer, R. The development of language and cognition: The cognition hypothesis. In B. Foss (Ed.), *New perspectives in child development.* Harmondsworth, Middlesex: Penguin, 1974.

Cromer, R. The cognitive hypothesis of language acquisition and its implications for child language deficiency. In D. Morehead & A. Morehead (Eds.), *Normal and deficient child language.* Baltimore: University Park Press, 1976.

Cromer, R. The basis of childhood dysphasia: A linguistic approach. In M. Wyke (Ed.), *Developmental dysphasia.* New York: Academic Press, 1978.

Dalby, M. *Air studies in language-retarded children: Evidence of early lateralization of language function.* Paper presented at International Congress of Child Neurology, Toronto, 1975.

deAjuriaguerra, J., Jaeggi, A., Guignard, F., Kocher, F., Maquard, M., Roth, S., & Schmid, E. Evolution et prognostic de la dysphasie chez l'enfant. *La Psychiatrie de l'Enfant,* 1965, *8,* 291-352.

Dihoff, R., & Chapman, R. *First words: Their origins in action.* Paper presented at the Stanford Child Language Research Forum, Stanford, 1977.

Edwards, M., & Bernhardt, B. *Phonological analysis of the speech of four children with language disorders.* Unpublished paper, Stanford University, 1973.

Eisenson, J. *Aphasia in children.* New York: Harper & Row, 1972.

Farwell, C. A note on the production of fricatives in linguistically deviant children. *Papers and Reports on Child Language Development,* 1972, *4,* 93-102.

Fey, M., Leonard, L., Fey, S., & O'Connor, C. *The intent to communicate in language impaired children.* Paper presented at Boston University Conference on Language Development, Boston, 1978.

Fillmore, C. The case for case. In E. Bach & R. Harms (Eds.), *Universals in linguistic theory.* New York: Holt, Rinehart & Winston, 1968.

Fillmore, C. Some problems for case grammar. *Georgetown University Monographs for Languages and Linguistics,* 1971, *24,* 35-56.

Folger, M., & Leonard, L. Language and sensorimotor development during the early period of referential speech. *Journal of Speech and Hearing Research,* 1978, *21,* 519-528.

Freedman, P., & Carpenter, R. Semantic relations used by normal and language-impaired children at Stage I. *Journal of Speech and Hearing Research,* 1976, *19,* 784-795.

Gall, F. *Organology.* Boston: Marsh, Capen & Lyon, 1835.

Gallagher, T. Revision behaviors in the speech of normal children developing language. *Journal of Speech and Hearing Research,* 1977, *20,* 303-318.

Gallagher, T., & Darnton, B. *Revision behaviors in the speech of language disordered children.* Paper presented to American Speech and Hearing Association, Chicago, 1977.
Goodglass, H., & Geschwind, N. Language disorders. In E. Carterette & M. Friedman (Eds.), *Handbook of perception: Language and speech.* New York: Academic Press, 1976.
Greenfield, P. Who is "dada"? Some aspects of the semantic and phonological development of a child's first words. *Language and Speech,* 1973, *16,* 34–43.
Guillaume, P. Les debuts de la phrase dans le langage de l'enfant. *Journal de Psychologie,* 1927, *24,* 1–25.
Haas, W. Phonological analysis of a case of dyslalia. *Journal of Speech and Hearing Disorders,* 1963, *28,* 239–246.
Haber, L. *A syntactic study of language-impaired children.* Paper presented to Linguistic Society of America, Chicago, 1977.
Hinckley, A. A case of retarded speech development. *Pediatric Seminary,* 1915, *22,* 121–146.
Hoar, N. *Paraphrase capabilities of language impaired children.* Paper presented to Boston University Conference on Language Development, Boston, 1977.
Ingram, D. The acquisition of the English verbal auxiliary and copula in normal and linguistically deviant children. *Papers and Reports on Child Language Development,* 1972, *4,* 79–92. (a)
Ingram, D. The acquisition of questions and its relation to cognitive development in normal and linguistically deviant children: A pilot study. *Papers and Reports on Child Language Development,* 1972, *4,* 13–18. (b)
Ingram, D. *Phonological disability in children.* London: Edward Arnold, 1976.
Ingram, D. Sensorimotor intelligence and language development. In A. Lock (Ed.), *Action, gesture and symbol: The emergence of language.* New York: Academic Press, 1977.
Ingram, T. The classification of speech and language disorders in young children. In M. Rutter & J. Martin (Eds.), *The child with delayed speech.* Philadelphia: Lippincott, 1972.
Inhelder, B. Observations sur les aspects operatifs et figuratifs de la pensee chez des enfants dysphasiques. *Problemes de Psycholinguistique,* 1963, *6,* 143–153.
Johnston, J. The language disordered child. In N. Lass, J. Northern, D. Yoder, & L. McReynolds (Eds.), *Speech, language and hearing.* Philadelphia: Saunders, in press.
Johnston, J., & Kamhi, A. *The same equals less: Syntactic and semantic aspects of the language of language disordered children.* Paper presented at Symposium on Research in Child Language Disorders, Madison, 1980.
Johnston, J., & Ramstad, V. *Cognitive development in preadolescent language-impaired children.* Paper presented to American Speech and Hearing Association, Chicago, 1977.
Johnston, J., & Schery, T. The use of grammatical morphemes by children with communication disorders. In D. Morehead & A. Morehead (Eds.), *Normal and deficient child language.* Baltimore: University Park Press, 1976.
Kamhi, A., & Johnston, J. *Symbolic and conceptual abilities in language-impaired and MA- and MLU-matched controls.* Paper presented to American Speech and Hearing Association, Atlanta, 1979.
Kerschensteiner, M., & Huber, W. Grammatical impairment in developmental aphasia. *Cortex,* 1975, *11,* 264–282.
Kessler, C. Postsemantic processes in delayed child language related to first and second language learning. In D. Dato (Ed.), *Georgetown University roundtable on language and linguistics.* Washington, D.C.: Georgetown University Press, 1975.
Kracke, I. Perception of rhythmic sequences by receptive aphasic and deaf children. *British Journal of Disorders of Communication,* 1975, *10,* 43–51.
Landau, W., Goldstein, R., & Kleffner, F. Congenital aphasia: A clinicopathologic study. *Neurology,* 1960, *10,* 915–921.
Lee, L. Development sentence types: A method for comparing normal and deviant syntactic development. *Journal of Speech and Hearing Disorders,* 1966, *31,* 311–330.

Lee, L., & Canter, S. Developmental sentence scoring: A clinical procedure for estimating syntactic development in children's spontaneous speech. *Journal of Speech and Hearing Disorders,* 1971, *36,* 315-340.

Leonard, L. What is deviant language? *Journal of Speech and Hearing Disorders,* 1972, *37,* 427-446.

Leonard, L. Language impairment in children. *Merrill-Palmer Quarterly,* 1979, *25,* 205-232.

Leonard, L., Bolders, J., & Miller, J. An examination of the semantic relations reflected in the language usage of normal and language disordered children. *Journal of Speech and Hearing Research,* 1976, *19,* 371-392.

Leonard, L., Miller, J., & Brown, H. Consonant and syllable harmony in the speech of language disordered children. *Journal of Speech and Hearing Disorders,* 1980, *45,* 336-345.

Leonard, L., Steckol, K., & Schwartz, R. Semantic relations and utterance length in child language. In F. Peng & W. von Raffler-Engel (Eds.), *Language acquistion and developmental kinesics.* Tokyo: Bunka Hyoron Press, 1978.

Liles, B., Shulman, M., & Bartlett, S. Judgments of grammaticality by normal and language-disordered children. *Journal of Speech and Hearing Disorders,* 1977, *42,* 199-209.

Lorentz, J. *An analysis of some deviant phonological rules of English.* Unpublished paper, University of California, Berkeley, 1972.

Lorentz, J. A deviant phonological system of English. *Papers and Reports on Child Language Development,* 1974, *8,* 55-64.

Lovell, K., Hoyle, H., & Siddall, H. A study of some aspects of the play and language of young children with delayed speech. *Journal of Child Psychology and Psychiatry,* 1968, *9,* 41-50.

Lowe, A., & Campbell, R. Temporal discrimination in aphasoid and normal children. *Journal of Speech and Hearing Research,* 1965, *8,* 313-314.

Mackworth, N., Grandstaff, N., & Pribram, K. Orientation to pictorial novelty by speech-disordered children. *Neuropsychologia,* 1973, *11,* 443-450.

Martin, J. Rhythmic (hierarchical) versus serial structure in speech and other behavior. *Psychological Review,* 1972, *79,* 487-509.

Meline, T. *Referential communication by normal- and deficient-language children.* Paper presented to American Speech and Hearing Association, San Francisco, 1978.

Menyuk, P. Comparison of grammar of children with functionally deviant and normal speech. *Journal of Speech and Hearing Research,* 1964, *7,* 109-121.

Menyuk, P. The language-impaired child: Linguistic or cognitive impairment? *Annals of the New York Academy of Sciences,* 1975, *263,* 59-69.

Menyuk, P. Linguistic problems in children with developmental dysphasia. In M. Wyke (Ed.), *Developmental dysphasia.* New York: Academic Press, 1978.

Morehead, D., & Ingram, D. The development of base syntax in normal and linguistically deviant children. *Papers and Reports on Child Language Development,* 1970, *2,* 55-75.

Morley, M. Receptive/expressive developmental aphasia. *British Journal of Disorders of Communication,* 1973, *8,* 47-54.

Morley, M., Court, D., Miller, H., & Garside, R. Delayed speech and developmental aphasia. *British Medical Journal,* 1955, *2,* 463-467.

Nice, M. A child who would not talk. *Pedagogical Seminary,* 1925, *32,* 105-144.

Oller, D. Regularities in abnormal child phonology. *Journal of Speech and Hearing Disorders,* 1973, *38,* 36-47.

Oller, D., Anderson, D., Augustine, L., Groher, M., Hedrick, D., Holder, R., Levinson, P., Marquardt, T., Peterson, C., Prather, E., Schubert, G., Winstead, L., & Woodle, A. *Five studies in abnormal child phonology.* Unpublished paper, University of Washington, 1972.

Patti, S. *The interface of selected verbal and nonverbal behaviors in mother-child dyadic interactions with normal and language disordered children.* Unpublished doctoral dissertation, Purdue University, 1978.

Petrie, I. Characteristics and progress of a group of language disordered children with severe receptive difficulties. *British Journal of Disorders of Communication,* 1975, *10,* 123–133.

Piaget, J. *Play, dream and imitation.* New York: Norton, 1962.

Pollack, E., & Rees, N. Disorders of articulation: Some clinical applications of distinctive feature theory. *Journal of Speech and Hearing Disorders,* 1972, *37,* 451–461.

Poppen, R., Stark, J., Eisenson, J., Forrest, T., & Wertheim, G. Visual sequencing performance of aphasic children. *Journal of Speech and Hearing Research,* 1969, *12,* 288–300.

Prinz, P. *Comprehension and production of requests in language-disordered children.* Paper presented to Boston University Conference on Language Development, Boston, 1977.

Rapin, I., & Wilson, B. Children with developmental language disability: Neurological aspects and assessment. In M. Wyke (Ed.), *Developmental dysphasia.* New York: Academic Press, 1978.

Rees, N. Auditory processing factors in language disorders: The view from Procrustes' bed. *Journal of Speech and Hearing Disorders,* 1973, *38,* 305–315.

Sachs, J., & Devin, J. Young children's use of age-appropriate speech styles in social interaction and role-playing. *Journal of Child Language,* 1976, *3,* 81–98.

Schwartz, R., Leonard, L., Folger, M., & Wilcox, M. Evidence for a synergistic view of language disorders: Early phonoglical behavior in normal and language disordered children. *Journal of Speech and Hearing Disorders,* 1980, *45,* 357–377.

Scott, C., & MacVean, M. *Phonological residual in a ten year old with language-learning problems.* Paper presented to American Speech and Hearing Association, San Francisco, 1978.

Shatz, M., & Gelman, R. The development of communication skills: Modifications in the speech of young children as a function of listener. *Monographs of the Society for Research in Child Development,* 1973, *38.*

Shatz, M., Bernstein, D., & Shulman, M. The responses of language disordered children to indirect directives in varying contexts. *Applied Psycholinguistics,* 1980, *1,* 295–306.

Siegel, L., Cunningham, C., & van der Spuy, H. *Interactions of language delayed and normal preschool children with their mothers.* Paper presented to Society for Research in Child Development, San Francisco, 1979.

Skarakis, E., & Greenfield, P. *The role of old and new information in the linguistic expression of language-disabled children.* Paper presented at the Boston University Conference on Language Development, Boston, 1979.

Snyder, L. The early presuppositions and performatives of normal and language disabled children. *Papers and Reports on Child Language Development,* 1976, *12,* 221–229.

Stark, J. A comparison of the performance of aphasic children on three sequencing tasks. *Journal of Communication Disorders,* 1967, *1,* 31–34.

Stark, J., Poppen, R., & May, M. Effects of alterations of prosodic features on the sequencing performance of aphasic children. *Journal of Speech and Hearing Research,* 1967, *10,* 849–855.

Steckol, K., & Leonard, L. The use of grammatical morphemes by normal and language impaired children. *Journal of Communication Disorders,* 1979, *12,* 291–302.

Stevenson, J., & Richman, N. The prevalence of language delay in a population of three-year-old children and its association with general retardation. *Developmental Medicine and Child Neurology,* 1976, *18,* 431–441.

Stumpf, C. Eigenartiga sprachliche entwicklung eines kindes. *Zeitschrift für päd. Psychol.,* 1901, *6,* 420–447.

Tager-Flusberg, H. *Early infantile autism: The relationship between a cognitive deficit and language dysfunction.* Paper presented to Society for Research in Child Development, San Francisco, 1979.

Tallal, P., & Piercy, M. Defects on nonverbal auditory perception in children with developmental aphasia. *Nature,* 1973, *241,* 468–469. (a)

Tallal, P., & Piercy M. Developmental aphasia: Impaired rate of non-verbal processing as a function of sensory modality. *Neuropsychologia,* 1973, *11,* 389–398. (b)

Tallal, P., & Piercy, M. Developmental aphasia: Rate of auditory processing and selective impairment of consonant perception. *Neuropsychologia,* 1974, *12,* 83-93.

Tallal, P., & Piercy, M. Developmental aphasia: The perception of brief vowels and extended stop consonants. *Neuropsychologia,* 1975, *13,* 69-74.

Tallal, P., & Stark, R. Speech perception of language-delayed children. In G. Yeni-Komshian, J. Kavanaugh, & C. Ferguson (Eds.), *Child Phonology: Volume 2.* Cambridge, Mass.: MIT Press, 1980.

Tallal, P., Stark, R., & Curtis, B. The relation between speech perception impairment and speech production impairment in children with developmental dysphasia. *Brain and Language,* 1976, *3,* 305-317.

Trantham, C., & Pedersen, J. *Normal language development.* Baltimore: Williams & Wilkins, 1976.

Uzgiris, I., & Hunt, J. *Assessment in infancy: Ordinal scales of psychological development.* Champaign, Ill.: University of Illinois Press, 1975.

Vaisse, L. Des sourds—muets et de certains cas d' aphasie congenitale. *Bulletin de la Societe Anthropologique de Paris,* 1866, *1,* 146-150.

Van Kleeck, A., & Carpenter, R. *Effects of children's language comprehension level on language addressed to them.* Paper presented to American Speech and Hearing Association, San Francisco, 1978.

Van Kleeck, A., & Frankel, T. Discourse devices used by language disordered children: A preliminary investigation. *Journal of Speech and Hearing Disorders,* 1981, *46,* 250-257.

Watson, L. *Conversational participation by language-deficient and normal children.* Paper presented to American Speech and Hearing Association, Chicago, 1977.

Weber, J. Patterning of deviant articulation behavior. *Journal of Speech and Hearing Disorders,* 1970, *35,* 135-141.

Weeks, T. *The slow speech development of a bright child.* Lexington, Mass.: Heath, 1974.

Weeks, T. The use of nonverbal communication by a slow speech developer. *Word,* 1975, *27,* 460-472.

Weiner, P. The perceptual level of functioning of dysphasic children. *Cortex,* 1969, *5,* 440-457.

Weiner, P. The perceptual level functioning of dysphasic children: A follow-up study. *Journal of Speech and Hearing Research,* 1972, *15,* 423-438.

Weiner, P. A language-delayed child at adolescence. *Journal of Speech and Hearing Disorders,* 1974, *39,* 202-212.

Weiner, P. Developmental language disorders. In H. Rie & E. Rie (Eds.), *Handbook of minimal brain dysfunction.* New York: Wiley, in press.

Werner, L. Treatment of a child with delayed speech. *Journal of Speech Disorders,* 1945, *10,* 329-334.

Whitehurst, G., Novak, G., & Zorn, G. Delayed speech studied in the home. *Developmental Psychology,* 1972, *7,* 169-177.

Wilde, W. *Practical observations on aural surgery.* Philadelphia: Blanchard and Lea, 1853.

Williams, R. *Play behavior of language-handicapped and normal-speaking preschool children.* Paper presented to American Speech and Hearing Association, San Francisco, 1978.

Wolpaw, T., & Nation, J. *Developmental language disorders: A follow-up study.* Paper presented to American Speech and Hearing Association, Chicago, 1977.

Wulbert, M., Inglis, S., Kriegsmann, E., & Mills, B. Language delay and associated mother-child interactions. *Developmental Psychology,* 1975, *11,* 61-70.

7 The Language of the Mentally Retarded: Development, Processes, and Intervention

Sheldon Rosenberg
University of Illinois at Chicago Circle

INTRODUCTION

I originally intended to limit my review of the literature on the language of the mentally retarded to the period from 1974 to the present, in order to avoid overlap with the work of such earlier reviewers as Cromer (1974), Rosenberg (1970), Schiefelbusch (1974), and Yoder and Miller (1972). It turned out not to be possible to limit myself in this fashion, however. Thus I had to examine, albeit selectively, the earlier literature in the course of examining the more recent work.

An attempt was made to organize the present chapter along lines suggested by contemporary linguistics, psycholinguistics, and cognitive psychology. Thus there are separate sections on syntactic, semantic, phonological, and pragmatic linguistic knowledge and development, as well as a section on the impact of the linguistic environment on language development, and one on linguistic performance. Finally, because our ultimate interest as applied psycholinguists is in raising the communicative capabilities of mentally retarded individuals, there is a section on language training.

Some Preliminaries

Although attempts have been made (Grossman, 1973) to lessen our dependence on measures of intellectual functioning to describe mental retardation, the use of the psychometrically based concepts of mental age (MA) and IQ continues to be strong (Smith & Polloway, 1979). As a result, the definition of mental retardation continues to be grounded in the characterizations of the ability dimensions that are thought to underly individual differences in performance on the instruments used to assess MA and IQ, the most frequently cited dimensions being those of verbal and performance intelligence.

Although the attempts to broaden the definition of mental retardation (so as to include both intellectual and adaptive behaviors) are commendable, inasmuch as mentally retarded individuals regardless of etiology continue to present a picture of retardation in both linguistic and nonlinguistic abilities, investigators are likely to continue to describe mental retardation in terms mainly of verbal and performance intellectual capabilities.

It should be pointed out here that progress has been made in recent years in our understanding of the organization of human abilities (Horn, 1976), and as a result the traditional concepts of verbal and performance intelligence are beginning to be replaced by the concepts of *crystallized* and *fluid intelligence* and related information-processing capabilities (Carroll, 1976).[1] *Crystallized intelligence,* according to Horn (1976) is evident in an "Awareness of concepts and terms pertaining to a broad variety of topics, as measured in general information and vocabulary tests and in tests which measure knowledge ... [p. 445]" in a variety of subjects taught in the schools. Comprehension and the ability to perceive similarities in the meanings of words are also thought to be a reflection of this aspect of intelligence. *Fluid intelligence,* on the other hand, involves mainly facility in nonverbal reasoning.

Although the emphasis here is on mental retardation as a cognitive disorder, I do not wish to claim that it is exclusively a cognitive disorder. Indeed, I would like to suggest that we consider the possibility that mental retardation has associated with it the noncognitive characteristic of *passivity*.

O'Connor (1975) has made much of his observation, based upon years of research, that mentally retarded individuals suffer from an "inertia" in regard to linguistic coding. In other words, they tend not to use language, particularly its semantic component, to facilitate information processing. This tendency, I would like to suggest, is part of a general trait of passivity that is also operating when, for example, a retarded individual fails to utilize spontaneously available memorial strategies (Brown & Barclay, 1976). In addition, it seems reasonable to speculate that passivity is one of the factors responsible for the slow rate of development of linguistic and other cognitive capabilities in the mentally retarded. Should this claim regarding passivity be substantiated by future observation, it will become important to determine why a cognitive disorder should have associated with it a motivational trait.

---

[1]The information-processing capabilities that appear frequently in the literature are noncategorial sensory encoding, sensory storage, pattern recognition, short-term memory, rehearsal, input organization, input assimilation, long-term storage, memory retrieval, and the monitoring of information-processing activities.

To return to our main concern, when we compare mentally retarded individuals with nonretarded individuals in the same chronological age (CA) range in regard to cognitive development in areas other than language (Klein & Safford, 1977), we find that: (1) recognizeable landmarks begin to appear at a later age; (2) development is slower generally; (3) final achievements are lower; but (4) the "stages" they go through as well as the order of stages do not distinguish them from nonretarded individuals. Because of the relationship that exists between verbal and nonverbal intelligence in the mentally retarded, it was anticipated that a similar picture would emerge from an examination of language development in mentally retarded and nonretarded individuals.

MULTIDIMENSIONAL STUDIES OF LANGUAGE BEHAVIOR

Before we turn our attention to specific aspects of linguistic knowledge and performance, studies in which a variety of measures were employed are reviewed.

After noting that his (Lyle, 1959) sample of institutionalized mentally retarded individuals tended to score lower than his sample of noninstitutionalized (day school) mentally retarded individuals on verbal intelligence, Lyle (1960) proceeded to compare the two on a number of measures of linguistic behavior. The contrast institutionalized/noninstitutionalized is thought by many investigators to sample differences in environmental variables (linguistic and nonlinguistic) that may influence the development of linguistic knowledge and performance. The main measures Lyle used were common object and action labeling, word comprehension, word definition, speech–sound production (as measured by word repetition), and sentence complexity. Unfortunately, no details were supplied that would allow a reader to evaluate the validity of the sentence complexity and speech–sound production measures. Moreover, the remaining measures represent a rather small sampling of lexicosemantic knowledge. Furthermore, the selection of measures generally was not based upon any systematic characterization of linguistic knowledge and performance. Indeed, Lyle describes his measures as being "ad hoc". Form A of the Minnesota Preschool Scale was used to estimate verbal and nonverbal intelligence.

Etiology was variable in Lyle's sample, which included both boys and girls. CA ranged from 6;6 to 14;0 in the institutional group and from 6;6 to 13;6 in the day school group. The nonverbal MA range was identical for both groups (2;6–5;6). Mean nonverbal IQ was 35.05 (range 20–54) in the institutional sample and 35.34 (range 20–49) in the day school sample.

Performance distributions and CA for the two samples combined were dichotomized by median splits and results analyzed using *phi coefficients*. The analysis also included the dichotomies institution/day school, male/female, and Down's syndrome/all other etiologies.

As for the results, it was noted, first of all, that the correlations for the measures of linguistic behavior ranged from .588 to .804. Second, verbal MA predicted linguistic performance better than did nonverbal MA, and both MA scores predicted linguistic performance better than did CA. Third, Down's syndrome subjects scored lower than non-Down's-syndrome subjects on all the linguistic scales except labeling and word comprehension. What is more, they also scored lower on verbal MA. Fourth, sex was found to be a poor predictor of linguistic performance and MA. The last finding of interest here was that the institutional sample tended to score lower than the day school sample on all the linguistic measures and on verbal MA. Other findings from this investigation are not presented here.

Fifty-eight MA-matched (nonverbal) pairs of nonretarded and mentally retarded children were studied in another investigation by Lyle (1961), using the ad hoc linguistic measures of the previous investigation. CA ranged from 6;6 to 13;6 in the retarded sample and from 2;6 to 4;6 in the nonretarded sample. Median MA was approximately 3;8 in both groups. Although no specific figures were given, it is clear from the introduction of this article that the mentally retarded and nonretarded subjects differed in verbal MA. The mentally retarded subjects were being reared at home by their parents and were attending day school.

A preliminary analysis failed to find differences between Down's syndrome and other mentally retarded children. Nonretarded subjects, however, performed at a significantly higher level than mentally retarded subjects on word definition, speech-sound production, and sentence complexity but not on labeling and word comprehension. Moreover, on some of the measures, Lyle observed a difference in favor of the nonretarded subjects at the lower MA levels only.

Lyle ordered his tasks developmentally and reported that, with one exception, the largest differences between the nonretarded and mentally retarded subjects occurred on the developmentally more advanced tests. Unfortunately, the nature of the tasks used makes it impossible to determine the relative contributions of linguistic knowledge, linguistic performance strategies, general information-processing capabilities, and the like to these findings (and, of course, to the overall differences as well). And, what is more, there are conceptual and empirical problems with the developmental ordering itself.

More interesting results were produced with an analysis of characteristics of the responses subjects made to the various task items. In this analysis, responses were sorted into the categories no response, jargon (babbling, grunting, nonsense), echolalia, sign language (meaningful gestures), irrelevant verbal responses (linguistically but not semantically acceptable), and speech only (linguistically and semantically acceptable and none of the other categories of response present). Moreover, these categories, as I have listed them, were thought by Lyle to be ordered developmentally. This claim was supported by the finding of a positive relationship between the presumed developmental level of a category and mean verbal MA for the mentally retarded children. The nonretarded subjects produced virtually no responses in the first three categories, giving mainly speech-only responses. On the basis of these observations, Lyle (1961) concluded that "the normal children were considerably more advanced linguistically than imbeciles of the same non-verbal MA [p. 47]" and suggested that the language retardation of his mentally retarded subjects was ". . . . due partly to a lower terminal achievement and partly to a slower rate of verbal development [p. 48]."

Lyle also paired his noninstitutionalized mentally retarded subjects with institutionalized subjects on the basis of etiology and nonverbal MA and CA and found that the institutionalized subjects performed at a developmentally lower level than the noninstitutionalized subjects on these measures.

One of the best known studies of language development in the mentally retarded—specifically, in Down's syndrome individuals—is the one by Lenneberg, Nichols, and Rosenberger (1964). Their subjects were 61 Down's syndrome individuals in the CA range 3;0 to 22;0 who were being raised at home by their parents. The subjects were observed at various times over a period of 3 years (although no longitudinal findings were presented). The observations included medical, neurological, and psychological testing, measures of spontaneous speech, and articulatory, sentence-repetition, vocabulary, command-understanding, and vocalization testing. Details of the observation procedures were not supplied by these investigators. The IQs in this sample ranged from the 20s to the 70s. Three different IQ tests were employed.

In order to determine the relationship between IQ and the stage of language development a subject appeared to have reached (based presumably on the spontaneous speech data), Lenneberg et al. reduced their sample to subjects in the CA range 5;6 to 13;6. This was done to adjust for an observed negative relationship between CA and IQ as well as to offset the possible effects of differences between the IQ tests. The authors did not supply information on the characteristics of the adjusted sample, except to indicate that the IQ distribution was broken down into quartiles. Of use would have been, for example, data on CA and MA for each of the IQ quartiles. Moreover, their scale of language development contained rather rough categories (mostly babble, mostly words, primitive phrases, sentences) and no details were given regarding the categorization procedures themselves. Finally, the subjects in their adjusted sample ($N = 35$) tended to bunch up ($N = 32$) in the two middle categories on stage of language development.

Lenneberg et al. reported finding no relationship between IQ and stage of language development. They did, however, find positive relationships between stage of language development and CA and motor maturity, but without data on the relationship between stage of language development and MA it is difficult to evaluate these findings. Moreover, the specific figures in their scatter diagram for CA and stage of language development do not appear to be reliable or at least are not accounted for by information in the body of the article. The reported trend, however, I would guess to be reliable.

From another analysis, these investigators reported that articulation tended to lag behind other aspects of language development and performance. However, the generality of this finding for articulation, which was based upon an analysis of spontaneous speech, was questioned after it was noted in a separate study that a sample of Down's syndrome children (details not given) performed "considerably better" on a test of speech-sound articulation than it did during spontaneous speech.

Sentence repetition performance was the subject of another analysis based on a selected sample of 25 children (characteristics unspecified) and a new scale of language development that ran from "few phrases only" to "mistakes only in complex sentences." In this analysis, with one exception, the tendency to parrot (i.e., to repeat the last item or items in a presented sentence) was found to be inversely related to stage of language development. Parroting was also found to occur more often on syntactically complex than on syntactically simple sentences. Finally, these authors mentioned briefly, without going into details, that sentence-repetition performance in nonretarded children (CA 24-30 months) was similar to what it was in their retarded sample.

Generally speaking, Lenneberg et al. found no evidence of qualitative differences in language behavior between their mentally retarded subjects and nonretarded children but rather developmental arrest at earlier stages of normal language development.

A large-scale study of language behavior in mentally retarded and nonretarded children by Ryan has been reported on informally on two occasions (1975, 1977). Thus many important details are missing in these reports. Three groups of children matched on Stanford-Binet MA ($\bar{x} = 3;1$) were studied, a nonretarded group ($\bar{x}$ IQ = 103, $\bar{x}$ CA = 2;11), a Down's syndrome sample ($\bar{x}$ IQ = 40, CA between 5;0 and 9;0), and a group of mentally retarded children with etiologies other than Down's syndrome ($\bar{x}$ IQ and CA range same as Down's sample). All the subjects were attending some kind of school and were living at home. In addition, the groups were balanced on social class and sex. Observations were carried out over a period of 2 weeks and included spontaneous speech sampling and linguistic and other tests. The mentally retarded children were observed again 14 months later and the nonretarded children 3.5 months later (to control for differences in rate of development).

As for results (Ryan, 1975), we are told that when subgroups were matched on mean length of utterance (MLU), an estimate of overall linguistic maturity:

> ... no differences were found between the groups as regards the proportion of complete sentences (noun phrase + verb phrase) in their speech, of incomplete ones, or of cliches and "ready-made" utterances. ... No differences were found in the range and variety of verb transformations used. Similar errors of omission, of

substitution, and of overgeneralization of the various inflections were made in all groups.... Other errors, such as inversion of word order and omission of auxiliaries occurred in all groups [p. 272].

Presumably, a sample of severely retarded children can contain a number who have reached final level of achievement in both MA and linguistic maturity prior to testing. Thus in order to equate nonretarded and mentally retarded children on MLU, which is an estimate of overall level of linguistic maturity during the early years of language development, it is necessary to select mentally retarded subjects whose MAs are higher on the average than those of their MLU-matched nonretarded controls. It is not surprising, therefore, that Ryan's MLU-matched retarded subjects had higher MAs than their nonretarded controls.

One area in which the nonretarded subjects were superior to the MLU-matched retarded subjects was articulation, and Ryan suggests that this may have been due to the presence in her mentally retarded sample of children with, for example, central nervous system damage or some hearing loss.

When the nonretarded and mentally retarded children were matched on MA, differences in favor of the nonretarded children did occur on measures of grammatical behavior but not on measures of single-word vocabulary, at least as far as nouns were concerned (the same was not true of prepositions). The finding of a difference in grammatical behavior was not surprising, given the low level of Ryan's mentally retarded subjects.

Additional findings from this study were presented in the 1977 article. Briefly, Ryan noted that: (1) differences between the retarded groups were minimal; (2) auditory and respiratory difficulties characterized the Down's children; (3) intercorrelations between measures were higher for the nonretarded children than they were for the mentally retarded children; (4) the grammatical performance of the mentally retarded subjects did not improve over the 14-month period, with some children showing poorer performance, but the nonretarded children did show development over a period of 3.5 months; and (5) nonretarded and mentally retarded children showed similar development in vocabulary over their respective observation periods.

A correlational study of language abilities in Down's syndrome individuals ($N = 101$) was carried out by Evans (1977). Evans' subjects varied in sex, placement (day versus hospital), CA (8;4-31;1), and Stanford-Binet (presumably full-scale) MA (2;6-7;10). The measures used included several aspects of spontaneous speech, a modified version of Berko's Test of Morphology, the experimental edition of the Illinois Test of Psycholinguistic Abilities (ITPA), vocabulary tests, and two tests of intellectual functioning. Evans indicated an awareness of the serious limitations of the ITPA but chose to use it anyway.

Because of generally poor performance on Berko's Test, it became necessary to eliminate the data it produced from the analysis. Some additional measures had to be eliminated for the same and other reasons.

The problems Evans encountered in formal testing are not surprising, given the number of relatively low-level individuals in his sample. What one requires for a variable such as morphological knowledge is samples of spontaneous naturalistic conversations adequate to perform the sorts of analyses carried out by Brown (1973) and others with nonretarded children. Brown has observed that controlled observation procedures such as Berko's tend to date mastery of grammatical morphemes later than measures derived from samples of spontaneous naturalistic speech, a major reason being, presumably, the linguistic performance and information-processing demands of controlled observation. Brown's observation is made all the more interesting by the fact that his criterion for mastery of a grammatical morpheme is a lot tougher than the criteria of controlled observation procedures. Of course, other things being equal, one would expect a greater discrepancy between controlled observation and naturalistic estimates of linguistic mastery for mentally retarded than for nonretarded children.

Evans' measures were intercorrelated and the correlations factor analyzed using Principal Components, Varimax, and oblique (Promax) procedures. The Principal Components analysis revealed a general language factor, a dysfluency factor, and a factor difficult to interpret. However, this picture was clarified by rotation, which produced a general verbal ability factor that included Stanford–Binet MA, a dysfluency factor, and a structural speech production factor. CA, it is to be noted, loaded more highly than Stanford–Binet MA on this last factor.

Details of administration and scoring of the ad hoc linguistic measures in this study were not supplied, so it is difficult to interpret fully the findings. Moreover, the reader was not given an opportunity to examine the matrix of intercorrelations from this study.

An extensive study ($N = 78$) of the relationship among MA, CA, etiology, and linguistic and communicative maturity has been conducted by Miller, Chapman, and Bedrosian (1978) using assessment procedures based upon a program of research (Miller, 1978). Of particular interest to these investigators was the question of whether, developmentally, cognitive achievements predict linguistic achievements in the mentally retarded in the way they do in nonretarded individuals. In addition to their interest in cognition and etiology, these investigators were interested in whether comprehension performance matches production performance in the mentally retarded.

Clinical evaluations of children for possible developmental disabilities produced the data for the present study, which included both nonretarded and mentally retarded subjects. Nonlinguistic and linguistic developmental status were assessed using Piagetian tasks, standardized intellectual scales, syntax and vocabulary comprehension tasks, various measures of speech production (for semantics, syntax, and phonology), and a measure of communicative functions. Also included in this battery were measures of motor maturity, hearing, and speech mechanism defects. Intellectual assessment was limited as far as possible to a nonverbal performance mode. The developmental status of linguistic variables was estimated by examining the basic literature on normal language development.

CA and IQ both varied considerably at each cognitive level (Piagetian tasks). In the main, developmental level of language functioning tended to correspond to developmental level of nonlinguistic cognitive functioning. This finding led these authors to conclude that in mentally retarded and nonretarded individuals, over a wide CA range, nonlinguistic cognitive maturity is a factor that limits linguistic maturity, whereas linguistic maturity has no effect on nonlinguistic cognitive status.

Unfortunately, there are problems with this conclusion. For one thing, it is based on correlational data. Second, the study is not analytic enough. If one is to make even correlational claims, one must be able to relate specific nonlinguistic cognitive achievements and operations to specific achievements in language development (i.e., in syntax, phonology, etc.) throughout the course of language development and to do so in a manner that will differentiate between linguistic and communicative knowledge on the one hand and linguistic and communicative performance on the other. Third, studies of the relationship between Piagetian stage of cognitive development and stage of language development in normal children have not demonstrated the kind of correspondence between the two that one would expect to find on the view that nonlinguistic cognitive development is a factor that paces language development (Corrigan, 1978; Folger & Leonard, 1978; Miller, Chapman, Branston, & Reichle, 1980). Fourth, a number of Piagetian tasks are clearly not free of linguistic confounding (Donaldson, 1978). Last, it has by no means been established empirically that linguistic achievements have no effect on nonlinguistic cognitive development (Blank, 1975; Bowerman, 1978).

Miller et al. found no evidence to suggest that general etiological groupings predict language behavior. They were quick to point out, however, that their findings are limited by small numbers of subjects in the various etiological groups and the broad nature of the groupings.

Surprisingly, language production performance was not found to predict language comprehension performance in this study. Individuals with similar production profiles showed considerable variability on comprehension measures. In addition, production performance did not predict "cognitive performance consistently."

The relationship between the achievements of Piagetian sensorimotor intelligence and language acquisition in profoundly retarded children was the topic of a study by Kahn (1975), using a rough measure of language production, the ability "to use language to ask for various objects [p. 641]." Unfortunately, whether any of the children produced anything more than one-word utterances and how, precisely, their linguistic performance was assessed were not specified in this article. Moreover, it was apparently the case that no attempt was made to assess the children's language comprehension performance. In addition, no attempt was made to determine whether the utterances that were observed were productive or object-specific.

The subjects ($N = 16$) in this study were from day-care schools; 8 "were able to use language to ask for various objects" [p. 641]" ($\bar{X}$ CA = 71 months, range 53-98) and 8 evidenced no sign of expressive language ($\bar{X}$ CA = 67 months, range 47-92). MA and IQ data had not been collected on these children because of their low level of cognitive functioning. Stage of sensorimotor functioning was assessed using subtests from Uzgiris and Hunt's (1966) test.

The investigation was inspired by the Piagetian view that the achievements of Stage 6 of sensorimotor cognitive functioning are necessary but not sufficient for the acquisition of language that is meaningful, which led to the formulation of the following hypothesis: "(a) all of the children exhibiting meaningful expressive language will be, at least, at Stage 6 of Piaget's sensorimotor period; (b) some of the children not exhibiting any meaningful expressive language will be at Stage 6, but some will be below Stage 6 . . . [pp. 640-641]."

Kahn's (1975) findings were consistent with expectation and were offered in support of "the hypothesis that Stage 6 functioning is a necessary, though not sufficient, prerequisite for learning meaningful expressive language [p. 642]."

Unfortunately, one must object to this conclusion on a number of grounds. First, it is based upon the findings of a single *correlational* study and not one that was designed to show a causal relationship between antecedent sensorimotor achievements and subsequent linguistic achievements. Second, the study does not even show a noncausal relationship between *prior* sensorimotor achievements and subsequent linguistic achievements, but only that Stage 6 functioning and linguistic functioning were present *simultaneously* in the same individuals. Third, no attempt was made to determine whether or not any of the children who did not meet the expressive language criterion could *comprehend* linguistic input. Finally, it is not at all clear what were actually determined to be instances of "meaningful expressive language."

Conclusions

Despite the limitations of the research reviewed thus far, some tentative conclusions and hypotheses are worth noting.

1. MA in the mentally retarded tends to predict performance on linguistic tasks better than CA.
2. Institutionalized mentally retarded individuals may be at a disadvantage in the area of language functioning.
3. Except in the area of articulation, and only to a limited extent there, etiology does not predict linguistic performance in the mentally retarded.

4. In comparison to nonretarded individuals in the same CA range, language development in the mentally retarded shows the following characteristics: later onset, slower progress, lower final level of achievement, retardation in all aspects of language functioning, but similar stages of acquisition. Thus it appears that the *developmental lag hypothesis* describes not only nonlinguistic cognitive development in the mentally retarded but linguistic cognitive development as well.
5. Ryan's observation that MLU-matched nonretarded and mentally retarded children show "similar errors of omission, of substitution, and of overgeneralization of the various inflections" plus similar word-order inversions and auxiliary omissions suggests that language acquisition strategies may be similar in the two populations.

A Longitudinal Study of Two Down's Children

In the course of my literature search I found only one longitudinal study that looked at a number of specific aspects of language development, in light of the findings of research on normal language development and reported findings in detail, a dissertation by Dooley (1976). I therefore decided to review this study apart from other multidimensional studies.

Dooley studied two Down's syndrome children, a boy (Timmy) and a girl (Sharon), who were being raised at home by their parents. Neither child displayed any complicating conditions and their IQs were average for Down's children (51 for Timmy and 44 for Sharon) with a starting MA and CA of 2;5 and 3;10 in the case of Timmy and 2;11 and 5;2 in the case of Sharon. Both showed MLUs in the early sessions of the study that placed them in Brown's (1973) developmental Stage I. Timmy's was 1.48 and Sharon's was 1.84. Recordings of spontaneous speech were made in the children's homes every 2 weeks or so mainly during free play with an investigator. Parents and others were also present at various times. Dooley also took notes on the nonlinguistic context. In the case of both children, the corpus of utterances he analyzed consisted of the first three (Sample I) and the last three (Sample II) sessions of 12 months of recording. He was interested mainly in tabulating fully audible nonimitative single-word and multiword utterances in order to determine MLU, diversity of utterances (type and token frequencies and their ratios), the children's lexicons, the *routines* the children used (i.e., the unanalyzed multimorphemic utterances that on certain criteria appeared not to be "analyzed or constructed syntactically" but functioned as lexical items), Brown's (1973) basic semantic relations in multiword utterances, and the use in obligatory contexts of the 14 grammatical morphemes studied by Brown (1973). The morphemes in question serve to modulate and enrich the meanings of multiword utterances.

Timmy's MLU grew from 1.48 in Sample I to 1.75 in Sample II. Sharon's MLU declined somewhat (1.84–1.73) during the same period. Both children, however, were found to be talkative. Performance on the measure of utterance diversity rose from .18 to .26 for Timmy and from .29 to .39 for Sharon from Sample I to Sample II. The children's lexicons also grew over the period of observation.

In the case of both Timmy and Sharon, the percentage of multiword utterances in Samples I and II accounted for by the basic semantic relations (e.g., recurrence, nonexistence, agent and action, entity and attribute, agent-action-object) was appreciable, although higher in Sharon's case.

After examining a set of cross-linguistic samples of multiword utterances from studies of normal language development during the early stages, Bowerman (1975) concluded that for the most part "word order corresponds to the dominant (or only) adult order [p. 280]." Although Dooley did not examine his multiword samples for word-order regularities, I found it possible to estimate such regularities myself from data presented in Appendix B of his dissertation. Briefly, what I found for these Down's children does not contradict what Bowerman found for nonretarded children. Both Sharon and Timmy appear to have been sensitive to word-order constraints in expressing semantic relations in the earliest stage of combinatorial speech.

As regards the grammatical morphemes (e.g., present progressive, plural, possessive, articles, past tense regular, contractible auxiliary), Dooley (1976) reports in a summary statement that:

> By the criterion of acquisition of the usage of grammatical morphemes used in Brown (1973), Timmy and Sharon had not acquired productive usage of any of fourteen grammatical morphemes considered, as was the case also with the nonretarded children studied by Brown and his associates when the non-retarded children were at Stage I [p. 98].

However, when one looks at the raw percentage usages in obligatory contexts for these grammatical morphemes, there is evidence, as Dooley points out, that these Down's children were mastering them in an order not unlike the order in which Brown's (1973) three nonretarded children mastered them.

Dooley compared his findings with the findings of studies of young nonretarded children acquiring their first language and found that in the main his Down's subjects were acquiring language at a considerably slower rate. On measures of utterance length, Sharon showed no gain from Sample I to Sample II, and Timmy showed a gain "approximating . . . the equivalent of one month's growth for a non-retarded child [p. 80]." As regards utterance diversity and size of lexicon, Timmy and Sharon were similar to nonretarded children of similar MLUs. Moreover, their performance vis-à-vis the basic semantic relations, although it showed less change developmentally, was similar to that of nonretarded children in Stage I. Timmy's and Sharon's retardation relative to nonretarded children was quite apparent on the grammatical morphemes, but there was no evidence of qualitative differences.

Dooley considered carefully the import of the finding that the diversity of the types of multiword utterances that expressed the basic and other semantic relations Brown (1973) studied was less in his retarded children, due to the use of routines, that is, unanalyzed multiword utterances that appear to act as single lexical items. This, plus the use of certain proforms (e.g., *it, they, here, there, do*) suggested that the language acquisition strategies of his Down's children may have differed from those of nonretarded children acquiring their first language. He points out, however, that some of the proforms in question were probably being used productively and that there is evidence in the normal literature of the use of routines during the early period of syntactic growth.

Thus, in the final analysis, Dooley appears to have rejected the possibility that the phenomena in question are unique to retarded children. Moreover, he speculated that individual differences in the use of routines and proforms might reflect individual differences in language acquisition strategies in both nonretarded and mentally retarded children.

The suggestion that the use of routines represents a stage in language aquisition seems plausible (see the article by R. Clark, 1974, also cited by Dooley). What may happen is that initially children compute and store the meaning of a syntactically unanalyzed multiword utterance of an adult or map such an utterance onto an already established percept, action, or thought, after which they begin to identify and internalize the syntactic rules that free individual lexical items from the routines they have been occurring in and make true sentential productivity possible. The fact that mentally retarded children tend to spend more time depending on routines than nonretarded children do may mean that it takes them longer to acquire the semantic-routine pairings or longer to analyze the routines syntactically, or both.

Thus it will be important to continue and extend the line of longitudinal research begun by Dooley in order to determine the full extent of a mentally retarded child's dependence on routines relative to a nonretarded child's use of such utterances.

STUDIES OF SYNTACTIC BEHAVIOR IN THE MENTALLY RETARDED

In this section I review research that was concerned primarily or exclusively with the syntactic capabilities of mentally retarded individuals, beginning with studies that examined a number of facets of English syntax.

Lozar, Wepman, and Hass (1973) used TAT cards to elicit speech samples from 30 nonretarded and 20 high-level mentally retarded children (both institutionalized and noninstitutionalized) matched on mean CA (11 years approximately). Mean MA was 7;0 in both groups of mentally retarded children, and their IQ means were approximately 61. The nonretarded children had PPVT IQ scores of 90 or higher. The nonretarded children produced larger speech samples than did the mentally retarded children and this prompted Lozar et al. to identify a subsample of 10 nonretarded children whose output matched that of the mentally retarded subjects.

Each child's corpus was segmented into constituent simple, compound, and coordinated sentences for purposes of anlaysis. Words were sorted into the categories common and uncommon according to TAT norms and subjected to a traditional syntactic category analysis. A second measure had to do with the complexity of produced sentences, verb phrases, and noun phrases. Verb phrases increased in complexity as a function of tense and auxiliary markers, noun phrase complexity was determined by length, and sentence complexity by a measure that appears to be reduceable to relative number of embedded clauses per sentence.

It should be mentioned here that complexity measures are notoriously difficult to justify on independent grounds (Rosenberg, 1977). The previous phrasal and sentential complexity metrics very likely represent a confound of syntactic knowledge, semantic knowledge, and information-processing (e.g., computational) load. A third measure used was one of syntactic structure diversity, sentential and phrasal, as represented by H (utterance-type redundancy) and relative H.

Although the nonretarded and mentally retarded children differed on verbal output, both groups produced mainly common words. However, a measure of lexical productivity based on speech samples is likely to underestimate nonretarded children's lexical knowledge and, to a lesser extent, retarded children's as well. Thus when one is interested in assessing lexical knowledge, speech samples should be supplemented with measures of lexical comprehension and a controlled production task in which subjects are asked to use a given word in a sentence.

In the main, the nonretarded and mentally retarded children did not differ in the percentages of words in the various syntactic form classes. (But, see the papers by Mein & O'Connor, 1960, and Mein, 1961, for some information on the lexicon in lower level mentally retarded individuals.) Unfortunately, no error data were reported for the syntactic form classes. As was the case with syntatic form class, nothing of interest emerged from the analysis of phrasal complexity.

It has been noted (Rosenberg, 1974) that the tendency to combine simple sentences through embedding and the use of subordinating conjunctions increases reliably over the elementary school years in nonretarded children. Thus one would expect that mentally retarded children whose mean MA is 7;0 should use embedding less often than nonretarded children whose mean MA is approximately 11;0, which is exactly what Lozar et al. found.

It is interesting to note that the institutionalized mentally retarded children in this study did not perform as well as their noninstitutionalized counterparts on the measure in question.

This is as much of this study as we need to review here. It should be mentioned in passing, however, that Lozar and her associates caution the reader

7. THE LANGUAGE OF THE MENTALLY RETARDED

about the limitations of their study vis-à-vis the problem of estimating linguistic knowledge from limited observation procedures.

The Carrow (1968) Experimental Test of Linguistic Comprehension (picture identification) was used by Bartel, Bryen, and Keehn (1973) to assess syntactic form class, grammatical morpheme, and sentential knowledge in a sample of special-class retarded individuals. Carrow in her study had used nonretarded children in the CA range 2;10 to 7;9. CA ranged from approximately 9 to 13, MA from 2;8 to 6;0, and IQ from 23 to 50 in Bartel et al.'s mentally retarded sample. Thus the present sample was not very different from the sample of nonretarded children studied by Carrow on MA range.

Overall, the performance of the mentally retarded children was inferior to the performance of Carrow's nonretarded sample, particularly on certain grammatical morphemes and on the passive construction. Both IQ and MA correlated highly with raw score for the mentally retarded sample, the coefficients being .80 and .70, respectively. CA, on the other hand, did not correlate significantly with raw score (.17). Thus IQ and MA must have been related in the mentally retarded group.

It should be noted that the raw score hides the fact that performance did not increase with increased MA in the mentally retarded group on certain items (e.g., the ones having to do with pronominalization, negation, and passivization). It is not possible to determine, however, to what extent these findings represented the operation of factors other than linguistic knowledge in comprehension performance.

A comprehension test was used by Wheldall (1976) to study knowledge of a variety of syntactic structures in mentally retarded (special class) and nonretarded children. The test contained sentences varying in length and "grammatical complexity" that illustrated 15 syntactic structures, four sentences for each structure. Comprehension of each sentence was evaluated by having a subject choose from among three or four simultaneously presented pictures the one that was appropriate semantically to the presented sentence. A child was assumed to have mastered a given structure when he or she performed correctly on at least three of the four sentences representing that structure. There were 86 retarded and 30 nonretarded (nursery school) children equated on mean vocabulary age (53 months in the case of the retarded and 51 months in the case of the nonretarded children). The mean CAs in these two groups were, respectively, 12;6 and 4;0. Thus the groups were equated on an estimate of verbal MA (the British version of the PPVT).

There were no instances in which a child, retarded or nonretarded, completed all the items on the test. Moreover, the nonretarded and the mentally retarded subjects did not differ on overall performance. Total score correlated .81 with vocabulary age for the retarded and .84 for the nonretarded children. It is also interesting to note that the order of difficulty of the structures was similar for these two groups ($r = .87$).

The order of difficulty of the various structures (nonretarded data only reported), it is to be noted, appears to be predictable to a considerable extent on the basis of nonretarded developmental order of mastery, with embedding, passivization, and tense and number proving to be the most difficult.

Thus in this investigation the performance of 12-year-old mentally retarded individuals was similar to that of nonretarded preschoolers. Further evidence of developmental lag among the mentally retarded in the more linguistically advanced aspects of syntax can be found in the results of research by Naremore and Dever (1975) and Shotick and Blue (1971) using indices derived from speech samples.

Syntactic performance in noninstitutionalized trainable and educable mentally retarded subjects was studied by Bliss, Allen, and Walker (1978) using a task (story completion) in which language comprehension and language production capabilities were confounded. Mean CA was between 10;0 and 11;0 for both groups, whereas IQs varied from 29 to 50 among the trainables and 51 to 78 among the educables. Thus the two groups differed on MA ($\bar{X} = 4;2$ and 6;0 for the trainables and educables, respectively). The task used here assessed 14 grammatical phenomena, 10 having to do with simple and complex sentential structures, 2 having to do with grammatical morphemes (number and future tense), and 2 having to do with adjective–noun structures. Subjects were given two choices on each structure.

On overall performance, as one would expect, the educable group was superior to the trainable group. As regards the individual items, 71% of the items that fell below the median of the performance distribution for the educable children fell below the median of the performance distribution for the trainable children, according to my calculation. The items that both groups found difficult on this criterion were doubly modified noun, number, comparative, embedding, and future tense. A slight lessening of this criterion would have brought the passive and the direct–indirect object structures into the category of items that both groups had problems with. Thus, not surprisingly, both sentence combining and grammatical morpheme structures were difficult for these mentally retarded children.

These authors found, in addition, among other things, both similarities and differences between their findings for the individual items and earlier findings for nonretarded children, with the similarities outweighing the differences.

One of the most convincing cases for the claim that mental retardation does not result in qualitatively different syntactic behavior and development has been presented by Lackner (1968) for the domain of phrase structure rules and transformations. His mentally retarded subjects were four institutional children and one home-reared special-school child in the MA range 2;3 to 8;10 and the CA range 6;5 to 16;2. Some nonretarded children were also studied for comparative purposes. The retarded children spent 8 weeks in a clinic during which time samples of spontaneous speech were recorded. In addition, the following tasks were administered to both the retarded and the nonretarded children: naming, sentence imitation, and sentence comprehension. The spontaneous speech samples were scored for, among other things, the following sentence types: declarative, question, negative, passive, negative passive, and negative passive question. The sentences used in the controlled observation procedures were consistent with the spontaneous speech and vocabulary data and syntactically more advanced than the structures apparent in the spontaneous speech data.

Without going into details, it is clear from Lackner's results that from the standpoint of the linguistic structures examined, and regardless of MA level, no qualitative differences were found between the mentally retarded and nonretarded children in the syntactic rules that were operating in spontaneous speech and in the controlled observation procedures. The mentally retarded children, however, evidenced less variety in their use of underlying syntactic rules. Whether this last finding represents a stable feature of linguistic performance in the mentally retarded or a characteristic of institutionalized retarded children (recall that all but one of Lackner's retarded subjects were institutionalized) remains to be determined.

Graham and Graham (1971) examined spontaneous speech samples of nine institutionalized mentally retarded individuals in the MA range 3;6 to 10;0 (CAs 10;0–18;0 and IQs 26–64) for, among other things, evidence of the use of sentence combining operations (e.g., embedding), with results that indicated that the higher MA subjects tended to combine simple sentences to a greater extent than did the lower MA subjects.

Morphological Behavior

Morphology has been the topic of four investigations, none of them, however, involving longitudinal comparisons. Moreover, as we soon see, the findings of controlled observation were checked against the findings of an analysis of speech samples in only one of these investigations.

Special-school mentally retarded children ($N = 160$) in the CA range 8 to 15 were studied by Lovell and Bradbury (1967). The children did not suffer from speech defects and their mean IQ was 70.1 (SD = 6.2) on the Stanford–Binet scale. Some minor changes were made in Berko's (1958) test, mainly by increasing the number of real words used. In Berko's test, in order to increase the likelihood that a child has productive mastery of an inflection, most of the items the children are required to inflect are nonsense words.

The following sequence (along with an appropriate picture) would be an example of the items Berko used.

    This is a wug.
    Now there is another one.
    There are two of them.
    There are two _____.

The reader interested in Berko's test should examine Brown's (1973) detailed discussion of its limitations. Berko studied nonretarded preschoolers' and first-graders' knowledge of English morphological rules and found, among other things, age-related improvements on a number of inflections (40% of the plural items, 38% of the past tense items, 67% of the possessives, and the single progressive item). Age was not related to performance on the two third-person-singular items, however. Thus there was considerable variability in performance within an inflectional class.

Lovell and Bradbury found, among other things, that their 14- and 15-year-old mentally retarded subjects did not perform as well as Berko's first graders did on the nonsense items used to test pluralization, the past tense, possession, the third-person singular, and the present participle. Moreover, the mentally retarded children did not perform as well on the real words as Berko's younger nonretarded children performed on the nonsense words. Third, the performance of the mentally retarded children showed little improvement with age. What improvement did occur appeared to be limited to certain of the real words. Fourth, IQ correlated significantly (.42) with the ability to inflect the nonsense words. Unfortunately, no MA data were supplied. Finally, in all instances in which a comparison was possible, performance on real words was superior to performance on nonsense items.

Thirty educable residents of a State school were the mentally retarded subjects in a study of morphological performance by Newfield and Schlanger (1968). Mean CA was 10;4 (range 8;10–12;1) in this sample and mean MA (test not specified) was 6;2 (range 4;10–8;0). Mean IQ was 60 (range 44–76). A sample of 30 nonretarded elementary school children ($\bar{X}$ CA = 6;10, range 5;8–8;4) was also included in this study. The PPVT was given to both groups. On this scale, mean MAs for the retarded and nonretarded children, respectively, were 5;10 (range 3;6–9;8) and 7;9 (range 5;1–10;8). Thus Newfield and Schlanger's mentally retarded sample was not on the average very different from Lovell and Bradbury's on CA and IQ. Most of Berko's nonsense and real words were used by Newfield and Schlanger as well as some additional lexical items. Scoring differed from Berko's in only one case.

In general, the performance of the nonretarded children was superior to that of the retarded children on both the real (90% versus 48% correct) and the nonsense words (72% versus 29% correct). Both groups, however, showed better performance on the real words than they did on the nonsense items. Moreover, the order of difficulty of nonsense items (but not real words) was quite similar for the nonretarded and retarded subjects ($r = .91$). (The finding for real words was most likely the result of a ceiling effect in the case of the nonretarded subjects.) Newfield and Schlanger reported also that the order of difficulty of the inflected nonsense items in their groups was similar to Berko's (1958).

In view of Brown's (1973) finding of a similarity in the order of difficulty of the morphemes he and Berko had both studied, this finding of Newfield and

Schlanger becomes an important one, for it suggests that the variables that are responsible for the order of acquisition of grammatical morphemes in spontaneous speech and their order of difficulty on Berko's test are the same for nonretarded and mentally retarded children in spite of the fact that development in this area is very slow in the mentally retarded.

In order to check this finding of Newfield and Schlanger against Brown's findings from analyses of spontaneous speech, I determined as best I could the order of difficulty of the five morphemes that had been studied by both Brown and Berko from data on percentage correct in Table 1 of Newfield and Schlanger's article and compared this data with Brown's results. The morphemes in question in their order of difficulty from easiest to most difficult in spontaneous speech were the following:

Progressive
Plural
Possessive
Past, regular
Third person, regular

In the case of Newfield and Schlanger's mentally retarded subjects, order of difficulty on Berko's procedure matched order of mastery in spontaneous speech *perfectly* for both the nonsense and the real words. The nonretarded subjects in Newfield and Schlanger's study showed a similar trend, with one reversal on the nonsense items and one on the real words.

Thus although it might be the case that Berko's test tends to underestimate the degree of mastery of a grammatical morpheme (due to its demand and other characteristics), it does have validity as a predictor of order of mastery of certain inflections in spontaneous speech for both nonretarded and mentally retarded children.

To return to Newfield and Schlanger's findings, in the nonretarded group, MA (PPVT) predicted performance on the nonsense word plural and verb tense items ($r = .46$ and $.41$, respectively) and CA predicted performance on the nonsense word possessive task ($r = .37$). CA did not predict performance on any of the items in the retarded group but MA was significantly related to performance in the case of real-word pluralization (.45), real-word verb tense (.38), and real-word possession (.46).

With MA held constant statistically, the nonretarded children were found to perform better than the retarded children on all the nonsense and real-word subtests used in this study. One final note, there appeared to be more similarities than differences in the pattern of results reported by Newfield and Schlanger and by Lovell and Bradbury (1967).

Most of Berko's test was presented by Dever and Gardner (1970) to nonretarded boys and CA- and MA-matched educable mentally retarded boys, using as a scoring criterion the performance of a group of teachers. Overall differences in favor of the nonretarded subjects were found with both CA and MA matching, but the difference between nonretarded and mentally retarded children was greatest when matching was by CA. There were also indications that performance had to some extent increased with CA under both matchings for both nonretarded and mentally retarded children.

These investigators also reported their results by individual items, but there is no need to discuss these findings here. Their discussion section, it should be pointed out here, contains some useful ideas vis-à-vis the validity and reliability of Berko's test.

Dever (1972) modified Berko's test along lines suggested by the earlier research findings for the purpose of determining whether it would predict morphological usage in free speech. His subjects for this study were special-school mentally retarded children in the IQ range 60 to 84 and at the MA levels 6, 7, 8, 9, and 10. Dever collected two speech samples from each child, each one lasting 5 minutes. Questions and prompts were used in the second speech session in an effort to elicit forms that were not used in the first session. Dever recorded both correct usages and errors on the various inflections and found that in the main getting an item correct on the test, regardless of whether it was part of a real or a nonsense word, did not mean that it would be used correctly during speech. Indeed, an error was less likely to occur on an item used during speech than it was on an item used on the test. Thus, working with a limited speech sample and a modified version of Berko's test, Dever found that the test tends to underestimate a high-level mentally retarded child's mastery of a grammatical morpheme. Unfortunately, Dever did not report the kinds of descriptive data that would allow us to compare his findings with those of Brown (1973).

As a summary statement, I would like to say that the studies I have just reviewed confirm what others have found (Bartel et al., 1973, using comprehension; Bliss et al., 1978, with a task that involved elements of both comprehension and production; Dooley, 1976, in a longitudinal study of spontaneous speech; Evans, 1977, with Berko's test; Wheldall, 1976, using comprehension), namely, that inflectional morphology is an area of poor performance for mentally retarded children in general and one that develops at a slower rate than some of the other aspects of linguistic structure.[2]

Actually, the difficulty mentally retarded individuals have with grammatical morphemes is not surprising, given the likelihood that both grammatical and semantic complexity predict order of acquisition for these morphemes (Brown,

---

[2]The reader has noted, I am sure, that there has been some variability in the literature as regards the relationship between CA and grammatical morphological development in mentally retarded children. Differences between the studies in the CA range sampled, however, may have been responsible for this variability. Overall, CA was observed to be a rather weak predictor of the mastery of grammatical morphemes.

1973). Keep in mind as well the fact that the grammatical morphemes require, for their mastery and use, mastery of the linguistic structures that express the semantic phenomena they modulate.

Studies of Sentence Behavior

Not surprisingly, workers interested in the language of the mentally retarded turned to transformational grammar for ideas about possible predictors of linguistic performance complexity. Semmel and Dolley (1971), for example (also Greenough, 1968), studied the comprehension and imitation of simple sentences varying in transformational complexity by special-class trainable Down's children and found no evidence of a systematic relationship between sentence complexity and performance in either task. Task-related factors evidently interferred with performance in this investigation (Lamberts & Weener, 1976).

The comprehension (picture choice) and imitation of reversible and nonreversible positive and negative sentences by institutionalized trainable mentally retarded individuals (of unspecified etiology) were studied by Lamberts and Weener (1976). The means for CA and IQ, respectively, were 17;5 and 30 in this study. For semantic reasons, nonreversible sentences were expected to be easier to comprehend than reversible sentences, whereas positives were favored over negatives for both syntactic and semantic reasons. Lamberts and Weener's findings supported these expectations. Moreover, these investigators found a significant positive correlation between total comprehension performance and MA (.47) for their subjects. CA, on the other hand, did not predict comprehension performance. The easiest sentences in their study, the nonreversible positives, did not contribute to the significant correlation between MA and comprehension performance. The findings for imitation were not reported systematically, so they are not discussed here.

Unfortunately, studies such as the one just reviewed can tell us nothing about the course of productive mastery of negation, nor whether even high-level mentally retarded individuals are capable of mastering all the complexities of negation in the English language, both syntactic and semantic (Klima, 1964).

Imitation and comprehension performance in relation to transformational complexity were studied by Berry and Foxen (1975) using subjects with a mean vocabulary age of 5;6, but the presence of theoretical, task, and procedural problems in this investigation make the findings difficult to interpret.

Systematic investigations of the types of complex sentences that nonretarded children tend to master late are virtually nonexistent in the area of mental retardation. Such sentences tend to be difficult, evidently, not only because of the complexity of the kinds of semantic notions they express but because of their syntactic characteristics (and possibly their information-processing demands) as well and are likely therefore to cause difficulty for even high-level mentally retarded individuals.

Cromer (see his 1975 review chapter) is one of the few investigators interested in this aspect of language acquisition in the mentally retarded. Using hand puppets that the child operated, Cromer studied the ability to comprehend the type of embedded complement sentence (which I call Type S) in which the subject of the embedded sentence is present (e.g., *The wolf is willing to bite; The duck is glad to bite*) and the type of embedded complement sentence (Type O) in which the subject of the embedded sentence is *not* expressed (e.g., *The wolf is hard to bite; The duck is fun to bite*). Thus, except for the difference in the adjectives they can take, these two sentence types have identical surface syntactic phrase structures. Their syntactic difference, then, is to be found at an abstract level of linguistic structure.

Cromer's earlier research with nonretarded children had indicated that prior to an MA (as estimated from a picture vocabulary test) of 6;3, most children used what he called "the primitive rule" to interpret all the sentences presented to them, both Type S and Type O, on at least one of two testings. A child using the primitive rule identified the noun in both Type S and Type O sentences as being the animal that did the biting, thus failing to note the difference between the two sentence types. Children whose MAs were above 6;3 almost never used the primitive rule. When Cromer administered his task to mentally retarded children (CAs 7;1–16;6 and IQs 36–88), he found the same relationship with MA as he had noted for nonretarded children: use of the primitive rule below MA 6;3 and absence of same above MA 6;3.

Cromer detected an intermediate stage in the mastery of the distinction between Type S and Type O structures from his analysis of inconsistencies in performance from the first to the second testing in both nonretarded and mentally retarded subjects. Moreover, as one would expect, more errors were made on Type O sentences than were made on Type S sentences.

Cromer went on to examine hypotheses regarding the acquisition of these structures using an artificial learning paradigm, but I do not discuss this research here. Some critical comments on this research and the work I reviewed previously can be found in Johnson-Laird (1975).

Some interesting preliminary observations on complex sentence behavior in Down's children in relation to vocabulary development have been reported by Parisi and Giannelli (1979), but not enough information is presented by these authors to warrant discussion at this time.

Conclusions

Methodological issues aside, the picture of syntactic functioning in the mentally retarded that emerges from an examination of performance on specific syntactic structures using both production and comprehension tasks is one of developmental lag, particularly as regards the mastery of grammatical morphemes and sentence-combining operations. As a result, MA tends, in the main, to predict syntactic performance better than CA in the mentally retarded. Little is known, however, about the details of syntactic development or the final achievements of syntactic development, due to the absence of longitudinal observations beyond the earliest stages of syntactic development and the absence of comprehensive studies of the syntactic capabilities of mentally retarded adults.

SEMANTICS

Semantics is the study of those categories and relations of perception, action, and thought, and their interrelations that can be expressed linguistically. Some have their origin in the achievements of nonlinguistic cognitive development; others, apparently, in the impact of adult language on nonlinguistic cognitive development (Blank, 1975; Bowerman, 1978). Of interest in this domain have been such phenomena as: (1) lexical meaning (i.e., the content and organization of the meanings expressed by individual words); (2) the semantic relations or propositions expressed in simple sentences (e.g., agent–action–object; object–attribute; object–location; agent–action–instrument); (3) the topic–comment (given–new) relation expressed through contrastive stress, word order, and syntactic structure; (4) the semantic dependency relations that are expressed when simple sentences are combined through embedding and the use of subordinating conjunctions; (5) the semantic dependency relations that are expressed in connected discourse through the use of anaphora (e.g., pronominalization); (6) meaning ambiguity; (7) metaphor; and (8) inferential meaning.

The importance of semantics in language should have produced a considerable amount of literature on semantic behavior and semantic development in the mentally retarded, but for unknown reasons it has not. Moreover, among the studies that are available, one finds a relatively limited number that reflect the developments that have taken place in basic psycholinguistics in this area over the years.

Some of the studies reviewed earlier examined aspects of semantic behavior and its development. Dooley (1976) included in his longitudinal study of two Down's syndrome children a measure of their use in early multiword utterances of the semantic relations that Brown (1973) had studied in nonretarded children and found evidence of developmental lag but no evidence of qualitative differences between his subjects and nonretarded children on this aspect of early semantic development. Sentence negation appeared to create problems on a comprehension task for the retarded children in the investigation by Lamberts and Weener (1976). Finally, more than one of the investigations reviewed earlier has shown that sentences that are syntactically and semantically complex tend to be mastered late by both retarded and nonretarded children.

Duchan and Erickson (1976) studied the ability of mentally retarded (special class) and nonretarded children to identify (through object manipulation) the semantic relations (agent–action, action–object, possessive, locative) expressed in telegraphic (grammatical morphemes absent) two-word, expanded (grammatical morphemes present), and partially nonsensical utterances. They were interested mainly in the question of whether children who were producing mostly one- and two-word (telegraphic) utterances could understand developmentally more advanced utterances. Twelve retarded (IQ range 50–80) and 12 nonretarded children whose MLUs fell between 1 and 2.5 morphemes were selected for this study. Mean MLU was 1.67 (CA 4;0–7;9) in the retarded sample and 1.56 (CA 1;6–2;7) in the nonretarded sample.

The various utterance types arranged themselves in the order (from easiest to most difficult) expansion, telegraphic, and nonsense for both the retarded and the nonretarded subjects, with a significant pairwise difference between expansion and nonsense items only. Differences were found between the various semantic relation types but the main finding of interest to the present review was that the retarded and nonretarded children performed similarly.

Thus Duchan and Erickson, using a comprehension task, have confirmed the observation made by Dooley to the effect that in the early sessions of his study his retarded children were functioning at the same level as nonretarded children of similar MLU as regards their use of semantic relations in multiword speech.

Layton and Sharifi (1979) used Chafe's (1970) model of semantic competence to study semantic relations and other semantic phenomena expressed in the spontaneous sentences of nonretarded and Down's syndrome children. The nine home-reared Down's children and nine nonretarded children of this study, who were matched on PPVT MA, displayed the following characteristics, respectively: CA 7;4 to 12;2, IQ 39 to 61, MA 38 to 69 months ($\bar{X} = 55$); and CA 2;10 to 5;4, MA 42 to 59 months ($\bar{X} = 53$). A speech sample was collected from each child during conversation with a speech pathologist. Two groups were identified in the nonretarded sample on the basis of MLU (low MLU group = 4.63, range 3.79–5.40; high MLU group = 7.66, range 7.19–8.00) that were comparable on CA and MA. MLU was 5.37 (range 4.63–6.65) in the Down's sample.[3]

Some quantitative differences were noted between the Down's children and the two nonretarded groups but no apparent qualitative differences. For example, in the case of the basic semantic relations expressed in noun–verb combinations, the Down's children tended to express more agent–action relations but fewer patient–process relations than did the two nonretarded samples. Overall, the similarities between the three groups outweighed the differences. It is interesting to note that the Down's and the low MLU nonretarded children showed less consistency in their use of the modulators of semantic relational meaning than did the high MLU nonretarded children. Evidently the linguistically less mature children in this study were still in the process of attempting to master the grammatical morphemes of modulation in question.

---

[3]The MLUs for the retarded sample seem higher than one would have expected. Moreover, it is questionable whether the MLUs of the high MLU group were predictive of their linguistic maturity (Brown, 1973).

Coggins (1979) examined the "two-word non-imitated, spontaneous utterances" of four Down's syndrome children whose MLUs ranged from 1.22 to 2.06 and whose CAs ranged from 3;10 to 6;3. The language samples were collected over a period of 4 weeks in a variety of contexts using videotape and subjected to an analysis similar to the one used by Dooley (1976) to study the semantic relations expressed in multiword utterances. The main results of this study and their implications are summarized by Coggins in the following passage from his article.

> Findings from this study suggest that Down's syndrome children at Stage 1 of linguistic development do indeed concentrate on the same, rather small set of relational meanings as in normal children's early two-word combinations.... The findings also suggest the possibility that the processes and structures by which meaning is known, represented and created in the sensorimotor period, may be quite similar to that of normal children. Of course this contention is necessarily tentative because the present study did not try and determine the underlying processes used to encode those meanings [p. 176].

The question of how lexical semantic knowledge develops and the question of how it is organized in mentally retarded individuals are issues that have seldom been systematically studied. The older literature concentrated, to a large extent, on trying to identify the level of abstraction of mentally retarded children's definitions of concrete nouns, by attempting to sort them into the categories descriptive or concrete (e.g., *A banana is yellow*), functional (e.g., *You eat a banana*), and abstract (e.g., *A banana is a fruit*). It was usually assumed in this research that abstract definitions were developmentally more advanced than functional definitions that, in turn, were developmentally more advanced than descriptive definitions. What this assumption involves, of course, is the belief that the use of a category label to define a concrete noun signifies that its underlying semantic representation has not changed; the individual has simply acquired a *label* for that representation. Moreover, there is a further complication, which is a problem for both these interpretations: The definitional task is a production task and thus an individual's failure to produce an abstract category label does not necessarily signify that he or she cannot *comprehend* that label. (See Anglin's 1977 book for an example of how one might apply multiple procedures to the task of studying the development of category labels.)

A good example of the research on verbal definitions in the mentally retarded is the study by Papania (1954). Fifty retarded children ranging in MA from 6 through 10, with mean IQ of approximately 70, were asked to define Stanford–Binet vocabulary items. A nonretarded sample in basically the same CA range as the retarded children was also included in this study. The proportion of abstract definitions produced by the retarded children increased with MA (and evidently with CA as well), although the proportion of concrete definitions decreased. Moreover, abstract definitions were given relatively more frequently by the nonretarded children than by the retarded children. Just the opposite was the case for the definitions scored as concrete.

Evidence of a developmental lag in lexical categorial identification and formation in mentally retarded students has been found recently by Winters and Brzoska (1976); and Cornwell (1974) noted MA-related increases in, among other things, the ability of Down's children to designate the function of a concrete noun.

The application of the word association task to the study of the development of lexical knowledge is exemplified in the work of Semmel, Barritt, Bennett, and Perfetti (1968). These investigators found, among other things, evidence of developmental lag in educable mentally retarded children matched with nonretarded children on CA in the tendency to give same syntactic class (i.e., paradigmatic) responses on a word association task. Presumably, this difference reflects differential utilization of a semantic featural matching strategy, a difference in lexical semantic knowledge, or both (see Clark and Clark, 1977, pp. 477–482, for a recent discussion of word association phenomena).

Harrison, Budoff, and Greenberg (1975) utilized a continuous word association task with educable mentally retarded (EMR) school children in an attempt to determine "whether EMR children differed from nonretarded children in the productivity, speed, and quality of associative connections with vocabulary size controlled [p. 583]." Unfortunately, the scale these investigators used to determine the quality of associations is open to some serious criticisms, for example, having to do with the ordering of certain response categories and the fact that it is not possible to determine whether the scale in question reflects differences in associative performance strategies, lexical semantic knowledge, or both. What would be helpful would be to collect detailed stimulus-word definitional data from the subjects in a study of the content of word associations using an interview technique (Anglin, 1977).

Mean CA was between 13 and 15 years for both the EMR subjects ($N = 32$) and a nonretarded control group ($N = 32$). Mean IQ (WISC) was approximately 70 in the EMR children and 97 in the nonretarded sample, and these groups also differed on mean PPVT performance and mean reading grade. The stimulus materials were 10 words from the Kent-Rosanoff list, and each subject's task was to try to "produce up to 25 associations to each stimulus word [p. 585]." The experimenter repeated the stimulus word following each response.

The nonretarded and retarded subjects differed in the direction one would expect on response quantity and speed but only speed differences remained when data were corrected for a small difference in CA and a difference on an estimate of vocabulary size (the latter correction, of course, probably reduced the differences between the retarded and nonretarded children on verbal MA). As for response quality, some of the differences that were noted in favor of the nonretarded subjects disappeared when CA and vocabulary size were controlled for.

Two of the measures on which the nonretarded subjects were superior to the retarded subjects regardless of whether CA and vocabulary size were controlled for were the tendencies to give superordinate and subordinate responses. However, that the word association task underestimates EMR children's knowledge and/or ultilization of these classes of semantic attributes is clear from the results of a recent study of Bender and Johnson (1979). These investigators found evidence of both knowledge and utilization of hierarchic class-inclusion lexical-semantic concepts in EMR adolescents using a concept identification and a prompted recall task. Moreover, in the main, the performance of the EMR subjects in this study suggested a semantic organization in the domain of the concepts studied similar to that of nonretarded individuals.

Four other investigators have produced evidence of semantic categorial capabilities in mentally retarded individuals. In the first of two experiments, Sperber, Ragain, and McCauley (1976) asked special-class mentally retarded subjects to name as accurately and as quickly as possible pictures of objects, the labels of which they had already demonstrated a knowledge of. The second number of each successive pair of objects was either categorially related (e.g., *cat-horse*) or categorially unrelated to the first member (according to experimenter intuition). The question at issue was whether the presence of semantic categorial relatedness in a pair would reduce the naming latency for the second member of the pair. As these investigators point out, such a semantic categorial priming effect had already been noted in nonretarded adults and children. Twenty-two mentally retarded individuals served as subjects. Their IQs ranged from 41 to 74 ($\bar{X} = 60$), their MAs from 4;5 to 10;3 ($\bar{X} = 7;3$), and their CAs from 10;7 to 22;6 ($\bar{X} = 16;4$). The WISC and the WAIS had been used to assess MA and IQ.

A significant semantic categorial priming effect was noted by these investigators, the magnitude of which was not found to be correlated significantly with either MA or IQ. Moreover, as Sperber et al. point out, an analysis of performance over sessions did not indicate that the obtained effect was due to the creation over trials of an expectancy for categorially related items. The design of Experiment 1, however, did not rule out the possibility that the priming effect was due to interitem associations rather than categorial relatedness. Thus for this reason a second experiment was carried out in which only categorially related items low in normative (mentally retarded) associative strength (e.g., *necktie-dress*) were used, and category knowledge was further assessed through the use of a relatedness recognition task (pointing to the two pictures in a triplet that were thought to go together) and a task designed to assess retarded subjects' ability to verbalize the basis for item–pair relatedness.

Verbalization was scored by weighting a category label response more heavily than a function or property response. Unfortunately, as I pointed out earlier, the use of a category label does not necessarily signal that an item is no longer being assigned to a category on the basis of functional or descriptive attributes.

In the second experiment, subjects' IQs ranged from 40 to 76 ($\bar{X} = 59$), their MAs ranged from 4;6 to 10;4 ($\bar{X} = 7;1$), and their CAs from 7;11 to 22;5 ($\bar{X} = 15;5$).

Results on the semantic categorial priming task were identical to those of Experiment 1. In addition, as in the first study, the magnitude of the priming effect did not correlate significantly with IQ. However, as the investigators point out, the interpretation of this finding is complicated by the fact that MA and IQ were highly correlated in Experiment 2 (no information was given on correlations with CA). Significant positive correlations were found between IQ and the relatedness recognition and verbalization tasks but not between the magnitude of the priming effect and the recognition or verbalization tasks. Not surprisingly, a significant positive correlation was found between performance on the recognition and verbalization tasks. Finally, a large difference was noted between performance on the recognition and verbalization tasks; "subjects did not verbalize many of the relationships that they were capable of recognizing [p. 232]." Unfortunately, it is difficult to interpret this last finding, because data on the percentage of responses in the various scoring categories of the verbalization task (category label versus function or property versus incorrect or no response) were not presented.

In research by Glidden and Mar (1978), mentally retarded ($\bar{X}$ CA = 15;4, $\bar{X}$ IQ = 60) and CA-matched nonretarded ($\bar{X}$ CA = 14;8) students were required to retrieve instances of the categories SPORTS and ANIMALS from memory in what was referred to as an accessibility task and then to indicate, in an availability task, whether items selected on the basis of retarded and nonretarded norms, and varying in accessibility frequency, were instances of these categories. Instances of these categories were significantly more accessible to the nonretarded subjects than they were to the retarded subjects. The absolute mean differences between the two groups on the availability task were very small and in favor of the nonretarded subjects, although Glidden and Mar reported finding significance at two levels of normative instance frequency, moderate and low. The statistical analyses they used were questionable, however. Moreover, according to Weil, McCauley, and Sperber (1978), their retarded subjects may not have known the meanings of some of the low-frequency instances used in the availability task.

Problems of data analysis and item selection aside, it did appear that the retarded subjects in this experiment differed from their CA-matched nonretarded counterparts more in their ability to retrieve lexical category instances from semantic memory than in their underlying knowledge of lexical category instances.

Of course, this pattern of results is limited to the concrete categories and instances used in this experiment. It remains to be determined whether it will generalize to more abstract domains of lexical semantic knowledge.

The use of subcategory cues in a second experiment conducted by Glidden and Mar facilitated retrieval of category instances from semantic memory in educable special-class retarded adolescents ($\bar{X}$ CA approximately 16;0, $\bar{X}$ IQ approximately 64). However, when these cues were no longer made available, their performance returned to its precuing level, thus suggesting that these subjects did not spontaneously adopt an efficient retrieval strategy.

A semantic priming (picture naming) task was used in another investigation (Weil et al., 1978) in order to study educable special-class retarded adolescents' ($\bar{X}$ CA = 17;0, $\bar{X}$ IQ = 67) knowledge of the typicality of semantic catgory instances. As in the case with nonretarded individuals in earlier investigations, the retarded subjects in Weil et al.'s study showed both item relatedness and item typicality effects.

Finally, in a study by McCauley, Sperber, and Roaden (1978) of the verification of true and false semantic property statements by educable mentally retarded ($\bar{X}$ IQ = 68.5) and nonretarded adolescents matched on CA ($\bar{X}$'s approximately 17;0), the following results were reported. True statements: (1) Response times were slower in retarded adolescents; (2) statements that contained high strength properties (e.g., *Bees can sting*) were verified faster than statements that contained low strength properties (e.g., *Sheep can walk*) by both the retarded and the nonretarded adolescents; (3) for the retarded subjects only, response times to sentences containing action properties of the extrinsic type (e.g., *Beans can be eaten*) were faster than they were to sentences containing static properties (e.g., *Camels have humps*), although it could not be determined from the available data whether action properties might have been more salient for the retarded subjects than they were for the nonretarded subjects. False statements: The retarded subjects responded slower than the nonretarded subjects. A developmental lag hypothesis was invoked to account for this pattern of results.

The development of lexical semantics is reflected in part in the ability to correctly name or label pictured objects and in the speed with which the correct label is retrieved from lexical memory. Moreover, similarities between mentally retarded and nonretarded individuals in labeling difficulty and latency of correct labeling for a set of words would suggest similarities in the acquisition processes for this set of words. Winters and Cundari (1979), in a recent investigation (also Winters & Brzoska, 1975), studied labeling of pictured objects in 36 institutionalized mentally retarded students ($\bar{X}$ CA = 17;3, $\bar{X}$ MA = 8;11, and $\bar{X}$ IQ = 57). The stimuli were 48 colored pictures of objects selected from a set of items for which there existed estimates of age of acquisition of their names from nonretarded adults. The task given each subject was to name each picture "as fast and as accurately as possible."

Labeling accuracy was best for lower age-of-acquisition items. The adult age-of-acquisition norms predicted group accuracy for the retarded subjects with an r of $-.84$. (The same correlation for a group of noninstitutionalized adolescent retarded individuals from the Winters & Brzoska study was found to be $-.82$.) Item labeling latency decreased as item labeling accuracy increased for both the institutionalized ($r = -.81$) and the noninstitutionalized ($r = -.79$) retarded subjects. Moreover, it was observed "that names that were estimated to have been acquired earliest by [nonretarded adults] were retrieved fastest by the retarded group [p. 569]'' in the study by Winters and Cundari. It is to be noted that a similar finding for nonretarded subjects had been reported previously in the literature.

Further evidence that semantic development in mentally retarded children runs a course similar to that in nonretarded children has been provided by Leonard, Cole, and Steckol (1979) in a study of informativeness constraints on lexical usage in mentally retarded children in the CA range 27 to 46 months and the Bailey Infant Scale range of 14 to 24 months (see, however, Pea, 1979, for a recent discussion of the problems of studying informativeness in young children).

Conclusions

Although much remains to be done on the problem of semantic development and performance in the mentally retarded, the research that is available does permit some tentative conclusions to be drawn. First, although semantic knowledge tends to develop at a slower rate in the mentally retarded than it does in the nonretarded (at least when they are matched on CA), the course of development and the knowledge achieved appear to be similar in the two populations. This conclusion, of course, is based largely on research on concrete referential nomenclature and early concrete semantic relations; we know nothing about the development and organization of, for example, abstract lexicon (e.g., *truth, justice, ambiguity*) in the mentally retarded. I might point out here that it is surprising that this is the case, inasmuch as one would expect to find interesting differences between retarded and nonretarded individuals in the domain of abstract lexicon. Second, there are some observations in the literature that suggest that mentally retarded individuals sometimes encounter strategic and/or motivational difficulties in utilizing their semantic knowledge.

PHONOLOGY

We turn our attention now to a review of recent work on phonological functioning in the mentally retarded as evidenced in studies of speech–sound articulation and perception and related phenomena, in order to determine whether the trends we have observed in other domains of linguistic structure appear in the area of phonology as well. Before we do so, however, we will look briefly at the findings reported in a sample of earlier reviews.

According to Schlanger's (1973) review of speech and language disorders in mentally retarded individuals, disorders of articulation, voice, and rhythm, including slurred speech, are found among the mildly retarded (IQs of 50–70), but the incidence of such problems is not so great at this level of intellectual functioning as it is at lower levels of IQ. Moreover, the research reviewed by Schlanger suggested that disorders of articulation, voice, and rhythm occur more frequently in samples of Down's syndrome individuals than they do in other etiological categories.

Ingram (1976) looked more directly at phonological processes in his review of studies of speech–sound substitution and omission errors in non-Down's syndrome and Down's syndrome mentally retarded children (see also Smith, 1975). The available research on non-Down's-syndrome mentally retarded children appeared to indicate that such children "show similar substitution patterns to those of normal children... [p. 122]" and, possibly, a heightened use of errors of omission.

Unfortunately, no such picture of articulatory functioning emerged from the available research with Down's children, due perhaps to the high incidence of speech deficiencies in this population. According to Ingram (1976), "children with Down's syndrome are generally considered to have harsh voice qualities..., abnormal intonation, and a predominance of grunts in their speech [pp. 125–126]." Moreover, speech intelligibility is frequently reported to be low in members of this population, due to their tongue size. However, the grunt's of some Down's children have been observed to be systematically communicative. As for phonological processes, both similarities and differences between Down's and nonretarded children in substitution patterns have been reported.

In the recent literature, the oft-cited voice problems of Down's syndrome individuals was the topic of an investigation by Montague, Brown, and Hollien (1974) of vocal fundamental frequency (VFF) in institutionalized subjects ($N = 20$, $\bar{X}$ CA = 10;5, $\bar{X}$ IQ = 32.2). Twenty CA-matched intellectually average public school children served as a control group. Auditory acuity was somewhat better in the Down's sample. Voice samples were collected by having each subject name the objects in a series of pictures after the experimenter had named them. The pictures, each of which contained a single object, were presented one at a time. A set of three words that "offered a wide sampling of vowel contrasts [p. 416]" was selected from the picture-naming responses for analysis. Although a significant interaction was found between the groups in this study and the sex of their members, the main effects of group and sex were not found to be significant. An analysis of simple effects revealed that the males in the Down's sample had a significantly higher fundamental frequency than both the nonretarded males and the Down's females. Finally, none of the correlations that were computed between IQ and fundamental frequency was found to be significant. The authors concluded that some attribute other than fundamental frequency may be responsible for the frequent clinical observation that Down's children in general display vocal problems.

The origin of the speech articulatory problems of Down's children was the topic of a study by Dodd (1975) but, unfortunately, her results are impossible to interpret due to materials, task, and conceptual problems in the design of the study. I just comment briefly here on the rationale for her study.

Dodd cites observations (Smith, 1975; see also the following discussion of Dodd, 1976) to the effect that Down's children make fewer articulation errors in imitating words than in producing them spontaneously, a finding that she interprets as indicating that their vocal apparatus is not disabled. This leads her to speculate that "the spontaneous articulatory disorder of the Down's syndrome children must be due either to a deficit in auditory processing and storage or to a disability in the motor programming of the speech act [p. 306]." Dodd does not point out, however, that what her speculation implies is that the internal phonological *representations* of lexical items are intact in Down's children and therefore the defect in auditory processing and storage (or more properly auditory processing *and/or* storage; from an information-processing standpoint these should be treated separately) could not be a serious one, otherwise *the acquisition of the representations would have been affected*. Moreover, there is no mention of the fact that both imitation (of heard lexical items) and spontaneous production (e.g., in conversation or in naming the objects in pictures) must involve in the final stages of speech planning, articulatory programming. Lastly, there is no indication of how auditory processing and storage can be involved in spontaneous speech planning. If anything, if Down's syndrome children do suffer from a deficit in auditory processing and storage, this would be more likely to show up in an imitation task where there are obvious auditory processing and storage demands than in a spontaneous speech task. Given the greater dependence on auditory processing and storage in speech imitation and the involvement of articulatory programming in both spontaneous speech and imitation, Dodd should have been surprised at the observation that imitation articulatory performance was not *worse* than spontaneous articulatory performance in Down's children.

Dodd's claims regarding imitation and spontaneous articulation were evidently based upon the findings of a study that she herself had conducted that did not appear until 1976. In it she studied the phonological (consonant) errors made by Down's syndrome mentally retarded, non-Down's syndrome mentally retarded, and nonretarded children during elicited picture naming (Dodd's "spontaneous" production task) and elicited lexical imitation. The items used in the elicited imitation task were the names of the pictures. The three groups ($N = 10$ in each) were matched on Stanford–Binet MA and social background. Moreover, the subjects were all determined to be free of sensory, neurological, and gross motor impairments that might have interfered with performance. In addition, each group included both home-reared and residential children. The means for MA fell between 3;0 and 4;0. Mean CA was approximately 3;7 in the nonretarded sample and 10;8 in the two retarded samples. Thus mean IQ was low in both retarded samples.

It should be noted here that given the fact that language development in the mentally retarded tends to lag behind MA in certain areas, it is likely that the overall linguistic maturity of Dodd's Down's and non-Down's retarded children was lower than what it was in her nonretarded children. Moreover, it is unlikely the children in the retarded samples were functioning much beyond the earliest stage of language acquisition.

Subjects named the pictures first, performed the elicited imitation task second, and were then required to name the pictures a second time. The identical phonetic transcriptions of taped responses by two independent speech therapists constituted the data for this investigation. Errors were sorted into three categories identified by Smith (1973): cluster reduction, production of consonant harmony, and simplification of the phonological system. All other errors were treated separately.

It needs to be mentioned here that the naming and imitation tasks were not presented in a balanced fashion as regards order and frequency and no attempt was made to examine individual differences. Furthermore, no direct comparisons were made between naming and imitation on a word-to-word basis. Finally, questions can be raised concerning the appropriateness of some of Dodd's statistical analyses and as a result I have nothing to say here about the results for the comparisons between imitation and naming or between naming1 and naming2, including the finding that the Down's subjects made more errors in elicited picture naming than they did in elicited imitation.

In the case of the three main error categories under investigation, analysis revealed that overall the Down's sample made more errors and "produced a greater number of different error types [p. 40]" than either of the other two groups. The Down's sample also made more noncategorized errors than either of the other two groups. The nonretarded and non-Down's syndrome groups did not differ in any of these analyses.

Bartolucci and Pierce (1977) were interested in studying phonological performance in autistic children but included a mentally retarded (etiology unspecified) and a nonretarded sample in their study for control purposes. I have nothing to say here concerning their autistic sample. Mean CA was 10;6 in the retarded group ($N = 10$) and 6;3 in the nonretarded group ($N = 10$) but the groups were matched on mean nonverbal MA (6;1 and 6;4, respectively). Thus mean MA and mean IQ were higher in Bartolucci and Pierce's retarded sample than they were in Dodd's (1976) retarded samples, whereas mean CA was lower in Dodd's nonretarded sample. Bartolucci and Pierce estimated overall linguistic maturity in their subjects using Lee's (1974) Developmental Sentence Scoring technique. Not surprisingly, mean performance was highest in the nonretarded sample on this scale. All subjects were free of conditions that might have complicated articulation or perception.

These investigators used a picture-naming test to assess articulation, but one that was "constructed in such a way as to elicit examples of the 24 consonant phonemes of English in initial, final, preconsonantal, postconsonantal, and intervocalic positions, as far as the phonotactics of the language and the picturability of the words permitted (p. 140)." In addition, appropriate tests were administered to assess perception of the phonemes.

Performance on the production test varied as a function of phoneme class and subject group, with the retarded group producing proportionally more errors overall than the nonretarded group. Differences were evident in fricatives, affricates, and liquids. The pattern of error percentages also differed in certain respects for the two groups. Furthermore, nonverbal MA was not found to correlate with number of production errors in either group, but there was a significant negative correlation between Developmental Sentence Scoring performance and number of production errors in the mentally retarded group. Thus, in the retarded sample, articulatory performance improved with language development generally but not with nonverbal MA. The failure to find a significant correlation between MA and phonological performance in the retarded group may have been due to the sample size and other (unknown) characteristics of this group. Earlier investigators (Schlanger, 1973) have reported such a correlation for both speech–sound production and discrimination.

Evidently, because of differential information-processing demands, both retarded and nonretarded subjects made more errors on phoneme perception than they did on phoneme production. More important, the error percentages and error patterns of the two groups differed little on the perception tasks. Furthermore, the correlations between phoneme perception errors and nonverbal MA and Developmental Sentence Scoring were not significant in either of the two groups.

If Bartolucci and Pierce's retarded sample did not contain any Down's children, their results for phoneme production question those of Dodd (1976) for the subject contrast nonretarded/non-Down's syndrome retarded children. One can speculate that the differences in the findings of these two studies were due to materials and dependent variable differences. It is unlikely that they were due to subject-related differences, because Bartolucci and Pierce used a higher level retarded sample than did Dodd.

The most detailed analysis of phonological repertoires and processes in Down's syndrome children in the literature is perhaps to be found in a recent study of Stoel-Gammon (1980). Her subjects were four mildly mentally retarded Down's children in the CA range 3;10 to 6;3 who were being "raised at home by their natural parents [p. 4]." English was the only language spoken; vision and audition were determined to be normal; they were involved in preschool programs; and records did not indicate presence of complicating neurological problems. Three hours of the spontaneous speech of each child were recorded over a period of a month during various interactions in the home and preschool. The subjects' MLUs (Coggins, 1979) ranged from 1.22 to 2.06 (Brown's, 1973, Stage I). Phonetic transcriptions of 250–300 glossed utterances comprised the data base for each child. Vowel errors were infrequent (less than 10%); therefore the analysis was limited to consonants. Other scoring criteria can be found in the article.

Stoel-Gammon reported three major findings from her analysis of consonant productions. First, "although they made many pronunciation errors, the subjects were *capable* of producing nearly all the phonemes of English [p. 25]." According to Stoel-Gammon, "This finding makes it difficult to attribute the errors to abnormalities of the oral structure... [p. 25]." The second major finding was that the childrens' mispronunciations "were systematically related to the adult forms in regular and predictable ways... [p. 25]." Finally, Stoel-Gammon noted that the pronunciation patterns of her Down's children were "consistent with patterns reported in studies of the speech of children developing language normally.... [p. 25]." The only departure was for the phenomenon of consonant harmony.

Thus the frequent observation in the literature that Down's syndrome childrens' articulatory development lags behind the development of other aspects of language performance is not supported by Stoel-Gammon's findings. Moreover, although they may develop articulatory skills at a slower rate than their nonretarded CA mates, when they are compared with MLU-matched nonretarded children on phonological abilities, they "are as good as, if not better than, the normal population [p. 27]." It is hoped that the generality of Stoel-Gammon's findings will be evaluated in the near future using a larger sample and a wider range of cognitive ability levels and CA.

Conclusions

In spite of the differences in method and data analysis as well as some differences in findings that were noted previously in the recent studies of phonological behavior and development in the mentally retarded, some tentative conclusions are possible.

The results of the investigation by Bartolucci and Pierce (1977) and the portion of Dodd's (1976) study reviewed here, like earlier investigations, paint a picture of developmental delay rather than one of developmental deviance in the domain of phonological production in non-Down's syndrome mentally retarded children. The phonological productions of the Down's syndrome mentally retarded children in Stoel-Gammon's (1980) study also appeared to be characterized by development delay rather than developmental deviance. Moreover, the results of Stoel-Gammon's study suggest that earlier investigations underestimated the rate of development of the phonological system in Down's syndrome mentally retarded children relative to the rate of development of other aspects of their linguistic competence.

PRAGMATICS

The study of pragmatic or communicative competence is a recent interest in the area of mental retardation as well as in basic psycholinguistics (see, for example, the reviews of Bates, 1976; Clark & Clark, 1977; and Rees, 1978). Pragmatics recognizes that most utterances are created to serve communicative functions (e.g., to obtain information, to give information, to negate previously asserted propositions, to demand or request action, and to signal the given and new information in an utterance) and, moreover, that these functions are mapped directly or indirectly onto certain syntactic (e.g., interrogatives) and other (e.g., intonational) linguistic structures. Furthermore, it is recognized that such communicative functions can be represented not only in terms of speakers' intentions but in terms of listeners' obligations as well. In addition, it is apparently the case that the "natural" context for the exercise of pragmatic competence is face-to-face conversational interaction, although there is also interest in conversational interaction at a distance, as in the case of referential communication where the participants are physically separated and receive only verbal cues from each other, and in instruction giving (face to face and at a distance). Finally, a thorough treatment of speaker–listener pragmatic capabilities would have to include a discussion of the contribution of nonlinguistic cognitive capabilities as well as the contribution of not specifically pragmatic aspects of phonological, syntactic, and semantic knowledge and performance skills.

In the present section, I review recent research on pragmatics in the area of mental retardation. The range of phenomena studied, however, as the reader will see, has been quite limited and not productive of more than a few tentative generalizations.

Non-face-to-face referential communication in mentally retarded adolescents was the topic of a series of studies by Longhurst (1974). The basic task used was one that required a listener to select from a visual array of nonsense designs, the one that was being described by a speaker. Speakers received no feedback regarding the listeners' responses on the basic task. The subjects were 60 institutionalized mentally retarded individuals in the CA range 11;6 to 18;2 who were paired on the basis of sex and IQ matching (at three levels; IQ 70–90, 56–69, and 40–55). The various subgroups produced by this procedure were comparable in CA; thus IQ and MA were positively correlated in this sample. Extensive pretesting and pretraining ensured that subjects could discriminate the stimuli and engage in the basic referential communication task. The dependent variables in the first study were number of correct choices by listeners, length of speakers' descriptions of the stimuli, and a type-token ratio (a measure of vocabulary diversity in the speakers' descriptions).

Mean performance on these measures increased with increased mean IQ. On number of correct choices, the two higher IQ groups differed significantly from the lowest IQ group but not from each other. On the remaining measures, the highest IQ group differed significantly from the other groups that did not differ. None of the differences due to sex was significant. The mean percent correct for the highest IQ group was 54.21. According to Longhurst, the performance of listeners from adult nonretarded dyads is essentially perfect.

Longhurst conducted three additional studies in an attempt to estimate the relative contributions of speakers and listeners to the results of the first study, the results of which he interpreted to suggest that the performance of listeners in the first study as regards number of correct choices was due mainly to poor speaker-communication skills. The presence of some confoundings, however, in Experiments 2, 3, and 4 makes this suggestion a tentative one. Moreover, given the nature of the basic task itself, it would be impossible to identify (as Longhurst himself realizes) the specific characteristics of retarded speakers and listeners that might make for unsuccessful non-face-to-face referential communication. Furthermore, it is questionable whether anything of interest regarding mentally retarded individuals' capacity for everyday non-face-to-face referential communication is likely to come out of studies using stimuli of the sort that were used in this investigation. Finally, on the basis of the results of the pretesting and pretraining tasks, one must conclude that the information processing demands of Longhurst's task were inordinately high for the lower level mentally retarded subjects.

Retarded adolescents' ability to utilize feedback in a nonsense referential communication task was studied by Longhurst and Berry (1975). These investigators found, among other things, and not surprisingly, a positive relationship between IQ and the likelihood that retarded speakers would adjust their descriptions on the basis of listener feedback following communication failure.

Beveridge and Tatham (1976) attempted to overcome some of the limitations of Longhurst's (1974) study of non-face-to-face referential communication through the use of pictures depicting simple scenes (e.g., "a girl cutting a cake"). The subjects were six noninstitutionalized mentally retarded males ($\bar{X}$ CA = 14;10, $\bar{X}$ IQ = 50). Thus they were comparable in IQ to Longhurst's lowest level subjects. All subjects demonstrated in pretesting an ability to describe the individual pictures appropriately and to comprehend appropriate descriptions of the pictures. Identical sets of three related pictures were constructed for speakers and listeners that allowed for the communication of subject, verb, and object roles. Each subject served with every other subject as both a speaker and a listener. The task of the speaker was to describe one member of each set of three pictures so that the listener could pick it out from among the same three pictures. The speaker was scored for transmitting the information necessary for a correct selection by the listener, the listener for the correctness of his selection.

It is interesting to note that "subjects who were good listeners were also good speakers, and vice versa [p. 98]." Moreover, the subjects whose performance was poor as speakers and listeners initially showed considerable improvement over trials in both roles. Third, speakers encountered their greatest difficulty describing target pictures in which the verb was the crucial element, and listeners encountered their greatest difficulty selecting pictures for which the verb was crucial. Finally, it is necessary to note that the results of this study "suggest that being able to produce and comprehend a particular sentence does not guarantee its appropriate use in a dyadic referential task [p. 98]."

Although the results of this investigation are interesting, they could have been made more illuminating if control data had been collected from nonretarded subjects, if the subject sample had been larger and had included institutionalized retarded individuals and if speaker–listener item contigency data had been reported.

Arrays of meaningful stimuli, each of whose label was determined to be in the productive and receptive vocabularies of a group of mentally retarded teenagers, were used by Beveridge and Mittler (1977) to study "the effect of immediate corrective feedback to retarded listeners from retarded speakers [p. 150]" in a non-face-to-face referential communication task. Three severely retarded Down's syndrome children (CA range approximately 11;0–16;0, performance MA range 3;0–3;6, and verbal age range 2;11–3;7) served as listeners and two other retarded children (etiology unspecified, CAs between 15 and 16, IQs 48 and 55) served as speakers. The procedure employed by these investigators called for the collection of baseline data (without feedback), to be followed by a period of verbal feedback from the speaker (both positive and negative) concerning choice correctness and then a period in which speakers reverted to the no feedback condition.

Listener performance was best during the feedback trials in this study but, in that no control group was used, one must be cautious in drawing conclusions. Moreover, the small number of subjects used by these investigators must also be a matter for concern.

The mentally retarded individual's ability to take into account characteristics of the listener in a face-to-face communication task was studied by Hoy and McKnight (1977). The subjects were 20 residential and 20 day-school mentally retarded individuals, 9 of whom had Down's syndrome, in the CA range 6 to 18 years and the MA (Stanford–Binet) range 2 to 8 years. They were assigned to dyadic subgroups of varying speaker–listener intellectual (MA and IQ) levels; specifically, high speaker–high listener, high speaker–low listener, low speaker–high listener, and low speaker–low listener. The task was a board game that pretrained speakers were required to try to teach to naive listeners. The speaker communication channels recorded were verbal, gestural, and manipulative. Listener understanding was also recorded as well as measures of speaker and listener speech style (verbal productivity, vocabulary diversity, and sensitivity to partner as evidenced, for example, in attention-getting utterances).

As for the results, high speakers' game explanation time was significantly lower than low speakers' game explanation time; the combination of low speaker and high listener led to significantly fewer item explanations than any of the other combinations, which did not differ from each other; the verbal channel alone was used to communicate most often (relatively speaking) by speakers in the high speaker–high listener dyads, whereas manipulation and gestures occurred least frequently in this condition; speakers in the low speaker–low listener group used a combination of verbal and manipulative communications with appreciable frequency (relative to the other groups); some differences were noted in favor of the speakers in the high groups on the measures of communication style; there was evidence that both high and low speakers adjusted their communications to the level of their listeners; and "the percentage of items understood was significantly lower for low-level listeners instructed by high-level speakers . . . than for listeners in the other three groups. . . [p. 594]." Thus "low-level speakers were understood equally well by listeners at both levels [p. 594]." Other results were reported, but these appear to be the main findings.

These findings suggest that communicative effectiveness in dyads of mentally retarded individuals is likely to be a complex function of a variety of factors, not the least of which is the particular measure of communicative effectiveness adopted. The question of the generality of Hoy and McKnight's findings, however, must be held in abeyance until a variety of tasks are investigated and performance is related to a subject's mastery of specific linguistic and nonlinguistic communicative processes as well as a subject's information processing and social interactive capabilities.

The last two studies to be included in the present section were concerned with conversational interaction. Bedrosian and Prutting (1978) investigated the conversational performance of mentally retarded adults in four settings: conversation with a speech-language pathologist, parents (or guardian), peers, and a six-year-old nonretarded male. The subjects were three males and one female in the CA range 23 to 28 years from a day-training center who were involved in speech and language remediation. Three of the subjects had Stanford-Binet IQs of 29, 36, and 31. An IQ score was not available for the fourth subject. One of the male subjects had Down's syndrome. Conversations during "natural unstructured discourse" were recorded over a 3-month period in the various settings for each subject.

Results indicated for the measures studied (which were only a subset of possible conversational dependent variables) the following. First, only one subject held the dominant position in conversation (specifically, in the peer and child settings); in other words the majority of the mentally retarded subjects did not even dominate the conversations with the child. Second, all the subjects were able to signal "communicative distress" throught the use of "requests for restatement." Third, individual differences and differences due to conversational setting notwithstanding, an ability to control conversations in ways similar to those of nonretarded adults was evident in the present mentally retarded subjects. Thus, despite the intellectual (and linguistic) limitations of the mentally retarded individuals in this study, they were able to engage in interactive linguistic performance. However, how thoroughly this investigation was able to assess their conversational competence is impossible to determine.

Price-Williams and Sabsay (1979) examined a number of aspects of conversational interaction in nine male institutionalized Down's syndrome adults (CAs 29–49 years, IQs 17–26, lengths of institutionalization 20–35 years). Language skills varied considerably in this sample, which included "men known to be friends." Conversations between members of this sample (both spontaneous and elicited) and between the members and hospital research staff were audio- and video-recorded in various settings. Unfortunately, although this study was a substantial one (15 hours of conversation were recorded), the investigators reported only illustrative findings, so the following summary statements must be treated cautiously. First, in spite of intelligibility difficulties due to articulatory and linguistic difficulties, the communicative interactions of the subjects were reported to be mostly successful. A variety of communicative functions were served by the utterances they produced; conversational turn-taking, greeting exchanges, question–answer interactions, etc., were in evidence. Second, speakers were observed to employ a variety of linguistic and nonlinguistic devices to attract the attention of their intended listeners. Third, there was evidence in the protocols of successful treatment of contexts relevant to the conversations. Fourth, there was also evidence of appropriate responses to requests for clarification on the part of speakers.

The hypothesis suggested by the findings of these last two studies, of course, is that the conversational competence and performance capabilities of low-level mentally retarded individuals in face-to-face conversational activities may in many respects be greater than one would predict on the basis of their basic linguistic competence and performance capabilities. Needless to say, this is a hypothesis that is worthy of careful evaluation with developmental samples of varying linguistic and other cognitive capabilities.

Given the sparcity of interesting work on pragmatic aspects of language functioning in the mentally retarded, it would be premature to attempt to integrate what is available at this time.

LINGUISTIC PERFORMANCE

Thus far in the present review we have been interested mainly in attempting to map the course and achievements of language development in the mentally retarded. In order to do so, we have had to examine the products of linguistic performance, that is, the products of the interaction among linguistic knowledge, nonlinguistic knowledge, linguistic and other information-processing skills, and motivation in the domains of speech production, speech comprehension, and memory for linguistic input, recognizing full well that in a number of instances it was impossible to determine whether these products revealed the level of linguistic knowledge achieved or something about the other determinants of linguistic performance.

In the present section, we examine work that bears on questions concerning linguistic performance processes in the mentally retarded. Much of what we know and can reasonably surmise regarding linguistic performance in nonretarded language users has been summarized by Clark and Clark (1977) and by Foss and Hakes (1978).

Passivity

The reader will recall that at the beginning of this chapter, I cited evidence in support of the claim that mental retardation has a motivational component, that of passivity. One could also cite in its support the observation of Glidden and Mar (1978) of a "failure to use spontaneously mnemonic strategies that were consistent with... semantic organization [p. 33]" in educable mentally retarded adolescents. Moreover, one might speculate that at least some of the difficulties mentally retarded individuals are sometimes observed to encounter in referential communication tasks (see the discussion in the previous section) are a reflection of a passive attitude and that to some extent their productivity when generating monologues (Lozar et al., 1973) is also a reflection of this attitude.

The presence of passivity in the mentally retarded reduces, among other things, our ability to assess their linguistic-communicative competence and performance reliably. It becomes important, therefore, to identify the source or sources of this attitude. Unfortunately, there appears to be nothing one can say at present about this matter, except to suggest that the source or sources of passivity may be found eventually by examining conditions (i.e., experimental interventions) that increase the likelihood that a mentally retarded individual will utilize his or her underlying linguistic, communicative, and other cognitive capabilities.

Speech Production

The study of speech planning and execution processes in nonretarded individuals has been limited mainly to research on pausal and other hesitation phenomena, research using certain experimental paradigms to access putative components of these processes, research on naturally occurring speech errors, and research in experimental phonetics (see, for example, the reviews in Clark & Clark, 1977; Rosenberg, 1977; and Foss & Hakes, 1978). Moreover, most of the research in question has been with mature language users; little is known about the development of speech planning and execution processes.

Some hesitation phenomena were investigated by Naremore and Dever (1975) in a study of short spontaneous speech samples of nonretarded and educable mentally retarded children, but the results were not presented in a fashion that would allow us to make comparisons with results of studies of nonretarded individuals in which hesitation phenomena served as the basis for characterizing aspects of speech planning and execution. Unfortunately this was the only study I uncovered during my literature search that had something to do with the topic of speech production processes. Consequently, there is much need for research with mentally retarded individuals on the pragmatic and semantic propositional decisions of speech planning, the syntactic packaging of ideas, the use of syntactic routines, lexical selection in speech planning, the planning unit (or units) of speech, speech errors (their organization, detection, and correction), articulatory control processes, monitoring generally, breath control and other pausal phenomena, and shortcutting and listener-sensitive strategies.

Speech Comprehension

In the mature language user, speech comprehension, the intent of which is to recover the meanings and communicative intentions of speakers, is a complex process that involves making decisions (both serially and in parallel) at a rapid rate on a number of levels (acoustic, phonological, lexical, intonational, syntactic, semantic propositional, pragmatic) on the basis of linguistic knowledge, knowledge of the world, linguistic and nonlinguistic contextual information, linguistic and general-purpose information processing capabilities and strategies, and the like. However, in spite of its complexity, the richness of the input to the speech comprehension process, in combination with the extent of the knowledge and skills that listeners bring to it, means that the response is overdetermined and, as a result, listeners are rarely at a disadvantage when either the input is degraded or they are unable to marshall all their resources for speech comprehension.

The fact that, as we saw earlier, many mentally retarded individuals can engage in conversation, be guided by instructions, and show a mastery of linguistic knowledge on comprehension tasks and tests that tends to mirror their productive linguistic knowledge, suggests that their performance capabilities in the comprehension mode keep pace with their other achievements in the domain of language. Interest in specific aspects of the speech comprehension process in the mentally retarded, however, has been growing. One aspect of the input to everyday speech comprehension, namely, that it frequently contains deletions or is otherwise degraded, is modeled by the familiar cloze procedure.

Semmel, Barritt, and Bennett (1970) employed this procedure with institutionalized ($\bar{X}$ CA = 11;9, $\bar{X}$ MA = 8;3, $\bar{X}$ IQ = 70.15) and public school ($\bar{X}$ CA = 11;9, $\bar{X}$ MA = 8;2, $\bar{X}$ IQ = 69.60) mentally retarded children and MA- and CA-matched nonretarded children. The groups contained 20 subjects each and were balanced for sex. One word at a time was deleted from various positions in five different sentence types and subjects had to attempt to supply the missing items. The findings of interest here are that the nonretarded groups were superior to the retarded groups overall and that there were no differences between the retarded or the nonretarded subgroups. Moreover, both retarded groups showed appreciable improvement on the last of the deleted positions in the sentences, a fact that these investigators discussed at length.

Unfortunately, it is not possible to determine whether these findings reflected differences in linguistic competence or linguistic performance or both. In order to begin to identify the performance factors involved, one would have to establish first, *on independent grounds,* that the mentally retarded subjects possess the linguistic knowledge required for the comprehension of the nondeleted versions of the experimental sentences and can utilize it under optimal conditions of comprehension (i.e, when there are no deletions or other degradations in the input). Then and only then can one turn his or her attention to the task of identifying individual differences and the sources of individual differences in degraded-input reconstruction.

It should be noted in passing that some of the problems with the interpretation of cloze data are also to be found in the task in which subjects attempt to identify the meaning of a nonsense word embedded in grammatical and meaningful linguistic context (Lieber & Spitz, 1976) and in studies of word intelligibility under distorted conditions, where no attempt is made to determine beforehand whether or not all the words are known to the mentally retarded subjects (Flowers, 1974).

Sommers and Starkey (1977) searched for evidence of differences in the lateralization of verbal (word) processing in mentally retarded Down's and nonretarded children. Pretesting determined that all subjects had normal hearing and could identify the experimental words and distractors under optimal conditions. The mean CA in the nonretarded sample ($N = 20$) was 4;3 (range 3;0–5;5) and mean MA (PPVT), 5;1. The Down's children ($N = 29$), who were determined through extensive pretesting to vary in linguistic maturity, were selected from a population of special day-school students. Right-handedness predominated in both groups. The Down's children were divided into a high language performance group ($N = 14$) and a low language performance group ($N = 15$) on the basis of the pretesting. The highs displayed the following characteristics: $\bar{X}$ CA = 13;2, $\bar{X}$ IQ (Stanford–Binet) = 46.0, $\bar{X}$ MA = 5;4. For the lows, these values were $\bar{X}$ CA = 14;5, $\bar{X}$ IQ = 39, $\bar{X}$ MA = 4;3. (Note that mean IQ and MA were both lower in the lows.) Dichotic word perception was tested using a four-choice picture verification task. Test–retest reliability was found to be extremely high on the dichotic task for both the nonretarded and the retarded subjects.

As for the results, the nonretarded subjects evidenced "a 23 percent right-ear preference while no ear preference was found for the subjects in the [p. 49]" high and low linguistic performance Down's groups. An analysis of performance on the basis of initial phonemes revealed a greater similarity between the highs and the nonretarded samples than between the highs and the lows. In addition, CA, MA, IQ, and measures of linguistic maturity were not found to correlate significantly with right-ear scores in the mentally retarded sample.

Clearly, only the nonretarded subjects in this study showed a preference for words presented to the right ear. It is not at all clear, however, how one is to interpret this finding. Is it due to some subtle differences in linguistic knowledge or to unknown performance constraints? We shall surely be rewarded by additional research on the lateralization of linguistic functions in mentally retarded individuals.

An interest in the variables that might influence the sentence comprehension test performance of mentally retarded children motivated research by Wheldall and Swann (1976) and Wheldall and Mittler (1977). Intonational emphasis was the variable of interest in the first article and order of presentation of pictures and sentences was the topic of the second. No useful generalizations emerged from these investigations, however, due clearly to theoretical and methodological problems.

A recent study by Dewart (1979) attempted to identify the performance strategies mentally retarded children employ in comprehending sentences (e.g., whether, like young nonretarded children, they tend to assign the role of actor to the first noun of a reversible passive sentence or to assign interpretations based upon the real-world probabilities of occurrence of the events described in a sentence). Rather than use a picture verification task, which Dewart felt adds the task of picture interpretation to sentence interpretation, she required the subjects to act out the contents of the sentences using various objects. In this investigation, "There were two between-subjects variables, subject group (retarded vs. nonretarded) and mental age (MA) (higher vs. lower MA group) and two within-subjects variables, sentence voice (either active, passive with the auxiliary verb *is,* or passive with the auxiliary verb *gets*) and semantic constraints (either neutral, probable, or improbable) [p. 178]." The sentences contained words selected from vocabulary norms for retarded subjects but experimenter judgement was the basis for the manipulation of semantic constraints. Thus it is possible that the neutral list contained some probable sentences. Moreover, it was clear from an examination of the sentences used that included among the improbable sentences were some semantically anomalous sentences that might have caused difficulties independent of their low probabilities of occurrence. In addition, in this study, semantic constraint was clearly confounded with comprehensibility (and, very likely, with imageability as well).

Although having subjects act out the content of a sentence may have some advantages over picture verification, it is not a task that is without its problems for a subject; one being the necessity of maintaining in short-term memory the content of a sentence during acting out; another being the problem of determining reliably whether the content has in fact been acted out. In regard to the first problem, because semantic constraint was very likely confounded with comprehensibility and imageability, the lower the semantic constraint, the greater the difficulty of remembering the content of a sentence. As for the second problem, one has to be concerned when he or she reads that the criterion for correctness in acting out was whether "the experimenter could see clearly that the appropriate toy was made to act on the other, regardless of the exact nature of the action carried out [p. 179]."

MA-matched (PPVT) special-school retarded and nonretarded children served as subjects. Etiology was heterogeneous in the retarded sample. The pairs were divided into two groups on the basis of MA, a group whose MAs ranged from 1;10 to 3;0 and a group whose MAs ranged from 3;2 to 7;1. The retarded subjects had CAs that were on the average more than twice those of the nonretarded subjects and spontaneous speech capabilities that varied considerably.

The nonretarded subjects performed at a significantly higher level on frequency of correct responses overall; actives were significantly easier than passives; and increased semantic constraint facilitated performance significantly. Subject group did not interact with sentence voice but it did interact with semantic constraint such that there was a greater effect of this variable for the retarded subjects, with a significant difference in favor of the nonretarded subjects on the neutral and improbable sentences but not on the probable sentences. Interactions showed, further, that sentence voice did not affect the performance of the low-MA retarded group, whose performance was below chance generally.

Subjects had been administered a memory span test in addition to the comprehension task, but performance on these two measures did not correlate significantly.

There was some evidence in this study that as verbal cognitive maturity increased, retarded children went from random performance to the use of a word-order strategy for both active and passive sentences not unlike what nonretarded children have been observed to use for a time during development. Unfortunately, interpretation of the findings for semantic constraint must await further research because of the confoundings mentioned earlier.

Memory for Linguistic Input

The particular interest of this section is memory for linguistic input. However, we might consider briefly whether there is any evidence that memory is in general impaired in the mentally retarded, because memory impairment would be expected to affect not only linguistic performance but language acquisition as well.

For obvious reasons, memorial performance has been studied extensively in the mentally retarded (see, for example, Butterfield & Belmont, 1972; Cohen & Sandberg, 1977; Dugas & Kellas, 1974; Pennington & Luszcz, 1975; as well as the references contained in these articles), sometimes with conflicting findings. Nevertheless, it seems reasonable to claim from this work that mentally retarded individuals tend to show memorial performance that resembles that of younger nonretarded individuals. The reasons for this lag in the development of memorial capabilities in the mentally retarded are still being investigated, however. Strategic factors (encoding, rehearsal, organization, retrieval) appear to be implicated in tasks that are reasonably demanding, but I would not want to rule out as yet, on the basis of the available evidence, possible capacity differences as well. And, of course, one would want to explore thoroughly the possible role of the trait of passivity discussed earlier.

For whatever reasons, working or short-term memory is likely to be overloaded more readily in mentally retarded individuals than in nonretarded individuals in speech production and comprehension performance and in memorizing linguistic input, and this possibility needs to be kept in mind whenever one attempts to plan and/or to interpret the results of studies of linguistic competence and performance.

Strings of unstructured and syntactically structured words were presented by Graham (1968) one at a time for immediate repetition to 44 special-school mentally retarded children in the CA range of 6 to 11 years ($\bar{X} = 9;0$) and the IQ (Stanford–Binet or WISC) range of 47 to 82 ($\bar{X} = 62$). The unstructured strings varied in length from two to six words and were made up of a random selection of words from the list of grammatical strings (i.e., sentences). These strings were used to assess short-term memory span. The grammatical sentences, which were presented in two parallel lists, varied considerably in syntactic complexity but they were all eight words in length. Of course, in order to hold length constant, syntactic structures of different types needed to be combined. Moreover, although there was an attempt to use vocabulary that mentally retarded subjects would be expected to be familiar with, there was no indication that Graham controlled for semantic constraint within the structured strings. Further, it was impossible to assess semantic constraint informally, because the materials used in this study were not reproduced in the article.

The procedure required subjects to repeat each sentence or string verbatim immediately after a single presentation. Thus there was no attempt to ensure that subjects would attempt to process the syntax and semantic content of each sentence. Given the frequent observation that mentally retarded individuals do not encode linguistic input semantically as fully as do nonretarded individuals, one has to be cautious in interpreting stimulus repetition (and comprehension) data. In addition, interpretation of stimulus repetition data is further complicated by the observation that a rather shallow encoding of linguistic input is frequently adequate for purposes of immediate recall (Rosenberg & Jarvella, 1970; Treisman & Tuxworth, 1974). This is not to say, of course, that repetition (or immediate elicited imitation) data are not useful, only that they need to be interpreted cautiously due to the possible presence of uncontrolled variables.

Subjects' short-term memory scores for the unstructured strings correlated highly with their sentence recall scores, even with CA and IQ partialled out. Moreover, the sentences varied significantly in difficulty, with the least variability occurring for the subjects with the higher short-term memory scores (this due, evidently, at least in part, to a ceiling effect for the length of sentences used).

Unfortunately, no attempt was made to analyze the errors that subjects made in recalling the sentences. Further, in the absence of information on how the sentences were actually encoded, response latency, and the subjects' linguistic maturity vis-à-vis the syntactic and semantic structures used, it is difficult to interpret the relationship between short-term memory score and sentence recall.

Some information on short-term memory and language test performance in the mentally retarded can be found in an article by Walker, Roodin, and Lamb (1975), but problems of interpretation of positive correlations are present there as well.

A more systematic approach to the study of short-term recall of linguistic input is evident in the work of Berry (Berry, 1976; Berry & Taylor, 1976). Berry and Taylor studied the relationship between elicited imitation and production to determine whether these performance tasks would produce similar assessments of linguistic knowledge. The subjects were 17 special-school mentally retarded children with a mean CA of 137.12 months and a mean picture vocabulary age of 43.47 months. Thus mean IQ was not much over 30 in this sample. The imitation task consisted of a number of subtests including one that required sentence completion. Included in this task was input that varied in syntactic complexity. Moreover, most of the task responses were weighted in scoring so as to take into account systematic syntactic and semantic errors.

Pictures were used to elicit speech production from the children. The pictures depicted a variety of objects and events, some of them anomalous. Needless to say, performance on such a task depends heavily on the perceptual encoding capabilities, strategies, and styles of subjects. The productions were weighted in scoring so as to reflect differing levels of linguistic competence; for example, a relevant telegraphic response was not assigned as high a score as was a relevant expanded grammatical response.

CA was not found to predict either imitation or production performance in this study but the estimate of verbal MA was significantly related to both imitation and production. In addition, imitation task performance correlated significantly with production (r's varied from .605 to .806 between the overall imitation score and the situations depicted in the pictures). Finally, Berry and Taylor reported, without presenting detailed data, however, similarities between specific features of performance on both imitation and production.

Thus these findings suggest that individual differences in linguistic competence are a factor in linguistic elicited imitation performance. Presumably, however, short-term memory capabilities also contributed to imitation performance in this study (but see Berry's discussion of short-term memory and imitation performance in his 1976 book and the study by Lamberts & Burns, 1979).

Basic research has established that a major factor in memory for linguistic input is the extent to which the content of the input is assimilated to established knowledge schemata (see, for example, the review by Bransford & McCarrell, 1974). Furthermore, this work has indicated that language users typically make use of all their constructive comprehension capabilities, including inference making and input integration, in this assimilation process.

Similar phenomena have been observed to occur in nonretarded elementary school-age children, as Paris, Mahoney, and Buckholt (1974) pointed out in the introduction to an article on semantic integration in the sentence memory of special-class and potential special-class mentally retarded children. These investigators tested 20 retarded children in the CA range 127 to 161 months (IQs 62–88) and 20 in the CA range 89 to 126 months (IQs 52–78) who were subdivided into CA- and MA-matched experimental and control groups. The experimental/control contrast here was the presence or absence of imagery instructions in a second task. Task 1 involved the memorization and subsequent recognition of sentences presented in story contexts. A recognition set contained a sentence that was true (with reference to the original story), one that was false, a true inference, and a false inference. Task 2 was identical to Task 1 with the exception that different acquisition stories were presented and the experimental subjects were instructed to use imagery in encoding the acquisition sentences.

The effects of age and group (experimental versus control) were nonsignificant on Task 1. The retarded subjects in this study, however, demonstrated a significant tendency to incorrectly recognize "nonpresented true inferences as original acquisition sentences [p. 717]," thus supporting earlier observations with nonretarded adults and children. On Task 2, recognition errors on true inferences occurred significantly more frequently in the experimental group than they did in the control group. Such errors, however, dominated recognition responding in both groups. Other findings indicated that the imagery instructions had facilitated original learning (see, in addition, the results of a study by Riding & Shore, 1974).

The studies reviewed here were those that it was thought might tell us something about basic processes in the mentally retarded in memory for linguistic input. Other aspects of memory as it relates to language have been investigated by Lent, Holvoet, Ferneti, Keilitz, and Tucker (1973), Reid and Kiernan (1979), and Bryant (1965a, 1965b, 1967). It should be clear, on the basis of the studies we have been discussing, that investigators have only just begun to scratch the surface of the problem of memory for linguistic input in mentally retarded individuals.

Discussion

Has our understanding of language competence and the development of language competence in the mentally retarded been enhanced by research on language performance processes? Clearly, on the basis of the research reviewed here, only to a limited extent. We have seen that we are far from a thorough understanding of the presumed passivity of mentally retarded individuals; that, for all intents and purposes, speech planning and execution processes have yet to be investigated in the area of mental retardation; that, frequently, performance processes cannot be assessed due to failure to control for differences in linguistic competence between retarded and nonretarded subjects; and that we have only just begun to examine speech comprehension processes and memory for linguistic input in a reliable fashion.

There are some positive notes to sound, however. First, I found facinating the observation by Paris, Mahoney, and Buckholt (1974) that memory for concrete sentences is inferential in mildly retarded children varying in CA and facilitated by an imagery mnemonic, for it is inconsistent with expectations derived from the passivity hypothesis. Thus linguistic inference making and the variables that influence it need to be thoroughly investigated in the area of mental retardation. Second, the use of elicited imitation procedures to assess linguistic knowledge in mentally retarded children has been to some extent validated by the research of Berry and Taylor (1976). Third, what little we know about language performance processes in the mentally retarded has not infirmed the developmental lag hypothesis; that is, language production and comprehension skills appear to keep pace with each other. Finally, we should be encouraged to study further the relationship between cerebral lateralization and language functioning in the mentally retarded, given the findings reported by Sommers and Starkey (1977).

THE LINGUISTIC ENVIRONMENT

Much interest has been shown in recent years in the nature of the linguistic input the young nonretarded language learning child receives. Behind this interest is, in many instances, the hope that language acquisition will be found to be the result, mainly, of environmental shaping. This work has indicated that contrary to earlier rationalist claims (Chomsky, 1965) the linguistic input in early language acquisition is not complex, ill-formed, filled with dysfluencies, and variable but, rather, displays much that is simple, well-formed, fluent, and stable. Mothers have been observed to make a variety of adjustments in their speech to their young language learning children (Snow & Ferguson, 1977).

It seems likely, however, that the adjustments mothers make in talking to their young language learning babies serve mainly to establish and maintain conversation (Brown, 1977; Snow, 1977) rather than to teach the local language, If some of these adjustments do serve to facilitate language acquisition, then they appear to do so in a complex manner that is to a significant extent filtered through whatever cognitive biases (linguistic and nonlinguistic) the child brings to the situation (Newport, Gleitman, & Gleitman, 1977). Thus the literature on mother–child interactions in language acquisition has not produced evidence of *simple functional relations* between aspects of linguistic input and features of language acquisition. This is not to say, of course, that linguistic environments cannot be more or less adequate vis-à-vis language acquisition. Clearly, aspects of what mothers say to their children during the early stages of language acquisition, the manner in which they speak, and the circumstances under which they speak must constitute a significant portion of the *raw material* for language acquisition.

Interest in studying the linguistic environment of young mentally retarded individuals has increased as a result of the amount of effort directed toward this topic in developmental psycholinguistics. Buium, Rynders, and Turnure (1974) studied five mother–nonretarded child and six mother–retarded (Down's syndrome) child pairs. The children were 24 months of age in both groups. Moreover, the groups were matched on the family variables of socioeconomic status, maternal IQ (at least 90), bilingualism/monolingualism (all subjects were monolingual), and sensory status. Recordings on audiovideo tape were made of mother–child interactions in various situations. The data analyzed consisted of a random sample of utterances of equal length from each mother's corpus of utterances. The total data base, however, was relatively small. The grammatical structures produced were assigned to developmental levels based upon results of developmental findings with nonretarded children. In addition, these investigators examined certain sentential structures, vocabulary diversity, and measures of productivity. Unfortunately, no attempt was made to examine the children's utterances that, one would have to assume based upon previous research, were *substantially more mature in the group that contained the nonretarded children.* Thus any differences between the two groups could reflect the impact of disability status (or labeling) or differences in developmental status. What is needed, of course, is a group of mothers with Down's children whose children's MLUs match those of the nonretarded children.

By and large, the mothers in both groups produced utterances that are believed to be among the early achievements of language development. Among the significant differences reported by these investigators were: (1) lower MLUs; (2) more grammatically incomplete sentences; and (3) more single-word sentences in two situations among the mothers of the Down's children. On the basis of their findings, Buium et al. concluded that Down's children must make use of "linguistic data that are somewhat different than the data provided to normal children [p. 57]." Unfortunately, this conclusion does not follow from the differences observed. For one thing, we do not know what such differences mean vis-à-vis the language acquisition process; second, we have no way of knowing whether the differences in question were a reflection of the lower developmental status of the Down's children or the fact that their parents knew they were Down's children.

The linguistic environment of a severely language-delayed male child between the ages of 4;0 and 5;0, who may have been mentally retarded as well, was studied by Cramblit and Siegel (1977). He was compared with a normal female cousin of similar CA. The adults in the study were the language-delayed child's parents and a young aunt. The adults' speech was recorded in short free-play and storytelling situations as well as during a conversation with the experimenter. In the main, the adults in this study tended to make adjustments in their speech to the language-delayed child that "are similar to the kinds of adjustments mothers are reported to make when talking with their young [normal] language-learning children [p. 480]."

Mother–infant interactions were observed by Buckholt, Rutherford, and Goldberg (1978). The subjects were 10 mother–Down's syndrome retarded and 10 mother–nonretarded pairs. The mothers in the two groups, as well as the infants, did not differ significantly in CA. Mean CA was 13.5 months (SD = 2.63) for the Down's infants and 12.5 months (SD = 3.79) for the nonretarded infants, and each group contained both males and females. Mean MA (estimated from the Bayley Mental Development Index) was 13.6 and 8.0 months, respectively, for the nonretarded and Down's syndrome infants. All the subjects were from middle-income families. Observations were made of both linguistic and nonlinguistic interactions. Of particular interest was the mothers' performance during a "direct teaching task."

Although the mothers of the Down's infants produced significantly more utterances than did the mothers of the nonretarded infants in the teaching situation, the two groups of mothers did not differ in MLU (the measure of language complexity). Moreover, infants' MAs, but not CAs, correlated positively with MLUs in both groups. Similar correlations were reported for another measure, number of utterances, although the r did not reach significance in the Down's group. The behavior of the mothers vis-à-vis responsiveness did not differ in a noninstructional situation, although the Down's infants appear to have been less responsive to their mothers than were the nonretarded infants to theirs. In addition, there was evidence that in this situation "mothers did more talking to older and more competent babies within groups [p. 341]."

As far as the measure of language complexity (mothers' MLUs) is concerned, the present study did not confirm Buium et al.'s (1974) finding for 24-month-old nonretarded children, who were observed to receive longer utterances on the average. Thus mothers' linguistic adjustments appear to reflect the developmental maturity of their children regardless of whether they are nonretarded or retarded. This finding, moreover, was confirmed by Rondal (1978) in a more extensive investigation of nonretarded and Down's syndrome children and their mothers in the home environment (see also Guralnick & Paul-Brown, 1977, 1980; Gutmann & Rondal, 1979).

Conclusions

It seems likely on the basis of these findings that mothers adjust their speech to young language learning mentally retarded children in a fashion similar to the way in which they adjust their speech to young language learning nonretarded children. Moreover, there is evidence that the complexity of mothers' speech increases as a function of the developmental status of their children regardless of whether they are nonretarded or retarded. Finally, although there is some evidence that young retarded Down's children are less responsive to their mothers than are young nonretarded children, there is no way at present to determine the role reduced responsiveness may play in language acquisition. The fact of its occurrence, of course, is consistent with the presumed trait of passivity.

LANGUAGE TRAINING

We have in the area of language intervention a serious programmatic literature (see, for example, the many chapters that deal with language training in Schiefelbusch, 1978; Schiefelbusch & Lloyd, 1974) that has been generated by behavioral scientists and language clinicians. I shall not attempt, however, to describe and evaluate this work within the confines of a short section on language intervention in the mentally retarded. Instead I shall attempt to provide the reader with a picture of what I believe to be a representative sample of the journal research literature I came across during the course of my literature search for the present chapter. Some reviews of the earlier research using operant procedures are available (Cooke, Cooke, & Apolloni, 1976; Snyder, Lovitt, & Smith, 1975).

An excellent example of the application of operant conditioning procedures to language training in severely retarded children can be found in a study by Baer and Guess (1973; see also their references) in which an attempt was made to train four severely retarded children (CAs 11-16) in the productive use of nouns derived from verbs (e.g., *farms-farmer, hunts-hunter*) by the addition of the bound morpheme *er*. Pictures displaying the actions depicted by 57 verbs were used in training. Procedures were used to determine ahead of time that each subject could imitate examples of nominals ending in *er* and *ist*. Subsequent pretesting established that the subjects could not produce, where called for, a sample of derived nominals ending in *er*. A variety of social and other stimuli were used as reinforcers for correct responding.

In the first of three conditions, training involved the following (1) The experimenter described the action in a presented picture (e.g., "This man writes."). (2) The experimenter then provided, for example, the stimulus "He is a . . . ?", to which the subject was expected to respond with the appropriate nominal (e.g., "writer"). (3) A correct response was reinforced by the experimenter; in the case of an incorrect response, he uttered "No" and followed this with the correct noun and, 10 sec later, with another presentation of picture and verbal description. (4) Although rarely used, "If no response was given within 10 seconds on any trial, the experimenter would model the correct verb-suffix label, and reinforce the subject for a correct imitation [p. 500]." (5) "Criterion for each word trained was five correct consecutive responses" and "Training continued in this way until it appeared that the subject would reliably give the correct noun on the first five trials of each new verb presented [p. 500]."

Condition II involved training on the verbs with the incorrect suffix *ist* in order to identify the general effectiveness of the operant procedures. Condition III was a repetition of Condition I.

Scoring reliability for subjects' responses was found to be quite high (94–100%). Training under each condition was considered to have been successful. Moreover, all subjects were able eventually to use the trained suffix on new verbs without error.

Unfortunately, these findings are not without their problems, some of which the authors themselves were quick to point out. First, no attempt was made to assess generalization beyond the conditions of the study or to assess "the durability of training effects over time [p. 505]." Second, no attempt was made to evaluate the contribution of the pictures and their relation to the comprehension of the linguistic input. Third, there is no way to identify the contribution of the subjects in this study. Fourth, we have no way of knowing whether the subjects had any appreciation of the complex semantics of the derived nominals used in this study. Fifth, there is always the possibility, given what we know about language acquisition generally, that there exist interventions that are more effective than operant procedures that, in addition, may not necessarily require overt responding during training. It would have been interesting, for example, to have presented the essential information regarding the derived nominals (and the verbs themselves, of course) in the context of a narrated motion picture film prior to testing. Sixth, it needs to be pointed out that no attempt was made to assess systematically the linguistic competence of the children in this study prior to training to determine what progress, if any, they were making with the development of grammatical morphemes generally and the precursors (sentential and lexical) of the mastery of grammatical morphology. Finally, it is not clear whether the reinforcement served to strengthen the linguistic behavior or to increase the likelihood that the subjects would actively process the linguistic (and situational) input (i.e., that their presumed passivity would be attenuated).

Thus there is no way to determine whether the subjects in this study (and in many others like it, for that matter; see, for example, Smeets & Striefel, 1976, and references cited by Baer & Guess) were learning language at all.

The use of modeling, imitation, reinforcement, and multiple examples in a situation in which nonlinguistic contextual cues to meaning were available was demonstrated by Jeffree, Wheldall, and Mittler (1973) in an attempt to facilitate two-word utterances in two Down's syndrome boys who were functioning at the stage of single-word utterances at the beginning of the study. Of particular interest in this study was the experimental development of two-word utterances of the "open-pivot" variety (e.g., *shoe gone, bus gone*). Unfortunately, sample size, absence of a control condition in which no training occurred, and limited opportunity to observe transfer outside the experimental situation made it difficult to evaluate fully the effectiveness of the training procedures in this study. The investigators reported that the program was effective during original training and in facilitating production of novel "open-pivot" constructions in the experimental situation.

Verb–noun instruction-following skills in two institutionalized severely retarded boys (12-year-olds) were trained by Striefel, Wetherby, and Karlan (1976) and observed to generalize to untrained verb–noun instructions using an elaborately controlled program. Correct responses (actions on objects) were reinforced throughout the study. Modeling and guidance facilitated establishment of the required nonlinguistic behaviors as well as their transfer to the verbal instructions. A limitation of this study, however, as the authors point out, is that the subjects had "had a history of about 2 consecutive years of training [p. 259]." Thus it remains to be determined whether subjects without such a history can benefit from the verbal comprehension training employed in this study.

Parent-assisted language intervention procedures involving imitation, conversation, and play have been utilized by MacDonald, Blott, Gordon, Speigel, and Hartmann (1974) in an attempt to facilitate development in utterance length and complexity beyond the two-word stage of language acquisition in an experimental and a control group of Down's children. However, although these investigators reported positive achievements, some important details were omitted from the description of their study, and as a result it is not possible to evaluate fully the outcome of their efforts. I did not find it possible, for example, to determine the extent of their trained subjects' *productive* control of the multimorphemic semantic relational types under investigation. Were the children acquiring rules or increasing their repertoires of routines (see my earlier discussion of Dooley's 1976 dissertation)?

Twenty-four mildly retarded language-delayed children in the CA range 3;1 to 4;9 from the clinical population of a speech and hearing facility participated in a training study by Leonard (1975) involving basic two-word semantic relational structures. At the beginning of the study, the children were functioning at the one-word stage of language development. Modeling and reinforcement procedures were combined in a traditional experimental design (rather than a single-subject operant procedure) in order to study the effects of nonlinguistic situational support and number of semantic relations underlying subject–verb utterances on the acquisition of semantic relational structures. In this investigation, situational support was found to facilitate the mildly retarded children's use of subject–verb utterances. Thus, not surprisingly, exposure to appropriate lexical items and word order alone was not enough to ensure acquisition of semantic relational forms.

Other studies identified during the course of my literature search for the present chapter that were concerned with language intervention in the mentally retarded were, for example, a study by Taylor, Thurlow, and Turnure (1977) of vocabulary training through verbal elaboration, one by Cheseldine and McConkey (1979) in which parents participated, one by Palyo, Cooke, Schuler, and Apolloni (1979) that was concerned with the modification of echolalic speech, and finally an investigation by Walsh and Lamberts (1979) of procedures for teaching sight words.

Discussion

The research we have reviewed in the present section (in combination with what we already know and suspect regarding language development and functioning in the mentally retarded) has revealed many more questions and proposals for future research than it has conclusions that we can feel confident about. Some of the more obvious questions and proposals are listed below.

1. Because linguistic input does not appear to be impoverished in the case of retarded children who are being raised by their parents at home, research in language training should concentrate on identifying child-environment interactions that can compensate to whatever extent is possible for internal limitations. The question, in other words, is how can a retarded child be led to engage in linguistic and other information processing activities that will facilitate language acquisition?
2. How do retarded children's cognitive capacities generally interact with language intervention procedures? Will it become necessary, in other words, to adapt such procedures to a retarded child's developmental potential?
3. Language training programs for the retarded should include procedures for compensating to whatever extent is possible for such performance limitations as memory and passivity.
4. Do mentally retarded children at a given cognitive level display similar or different language acquisition strategies?
5. The short-range goals of laboratory language training studies should be augmented to include generalization to representative everyday language performance.
6. What is the role of language comprehension training in the acquisition of linguistic productive capabilities?
7. Should linguistic structures be trained one at a time or simultaneously so as to reflect the course of language development in retarded children who develop appreciable linguistic competence?
8. Language training procedures for the mentally retarded should reflect what we know about the differential rates of development of different features of language (recall, for example, our earlier observations regarding the development of the grammatical morphemes and complex sentence-combining operations).
9. Can language training procedures make possible the achievement of ma-

ture linguistic and communicative competence in mildly retarded individuals?
10. More attention should be paid to the experimental evaluation of alternatives to operant conditioning procedures for language training. The use of second-language learning procedures in the case of moderately and mildly retarded adolescents, for example, to enhance language development should be examined.
11. In view of the fact that language appears to develop in a similar fashion in nonretarded and mentally retarded children, it may prove possible to evaluate experimentally hypotheses concerning language training procedures for the mentally retarded more easily and in less time in MLU-matched nonretarded children, with only occasional checks for generalizability with retarded subjects.

It should be obvious from the nature of these questions and proposals that we have our work cut out for us in the field of language training for the mentally retarded.

GENERAL DISCUSSION

Many methodological and other problems were uncovered during the course of my examination of a number of the recent and earlier studies of the language of the mentally retarded. I have nothing more to say about these problems, however, because I believe it is more important at this point to offer some summary statements on what appears to be needed in the way of future research in this area. The more pressing needs are for the following:

1. More detailed information on the course of development of specific features of all aspects of linguistic and communicative knowledge and performance in individual mentally retarded children.
2. A thorough assessment of the final achievements in linguistic and communicative knowledge and performance in moderately and mildly retarded adults.
3. Research that will identify the source or sources of the mentally retarded individual's difficulties in the domains of grammatical morphology and sentence-combining operations.
4. Analytic research on the relations between specific features of mothers' speech to young language learning mentally retarded children and specific features of their retarded children's speech.
5. Studies of the development of abstract lexical items.
6. Information on the relationship between linguistic and communicative capabilities in the mentally retarded.

7. Research into the correlates and antecedents of the observed memorial limitations and passivity of the mentally retarded.
8. Research that will reveal the strategies mentally retarded children employ in acquiring language.
9. A thorough examination of the relations between specific aspects of nonlinguistic and linguistic cognitive development and functioning in the mentally retarded.
10. More experimental *psycholinguistic* research on language intervention.

Problems and research needs aside, it seems reasonable to offer as a working conclusion, on the basis of the work reviewed in the present chapter, the generalization that mental retardation is a disorder that involves a quantitative lag in the development of nonlinguistic, linguistic, and communicative cognitive knowledge with associated performance deficits. The performance deficits that have been tentatively identified are memorial and motivational. Moreover, particularly at risk as far as linguistic knowledge is concerned are grammatical morphology and sentence-combining operations.

Other working conclusions that should be mentioned here are listed.

1. No convincing case has been made for the frequent claim that certain nonlinguistic achievements necessarily antedate and/or pace language development in the mentally retarded.
2. Mothers' speech to young language learning mentally retarded children has not been shown to differ from mothers' speech to young language learning nonretarded children.
3. Etiology per se does not appear to be implicated in language development and functioning in the mentally retarded.
4. There is no evidence thus far that mentally retarded children who acquire some degree of mastery of syntactic, semantic, phonological, and pragmatic knowledge utilize language acquisition strategies that differ from those that nonretarded children appear to use.

At this point, it would be constructive to compare the previous conclusions with those of earlier reviewers (Cromer, 1974; Rosenberg, 1970; Schiefelbusch, 1974; Yoder & Miller, 1972). Constraints on space and time, however, dictate that I leave the task of comparing reviewers' conclusions to the interested reader.

ACKNOWLEDGMENTS

Work on this chapter was supported in part by the Illinois Institute for Developmental Disabilities, Dr. Kenneth R. Swiatek, Director. I am indebted to Leonard Abbeduto for his critical reading of the manuscript.

REFERENCES

Anglin, J. M. *Word, object, and conceptual development.* New York: Norton, 1977.
Baer, D. M., & Guess, D. Teaching productive noun suffixes to severely retarded children. *American Journal of Mental Deficiency,* 1973, *77,* 498-505.
Bartel, N. R., Bryen, D., & Keehn, S. Language comprehension in the mentally retarded child. *Exceptional Children,* 1973, *39,* 375-382.
Bartolucci, G., & Pierce, S. J. A preliminary comparison of phonological development in autistic, normal, and mentally retarded subjects. *British Journal of Disorders of Communication,* 1977, *12,* 137-147.
Bates, E. Pragmatics and sociolinguistics in child language. In D. M. Morehead & A. E. Morehead (Eds.), *Normal and deficient child language.* Baltimore, Md.: University Park Press, 1976.
Bedrosian, J. L., & Prutting, C. A. Communicative performance of mentally retarded adults in four conversational settings. *Journal of Speech and Hearing Research,* 1978, *21,* 79-95.
Bender, N. L., & Johnson, N. S. Hierarchical semantic organization in educable mentally retarded children. *Journal of Experimental Child Psychology,* 1979, *27,* 277-285.
Berko, J. The child's learning of English morphology. *Word,* 1958, *14,* 150-177.
Berry, P. (Ed.). *Language and communication in the mentally handicapped.* London: Edward Arnold, 1976.
Berry, P., & Foxen, T. Imitation and comprehension of language in severe subnormality. *Language and Speech,* 1975, *18,* 195-203.
Berry, P., & Taylor, J. Elicited imitation and production of language in severely subnormal children. *Language and Speech,* 1976, *19,* 160-172.
Beveridge, M. C., & Mittler, P. Feedback, language and listener performance in severely retarded children. *British Journal of Disorders of Communication,* 1977, *12,* 149-157.
Beveridge, M. C., & Tatham, A. Communication in retarded adolescents: Utilization of known language skills. *American Journal of Mental Deficiency,* 1976, *81,* 96-99.
Blank, M. Mastering the intangible through language. In D. Aaronson & R. W. Rieber (Eds.), *Developmental psycholinguistics and communication disorders. Annals of the New York Academy of Sciences,* 1975, *263,* 44-58.
Bliss, L. S., Allen, D. V., & Walker, G. Sentence structures of trainable and educable mentally retarded subjects. *Journal of Speech and Hearing Research,* 1978, *21,* 722-731.
Bowerman, M. F. Cross-linguistic similarities at two stages of syntactic development. In E. H. Lenneberg & E. Lenneberg (Eds.), *Foundations of language development* (Vol. 1). New York: Academic Press, 1975.
Bowerman, M. F. Semantic and syntactic development. In R. L. Schiefelbusch (Ed.), *Bases of language intervention.* Baltimore, Md.: University Park Press, 1978.
Bransford, J. D., & McCarrell, N. S. A sketch of a cognitive approach to comprehension: Some thoughts about understanding what it means to comprehend. In W. B. Weimer & D. S. Palermo (Eds.), *Cognition and the symbolic processes.* Hillsdale, N.J.: Lawrence Erlbaum Associates, 1974.
Brown, A. L., & Barclay, C. R. The effects of training specific mnemonics on the metamnemonic efficiency of retarded children. *Child Development,* 1976, *47,* 71-80.
Brown, R. *A first language: The early stages.* Cambridge, Mass.: Harvard University Press, 1973.
Brown, R. Introduction. In C. E. Snow & C. A. Ferguson (Eds.), *Talking to children.* Cambridge: Cambridge University Press, 1977.
Bryant, P. E. The effects of verbal labelling on recall and recognition in severely subnormal and normal children. *Journal of Mental Deficiency Research,* 1965, *9,* 229-236. (a)
Bryant, P. E. The effects of verbal labelling on recognition of pictures and names in severely subnormal and normal children. *Journal of Mental Deficiency Research,* 1965, *9,* 237-244. (b)

Bryant, P. E. Verbalization and immediate memory of complex stimuli in normal and severely subnormal children. *British Journal of Social and Clinical Psychology,* 1967, *6,* 212-219.

Buckholt, J. A., Rutherford, R. B., & Goldberg, K. E. Verbal and nonverbal interaction of mothers with their Down's syndrome and nonretarded infants. *American Journal of Mental Deficiency,* 1978, *82,* 337-343.

Buium, N., Rynders, J., & Turnure, J. Early maternal linguistic environment of normal and Down's syndrome language-learning children. *American Journal of Mental Deficiency,* 1974, *79,* 52-58.

Butterfield, E. C., & Belmont, J. M. The role of verbal processes in short-term memory. In R. L. Schiefelbusch (Ed.), *Language of the mentally retarded.* Baltimore, Md.: University Park Press, 1972.

Carroll, J. B. Psychometric tests as cognitive tasks: A new "structure of intellect." In L. B. Resnick (Ed.), *The nature of intelligence.* Hillsdale, N.J.: Lawrence Erlbaum Associates, 1976.

Carrow, M. A. The development of auditory comprehension of language structure in children. *Journal of Speech and Hearing Disorders,* 1968, *33,* 99-111.

Chafe, W. L. *Meaning and the structure of language.* Chicago: University of Chicago Press, 1970.

Cheseldine, S., & McConkey, R. Parental speech to young Down's syndrome children: An intervention study. *American Journal of Mental Deficiency,* 1979, *83,* 612-620.

Chomsky, N. *Aspects of the theory of syntax.* Cambridge, Mass.: MIT Press, 1965.

Clark, R. Performing without competence. *Journal of Child Language,* 1974, *1,* 1-10.

Clark, H. H., & Clark, E. V. *Psychology and language.* New York: Harcourt Brace Jovanovich, 1977.

Coggins, T. E. Relational meaning encoded in the two-word utterances of Stage 1 Down's syndrome children. *Journal of Speech and Hearing Research,* 1979, *22,* 166-178.

Cohen, R. L., & Sandberg, T. Relation between intelligence and short-term memory. *Cognitive Psychology,* 1977, *9,* 534-554.

Cooke, S., Cooke, T. P., & Apolloni, T. Generalization of language training with the mentally retarded. *Journal of Special Education,* 1976, *10,* 299-304.

Cornwell, A. C. Development of language, abstraction, and numerical concept formation in Down's syndrome children. *American Journal of Mental Deficiency,* 1974, *79,* 179-190.

Corrigan, R. Language development as related to stage 6 object permanence development. *Journal of Child Language,* 1978, *5,* 173-190.

Cramblit, N. S., & Siegel, G. M. The verbal environment of a language-impaired child. *Journal of Speech and Hearing Disorders,* 1977, *42,* 474-483.

Cromer, R. F. Receptive language in the mentally retarded: Processes and diagnostic distinctions. In R. L. Schiefelbusch & L. L. Lyoyd (Eds.), *Language perspectives—Acquisition, retardation, and intervention.* Baltimore, Md.: University Park Press, 1974.

Cromer, R. F. Are subnormals linguistic adults? In N. O'Connor (Ed.), *Language, cognitive deficits, and retardation.* London: Butterworths, 1975.

Dever, R. A comparison of the results of a revised version of Berko's test of morphology with the free speech of mentally retarded children. *Journal of Speech and Hearing Research,* 1972, *15,* 169-178.

Dever, R., & Gardner, W. I. Performance of normal and retarded boys on Berko's test of morphology. *Language and Speech,* 1970, *13,* 162-181.

Dewart, M. H. Language comprehension processes of mentally retarded children. *American Journal of Mental Deficiency,* 1979, *84,* 177-183.

Dodd, B. Recognition and reproduction of words by Down's syndrome and non-Down's syndrome retarded children. *American Journal of Mental Deficiency,* 1975, *80,* 306-311.

Dodd, B. A comparison of the phonological systems of mental age matched normal, severely subnormal and Down's syndrome children. *British Journal of Disorders of Communication,* 1976, *11,* 27-42.

Donaldson, M. *Children's minds.* Glasgow: Fontana/Collins, 1978.

Dooley, J. F. *Language acquisition and Down's syndrome: A study of early semantics and syntax.* Unpublished doctoral dissertation. Harvard University, 1976.

Duchan, J. F., & Erickson, J. G. Normal and retarded children's understanding of semantic relations in different verbal contexts. *Journal of Speech and Hearing Research,* 1976, *19,* 767-776.

Dugas, J. L., & Kellas, G. Encoding and retrieval processes in normal children and retarded adolescents. *Journal of Experimental Child Psychology,* 1974, *17,* 177-185.

Evans, D. The development of language abilities in mongols: A correlational study. *Journal of Mental Deficiency Research,* 1977, *21,* 103-117.

Flowers, D. M. Expansion and the intelligibility of speech by blind and sighted, nonretarded and retarded individuals. *American Journal of Mental Deficiency,* 1974, *78,* 619-624.

Folger, M. K., & Leonard, L. B. Language and sensorimotor development during the early period of referential speech. *Journal of Speech and Hearing Research,* 1978, *21,* 519-527.

Foss, D. J., & Hakes, D. T. *Psycholinguistics.* Englewood Cliffs, N.J.: Prentice-Hall, 1978.

Glidden, L. M., & Mar, H. H. Availability and accessibility of information in the semantic memory of retarded and nonretarded adolescents. *Journal of Experimental Child Psychology,* 1978, *25,* 33-40.

Graham, N. C. Short term memory and syntactic structure in educationally subnormal children. *Language and Speech,* 1968, *11,* 209-219.

Graham, J. T., & Graham, L. W. Language behavior of the mentally retarded: Syntactic characteristics. *American Journal of Mental Deficiency,* 1971, *75,* 623-629.

Greenough, D. *Comprehension and imitation of sentences by institutionalized trainable mentally retarded children as a function of transformational complexity.* Ann Arbor: Center for Research on Language and Language Behavior (University of Michigan), 1968, (ERIC Document Reproduction Service No. ED 030 235).

Grossman, H. J. (Ed.). *Manual on terminology and classification in mental retardation.* Washington, D.C.: American Association on Mental Deficiency, 1973.

Guralnick, M. J., & Paul-Brown, D. The nature of verbal interactions among handicapped and nonhandicapped preschool children. *Child Development,* 1977, *48,* 254-260.

Guralnick, M. J., & Paul-Brown, D. Functional and discourse analyses of nonhandicapped preschool children's speech to handicapped children. *American Journal of Mental Deficiency,* 1980, *84,* 444-454.

Gutmann, A. J., & Rondal, J. A. Verbal operants in mothers' speech to nonretarded and Down's syndrome children matched for linguistic level. *American Journal of Mental Deficiency,* 1979, *83,* 446-452.

Harrison, R. H., Budoff, M., & Greenberg, G. Differences between EMR and nonretarded children in fluency and quality of verbal associations. *American Journal of Mental Deficiency,* 1975, *79,* 583-591.

Horn, J. L. Human abilities: A review of research and theory in the early 1970s. *Annual Review of Psychology,* 1976, *27,* 437-485.

Hoy, E. A., & McKnight, J. R. Communication style and effectiveness in homogeneous dyads of retarded children. *American Journal of Mental Deficiency,* 1977, *81,* 587-598.

Ingram, D. *Phonological disability in children.* New York: Elsevier, 1976.

Jeffree, D., Wheldall, K., & Mittler, P. Facilitating two-word utterances in two Down's syndrome boys. *American Journal of Mental Deficiency,* 1973, *78,* 117-122.

Johnson-Laird, P. N. Commentary. In N. O'Connor (Ed.), *Language, cognitive deficits, and retardation.* London: Butterworths, 1975.

Kahn, J. V. Relationship of Piaget's sensorimotor period to language acquisition of profoundly retarded children. *American Journal of Mental Deficiency,* 1975, *79,* 640-643.

Klein, N. K., & Safford, P. L. Application of Piaget's theory to the study of thinking of the mentally retarded: A review of research. *Journal of Special Education,* 1977, *11,* 201-216.

Klima, E. Negation in English. In J. A. Fodor & J. J. Katz (Eds.), *The structure of language: Readings in the philosophy of language.* Englewood Cliffs, N.J.: Prentice-Hall, 1964.

Lackner, J. R. A developmental study of language behavior in retarded children. *Neuropsychologia,* 1968, *6,* 301–320.
Lamberts, F., & Burns, M. Observations on elicited language imitation with the severely retarded. *Language and Speech,* 1979, *22,* 21–35.
Lamberts, F., & Weener, P. D. TMR children's competence in processing negation. *American Journal of Mental Deficiency,* 1976, *81,* 181–186.
Layton, T. L., & Sharifi, H. Meaning and structure of Down's syndrome and nonretarded children's spontaneous speech. *American Journal of Mental Deficiency,* 1979, *83,* 439–445.
Lee, L. L. *Developmental sentence analysis.* Evanston, Ill.: Northwestern University Press, 1974.
Lenneberg, E. H., Nichols, I. A., & Rosenberger, E. F. Primitive stages of language development in mongolism. *Disorders of Communication,* 1964, Vol. XLII: Research Publications, A.R.N.M.D., 119–137.
Lent, J. R., Holvoet, J. F., Ferneti, C. I., Keilitz, I., & Tucker, D. J. Direction following of retarded and nonretarded adolescents. *American Journal of Mental Deficiency,* 1973, *78,* 316–322.
Leonard, L. B. Relational meaning and the facilitation of slow-learning children's language. *American Journal of Mental Deficiency,* 1975, *80,* 180–185.
Leonard, L. B., Cole, B., & Steckol, K. F. Lexical usage of retarded children: An examination of informativeness. *American Journal of Mental Deficiency,* 1979, *84,* 49–54.
Lieber, C. W., & Spitz, H. H. Inference of word meaning from syntax structure by normal children and retarded adolescents. *Journal of Psychology,* 1976, *93,* 3–12.
Longhurst, T. M. Communication in retarded adolescents: Sex and intelligence level. *American Journal of Mental Deficiency,* 1974, *78,* 607–618.
Longhurst, T. M., & Berry, G. W. Communication in retarded adolescents: Response to listener feedback. *American Journal of Mental Deficiency,* 1975, *80,* 158–164.
Lovell, K., & Bradbury, B. The learning of English morphology in educationally subnormal special school children. *American Journal of Mental Deficiency,* 1967, *72,* 609–615.
Lozar, B., Wepman, J. M., & Hass, W. Syntactic indices of language use of mentally retarded and normal children. *Language and Speech,* 1973, *16,* 22–33.
Lyle, J. G. The effect of an institution environment upon the verbal development of imbecile children: I. Verbal intelligence. *Journal of Mental Deficiency Research,* 1959, *3,* 122–128.
Lyle, J. G. The effect of an institution environment upon the verbal development of imbecile children. II. Speech and language. *Journal of Mental Deficiency Research,* 1960, *4,* 1–13.
Lyle, J. G. Comparison of language of normal and imbecile children. *Journal of Mental Deficiency Research,* 1961, *5,* 40–51.
MacDonald, J. D., Blott, J. P., Gordon, K., Spiegel, B., & Hartmann, M. An experimental parent-assisted treatment program for preschool language-delayed children. *Journal of Speech and Hearing Disorders,* 1974, *39,* 395–415.
McCauley, C., Sperber, R. D., & Roaden, S. K. Verification of property statements by retarded and nonretarded adolescents. *American Journal of Mental Deficiency,* 1978, *83,* 276–282.
Miller, J. F. *Assessing children's language behavior.* In R. L. Schiefelbusch (Ed.), *Bases of language intervention.* Baltimore, Md.: University Park Press, 1978.
Miller, J. F., Chapman, R. S., & Bedrosian, J. L. The relationship between cognitive development and language and communicative performance. *New Zealand Speech Therapist's Journal,* Nov. 1978.
Miller, J. F., Chapman, R. S., Branston, M. B., & Reichle, J. Language comprehension in sensorimotor stages V and VI. *Journal of Speech and Hearing Research,* 1980, *23,* 284–311.
Mein, R., & O'Connor, N. A study of oral vocabularies of severely subnormal patients. *Journal of Mental Deficiency Research,* 1960, *4,* 130–143.
Mein, R. A study of the oral vocabularies of severely subnormal patients. II. Grammatical analysis of speech samples. *Journal of Mental Deficiency Research,* 1961, *5,* 52–59.

Montague, J. C., Jr., Brown, W. S., Jr., & Hollien, H. Vocal fundamental frequency characteristics of institutionalized Down's syndrome children. *American Journal of Mental Deficiency,* 1974, *78,* 414–418.

Naremore, R. C., & Dever, R. B. Language performance of educable mentally retarded and normal children at five age levels. *Journal of Speech and Hearing Research,* 1975, *18,* 82–95.

Newfield, M. U., & Schlanger, B. B. The acquisition of English morphology by normal and educable mentally retarded children. *Journal of Speech and Hearing Research,* 1968, *11,* 693–706.

Newport, E. L., Gleitman, H., & Gleitman, L. R. Mother, I'd rather do it myself: Some effects and non-effects of maternal speech style. In C. E. Snow & C. A. Ferguson (Eds.), *Talking to children.* Cambridge: Cambridge University Press, 1977.

O'Connor, N. Cognitive processes and language ability in the severely retarded. In E. H. Lenneberg, & E. Lenneberg (Eds.), *Foundations of language development* (Vol. 1). New York: Academic Press, 1975.

Palyo, W. J., Cooke, T. P., Schuler, A. L., & Apolloni, T. Modifying echolalic speech in preschool children: Training and generalization. *American Journal of Mental Deficiency,* 1979, *83,* 480–489.

Papania, N. A qualitative analysis of vocabulary responses of institutionalized mentally retarded children. *Journal of Clinical Psychology,* 1954, *10,* 361–365.

Paris, S. G., Mahoney, G. J., & Buckholt, J. A. Facilitation of semantic integration in sentence memory of retarded children. *American Journal of Mental Deficiency,* 1974, *78,* 714–720.

Parisi, D., & Giannelli, W. Language and social environment at 2 years. *Merrill-Palmer Quarterly,* 1979, *25,* 61–75.

Pea, R. D. Can information theory explain early word choice? *Journal of Child Language,* 1979, *6,* 397–410.

Pennington, F. M., & Luszcz, M. A. Some fundamental properties of iconic storage in retarded and nonretarded subjects. *Memory & Cognition,* 1975, *3,* 295–301.

Price-Williams, D., & Sabsay, S. Communicative competence among severely retarded persons. *Semiotica,* 1979, *26,* 35–63.

Rees, N. S. Pragmatics of language. In R. L. Schiefelbusch (Ed.), *Bases of language intervention.* Baltimore, Md.: University Park Press, 1978.

Reid, B., & Kiernan, C. Spoken words and manual signs as encoding categories in short-term memory for mentally retarded children. *American Journal of Mental Deficiency,* 1979, *84,* 200–203.

Riding, R. J., & Shore, J. M. A comparison of two methods of improving prose comprehension in educationally subnormal children. *British Journal of Educational Psychology,* 1974, *44,* 300–303.

Rondal, J. A. Patterns of correlations for various language measures in mother-child interactions for normal and Down's syndrome children. *Language and Speech,* 1978, *21,* 242–252.

Rosenberg, S. Problems of language development in the retarded. In H. C. Haywood (Ed.), *Socialcultural aspects of mental retardation.* New York: Appleton-Century-Crofts, 1970.

Rosenberg, S. *Linguistic maturity and language development in elementary school-age children.* Chicago: Computer Psychometrics Affiliates, 1974. Mimeo.

Rosenberg, S. Semantic constraints on sentence production: An experimental approach. In S. Rosenberg (Ed.), *Sentence production: Developments in research and theory.* Hillsdale, N.J.: Lawrence Erlbaum Associates, 1977.

Rosenberg, S., & Jarvella, R. J. Semantic integration and sentence perception. *Journal of Verbal Learning and Verbal Behavior,* 1970, *9,* 548–553.

Ryan, J. Mental subnormality and language development. In E. H. Lenneberg & E. Lenneberg (Eds.), *Foundations of language development* (Vol. 2). New York: Academic Press, 1975.

Ryan, J. The silence of stupidity. In J. Morton & J. C. Marshall (Eds.), *Psycholinguistics: Developmental and pathological.* Ithaca, N.Y.: Cornell University Press, 1977.

Schiefelbusch, R. L. Language. In J. Wortis (Ed.), *Mental retardation and developmental disabilities: An annual review* (VI). New York: Bruner/Mazel, 1974.

Schiefelbusch, R. L. (Ed.). *Bases of language intervention.* Baltimore, Md.: University Park Press, 1978.

Schiefelbusch, R. L., & Lloyd, L. L. (Eds.). *Language perspectives—Acquisition, retardation, and intervention.* Baltimore, Md.: University Park Press, 1974.

Schlanger, B. B. *Mental retardation.* New York: Bobbs-Merrill, 1973.

Semmel, M. I., Barritt, L. S., & Bennett, S. W. Performance of EMR and nonretarded children in a modified cloze task. *American Journal of Mental Deficiency,* 1970, *74,* 681-688.

Semmel, M. I., Barritt, L. S., Bennett, S. W., & Perfetti, C. A. A grammatical analysis of word associations of educable mentally retarded and normal children. *American Journal of Mental Deficiency,* 1968, *72,* 567-576.

Semmel, M. I., & Dolley, D. G. Comprehension and imitation of sentences by Down's syndrome children as a function of transformational complexity. *American Journal of Mental Deficiency,* 1971, *75,* 739-745.

Shotick, A., & Blue, M. Influence of CA and IQ levels on structure and amount of spontaneous verbalization. *Psychological Reports,* 1971, *29,* 275-281.

Smeets, P. M., & Striefel, S. Training the generative usage of article-noun responses in severely retarded males. *Journal of Mental Deficiency Research,* 1976, *20,* 121-127.

Smith, N. V. *The acquisition of phonology.* Cambridge: Cambridge University Press, 1973.

Smith, N. V. Universal tendencies in the child's acquisition of phonology. In N. O'Connor (Ed.), *Language, cognitive deficits, and retardation.* London: Butterworths, 1975.

Smith, J. D., & Polloway, E. The dimension of adaptive behavior in mental retardation research: An analysis of recent practices. *American Journal of Mental Deficiency,* 1979, *84,* 203-206.

Snow, C. E. The development of conversation between mothers and babies. *Journal of Child Language,* 1977, *4,* 1-22.

Snow, C. E., & Ferguson, C. A. (Eds.). *Talking to children.* Cambridge: Cambridge University Press, 1977.

Sommers, R. K., & Starkey, K. L. Dichotic verbal processing in Down's syndrome children having qualitatively different speech and language skills. *American Journal of Mental Deficiency,* 1977, *82,* 44-53.

Snyder, L. K., Lovitt, T. C., & Smith, J. O. Language training for the severely retarded: Five years of behavior analysis research. *Exceptional Children,* 1975, *42,* 7-15.

Sperber, R. D., Ragain, R. D., & McCauley, C. Reassessment of category knowledge in retarded individuals. *American Journal of Mental Deficiency,* 1976, *81,* 227-234.

Stoel-Gammon, C. Phonological analysis of four Down's syndrome children. *Applied Psycholinguistics,* 1980, *1,* 31-48.

Striefel, S., Wetherby, B., & Karlan, G. R. Establishing generalized verb-noun instruction-following skills in retarded children. *Journal of Experimental Child Psychology,* 1976, *22,* 247-260.

Taylor, A. M., Thurlow, M. L., & Turnure, J. E. Vocabulary development of educable retarded children. *Exceptional Children,* 1977, *43,* 444-450.

Treisman, A., & Tuxworth, J. Immediate and delayed recall of sentences after perceptual processing at different levels. *Journal of Verbal Learning and Verbal Behavior,* 1974, *13,* 38-44.

Uzgiris, I. C., & Hunt, J. McV. *An instrument for assessing infant psychological development.* Unpublished manuscript, University of Illinois, 1966.

Walker, H. J., Roodin, P. A., & Lamb, M. J. Relationship between linguistic performance and memory deficits in retarded children. *American Journal of Mental Deficiency,* 1975, *79,* 545-552.

Walsh, B. F., & Lamberts, F. Errorless discrimination and picture fading as techniques for teaching sight words to TMR students. *American Journal of Mental Deficiency,* 1979, *83,* 473-479.

Weil, C., McCauley, C., & Sperber, R. D. Category structure and semantic priming in retarded adolescents. *American Journal of Mental Deficiency,* 1978, *83,* 110-115.

Wheldall, K. Receptive language development in the mentally handicapped. In P. Berry (Ed.), *Language and communication in the mentally handicapped.* London: Edward Arnold, 1976.

Wheldall, K., & Mittler, P. On presenting pictures and sentences: The effect of presentation order on sentence comprehension in normal and mentally handicapped children. *British Journal of Educational Psychology,* 1977, *47,* 322-326.

Wheldall, K., & Swann, W. The effect of intonational emphasis on sentence comprehension in severely subnormal and normal children. *Language and Speech,* 1976, *19,* 87-99.

Winters, J. J., & Brzoska, M. A. Development of lexicon in normal and retarded persons. *Psychological Reports,* 1975, *37,* 391-402.

Winters, J. J., & Brzoska, M. A. Development of formation of categories by normal and retarded persons. *Developmental Psychology,* 1976, *12,* 125-131.

Winters, J. J., Jr., & Cundari, L. Speed of retrieving information from the lexicon of mentally retarded adolescents. *American Journal of Mental Deficiency,* 1979, *83,* 566-570.

Yoder, D. E., & Miller, J. F. What we may know and what we can do. In J. E. McLean, D. E. Yoder, & R. L. Schiefelbusch (Eds.), *Language intervention with the retarded.* Baltimore, Md.: University Park Press, 1972.

8 Language in Infantile Autism

David Fay
Bell Laboratories Illinois

Rebecca Mermelstein
University of Illinois, Chicago

INTRODUCTION

In Leo Kanner's (1943, 1946) original descriptions of infantile autism, language disability played a prominent role. Kanner reported that none of his first 11 cases developed language normally: Three were mute; the other 8 developed speech at the usual age or after some delay, but the speech could hardly be considered normal. As Kanner described it, autistic speech, although clearly articulated for the most part, served no communicative function. Instead it consisted of memorized lists or words originally spoken by someone else. The autistic child was not even creating his or her own utterances, much less using them to convey a meaning. Rather, he or she was parroting speech directed to him or her. Furthermore, there was no evidence of the child comprehending the speech of others.

Kanner interpreted autistic speech in light of the other symptoms he observed in his patients. He attributed the failure to communicate to a general social withdrawal, the predominant characteristic of autism and the one that gives the syndrome its name. The autistic child is profoundly alone, treating people as if they were objects and showing no interest in interacting in any personal way. The failure to establish social contact through language, thought Kanner, followed directly. Kanner also related the repetitiveness of autistic speech to his observations that autistic children were obsessed with maintaining the sameness of their environment, often becoming upset when anything new or unexpected was introduced into their daily routines. For the same reason, he thought, the children failed to respond when spoken to, resisting speech as another intrusion into their private world. The autistic child's echoing of other's speech was interpreted as an indication of a prodigious memory ability, an ability that was apparently cultivated with words, numbers, and poems by parents trying to exercise what speech ability the child possessed. Kanner even considered the possibility that what he saw as highly intelligent but compulsive parents were interfering in this way with the autistic child's development of language.

Kanner had good reason to pin the autistic child's failure to use language on his or her self-imposed social isolation, for one of language's primary uses is as a vehicle of social communication. But he had another reason as well. The children were of high intelligence (or so Kanner thought), had excellent memories, and came from well-educated, highly verbal families. If the children, possessed of all the requisite cognitive equipment and linguistic experience, still failed to use language, it could only be that they had, in their private worlds, no reason to learn to use it.

In the nearly 4 decades since Kanner first described autism, many new facts about the disorder have come to light. But abnormal language development has remained one of its defining characteristics, even though the new facts have altered greatly recent thinking about the causes of the syndrome and its attendant linguistic disorder. In this review, our focus is on language. We describe what is known about the language abilities of autistic children as well as theories of the etiology of the language disorder and attempts that have been made to treat it. It is now known that autism is a disorder of cognition, affect, and social relations as well as of language. But these other aspects of the syndrome are described only insofar as they shed light on some aspect of the language disability. The reader should be aware that we are neglecting many important and interesting nonlinguistic aspects of autism.

Before autistic language is described, it is useful to mention some of the theoretical and methodological issues that ought to be kept in mind when considering autism as a developmental language disorder. The first distinction that must be observed is between language knowledge and language use. A person can have knowledge of the rules of language without any means of or interst in putting them to use in speaking or understanding. A child that does not speak might well not have acquired any knowledge of English. But it is also possible that he knows English quite well but fails to speak because, for example, his attention is continually and uncontrollably drawn away from those he would speak to. Although Kanner was not explicit on this point, he gives the impression that the autistic child's difficulty with language is in using it rather than acquiring its rules. We are concerned in this review to determine whether the peculiar aspects of autistic language are due to an inability to acquire the rules of English or alternatively to a failure to deploy linguistic knowledge to communicate.

With regard to language use, there is a second important distinction to be observed between comprehension and production of language. Although the two processes are guided by the same linguistic rules, they may well employ different psychological mechanisms (e.g., memory or attention). It is possible then for one or the other to be affected differentially in a disorder, as is apparently the case in the different varieties of adult aphasia. In considering autism it is important then to determine separately whether each ability is affected and to keep in mind that they might be affected differently.

Another important issue concerns the generality of a language disorder. Language is an extraordinarily complex system with many different levels of organization. It is possible in theory for one level (e.g., the sound system) to be affected independently of other levels (e.g., syntax). Alternatively, a language disorder may affect language across the board, with each level being diminished. Although it is often difficult to separate the deficits at different linguistic levels, such analysis is necessary for a full understanding of a language disability and, especially, for a rational treatment program.

A final theoretical issue related to this is the question of delay versus deviancy in the development of language. A level of language may be delayed relative to normal development, in which case that aspect of language will show all the characteristics of normal language at an earlier developmental stage, or it may be deviant in that the affected level has characteristics not normally found at any stage of normal development. It is generally thought, for example, that language in the mentally retarded is delayed rather than deviant (Cromer, 1974; Lackner, 1968), whereas at least some aspects of aphasic language use are most likely deviant (Bradley, 1978). We consider which of these two models autistic language patterns after.

In addition to these theoretical issues there are several methodological points to be kept in mind in evaluating research on autism. As Kanner (1943) pointed out, there are other childhood disorders that might be confused with autism. He mentioned mental retardation and childhood schizophrenia, but he thought autistic children to be sharply distinguished from these two groups by, on the one hand, their high intelligence and, on the other, the onset of the disorder shortly after birth. In the ensuing years, the distinction between autism and other developmental disorders, including ones discovered subsequent to Kanner's paper, has been considerably muddied.

In the case of mental retardation, the change is necessitated by the discovery that Kanner was simply wrong about autistic intelligence. It turns out that autsitic children are rarely of high intelligence even when measured on nonverbal intelligence tests, and in fact two-thirds are mentally retarded (Rutter, 1970). Any investigation of autistic language then ought to include a control group of retardates so that it can be determined which of the language characteristics are unique to autism and which are due simply to the accompanying mental retardation. Another solution to this problem is to study the subset of autistic children who have normal intelligence (Bartak, Rutter, & Cox, 1975), in which case the effects of low mental age are not at issue. The only danger here is the possibility that autistic children with normal IQs might be unrepresentative of the syndrome in respects other than their nonverbal intelligence.

Kanner's differentiation of autism from childhood schizophrenia has been borne out by subsequent research, even though the two syndromes have been persistently confused in the literature in the intervening years. (Autistic children are often referred to as childhood schizophrenics in the older literature.) But it now appears that there are really two varieties of childhood psychosis, distinguished primarily by the age of onset (Kolvin, 1971). The early-onset disorder, identified usually by 30 months, is infantile autism, and the late-onset psychosis, diagnosed most often in early adolescence after a period of fairly normal development, is childhood schizophrenia. This distinction has been incorporated into recent diagnostic criteria by requiring that an autistic child show the symptoms of the disorder by 30 months of age (Rutter, 1971). By adhering to this criterion, researchers can be confident that they are studying autistic rather than schizophrenic language.

Another disorder that has been compared to autism is developmental dysphasia (Bartak et al., 1975), the primary characteristic of which is an abnormal development of language similar in many respects to that found in autism. Nevertheless, the syndromes can be clearly differentiated on other criteria (Bartak, Rutter, & Cox, 1977; Cantwell, Baker, & Rutter, 1978), so they must be maintained as separate disorders. It is important then for a study of autistic language to include a control group of developmental dysphasics to determine which linguistic characterists are unique to the autistic syndrome, if any.

Finally, autistic language ought to be compared to a control group of normals at the appropriate developmental levels to determine whether the features of autistic language are deviant or delayed in any way.

In summary, the most useful study of autistic language includes control groups of normals, mental retardates, and developmental dysphasics, each matched with the autistic subjects on nonlinguistic mental age. If the study is designed to detect delays in autistic language relative to normals, then an additional normal control group is required that is matched with autistic subjects on chronological age. Although all these groups are important for a full interpretation of the obtained data, it is often impractical to obtain the necessary subjects. As seen, many of the studies in this area have had to make such concessions to practicality. To the extent that they do, their results are less than informative.

THE AUTISTIC LANGUAGE DISORDER

Recent descriptions of autism have converged on the following diagnostic criteria for the syndrome (Rutter, 1971):

1. Lack of responsiveness to humans, including avoidance of eye contact.
2. An obsession with sameness in the environment characterized by ritualistic behavior and tantrums or panic in response to changes in the child's surroundings or daily routines.
3. Language disability including abnormally slow development and echolalic speech.
4. Onset before 30 months.

The centrality of the language disorder for defining autism is supported by studies on recovery from infantile autism (Rutter, Greenfield & Lockyer, 1967). Degree of language impairment has been observed to be the single best predictor of outcome. Unfortunately, the prognosis for autism is not very favorable and about half the cases have no speech at all at adolescence (Kanner & Eisenberg, 1955; Rutter et al., 1967).

In what follows, the autistic language disorder is examined with respect to four levels of language organization: phonology, syntax, semantics, and pragmatics. Phonology concerns the sound patterns of a language, including not only the pronunciation of individual sound segments but also such suprasegmental factors as intonation, stress, and rhythm. The syntax of a language consists of the rules for determining the ordering and grouping of words in a sentence. Semantic principles govern the meanings of individual words and how those meanings can be combined to give a meaning to a sentence. Finally, pragmatics is the set of conventions governing language use, particularly the functions of language in various social contexts. Although there are other levels to language, these are the principle ones and have been the focus of studies on autistic language.

Phonology

Only two systematic studies have been carried out on the phonological abilities of autistic children, one comparing them to retardates and the other to language-delayed children and developmental dysphasics. Bartolucci, Pierce, Streiner, and Eppel (1976) examined the pronunciation of words by autistic children both in their spontaneous speech and in the Edinburgh Articulation Test (EAT), a test in which subjects name pictures of common objects. The sound segments used by autistic children in spontaneous speech were found to be nearly identical to MA-matched retardates and normals, indicating that there are no gaps in their use of the sounds of English. Furthermore, the distribution of errors in pronunciation on the EAT was similar in autistic and retarded subjects, with more errors being made in both groups on the less frequent sounds. At the same time, the pronunciation of autistic subjects is much poorer than normals; autistic children with a mean age of 11 perform at the level of a normal 4-year-old (Boucher, 1976).

Bartolucci et al. carefully examined the pattern of errors made by their subjects and found that, in substitution errors, autistics show the same tendency to replace sounds with ones differing by only a single distinctive feature as do retardates and normals. This is a significant finding, for distinctive features describe the underlying structure of the sound system of English (Chomsky & Halle, 1968). The fact that autistic errors are guided by this feature system shows that they perceive the same similarities among sound segments as do normals. In other words, they have apparently grasped a fundamental organizing principle for this aspect of language.

The only difference found by Bartolucci et al. between autistic subjects and retardates concerned marked versus unmarked sounds, where the latter are assumed to be simpler than the former. Autistic children do not show the expected tendency to replace marked sounds with unmarked, whereas retardates do. But recent evidence shows that even adult normals do not favor unmarked speech sounds in their speech (Shattuck-Hufnagel & Klatt, 1979), so the significance of this finding is unclear.

Despite the considerable deficit in pronunciation by autistic children, they are still considerably better than developmental dysphasics matched on chronological age and receptive vocabulary, scoring about 25% higher on the EAT (Boucher, 1976).

The picture that emerges from these studies is that the phonological abilities of autistic children are severely delayed, although no more so than would be expected from their mental ages. There is no sign of anything deviant about their abilities; indeed, they seem to have grasped the basic principles. Thus, if autistic children seem to have some unique language difficulty, it does not seem to extend to phonology. This observation is in accord with clinical observations of generally good pronunciation in autism relative to their general language level. Dysphasics, by way of contrast, seem to have a more severe problem in this area.

This conclusion may hold as well for suprasegmental phonology. Aurnhammer-Frith (1969), in a study of the recall of normal and scrambled sentences presented with either normal or abnormal stress, found that autistic children showed the same sensitivity to stress as normals. Specifically, stressed content words are remembered better than unstressed ones, whereas stressed and unstressed function words are remembered equally well.

Two caveats must be noted here. First, the studies on segmental phonology have focused only on speech production abilities. It is unknown whether autistic children might have special phonological problems in the perception of speech that might distinguish them from other groups. Second, outside of Frith's work there has been no systematic study of suprasegmental aspects of autistic speech. This omission is especially serious because this feature of autistic speech is often noted as deviant in clinical reports. Some autistic children are reported to have flat, expressionless speech; others are said to have an unusual stacato delivery and lack of rhythm (Rutter, 1970); others, a singsong intonation. It is hoped that future investigations will examine this neglected aspect of autistic speech.

Syntax

One difficult problem in studying the developing syntactic knowledge of young normal children is the existence of frozen unanalyzed forms in their speech (Brown, 1973). Children are often able to pick up adultlike expressions and use them appropriately before they have analyzed them into their component words. In this way, the child's speech gives the impression of far more linguistic sophistication than the child really possesses. For example, children just learning to speak may ask for the names of objects with *what is that?* Although it might appear that the child knows how to use the verb *is,* this may be the only expression in which *is* appears for many months. A more reasonable conclusion is that the child doesn't really understand the syntax of his utterance the way an adult would when using the same words.

The problem for the investigator of child speech then is to determine which aspects of the child's speech are reflections of his internalized linguistic knowledge and which are simply routines imitated from adult speech. This same problem applies to the study of autistic speech. In fact it is compounded by the frequently noted echolalia in autistic children. Echolalia, which is considered in more detail later, is the repetition by the child of phrases or sentences addressed to him by adults or even heard from a television. It is reported that autistic children may echo an expression days or even years after it was uttered. This means that special precautions must be taken in studying autistic speech to separate out echolalic speech from the child's spontaneous creations.

There are several methods for overcoming this problem. One is to study the comprehension of language by autistic children rather than their speech production. Knowledge of the syntax of English is just as necessary for comprehension as for production, but the problem of echolalia is avoided. Second, it is possible to focus on only those utterances in autistic speech that are incorrect by adult standards. Syntactic errors are almost certainly products of the child's own linguistic system rather than copies of an adult utterance because adult speech to children is almost error-free (Brown & Bellugi, 1964). Errors created by the autistic child can give much insight into the rules underlying his or her speech.

A third solution is to do a detailed study of each autistic child's speech, as is done with normals (Brown, 1973), to determine which syntactic structures are used widely and productively. With a large enough corpus of speech, it is possible to identify echolalic expressions by their repeated occurrence in the same form and the child's failure to use any other expressions with comparable syntactic structure. Although relatively few studies of the syntactic knowledge of autistic children have been carried out, all three of these techniques have been exploited to some degree.

In an interesting study of speech produced by a single female autistic child while alone in bed before falling asleep, Baltaxe and Simmons (1977) examined ungrammatical expressions as an indication of tacit linguistic knowledge. Except for the bedtime soliloquies, the child's speech was judged to be primarily echolalic. In the soliloquies themselves, however, Baltaxe and Simmons found it impossible to distinguish echolalic from propositional (creative) speech. Analysis of her ungrammatical expressions indicated that they deviated from adult English in ways narrowly circumscribed by the rules of English. For example, the subject was heard to say *I want a water,* presumably for *I want some water.* As Baltaxe & Simmons note, *a* would be perfectly correct if *water* were a count noun, like *cracker,* for example. In other respects, *a* has all the linguistic properties of the correct word *some.* So this error is a highly natural one and, in fact, is just the kind made by normal children learning English (Menyuk, 1969). This pattern held across a wide variety of errors observed in the soliloquies.

The only difference observed by Baltaxe and Simmons between their subject and a normal subject studied previously by Weir (1962), under similar conditions, was a tendency to concatenate two phrases together without making the appropriate grammatical adjustments. Baltaxe and Simmons make much of this difference arguing that it supports their view that the autistic child learns language through echolalic patterns, which are "only gradually broken down into individual chunks of varying sizes [p. 392]" and then recombined, a strategy they believe to be quite different from that employed by normal children. Before accepting such a dramatic conclusion, though, it would be wise to compare more than a single autistic child with a single normal, especially because the analysis of the normal child specifically excluded delayed imitations of adult speech (what Weir [1962] calls "quotations"), whereas Baltaxe and Simmons' study did not.

Baltaxe and Simmons' finding of a surprising degree of linguistic knowledge in an autistic child who gave little indication of that knowledge in interactions with others is supported by an imitation study of Voeltz (1976). Voeltz had autistic children repeat grammatical sentences of varying lengths and structures and their scrambled equivalents. She found that the children were able to repeat more of the structured sentences than the scrambled ones, demonstrating a sensitivity in autistic children to syntactic structure that parallels that found in normals.

This aspect of Voeltz' study replicates earlier work by Aurnhammer-Frith (1969) who also found that autistic children recalled more of normal than scrambled sentences. In addition, Aurnhammer-Firth found that autistic children were not so sensitive to grammatical structure in their recall as normals, although high-digit-span autistics, presumably those with more language ability, were more sensitive then low-digit-span individuals.

Voeltz (1976) also analyzed the errors made by her autistic subjects and concluded that they showed a rule mediation that was "grossly reflective" of the normal language development sequence.

Similar conclusions can be found in the work of Pierce and Bartolucci (1977), who compared the spontaneous speech of autistic children to that of retarded and normal children matched with them on nonlinguistic mental age. In one analysis, using a scoring system developed by Lee (1974), they found that the overall level of syntactic development in autistic children with an average nonlinguistic mental age of 6 and chronological age of almost 11 was comparable to that of a normal 3½-year-old. Their linguistic performance was lower than the MA-matched retarded group that in turn was lower than the MA-matched normals. A transformational grammar (Chomsky, 1957) was also written for the corpus of each subject. These grammars indicated that autistic speech is less complex than that found in either retardates or normals. However, the syntactic structures and rules used by the autistic group did not differ in kind from the other two groups.

Pierce and Bartolucci conclude that autistic speech is just as rule-governed as normal speech but is delayed to an extreme degree, a fact that may account in part for the many clinical descriptions of autistic speech as "bizarre."

One further comparison of autistic speech with that of developmental dysphasics is necessary to obtain a full picture of syntactic abilities in autism. This comparison is provided by Cantwell et al. (1978), who studied autistic and dysphasic children of normal nonverbal intelligence. They analyzed the spontaneous speech of the two groups for syntactic differences and found absolutely none, although the syntax of both groups was considerably delayed relative to normals. As a check on this finding, we can predict from this similarity and the qualitative similarity between autistic children and normals found by Pierce and Bartolucci that the syntax of dysphasic speech will be qualitatively similar to that of normals, a prediction that has been confirmed by Morehead and Ingram (1973).

It should be noted that the autistic and dysphasic children reported on in Caldwell et al. (1978) were studied earlier in Bartak et al. (1975) with somewhat different results. In that study, Bartak et al. report that autistic children have a more severe grammatical disability than dysphasic children. There are two possible causes for this discrepancy. First, Bartak et al. used a standardized language test (Reynell, 1969) to measure the abilities of the two groups. It may be that the scores of autistic children were lowered with this method of testing by the behavioral problems associated with their syndrome. Alternatively, because the test used by Bartak et al. measured comprehension of language rather than production, it may be that autistic children have as much linguistic knowledge as dysphasics (as shown by similar speech production abilities) but have more difficulty employing this knowledge in the comprehension of speech. Whatever may be the case, this issue needs to be examined further.

The studies we have reviewed in this section provide a remarkably consistent picture of autistic syntax. It is delayed in the extreme relative to normal language development. At least in part this must be due to the general cognitive retardation often found in autistic children. But there is an additional, specifically linguistic, delay that is comparable to that found in developmental dysphasia. There seems to be no evidence for any syntactic deviance in autistic speech, aside from Baltaxe and Simmons' finding of an unusual combinatorial strategy. This lump in an otherwise homogeneous set of findings deserves additional investigation.

The suggestion has been made that the special disability autistic children have in acquiring syntactic rules might be due to a more general cognitive deficit in ordering, cross-model matching, immediate memory, or cue matching (Hermelin & O'Connor, 1970). In a series of experiments involving these abilities, O'Connor and Hermelin (1965) compared autistic children with normals and retardates matched roughly with them on a perceptual-motor test. The pattern of results on the four tasks indicated the same relative difficulty of the tasks for the three groups, with one exception. The ordering task, which required the children to order five cardboard squares by size, was the easiest for the normal and retarded subjects, who performed nearly perfectly, whereas it was the hardest for the autistic children, who did no better than chance. Hermelin and O'Connor (1970) point out the relevance of ordering for learning the syntax of a language, although they equivocate on just how seriously one should take the analogy between ordering squares and ordering words. In any event, their results suggest that the autistic child's special deficit in ordering elements might underlie his or her problems learning syntax.

This suggestion, although an appealing one, runs into two difficulties. First, the syntax of a natural language consists of far more than the ordering of words, including as it does such abstract characteristics as hierarchical structure, grammatical relations, and rules of agreement. Even if ordering held special difficulty for autistic children, that wouldn't explain the severe, across-the-board delay in their development of syntax. A second problem is that ordering does not even seem to be one of their special difficulties. If it were, one would expect to find reports of deviant orderings in autistic syntax, above and beyond what one would expect on the basis of their overall language ability. However, that does not seem to be the case.

More recenltly, Hermelin (1978) has suggested another possibility as a cognitive basis for the autistic language disorder. She argues that autistic children suffer from an inability to construct and use abstract internal representations of their sensory experiences. Their impairment thus goes beyond the specific symbolic system of natural language to general symbolic representations upon which all cognitive activity is dependent. Taking a Piagetian point of view, Hermelin implies that the language deficit in autism is not just a concomitant but, in fact, a consequence of this more general cognitive defect.

The evidence Hermelin cites to support her view comes from a series of studies comparing normal, congenitally blind, and autistic children on a variety of perceptual-motor tasks (Hermelin & O'Connor, 1971, 1975; O'Connor & Hermelin, 1973). These findings indicate that autistic children act in many ways like blind children who, Hermelin assumes, have no mental representation of spatial world. It seems then that autistic children, like blind children, fail to form the internal spatial representations possessed by normals, although for reasons of cognitive defect rather than deprivation of visual input.

The difficulty with this conclusion is the lack of a retarded control group in these studies. It could well be whatever disabilities autistic children suffer from in this area may not be specific to autism but due rather to their general retardation. Hermelin (1978) does mention that retarded controls were run in some of the studies and performed like normals rather than blind and autistic subjects. However, these results are not reported anywhere in detail, so they are difficult to evaluate. Until the appropriate control group is included, Hermelin's position will have to be regarded with some caution.

The possible cognitive basis for autistic language problems is an important and intriguing problem that deserves to be investigated in great detail. Hermelin and O'Connor have provided a start in that direction but have not as yet provided a convincing case. It is likely that the investigation of this issue will prove every bit as knotty as it has been in the parallel case of normal language development (Fremgen & Fay, 1980; Sinclair, 1971).

Semantics

There are few published studies on the semantics of autistic language. However, one study by Hermelin and O'Connor (1967) did compare autistic and retarded children matched on digit span and vocabulary (although not on nonlinguistic mental age) on the amount of semantic clustering in their immediate recall of sequences of words. Retardates showed significantly more clustering than autistic subjects. It's not clear whether this result is due to some deficit in the immediate memory of autistic children or whether they simply didn't know the words used in the experiment as well as the retardates, despite the fact that the groups were matched on overall vocabulary. Baltaxe & Simmons (1977) also found evidence for some awareness of semantic relationships in the soliloquies of their autistic subject. Adjacent utterances in the soliloquy were occasionally in semantic opposition, as in *You sleep at daytime/You sleep at nighttime*. It's not clear, though, whether these oppositions arose from specific semantic contrasts or whether they were a chance product of the organization of the soliloquy into topics. In any event there is clearly too little information at present to tell whether autistics are deviant in their semantic knowledge or only delayed or whether they have any unique deficit in dealing with word or sentence meanings that would distinguish them from retardates or developmental dysphasics.

Pragmatics

Pragmatics covers a tremendous variety of topics in the use of language, most of which have not been investigated in the autistic syndrome. Most studies have focused on two aspects of pragmatics: the notion that language can serve to convey a message to another person and the idea of an interchange of information in conversation. Both of these functions of language are present in the normal child when he uses his first words (Bates, 1976) and, some would claim, even prelinguistically in his gestures (Bates, Camaioni, & Volterra, 1975). In contrast, the clinical reports of autistic language stress repeatedly the deviant use of whatever language the child possesses.

These reports have been confirmed in systematic studies of language functions in autism. Cantwell et al. (1978) found several differences between autistic children and developmental dysphasics, matched on age and IQ, in their use of language even though the syntax of their speech was indistinguishable. Dysphasics showed more spontaneous remarks than autistics, although there were no differences in their use of questions, answers, or directions. This finding parallels that of Bartak et al. (1975) on the spontaneous use of language in these same children. In that study, parents of autistic children reported that they rarely "chattered" spontaneously, whereas most dysphasic children were reported to do so. In addition, parents reported far fewer instances of autistic children engaging in conversation or reporting their activities in answer to a question than of the same uses of language in dysphasic children.

This deficit in communication extended beyond language to gesture. Bartak et al. (1975) reported that only 11% of autistic children used complex gestures to communicate at home whereas over half of the dysphasic children did.

Other uses of language distinguished the two groups as well. More autistic children than dysphasics produced delayed echolalia, talked to themselves, and used uninterpretable, "metaphoric" language (like *A love from me* or *Boot 50;* see Cantwell et al., 1978; Cantwell, Howlin, & Rutter, 1977). What seems to characterize these types of utterances is their generally noncommunicative intent. In general then, autistic children communicate with language much less than dysphasic children and (presumably) normals.

Interestingly, this same deficit appeared in the bedtime soliloquies studied by Baltaxe and Simmons (1977). Even though soliloquies are noncommunicative, Weir (1962) reported that in a normal child they often take the form of a dialogue with an imaginary interlocuter, with the child alternating between the roles of speaker and listener. In contrast, the soliloquies of the autistic child showed no evidence of such dialogue, despite the fact that her soliloquies each had a definite topic or theme.

These studies show that the autistic child has a special disability in the communicative use of language, a disability that is more severe than would be expected from his overall command of language. Although his knowledge of the structure of language is the equal of the developmental dysphasic, he shows much less inclination to use that ability to interact with others. It is unclear, as yet, whether the autistic child's deficit is one of deviance or merely of extreme delay. Because pragmatic aspects of language develop in the child just as do syntax and phonology, the autistic child may be grossly retarded in developing this aspect of language relative to phonology, for example. Alternatively, he or she may simply approach the use of language in quite a different way from normals at any stage of development. Only detailed qualitative studies of the communicative attempts of autistic children and young normals will settle this question.

It is interesting to speculate on what the cause might be of this pragmatic disability. Three hypotheses suggest themselves, only one of which has currency. First, it might be that the child communicates little because he has little to say. Attributing the disability to an ideational deficit in this way seems unpromising because autistic children communicate less than dysphasics matched on nonverbal mental abilities (Cantwell et al., 1978).

A second possibility is that they have the ideas to communicate but don't know how to put them into words. But this is unlikely because, as pointed out in earlier sections, they have every bit as much linguistic knowledge as the more communicative dysphasics. Moreover, this hypothesis would be unable to account for the lack of communication by gesture for which knowledge of a natural language is not required.

A final hypothesis is that autistic children have something to say and have the means to express it but fail to communicate for lack of intent; that is, autistic children don't communicate because they don't want to or they haven't discovered that language can be used in that way. This seems the most likely of the three hypotheses. There is no evidence directly in support of it, but it does correlate with their failure to develop social relationships outside the linguistic domain. In fact, if their problem is the failure to learn the communicative use of language, their social withdrawal may help to explain that failure. Alternatively, their social isolation may prevent them from using whatever communicative abilities they may possess. Whatever the case may be, this seems a most profitable area in which to look for a greater understanding of the autistic syndrome.

ECHOLALIA

If there is any aspect of language use that is considered both characteristic of autism and deviant in nature, it is echolalia. Echolalia is defined as the repetition by the child of something heard in the speech of others. The repetition can be either immediate or delayed and can be either exact or changed somewhat from the original, in which case it is termed "mitigated echolalia." (It should be noted that the definition of mitigated echolalia has the unfortunate and bizarre consequence of applying to normal, appropriate responses to questions, e.g., Q: Is the sun shining? A: *Yes, the sun is shining.*) In addition, the echolalic utterance can be used either communicatively or without apparent communicative intent.

As mentioned earlier, even with normal children it is difficult to tell whether a child's expression is being produced with his own grammar or whether it is simply parroted from the language of adults. Likewise, echolalia is difficult to identify in autistic children. This difficulty depends to some degree on whether the echolalia is immediate, in which case the adult model is apparent, or whether it is delayed. There is disagreement on whether it is possible to identify delayed echolalia reliably just from the form of the child's speech, without additional information about what has been said to the child on previous occasions (Baltaxe & Simmons, 1977; Cantwell, Howlin, & Rutter, 1977). Because of the difficulties in identifying delayed echolalia, most studies have limited themselves to immediate echolalia.

Immediate echolalia, although characteristic of autism, is not unique to it. It is also observed in developmental dysphasics (Cantwell et al., 1978), retardates (Campbell & Grieve, 1978), and adult aphasics (Whitaker, 1976). In fact, the incidence of immediate echolalia in autism is the same as for dysphasia (Cantwell et al., 1978). What seems to distinguish the two groups is a higher incidence of delayed echolalia in autism (Cantwell et al., 1978), but the difficulty in identifying utterances of this type on the basis of a single language sample indicates that this finding should be viewed with some caution.

Echolalia is even found in normal children in the early stages of language development (Despert, 1946; Shapiro, Roberts, & Fish, 1970), a finding that may be significant for determining its cause. Shapiro et al. compared eight child schizophrenics (who had all the symptoms of autism) with groups of normal 2-, 3-, and 4-year-olds to determine how much and what type of echoing occurred in the spontaneous speech of each group. Their most significant finding is that the amount of "rigidly congruent echoes," echoes in which the words of all or part of the adult's utterance are repeated verbatim, accounts for over 6% of 2-year-old's utterances. The proportion of rigid echoes in 3- and 4-year-olds decreases to 2% and 1%, respectively. In autistic children, with a mean age of 4.5, on the other hand, rigid echoes comprised 14% of their speech. It appears then that immediate echolalia is a characteristic of normal speech that disappears with increasing age or sophistication with language. So echolalic autistic children may be the equivalent of very young normals in their use of echolalia.

Another significant fact about echolalia is that it is selective. Echolalic children apparently imitate speech addressed directly to the child but not sounds in their environment nor speech overheard (Stengel, 1947). In one carefully controlled study of the immediate echoes of mentally retarded subjects, Campbell and Grieve (1978) found that more echoing occurs when the experimenter addressed the subject than when he spoke to someone else or spoke to himself. The same is apparently true in a case of presenile dementia with severe echolalia studied by Whitaker (1976), who reports that the subject would echo only when the speaker was directly in front of her, engaged her attention, and then spoke directly at her. Otherwise, the patient remained totally silent.

Another characteristic of echolalia is its association with a failure to understand the utterance being echoed. It has been suggested that echolalia is related to a low level of linguistic development (Stengel, 1947), but recently Paccia Cooper and Curcio (1979) have demonstrated that it is specifically related to comprehension difficulty. They determined the amount of echolalic responses to questions based on sentences previously determined to be either understood by autistic subjects or not. They found roughly a 50% increase in echolalic responses to questions incomprehensible to their subjects. It should be noted, though, that echolalic responses to comprehensible questions were still frequent. Many of these responses had an intonational change from what was originally presented suggesting that the child actually understood the question and was using his echo as an affirmative reply to the question.

One final fact that may be of significance is the often reported ability of echolalic subjects to complete phrases spoken to them (Stengel, 1947; Whitaker, 1976). Whitaker's patient was remarkable in this regard because she showed no spontaneous speech whatsoever but could easily provide grammatically correct, even semantically novel completions, to sentences like *What did you have for _____?* and *I would like an order of _____* as well as to proverbs and song titles. This ability has not been described in autistic children, although Paccia Cooper and Curcio (1979) do report little echolalia in the partial sentences they gave their subjects to complete. This suggests that the subjects may have provided completions comparable to other echolalic groups.

Having mentioned the major characteristics of echolalia, we can now consider what its cause might be. Two major hypotheses are suggested by the pattern of facts, one related to delay in the acquisition of language and the other to deviance. The delay hypothesis suggests that echolalia is characteristic of the first stages of normal language development. Presumably, it results from a child's attempt to converse with an adult he doesn't fully understand. Utterances the child is not capable of analyzing with his limited grammatical abilities are repeated back to the adult so that the conversational stream is not broken.

This view of echolalia is supported by Shapiro et al.'s finding of significant amounts of echolalia in very young normals and decreasing amounts as the child acquires more language. It is also supported by Paccia Cooper and Curcio's (1979) association of echoing with a failure to comprehend, as well as by clinical observations that echolalia occurs more frequently in younger autistic children and in the most severely affected among those who have any speech at all.

If correct, this view has an interesting implication for the apparent deficit autistic children have in using language communicatively. If we view echolalia as an attempt to respond communicatively to a situation in which the speaker may not be fully understood and the child may have little in the way of expressive capabilities, we may be led to question how severe the communicative deficit in autism really is. In echolalic responses the child seems to understand the principles of conversation reasonably well and seems limited more by his grammatical or cognitive deficits.

However, this revised view of the function of echolalia does not explain the failure of autistic children to initiate communication either linguistically or gesturally. So if further study of echolalic responses show that autistic children indeed understand conversational principles, we may have to look elsewhere for an explanation of why they don't inititate communication.

The hypothesis based on the deviancy of echolalia does not deny that autistic children are at a low level of grammatical knowledge, but it suggests that echolalic responses are a separate and unrelated deviancy of language use that cannot be explained by simple linguistic immaturity. This possibility is suggested by Whitaker's study of a severely echolalic patient with known brain damage due to presenile dementia. This patient was rendered echolalic after acquiring normal adult linguistic knowledge. This knowledge apparently remained with her during her echolalic performances for she revealed a remarkable ability to correct grammatical mistakes in sentences she repeated. For example, she repeated *He buy a dress yesterday* as *He bought a dress yesterday* and *He ate he dinner* as *He ate his dinner*. This ability extended to nearly every aspect of syntax and phonology tested. (In contrast, she never corrected semantic anomalies like *The stone tasted the coffee.*)

The occurrence of echolalia in the presence of apparently intact adult grammatical knowledge suggests that it may be wrong to associate echolalia with linguistic immaturity. Instead, the brain damage associated with presenile dementia (or carbon monoxide poisoning; Geschwind, Quadfasel, & Segarra, 1968) that results in echolalia might be a specific etiological factor underlying infantile autism. Before the parallels between autism and echolalic aphasics are to be taken seriously though, further investigations are needed to determine whether the two echolalias really represent the same phenomenon. By the same token, more detailed studies are necessary to determine whether the echolalia of autism is to be identified with that found in early normal development.

Summary

We can now summarize the characteristics of autistic language. The autistic child suffers from a severe delay in the development of language. Some of this delay is due to general mental retardation, but some is also due to a special language disability associated with autism. The delay in language development does not seem uniformly distributed over the various levels of language. The autistic child seems to be less impaired in phonology than developmental dysphasics. On the other hand they are about the same in syntax. The autistic child is also more impaired in comprehension than the dysphasic, although it is not clear at what level of language that impairment lies. Finally, the autistic child seems most severely impaired in pragmatic aspects of language, a deficit in keeping with the social isolation characteristic of the syndrome. The only hint that autistic language use may be deviant, in addition to being delayed, is to be found in echolalia, but even echolalia can be reasonably interpreted, given present evidence, as indicative of an early stage of language acquisition comparable to that associated with normal development.

ETIOLOGY

Theories on the cause of autism fall into two classes according to whether they take a psychological or biological approach to the disorder. Psychological approaches, often called psychogenic theories, focus on parental influences on the autistic child. Although there are many varieties of this view, they all see the autistic child as a victim of abnormal treatment by the parents. In contrast, the biological view assumes that there is something wrong with the autistic child's brain, eigher structurally or functionally, and attributes the defect to inheritance, prenatal disease, birth trauma, and the like.

Most of the etiological theories, both psychological and biological, have nothing specific to say about the language defect in autism, so we do not discuss them here (see Ornitz & Ritvo, 1976, and Rutter & Bartak, 1971, for reviews). There are two hypotheses though, one from each camp, that attempt to explain directly the autistic language disability. The psychological hypothesis attributes the disability to a poor language model provided by the parents and the biological hypothesis to structural damage to the language dominant cerebral hemisphere. These theories are discussed in turn.

The psychological hypothesis has been advocated primarily by Goldfarb and his colleagues (Goldfarb, Goldfarb, & Scholl, 1966; Goldfarb, Levy, & Meyers, 1966; Goldfarb, Levy, & Meyers, 1972; Meyers & Goldfarb, 1961). They have found that the parents of schizophrenic children (some, but probably not all, of whom are autistic) use abnormal language both to other adults and to their children. For example, in one study (Goldfarb, Goldfarb, & Scholl, 1966) a speech pathologist rated the speech of mothers of schizophrenic and normal children produced during an interview about the "maternal role." Ratings were made of volume, pitch, voice quality, rate, phrasing, fluency, stress, intonation, articulation, and finally communication of meaning and mood. The speech of the mothers of autistic children was found to be significantly poorer (in a summary rating) than that of mothers of normals. This result is especially striking in that the rater was blind as to the type of mother being rated because all identifying information was removed from the tape recordings.

In a similar study Lennard, Beaulieu, and Embry (1965) found that parents of childhood schizophrenics (again presumably including at least some autistic children) asked more questions of the child than parents of normal controls. This excess of questions they interpreted as an attempt to exert control over the child, taking away his opportunity to initiate behavior.

These studies, and others like them, have been criticized severely for the vague and impressionistic categories used to rate parental speech, the poor diagnosis of the children studied, small samples of speech analyzed, and the unnatural circumstances in which the speech was recorded (Baker, Cantwell, Rutter, & Bartak, 1976; Klein & Pollack, 1966). But the most important failing mentioned by these critics is the lack of a proper control group. In comparing the speech of parents of autistic children with that of the parents of normals, it is possible that the parental speech will be not so much the cause of the child's disability as an effect of it. Even in Goldfarb, Goldfarb, and School's study of blind ratings of mother's speech to another adult, it is quite conceivable that the mother of a disabled child will speak differently than the mother of a normal child, especially when discussing the "maternal role," perhaps with someone that blames the mother for the child's problems. The remedy for these difficulties is to compare the speech of mothers of autistic children with that of mothers of the most comparable language-disabled group, in this case, developmental dysphasics.

This comparison has been carried out by Cantwell, Baker, and Rutter (1977). They analyzed the speech of mothers to the autistic and dysphasic children of near normal IQ studied previously by Bartak et al. (1975). Mothers speech was analyzed for the type of utterance directed to the child (including categories that may be significant for language acquisition such as imitations, expansions, corrections, and prompts), its grammatical complexity and correctness, clarity in the sense of Goldfarb, Levy and Meyers (1966), and tone of voice. These exhaustive analyses showed virtually no differences in the speech of the two types of mothers. Where differences existed (e.g., in number of affectionate remarks), they were usually more favorable to the autistic child.

The results of the Cantwell et al. study provide strong evidence against the psychogenic views of the autistic language disorder, demonstrating once again the importance of using the appropriate control group. Although mothers of autistic children might speak differently to their children than mothers of normals, that difference is most likely a result of who they are speaking to than anything intrinsic to the mothers. We turn now to the biological hypothesis on the origin of autistic language.

This theory can be called the Hemispheric Dysfunction Theory. It is related to the fact that many cognitive functions, language included, are lateralized to one cerebral hemisphere or the other in most normal people. Evidence has accumulated over the past few years that autistic children may not have the same lateralization as normals, suggesting that language disabilities in autism may be caused by the abnormal functioning of the left hemisphere, where language usually resides.

The strongest evidence for the Hemispheric Dysfunction Theory comes frm a study of lateral biases in motoric behavior and sensory responsiveness, by Levy, Meck, and Staikoff (1979). Their study was based on the finding with certain kinds of patients having known unilateral brain damage that they tend to disregard the contralateral sensory field and have a motoric bias toward the side ipsilateral to the damage (Heilman & Watson, 1977). Levy et al. found the same to be true of autistic children. For example, autistic children, but not a retarded control group, tended to draw on the left half of a paper and tended to turn to the left to circumvent a barrier placed at the entrance to a room. In light of this bias, they suggest that autism is related to some disorder of the left hemisphere. They point out that their hypothesis can account for a variety of facts related to autism including the increased incidence of autism in males. Because females are believed to have less strongly lateralized hemispheric functions (Witelson, 1976), left-hemisphere damage would not be so serious for them. But more important for present purposes, the hypothesis would also account for the diminished language abilities in autistic children, either because the left himisphere tries to assume the language function but cannot support normal language development or because language becomes lateralized to the right hemisphere, which has severely dminished language abilities (Searleman, 1977).

Added support for this theory comes from two studies of the anatomical structure of the brains of autistic children. Hauser, DeLong, and Rosman (1975) found that the left lateral ventricle is enlarged in autistic children and Hier, LeMay, and Rosenberger (1979) report that the left cerebral hemisphere in autism is deficient in function because of fundamental anatomical abnormalities.

One objection to the Cerebral Dysfunction Theory needs to be mentioned. It is known that damage to the left hemisphere or even its complete removal is compensated for by the right hemisphere assuming left-hemisphere functions when the left hemisphere is affected at an early enough age (Lenneberg, 1967). Because autism is, by definition, present within the first few years of life, the question arises as to why the right hemisphere doesn't take over left-hemisphere functions and allow normal development. The only answer to this objection at present is that little is known about the conditions under which the right hemisphere will take over (Searleman, 1977). Current conceptions of brain lateralization suggest that during normal development the left hemisphere inhibits the corresponding functions in the right hemisphere (Kinsbourne, 1970). It's not clear whether that inhibition will be removed when the left-hemisphere damage is congenital as opposed to being acquired traumatically sometime after birth. The possibility exists that the malfunctioning left hemisphere in autism can still inhibit the right hemisphere from developing normal functions.

There is one piece of evidence that Levy et al. (1979) cite in favor of the Cerebral Dysfunction Theory that recent evidence has disputed. Both Levy et al. and Colby and Parkison (1977) found a high proportion of left-handedness and ambilaterality in their autistic subjects relative to normals. An elevation of sinistrality has been connected to early brain insult (Satz, 1973) supporting Levy et al.'s hypothesis. However, neither study included carefully matched retarded or normal control groups so it's not known whether the elevated handedness is really present or if it is whether it may be uniquely associated with autism rather than general retardation. When the appropriate controls are included (Barry & James, 1978; Boucher, 1977), no evidence is found for decreased right-handedness. This failure to find the predicted elevation in sinistrality must be counted against the Cerebral Dysfunction Theory.

Although the evidence in favor of the Cerebral Dysfunction Theory is not overwhelming at present, its initial successes suggest that it should be investigated in more detail. Of particular interest will be whether the theory can account for the details of the language disorder in autism, in particular the severe disabilities in the pragmatics language and other aspects of the autistic syndrome, including the failure to relate socially. In trying to meet these challenges to its explanatory power, the Cerebral Dysfunction Theory promises to provide new insights into the language abilities of autistic children.

TREATMENT

The remediation of the language deficits has been a goal of every intervention program designed to help autistic children. The means employed in reaching this goal vary widely across the different programs. Language intervention programs fall into two broad categories. The earliest kind of treatment for autistic children was developed by psychotherapists who classify autism as an emotional disorder. Their interventions followed logically from their theoretical positions on the etiology of autism, as well as their understanding of the normal course of development. Like Kanner, they believed that the deviant language observed in autistic children was a direct result of their general social withdrawal. As a consequence of this view they directed their remediation efforts toward the child's social development only. It was assumed that the child would begin talking appropriately as he began to function more appropriately in general. As this mode of treatment is not of particular interest to the psycholinguist, our discussion is brief.

The second category of treatment programs is in sharp contrast to the approach just described. The developers of these newer programs do not adhere to any one theoretical position on the etiology of autism nor do they take any position on the primacy of social versus cognitive deficits. They have focused exclusively on the language of the autistic children and are concerned with the development of the most efficient method for teaching functional linguistic skills to children who are able to learn these skills on their own. Underlying these approaches is the belief that the gains that the child makes in the linguistic realm will positively affect his social and emotional difficulties. In this chapter we discuss two representative approaches in this category: behavior modification and sign language therapy.

Psychotherapeutic Approach

The first treatment approach to be used with autistic children was a psychotherapeutic one. This was due in part to the influence of Kanner declassified autism as an "affective" disorder. As mentioned earlier, Kanner described the striking social withdrawal of the autistic children, their lack of appropriate eye contact, their preference for objects over people, and their self-stimulating body movements.

An early popular hypothesis proposed to explain these deviant behaviors was that autism resulted from the failure of the child during the first few weeks of life to develop a relationship with his mother, the first important human in his environment. As a result of the early failure, the child never develops the capacity for social interaction of any kind and shies away from all human contacts. Given this bizarre emotional development, the theory claims, it is to be expected that the child will not be motivated to learn to communicate.

There is some dispute about the underlying cause of the failure of the child to develop human relationships. Bettelheim (1967) places the majority of the blame on the parent. Most theorists, though, speculate that there may be some constitutional sensitivity (Mahler, 1968) or neurological imbalance (DesLaurier & Carlson, 1969) that prevents the child from making use of the adequate mothering that he receives.

Despite these theoretical disagreements, the therapeutic goal remains the same, namely, to break through the autistic defense against the social world by coaxing the child into entering a satisfying therapeutic relationship. Once this is accomplished, it is believed, the developmental process that was arrested so early will be stimulated and change will occur in all areas. (The therapist is, of course, most concerned with personality development.)

The style of therapy as well as the intensity varies across the different approaches. Bettelheim, for one, requires that the child be removed from his parents' home and have no further contact with them for the duration of treatment. Children live in an institutional setting and are assigned a therapist who provides the vast majority of their care and controls all aspects of their environment. Other therapists (DesLaurier & Carlson, 1969; Mahler, 1968) include the mothers in their treatment and see the children four times a week for 2-3 hour sessions. In all cases it is believed that effective treatment will take at least 3 to 4 years.

Despite the methodological variations, there is one relevant area of agreement among proponents of the psychotherapeutic approach. They are all highly critical of the kinds of language training programs that we describe in the remainder of the chapter because of their belief that the child should not be taught anything directly until he is "ready" for it emotionally. Thus Mahler (1968) cautions against enrolling the child in an education facility until the child has reached the point in his or her development where he or she can handle a group experience. In addition, psychotherapists are pessimistic about the success of training programs that try to teach language to the autistic child without first dealing with the underlying factors (e.g., the social withdrawal) that are responsible for the child's failure to develop language normally.

Bettelheim (1967) is most explicit on this point. He is particularly opposed to the training of autistic children using operant conditioning techniques, for these elicit from the child a response that the experimenter has chosen, whereas the desired situation is one in which the child willingly and spontaneously responds to his therapist in the context of a warm relationship. He believes—and most therapists tend to agree—that it is impossible to teach language in this way, for true communication must be the result of a human relationship and can not be forced out of a child.

After our discussion of two representative training approaches, we return to the doubts raised by psychotherapists and judge whether their pessimism is justified.

Psychotherapy for autistic children is still quite widespread although it no longer dominates the field. It is far more common to find a psychotherapeutic approach combined with another training program that is more directly concerned with changing behavior or teaching skills.

It is very difficult to evaluate the success of psychotherapy for autistic children because the clinicians involved have provided very little data. The concepts employed in their theories do not refer directly to observable behavior and therefore do not lend themselves easily to empirical validation. Research in this area is frought with methodological difficulties ranging from disagreements about relevant outcome measures to difficulties in finding appropriately matched control groups. In addition, ethical concerns constrain the use of treatment programs for research purposes.

As a consequence, in evaluating their therapies, psychotherapsits have relied, for the most part, on anectodal reports of case studies. The improvements noted in these reports (Bettelheim, 1967) are described in vague global terms that are difficult to evaluate. There are usually no pretests or posttests or control groups. The one exception to this is DesLaurier and Carlson ((1969) who provides some data on five autistic children before and after treatment in his program for 1 year. He found a significant pattern of change in a positive direction on the Fels Behavior Scale and on the Vineland Social Maturity Scale, neither of which measure language development. In any case, because there was no control group, it is difficult to determine the cause of this change.

BEHAVIOR MODIFICATION

From 1943 until the mid-1960s, there were few alternatives for parents of autistic children to psychotherapeutic treatment, which was very expensive and took a very long time. Because it is so intense, very few children could be treated at any given time.

In the late 1960s, Lovaas (1969) produced a film demonstrating that through the use of behavior modification techniques the behavior of autistic children could be brought under stimulus control. Most important, Lovaas showed that he could take previously mute autistic children and teach them to say some words.

Lovaas' film met with tremendous excitement. Behavior modification programs were set up across the country and many institutions and schools for autistic children began to incorporate some aspects of Lovaas' programs.

Lovaas did not enter this field with any special interest in autism. He did not base his work on any particular etiological theory nor is he interested in relating the language deficits to the other symptoms of the children. He was simply concerned with the "teaching of language to nonspeaking children" and chose autistic children as subjects.

In designing his language training programs, Lovaas and his followers drew heavily on the theoretical work of B. F. Skinner. They began with the assumption that normal children acquire language through imitation and reinforcement.

It should be noted that in the years since these programs were initiated developmental psychologists have challenged the reinforcement view of language acquisition (Dale, 1976, pp. 115-118). As a result many behaviorists have modified their views. For example, Stark (1972) denies that behaviorists are claiming that the learning of language in the normal child can be explained by reinforcement paradigms. They are merely providing evidence about the most efficient way to teach new behaviors to children who do not learn in the usual way. Similarly Lovaas (1977) describes his program as nothing more than a "technology ... on how to teach language to nonspeaking children" and explains the reliance on operant conditioning procedures as stemming from the following concern: "If one seeks to manipulate the child's environment to facilitate language training, then one is largely restricted to those operations specified within modern learning theory, certainly if one wants to base one's teaching efforts on experimental validated procedures [p. 10]."

Given Lovaas' theoretical bias, an effort to increase vocal imitation was a natural starting point for his program. The first part of the program was a discrimination training procedure with four steps:

1. The child is reinforced with food for any vocalization or for visually fixating on the adult's mouth. When the child reaches an achievement level of one vocalization every 5 sec and is fixating on the mouth more than 50% of the time, he moves on to step 2.
2. This step involves a temporal discrimination in which the child is required to make a vocal response within 6 sec after the adult's vocalization. Step 3 is introduced when the frequency of the child's vocal responses is three times the baseline rate.
3. Step 3 requires that the child match the adult vocalization. Initially the vocal behaviors in this step are prompted by manually moving the child through the behavior. Eventually these prompts are faded.
4. Step 4 involves the introduction of new sounds and words requiring increasingly finer discriminations. As the child begins to learn words, he is required to use the words appropriately. Accordingly he is not given water unless he says the word *water*.

Once the children are clearly imitative, Lovaas will move them into the second part of his program, which is designed to help establish meaningful speech. There are a number of aspects to this part of the program. Discrimination training of the kind just described is used to teach the child labels for the objects and people in his environment, as well as the use of pronouns, prepositions, and time-related concepts. The next step, the move from single words or isolated phrases to complete sentences, is probably the most problematic and challenging aspect of the program.

Originally, Lovaas attacked the problem of teaching the child to go beyond one-word speech to produce grammatical sentences by simply teaching the child to use a sentence frame of the form *I want* _____. This can be accomplished fairly easily using a response-chaining paradigm in which the last item is taught first and the earlier words are gradually prompted and reinforced.

As the program developed, the trainers were faced with the question of whether the child was actually learning syntactical rules or merely learning to parrot a certain specific response. This is a crucial question, for if the language taught is to be functional, the child must be able to produce new sentences based on some rule that he has internalized from the data presented to him. Behaviorists have recognized this problem in the notion of "response class." They are now concerned with demonstrating that the manipulation of a certain response in treatment will affect an entire class of responses that are similar in some way. Lovaas (1977) reports only a few examples of this.

For instance, he developed a program to teach the *ed* form of the past tense. Three children were taught to label 10 actions (e.g., walking, dancing) in the present tense and then trained to answer the question *What did you just do?* by transforming the present form of the verb to the past tense.

As a result of the new concern to demonstrate response generalization, the three subjects were then tested for use of the past tense with 10 new verbs. Data are presented in Lovaas (1977) for three echolalic children whose performance was errorless on the generalization test, suggesting that Lovaas' techniques are successful in getting the child to use syntactic rules rather than to simply memorize responses. The limitations of this kind of data are considered in the following.

Other behaviorists working with autistic children have reported similar successes. Wheeler and Sulzer (1970) report a study in which they trained a speech-deficient child who was already using "telegraphic speech," to use a particular sentence form.

Training involved reinforcement for correctly using sentences to describe pictures, with initial prompting of the sentences. Their results indicate that sentences were learned and applied to new pictures, although at a somewhat lower level of responding. The training involved no new vocabulary, only the recombination of words already in the child's repertoire. Therefore, the authors claim that it was the syntax of this sentence type that was learned and generalized to new situations.

Stevens-Long and Rasmussen (1974) and Stevens-Long, et al. (1976) present another series of studies demonstrating generalization across a response class.

Using a similar procedure to Wheeler and Sulzer (1970), they trained an autistic child to combine two simple sentences that he had been using with the word *and* and then tested for generalization using new pictures. They interpret their positive results as a demonstration of the efficiency of operant training procedures in teaching the productive use of simple and compound sentence structure to an autistic child.

Although this is an interesting study, it is unfortunate that the authors only probed for generalization of the insertion of the word *and*, for it is difficult to know from this whether the child has simply learned a rote response or has really learned a rule for compounds. Their results would have been much more convincing had they probed for the use of other conjunctions known to be part of the child's vocabulary (such as *but* and *or*) or tested on the use of compound nouns and verbs.

These few generalization studies represent a promising new direction in the research in this area that reflects a more sophisticated understanding of the complexity of language and a recognition of the need to take this into account in designing training programs.

The last part of Lovaas' program was designed in response to another frequent criticism of the program. The question was raised (Weiss & Born, 1967) whether their subjects were capable of using the language they had learned communicatively. Lovaas (1977) recognized the need to address this point [p. 85]:

> It is important to point out that the principal disadvantage of our training program centered on its failure to produce the kinds of spontaneous, cross-situational, generalized speech that normal children display.... Most of the children seemed not to want to speak, except in a situation where there was a powerful reinforcer available such as food.

In response, Lovaas began to incorporate programs to teach conversations, spontaneous communications, storytelling, and recall. An example of a "spontaneoty" session is as follows: The trainer would present a poster on which a picture of one object was posted and ask, *What do you see?* At first the answer would be prompted. The number of pictures was increased reinforcement became contingent on larger and larger responses. When the child was able to label all the pictures on the poster without any requests by the trainer, he was considered to have mastered this portion of the program. In the same way two-way conversations were systematically trained.

It is not necessary to point out that this is not what most people understand by spontaneous communication.

There are a number of ways that one can judge the success of the behavior modification program. Attention must be paid to at least three kinds of questions:

1. Are these specific interventions (reinforcement contingencies, etc.) directly responsible for the observed change in behavior or is there a third variable responsible?

2. Given that behaviorists have satisfied criterion (1), can these observed behavior changes be considered "language" training? In other words, do the new behaviors learned in the laboratory by the autistic children generalize in such a way that we would be justified in saying that they have learned communicative speech?
3. Is this the most efficient method for all autistic children, or is there a subset of autistic children who do not benefit from this approach?

Unlike the psychotherapists just discussed, behaviorists have been very concerned with Question 1. A standard ABA design is used to demonstrate the effects of training. There are many reports in the literature by behaviorists of successful training programs (Hartung, 1970; Lovaas, Schreibam, & Koegal 1974; Risley & Wolf, 1967; Stark, Giddan, & Mersel, 1968).

Lovaas, Berberich, Perloff, & Schaeffer (1966) used a variant of this approach in his evaluation of his own program. He introduced a second phase of treatment in which rewards were no longer response contingent. Instead they were made time contingent regardless of the child's behavior. As expected, the data show a deterioration in correct responding in the time-contingent condition.

It seems clear that these procedures are effective in increasing speech in the laboratory with at least some autistic children. But perhaps the most serious and widely raised question concerning the behavior modification technique focuses on Question 2, the generalization of their results. Thus Stark (1972) writes:

> The difficulties of teaching syntax and even simple transformations to children who have little or no functional speech is apparent to any clinician who has worked with a nonverbal autistic child. Whether a child will be able to generalize what he has learned in the clinic so that his language will be functional and whether he will be able to generate novel utterances based upon a program of systematically presented hierarchies of language stimuli remains an enigma [p. 192].

Behaviorists have conceptualized the generalization problem in three ways (Lovaas Koegal, Simmons, & Stevens-Long, 1973): (1) stimulus generalization, the extent to which the behavior changed in treatment transfers to different settings; (2) generalization over time; (3) response generalization, the extent to which the changes that occurred in treatment will effect other behaviors.

Lovaas et al. (1973) reported some follow-up measures on the first 10 children to be treated. Briefly, they found that children who lived with their parents maintained their gains (stimulus generalization plus generalization over time), whereas the children who were discharged to state institutions lost what they had learned in treatment. As a measure of response generalization, Lovaas et al. report Stanford Binet IQ scores and Vineland Social Quotient scores. All the children showed increases in these scores during treatment despite the fact that they were not explicitly trained on these tests. It should be noted that this demonstration of response generalization is of doubtful relevance because neither of these tests measure language.

In addition, behaviorists are now becoming interested in demonstrating more relevant types of response generalization. They have begun to train specific syntactic rules, which, it is expected, will generalize to new instances.

The evaluation of Question 3 is most difficult, for here the behaviorists have not provided the relevant data. They do not report failures in any detail nor do they compare their successes to control groups. Thus one cannot deduce precisely what the proportion of success is. Nor can one determine how this treatment compares with any other approach (or with a no-treatment control).

There certainly has been some discouragement with the behavior modification paradigm. Hingtgen and Churchill (1966) wondered if the small gains that had been demonstrated were worth the inordinate amount of time and effort that was necessary for their achievement. In their study, after 600 hours of training, half their subjects had not learned the simple visual-auditory association of picking up an object upon hearing the verbal label. Miller (1969) discontinued training after 1 year of daily sessions with an autistic boy when it became apparent that the child was merely forming rituals that were difficult to separate from the desired language response. She reported that no spontaneous speech resulted from the mastery of sounds and words.

From the bits of data presented by Lovaas and his colleagues, it appears that the probability that the training of a given child will be successful depends on his level at the outset. By 1974, Lovaas (1974) reported that his program was having little success in teaching mute, autistic children anything beyond simple imitation skills. The positive results that have been mentioned occurred primarily with children who were echolalic at the beginning of treatment. (Again, it is unknown what proportion of echolalic children this represents.)

There are a number of possible explanations for this limitation in Lovaas' training program. Lovaas (1977), and Lovaas, Varni, Koegel, and Lorsch (1977) claim that language behavior in the normal child once learned is not maintained by extrinsic reinforcement alone but is influenced by internal reinforcement. In other words, private language may have its own reward. Although his program can teach a child the rudiments of language, he believes that his failures with some autistic children are due to the inability of these children to make use of internal reinforcement to maintain their behavior when external reinforcement is not available. Lovaas does not offer any explanation for this deficit.

An alternate explanation for the observed discrepancy in the treatment gains made by mute versus echolalic children is the possibility that echolalic children know more about language than they spontaneously display. (This is, or course, the position taken by the psychotherapists and is certainly consonant with what is known about autistic language abilities.) Lovaas' program, then, is successful because it can motivate the children to talk and can draw them out of their autistic isolation through the use of intrusive measures (food reinforcers, negative reinforcement, physical punishment). As the autistic withdrawal is broken down, the echolalic children begin to display the knowledge of language that they had all along. The failure of Lovaas' program to teach language to mute subjects would then be due to their relative lack of linguistic knowledge upon entering training.

These opposing views can only be adjudicated when more is known about the nature of the autistic deficits and a theory is developed to explain their etiology. The lack of a position on these points is a major disadvantage of the behavior modification approach, for it provides no explanation of its successes and little understanding of its failures.

Sign Language Therapy

Because behavior modification programs are relatively unsuccessful with mute autistic children, clinicians began to seek alternative language training procedures. By the early 1970s, there were several reports in the literature of attempts by individual clinicians to teach sign language to mute autistic children. The initial results were encouraging and have stimulated quite a bit of research.

The decision to teach a sign language, as opposed to speech, was based in part on dissatisfaction with behavior modification as well as the recognition of the advantages of a visual language. Bonvillian and Nelson (1976) argue that the child's inability to learn to speak may be due to a very specific impairment in the speech areas that would leave the visual motor areas intact. Because there are a number of manifestations of language—written, spoken, and signed—the failure of the child to learn a spoken language suggests that one should try a different approach that might capitalize on the autistic child's presumed strengths.

Unfortunately, some of the alleged "strengths" cited by proponents of sign language therapy are not found in autistic children. For instance, Fulwiler and Fonts (1976) claim that sign language is appropriate for autistic children because these children naturally communicate with gestures. Bartak et al. (1975), however, investigated this point and found little use of spontaneous gesturing in autistic children.

These authors make another erroneous assumption about sign language that they cite as an advantage. They claim that the autistic child has difficulty learning a verbal language because it involves cross-modal associations; that is, the child must associate an auditory stimulus with a visually perceived object. Sign language on the other hand, claim Fulwiler and Fonts, is an easier system because it is unimodal—both sign and referent are visually perceived. This argument is dubious because only a small part of language is used to refer to concrete objects that can be seen. Thus the question of number of modalities employed does not distinguish between spoken and sign language most of the time.

Many of the reports of sign language programs are case studies in which one or two children were taught to use American Sign Language (Ameslan) (Bonvillian & Nelson, 1976), Ameslan with speech (Fulwiler & Fonts, 1976), signed speech (Schaeffer et al., 1977; Webster, McPherson, Sloman, Evans, & Kuchar,

1973), or simultaneous communication (Creedon, cited in Webster et al., 1973). These programs differ from one another primarily in the degree to which they include speech in their therapy.

A typical case study is described by Bonvillian and Nelson (1976). They trained a 5-year-old nonverbal autistic child to use American Sign Language in daily half-hour sessions. Two teaching methods were used, molding the signs for the child and requiring the child to imitate his teacher's signs. The teacher usually said the word that was associated with the sign as he presented it. A token reward system was used to motivate performance.

After 6 months in the program, the child learned 56 different signs and used the signs spontaneously (as reported by an objective observer). Most of his sign utterances were two-word combinations that seemed to resemble the range of two-word sentences of normal young children in their grammatical structure and semantic relationships.

Single case studies are interesting but their results may have limited generalizability. Benaroya, Wesley, Ogilvie, Klein, and Meaney (1977) report the results of a simultaneous communication program that was tried with six autistic children. This program had a number of steps:

1. Initially the teacher engaged the child in intrusion play (tickling, slapping, roughing, and rolling) in an effort to make him aware of her presence.
2. The second step involved teaching the child to imitate body movements.
3. Once the child could imitate, the teacher began to pair objects with both their manual sign and the verbal equivalent. Molding of the child's hands and reinforcement of successive approximations were primary teaching methods.
4. As the child began to learn some signs, an audiovisual teaching machine was introduced. The child was expected to sign appropriate answers to the stimuli presented by the machine.

Results indicate that four of the six children displayed spontaneous use of signs and five of the six combined the simple signs into two or more sign phrases.

The reports just described provide clear evidence that mute autistic children can learn to use some sign language. Many of the studies report an increase in verbal communication as well. However, the basis for the effectiveness of this form of treatment remains to be clarified. There has been some speculation, mentioned previously, about specific kinds of sensory mode deficits in autistic children that are avoided in sign language therapy. To shed light on these questions, Brady and Simouse (1978) designed a study in which three types of communication, vocalization, signing, and a combination of the first two, were compared. These three treatments were administered concurrently to one 6-year-old autistic boy. The study used a nine-word experimental language that had been developed by Churchill (1972). Results indicated that the simultaneous or total communication training, in which both vocalization and signing were taught, was most effective. There was a significant decrease from baseline responding in the vocalization-only condition.

On the basis of their results, Brady and Simouse question the notion that autistic children have a deficit in cross-modal association that hinders them in learning to speak. Rather they speculate that simultaneous communication is effective because it combines all the sense modes. Certainly more research of this kind with larger populations is necessary before a definitive explanation of the efficacy of treatment can be given.

Simultaneous communication programs seem to be rapidly replacing behavior modification as the treatment of choice for mute autistic children. That simulteneous communication can be successful where speech therapy has failed is interesting and not easily explained. Research on this question is exciting, for it offers new possibilities for shedding light on the nature of autistic deficits.

We began this section on treatment by noting some beliefs strongly held by psychotherapists about the kinds of treatments that can be successful with autistic children. Psychotherapists cautioned against formal training and were pessimistic about the possibility of teaching language without first attacking the sockal withdrawal. Behaviorist and sign language therapists have clearly demonstrated that their procedures can teach some language to certain subgroups of autistic children. Comparatively clear results have not been demonstrated by psychotherapists. Whether psychotherapists would consider the language taught to be truly communicative and spontaneous remains an open question.

In response to psychotherapists, language therapists have been concerned to demonstrate that their procedures result in positive changes in the social behavior of the autistic children. Thus Lovaas et al. (1974) reports improvements on the Vineland Social Maturity Scale as a result of behavior modification training and Casey (1978) and Benroya et al. (1977) report decreases in many inappropriate social behaviors as a result of sign language therapy.

There is much additional research to be done. Language therapists have been overly pragmatic in their approach. They have been content merely to demonstrate that a given program works. It is now necessary to direct research toward a better understanding of *why* certain programs work so that we can make judgments about the treatment of choice for a given autistic child. Therapy for autistic children will never reach this level of sophistication until more is known about autism.

CONCLUSIONS

We can now return to the theoretical issues raised in the introduction to this review to summarize our view of the language deficit in infantile autism.

The first distinction we introduced was between language knowledge and language use. The issue here is whether the autistic child acquires knowledge of language but fails to use it or whether he or she never learns language in the first place. The former hypothesis is implied by some psychogenic theories; the latter seems most compatible with etiological theories based on congenital damage to the central nervous system.

The evidence on this point indicates that the acquisition of language is the fundamental difficulty in autism. The autistic language deficit seems to hold across all facets of language organization and apparently affects both production and comprehension of language, although the evidence is weak on this point. This pattern suggests that it is the underlying knowledge rather than the mode of use that is deficient in the autistic child.

It must be admitted that there is no direct way to examine linguistic knowledge by itself. Any technique that requires a response from the child will reflect the mechanisms of language use in addition to linguistic knowledge. Nevertheless, the breadth of the language deficit in autism and its similarity to that of other disabled groups suggests strongly that the autistic child's principle difficulty is a failure to acquire language rather than difficulty in employing what knowledge the child possesses.

It is worth noting that this conclusion is limited to language use in the narrow sense of being able to articulate an idea. In the wider sense of being able and willing to communicate socially, autistic children have special difficulties that go beyond their deficit in linguistic knowledge.

A second important distinction concerns the two modes of language use, comprehension and production. Given the conclusion that the autistic language deficit does not involve language use, one would expect that comprehension and production abilities in autistic children should be equally deficient. There have been no studies specifically addressed to this issue, so no firm conclusion can be reached. If there is a difference between comprehension and production, however, it is not striking enough to show up in clinical reports.

It should be noted, though, that there was one hint that comprehension might be more severely affected than production in autism. Recall that the syntax of autistic children's spontaneous speech was comparable to that of developmental dysphasics, although, in a different study on the same children, it was found that their comprehension was not so good. This difference should be investigated further not only because of its theoretical interest but because of the potential practical value it has for language training programs with autistic children.

A third theoretical issue is whether autism involves a general language disorder or whether it is limited to certain facets of language. On the basis of the evidence reviewed here the answer to this question must be both. There is no area of language unaffected in autism; yet some areas are affected more than others. No study has found language abilities in autism equal to chronological age-matched normals. (Although this is true for the group as a whole, it may not be true of every individual child.) Because the majority of autistic children are mentally retarded, however, much of this nonspecific language disability may be accounted for by this fact alone. In the area of phonology, for example, there seems to be no further deficit beyond that due to retardation.

Although we have too little information about semantics to make a judgment, syntax and pragmatics, in contrast to phonology, seem to be specially affected in autism, above and beyond what one would expect on the basis of retardation. This raises the interesting question of what the cause of these differences might be. We would like to know, for example, whether there is some common factor underlying syntax and pragmatics that could be affected without at the same time diminishing phonological abilities. That this common factor might be related to brain localization is one possibility that might be investigated. Whatever the answer turns out to be, it will surely provide insight into the autistic syndrome.

The final issue to be considered is that of delay versus deviancy in autistic language disabilities. Our review of the literature indicates that, by and large, autistic language is severely delayed but not apparently deviant. Detailed studies of phonology and syntax have shown that autistic errors are identical to appropriately matched retardates and normals. Little evidence of deviancy was found in these studies suggesting that language acquisition proceeds on the same basis in autistic children as in other groups.

The only area in which deviance may be indicated is in the pragmatics of language, particularly in the use of echolalia. But as pointed out in our discussion of this phenomenon, it is not clear yet how deviant such language is. Echolalia is found in very young normal children and in other disabled groups, including retardates and certain varieties of aphasia. So if autistic echolalia is deviant at all, it is probably not uniquely so and may not provide any special insight into the nature of the autistic syndrome.

Consideration of these theoretical issues leads to the following rough picture of autistic language: There is an across-the-board delay in the acquisition of language with special severity in the areas of syntax and pragmatics. Although this is the picture that emerges from research on autistic language to date, there are enough uninvestigated areas that it could change substantially in the future. We expect that future advances in our understanding of the autistic language disorder will both illuminate nonlinguistic aspects of autism and provide a solid theoretical basis for effective treatment of the disorder.

REFERENCES

Aurnhammer-Frith, U. Emphasis and meaning in recall in normal and autistic children. *Language and Speech*, 1969, *12*, 29–38.

Baker, L., Cantwell, D. P., Rietter, M., & Bartak, L. Language and autism. In Ritvo, E., Freeman, B. J., Ornitz, E. M., Tanguay, P. E. (Eds), *Autism: Diagnosis, current research and management*. New York: Spectrum, 1976.

Baltaxe, C., & Simmons, J. Bedtime soliloquies and linguistic competence in autism. *Journal of Speech and Hearing Disorders*, 1977, *42*, 376–393.

Barry, R. J., & James, A. L. Handedness in autistics, retardates, and normals of a wide age range. *Journal of Autism and Childhood Schizophrenia,* 1978, *8,* 315-323.

Bartak, L., Rutter, M., & Cox, A. A comparative study of infantile autism and specific developmental receptive language disorder. I. The children. *British Journal of Psychiatry,* 1975, *126,* 127-145.

Bartak, L., Rutter, M., & Cox, A. A comparative study of infantile autism and specific developmental receptive language disorder. III. Discriminant functions analysis. *Journal of Autism and Childhood Schizophrenia,* 1977, *7,* 383-396.

Bartolucci, G., Pierce, S., Streiner, D., & Eppel, P. Phonological investigation of verbal autistic and mentally retarded subjects. *Journal of Autism and Childhood Schizophrenia,* 1976, *6,* 303-316.

Bates, E. Pragmatics and sociolinguistics in child language. In D. Morehead & A. Morehead (Eds.), *Normal and deficient child language.* Baltimore: University Park Press, 1976.

Bates, E., Camaioni, L., & Volterra, V. The acquisition of performatives prior to speech. *Merrill-Palmer Quarterly,* 1975, *21,* 205-226.

Benaroya, S., Wesley, S., Ogilvie, H., Klein, L. S., & Meaney, M. Sign language and multisensory input training of children with communication and related developmental disorders. *Journal of Autism and Childhood Schizophrenia,* 1977, *7,* 23-31.

Bettelheim, B. *The empty fortress: Infantile autism and the birth of the self.* New York: Free Press, 1967.

Bonvillian, J. D., & Nelson, K. E. Sign language acquisition in a mute autistic boy. *Journal of Speech and Hearing Disorders,* 1976, *61,* 333-338.

Boucher, J. Articulation in early childhood autism. *Journal of Autism and Childhood Schizophrenia,* 1976, *6,* 297-302.

Boucher, J. Hand preference in autistic children and their parents. *Journal of Autism and Childhood Schizophrenia,* 1977, *7,* 177-187.

Bradley, D. *Computational distinctions of vocabulary type.* Doctoral dissertation, Massachusetts Institute of Technology, 1978.

Brady, D. O., & Simouse, A. D. A simultaneous comparison of three methods for language training with an autistic child: An experimental single case analysis. *Journal of Autism and Childhood Schizophrenia,* 1978, *8,* 271-279.

Brown, R. *A first language.* Cambridge, Mass.: Harvard University Press, 1973.

Brown, R., & Bellugi, U. Three processes in the acquisition of syntax. *Harvard Educational Review,* 1964, *34,* 133-151.

Campbell, B., & Grieve, R. Social and attentional aspects of echolalia in highly echolalic mentally retarded persons. *American Journal of Mental Deficiency,* 1978, *82,* 414-416.

Cantwell, D., Baker, L., & Rutter, M. A comparative study of infantile autism and specific developmental receptive language disorder. IV. Analysis of syntax and language function. *Journal of Child Psychology and Psychiatry,* 1978, *19,* 351-362.

Cantwell, D., Howlin, P., & Rutter, M. The analysis of language level and language function: A methodological study. *British Journal of Disorders of Communication,* 1977, *12,* 119-135.

Cantwell, D. P., Baker, L., & Rutter, M. Families of autistic and dysphasic children. II. Mothers' speech to the children. *Journal of Autism and Childhood Schizophrenia,* 1977, *7,* 313-327.

Casey, L. D. Development of communicative behavior in autistic children: A parent program using manual signs. *Journal of Autism and Childhood Schizophrenia,* 1978, *8,* 45-59.

Chomsky, N. *Syntactic structures.* The Hague: Mouton, 1957.

Chomsky, N., & Halle, M. *The sound pattern of English.* New York: Harper & Row, 1968.

Churchill, D. W. The relation of infantile autism and early childhood schizophrenia to developmental language disorders of childhood. *Journal of Autism and Childhood Schizophrenia,* 1972, *2,* 182-197.

Colby, K. M., & Parkison, C. Handedness in autistic children. *Journal of Autism and Childhood Schizophrenia,* 1977, *7,* 3-9.

Cromer, R. Receptive language in the mentally retarded: Processes and diagnostic distinctions. In R. Schiefelbusch & L. Lloyd (Eds.), *Language perspectives—Acquisition, retardation, intervention*. Baltimore: University Park Press, 1974.

Dale, P. *Language development: Structure and function* (2nd ed.). New York: Holt, Rinehart & Winston, 1976.

DesLauriers, A. M., & Carlson, C. F. *Your child is asleep: Early infantile autism*. Homewood, Ill.: Dorsey Press, 1969.

Despert, J. L. Discussion. *American Journal of Psychiatry*, 1946, *103*, 245-246.

Fremgen, A., & Fay, D. *Linguistic reversibility without cognitive reversibility*. Unpublished manuscript, University of Illinois at Chicago, 1980.

Fulwiler, R. L., & Fouts, R. S. Acquisition of American sign languages by a noncommunicating autistic child. *Journal of Autism and Childhood Schizophrenia*, 1976, *6*, 43-51.

Geschwind, N., Quadfasel, F. A., & Segarra, J. M. Isolation of the speech area. *Neuropsychologia*, 1968, *6*, 327-340.

Goldfarb, W., Goldfarb, N., & Scholl, M. The speech of mothers of schizophrenic children. *American Journal of Psychiatry*, 1966, *122*, 1220-1227.

Goldfarb, W., Levy, D., & Meyers, D. The verbal encounter between the schizophrenic child and his mother. In G. Goldman & D. Shapiro (Eds.), *Developments in psychoanalysis at Columbia University*. New York: Hafner, 1966.

Goldfarb, W., Levy, D., & Meyers, D. The mother speaks to her schizophrenic child: Language in childhood schizophrenia. *Psychiatry*, 1972, *35*, 217-26.

Hartung, J. A review of procedures to increase verbal imitation skills and functional speech in autistic children. *Journal of Speech and Hearing Disorders*, 1970, *35*, 203-217.

Hauser, S. L., DeLong, G. R., & Rosman, N. P. Pneumogrpahic finding in the infantile autism syndrome. *Brain*, 1975, *98*, 667-688.

Heilman, K. M., & Watson, R. T. The neglect syndrome—A unilateral defect of the orienting response. In S. Harnad, R. W. Doty, L. Goldstein, J. Jaynes, & G. Krauthamer (Eds.), *Lateralization in the nervous system*. New York: Academic Press, 1977.

Hermelin, B. Images and language. In M. Rutter & E. Schopler (Eds.) *Autism: A reappraisal of concepts and treatment*. New York: Plenum, 1978.

Hermelin, B., & O'Connor, N. Spatial coding in normal, autistic, and blind children. *Perceptual Motor Skills*, 1971, *33*, 127-132.

Hermelin, B., & O'Connor, N. Remembering of words by psychotic and subnormal children. *British Journal of Psychology*, 1967, *58*, 213-218.

Hermelin, B., & O'Connor, N. *Psychological experiments with autistic children*. Oxford: Pergamon Press, 1970.

Hermelin, B., & O'Connor, N. Location and distance estimates of blind and sighted children. *Quarterly Journal of Experimental Psychology*, 1975, *27*, 295-301.

Hier, D. B., LeMay, M., & Rosenberger, P. B. Autism and unfavorable left-right asymmetries of the brain. *Journal of Autism and Developmental Disorders*, 1979, *9*, 153-159.

Hingtgen, J., & Churchill, D. Identification of perceptual limitations in mute autistic children. *Archives of General Psychiatry*, 1969, *21*, 68-71.

Kanner, L. Autistic disturbances of affective contact. *Nervous Child*, 1943, *2*, 217-250.

Kanner, L. Irrelevant and metaphorical language in early infantile autism. *American Journal of Psychiatry*, 1946, *103*, 242-245.

Kanner, L., & L. Eisenberg. Notes on the follow-up of autistic children. In P. H. Hoch & J. Zubin (Eds.), *Psychopathology of childhood*. New York: Grune & Stratton, 1955.

Kinsbourne, M. The cerebral basis of lateral asymmetries in attention. *Acta Psychologica*, 1970, *33*, 193-201.

Klein, D., & Pollack, M. Schizophrenic children and maternal speech facility. *American Journal of Psychiatry*, 1966, *123*, 232.

Kolvin, I. Psychoses in childhood—A comparative study. In M. Rutter (Ed.), *Infantile autism: Concepts, characteristics, and treatment.* London: Churchill-Livingstone, 1971.
Lackner, J. R. A developmental study of language behavior in retarded children. *Neuropsychologia,* 1968, *6,* 301-320.
Lee, L. *Developmental sentence analysis.* Evanston, Ill.: Northwestern University Press, 1974.
Lennard, H., Beaulieu, M., & Embry, M. Interaction in families with a schizophrenic child. *Archives of General Psychiatry,* 1965, *12,* 166-183.
Lenneberg, E. *Biological foundations of language.* New York: Wiley, 1967.
Levy, J., Beck, B., & Staikoff, J. *Dysfunction of the left cerebral hemisphere in autistic children.* Unpublished manuscript, University of Chicago, 1979.
Lovaas, O. I. (Producer). *Behavior modification: Teaching language to psychotic children.* New York: Appleton-Century-Crofts, 1969. (Film)
Lovaas, O. I. *The autistic child: Language development through behavior modification.* New York: Irvington Pub., 1977.
Lovaas, O. I., Berberich, J. P., Perloff, B. F., & Schaeffer, B. Acquisition of imitative speech in schizophrenic children. *Science,* 1966, *151,* 705-707.
Lovaas, O. I., Koegel, R., Simmons, J. Q., & Stevens-Long, J. Some generalization and follow-up measures on autistic children in behavior therapy. *Journal of Applied Behavior Analysis,* 1973, *6,* 131-165.
Lovaas, O. I., Schreibman, L., & Koegel, R. L. A behavior modification approach to the treatment of autistic children. *Journal of Autism and Childhood Schizophrenia,* 1974, *4,* 111-129.
Lovaas, O. I., Varni, J. W., Koegel, R. L., & Lorsch, N. Some observations on the nonextinguishability of children's speech. *Child Development,* 1977, *48,* 1121-1127.
Mahler, M. S. *On human symbiosis and the vicissitudes of individuation: Infantile psychosis.* New York: International Universities Press, 1968.
Menyuk, P. *Sentences children use.* Cambridge, Mass.: MIT Press, 1969.
Meyers, D., & Goldfarb, W. Studies of perplexity in mothers of schizophrenic children. *American Journal of Orthopsychiatry,* 1961, *31,* 551-564.
Miller, N. Language therapy with an autistic nonverbal boy. *Exceptional Children,* 1969, *35,* 555-557.
Morehead, D., & Ingram, D. The development of base syntax in normal and linguistically deviant children. *Journal of Speech and Hearing Disorders,* 1973, *16,* 330-352.
O'Connor, N., & Hermelin, B. Visual analogies of verbal operations. *Language and Speech,* 1965, *8,* 197-207.
O'Connor, N., & Hermelin, B. The spatial or temporal organization of short term memory. *Quarterly Journal of Experimental Psychology,* 1973, *25,* 335-343.
Ornitz, E. M., & Ritvo, E. R. The syndrome of autism: A critical review. *American Journal of Psychiatry,* 1976, *133,* 609-621.
Paccia Cooper, J., & Curcio, F. *Language processing and forms of echolalia in severely disturbed children.* Unpublished manuscript, Boston University, 1979.
Pierce, S., & Bartolucci, G. A syntactic investigation of verbal autistic, mentally retarded, and normal children. *Journal of Autism and Childhood Schizophrenia,* 1977, *7,* 121-134.
Reynell, J. *Reynell developmental language scales.* NFER Publishing Co., Ltd: Windsor, England, 1969.
Risley, T., & Wolf, M. Establishing functional speech in echolalic children. *Behaviour Research and Therapy,* 1967, *5,* 73-88.
Rutter, M. Autistic children: Infancy to adulthood. *Seminars in Psychiatry,* 1970, *2,* 435-450.
Rutter, M. The description and classification of infantile autism. In D. Churchill, G. Alpern, & M. DeMeyer (Eds.), *Infantile autism.* Springfield, Ill.: Charles C. Thomas, 1971.
Rutter, M., & Bartak, L. Causes of infantile autism: Some considerations from recent research. *Journal of Autism and Childhood Schizophrenia,* 1971, *1,* 20-32.

Rutter, M., Greenfield, D., & Lockyer, L. A five to fifteen year follow-up study of infantile psychosis. II. Social and behavioral outcome. *British Journal of Psychiatry,* 1967, *113,* 1183–1199.

Satz, P. Left-handedness and early brain insult: An explanation. *Neuropsychologia,* 1973, *11,* 115–117.

Schaeffer, B., Kallingas, G., Musil, A., & McDowell, P. Spontaneous verbal language for autistic children through signed speech. *Sign Language Studies,* 1977, 287–328.

Searleman, A. A review of right hemisphere linguistic capabilities. *Psychological Bulletin,* 1977, *84,* 503–528.

Shapiro, T., Roberts, A., & Fish, B. Imitation and echoing in schizophrenic children. *Journal of the American Academy of Child Psychiatry,* 1970, *9,* 548–567.

Shattuck-Hufnagel, S., & Klatt, D. The limited use of distinctive features and markedness in speech production: Evidence from speech error data. *Journal of Verbal Learning and Verbal Behavior,* 1979, *18,* 41–55.

Sinclair, H. Sensorimotor action patterns as a condition for the acquisition of syntax. In R. Huxley & E. Ingram (Eds.), *Language acquisition: models and methods.* New York: Academic Press, 1971.

Stark, J. Language training for the autistic child using operant conditioning procedures. *Journal of Communicative Disorders,* 1972, *5,* 183–194.

Stark, J., Giddan, J., & Mersel, J. Increasing verbal behavior in an autistic child. *Journal of Speech and Hearing Disorders,* 1968, *33,* 42–48.

Stengel, E. A clinical and psychological study of echo-reactions. *Journal of Mental Science,* 1947, *93,* 598–612.

Stevens-Long, J., & Rasmussen, M. The acquisition of simple and compound sentence structure in an autistic child. *Journal of Applied Behavior Analysis,* 1974, *7,* 473–479.

Stevens-Long, J., Schwartz, J., & Bliss, D. The acquisition and generalization of compound sentence structure in an autistic child. *Behavior Therapy,* 1976, *7,* 397–404.

Voeltz, L. An analysis of the linguistic behaviors of severely developmental handicapped children diagnosed as autistic. (Doctoral dissertation, Indiana University, 1976). *Dissertation Abstracts International,* 1977, *37,* 5045.

Webster, D. D., McPherson, H., Sloman, L., Evans, M. A., & Kuchar, E. Communicating with an autistic boy by gestures. *Journal of Autism and Childhood Schizophrenia,* 1973, *3,* 337–346.

Weir, R. *Language in the crib.* The Hague: Mouton, 1962.

Weiss, H., & Born, B. Speech training or language acquisition? *American Journal of Orthopsychiatry,* 1967, *37,* 49–55.

Wheeler, A., & Sulzer, B. Operant training and generalization of a verbal response form in a speech deficient child. *Journal of Applied Behavior Analysis,* 1970, *3,* 139–147.

Whitaker, H. A case of isolation of the language function. In H. Whitaker & H. A. Whitaker (Eds.), *Studies in Neurolinguistics* (Vol. 2). New York: Academic Press, 1976.

Witelson, S. Sex and the single hemisphere: Specialization of the right hemisphere for spatial processing. *Science,* 1976, *193,* 425–427.

9 The Language Development of Deaf Children and Youth

Stephen P. Quigley
Cynthia M. King
University of Illinois at Urbana-Champaign

INTRODUCTION

The plan for the chapter involves: (1) dicussion of the terms *deaf* and *language development* in order to define the population and the problem with which we are concerned; (2) discussion of the present language status of deaf students to indicate the nature and extent of the language problem; (3) discussion of language development in deaf children through ASL, manual English, and oral English; and (4) a brief conclusion. Presentation of literature in the chapter is selective and is meant to be representative of issues and processes being discussed rather than exhaustive.

DEAFNESS AND LANGUAGE DEVELOPMENT

Deafness

Hearing is usually measured across a range of frequencies from 125 Hz to 8000 Hz on a continuous logarithmic scale, with the unit of measurement being the decibel (dB). Hearing impairment is represented on the audiogram, which graphs the hearing threshold level (HTL) for an individual in relation to a statistically defined normal threshold (ANSI, 1969) represented on the audiogram as zero at each of the frequencies measured. *Hearing impairment* is a generic term covering all degrees of hearing loss, with deafness being the extreme form of the impairment. HTL on the audiogram can be measured from -10 dB to 110 dB.

Hearing impairment is usually presented as the average of the HTL for the three frequencies considered to be most important for the reception of speech: 500, 1000, and 2000 Hz. Thus, an individual with HTLs of 45 dB at 500 Hz, 50 dB at 1000 Hz, and 55 dB at 2000 Hz is said to have a HTL or hearing impairment of 50 dB. The degree of hearing impairment, thus measured, is the primary descriptive variable for hearing-impaired populations. Next in importance to degree of impairment is the age at onset of impairment. Particularly with what is defined later as deaf persons, the age at which the impairment occurred can have a profound influence on various aspects of the individual's functioning.

Other important descriptive variables are etiology and type of hearing impairment and hearing status of parents and siblings of the hearing-impaired individual. Etiology is important because some of the causes of hearing impairment (such as maternal rubella and anoxia) often result in problems in addition to deafness. As many as 25% of what we define as the deaf population might have complicating factors such as visual problems, retardation, and cerebral palsy (Vernon, 1969). Type of hearing impairment refers to whether the impairment is conductive, sensorineural, mixed, or central in nature. In conductive impairment, all or some part of the impairment involves only the conductive mechanism of the middle and outer ear. This type of impairment often is treatable medically or by amplification (hearing aids). Sensorineural impairment results usually from damage to some portion of the inner ear in which most of the sensory mechanism of hearing is located. This type of impairment is usually medically irreversible and yields only partially to amplification. Combinations of sensory and conductive impairment are known as mixed. Damage to the auditory nerve that transmits sensory information from the inner ear to the auditory cortex, and to the auditory cortex itself, can produce central hearing impairment. Hearing status of parents and siblings is of special interest with the deaf population because the form of language and communication to which the deaf individual is exposed in infancy and early childhood can be quite different for the deaf child of deaf parents than for the deaf child of hearing parents. This factor alone can profoundly affect the language and educational development of the child and his social and personal functioning. A good source for readable technical detail on hearing and hearing impairment is Davis and Silverman (1970).

Complete description of a hearing-impaired individual or population, therefore, should include hearing threshold level, age at onset of hearing impairment, type and etiology of the impairment, and hearing status of parents and siblings. All the variables important to description of hearing populations are, of course, similarly important with hearing-impaired populations, such as IQ and socioeconomic status of family. Much of the confusion in studying and interpreting the language and communication of deaf children arises from incomplete descriptions of the populations under consideration and generalization of findings to dissimilar populations.

Although all the variables just described are important to an understanding of deafness, classification systems for hearing impairment usually are one-dimensional. Table 9.1 presents a classification that has been used by the Department of Public Health in the state of Illinois and is based on a system proposed by Davis (1965). There are five categories of impairment in this classification, each of which is supposed to represent a different type or degree of language and communication problem. When we refer to deaf individuals, or groups, or populations in this chapter, we are referring to the fourth and fifth categories only, and primarily to the fifth. The first three categories will be excluded as representing hard of hearing individuals. The fourth category represents a zone between hard of hearing and deaf. Most individuals with this degree of impairment should be able to benefit substantially from their remaining hear-

TABLE 9.1
Relationship of Degree of Handicap to Educational Needs[a]

Degree of Handicap	Effect of Hearing Loss on the Understanding of Language and Speech	Educational Needs and Programs
Slight 16 to 29dB (ASA) or 27 to 40dB (ISO)	May have difficulty hearing faint or distant speech. Will not usually experience difficulty in school situations.	May benefit from a hearing aid as loss approaches 30dB (ASA) or 40dB (ISO). Attention to vocabulary development. Needs favorable seating and lighting. May need lip reading instruction. May need speech correction.
Mild 30 to 44dB (ASA) or 41 to 55dB (ISO)	Understands conversational speech at a distance of 3-5 feet (face-to-face). May miss as much as 50% of class discussions if voices are faint or not in line of vision. May exhibit limited vocabulary and speech anomalies.	Child should be referred to special education for educational follow-up if such service is available. Individual hearing aid by evaluation and training in its use. Favorable seating and possible special class placement, especially for primary children. Attention to vocabulary and reading. May need lip reading instruction. Speech conservation and correction, if indicated.
Marked 45 to 59dB (ASA) or 56 to 70dB (ISO)	Conversation must be loud to be understood. Will have increasing difficulty with school situations requiring participation in group discussions. Is likely to have defective speech. Is likely to be deficient in language usage and comprehension. Will have evidence of limited vocabulary.	Will need resource teacher or special class. Special help in language skills, vocabulary development, usage, reading, writing, grammar, etc. Individual hearing aid by evaluation and auditory training. Lip reading instruction. Speech conservation and speech correction. Attention to auditory and visual situations at all times.

(continued)

TABLE 9.1. (*Continued*)

Degree of Handicap	Effect of Hearing Loss on the Understanding of Language and Speech	Educational Needs and Programs
Severe 60 to 79dB (ASA) or 71 to 90dB (ISO)	May hear loud voices about one foot from the ear. May be able to identify environmental sounds. May be able to discriminate vowels but not all consonants. Speech and language defective and likely to deteriorate. Speech and language will not develop spontaneously if loss is present before one year of age.	Will need full-time special program for deaf children, with emphasis on all language skills, concept development, lip reading and speech. Program needs specialized supervision and comprehensive supporting services. Individual hearing aid by evaluation. Auditory training on individual and group aids. Part-time in regular classes only as profitable.
Extreme 80dB or more (ASA) or 91dB or more (ISO)	May hear some loud noises but is aware of vibrations more than tonal pattern. Relies on vision rather than hearing as primary avenue for communication. Speech and language defective and likely to deteriorate. Speech and language will not develop spontaneously if loss is present before one year.	Will need full-time in special program for deaf children, with emphasis on all language skills, concept development, lip reading and speech. Program needs specialized supervision and comprehensive supporting services. Continuous appraisal of needs in regard to oral and manual communication. Auditory training on group and individual aid. Part-time in regular classes only for carefully selected children.

[a]Bernero, Raymond J. and Bothwell, Hazel. *Relationship of Hearing Impairment to Educational Needs,* Illinois Dept. of Public Health and Office of the Superintendent of Public Instruction, 1966.

ing, but additional factors sometimes make their linguistic performance more like deaf than hard of hearing individuals.

The key factor in delimiting the deaf population is contained in a statement in the second column of the fifth category in Table 9.1: "Relies on vision rather than hearing as primary avenue for communication." More than any other factor, this serves to define deaf people. Although hearing impairment can be considered a continuum on the decibel scale, at some point along that continuum the individual ceases to be linked to the world of communication primarily through his ears and becomes linked to it primarily through his eyes. The point where "hard of hearing" becomes "deaf" seems to be at about 90 dB (ANSI, 1969). Studies by Conrad (1979), Ling (1976), Quigley, Steinkamp, Power, and Jones (1978) and others have indicated that for speech and various aspects of reading and written language there is a discontinuity in performance at this point on the hearing impairment scale.

In addition to having hearing impairment usually of 90 dB (ANSI, 1969) or greater, the population we consider as deaf for studying language development consists mostly of individuals who have sensorineural impairment and suffered the impairment prior to the age of 2 years. This does not limit the population much more than the degree of impairment does. Most individuals who have profound hearing impairment have sensorineural impairment, and medical advances during the past few decades have reduced sharply the incidence of adventitious deafness, so that most instances of profound deafness now occur prenatally or during the first 2 or 3 years of life. Thus, we are considering the language development of individuals who have profound sensorineural hearing impairment of almost 90 dB (ANSI, 1969) or greater and suffered it prior to the age of 2 years. Available statistics (Karchmer, Milon, & Wolk, 1979) indicate that there are about 54,000 students in identifiable school programs who roughly match this definition.

Language Development

Bloom and Lahey (1978) define language as "a code whereby ideas about the world are represented through a conventional system of signals for communication [p. 4]." For most human languages, spoken words are the primary signals to convey ideas about the world. Many deaf persons, however, use a conventionalized system of gestures, known as American Sign Language (ASL or Ameslan), which seems to meet the criteria of the Bloom and Lahey definition of language. The conventionalized system of signals in ASL is composed of signs made by the hands and arms in relation to various parts of the body.

The young hearing child learns the communication code (language) used by the people around him primarily through an easy interactive process with a language model (usually the mother). For the deaf child, however, the matter is much more complex because he is deprived of the primary channel by which language is normally and easily acquired. Although the auditory channel is used in language development with deaf children, other sensory channels, primarily the visual, assume major importance.

A small percentage of deaf children have deaf parents (about 4% according to Rawlings & Jensema, 1977). For these children, the combination of early identification (which commonly occurs), parental acceptance, and early communication provide an environment in which language often can be acquired in the fluent and easy interactive manner in which it is acquired by hearing children from their hearing parents. As discussed later, some of these children have oral deaf parents who attempt to communicate with the child only by aural-oral methods, some have deaf parents who use some form of manual English in communicating with and around the child, and some have deaf parents who use colloquial ASL. But, whatever the communication system used by the parents, the fact that those children have deaf parents is a significant positive factor in their language development. The majority of deaf children, however, have hearing parents and they do not acquire the language of their parents in an easy, interactive manner.

Thus, language development for deaf children, besides involving the factors usually associated with language development in hearing children, also involves the visual-manual channel and the hearing status and communication practices of the parents. This means that language cannot be considered as developing only in the aural-oral modality and only with speaking parents. The combinations of aural-oral and visual-manual channels with speaking and signing parents result in three major paths of language development for deaf children: (1) American Sign Language; (2) manual English that uses manual codes for spoken or written English; and (3) oral English. The problem is further complicated by the fact that, for the majority of deaf children (about 95%) who have hearing parents, language acquisition at present usually involves some formal intervention system. Some of the best known are described because they can play a vital role in the deaf child's language attainments.

LANGUAGE INTERVENTION SYSTEMS

American Sign Language

Probably most deaf persons use American Sign Language (ASL or Ameslan) to communicate with each other and with hearing people who know the language. Although there is still some question whether ASL is a bonafide language or another signal system such as Morse code (Schlesinger & Namir, 1978), many language researchers (Friedman, 1977; Klima & Bellugi, 1979; Siple, 1978; Stokoe, 1960; Wilbur, 1979) present evidence for its status as a genuine language. There is, however, considerable influence exerted by English on the manual communication of many deaf people. Many adventitiously or well-educated deaf people use varying amounts of English syntax when communicating manually, and finger spelling is used frequently to spell English words for which there are no signs. This combining of the two languages (ASL and English) has been termed *Ameslish* (Bragg, 1973). Stokoe (1971, 1972) has described the diglossic continuum that characterizes ASL usage in the United States. The continuum ranges from colloquial ASL to a form of signed English in which the ASL vocabulary is used in precise English word order. Deaf children of deaf parents frequently are exposed to ASL in some form in early childhood, paralleling the normal interactive language learning process of hearing children.

Manual English

Several systems have been devised to represent English manually. Six of the best known are described here in their order of approximation to English with the closest approximation (finger spelling) being first.

Finger Spelling. Finger spelling is a manual representation of written English that provides a one-to-one correspondence between written letters and hand configurations representing the letters. The user simply spells English words, in English word order, with his fingers rather than with written letters. The combination of finger spelling and speech is known as the Rochester Method (Quigley, 1969).

Cued Speech. This is a manual representation of those syllables and phones of spoken English that are not visible for speechreading. Eight hand shapes are used in four positions to represent phonetic elements that are difficult to speechread. The system is used to supplement speechreading and was deliberately constructed in such manner that it could not function alone as a manual system of communication (Cornett, 1967). This system could also be classified as a form of oral English.

L.O.V.E. (Linguistics of Visual English). This was designed for preschool and kindergarten deaf children. According to Bornstein (1973), L.O.V.E. signs are supposed to parallel speech rhythm (i.e., a three-syllable word would be represented by a three-movement sign). Materials for this system are difficult to obtain and it is not widely used. L.O.V.E. signs resemble ASL signs much less than do the other systems of manual English.

S.E.E. I (Seeing Essential English). S.E.E. I was created by Anthony (1966). Three criteria were established to determine the use of ASL signs for a particular English word: *meaning, spelling,* and *sound.* A single sign is used when any two out of the three criteria are the same for two English words. For example, the English word *right* has three common *meanings* (correct, direction, privilege) but, because the *spelling* and *sound* are the same, one sign is used in S.E.E. I, whereas ASL has separate signs for each of the three English meanings. Compound words, such as *butterfly,* are signed using the ASL signs for the component words (the sign for *butter* followed by the sign for *fly*). Markers are used to represent the English inflectional system. S.E.E. I is supplemented by finger spelling for words that have no ASL sign equivalent.

S.E.E. II (Signing Exact English). S.E.E. II considers English words in three groups: (1) basic; (2) compounds; and (3) complex. S.E.E. II differs from S.E.E. I mostly on its treatment of compound words. Basic words are subject to the same "two out of three" criteria rules as used in S.E.E. I and markers are used to represent the English inflectional systems for complex words. Compound words such as *butterfly* for which there is no relation to the words *butter* and *fly* are represented with a single sign (the ASL sign for *butterfly*). However, if the meaning of the words separately (*under* and *line*) is consistent with the meaning of the compound word (*underline*), the component words are signed separately

(Gustason, Pfetzing, & Zawolkow, 1972, 1975). Finger spelling is used as a supplement for words not included in the dictionary. Bornstein (1973) noted that the Signing Exact English (S.E.E. II) system is composed of 61% ASL signs, 18% modified ASL signs, and 21% new signs.

Signed English. This system is a semantic representation of English (Bornstein, 1973, 1974). The objective of Signed English is to cover the needs of the syntax and vocabulary used with children between the ages of 1 and 6 years. ASL signs are placed in English word order and 14 sign markers are added to represent English inflections. Finger spelling is used for words not included in the dictionary and the storybooks that are available for this system. This system remains closer to the ASL use of signs than any of the preceding systems.

Siglish, Ameslish. These names represent the systems that use ASL signs in English word order without use of English inflections. Aspects of ASL grammar, such as sign space, pluralization, and directionality, are used. Finger spelling is used for words that do not have ASL signs. This system is used by most well-educated deaf people when they wish to approximate English using signs and finger spelling (Bragg, 1973).

It should be noted that, although the systems have been discussed here as discrete entities, there is frequent borrowing among systems. In addition, many communities have local signs that have evolved or have been created for specific purposes. Most of the manual English systems are used in combination with aural–oral communication and are most frequently used as teaching devices. The combination of manual and oral communication in English word order is known as the *Simultaneous Method.* As stated previously, finger spelling and speech are known as the *Rochester Method,* after the Rochester School for the Deaf where it was first used extensively in 1878.

Oral English

This is simply the use of English in oral form—the common method of communication used among hearing people. Two methodologies employed with deaf children rely solely on oral communication, the *Aural–Oral Method* and the *Acoupedic (or Unisensory) Method.* The *Aural–Oral Method* actively utilizes speech and speechreading for communication between child and teacher. Great emphasis is placed on the early and consistent use of high-quality amplification devices and auditory training. The *Acoupedic Method* (Pollack, 1964) minimizes speechreading and places major emphasis on amplification and auditory training to utilize as fully as possible the residual hearing that most deaf children have to varying extents.

The other common term that the reader should know is *Total Communication.* This has been defined in various ways, but the most commonly accepted definition now seems to be that it is a system that allows use of any means of communication between the child and teacher and between the child and parents. Thus, it could include any or all of the methods and systems that have just been discussed.

To summarize to this point, the language development of deaf children cannot be studied in the relatively uncomplicated manner in which the aural-oral system of hearing children can be studied. Probably the only close parallel is the population of deaf children whose parents use manual communication in some form with and around the child from infancy in the same manner that the hearing child is constantly exposed to oral language. This usually happens only with deaf children who have deaf parents, and not even with all of those. This type of child probably forms fewer than 5% of the total population of deaf children and youth. Most deaf children are exposed in infancy and early childhood to a variety of systems, the relative merits and effectiveness of which are continually being debated.

PRESENT STATUS OF LANGUAGE PERFORMANCE

Although there are various schools of thought as to how language should be developed in deaf children, there is general agreement that competence in reading and writing English are desirable goals. Reading and writing tend to function as common denominators in the education of deaf children and youth. They are indicators of language achievement and measures of the effectiveness of various communication approaches and curriculum practices. The studies to be presented serve to establish the extent of the language problem of deaf children and the lack of success in language development attained by most approaches.

Reading

Most studies of the reading levels of deaf students have used reading tests standardized on nondeaf children. Whether the studies have been performed in a single school or have involved stratified random samples of the national student population, the results are almost invariably the same. Most deaf students upon leaving school read below the fifth-grade level as measured on standardized tests.

Some of the earliest research in this area was reported by Pintner and Patterson (1917) more than 60 years ago. Their results showed that the median reading scores of deaf students at any age never reached the median for 8-year-old hearing children. Pugh (1946) reported that the groups she examined never obtained median scores as high as sixth-grade level on the *Iowa Silent Reading Test*. More recently, Furth (1966) reanalyzed the data collected on the *Metropolitan Achievement Test* by Wrightstone, Aronow, and Moskowitz (1963) in a survey of the reading abilities of 4624 deaf students between the ages of 10½ and 16½ years of age and found that the mean reading achievement rose from a grade level of only 2.7 at age 11 years to only 3.5 at age 16. An even larger national study by DiFrancesca (1972) produced similar results. Results on the Paragraph Meaning subtest of the *Stanford Achievement Test* administered to approximately 17,000 deaf students between 6 and 21 years of age revealed that the highest average grade equivalent score was 4.3 at age 19 years and that the average reading growth was 0.2 grade levels per year of schooling. The most recent national study (Trybus & Karchmer, 1977) studied reading scores in a stratified, random sample of 6871 deaf students and found that the median reading score at age 20 years and older was a grade equivalent of 4.5. Only 10% of the best reading group (18 years of age) could read at or above the eighth-grade level.

These low levels of achievement are not confined to students nor to the American deaf population. Hammermeister (1971) compared scores on the Paragraph Meaning and Word Meaning subtests of the *Stanford Achievement Test* for 60 deaf adults, 7–13 years after leaving school, with scores on the same tests for the same subjects from their last year in school. There was no change in the Paragraph Meaning scores but significant increase in Word Meaning. This indicates that although vocabulary increased for these deaf individuals, their ability to read connected language material did not improve. Conrad (1979) used the *Wide-Span Reading Test* (Brimer, 1972) to study reading levels in all deaf school leavers in England and Wales in 1976. The 468 students, who were between 15 and 16 years of age at testing, had a mean reading age equivalent to 9-year-old hearing children. Conrad also cites a number of studies conducted in Sweden, Denmark, and New Zealand, showing performance of school leavers at 16 years or so to be no higher usually than the level of 10-year-old hearing children. So the poor reading performance of deaf people seems to be universal. It is interesting to note that Conrad found only five profoundly deaf students among his 468 school leavers who had reading ages comparable to their chronological ages. Of these five, two were students whose parents were both deaf.

Results of other studies confirm these findings of very low levels of performance by deaf students on standardized reading tests. Studies of a different type, however, reveal that though the levels on standardized tests for deaf students are very low, actual reading performance might be even lower. Experienced teachers claim that many deaf students cannot read books graded at the level of their reading achievement as indicated by standardized tests. Support for this observation is provided by Moores (1967) who used the cloze procedure to study the reading performance of an experimental group of 37 deaf students matched with a comparison group of 37 hearing students on reading scores on the *Stanford Achievement Test*. Subjects were required to read passages of 250 words each, selected from fourth-, sixth-, and eighth-grade reading texts and to replace words that had been deleted from the passages. Measures were derived to indicate the ability of the deaf and hearing subjects to utilize their knowledge of vocabulary and syntax in the replacement of missing words. Results indicated substantial deficiencies in vocabulary and syntax for the deaf subjects in comparison to the hearing subjects, even though the two groups had been matched on reading ahcievement level on the *Stanford Achievement Test*. Moores' conclusions were confirmed by O'Neill (1973) in a study of deaf and hearing children's knowledge of phrase structure. She found deaf children to be significantly inferior to hearing children on the ability to judge correctly the grammaticality of pairs of grammatical and ungrammatical sentences, despite the fact that the deaf and hearing groups had been matched on reading achievement level. Both studies indicate that standardized reading tests give spuriously high estimates of the reading levels of deaf individuals, even though those estimates are distressingly low.

Syntax

Reading tests have definite but limited value for studying the language of deaf children. The tests are used primarily to classify children and to provide a measure of improvement in reading performance over time. As Chall (1967) has pointed out, reading tests cover a conglomerate of skills and there is need for single component tests to assess the various aspects of the reading process. This is particularly important for deaf children. Reading level is generally assessed for these children by tests that consist of subtests of Paragraph Meaning and Word Meaning. Although the Word Meaning subtest provides a measure of vocabulary functioning, there has been no similar test for syntax, and the syntax of English presents such great difficulty for deaf students that they rarely ever achieve even adequacy in its use.

Schmitt (1968) conducted one of the first investigations into comprehension and production of specific syntactic structures by deaf students. These types of investigations were further developed by Power and Quigley (1973); Quigley, Smith, and Wilbur (1974); Quigley, Wilbur, and Montanelli (1974, 1976); Wilbur, Quigley, and Montanelli (1975); Wilbur and Quigley (1975); Wilbur, Montanelli, and Quigley (1976); Quigley, Montanelli, and Wilbur (1976); Quigley, Power, and Steinkamp (1977); and Steinkamp and Quigley (1977). This group of investigators used a number of formats to study the ability of deaf students between the ages of 10 and 19 years to comprehend sentences with a variety of syntactic constructions: negation, conjunction, determiners, verb processes, pronominalization, question formation, relativization, and complementation. A preliminary version of the *Test of Syntactic Abilities* (Quigley, Steinkamp, Power, & Jones, 1978) was utilized as the main instrument of measurement. It was found that even when the deaf students understood the vocabulary in the sentences and understood the concepts involved when they were expressed in simple sentences, they had limited success in comprehending the test items. For example, when given the two sentences, *The boy kissed the girl* and *The boy ran away*, most students understood them; but when one sentence was embedded within the other to form the relativized sentence, *The boy who kissed the girl ran away*, most students, even at advanced ages, believed that it was the girl rather than the boy who ran away. Using a series to similar techniques, these investigators were able to determine: (1) the extent to which different syntactic structures posed difficulty in comprehension for deaf students; (2) the extent to which deaf students' comprehension of common syntactic structures was below the level needed for understanding common reading materials; and (3) a series of syntactic constructions that seemed to be distinct to deaf students.

Table 9.2 shows: (1) the order of difficulty of various syntactic structures for deaf students between 10 and 19 years of age; (2) the order of the same structures for hearing students aged 8 through 10 years; and (3) the frequency of occurrence of each structure in a reading series from Houghton–Mifflin titled, *Reading for Meaning* (McKee, Harrison, McCowen, Lehr, & Dunn, 1966). The orders of difficulty for deaf and hearing students are similar but not identical. The order of difficulty is also what would be predicted from psycholinguistic observations of the development of language in young hearing children. It is of interest to note that the average 18-year-old deaf student performed at a lower level than the average 8-year-old hearing student.

It can also be seen in Table 9.2 that the gap between the deaf students' comprehension of specific syntactic structures and the appearance of those structures in the Houghton-Mifflin reading series is so large that the investigators concluded that many deaf students cannot read the books they are supposed to be reading and from which they are supposed to be learning. For example, when *for-to* and *POSS-ing* complements occur at the rate of 32 times per 100 sentences in the sixth-grade text, and when the research data show that even the oldest deaf students barely scored above the chance level in understanding sentences containing those structures, a reading problem of major proportions obviously exists based on this structure alone. Similar findings can be seen for the other structures in Table 9.2.

Table 9.3 presents a list of distinct syntactic structures that appear consistently in the writing of many deaf students. These structures were also used as distractors in the *Test of Syntactic Abilities*. Quigley, Wilbur, Montanelli, Power, & Steinkamp (1976) found that these structures not only appeared in the written language of deaf students but were accepted by those students as grammatical when used as test items. Many consistent misinterpretations of sentences by deaf students were revealed in this study. The most general pattern found was the strong and widely prevalent tendency to impose a subject–verb–object (S–V–O) pattern on sentences, to see English as a linear rather than a heirarchical structure, even when this led to complete misinterpretation of the sentences. The following examples from Quigley et al. (1976) illustrate this problem.

TABLE 9.2
Summary of Performance on Syntactic Structures and Their Frequency of Occurrence Per 100 Sentences in the *Reading for Meaning* Series

Structure	Deaf Students (%)				Hearing Students (%)	Frequency of Occurrence	
	Average across Ages	Age 10	Age 18	Increase	Average across Ages	Level at which Structure First Appeared	Frequency in Sixth Grade Text
Negation							
Be	79	60	86	26	92	1st primer-13	9
Do	71	53	82	28	92		
Have	74	57	78	21	86		
Modals	78	58	87	29	90		
Means	76	57	83	26	90		
Conjunction							
Conjunction	72	56	86	30	92	1st primer-11	36
Deletion	74	59	86	27	94		
Means	73	57	86	29	92		
Question Formation							
WH-questions:							
Comprehension	66	44	80	36	98	2nd primer-5	6
Yes/no questions:							
Comprehension	74	48	90	42	99	1st primer-5	3
Tag questions	57	46	63	17	98		
Means	66	46	78	32	98		
Pronominalization							
Personal pronouns	67	51	88	37	78		
Backward Pronominalization	70	49	85	36	94	4th grade-1	0 (4 per 1000)
Possessive adjectives	65	42	82	40	98	1st grade-4	27
Possessive pronouns	48	34	64	30	99	3rd primer-1	0 (3 per 1000)
Reflexivization	50	21	73	52	80	2nd grade-1	2
Means	60	39	78	39	90		
Verbs							
Verb auxiliaries	54	52	71	19	81	1st grade-1	18
Tense sequencing	63	54	72	18	78		
Means	58	53	71	18	79		
Complementation							
Infinitives and gerunds	55	50	63	13	88	2nd primer-4	32
Relativization							
Processing	68	59	76	17	78	3rd primer-2	12
Embedding	53	51	59	8	84		
Relative pronoun referents	42	27	56	29	82		
Means	54	46	63	18	82		
Disjunction and Alternation	36	22	59	37	84	1st grade-1	7

Source: Adapted from Quigley et al. (1976).

TABLE 9.3
Some Distinct Syntactic Constructions in the Language of Deaf Students

Structural Environment in which Construction Occurs	Description of Construction	Example Sentences
Verb system	Verb deletion	The cat under the table.
	Be or *have* deletion	John sick. The girl a ball.
	Be-have confusion	Jim have sick.
	Incorrect pairing of auxiliary with verb markers	Tom has pushing the wagon.
	By deletion (passive voice)	The boy was pushed the girl.
Negation	Negative outside the sentence	Beth made candy no.
Conjunction	Marking only first verb	Beth threw the ball and Jean catch it.
	Conjunction deletion	Joe bought ate the apple.
Complementation	Extra *for*	For to play baseball is fun.
	Extra *to* in POSS-ing complement	John goes to fishing.
	Infinitive in place of gerund	John goes to fish.
	Incorrectly inflected infinitive	Bill liked to played baseball.
	Unmarked infinitive without *to*	Jim wanted go.
Relativization	NPs where whose is required	I helped the boy's mother was sick.
	Copying of referent	John saw the boy who the boy kicked the ball.
Question formation	Copying	Who a boy gave you a ball?
	Failure to apply subject-auxiliary inversion	Who the baby did love?
	Incorrect inversion	Who TV watched
Question formation, Negation	Overgeneralization of contraction rule	I amn't tired. Bill willn't go.
Relativization, Conjunction	Object-object deletion	John chased the girl and he scared. (John chased the girl. He scared the girl.)
	Object-subject deletion	The dog chased the girl had on a red dress. (The dog chased the girl. The girl had on a red dress.)
All types of sentences	Forced subject-verb-object pattern	The boy pushed the girl. (The boy was pushed by the girl.)

Source: Adapted from Quigley et al. (1976).

Passive	The boy was helped by the girl.
Relative	The boy who kissed the girl ran away.
Complement	The boy learned the ball broke the window.
Nominal	The opening of the door surprised the cat.

Surface order reading (S-V-O) led many deaf students to interpret these sentences as having the following meanings.

The boy helped the girl.
The girl ran away.
The boy learned the ball.
The door surprised the cat.

Because the students knew the vocabulary used in the sentences, and because they could understand the concepts involved when they were expressed in single declarative sentences, their misunderstandings were interpreted as indicative of inability to comprehend the meaning conveyed by the syntactic structure of the original sentences.

Written Language

Probably the best single indicator of a deaf child's command of English is the quality of his spontaneously produced written language. Unfortunately, instruments and methods for eliciting and measuring samples of written language are not well developed. Various visual stimuli (pictures, picture sequences, filmed stories) have been used in attempts to standardize the language eliciting process, and measurement usually has consisted of the counting of "errors" as indicated by some grammatical framework. The validity and reliability of these procedures have usually not been established.

Until about 15 years ago, most analysis of the written language of deaf students was conducted within the framework of traditional grammar. Investigators such as Heider and Heider (1940), Simmons (1962), Myklebust (1964), and Stuckless and Marks (1966) produced various counts of sentence length, type-token ratio, distribution of parts of speech, and kinds of grammatical "errors." The results of these investigations have been concisely summarized by Cooper and Rosenstein (1966).

> (Deaf childrens') written language, compared to that of hearing children, was found to contain shorter and simpler sentences, to display a somewhat different distribution of the parts of speech, to appear more rigid and more stereotyped and to exhibit numerous errors or departures from Standard English use [p. 66].

Since the time of Cooper and Rosenstein's summarization, research analysis on both receptive (reading) and expressive (written) aspects of deaf children's language has tended to be influenced by recent developments in linguistics, primarily by the theory of transformational generative grammar (Chomsky, 1957, 1965, 1976). The investigations of Taylor (1969), Marshall and Quigley (1970), and Quigley et al. (1976) are illustrative of this approach. Rather than viewing the written productions of deaf persons (as typified by the samples on p. 444) as merely garbled or stereotyped versions of standard English, these investigators presupposed that, deviant though it might seem, the written language of deaf persons is nonetheless generated by a grammar of rules and that the rules could be described within the framework of transformational generative grammar. They attempted to describe the growth of specific syntactic structures in the language of deaf students, the deviant structures that appeared consistently and persistently in the written language, and the rules that would generate those deviant structures.

Details of the findings by Quigley et al. (1976) have been presented in the section "Reading." It should be emphasized that these structures were products of the expressive language process (writing) as well as the receptive process (reading). Taylor's findings (1969) were similar in nature. Her research showed that deaf children's written productions, even at 16 years of age, still deviate greatly from standard English usage. In general, it may be said that at 16 deaf students have achieved mastery over some aspects of the production of simple active declarative sentences; that is, they only infrequently make errors of substituting major categories incorrectly, as in *The boy played a happy;* rarely do they disturb the standard subject-verb-object order of the simple sentence; and very rarely do they violate selectional restrictions, as in *The rock sang a song.* However, even at this advanced age, they still have many problems with the morphology of English, particularly as regards verb and noun inflections. They still have many problems in handling the determiner and auxiliary systems of English—indeed, they seem to have more deviancies in these areas than in any others. They make relatively few mistakes in producing complex transformations only because they rarely attempt such difficult productions. It would seem from Taylor's analysis that most 16-year-old deaf students know little about the relativization and nominalization rules of English and that when they attempt usages of such structures, they produce many deviant structures. They are, at this age, beginning to attain reasonably correct use of conjunction rules but, even so, still produce many conjoined sentences that are not standard English.

Although recent studies have provided some insight into the dynamics of the written language of deaf children, the best way to illustrate the problems of written language for these children is simply to present a few samples. The following are "typical" language samples produced by deaf students aged 10, 14, and 18 years of age. They illustrate far better than detailed research descriptions the present status of the written language performance of deaf students.

> We went to family camp today. She will be good family camp dog food. Boy went family fun dog friend car look. The played outuroor camp family good eat afternoon. The played eat fun camp after home. We perttey fun camp after home. The will week fun camp after car. We family will eat and aftrnoon. (10-year-old male, Performance IQ of 129, born deaf, Better Ear Average of 100 dB [ASA].)
>
> We will go to pinic. the woman package. A boy give to a dog eat the bread. The dog barked. the boy look at dog. the boy told a woman stop at car. He carried to the

pinic dog sa. the mother told her sister put on the table. She park a car. He was fun. Her brothers played baskeball. the dog played with the boy. after whith. He will go home at 6:45. his mother drive a car. (14-year-old male, Performance IQ of 104, born deaf, Better Ear Average of 90 [ASA].)

Everyone is packing the food in the basket for a picnic. They are very exciting to go to the picnic for their pleasure. A girl gives a sandwich to a little dog to eat. Father carries a bat to play with his girl & boy. Then they have everythings in the car what they want.

After a while the car is leaving out but one boy saw his little dog alone. He told his father to stop to see the dog. He went out of a car. Everyone is laughing. He pats his dog and brings him in the car to go with them too. Then they arrive at a picnic. Mother cooks the food for them. A girl put any dishes on the picnic table. Father and a boy play a softball. Everyone is enjoying today for a picnic. (18-year-old female, Performance IQ of 97, born deaf, Better Ear Average of 100 dB [ASA].)

Speech Intelligibility

Although we have nominated reading and written language ability as the common denominators in the education of deaf children and as the variables by which to judge the ultimate educational success of various methods of language acquisition and development, speech intelligibility deserves major attention also. Spoken language is the form of communication used by almost all the human race and facility in it is of importance for almost all areas of human functioning. There are some studies that provide information on this important variable with deaf children nationally.

As part of a study of the effects of finger spelling on educational development, Quigley (1969) measured the speech intelligibility of 163 students in six residential schools each year from 1963 through 1967. Intelligibility was measured by tape-recording lists of selected words from each student in each of the 5 years and having a panel of listeners identify the words from the recordings. Babbini and Quigley (1970) reported on the results of this study and concluded that the students "... could speak no more intelligibly at the end of the five-year study than they could at the beginning, regardless of the amount of training they received in between, if any [p. 12]."

Jensema, Karchmer, and Trybus (1978) reported extensively on speech intelligibility in a random sample of 1362 hearing-impaired students in all types of special programs in all parts of the United States. Intelligibility ratings were obtained for 978 of the students on a five-point scale. The investigators report extensively on the degree of intelligibility in various educational environments and its relationships with a variety of variables such as degree of hearing impairment and hearing aid usage. Of importance here is the finding that intelligibility did not improve with age in a cross-sectional analysis of the data. This agrees with the longitudinal findings of Babbini and Quigley. Analysis of the data by category of hearing impairment revealed that for impairment greater than 91 dB (ANSI, 1969) only 23.1% of the students had speech rated as intelligible or very intelligible, 28.2% as barely intelligible, and 48.6% as unintelligible or not speaking at all. This is the category we have defined as deaf for the purpose of this chapter. The data further showed that speech intelligibility increased as hearing impairment decreased among the six categories used for the study. The investigators concluded "... speech intelligibility appeared to be related primarily to the extent and quality of auditory input as reflected by the degree of hearing loss, usage of hearing aids, and the frequency of speech communication." It would seem that the type of educational program and formal teaching had little effect on intelligibility, making the situation about the same as for reading and written language performance.

Conrad (1979) used a rating scale with deaf school leavers in England, similar to the one used by Jensema and Trybus (1978), and compared results of the two studies. Table 9.4 compares the percentages of children in the two studies whose speech was no better than barely intelligible. The strong relationship between degree of hearing impairment and speech intelligibility can be clearly seen. Of more interest, however, is that the percentages of students in the 91+ dB category are almost identical for the two studies. This is the category termed *deaf* for this chapter and about three-fourths of such students in both countries have speech that for most practical purposes is rated as unintelligible. A good source for detailed information on the speech capabilities of deaf children and strategies used to teach speech is Ling (1976).

TABLE 9.4
Speech Intelligibility of Deaf Students in England and Wales and in the United States

	England and Wales (Conrad 1979)	*United States* (Jensema & Trybus 1978)
− 70 dB	6.3%	16.5%
71 − 90 dB	31.4%	45.0%
91 +	73.5%	76.8%

Summary of Present Language Status Studies

The present situation for reading is one of low performance on standardized reading tests, with large numbers of deaf students never reaching the level of functional literacy (fourth-grade reading level); even lower performance when more precise and diagnostic measures of vocabulary and syntax are used; and large gaps between deaf students' comprehension of specific syntactic structures and the appearance of those structures in commonly used reading materials. Studies of written language show similar low levels of performance. It is apparent that deaf children neither read nor write the English language even adequately. And the data for speech intelligibility show a similar situation where most children who are deaf (as defined in this chapter) cannot speak intelligibly.

LANGUAGE AND COGNITION

Psychological investigators have frequently utilized deaf subjects in research to investigate the relationships between thinking and language. Major contributors to this research during the past 20 years have been Hans Furth and a group of collaborators at the Catholic University; Odom, Blanton, Nunnally, and others at Vanderbilt University; Locke at the University of Illinois; and Conrad at Cambridge University. Their work can be reviewed here only briefly, and in relation primarily to the language development of deaf individuals, but is worthy of more intensive study for the insights it provides on language and the cognitive processes in hearing as well as in deaf people.

Research on language and cognition with deaf people has frequently used them as control subjects on the assumption that they are practically devoid of verbal language as used by hearing people. Furth (1966) cites as substantiation for this the various studies that have determined the reading level of most deaf students, even by school leaving age, to be below the fourth-grade, a level he considers to be functional illiteracy. Furth and Youniss (1971) emphasize the contention that deaf children have not acquired the use of an inner language that comes from internalization of an externally transmitted language such as speech. Having accepted this premise, researchers predict that on cognitive tasks that can be performed without the use of language deaf subjects will perform as well as hearing subjects and on cognitive tasks requiring verbal language they will not. Much of the work of Furth and his colleagues is contained in the book, *Thinking Without Language* (1966). In this and subsequent works, Furth summarizes his studies as showing that the cognitive development of deaf people is similar to that of hearing people when verbal language is not a factor in the cognitive task. He argues from this that the linguistic and educational deprivation of deaf children is not a result of deafness or cognitive deficit but of misguided educational practices, especially in the early childhood years. He argues for sign language as the basic language of deaf children on which thinking and the educational process can be based.

The work of Furth and his colleagues has made a significant contribution to the question of language and thought, largely relying on deaf subjects as the language control, but their conclusions need to be tempered by several substantial questions about procedure. First, Furth set a level of 60 dB (ANSI, 1969) as the defining criterion of deafness in some of his studies and in others did not specify a level at all. According to the definition established at the beginning of this chapter, at least some of the subjects used in the studies would not be considered deaf. Second, when, as was the case in some studies, the investigators did not find deaf subjects performing as well as hearing subjects on nonverbal tasks, the findings were ascribed to an experiential deficit resulting from lack of an adequate internalized language system rather than to cognitive deficit. Third, Conrad (1979) has stressed the importance of even a small amount of internal speech in the functioning of deaf individuals on cognitive and language tasks. His work indicates that lack of internal verbal language cannot be assumed in deaf individuals; it must be established by test. Conrad has shown that even deaf individuals as defined in this chapter, with HTL of 90 dB or greater, can have some internalized speech that can aid them significantly in the performance of various cognitive and language tasks. This finding, if substantiated, has significance for reinterpretation of much past research and for the control of future studies. Presence of internal speech might be a more significant factor for research than degree of hearing impairment.

Inner Language

At roughly the same time as Furth and his colleagues were studying cognitive processes in deaf people, a group at Vanderbilt University was considering the internal language functioning of deaf persons. Whereas Furth was interested in internal language with deaf people primarily to assert that it was not verbal, the Vanderbilt group was interested in studying the nature of whatever internal language did exist. Odom, Blanton, and McIntyre (1970) found that deaf subjects could understand connected prose better when the syntax of printed messages had been changed from English to the syntactical order of American Sign Language, thus indicating that the subjects were using an internalized language system but not that of English. They also found that deaf children had no difficulty memorizing words in signs whereas they had difficulty memorizing words for which signs did not exist. Odom et al. also found, as did Bellugi, Klima, and Siple (1974), that deaf children are quite capable of remembering in signs rather than recoding into words. These studies indicate that many deaf individuals use an internalized language system which is not the spoken language of the general population.

The internalized auditory verbal language of the hearing child, besides providing the major cognitive tool for thinking, is the base on which reading and writing are developed. The lack of such internalization of the externally transmitted spoken language of hearing people has been blamed as the primary cause of the deaf child's major deprivation in reading and writing. Kavanagh (1968) and Kavanagh and Mattingly (1972), among others, have shown that speech is important to reading. Electromyographic studies by Hardyck and Petrovinovich (1970) and McGuigan (1970); studies of reaction times to multisyllabic and monosyllabic words of identical graphemic length by Erikson, Pollack, and

Montague (1970), and Klapp (1972); and studies of readers' abilities to identify all instances of a specific letter in prose passages in which the letter appears in both pronounced (e.g., ra*g*) and silent (e.g., rou*g*h) forms have provided substantial evidence of the importance of phonetic recoding in the silent reading process. The typical reader does not go directly from the visual form of the printed message to meaning but somehow converts the visual stimulus to its phonemic counterpart in speech as a mediating process between print and meaning. But what mediating system (if any) does the deaf child work through when he goes from print to meaning? Locke in the United States and Conrad in Englad have addressed this question in some detail.

Locke and Locke (1971) studied the abilities of deaf and hearing children to recall lists of letters paired on the basis of phonetic, visual, or dactylic (finger spelling) similarity on the assumption that the internal coding activity of the subjects could be inferred from their recall and forgetting patterns of the various tasks. They found that the hearing controls (HCs) committed the most errors explainable on the basis of phonetic similarity, followed by deaf subjects with intelligible spoken language (ID), and finally deaf subjects who had unintelligible spoken language (UD). Confusions in visually similar letters were most frequent in UD subjects, followed by the ID and finally the HC subjects. UD subjects had the greatest proportion of dactylically similar confusions, followed by ID and HC subjects. Results were highly similar for both recall and forgetting patterns. It would appear that the hearing subjects and many of the deaf subjects with intelligible spoken language were recoding the visual stimuli phonetically, whereas the deaf subjects with unintelligible spoken language were recoding dactylically as well as visually.

Locke (1978) had 24 deaf and 24 hearing children silently read a specially prepared passage while crossing out all detected instances of specified target letters. The target letters appeared in phonemically modal and phonemically nonmodal forms. In phonemically modal forms, the pronunciation of the target letters involved a phoneme typically associated with the letter's name (e.g., the *g* in ra*g* and ra*g*e) is phonemically modal. In nonmodal forms, the pronunciation was of a type not commonly associated with the phoneme's name (e.g., the *g* in rou*g*h and in rin*g*). The hearing subjects detected significantly more of the modal forms than nonmodal forms indicating that they used speech in mediating the printed passage. Deaf subjects detected as many modal as nonmodal letters, indicating that they did not use speech effectively, as a group, to mediate print.

These studies indicate that many deaf individuals use internal codes other than internal speech. In the Locke study, these codes would appear to be dactylic or visual representations of the printed symbols. In the Odom et al. (1970) study, American Sign Language seemed to be the functioning internal code. In the Locke study, however, it was noted that some of the deaf subjects with intelligible speech apparently used phonetic coding. This issue of the use of internal speech by some deaf individuals has been explored by Conrad (1979) in a series of studies and has important implications for much of the research on cognitive and language development of deaf children.

Internal Speech

Hearing children babble extensively during the early months of life and progress from this to utterances and words by about 18 months. By the age of 24 months, these children typically have vocabularies of 50 words and are using two-word phrases. The 3-year-old typically has a vocabulary of 1000 words and has much of the grammatical complexity of adult speech. By the age of 5 years, the hearing child is thinking internally in speech and speech has become an important cognitive tool. Besides serving as a major tool for thinking, internal speech (as indicated by studies cited previously) is the base on which reading and writing are based. Without this base, the deaf child faces the problem not only of establishing some system of language for thinking and communication but also for the later development of reading and writing. This is perhaps the crux of the language problem of deaf children. What shall be the first language and system of communication they should be helped to develop? Shorn of the unfortunate emotionality that has surrounded it in the form of the oral–manual controversy, this is a highly significant problem for the language development of deaf children.

Although the studies of Odom et al. and Locke have substantiated the use of internal coding other than speech by many deaf individuals, the use of internal speech by some deaf subjects was also noted. In a series of studies, Conrad (1970, 1972a, 1972b, 1973) has shown that the use of internal speech by even profoundly deaf children (85 dB or greater) is fairly common. He also argues that the use of internal speech by deaf children should not be considered an all-or-none phenomenon—it can exist in varying degrees. And although it is linked strongly to externally intelligible speech, it also exists in some deaf children whose speech is relatively unintelligible. Conrad (1979) hypothesizes that the speech of a deaf child might be intelligible to the child for coding purposes, even when it is unintelligible externally to unsophisticated listeners. If the child has speech in which he or she uses a consistent articulatory and acoustic pattern for a particular word and if he or she has (for him or her) discriminable patterns for different words, then his or her speech could be functional to him or her as an internal code even though it might be externally unintelligible to others.

Conrad (1979) devised an Internal-Speech Ratio (I-S Ratio) that he believes provides a measure of the extent of usage of internal speech. The I-S Ratio is derived from the individual's response to memorizing and reproducing two lists of words, one of which is composed of phonetically similar words and the other of visually similar words. Individuals using an internal-speech code typically make many more confusions on the list of phonetically similar words than on the list of visually similar words. Those not using internal speech have the reverse pattern. The ratio of the scores on the two lists provides an index of the extent of use of internal speech. Conrad (1979) used this procedure with the deaf school leavers of England and Wales whose reading performance was discussed previously. He found that, for hearing threshold levels of less than 85 dB, more than 75% of the students were using internal speech to some extent; but, at about 85-dB hearing threshold, a striking difference emerged. Beyond this level only about 40% of the students seemed to use internal speech. As Conrad points out, the percentage would probably be much smaller if the task were more orally demanding than simply reproducing individual words. The use of internal speech is related to the external intelligibility of the deaf individual's speech, but the relation is imperfect. Although 40% of the deaf students with HTLs greater than 85 dB had some use of internal speech, only a very few had intelligible speech and beyond 95 dB not a single student had wholly intelligible speech.

If internal speech is essential to the development of reading skill, then many deaf children have an almost insurmountable handicap. Those deaf children who do develop effective use of internal speech as a cognitive tool should be able to learn to read in similar fashion to hearing children. It is important to know, however, what internal codes are used by those who do not develop adequate internal speech. If dactylic (finger spelling) codes are used by some, this might form an effective mediating tool between print and meaning because of the one-to-one relationship between the letters of the manual and the orthographic alphabet. But, if American Sign Language functions as the mediating tool, then learning to read might become a very difficult and complex process. Surely the methods of reading used with children who have internal speech are not likely to function well with children using a nonorthographic internal code. And likely some deaf children are functioning without any symbol system with which to mediate meaning—children who perhaps use imagery, some recalled part of the referent itself, to represent the objects and events of the world. Because the nonusers of internal speech probably form the majority of deaf children, and because most reading procedures are based on the presumption of internal speech, the low reading levels of deaf children is understandable.

The work of Conrad has another significance for research with deaf individuals. If internal speech is present to some degree in a substantial minority of deaf children and if it is a potent factor in the accomplishing of many cognitive and language tasks, then it must be taken into account as an experimental variable in research with deaf children. It might not be enough to define deaf children as done at the beginning of this chapter. Internal speech might be more important than degree of hearing impairment. If this be the case, then much of the previous work on the cognitive abilities of deaf children needs to be reexamined and future research must take account of the possible presence of internal speech in even profoundly hearing-impaired (deaf) children and its importance in much of the behavior of such children.

COMMUNICATION PATTERNS AND LANGUAGE DEVELOPMENT

Silverman (1971) indicated that in 1968 approximately 85% of deaf children enrolled in special schools were exposed to an exclusively oral method of communication at least in the early years of schooling. The situation has changed greatly in the ensuing decade, however, with Jordan, Gustason, and Rosen (1976) reporting that 64% of classes for hearing-impaired students in the United States were using "Total Communication" defined as "the use of manual signs, finger spelling, speechreading, and amplification." Jensema and Trybus (1978) conducted a national study of communication patterns and educational achievement of hearing-impaired students. They found a diversity of communication behaviors being used in the school and in the home involving speech, signs, finger spelling, writing, and various combinations thereof. The investigators concluded:

> ... there is much variability in the communication patterns employed with hearing impaired children; (2) combinations of methods, rather than single methods, are the rule in the classroom but far less so at home; (3) the use of speech alone is by far the single most common pattern at home, while a combination of speech, signs, finger spelling, writing, and gestures is the single most common pattern at school; and (4) there is relatively little consistency between patterns of communication used at home and in school [p. 8].

This diversity of communication patterns makes the study of language development in deaf children extremely difficult except on a case-by-case or small-group basis. It should serve to emphasize the caution uttered several times in this chapter that precise definitions of the terms *deaf* and *language development* are of extreme importance in evaluating studies in the area. An attempt will be made in discussing the language development of deaf children through oral English, manual English, and American Sign Language to adhere to the definitions given early in the chapter, but this is not always possible.

ORAL ENGLISH AND LANGUAGE DEVELOPMENT

Oral English

Swisher (1976) provides a useful review of oral English research with hearing-impaired children; however, many of the studies cited included children who were exposed to manual forms of communication and children with hearing losses that would not be classified as deaf as defined in this chapter. The discussion in this section is limited as much as possible to studies of deaf children exposed primarily to oral English. Empirical (data-based) research studies are discussed dealing with the following topics: (1) oral language skills; (2) reading and written language skills; and (3) language skills of oral deaf children in regular classrooms.

Oral Language Skills of Oral Deaf Children. Several spontaneous (oral) language elicitation procedures developed for hearing children have been used to assess the oral language skills of deaf children. Presnell (1973) administered the *Northwestern Syntax Screening Test* (NSST) (Lee, 1969) to deaf and hearing children between the ages of 5 and 13 years. Spontaneous language samples were obtained from the same children. Some of the hearing-impaired children in this study did not meet the criterion of deafness (90-dB hearing threshold level) established in this chapter, but all subjects were prelingually hearing impaired. As expected, older hearing-impaired children performed better than younger ones, with the greater language changes occurring between 5 and 9 years of age. Differences in the rate of improvement in test scores indicated that syntactic ability is developed more slowly in hearing-impaired children than in hearing peers of the same age. Analysis of spontaneous language samples revealed no significant improvement with increases in chronological age for the hearing-impaired subjects. Hearing-impaired subjects of all ages were least successful in the use of verbs in their attempts at English syntax. Presnell hypothesized that this was due to the unnatural order of teaching verbs that has traditionally been used with hearing-impaired children.

Geers and Moog (1978) used the *Developmental Sentence Analysis* (Lee, 1974) to assess spontaneous language and the *Carrow Elicited Language Inventory* (CELI) (Carrow, 1974) to assess imitated language of hearing-impaired children, ages 4 to 15. Again, several of the subjects had hearing threshold levels of less than 90 dB. This study supports Presnell's finding of a spurt in language growth in the early school years (between 4 and 9 years of age). The Developmental Sentence Scores (DSS) of 56% of the hearing-impaired subjects were below the score of the average hearing 3-year-old. Hearing-impaired subjects also differed qualitatively from the hearing children norms in that they used more structurally complex sentences but with a greater number of grammatical errors. The differences between the ages of the hearing-impaired subjects (4 to 15) and the ages of the hearing children used to establish the norms (2 to 6) might account for the use of more structurally complex language by the hearing-impaired subjects. On the *Carrow Elicited Language Inventory,* 51% of hearing-impaired subjects made more errors than the average 3-year-old hearing child. Luterman (1976) also compared deaf children with normative data for hearing children. Performance on subtests of the *Illinois Test of Psycholinguistic Abilities* (ITPA) (Kirk, McCarthy, & Kirk, 1968) was compared for two groups of deaf children; one trained in a visual-oral method, the other trained in an auditory-oral method. Both groups were consistently below the test norms with one exception on the Visual Reception subtest where the auditory-oral group scored 7 months above the test norms. Deficiences ranged from 2 months below the test norms on Visual Reception (visual-oral group) to 4 years 8 months on the grammatic Closure subtest (visual-oral group).

Reading and Written Language Skills of Oral Deaf Children. Geers and Moog (1978) calculated correlations of the spontaneous language (DSS) and imitated language (CELI) scores of their subjects with reading scores as measured by the *American School Achievement Test.* The results indicated that "maturity of language structure used by deaf children in spoken language is not highly predictive of their reading vocabulary or comprehension [p. 388]." Correlations between reading level and spontaneous language tended to increase with age whereas correlations between reading level and imitated language tended to decrease. This seems to indicate that ability to imitate is a useful measure of beginning reading (and verbal) skill whereas maturity of spontaneous language becomes more important as reading (and verbal) abilities increase.

Magner (1964) reported that 8- to 10-year-old deaf students at the Clarke School for the Deaf (a private oral school) had average reading scores on the *Stanford Achievement Test* at the second- to third-grade level and 17- to 18-year-old students were reading at an average of sixth-grade level. Lane and Baker (1974) compared the performances of 132 former pupils of Central Institute for the Deaf (CID), another private oral school, with the data reported by Furth (1966). They reported that, between the ages of 10 and 16 years, mean reading levels increased by 2.5 grades compared to the 0.8 grade reported by Furth. This result was supported by Geers and Moog (1978) who reported reading scores for 52 students from the same institution. Average reading scores rose from second-grade level for 7- to 9-year-olds to almost fifth-grade level for 13- to 15-year-olds. These results, however, are difficult to evaluate because the reading test (*The American School Achievement Series*) used by CID is rarely used in other schools for deaf students and the reported IQ of 108 (Lane & Baker, 1974) was considerably higher than the average for the general population of deaf students.

Language Skills of Oral Deaf Children in Regular Classrooms. Geers and Moog (1978) and Presnell (1973) make the statement that oral deaf children with good language skills are integrated into regular classrooms with their hearing peers and thus are not included in studies of the language performance of oral deaf children in special schools and classes. Retesting of 14 children, some of whom had been integrated into regular classrooms, on the DSS and the CELI (Geers & Moog, 1978) indicated that children selected for integration scored significantly higher in their spontaneous language (gain = 2.45 points) whereas those who remained at CID showed little improvement (gain = 0.99 point). The opposite trend, however, was found for imitated language. Students who remained in special classes showed an average reduction in errors of 20 points. Integrated children, however, reduced their errors only by 4.5 points. No information is provided by which to determine if the integrated students were performing at the grade level appropriate for their age or whether they differed from nonintegrated deaf children on such significant factors as IQ and socioeconomic status of families. Doehring, Bonnycastle, and Ling (1978) assessed the reading and language skills of a group of hearing-impaired children enrolled in regular public school classes. Ten of the 21 subjects were classified as profoundly hearing impaired (90+ dB). These subjects were at or above normal grade level on 9 out of 11 reading related tests; however, all subjects were below normal grade level on at least four out of the five language measures. It is interesting to note that the profoundlly hearing-impaired subjects performed better than the severely hearing-impaired subjects. Doehring et al. attributed this result to the earlier identification and training that profoundly hearing-impaired children frequently obtain.

It is difficult to summarize the language development of deaf children trained primarily in oral English because of the paucity of data and because of problems in specifications of the populations involved in the studies. Although most parents seem to use spoken language with their deaf children (Jensema & Trybus, 1978) and a substantial number of educational programs still utilize it exclusively, the approach in these situations tends to be relatively passive. An active oral approach to language development probably is confined to a few private schools, a number of preschools, and some speech and hearing centers. Except for the few private schools, children progressing into the general school system are exposed either to relatively passive use of oral English or to a variety of communication patterns popularly known as "Total Communication."

The studies that have been cited here as representative indicate that deaf children in actively oral environments tend to develop better language skills as measured by various means, including reading and writing, than do deaf children in the general school population. This generalization must be qualified by the fact that the populations of deaf children considered often are more select in terms of IQ and socioeconomic status than deaf children in general. But even given the select nature of the populations, the degree of success in language development in actively oral English programs can be impressive. A study by Ogden (1979) provides perhaps the most extensive evidence of this.

Ogden (1979) identified 1102 graduates and former students of three major private oral schools for deaf children and youths in the United States. He obtained extensive information on 637 of them by use of a questionnaire and rating scale. Ninety percent of the subjects were prelingually hearing impaired and most of them met the definition of deafness established in this chapter. The subjects were found to be highly successful in terms of their academic and occupational accomplishments. A majority of the 441 subjects who were out of school were engaged in professional-level occupations, and 30.6% of them had completed at least undergraduate college education as compared with the national average of 19.6% and 11.6% for white men and women, respectively, in the United States. This figure becomes even more impressive when it is realized that 39.2% of the 196 subjects still in school at the time of the survey were in institutions of higher education.

The subjects attributed their academic and occupational success in large measure to their development of oral English. The great majority of the subjects felt that their speech was readily understood by others and that they could understand speech well through speechreading. They believed their communication and language skills had enabled them to participate successfully in the general society. It should be noted, however, that the subjects came from academically and occupationally elite families. More than 43% of the fathers and 30% of the mothers completed a 4-year college education. Of these fathers, 52.5% went on to studies ranging from graduate to postdoctoral, and 39.7% of the mothers did graduate to postdoctoral work. But, as stated earlier, in spite of the elite nature of the students involved, their success in acquiring oral English and the contributions of that skill to their later success in life are impressive.

MANUAL ENGLISH AND LANGUAGE DEVELOPMENT

The various forms of manual English, whereby finger spelling, signs, and combinations thereof are used with English syntax, were described earlier. Several studies exist of the effects of these communication forms on language development in deaf children. It should be remembered, however, that frequently there is borrowing among different systems of manual English and between ASL and manual English with the result that often deaf children are not exposed to a single system but to a combination of signs from various sign systems.

Schlesinger and Meadow (1972) describe the language acquisition of four deaf children. Three of their subjects were exposed to at least some Seeing Essential English (S.E.E. I) signs. These children, however, were not exposed to manual English from birth. The beginning of simultaneous sign–speech input ranged from 15 months to 3 years of age. Rapid development was observed in both syntactic development and vocabulary development. The subject who was first introduced to signs at age 3 had developed several English inflections, using the S.E.E. I inflectional markers, by age 4. In a 4-month period, beginning at age 3, 256 signs were added to the vocabulary of another deaf child. On the basis of spontaneous language samples and tests of grammatical competence (Fraser, Bellugi, & Brown, 1963), Schlesinger and Meadow concluded that the deaf children were acquiring grammatical competence in the same sequence as hearing children, although development was somewhat slower.

Morkovin (1960) reported on experiments in Russia with neo-oralism, which is similar to the Rochester Method—a combination of speech and finger spelling. Morkovin's translations indicated that the Russians claimed to have succeeded in developing vocabularies of 2000 or more words in deaf children from ages 2 to 6 years. The Russian investigators also claimed that the use of finger spelling fostered the development of speech and speechreading. Quigley (1969) investigated the use of a similar method in the United States. In two studies, one a longitudinal survey of finger spelling in several residential schools and the other an experimental comparison of the Rochester (finger spelling) Method and the Oral Method, he sought to determine the effects of finger spelling on the development of language, communication, and educational achievement in deaf children. In both studies, the students using finger spelling in class exceeded the comparison students on almost all the measures used and particularly in language related variables such as reading and written language.

Brasel and Quigley (1977) examined the effects of method of communication and type of language input on the language of deaf children. Four groups, each with 18 deaf students between 10 and 19 years of age, were tested with the *Test of Syntactic Abilities* and the reading subtests of the *Stanford Achievement Test*. The groups were differentiated by the type of language used by them in infancy and early childhood; Siglish, American Sign Language, Intensive Oral, and Average Oral. Students in the Siglish group had parents who were language-competent deaf persons who used signs and finger spelling in English word order with their children from birth. The ASL group was composed of students whose deaf parents used American Sign Language with their children from infancy. The parents of the students in the Intensive Oral group had normal hearing and reported that they expended every effort to obtain the most intensive oral training for their children and most of the parents obtained oral instruction so they could work with the children at home. The parents of the Average Oral group were hearing persons who left the education of their children to the schools.

The results showed significant superiority of the Siglish group over the two oral groups on five of the six major syntactic structures measured by the *Test of Syntactic Abilities*. On the *Stanford Achievement Test,* the Siglish group was significantly superior to the other three groups on all four subtests used, including Paragraph Meaning, where the superiority ranged from 1.76 grade levels over the Intensive Oral group to 2.23 grade levels over the Average Oral group. Brasel and Quigley interpreted the findings to mean that both type of communication and type of language input are important variables in the language development of deaf children.

Of the various systems of manual communication devised to conform to the grammatical structure of English, Signing Exact English (S.E.E. II, Gustason et al., 1975) is apparently the most widely used. Babb (1979) studied the effects of this form of communication on the development of language in deaf students. Using a design similar to that used by Brasel and Quigley, he tested two groups of 18 deaf students and a comparison group of 18 hearing students with the *Test of Syntactic Abilities* and several subtests of the *Stanford Achievement Test*.

Written language samples were also collected from the subjects. One group of deaf students had been using S.E.E. II in the classroom for 10 years or more and the parents of those students had also learned it and used it at home. The other group of deaf students had similar classroom experience, but their parents had not learned and used S.E.E. II in the home. The groups were compared with each other, with the hearing comparison group, with the groups in the Brasel and Quigley study, and with normative data for hearing-impaired students on the *Stanford Achievement Test for Hearing Impaired Students* (Office of Demographic Studies, 1972).

The deaf group that used S.E.E. II in the home and in school performed as well as the Siglish group from the Brasel and Quigley study on most of the common variables measured. The deaf group that used S.E.E. II only in school had much inferior performance to these two groups and, in fact, performed no better than the Average Oral group from the Brasel and Quigley study on common variables and no better than the norms for the general populations of deaf students on the *Stanford Achievement Test*. This would indicate that the method was effective only when used in the home as well as in the school. This finding, along with the findings of the Brasel and Quigley study and several studies to be discussed in the section on "ASL and Language Development", indicate that for many deaf children the family might have as much influence on language development as the school.

ASL AND LANGUAGE DEVELOPMENT

Approximately three-quarters of deaf American adults use American Sign Language (ASL) (Rainer, Altshuler, & Kallmann, 1969), but only a small percentage learn it through communicating with their parents in early childhood. Most deaf persons learn ASL through interacting with deaf peers who have deaf parents or with deaf adults, a process that normally begins after the individual has entered the school system. Deaf children of deaf parents (only about 4% of the deaf population), however, may acquire ASL natively in much the same way as hearing children learn the language spoken by their parents. But the language learned in the home by deaf children of deaf parents is not always ASL. Some deaf parents use a form of manual English or communicate orally (using speech and speechreading) with their children. Other parents alternate between ASL and English syntax. Most of the available studies of ASL in young deaf children are longitudinal observational studies of small groups or individual children. The children observed ranged in ages from 6 months to adolescence and were observed under both natural and laboratory conditions. Discussion of these studies covers prelinguistic behavior and gestural development and the stages of acquisition from one-word utterances to two-word utterances to more complex utterances.

Prelinguistic Behavior and Gestural Development

Meadow (1976) states that most deaf children, whether they receive formal sign input from their parents or not, have acquired some signs by age 11. Deaf children frequently develop homemade signs or gestures (not recognizble to the general signing community) to communicate with their parents and peers. Several parallels between the development of the gesture systems of deaf children and normal language development in hearing children has led investigators (Feldman, 1975; Goldin-Meadow, 1975; Goldin-Meadow & Feldman, 1977) to consider the gesture systems to be symbolic and highly organized behavior. Deictic gestures (pointing) preceded the use of specific gestures (which referred to an action or object). Nelson (1973) and Bates (1976) also found similar deictic gestures that preceded spoken language development in young hearing children. When specific gestures did appear, they were used to express action relationships before nonaction relationships, again paralleling normal language development. In addition, the child was often the initiator of the gesture communication with only about 25% of the signs being shared between mother and child. The children were also able to develop characterizing signs for new objects they had not previously encountered. At the multisign level, the deaf children were observed to express semantic relationships in a systematic way, thus supporting the contention by Goldin-Meadow and Feldman (1977) that "the human child reveals a natural inclination to develop a structured communication system [p. 403]."

The One-Word Stage of Language Acquisition

Hearing children normally utter their first word between the ages of 10 and 13 months. Deaf children learning ASL also produce their first signs around this age (Caccamise, Hatfield, & Brewer, 1978; Schlesinger & Meadow, 1972). There is some evidence, however, that first signs may actually be produced before first words (Boyes-Braem, 1973; McIntire, 1974). This finding is substantiated by studies of hearing children who learn ASL and English at the same time (Jones & Quigley, 1979; Schlesinger & Meadow, 1972).

Phonology. Spoken words can be divided into at least four phonemic elements: a supporting breath stream, oropharyngeal configurations, rhythm, and inflectional patterns (Collins-Ahlgren, 1975). Hearing children begin to use some speech elements before others and easier (unmarked) sounds are often substituted for more difficult (marked) sounds. ASL signs can be divided into cheremic (hand) elements (Stokoe, 1960). Each sign is composed of four parts: a hand configuration, a movement of the hand, placement of the hand in relation to the other hand, and hand placement in relation to the signer's body. Like their hearing peers, deaf children learn easier (unmarked) elements before more difficult (marked) elements. Boyes-Braem (1973) and McIntire (1974) studied the acquisition of handshapes in the signs of deaf children. Boyes-Braem (1973) postulated that the "A" handshape is the easiest to form and therefore is unmarked. Other handshapes are formed by adding the following features:

1. Opposition of the thumb.
2. Extension of one or more fingers.
3. Contact of a finger with the thumb.
4. Crossing of adjacent fingers.

McIntire (1974) found the following developmental pattern in the acquisition of handshapes for one deaf child:

Stage 1: 5, S, L, A, G, C, and "baby O"
Stage 2: B, F, and adult O
Stage 3: I, Y, D, P. 3, V, H, and W
Stage 4: 8, 7, X, R, T, M, N, and E

(*Note:* Handshapes are used in sign formations and do not denote use of finger spelling although the numerals and letters denote manual alphabet configurations.) This developmental pattern appears to support the hypothesis of Boyes-Braem (1973) concerning the marked characteristics of the handshapes and demonstrates a progression from easier to more difficult handshapes requiring increasingly finer motor control of the fingers.

Substitutions among the cheremic elements of a sign are found among learners of ASL—paralleling substitution of phonemic elements in hearing children. These substitutions occur for each cheremic element and appear to be less marked than the adult form for which they are substituted. Examples of substitutions from studies of deaf children acquiring ASL are provided in Table 9.5.

Thus, hearing and deaf children appear to go through similar processes in acquiring the phonological and cheremic elements of their language: progressing from easier, less-marked elements to more difficult more-marked elements; substituting easier elements for more difficult ones.

Semantics. The first words of children typically do not have the same meaning as adults attach to the words. Children frequently overextend the meaning of a word to include other similar objects. Schlesinger and Meadow (1972) report that one of their deaf subjects overextended the sign DOG to refer to all animate objects other than her parents. Clark (1973) also describes the overextension of the word DOG to mean four-legged animal among hearing children. The frequent overextension of "Mom" or "Dad" to refer to any caretaker among hearing children was also reported by Newman (1972) for his deaf daughter at 10 months of age.

TABLE 9.5
Examples of Substitution of Cheremic Elements in the Signs of
Deaf Children Acquiring ASL

Cheremic Element	Example	Source
Handshape	APPLE signed with "A" handshape rather than "X"	McIntire (1974)
	WRONG signed with "A" handshape rather than "Y"	Schlesinger and Meadow (1972)
Movement of the hand	CAR signed without steering motion	Schlesinger and Meadow (1972)
	SHOUT signed with wiggling movement rather than raising away from mouth (resulting in the sign CROSS)	Collins-Ahlgren (1974)
Placement of hand in relation to other hand	Right thumb placed in left hand instead of under left palm in signing TURTLE	Collins-Ahlgren (1974)
Location of hands in relation to body	MORE signed above head rather than at chest level	Schlesinger and Meadow (1972)
	DOG signed both on mother and father rather than on signer's body	Schlesinger and Meadow (1972)

Syntax. The term *holophrastic* has been applied to the one-word stage to indicate that the child is expressing syntactic relationships and means more than the one word expressed but is unable to produce more because of perceptual or linguistic limitations. Although some theorists dispute this description (see de-Villiers & deVilliers, 1978 for discussion), it is clear that the child may have several different meanings for a single-word utterance. Schlesinger and Meadow (1972) report that one of their deaf subjects used the sign SMELL to mean "I want to go to the bathroom"; "I am soiled, please change"; and "I want the pretty smelling flower."

The one-word stage in hearing children frequently ends around the age of 18 to 20 months with the appearance of two-word utterances. McIntire (1974), however, found two-sign utterances in the language of a 10-month-old deaf subject. In addition, hearing children generally know approximately 50 words at the end of the one-word stage (Dale, 1976), whereas Schlesinger and Meadow (1972) found that one of their subjects had a vocabulary of 117 signs and 5 letters at 19 months and a deaf child studied by Bellugi and Klima (1972) had a vocabulary of over 50 signs at 18 months of age. Thus, it appears that deaf children learning ASL may actually be ahead of their hearing peers at the early stages of language acquisition. Ahlgren (1977) makes this point quite strongly:

> The deaf child in an adequate linguistic surrounding, i.e. deaf parents... is using language on a developmental level comparable to his hearing peers but in fact on an even more advanced level. The deaf two year old appears to have a richer vocabu-

lary (granting the difficulty in estimating size of vocabulary), a more context free and informative use of language and a more conscious and analytical attitude toward language [p. 4].

The Two-Word Stage of Language Development

Dale (1976) states that two-word utterances begin to appear in the language of hearing children around 18 to 20 months. Brown, Cazden, and Bellugi (1969), however, found a wide range in the age that hearing children begin forming two-word utterances. Schlesinger and Meadow (1972) reported that one of their deaf subjects began putting together two-sign utterances at 17 months of age. McIntire (1974) reported the beginning of the two-sign stage for her subject at 10 months of age.

Mean length of utterance (MLU), measured in number of morphemes, appears to be a useful measure for describing language acquisition. Bellugi and Klima (1972) found that the rate of MLU increase for a deaf child of deaf parents learning ASL was comparable with that of three hearing children studied by Brown (1973). At the beginning of the study, the deaf child had a MLU of 1.7 signs per utterance (age 2.7) and at age 3.0 (5 months later) had achieved a MLU of 2.8 signs per utterance. Although more thorough studies with more children are needed, it appears that onset of the two-word stage of language development and progress in mean length of utterance might be comparable for deaf and hearing children.

Syntax. Braine's (1963) pivot grammar was among the first to recognize that children are not simply reproducing shortened (telegraphic) versions of adult language in their two-word utterances. Pivot grammar is based on positional categories—pivot and open words that can occur in various combinations. Schlesinger and Meadow (1972) subjected the language data from one of their subjects to a pivot-grammar analysis. The grammar proved inadequate to cover all the data and in fact made some false predictions. This finding supports the position of many current researchers (deVilliers & deVilliers, 1978) who have rejected pivot grammars in favor of a semantic interpretation of two-word utterances.

Semantics. Bloom (1970) and Bowerman (1973) hypothesized semantic rather than syntactic relationships to account for two-word utterances. It is clear that a limited number of relationships are expressed by the young hearing child and this set of relationships appears to have some universality. Brown (1973) found that a list of eight semantic relationships seemed to account for the majority of two-word utterances. Several of the studies of deaf children learning ASL (Bellugi & Klima, 1972; Collins-Ahlgren, 1975; Newport & Ashbrook, 1977) have shown that "for children acquiring American Sign Language, the sequence in which these semantic relations emerged was approximately the same as that for children learning English, despite the difference in the modality of the languages and the consequent differences in the syntactic means of expressions in the two languages [Newport & Ashbrook, 1977, p. 3]."

Complex Utterances in Language Acquisition

There is no stage level in which only one-, two-, and three-word utterances occur. Moskowitz (1978) explains this is a result of the fact that there are many binary semantic relationships but not many ternary relationships. Following the two-word (sign) stage, child language grows gradually more complex. Description of ASL structure is incomplete at present. (However, see Friedman, 1977, Klima & Bellugi, 1979; Schlesinger & Namir, 1978; Siple, 1978; and Wilbur, 1979, for currently available information.) Therefore, not many studies of development of ASL in older deaf children have been conducted. There are several patterns of development in learning ASL, however, that do not fit into the two-sign stage that have been reported in the literature.

Overgeneralization of a linguistic rule has been shown to be an important source of errors in hearing children's development of language. For example, hearing children go through six stages in developing the past-tense system of English (Moskowitz, 1978). Overgeneralization also is a major process in the development of ASL. Table 9.6 contains some examples of ASL syntax in which a linguistic rule is overgeneralized to situations in which the rule does not apply in adult grammar.

In addition, Collins-Ahlgren (1974) noted some substitutions and modulations of future tense for a deaf subject that do not occur in English. The subject combined the handshape and placement for the sign MOTHER with the movement of the temporal marker WILL to form one "sign" (mother + will). ASL also allows for differentiation between near future and distance future through variance in the distance of future temporal markers from the signer's body. Collin-Ahlgren's deaf subject of less than 4 years of age included this distinction in her signed utterances.

In the past, it was sometimes thought that ASL did not have required word order. Some studies of ASL structure, however, have claimed that whereas order is freer in ASL than in English, there is a definite word order (Fischer, 1975). This point is still debated by some researchers (Crystal & Craig, 1978). Newport and Ashbrook (1977) found that deaf children learning ASL do use fixed word order to express specific syntactic relationships and that "the young child seems not to make use of the syntactic devices particular to American Sign Language [p. 4]." This corresponds to hearing children's use of fixed word order to express syntactic relationships before learning the correct inflectional markers. Fischer (1974) has provided some information on the acquisition of negation and question formation in ASL. Deaf children learning ASL and hearing children learning

TABLE 9.6
Overgeneralization of Linguistic Rules in the Acquisition of ASL by Deaf Children with Deaf Parents

Structure	Example		Source
	Adult Form	Child Overgeneralization	
Negative marker incorporated into positive sign (downward movement away from signer)	DON'T + WANT DON'T + LIKE	Downward movement to negate some sentences	Bellugi and Klima (1972)
Signs change direction to incorporate subject and/or object	DON'T + KNOW I + LOOK + AT + YOU YOU + LOOK + AT + ME	DON'T + HAVE I + FINGER SPELL + TO + YOU YOU + FINGER SPELL + TO + ME (Sign that does not use directionality in the adult form)	Collins-Ahlgren (1974) Bellugi and Klima (1972) Collins-Ahlgren (1974)
Reduplication of sign to connote long duration or repetition of action or state	LOOK, LOOK, LOOK (different directons), FOUND	WORK, WORK, WORK, TIRED, TIRED I WANT READ, READ	Collins-Ahlgren (1974)

English seem to go through similar stages in the development of negation. At first, the negative element is external to the sentence, followed by the insertion of the negative element internally and the appearance of *can't* and *don't* (although *can* and *do* seem not to appear). Overgeneralizations occur in both English and ASL (see Table 9.6 for examples from ASL acquisition studies). In the third stage, overgeneralizations are corrected and negative elements are used appropriately.

The development of questions in ASL and English, however, differs slightly. Because adult yes–no questions in ASL are not complex, deaf children acquire this form quickly, whereas the hearing child goes through several stages to arrive at the adult form of English yes–no questions. The development of Wh-questions in ASL is more complex than for yes–no questions. The child first uses a generalized Wh-sign that Fischer (1974) translates as "Huh?" or "Well?" Receptive understanding of Wh-questions, however, is not demonstrated during this stage. In the second stage, the deaf child begins to differentiate three Wh-signs—*where, what,* and *who.* The most frequent of these is *where.* Receptively, the child usually only understands Wh-questions when the Wh-sign does not appear in initial position in the sentence. In later stages, other Wh-signs are added and the child learns to understand questions when the Wh-sign is in initial position. This process differs slightly from that demonstrated by hearing children, but the similarity of acquisition in the two languages is striking.

Collins-Ahlgren (1974) discusses the acquisition of English as a second language for a deaf child of deaf parents through the addition of signed English morphemes to her ASL utterances at age 3. Collins-Ahlgren reports that several English markers such as past-tense inflections and plurality became functional between the third and fourth year of life. In addition, the subject's signs were usually accompanied by speech. An interesting dichotomy between the speech code and the sign code was noted by Collins-Ahlgren (1974) and by Schlesinger (1978). Collins-Ahlgren's subject frequently used a sign that represented a wide semantic field (SEE), and the accompanying spoken utterance provided the specific meaning (WATCH, LOOK) or included English inflectional morphemes not included in the signed utterance ("What [do] you want?") (Collins-Ahlgren, 1974, p. 493). H. Schlesinger (1978) also found that some forms were expressed in the sign code but not in the spoken code and vice versa. The following examples illustrate the difference.

Top = signed utterance
Bottom = spoken utterance

Serjei	go	Lake Tahoe	J-S	fought	with Ruth yesterday
	going			fight	

(Examples taken from Schlesinger, 1978, pp. 86, 88)

The effects of having learned ASL in early childhood and the subsequent learning of English upon entering school have not been assessed in detail. Charrow and Fletcher (1974), however, offer some insight on this issue. Deaf adolescents with deaf and hearing parents were compared on the TOEFL (*Test of English as a Foreign Language*) and the SAT (*Stanford Achievement Test*). Performance of deaf subjects with deaf parents on the TOEFL was more highly correlated with performance by hearing foreign students than with the performance of deaf subjects with hearing parents. Charrow and Fletcher concluded that "the results indicated that English may be a second language for deaf children and that early experience with sign language may facilitate later learning of English [p. 463].''

Much more research is needed on the effects of having learned a first language on the later learning of English. From research conducted thus far, however, it appears according to Caccamise et al., (1978) that "the acquisition of language in a visual–manual modality parallels the acquisition of language in the oral–aural modality [p. 814]" and it is likely that learning some form of manual communication early in life might facilitate development of English skills later in life. Stokoe (1974), Kannapell (1974), and Hatfield, Caccamise, and Siple (1978) suggest that a bilingual approach to educating deaf children may facilitate both English and ASL acquisition.

Intervention Programs

Most of the research on the use of American Sign Language with deaf children has come from studies of the performance of deaf children of deaf parents as compared to the performance of deaf children of hearing parents. Many deaf children are exposed to manual communication simply because that is the way their parents communicate. Although some deaf parents will communicate with their deaf children orally or in Siglish, it is highly likely that most of them use American Sign Language. That assumption is implicit in most of the studies cited here.

One of the first studies of this type was a substudy in an investigation of educational environments by Quigley and Frisina (1961). They compared data on 16 students who had deaf parents with data on 70 deaf students who had no deaf relatives in their immediate families and found that the students with deaf parents had significantly superior scores in vocabulary and finger spelling and had higher scores in educational achievement. Stuckless and Birch (1966) compared two matched groups of deaf students, with one group having been exposed to manual communication early in life, primarily because of having deaf parents, and the other group not having had such exposure. Results showed that the group with early manual communication exposure was superior to the control group in reading, written language, and speechreading. Meadow (1967) investigated the development of self-concept in deaf children of deaf parents and deaf children of hearing parents, and she found that a group of deaf children with deaf parents had better development of self-concept, and better psychosocial development, than did a matched group of deaf children with hearing parents. The group with deaf parents also had significantly higher scores in reading, written language, finger spelling, and the use of American Sign Language. All of these investigators interpreted their findings as indicating that early exposure to manual communication (probably in the form of American Sign Language) was beneficial to language development in deaf children.

These studies have been criticized on various grounds: (1) the children of deaf parents were genetically deaf and thus were less likely to have the additional problems, such as brain damage, which are prevalent in other etiologies of hearing impairment; (2) the differences found in favor of deaf children of deaf parents, although statistically significant, were small; (3) the differences in favor of deaf children of deaf parents could have resulted from such parents being less traumatized by having a deaf child and providing a healthy emotional and learning environment in the home; and (4) the groups compared were not truly equivalent because the comparison groups of deaf children of hearing parents had not been provided with early and intensive exposure to language solely through oral communication. Some studies have addressed these criticisms.

Vernon and Koh (1970) provided an essential control for the genetic problem by comparing deaf children whose parents were deaf with deaf children with recessive genetic deafness whose parents were hearing. The children with deaf parents performed significantly better than those with hearing parents on measures of reading and educational achievement and on teacher ratings of written language performance. This would seem to indicate that the genetic factor was not responsible for the differences found in the earlier studies. The Brasel and Quigley (1977) study discussed previously would seem to have disposed of the criticism that the oral groups were not exposed to intensive enough oral communication input to be truly comparison groups for the groups of deaf children with deaf parents.

Corson (1973) investigated the factor of parental acceptance of the deaf child by comparing the performance of three groups: (1) a group of deaf children with deaf parents who used only oral communication with their deaf children; (2) a group of deaf children of deaf parents who used manual communication with their children; and (3) a group of deaf children with hearing parents. This controlled for the factor of communication. Corson found that both groups of deaf children with deaf parents outperformed the deaf children with hearing parents but that the group with oral deaf parents performed as well or better than the group with manual deaf parents on tests of reading, social adjustment, self-image, speech intelligibility, speechreading, and other variables. This would seem to indicate that parental acceptance is indeed an important factor.

The questions of: (1) the relative effectiveness of various communication approaches in the early language development of deaf children; and (2) what kinds of children seem to progress best with which kind of communication approach; are a long way from being answered. But the studies cited here represent a promising beginning in the search for answers. The search will certainly continue. It would seem, for example, that additional research on factors in the family environment that influence language development might be fruitful. The studies of Corson (1973), Brasel and Quigley (1977), and Babb (1979) indicate that deaf children exposed by their families to intensive communication in English later develop better use of English than deaf children who did not have such exposure. Because Corson studied oral English; Brasel and Quigley, Siglish; and Babb, Signing Exact English; a common factor in the communication seemed to be that each used English. Perhaps the common and important factors in the studies were the provision of a healthy emotional and learning climate in the home and a system of English communication between parents and children, resulting from a strong family involvement in the children and their problems.

IN CONCLUSION

The education of deaf children shared in the great expansion of educational programs of all types that took place during the late 1950s and the 1960s. Research on the language development of deaf children profited both from direct investment in specific language-research programs and training of personnel in hearing impairment and indirectly from new developments in language research resulting from the work of Chomsky (1957, 1965) and the explosive increase in the number of linguists and psycholinguists. Much of the present practice in language development of deaf children is the direct result of applications of quite recent psycholinguistic research. Perhaps the most notable recent development in language research with deaf children has been the great influx of linguists into research on American Sign Language. In addition to the outstanding pioneering linguistic research of Stokoe (1960) in the 1950s and 1960s, there are now a dozen or more books on the structure and teaching of ASL, a considerable body of research literature in professional journals, courses in a number of linguistics departments, and a cadre of linguistic researchers in a number of universities with major interest in ASL. Some of this interest is societal in nature, in much the same way as interest in Black English and the dialects and languages of other minorities was socially motivated in the 1960s, but much of it also arises from speculations about the place of gesture languages in the origins of human communication and from interest in the universals of language and cognition.

This fortunate involvement of linguists, psycholinguists, and cognitive psychologists in research on the language and cognitive development of deaf children has produced a substantial body of research, has directly influenced language development practices, and could provide the base for substantial future improvements in language attainments by deaf children. Although the survey data that have been cited have shown no improvements in recent years in the language performance of deaf students, the developments in linguistics and psycholinguistics have perhaps not been applied extensively enough nor long enough for their effects to become apparent. The same might be true of the intensive efforts in parent–infant and early childhood education with deaf children. The full effects of these efforts on language performance might not be apparent for some years yet, and it is possible that any emerging effects are obscured in large-scale surveys.

Nothing has been said in this chapter concerning the role of technology in the development of language in deaf children. This has been primarily because few accounts are available in the professionally published literature. There are, however, a number of recent and ongoing developments that can appropriately be mentioned in closing because they indicate future possible directions of research. The work of Suppes (Fletcher & Suppes, 1973) and a number of colleagues at Stanford University has demonstrated the effectiveness of computer-assisted instruction in the development of mathematical skills in deaf children. Quigley and a group of colleagues at the University of Illinois have used the PLATO computer education system to program linguistic materials for training teachers of deaf children (Russell, Quigley, & Power, 1976). Levitt and Newcomb (1978) have devised a process for utilizing computers in the grammatical analysis of the written language of deaf individuals. A promising project by Bates and Wilson (1979) at Boston University is using ILLIAD to generate sentences in an interactive manner with deaf children in an attempt to improve written language ability. The Media Development Project for the Hearing Impaired at the University of Nebraska (1978) is experimenting with the use of videodiscs, captioned television, and other technological approaches to language teaching and development. It is likely that this technological research will increase considerably in the next decade, and it is hoped that the wedding of the research contributions of linguistics, psycholinguistics, cognitive psychology, and infant and early childhood education with technological developments will result in greatly improved language development for deaf children.

REFERENCES

Ahlgren, I. Early linguistic cognitive development in the deaf and severely hard of hearing. *Proceedings of National Symposium on Sign Language Research and Training.* Chicago, Ill., May 30 to June 3, 1977.

American National Standards Institute. *American National Standard Specifications for Audiometers (ANSI S3.6-1969).* New York: American National Standards Institute, 1969.

Anthony, D. A. *Seeing essential English.* Unpublished master's thesis, Eastern Michigan University, 1966.

Babb, R. *A study of the academic achievement and language acquisition levels of deaf children of hearing parents in an educational environment using Signing Exact English as the primary mode of communication.* Unpublished doctoral dissertation, University of Illinois, 1979.

Babbini, B. E., & Quigley, S. P. *A study of the growth patterns in language, communication and educational achievement in six residential schools for deaf students.* Urbana, Ill.: Institute for Research on Exceptional Children, 1970.

Bates, E. *Language and context: The acquisition of pragmatics.* New York: Academic Press, 1976.

Bates, M., & Wilson, K. *A generative computer system to teach language to deaf children.* Paper presented at the Annual Conference of the Association for Development of Computer-Based Instructional Systems, Feb. 1979, San Diego.

Bellugi, U., & Klima, E. S. The roots of language in the sign talk of the deaf. *Psychology Today,* 1972, *6,* 60–64, 76.

Bellugi, U., Klima, E. S., & Siple, P. Remembering in signs. *Cognition,* 1974, *3,* 93–125.

Bernero, R., & Bothwell, H. *Relationship of hearing impairment to educational needs.* Illinois Department of Public Health and Office of the Superintendent of Public Instruction, 1966.

Bloom, L. *Language development: Form and function in emerging grammars.* Cambridge, Mass.: MIT Press, 1970.

Bloom, L., & Lahey, M. *Language development and language disorders.* New York: Wiley, 1978.

Bornstein, H. A description of some current sign systems designed to represent English. *American Annals of the Deaf,* 1973, *118,* 454–463.

Bornstein, H. Signed English: A manual approach to English language development. *Journal of Speech and Hearing Disorders,* 1974, *39,* 330–343.

Bowerman, M. *Early syntactic development: A cross-linguistic study with specific reference to Finnish.* New York: Cambridge University Press, 1973.

Boyes-Braem, P. *A study of the acquisition of the dez in the American Sign Language.* Working paper, Salk Institute for Biological Sciences, LaJolla, Calif., 1973.

Bragg, B. Amelish—Our American heritage: A testimony. *American Annals of the Deaf,* 1973, *118,* 672–674.

Braine, M. The ontogeny of English phrase structure: The first phase. *Language,* 1963, *39,* 1–13.

Brasel, K., & Quigley, S. The influence of certain language and communication environments in early childhood on the development of language in deaf individuals. *Journal of Speech and Hearing Research,* 1977, *20,* 95–107.

Brimer, A. *Wide-span reading test.* London: Nelson, 1972.

Brown, R. *A first language: The early stages.* Cambridge, Mass.: Harvard University Press, 1973.

Brown, R., Cazden, C., & Bellugi, U. The child's grammar from 1 to 3. In J. P. Hill (Ed.), *Minnesota symposium on child psychology* (Vol. 2). Minneapolis: University of Minnesota Press, 1969.

Caccamise, F., Hatfield, N., & Brewer, L. Manual/simultaneous communication (M/SC) research: Results and implications. *American Annals of the Deaf,* 1978, *123,* 803–823.

Carrow, E. A test using elicited imitation in assessing grammatical structure in children. *Journal of Speech and Hearing Disorders,* 1974, *39,* 437–444.

Chall, J. *Learning to read: The great debate.* New York: McGraw-Hill, 1967.

Charrow, V., & Fletcher, D. English as the second language of deaf children. *Developmental Psychology,* 1974, *10,* 463–470.

Chomsky, N. *Syntactic structures.* The Hague: Mouton, 1957.

Chomsky, N. *Aspects of the theory of syntax.* Cambridge, Mass.: MIT Press, 1965.

Chomsky, N. *Reflections on language.* London: Temple-Smith, 1976.

Clark, E. V. What's in a word? On the child's acquisition of semantics in his first language. In T. E. Moore (Ed.), *Cognitive development and the acquistion of language.* New York: Academic Press, 1973.

Collins-Algren, M. Teaching English as a second language to young deaf children: A case study. *Journal of Speech and Hearing Disorders,* 1974, *39,* 486–500.

Collins-Algren, M. Language development of two deaf children. *American Annals of the Deaf,* 1975, *120,* 524–539.

Conrad, R. Short-term memory processes in the deaf. *British Journal of Psychology,* 1970, *61,* 179-195.

Conrad, R. Short term memory in the deaf: A test for speech coding. *British Journal of Psychology,* 1972, *63,* 173-180. (a)

Conrad, R. Speech and reading. In J. F. Kavanagh & I. Mattingly (Eds.), *Language by ear and by eye: The relationships between speech and reading.* Cambridge, Mass.: MIT Press, 1972. (b)

Conrad, R. Some correlates of speech coding in short-term memory of the deaf. *Journal of Speech and Hearing Research,* 1973, *16,* 375-384.

Conrad, R. *The deaf school child: Language and cognitive function.* London: Harper & Row, 1979.

Cooper, R. L., & Rosenstein, J. Language acquistion of deaf children. *The Volta Review,* 1966, *68*(1), 58-67.

Cornett, O. Cued speech. *American Annals of the Deaf,* 1967, *112,* 3-13.

Corson, H. *Comparing deaf children of oral deaf parents and deaf parents using manual communication with deaf children of hearing parents on academic, social, and communication functioning.* Unpublished doctoral dissertation, University of Cincinnati, 1973.

Crystal, D., & Craig, E. Contrived sign language. In I. M. Schlesinger & L. Nomir (Eds.), *Sign language of the deaf.* New York: Academic Press, 1978.

Dale, P. *Language development structure and function.* New York: Holt, Rinehart & Winston, 1976.

Davis, H. Guide for the classification on education of hearing handicap in relation to the international audiometric zero. *Transactions of the American Academy of Ophtholmology and Otolaryngology,* July-Aug. 1965, 740-751.

Davis, H., & Silverman, S. R. *Hearing and deafness* (3rd ed.). New York: Holt, Rinehart & Winston, 1970.

deVilliers, J., & deVilliers, P. *Language acquisition.* Cambridge, Mass.: Harvard University Press, 1978.

DiFrancesca, S. *Academic achievement test results of a national testing program for hearing impaired students, United States, Spring, 1971.* Washington, D.C.: Gallaudet College, Office of Demographic Studies, 1972.

Doehring, D., Bonnycastle, D., & Ling, A. Rapid reading skills of integrated hearing-impaired children. *Volta Review,* 1978, *80*(6), 399-409.

Erikson, C. W., Pollack, M. D., & Montague, W. E. Implicit speech: Mechanism in perceptual encoding? *Journal of Experimental Psychology,* 1970, *84,* 502-507.

Feldman, H. *The development of a lexicon by deaf children of hearing parents or, there's more to language than meets the ear.* Unpublished doctoral dissertation, University of Pennsylvania, College Park, Pa., 1975.

Fischer, S. The otogenic development of language. In E. W. Straus (Ed.), *Language and language disturbances: The fifth Lexington conference on pure and applied phenomenology.* Pittsburgh: Duquesne University Press, 1974.

Fischer, S. Influences on word-order change in American Sign Language. In C. Li (Ed.), *Word order and word order change.* Austin: University of Texas Press, 1975.

Fletcher, J., & Suppes, P. *Computer-assisted instruction in mathematics and language arts for the deaf: Final report.* Project No. 14-2280, U.S. Dept. of Health, Education and Welfare. Stanford: Institute for Mathematical Studies in the Social Sciences, 1973.

Fraser, C., Bellugi, U., & Brown, R. Control of grammar in imitation, comprehension and production. *Journal of Verbal Learning and Verbal Behavior,* 1963, *3,* 121-135.

Friedman, L. *On the other hand.* New York: Academic Press, 1977.

Furth, H. *Thinking—Without language.* New York: Free Press, 1966.

Furth, H., & Youniss, J. Formal operations and language: A comparison of deaf and hearing adolescents. *International Journal of Psychology,* 1971, *6,* 49-64.

Geers, A., & Moog, J. Syntactic maturity of spontaneous speech and elicited imitations of hearing-impaired children. *Journal of Speech and Hearing Disorders,* 1978, *43,* 380-391.

Golden-Meadow, S. *The representation of semantic relations in a manual language created by deaf children of hearing parents: A language you can't dismiss out of hand.* Unpublished doctoral dissertation, University of Pennsylvania, College Park, Pa., 1975.

Golden-Meadow, S., & Feldman, H. The development of language-like communication without a language model. *Science,* 1977, *197,* 401–403.

Gustason, G., Pfetzing, D., & Zawolkow, E. *Signing exact English.* Rossmoor, Calif.: Modern Signs Press, 1972.

Gustason, G., Pfetzing, D., & Zawolkow, E. *Signing exact English* (Rev. ed. Rossmoor, Calif.: Modern Signs Press, 1975.

Hammermeister, F. Reading achievement in deaf adults. *American Annals of the Deaf,* 1971, *116,* 25–28.

Hardyck, C. D., & Petrinovich, L. F. Subvocal speech and comprehension level as a function of the difficulty level of reading material. *Journal of Verbal Learning and Verbal Behavior,* 1970, *9,* 647–652.

Hatfield, N., Caccamise, F., & Siple, P. Deaf students' language competency: A bilingual perspective. *American Annals of the Deaf,* 1978, *123,* 847–851.

Heider, F., & Heider, G. A comparison of sentence structure of deaf and hearing children. *Psychological Monographs,* 1940, *52,* 52–103.

Jensema, C., Karchmer, M., & Trybus, R. *The rated speech intelligibility of hearing impaired children: Basic relationships and a detailed analysis.* Series R, No. 6. Washington, D.C.: Gallaudet College, Office of Demographic Studies, 1978.

Jensema, C., & Trybus, R. *Communication patterns and educational achievement of hearing impaired children.* Series T, No. 2, Washington, D.C.: Gallaudet College, Office of Demographic Studies, 1978.

Jones, M., & Quigley, S. The acquisition of question formation in English and American Sign Language by two hearing children of deaf parents. *Journal of Speech and Hearing Disorders,* 1979, *44,* 196–208.

Jordon, I. K., Gustason, G., & Rosen, R. Current communication trends in programs for the deaf. *American Annals of the Deaf,* 1976, *121,* 527–532.

Kannapell, B. M. Bilingualism: A new direction in the education of the deaf. *Deaf American,* 1974, *26,* 9–15.

Karchmer, M., Milone, M., & Wolk, S. Educational significance of hearing loss at three levels of severity. *American Annals of the Deaf,* 1979, *124,* 97–109.

Kavanagh, J. F. (Ed.). *Communicating by language: The reading process.* Bethesda, Md.: U.S. Dept. of Health, Education and Welfare, 1968.

Kavanagh, J. F., & Mattingly, I. (Eds.). *Language by ear and by eye: The relationship between speech and reading.* Cambridge, Mass.: MIT Press, 1972.

Kirk, S., McCarthy, J., & Kirk, W. *Illinois test of psycholinguistic abilities.* Urbana, Ill.: University of Illinois Press, 1968.

Klapp, S. T. Implicit speech inferred from response latencies in same-different decisions. In J. F. Kavanaugh & I. G. Mattingly (Eds.), *Language by ear and eye: The relationship between speech and reading.* Cambridge, Mass.: MIT Press, 1972.

Klima, E., & Bellugi, U. *The signs of language.* Cambridge, Mass.: Harvard University Press, 1979.

Lane, H., & Baker, D. Reading achievement of the deaf: Another look. *The Volta Review,* 1974, *76,* 489–499.

Lee, L. *Northwestern syntax screening test.* Evanston, Ill.: Northwestern University Press, 1969.

Lee, L. *Developmental sentence analysis.* Evanston, Ill.: Northwestern University Press, 1974.

Levitt, H., & Newcomb, W. Computer-assisted analysis of written language: Assessing the written language of deaf children. *Journal of Communication Disorders,* 1978, *11,* 257–277.

Ling, D. *Speech and the hearing impaired child: Theory and practice.* Washington, D.C.: Alexander Graham Bell Association for the Deaf, Inc., 1976.

Locke, J. Phonemic effects in the silent reading of hearing and deaf children. *Cognition,* 1978, *6,* 175-187.
Locke, J., & Locke, V. Deaf children's phonetic, visual, and dactylic coding in a grapheme recall task. *Journal of Experimental Psychology,* 1971, *89,* 142-146.
Luterman, D. A comparison of language skills of hearing impaired children trained in a visual/oral method and an audiitory/oral method. *American Annals of the Deaf,* 1976, *121,* 389-393.
Magner, M. E. Reading: Goals and achievements at Clarke School for the Deaf. *Volta Review,* 1964, *66,* 464-468.
Marshall, W., & Quigley, S. *Quantitative and qualitative analysis of syntactic structure in the written language of deaf students.* Urbana, Ill.: Institute for Research on Exceptional Children, 1970.
McGuigan, F. J. Covert oral behavior during the silent performance of language tasks. *Psychological Bulletin,* 1970, *74,* 309-326.
McIntire, M. *A modified model for the description of language acquisition in a deaf child.* Unpublished master's thesis, California State University, Northridge, Calif., 1974.
McKee, P., Harrison, M. I., McCowen, A., Lehr, E., & Durr, W. K. *Reading for meaning* (4th ed.). Boston: Houghton-Mifflin, 1966.
Meadow, K. *The effect of early manual communication and family climate on the deaf child's development.* Unpublished doctoral dissertation, University of California, Berkeley, 1967.
Meadow, K. The development of deaf children. In E. Hetherington (Ed.), *Review of child development research* (Vol. 5). Chicago: University of Chicago Press, 1976.
Media Development Project for the Hearing Impaired. Papers from the symposium on research and utilization of educational media for teaching the deaf. *American Annals of the Deaf,* 1978, *123,* 615-884.
Moores, D. *Applications of "cloze" procedures to the assessment of psycholinguistic abilities of the deaf.* Unpublished doctoral dissertation, University of Illinois, 1967.
Morkovin, B. V. Experiment in teaching deaf preschool children in the Soviet Union. *The Volta Review,* 1960, *62,* 260-268.
Moskowitz, B. The acquisition of language. *Scientific American,* 1978, *239,* 92-108.
Myklebust, H. R. *The psychology of deafness* (2nd ed.). New York: Grune & Stratton, 1964.
Nelson, K. Structure and strategy in learning to talk. *Society for Research on Child Development* 1973, *38,* No. 1-2.
Newman, L. Cherry blossoms come to bloom. *The Deaf American,* 1972, *24,* 25-27.
Newport, E., & Ashbrook, E. The emergence of semantics in American Sign Language. *Papers and reports on child language development,* 1977, *13,* 16-21.
Odom, P. B., Blanton, A. L., & McIntyre, C. K. Coding medium and word recall by deaf and hearing subjects. *Journal of Speech and Hearing Research,* 1970, *13,* 54-58.
Office of Demographic Studies. *Academic achievement test results of a national testing program for hearing impaired students.* Washington, D.C.: Author, 1972.
Ogden, P. *Experiences and attitudes of oral deaf adults regarding oralism.* Unpublished doctoral dissertation, University of Illinois, 1979.
O'Neill, M. A. *The receptive language competence of deaf children in the use of the base structure rules of transformational generative grammar.* Unpublished doctoral dissertation, University of Pittsburgh, 1973.
Pinter, R., & Patterson, D. A measurement of the language ability of deaf children. *Psychological Review,* 1917, *23,* 413-436.
Pollack, D. Acoupedics: A uni-sensory approach to auditory training. *The Volta Review,* 1964, *66,* 400-409.
Power, D., & Quigley, S. Deaf children's acquisition of the passive voice. *Journal of Speech and Hearing Research,* 1973, *16,* 5-11.
Presnell, L. Hearing-impaired children's comprehension and production of syntax in oral language. *Journal of Speech and Hearing Research,* 1973, *16,* 12-21.

Pugh, G. A. Summaries from appraisal of the silent reading abilities of acoustically handicapped children. *American Annals of the Deaf,* 1946, *91,* 331–349.
Quigley, S. P. *The influence of finger spelling on the development of language, communication, and educational achievement in deaf children.* Urbana, Ill.: Institute for Research on Exceptional Children, 1969.
Quigley, S. P., & Frisina, D. R. Institutionalization and psychoeducational development of deaf children. *C.E.C. Research Monographs,* 1961.
Quigley, S., Montanelli, D., & Wilbur, R. Some aspects of the verb system in the language of deaf students. *Journal of Speech and Hearing Research,* 1976, *19,* 536–550.
Quigley, S., Power, D., & Steinkamp, M. The language structure of deaf children. *The Volta Review,* 1976, 79, 73–84.
Quigley, S., Smith, N., & Wilbur, R. Comprehension of relativized sentences by deaf students. *Journal of Speech and Hearing Research,* 1974, *17,* 325–341.
Quigley, S., Steinkamp, M., Power, D., & Jones, B. *Test of Syntactic Abilities.* Beaverton, Ore.: Dormac, 1978.
Quigley, S., Wilbur, R., & Montanelli, D. Question formation in the language of deaf students. *Journal of Speech and Hearing Research,* 1974, *17,* 699–713.
Quigley, S., Wilbur, R., & Montanelli, D. Complement structures in the language of deaf students. *Journal of Speech and Hearing Research,* 1976, *19,* 448–457.
Quigley, S., Wilbur, R., Power, D., Montanelli, D., & Steinkamp, M. *Syntactic structures in the language of deaf children.* Urbana, Ill.: Institute for Child Behavior and Development, 1976.
Rainer, J., Altschuler, K., & Kallmann, F. (Eds.). *Family and mental health problems in a deaf population* (2nd ed.). Springfield, Ill.: Thomas, 1969.
Rawlings, B., & Jensema, C. *Two studies of the families of hearing impaired children.* Series R, No. 5. Washington, D.C.: Gallaudet College, Office of Demographic Studies, 1977.
Russell, K., Quigley, S., & Power, D. *Linguistics and deaf children.* Washington, D.C.: Alexander Grahame Bell Association for the Deaf, Inc., 1976.
Schlesinger, H. The acquisition of bimodal language. In I. M. Schlesinger & L. Namir (Eds.), *Sign language of the deaf.* New York: Academic Press, 1978.
Schlesinger, H., & Meadow, K. *Sounds and sign.* Berkeley: University of California Press, 1972.
Schlesinger, I. M., & Namir, L. (Eds.). *Sign language of the deaf.* New York: Academic Press, 1978.
Schmitt, P. *Deaf children's comprehension and production of sentence transformations and verb tenses.* Unpublished doctoral dissertation, University of Illinois, 1968.
Silverman, S. R. The education of deaf children. In L. E. Travis (Ed.), *Handbook of speech pathology and audiology.* New York: Appleton, 1971.
Simmons, A. A comparison of the type-token ratio of spoken and written language of deaf and hearing children. *The Volta Review,* 1962, *64,* 117–121.
Siple, P. (Ed.). *Understanding language through sign language research.* New York: Academic Press, 1978.
Steinkamp, M., & Quigley, S. Assessing deaf children's written language. *The Volta Review,* 1977, *79,* 10–18.
Stokoe, W. C., Jr. Sign language structure: An outline of the visual communication systems of the American deaf. *Studies in Linguistics.* Occasional Paper No. 8, 1960. Reissued, Washington, D.C.: Gallaudet College Press.
Stokoe, W. C., Jr. *The study of sign language* (Rev. ed.). Linguistics Research Laboratory, Washington, D.C.: Gallaudet College, 1971.
Stokoe, W. C., Jr. *Semiotics and human sign languages.* The Hague: Mouton, 1972.
Stokoe, W. C., Jr. The view from the way: Two ways to English competence for the deaf. *Gallaudet Today,* Winter 1974–1975, *5,* 31–32.
Stuckless, E. R., & Birch, J. The influence of early manual communication on the linguistic development of deaf children. *American Annals of the Deaf,* 1966, *111,* 452–460, 499–504.

Stuckless, E. R., & Marks, C. H. *Assessment of the written language of deaf students.* (Cooperative Research Project No. 2544, Office of Education, U.S. Dept. of Health, Education and Welfare.) Pittsburgh: University of Pittsburgh, School of Education, Program in Special Education and Rehabilitation, 1966.

Swisher, L. The language performance of the oral deaf. In H. Whitaker & H. A. Whitaker (Eds.), *Studies in neurolinguistics* (Vol. 2). New York: Academic Press, 1976.

Taylor, L. *A language analysis of the writing of deaf children.* Unpublished doctoral dissertation, State University of Florida, 1969.

Trybus, R., & Karchmer, M. School achievement scores of hearing impaired children: National data on achievement status and growth patterns. *American Annals of the Deaf Director of Programs and Services,* 1977, *122,* 62-69.

Vernon, M. *Multiply handicapped deaf children: Medical, educational and psychological considerations.* Washington, D.C.: Council for Exceptional Children Research Monograph, 1969.

Vernon, M., & Koh, S. Effects of oral preschool compared to early manual communication on education and communication in deaf children. *American Annals of the Deaf,* 1970, *116,* 569-574.

Wilbur, R. B. *American sign language and sign systems.* Baltimore, Md.: University Park Press, 1979.

Wilbur, R., Montanelli, D., & Quigley, S. Pronominalization in the language of deaf students. *Journal of Speech and Hearing Research,* 1976, *19,* 120-140.

Wilbur, R., & Quigley, S. Syntactic structures in the written language of deaf children. *The Volta Review,* 1975, *77,* 194-203.

Wilbur, R., Quigley, S., & Montanelli, D. Conjoined structures in the language of deaf students. *Journal of Speech and Hearing Research,* 1975, *18,* 319-335.

Wrightstone, J. W., Arnow, M. S., & Moskowitz, S. Developing reading test norms for deaf children. *American Annals of the Deaf,* 1963, *108,* 311-316.

ADULT LANGUAGE DISORDERS

10 A Psycholinguistic Assessment of Adult Aphasia

Alfonso Caramazza
Rita Sloan Berndt
The Johns Hopkins University

INTRODUCTION

It has been observed repeatedly since the time of Hippocrates that damage to the brain can result in a disturbance of language capacities. In fact, most of the clinical forms of aphasia were described in detail prior to 1880 (Benton & Joynt, 1960). Despite this early interest in the topic, it was a discovery by Paul Broca reported around 1865 that marks the beginning of the study of aphasia in its present form.

Broca reported neuroanatomical evidence that destruction of the posterior part of the third frontal convolution in the left hemisphere (an area now known as "Broca's area") resulted in a language disturbance, whereas a corresponding lesion in the right hemisphere did not result in any observable language deficit. Broca's observations were soon verified by Charcot and other neurologists, thus confirming the claim that a part of the left hemisphere is the "center" for articulated speech. This discovery by Broca had three important components:

1. It was based on observations of disturbed language that occurred suddenly in previously normal individuals.
2. The observed language disturbance was associated with a focal brain lesion, as documented by postmortem examination.
3. The cortical lesion was localized in a specific region of the left hemisphere.

Despite the undisputed importance of Broca's discovery, his work failed to establish that there is a specific *type* of language disturbance associated with the lesion he described rather than simply an undifferentiated reduction in language capacity. It was the work of the German neurologist Carl Wernicke (1874) that provided the additional evidence for the modern study of aphasia (Eggert, 1977). Wernicke reported observations indicating that damage to the posterior regions of the temporal lobe in the left hemisphere (later known as "Wernicke's area") results in a type of language disturbance dramatically different from that produced by lesions in Broca's area (see Fig. 10-1). The symptoms associated with focal lesions to the posterior regions of the frontal lobe of the left hemisphere ("Broca's aphasia") involve articulatory or "expressive" aspects of language—a drastic reduction of speech output, distorted articulation, and slow, effortful, dysprosodic speech. The symptoms associated with lesions in the posterior parts of the temporal lobe ("Wernicke's aphasia") are primarily sensory or "receptive" in nature—patients experience a profound failure to understand written and oral language, although there is no indication of primary visual or auditory impairments. Thus, we are confronted with a remarkable dissociation: The Broca's aphasic has difficulties in speaking, although appearing to have a relatively preserved ability to comprehend language; the Wernicke's aphasic has difficulties in language comprehension but no apparent trouble articulating speech. These observations by Wernicke established two principles that can be added to those made on the basis of Broca's work:

1. Damage to the left hemisphere does not result in a unitary language deficit nor in complete disruption of language functions.

2. Damage to different areas of the left hemisphere results in remarkably different patterns of language disturbance.

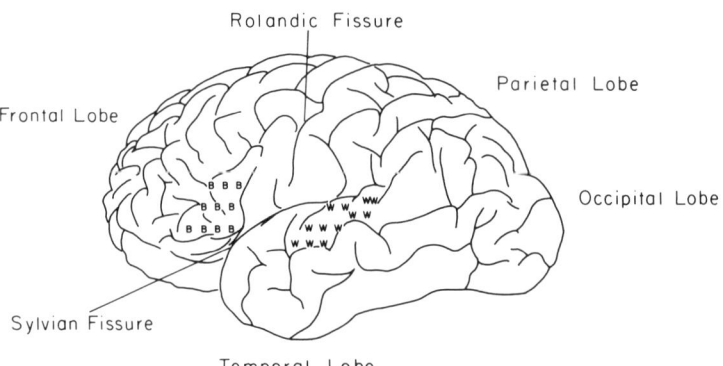

FIG. 10.1. Lateral surface of the left hemisphere (B = Broca's area; W = Wernicke's area).

This early work by Broca and by Wernicke provided empirical support for the notion of aphasic syndromes by showing that constellations of symptoms co-occur in relation to specific focal damage. In addition, this early work clarified the definition of aphasia itself by delimiting its scope to acquired language disorders consequent to focal brain damage, as distinguished from disturbances related to primary sensory or motor impairments.

Wernicke's contribution to the study of aphasia went beyond these general considerations. On the basis of the differential disruptions of language ability consequent to brain damage in different loci, he developed a neuropsychological theory of language based on the associationist principles and the neuroanatomical theories prevalent in his time. Wernicke assumed that specific components of language representation (sound or sensory "images," articulatory "gestures," etc.) are organized in cortical centers connected to one another. Language functions such as comprehension and speech production require the normal operation of these centers. Destruction of Broca's area, for example, will affect the articulatory images of words and will produce the articulatory defect noted in Broca's aphasia.

Wernicke's neuropsychological theory had predictive power in that it allowed neurologists to predict the site of a patient's lesion on the basis of behavioral data. More importantly, it provided the theoretical basis from which Wernicke described syndromes that had not yet been reported. In this regard, the most celebrated example is his prediction of the existence of the syndrome of conduction aphasia. He reasoned that a lesion that affected the connecting pathways between Broca's area (motor images) and Wernicke's area (sensory images) should result in a dissociation of two components of a word. Because Broca's and Wernicke's areas remain intact, the patient should have normal articulatory agility and comprehension but would show impairments in word choice and in repetition of speech. In 1885, Lichtheim provided empirical confirmation of the existence of this symptom pattern and the associated focal lesion that Wernicke had predicted.

Whatever the specific merits of Wernicke's neuropsychological theory (henceforth called the *classical* theory), it made two important assumptions that have remained central to most accounts of aphasia. On the psychological level, it assumed a componential view of the structure of language. This assumption allowed a detailed consideration of aphasic symptoms in terms of presumed dissociations among components or the "subtraction" of specific components from the normal process of language use. On the neuroanatomical level, and corresponding to the componential view of language structure, was the strict localizationist assumption that these psychological components are discretely represented in specific areas of the brain. This latter assumption provided the basis for the analysis of brain–behavior correlates.

Although the classical theory has been subjected to extensive criticisms almost from its inception (Freud, 1891; Jackson, 1878), it has recently regained a prominent place in neuropsychology primarily through the efforts of neurologist Norman Geschwind (1965). One reason for the resurgence of interest in the classical theory may be its superficial similarity to information-processing models of cognition. Specifically, a stage analysis of language processing is implied by the classical theory, which has been easily reinterpreted within the modern framework. However, some of the criticisms directed at the classical theory were not without foundation. These criticisms challenged the description of the observed language deficits and the psychological theory on which these were based, as well as the assumption that functional components of language are discretely represented in the brain. Two examples make clear the nature of these criticisms.

Pierre Marie (1906), in an article appropriately entitled "The Third Frontal Convolution does not Play any Special Role in Language Use" challenged the analysis of the Broca syndrome and the precise localization of its corresponding lesion. He maintained that the lesion associated with Broca's aphasia was much larger than originally claimed by Broca, thus undermining the basic neuroanatomical correlate of the syndrome. More important, he challenged the view that brain damage to the left hemisphere resulted in the differential impairment of components of language use. Instead he suggested that there is a single form of language disruption—Wernicke's aphasia—and that the other observed syndromes are merely different combinations of Wernicke's aphasia and disorders of peripheral language mechanisms. Thus, Broca's aphasia was simply Wernicke's aphasia plus disturbed articulation (dysarthria). The psychological theory implicit in Pierre Marie's analysis of aphasia is that language structure is indissoluble and, consequently, unanalyzable under conditions of brain damage—obviously a rather unproductive view.

A more interesting challenge to the classical theory was advanced by Goldstein (1948), who rejected the associationist psychological model of Wernicke in favor of a psychological theory based on the writings of the gestalt psychologists. Goldstein's analysis of the syndrome of conduction aphasia illustrates the nature of his criticism of the classical theory.

Goldstein assumed that the symptoms found in conduction aphasia (which he renamed "central aphasia") were the result of a disturbance of the mechanisms of "inner speech." He argued that the patient could not reproduce an orally presented model because, although the input was adequately processed, it could not be organized into an inner speech form that was adequate to serve as a model for repetition.

Whatever the value of the specific details of Goldstein's proposal, his theory had two general merits. First, he attempted to offer an alternative to the strict localizationist hypothesis in terms of a dynamic organization of language functions, that is, he argued that although specific parts of the brain are needed for the proper realization of some component process, a particular brain structure is not the actual repository of that process. Rather, the component process is a product of the normal activity of an integrated set of structures. Second, his challenge of the analysis of the syndromes described within the classical theory forced a reconsideration of the underlying psychological theory. He explicitly rejected the associationist model as offering too simplistic a view of the structure of language processes. Unfortunately, however, the alternative "theory" offered by Goldstein was unproductive because it was developed only in the most general terms.

The criticisms of the classical theory offered in the first half of this century by Goldstein and others (Head, 1926; Luria, 1947) questioned the adequacy of the psychological theory assumed to be part of theories of aphasia. In particular, these criticisms focused on the very simple analysis of the cognitive and linguistic operations involved in a specific language behavior. Furthermore, because of the strong symptom/pathology association that was assumed in the classical theory, it was relatively easy to undermine the strict localizationist hypothesis. For example, if it could be shown that a symptom such as comprehension failure resulted from lesions in markedly different areas of the brain, then it was concluded that the strict localizationist position was false. Indeed, this type of argument has been offered repeatedly in the literature. Such evidence, however, serves only to falsify one form of the localizationist hypothesis—the strict localization of complex functional components such as comprehension or repetition. It does not falsify a more interesting form of the localizationist hypothesis that argues that abstract processing mechanisms are localized. Specifically, within a modern componential view of language processing, a general symptom such as poor comprehension could result because of lexical, syntactic, or semantic integration problems. On the assumption that these various processes may be represented in different parts of the brain, lesions in different areas may have similar consequences on a single, grossly measured behavior such as comprehension.

In our view, then, the historical criticisms of the classical theory are most valuable not because of their rejection of the localizationist hypothesis but because of their arguments concerning the proper level of psycholinguistic analysis of aphasia.

The modern study of the neuropsychology of language has undergone a development similar to that of modern psycholinguistics. Indeed, psycholinguistic investigations of aphasia generally proceed along lines similar to those employed in the study of normal language processing and of language development. The work of Jakobson and of Goodglass can be singled out as the major contributions influencing the approach currently taken in the study of aphasia.

Jakobson's synthesis of the criticisms that had been leveled at the classical theory provided the basis for thinking of language dissolution in terms of the impairment of abstract linguistic mechanisms. Working from Luria's detailed description of aphasic symptoms, Jakobson (1964) offered a linguistic explanation of those syndromes based on a set of three dichotomies. The most useful of these involves the linguistic distinction between "selection" and "combination" and leads to the prediction that there should be two qualitatively different types of aphasic disorders. In one type, termed a *similarity* disorder, the patient has difficulty selecting from similar lexical entries (i.e., he has trouble finding the right word from the available alternatives). In the second type of disturbance (a "contiguity" disorder) the patient has difficulty combining and integrating words into a unified scheme. Jakobson was able to subdivide these two basic classes further using two other polar constructs so that he ultimately provided a linguistic explanation for the six types of aphasia that Luria described. For present purposes, it is necessary to note only that the basic division into "similarity" and "contiguity" disorder corresponds in several important respects to the classic division of aphasic types. Jakobson's contribution was to couch this division (and several even finer distinctions) in terms of abstract linguistic components. This advance provides a new basis for arguments about the localization of function, such that if there is any localization of function it will be these general linguistic operations that are localized rather than gross behavioral components such as repetition or comprehension.

The second major development in aphasia research was provided by Harold Goodglass, who shares Jakobson's general view of the level at which aphasic language should be analyzed. Goodglass added an important new dimension to aphasia research—the application of quasi-experimental methods and quantitative analysis to aphasic language. The value of this contribution goes far beyond the obvious advantages that accompany the quantification of aphasic performance. Rather, this new approach represents an implicit shift in the conceptualization of the problem of aphasic language. If, as Jakobson argues, aphasia is considered to be a reflection of the selective disturbance of abstract linguistic operations, it should be possible to perform task analyses to reveal the linguistic operations that are needed for the proper execution of various tasks. Furthermore, it should also be possible to test specific hypotheses about the nature of the impairment in various types of aphasia. Thus, if we assume that a particular type of aphasia results from the impairment of a specific linguistic component, we should be able to test our hypothesis by devising tasks that implicate the component in various ways. The value of this approach is that it forces a careful psycholinguistic analysis of patterns of aphasic symptoms; in addition, it provides an alternative to the traditional clinicopathological case study method that has dominated the field of aphasia research.

During the past 10 years there has been a gradual accumulation of studies that have taken such an approach. Working from theories of language developed within linguistics and psychology, and often employing techniques used to study normal language in the psycholinguistics laboratory, aphasiologists have attempted to explain aphasic symptoms as reflections of an impairment of one or more of the components of language processing. The primary purpose of this chapter is to provide a review of this recent literature. Before that review can be approached, however, the major aphasic syndromes must be described in some detail. In addition, we summarize in general terms the theory of normal language representation and processing that provides the basis for many of the recent studies of aphasia.

THE SYNDROMES OF APHASIA

The classical distinction between the two markedly different types of aphasia that can occur when the left hemisphere is damaged survives as the most important dichotomy among aphasic syndromes. Although explanations for the two symptom patterns differ widely, all major taxonomies of aphasia acknowledge the distinction proposed by Wernicke (but see Schuell & Jenkins, 1959, for an antitaxonomic approach). The original characterization of the primary difference between these two types of aphasia divided them neatly on the basis of gross behavioral differences: Patients with damage to the frontal lobe (''anterior'' to the Rolandic fissure) have difficulty *producing* speech; those with damage in the temporal lobe (in ''posterior'' regions) have trouble *comprehending* speech. This rough characterization was formalized by Weisenberg & McBride (1935), who divided all aphasic syndromes into ''expressive'' and ''receptive'' disorders. This distinction, which remains popular in some circles, glosses over many problems that are readily apparent even to a casual observer of aphasic patients. Most important, the description implies that patients with a ''receptive'' disorder (posterior-damaged patients) have normal speech output. On the contrary, many patients with a comprehension disorder (who would fit into the ''receptive'' category) have great difficulty producing a coherent and meaningful sentence. Although these patients typically do not have difficulty articulating speech, their fluent verbal productions are usually far from normal, a point that is developed in the following.

Another major dichotomy of aphasic syndromes, which tends to result in the same division between patients as the expressive/receptive distinction, is made on the basis of quantitative analysis of speech output. Goodglass, Quadfasel, and Timberlake (1964) divided patients into ''fluent'' and ''nonfluent'' based on the average number of words produced together within a phrase (see also Howes, 1967). This approach is atheoretical: It makes no assumptions about any language functions other than speech production, nor does it attempt to characterize qualitatively the type of speech that the patients produce. It is important because it provides an objective means for dividing patients into two groups that correspond fairly well to the neuroanatomic distinction between anterior and posterior lesion sites (Benson, 1967).

The importance of this single distinction between aphasic symptoms is based on long-standing evidence of two remarkably different manifestations of language disturbance that seem to be correlated quite well with differing lesion sites. As shown later, recent research has continued to focus on this basic distinction.

Nonetheless, this emphasis cannot be allowed to overwhelm the finer distinctions that have been made among aphasic syndromes. As might be expected, as the description of symptom patterns becomes more specific, it is increasingly difficult to find clear correspondences among types in the many taxonomies of aphasia that have been offered. Thus, it is necessary to limit our discussion of aphasic syndromes to the types identified in a single taxonomy.

Our discussion of aphasic syndromes follows the classification system developed by Goodglass and Kaplan (1972), which is based on the classical description of syndromes (Benson & Geschwind, 1977; Goodglass & Geschwind, 1976). This system has served as the classification model for many of the recent studies to be discussed. Unlike other taxonomies that might have been chosen, it offers a diagnostic means (the Boston Diagnostic Aphasia Examination) for classifying patients into types on the basis of a battery of objectively and subjectively scored measures.

Our emphasis on this classification scheme should not be interpreted as an indication of universal acceptance within the field, of the system itself, its underlying assumptions, or even of the division of patterns of symptoms into syndromes. There is considerable difference of opinion in all of these areas, especially with regard to assumptions concerning localization of function. The two major theoretical approaches to aphasia that differ markedly from the approach offered here are those of Luria (1964, 1970) and of Brown (1972, 1977). Both of these involve well-developed and complex arguments concerning the structure and localization of language functions, although neither approach has as yet spawned much empirical research. Table 10.1 demonstrates how the classification systems employed by Luria and by Brown correspond to the system discussed here, although the theoretical basis for their taxonomies is not elaborated (see Lesser, 1978, for a discussion of these and other approaches.)

The Major Syndromes

Broca's Aphasia. The syndrome known as "Broca's aphasia" was the first symptom pattern to be identified with damage to a particular cortical area. The most striking characteristic of this syndrome is effortful, dysprosodic, and tortuously articulated speech. These patients are the prototypical "nonfluent" or "expressive" type. The Broca's aphasic typically produces short phrases made up primarily of substantive words—concrete nouns, main verbs and important modifiers—that most often convey successfully the intended message. Broca speech is characterized as "agrammatic" because of the frequent omission of the grammatical "function words" (articles, prepositions, auxiliary verbs, conjunctions, and some pronouns) and "bound" grammatical morphemes such as number and tense markers. Significantly, repeated sequences may be somewhat more easily produced than spontaneous speech, and highly familiar material may be articulated without difficulty. The following is a sample of speech from a

TABLE 10.1
Some Classifications of The Major Syndromes of Aphasia

Goodglass & Kaplan, 1972	Wernicke (Lichtheim, 1885)	Goldstein, 1948	Weisenberg & McBride, 1935	Luria, 1976	Brown, 1972
Broca's aphasia	Cortical motor aphasia	Motor aphasia	Expressive aphasia	Efferent motor aphasia	Agrammatic aphasia
Wernicke's aphasia	Cortical sensory aphasia	Sensory aphasia	Receptive aphasia	Sensory (acoustic) aphasia	Semantic aphasia
Conduction aphasia	Conduction aphasia	Central aphasia		(1) Afferent motor aphasia (2) Acoustico-mnestic aphasia	Phonemic aphasia
Anomic aphasia		Amnesic aphasia		Amnestic aphasia	Nominal aphasia
Transcortical motor aphasia	Transcortical motor aphasia	Transcortical motor aphasia		Dynamic aphasia	
Transcortical sensory aphasia	Transcortical sensory aphasia	Transcortical sensory aphasia			

patient classified as a Broca's aphasic, who is attempting to describe the "cookie theft" picture from the Boston Diagnostic Aphasia Examination:[1]

girl is . . falling falling (6 sec) c-cookie /tsɑr/ fall . .
ah man ok / lady washin' . . eh . . /tʃɪtʃɪz/ ah man . .
boy . . ah . . /wɔʒ/ (7 sec) fall . . fall . . fall

Writing ability is usually at least as severely impaired as speech production in Broca's aphasia, indicating that more than pure articulation is involved. It is usually assumed that auditory comprehension is relatively preserved and that reading ability is largely intact. Recent research (reviewed following) has raised doubts about the Broca patient's abilities in these areas, however.

The neuroanatomical site associated with this syndrome is usually assumed to be the region identified by Broca that now bears his name (i.e., the third frontal convolution of the left hemisphere) (see Fig. 10.1). Mohr (1976) has argued recently that the full constellation of Broca symptoms results only when an area

---

[1]The picture to be described portrays a kitchen scene in which a boy is balanced precariously on a tilting stool as he reaches toward a cookie jar. A girl stands beside him reaching up as if to get a cookie. A woman stands with her back to the children, washing dishes, seemingly oblivious to the water running over the side of the sink and forming a puddle at her feet.

Questionable segments of the patients' speech are transcribed phonetically. Pauses of between 1 and 3 sec are noted by two dots. Longer pauses are noted in parentheses. Interjections by the experimenter are marked by a slash.

is damaged that is considerably larger than this circumscribed region. Recent studies using several new lesion localization techniques have supported Mohr's argument that a fairly extensive area anterior to the Rolandic fissure, including subcortical tissue, is usually damaged in cases of Broca's aphasia (Kertesz, Lesk, & McCabe, 1977; Naeser & Hayward, 1978).

Wernicke's Aphasia. The syndrome that is traditionally viewed as the contrast to Broca's aphasia bears the name of the neurologist who originally described it. The speech output of the Wernicke's aphasic is characteristically "fluent," and rate of speech may be even higher than normal. Patients articulate words without difficulty and produce utterances with normal voice quality and intonation.

The striking feature of the Wernicke's speech output is its characteristic failure to convey meaningful information. There is a relative lack of substantive elements; frequent use of indefinite, very general nouns; and a frequent resort to circumlocution to avoid making specific reference. Word-finding difficulty is a pervasive feature. Wernicke patients often employ complex grammatical constructions, but they sometimes apply grammatical rules incorrectly or produce syntactic errors (called "paragrammatism"). The following is a sample from the speech of a patient classified as a Wernicke's aphasic:

>   she's holdin' a plate 'n back she's holdin' it back . . /
>   she is ah . . wi - wi - wia /nɪs/overflowin' . . /
>   I can't /bɒv/ wha wha what it should do (8 sec)
>   what the other . . thing you see / /dʒɪk dʒə dʒɑmʌstʌd
>   /an' he f-fall down/ yeah it's fall down
>   its gonna fall down now . . see it's got the jar he's trying
>   kno-knock it out / an he's gonna /fɔt/ it . .
>   see he's gettin /æt/ done /raɪ/ he's grabbin' a thing

Wernicke's aphasics (and other patient types) often produce unintended elements ("paraphasia") in the course of fluent output. These may be limited to substitutions of single syllables or phonemes in the target utterance (e.g., dripping → dripsing), called *literal* or *phonemic* paraphasias. In some cases, the segment that is produced bears no discernable relationship to any word in the language, in which case the utterance is termed a *neologism*. In other cases, the unintended element produced by a patient involves the substitution of one word for another. These *verbal paraphasias* often involve the production of a semantically related word for the intended target (washing dishes → washing glasses), and these are termed *semantic* paraphasias. These paraphasic errors are not produced only by Wernicke's aphasics but are found to varying degrees in the speech of all varieties of "fluent" aphasics. Their frequent occurrence in the speech of Wernicke's patients, however, contributes to the relative unintelligibility of Wernicke speech, despite its fluency.

The hallmark of the Wernicke syndrome is its involvement of auditory comprehension: In the most severe cases, the patient may understand virtually nothing that is spoken to him. Other patients (or largely recovered patients) may understand all but complex utterances. The ability to repeat orally presented items is usually impaired in proportion to the patient's auditory comprehension deficit. Reading and writing are typically affected, and again the extent of the disturbance usually parallels the patient's comprehension impairment.

The neuroanatomical correlate of Wernicke's aphasia is the auditory association cortex of the left hemisphere (the posterior portion of the superior gyrus of the temporal lobe), which is adjacent to the primary auditory cortex (see Fig. 10.1).

Conduction Aphasia. Patients classified as Conduction aphasics are impaired in their ability to repeat orally presented material to an extent that is disproportionate to their other aphasic symptoms. Speech production is fluent, with normal intonation, although there may be marked hesitations for word finding and frequent literal paraphasias. Auditory comprehension is said to be near normal in some cases and only mildly impaired in others. Word-finding abilities may be disturbed in conduction aphasia, especially in confrontation naming tasks. Reading aloud may be very difficult, with many paraphasic errors, whereas silent reading for comprehension is done with relative ease. Writing ability is often disturbed, with frequent misspellings, omissions, reversals, and substitutions of letters. The repetition disturbance that is characteristic of this syndrome is most pronounced for polysyllabic and unfamiliar single words and low-probability (nonstereotyped) phrases and sentences. A sample of the speech of a conduction aphasic follows:

> and the girl and the girl is . . uh . . washin' dishes uh and uh and the uh I know what it is but it's uh goin' out goin' out and uh the water is (4 sec) going over over and to uh to uh to uh to the floor . . the floor uh the water going to the floor

The lesion site associated with Conduction aphasia has been somewhat controversial. The classical disconnection hypothesis of Wernicke located the damage as occurring to the arcuate fasciculus, a bundle of fibers connecting the Wernicke and Broca regions. This view is not shared universally, but there is considerable agreement that the general area implicated is the temperoparietal region (Benson, Sheremata, Bouchard, Segarra, Price, & Geschwind, 1973; Green & Howes, 1977). A lesion in this area, if deep enough, would affect the arcuate fasciculus.

Anomic Aphasia. The primary characteristic of this syndrome is the prominence of word-finding difficulty in otherwise fluent and well-formed speech. Substantive words, especially concrete nouns, occur infrequently. Paraphasic errors are not typical, but the patient may resort to frequent circumlocutions to avoid the production of an unavailable substantive:

well thus uh . . daughter . . she's (6 sec) has a cookie I guess already and . . and her . . son . . he's falling off the (11 sec) and he's . . trying to get his t-cookies . . and the mother she's washing . . the . . dishes and the water is overflowin' . . there's a couple of dishes . . there's (9 sec) can't think o' the names . . / and this is a (12 sec) um I know what they are because I can't tell . . this is a um um (10 sec) a house this is a house . .

Naming to confrontation is typically seriously impaired, although some patients perform significantly better in naming tasks than in producing substantive spontaneous speech. Repetition ability is most often intact. Auditory comprehension is relatively well-preserved in anomic aphasia, although many patients have a mild comprehension impairment, especially for isolated words. There is extensive variability among anomic patients in the areas of reading and writing. Some patients are seriously impaired in these abilities, whereas others read quite competently for meaning and write very much as they talk.

It is widely agreed that anomic aphasia is the most difficult syndrome to localize (Benson & Geschwind, 1977; Goodglass & Geschwind, 1976), and this may account for the variability within the syndrome complex. However, lesions in the temporal or parietal regions (angular gyrus) are the most commonly cited areas associated with this syndrome (Kertesz et al., 1977).

These four syndromes have been the focus of most recent aphasia research and are discussed further at some length. Several other syndromes have been described that have not been the subject of extensive research efforts, either because of a relative rarity of occurrence or severity of impairment.

Global Aphasia. As the name suggests, this syndrome describes the condition in which virtually all language functions are seriously impaired. Vocal productions may be limited to nonspeech sounds or, occasionally, to perseverated verbal stereotypies. Reading, writing, repetition, and naming are all severely affected. These patients have virtually no understanding of spoken speech, although they reportedly recognize differences between their native language and a foreign language and have retained some sense of when a response is required (Boller & Green, 1972).

As might be expected, the lesion associated with this syndrome is extensive, involving cortical and subcortical portions of the frontal, parietal, and temporal lobes (Naeser & Hayward, 1978).

Transcortical Motor Aphasia. The term *transcortical aphasia* was used by Wernicke to describe aphasic disorders in which the ability to repeat spoken language is spared in the context of other difficulties. The *transcortical motor* variety is characterized by a virtual absence of spontaneous speech, accompanied sometimes by a sparing of the ability to name objects to confrontation. The patient's major difficulty appears to be in the initiation of speech, but once initiated verbalizations are well-articulated. Auditory comprehension is typically fairly good, as is reading ability. In contrast, writing is most often impaired.

There is some agreement that the lesion associated with this syndrome is in the frontal lobe of the dominant hemisphere, anterior and/or superior to, but sparing, Broca's area (Benson & Geschwind, 1977; Naeser & Hayward, 1978).

Transcortical Sensory Aphasia. In this syndrome, the sparing of repetition ability occurs within a symptom complex that resembles Wernicke's aphasia. Patients of this type speak fluently when addressed but produce mostly neologisms and paraphasias. Confrontation naming tasks often yield paraphasic or grossly confabulatory responses, and reading and writing are destroyed. Repetition ability is remarkably intact and may even resemble severe echolalia in some instances. Many patients are also able to recite from memory long, overlearned passages, such as prayers.

This syndrome is said to be related to a posterior lesion in the border zone of the language area that spares Wernicke's area (Goodglass & Geschwind, 1976).

Alexia with Agraphia. *Alexia* and *agraphia* refer to acquired reading and writing disturbances (either partial or complete) that occur consequent to brain damage. In its most common form, impaired reading and writing ability is accompanied by mild anomia but no impairment of comprehension. A lesion to the dominant angular gyrus is implicated almost "without exception" (Benson & Geschwind, 1977, p. 12).

The Pure Aphasias

Several aphasic syndromes have been described in which language performance is affected in only a single modality, whereas all remaining language functions are left intact. The occurence of these cases is rare.

Pure Alexia (Alexia without Agraphia). Patients with this disorder can write normally but can read virtually nothing, even their own recent productions. In contrast, patients can spell aloud, recognize letters by touch, and understand orally spelled words and sentences. These patients may be able to recognize individual letters, and numbers are named without difficulty. The predominant neuroanatomical explanation for this disorder is that the left hemisphere primary visual association area is damaged, as well as the fibers of the corpus callosum (the splenium) that connect the visual association cortex of the right hemisphere to the language areas. Thus, although the language areas of the left hemisphere are intact, they are cut off from the only intact cortical area that could provide the visual input required for reading (Geschwind, 1965).

Pure Word Deafness. In this syndrome, auditory comprehension of speech is lost, although speech output, reading, and writing are normal. Despite preserved hearing, these patients react to speech as if they were deaf. They appear not to recognize speech as a familiar acoustic pattern and are consequently unable to repeat spoken models. This very rare condition is said to be caused by damage to the subcortical fibers that relay acoustic information from the primary auditory centers to Wernicke's area. Wernicke's area is spared, as well as at least one of the two primary auditory areas, because hearing is typically only mildly affected (Goodglass & Geschwind, 1976).

Aphemia (Pure Anarthria). This syndrome describes a pure articulation disorder, with no impairment of comprehension, reading, or writing. Unlike the verbal productions of the Broca's aphasic, the speech of the aphemic patient is not agrammatic and is not affected by factors such as familiarity or predictability. Repetition is as difficult as is spontaneous speech. Lesion site is believed to be largely subcortical, disconnecting an intact Broca's area from the articulatory system (Goodglass & Kaplan, 1972; Lecours & Lhermitte, 1976).

Some Caveats Concerning Classification and Localization

The syndromes that have been described are widely (though not universally) agreed upon as descriptions of qualitatively different types of aphasia that can occur in conditions of focal brain damage. It is not the case, however, that all cases of aphasia can be neatly classified into one of these syndromes. In fact, a large proportion of cases cannot be reliably diagnosed as exhibiting one of the major constellations of symptoms. Many patients suffer from symptoms that indicate the co-occurrence of more than one type of a deficit, a situation that would be expected in cases of multiple lesion sites or in conditions of diffuse cortical pathology. Most of the aphasias studied today result from cerebrovascular accident, and it may be that the structure of the vascular system (especially the distribution of the middle cerebral artery) is such that more than one of the hypothesized major language areas tends to be affected when the system is occluded. In any event, one reason for the occurrence of so many unclassifiable cases may be the relative rarity of clean focal lesions.

There are less obvious problems involved in classifying aphasic patients that may be of more interest to the psycholinguist. The first concerns the possibility that different patterns of performance may result from an interaction between the extent and site of lesion and the patient's premorbid abilities, emotional state, intelligence, and education. Patients may make use of residual abilities to differing degrees, using compensatory strategies that could produce different patterns of symptoms despite the same basic deficit. A related problem is that performance changes over the course of recovery (Kertesz, Harlock, & Coates, 1979), a situation that might logically be expected to reflect the amount and type of speech/language therapy that the patient has received.

Perhaps the most serious problem in classifying patients is the lack of precision in the syndrome classifications themselves. Each syndrome is defined by comparing performance in one type of task against performance in other tasks to arrive at a profile of "relative" abilities. At this time, there can be no set of absolute criteria for inclusion in any of the major syndromes, although obviously some patients are easier to identify than others. There is some hope that descriptions of syndromes will become better elaborated as tasks are designed to probe specific language functions, including those abilities that are not taken to be indicative of a particular syndrome.

In addition to the problems involved in classifying patients into types, there are other reasons why generalizations about brain/behavior relations based on data from aphasia must be made cautiously. First, the correlations between site of lesion and aphasic performance that are described here have been obtained only for a subset of the population at large. All of these results are specifically limited to individuals whose language functions are localized in the left hemisphere—a sample that is operationally defined as right-handed individuals. Little is known about language representation in left-handers, although the fact that unilateral lesions do not tend to cause aphasic symptoms suggests a more diffuse representation. A more subtle selection bias results from the fact that most research in aphasia has drawn patients from a predominantly male population. The brain/syndrome correlations noted here have been obtained primarily among male aphasics, and it has been suggested recently that they may not hold for female patients as a group (McGlone, 1978).

Evidence from outside the field of aphasia study suggests that there may be considerable variability in the way language is localized, even among right-handed males. Studies of morphological asymmetries between the two hemispheres, which usually assume a fairly direct link between asymmetries in structure and in function, have uncovered substantial variation in structure among individual brains (Whitaker & Selnes, 1976). Similarly, striking individual variability in localization of function has also been found in studies using electrical stimulation of the brain during surgery (Ojemann & Whitaker, 1978). Thus, it seems safe to assume that at least part of the "noise" in the classification of patients and in the syndrome/locus of damage correlations cannot be attributed to the classification problems discussed previously but results instead from actual differences among individuals in the way language functions are localized in their brains.

All of these problems are critically important to neuropsychological investigations of language, and it is especially important that readers who are unfamiliar with the field of aphasia research have a realistic picture of the data base from which we proceed. It is not our intention, however, to present a pessimistic account of a situation characterized by almost infinite potential for both biological and behavioral variability among aphasic patients. The fact is that, despite all of these problems, the syndromes that have been described are widely agreed upon as descriptions of qualitatively different types of aphasia that can be reliably identified in the clinic. Most of the types occur with some frequency among aphasic populations, and most have been found among speakers of languages other than English. More important, the association of these syndromes with particular neuroanatomical loci, though not perfect, is very strong among right-handed male patients. Many of the syndromes and their related lesions were described prior to 1900, and modern techniques of lesion localization have supported the early syndrome/site correlations. In short, the "classic" syndromes provide the best information available about how damage to a particular part of the brain would be expected to affect language capacities. Focus on these syndromes thus seems not only justified but required if we are to understand the extremely complex relationship between language and the brain.

A THEORETICAL MODEL OF LANGUAGE ORGANIZATION

Developments within linguistics and psycholinguistics in the past few decades have provided the theoretical basis for a redefinition of the major symptom constellations in aphasia. These developments have motivated the experimental search for deficits to abstract components of language processing that might provide an explanation for the symptom complexes that have been described. One result of this effort has been a change of thinking about precisely what language capacities are believed to be neuroanatomically localized. For example, psycholinguistic research has undermined the notion that "comprehension" is a unitary function and, therefore, discretely localizable in the brain. Instead, comprehension impairment might result from several kinds of problems: failure to process speech sounds adequately or a lack of understanding of individual words, for example. Most importantly, it is now understood that unless tasks are designed and interpreted very carefully, these two types of comprehension failure might be interpreted as reflections of the same deficit. The current approach is to search for the impaired component of language processing that yields a particular configuration of grossly described symptoms. Presumably, then, it is at this more abstract level that language would be expected to be localized in the brain.

The model of language that motivates much current research in aphasia differs little from the standard view that can be found in psycholinguistics textbooks (Clark & Clark, 1977; Foss & Hakes, 1978). A distinction that is central to this model, and very important in aphasia research, is that between structure and processing. The structure of language specifies the actual psychological representation of linguistic components that makes up a speaker's knowledge of the language. Processing considerations involve the mechanisms and procedures by which the speaker accesses and utilizes the structural components in producing and understanding language.

A question of central importance in aphasia research concerns the proper characterization of language deficits consequent to brain damage in terms of this structure/processing distinction. Specifically, considerable debate has focused on whether aphasic deficits involve an actual disruption of the structure of language (i.e., of some aspect of the form and content of the patient's knowledge system) (Caramazza & Berndt, 1978). This question is discussed at some length in the next several sections.

Historically, linguists have been concerned with describing the structure of language, whereas psychologists, working from linguistic theories, have attempted to validate empirically speakers' use of linguistic components in comprehension and production. The result has been a fairly widely accepted view of language as a system made up of at least three major structural components that function in a highly interactive fashion in the process of constructing a coherent verbal expression of some idea or of constructing a meaning representation for some set of speech sounds.

Linguistic descriptions of the language system (following Chomsky, 1965) have typically focused on three components. The phonological component of the language system describes the patterns of sounds that occur in a language. One primary concern within the study of phonology is the specification of how the speech stream is *segmented*—divided into discriminable elements within a language. At the phonetic level, segments are described (in articulatory or acoustic terms) as the basic elements of speech sounds that can be discriminated without reference to their meaningfulness within the language. At the phonemic level, the speech stream is segmented into combinations of phonetic features that bear on the meanings of words.

Another aspect of the speech stream that falls within the domain of phonology concerns suprasegmental aspects of speech: intonation contour, stress assignment, and prosodic elements in general. Although considerably less research has been directed at suprasegmental than at segmental aspects of speech in normal research, the description of prosodic aberrations in aphasic speech and investigations of the use of suprasegmental cues in aphasic comprehension have been relatively fruitful.

The syntactic component of language describes the structural rules governing the organization of words into meaningful utterances. One assumption in linguistic theories of syntactic organization is that sentences are made up of constituents—groups of words that are very closely related within the context of the sentence—arranged hierarchically rather than serially. An important question within psycholinguistics concerns the means that speakers and hearers employ to determine or to express these constitutent relationships among words. Several explanations have focused on the structure-marking role of the free grammatical morphemes—the "function words" such as articles, conjunctions, and prepositions—in segmenting utterances into structural constituents. Another feature of sentence processing that is often discussed as part of the syntactic component of language is the application of grammatical inflections (e.g., number and tense suffixes) that serve to mark and elaborate relations among words in sentences. Considerable research has been devoted to the possibility of syntactic impairments in aphasia.

The semantic component of language is concerned with the assignment and expression of meaning. There are two subcategories within the semantic component that must be distinguished. Lexical semantics deals with specifying the meaning of individual words. Considerable research within psycholinguistics has focused on determining how word meanings are represented in memory, that is, with the kind of information that is stored about a particular word and with how relationships among words are represented.

A second important aspect of semantics is concerned with the determination of sentence meanings. In constructing a sentence, or in extracting meaning from a sentence, the speaker or hearer must combine the lexical meanings of individual words and the syntactic relations among them to arrive at a unique semantic representation of the utterance. Very little attention has been devoted to this aspect of semantics by psycholinguists, so it is not clear how normal speakers construct meaning representations for sentences. It is possible, however, that the set of operations that combines the meanings of individual lexical items into more complex semantic structures is best characterized as an independent component of the system and, thus, potentially isolable under conditions of brain damage. We refer to this set of combinatorial processes as "semantic operations."

Psycholinguistic "processing" models have adapted these theoretical "structural" components in an attempt to describe how they are actually used in comprehension and production. Current psycholinguistic models of language comprehension, for example, describe the operation of four major processing components: a phonological analyzer, a syntactic parser, a lexicon, and a semantic interpreter (Clark & Clark, 1977). It is generally assumed that input to this system consists of two types of information—a set of speech sounds and a context. The context information feeds directly into the semantic interpreter, whereas the speech sounds must receive at least minimal phonological analysis before entering the other parts of the system. Once such minimal analysis has been achieved, the system operates in a staggered/parallel fashion so that interaction and feedback among all elements are possible. The components involved in the production of speech are essentially the same as those involved in comprehension. From the initial formulation of a proposition to be expressed, lexical items and a syntactic frame must be selected from available alternatives, combined into a semantically well-intergrated sentence and given the proper phonological realization.

Recent research in aphasia has focused on these components in attempting to characterize aphasic deficits within a theoretically viable linguistic framework.

PHONOLOGICAL FACTORS IN APHASIA

There are two distinct but related questions that have been addressed by researchers concerned with phonological factors in aphasia. The first concerns the extent to which aphasic symptoms that clearly involve a difficulty in processing or producing speech sounds can be said to involve a specific level of phonological representation; that is, attempts have been made to characterize various aphasic productive and perceptual disorders as involving specific levels of language organization that are theoretically part of the phonological system. These studies, which involve very careful acoustic and/or linguistic analysis of the speech stream, constitute a test of the theorized levels of phonological representation at the same time that they provide a much-enhanced description of the nature of aphasic deficits (Zurif & Caramazza, 1978). The second type of question addressed by phonological investigations of aphasia centers on defining the ultimate "cause" of aphasic symptoms that do not involve phonology in any obvious way. These studies seek to determine the extent to which fairly gross aphasic symptoms such as comprehension impairments or agrammatic speech can be attributed to a deficit at the level of phonological representation.

The primary distinction within the phonological system to receive attention in the first type of investigation is that between phonetic and phonemic levels of representation. The phonetic level is the most basic and involves, for the most part, physiological events: in production, the actual articulation of speech sounds; in perception, the processing of an acoustic event. The association of these physical events with phonological "meaning" within a language takes place at the "higher" (more abstract) phonemic level: in production, the organization of an articulated segment into an acceptable phonemic shape; in perception, the recovery from the acoustic event of a configuration of phonetic features that constitutes an acceptable phoneme.

Phonological analyses of speech production deficits in aphasia have been motivated by long-standing claims that the productive errors characteristic of different aphasic syndromes result from the involvement of different levels of phonological organization. The effortful, dysprosodic speech of the Broca's aphasic, which clearly involves at least some articulatory disturbance, has been described as a product of "phonetic disintegration" (Alajouanine, Ombredane, & Durand, 1939). Posterior patients, especially Wernicke's aphasics, are said to produce errors in their fluent speech that result from a "phonemic disintegration" (Hécaen & Angelergues, 1965); that is, these patients make errors in selecting the proper phoneme in a target item but articulate it correctly.

Although this analysis is intuitively appealing, close examination of aphasic speech reveals a situation that is considerably more complex. Blumstein (1973) analyzed spontaneous speech errors produced by 17 aphasic patients: 6 Broca's, 6 Wernicke's, and 5 Conduction aphasics. The analysis was limited to phonemic errors; phonetic transformations that maintained the phonemic shape of the target were excluded. Errors were classified into one of four types, and an analysis was carried out on all errors in which one phoneme was incorrectly substituted for another rather than simply added, deleted, or shifted within the target word. This analysis of substitution errors charted the phonological "distance" between the target and the substituted phoneme—the extent to which the error deviated from the intended utterance in terms of theoretical phonological distinctive features. The classification of error types yielded a pattern for all three types of aphasics that was similarly distributed across error types; further, substitution errors for all groups tended to differ from the target by only one distinctive feature.

These results support the idea that when brain damage leads to phonemic impairment, production breaks down in an orderly fashion that conforms to the theoretical organization of the phonological system. However, this analysis provides no information on the extent to which phonemic impairment rather than some other phonological deficit characterizes the various syndromes. The qualitative similarities among phoneme errors might be interpreted as an indication that similar phonological mechanisms are impaired in all three types of aphasia, that is, as evidence against the distinction between "phonetic" and "phonemic" disintegration. This interpretation is undermined by two factors. First, the quantitative differences in error production among the three groups was enormous, with Broca patients producing nine times more phonological errors than Wernicke's. Second, the errors that were excluded from the analysis (phonetic errors) were not produced equally by the three groups but were largely limited to the Broca's aphasics (Blumstein, 1980). It appears that the productive deficit characteristic of Wernicke's aphasics may indeed be limited to a difficulty with phonemic selection. The Broca patients (Blumstein, 1973), on the other hand, produce phonemic errors "as well as patterns of phonetic distortion superimposed upon the patient's entire speech production [p. 74]."

Blumstein's phonological investigation of production errors did not focus on the strict separation of phonetic from phonemic errors. Rather, it was an attempt to apply a linguistically motivated analysis to a corpus of phonemic errors. For that reason, any productive segment that could be characterized as a phonemic error was included as such; the phonetic errors that were excluded from the analysis were largely defined by default; that is, they could not be described as phonemic errors. Many of the errors classified as phonemic errors may in fact have been phonetic errors. For example, if a patient intended to say "bat" but instead produced "pat," the nature of the transformation of /b/ to /p/ could be either phonetic or phonemic; that is, the incorrect production of /p/ might reflect a phonetic error in which the correct phoneme was selected but misarticulated. Alternatively, the same error might reflect the correct articulation of an incorrectly selected phoneme (i.e., a phonemic error).

Blumstein and co-workers have attempted to differentiate between phonetic and phonemic errors of this type by subjecting the speech production of aphasic patients to an acoustic analysis and providing an operational definition of the two error types in terms of their acoustic realization (Blumstein, Cooper, Zurif, & Caramazza, 1977). This study exploited the phenomenon of categorical perception of stop consonants that is found in normal speech perception (Lisker & Abramson, 1964). The articulatory difference between the voiced consonant /b/ and the voiceless /p/ is characterized by a difference in voice onset time (VOT): the delay between the onset of vocal cord vibration ("voicing") and the release of the stop consonant. For the voiced consonants (e.g., /b/, /d/, /g/), there is a relatively short delay between voicing and release; for the voiceless consonants (/p/, /t/, /k/), there is a greater delay. The amount of delay between the two events constitutes a continuous variable, and synthetic speech sounds can be produced to sample values along this continuum. Values along the VOT continuum are not perceived as continuous, however, but as two discrete categories. When normal speakers are asked to identify values along the continuum, they consistently divide them into two nonoverlapping categories: voiced and voiceless. Within these categories, acoustic differences in VOT are not perceived (Liberman, Cooper, Shankweiler, & Studdert-Kennedy, 1967).

The normal production of stop consonants, when subjected to acoustic analysis, also describes two nonoverlapping categories of voiced and voiceless consonants, corresponding, for example, to the phonemes /da/ and /ta/. Blumstein and co-workers reasoned that an acoustic analysis of aphasic speech might uncover differences in acoustic segments that are not perceived as different by normal listeners, that is, VOT values falling *between* the two phonemic categories. These values were operationally defined as phonetic errors, whereas VOT values clearly falling in the wrong phonemic category were defined as phonemic errors. It must be noted that this latter error type cannot be unequivocally defined as phonemic rather than phonetic. It is certainly possible that a severe phonetic distortion might be realized as another phoneme entirely, as noted previously. Nonetheless, this method provides a rather rigorous means for identifying one class of errors that is clearly phonetic in nature.

Twelve aphasic patients were presented with six real-word monosyllabic stimuli to read, including three examples of voiced and three unvoiced alveolar stop consonants. The acoustic analysis of the resulting productions showed that the Wernicke's aphasics' articulations of these stop consonants defined a normal profile of two distinct categories of well-articulated voiced and voiceless syllables. Their errors were almost entirely phonemic (e.g., the clear utterance of /ta/ instead of /da/). The Broca patients' productions did not fall into distinct categories but described overlapping functions along the VOT continuum. They produced many VOT values that should have fallen between the two phonemic categories (i.e., phonetic errors). In addition, they produced errors that were classified as phonemic. It appears, then, that limited support has been obtained for the classic characterization of the speech output of these two aphasic types. Wernicke's aphasics have difficulty selecting the correct phoneme within a particular context. Broca's aphasics clearly demonstrate articulation impairments that produce phonetic distortions. It may be that they have difficulty at the phonemic level as well, but it is virtually impossible to define the point at which their phonetic difficulties end and their phonemic problems begin.

If the productive deficits that characterize different aphasic types can be said to involve these very specific levels of phonological representation, the question arises whether the same level of representation within the phonological system is impaired in speech *perception,* that is, to what extent is this phonetic or phonemic impairment a central deficit that is manifested in all modalities? Blumstein, Cooper, Zurif, and Caramazza (1977) addressed this question, again using linguistic stimuli that varied in voice onset time.

Several classes of aphasic patients were presented with synthetic speech stimuli from the VOT continuum that signaled the phonetic categories /da/ and /ta/. Patients performed two tasks: an identification test, in which they were asked to point to a printed "da" or "ta" corresponding to what they heard, and a discrimination task, in which they were asked to say whether a pair of stimulus sounds was the same. Eight patients performed normally on both tasks: They could discriminate between pairs of sounds and could label them correctly. Three other patients could neither discriminate between stimuli nor label them correctly. Most important, another four patients (three Wernicke's and one Broca's) performed normally on the discrimination task but were unable to label the sounds reliably. No patient who was able to label the sounds had difficulty discriminating between them. Blumstein et al. (1977) interpret this result as support for the hypothesis that the use of linguistic categories as discrete phonemic units depends on the auditory detection of properties that fall within a limited range of acoustic values. Thus, the ability to discriminate between stimuli within this critical range of values appears to be a more "basic" stage of processing on which the labeling of those values might be based (Zurif & Caramazza, 1978).

Three of four Wernicke patients tested exhibited this pattern of impaired phonemic labeling in the face of spared discrimination abilities. This might be taken as limited support for a central phonemic deficit, manifested both in production and in perception, for some Wernicke patients. The perceptual abilities of three of five Broca patients were intact in both tasks and appeared to be unrelated to the serious speech production errors that they produced; that is, there is little evidence that the "phonetic disintegration" characteristic of Broca speech is paralleled by perceptual problems at the phonetic level.

This brief review has demonstrated the difficulty of empirically validating suggestions that may be intuitively appealing. One primary problem involves the difficulty of distinguishing between two speech errors that are realized the same behaviorally but are based on impairments at different levels of processing. Actually, this review has not dealt with the enormous problems involved in categorizing speech errors, including the determination of what was actually said and what was intended (Lecours & Caplan, 1975, for discussion). It should be obvious that it becomes even more difficult to pinpoint the precise level of impairment as the speech units to be produced or perceived become larger than the single phoneme. The production of a sentence, a phrase, or even a word involves convergent inputs from several linguistic systems. Similarly, the understanding of spoken speech obviously requires more than just phonological processing. Nonetheless, several suggestions have been made that aphasic symptoms involving these broadly based observable behaviors are the result of a phonological impairment. Because phonological processing is the level of the linguistic system closest to the basic physiological events of articulation and acoustic reception of speech sounds, an impairment at this level would be expected to have a noticeable effect on more complex language behaviors. For example, a "phonetic disintegration" might be expected to result in a predictable pattern of speech output errors at the sentence level; phonemic imperception would provide an imperfect basis for syntactic and semantic analysis and might produce comprehension errors.

An argument of this type was made by Luria (1966, 1970), who defines the comprehension deficit characteristic of Wernicke's aphasia as an impairment of "phonemic hearing." He supports this argument with data showing that Wernicke's aphasics have difficulty discriminating between phonemes involving minimal contrasts. As might be expected, these patients have great difficulty selecting the correct depiction of an orally presented word when the alternative pictures involve phonemically similar items. The real question is whether this difficulty in discrimination between minimally different pairs underlies a larger comprehension deficit of these patients. Blumstein, Cooper, Zurif, and Caramazza (1977) addressed this question by comparing comprehension abilities as measured by the Boston Diagnostic Aphasia Examination (Goodglass & Kaplan, 1972) with patients' phoneme discrimination scores obtained as set forth previously. Although most of the patients with high comprehension scores performed well on the perceptual tasks, there were three patients with good comprehension who demonstrated marked difficulty either in labeling phonemes or in both discriminating and labeling. Conversely, patients with poor comprehension scores showed an entire range of abilities in the perceptual tasks. Most significantly, one Wernicke aphasic with a severe comprehension deficit performed normally on both the discrimination and the labeling tasks.

In a further demonstration that the hypothesized relationship between phonemic discimination and level of comprehension is not clear-cut, Blumstein, Baker, and Goodglass (1977) presented several diagnostic groups of aphasic patients with three discrimination tasks and then compared patients' scores with their comprehension abilities. The Wernicke's aphasics, the group with the most severe comprehension deficit, were not the most impaired group in the discrimination tasks. A group of mixed anterior aphasics, who had the most difficulty with phoneme discrimination, suffered only a moderate comprehension deficit. It seems clear that a speech perception problem at the level of phoneme discrimination cannot alone account for the serious comprehension difficulties found in Wernicke's aphasia, although it may be a contributing factor.

Another phonological factor that has been linked to auditory comprehension is the prosodic variable to stress assignment within phrases. Blumstein and Goodglass (1972) have shown that aphasic patients, even those with poor comprehension, can use stress assignment to differentiate between potentially ambiguous phrases (e.g., hótdog versus hot dóg). In fact, Kellar (1978) has shown that aphasic patients appear to rely on stress assignment within sentences when making metalinguistic judgments about sentence structure.

It can be tentatively concluded, therefore, that auditory comprehension deficits in aphasia cannot be attributed to a phonological deficit alone. Although many aphasic patients appear to have difficulty perceiving minimal speech contrasts, this deficit does not appear to be highly correlated with overall severity of comprehension impairment. Other phonological mechanisms are well preserved in aphasia and may even serve as aids in the comprehension of speech.

Another attempt to provide a phonologically based explanation for a major constellation of aphasic symptoms has been made by Kean (1977), who argues that the syndrome of Broca's aphasia is based on a phonological deficit. The agrammatic speech of the Broca patient is said to result from the phonological simplification of a sentence into the minimal string of items that serve as "phonological words" within the sentence. A phonological word is defined as "the string of segments marked by boundaries, which function in the assignment of stress to a word [p. 22]." The Broca's aphasic, it is argued, omits only nonphonological words, a category including, but not limited to, inflectional affixes and function words. Unstressed or reduced syllables (grammatical endings) and freestanding words that are neutral with respect to stress (the function words) are not produced. As noted previously, aphasic patients may be particularly sensitive to stress assignment in comprehension, and in production the use of a stressed word may be required to initiate speech (Goodglass, 1968). The question is whether the phonological conditioning of elements within sentences is sufficient to explain the entire constellation of symptoms that characterizes Broca's aphasia.

Kean presents linguistically rigorous arguments to support her contention, with appropriate modifications of the thesis when needed to account for what is known about the Broca syndrome. Kean's explanation of the deficit underlying Broca's aphasia has been challenged, however, particularly by supporters of the view that Broca's aphasia is the result of a syntactic deficit (Berndt & Caramazza, 1980a; Kolk, 1978a). Nonetheless, Kean's model represents a good example of the usefulness of linguistic theory when applied to an aphasic syndrome. It provides a systematic framework from which testable predictions can be made and ultimately measured against existing data.

SYNTACTIC BREAKDOWN IN APHASIA

One way of characterizing the distinction between anterior and posterior types of aphasia is in terms of a relative loss of, or sparing of, facility with syntax. The speech of many anterior aphasics (specifically the Broca-type patient) is classified as *agrammatic*. These patients tend to omit words and inflections that function as syntactic cues to the structural organization of sentences (the "grammatical morphemes"), although producing words with more "content." Posterior-damaged patients (especially Wernicke's aphasics) usually produce syntactically well-formed and often lengthy utterances that may be semantically deviant. The syntactic structure of the sentences produced by these patients is sometimes "paragrammatic": characterized by incorrectly applied (rather than omitted) grammatical morphemes. The paragrammatic speech produced by aphasic patients has not received extensive attention in the experimental literature. The most common view is that the incorrect juxtaposition of lexical items, or the selection of incorrect grammatical morphemes in a particular context, are not so much based on syntactic mechanisms as on the pervasive word-finding difficulties characteristic of the syndrome (Goodglass, 1976).

Broca's Aphasia

Far more extensive is the amount of research that has been directed at the agrammatic speech of the Broca's aphasic. As noted in the previous section, a theory of Broca's aphasia has been offered that explains agrammatic speech as an omission of the sentence items that do not constitute phonological words (Kean, 1977, 1978). This view is specifically offered in opposition to the widespread belief that the Broca syndrome results from a breakdown at the syntactic level of language organization. There is an impressive list of experimental results now available that seems to support this latter interpretation (Berndt & Caramazza, 1980a).

As pointed out previously, the speech of the Broca's aphasic is strikingly subject to a selective loss of vocabulary items. Speech output is composed almost entirely of nouns, adjectives, and uninflected main verbs, with relatively few pronouns, articles, prepositions, adverbs, auxiliary verbs, and conjunctions—the so-called "function words." Quantitative analyses have supported the impression that function words are significantly reduced in Broca speech (Howes, 1967).

Many of the earliest discussions of agrammatic speech explained the patient's reliance on content words as an effort to communicate the maximum amount of information with a minimum of effort (Isserlin, 1922). The patient was viewed as monitoring his output in a cost/benefit-type analysis, omitting those elements not absolutely necessary to the transmission of the message. This view, modified in only minor respects, remained the dominant explanation for agrammatic speech until quite recently (Lenneberg, 1973; Locke, Caplan, & Kellar, 1973). Broca's aphasia was thus believed to affect only the patient's ability to speak, leaving intact his "knowledge of language." In linguistic terms (Chomsky, 1965), the patient's "competence" is intact, but his "performance" is faulty (Weigl & Bierwisch, 1970).

In opposition to this hypothesis, many authors have argued that the speech characteristic of Broca's aphasia can be attributed to selective disruptions of specific linguistic faculties. Rules governing the relationships among words are lost, as well as the words whose function is to signal those relationships (Jakobson, 1956; Luria, 1970). The patient's agrammatic speech is viewed as a reflection of his loss of knowledge of some aspect of the form or content of his language rather than his inability to express his intact knowledge (Whitaker, 1970). Support for this hypothesis comes from recent work that has expanded the concept of "agrammatism" to the comprehension of language and to the patient's ability to make judgments about language structure (Caramazza & Zurif, 1976; Zurif & Caramazza, 1976).

Any attempt to decide between these competing interpretations must necessarily be based on a very careful description of the characteristic features of agrammatic speech. The omission of grammatical morphemes is rarely total: Some function words and inflections may always be produced; others may be produced inconsistently; still others may never be used. It is reasonable to expect that if the pattern of omissions in Broca speech can be adequately described, it should reveal something about the nature of the underlying deficit.

Goodglass, Fodor, and Schulhoff (1967) found that the probability that a function word will be omitted when a sentence is repeated depends on a combination of phonological salience (stress) and its position in the sentence. These authors systematically varied grammatical form, stress pattern, and position of functor in a series of three-word phrases. Broca's aphasics proved far more likely to omit a function word when it occurred in initial position, regardless of the syntactic form of the sentence. The only instances in which initially placed function words were produced occurred when they were stressed. The negative interrogative "don't" (which is stressed in initial position) was omitted less often than the corresponding (unstressed) affirmative, despite the fact that it is syntactically more complex. Similar results were obtained from a single agrammatic patient whose speech was elicited by a sentence completion technique: Stressed words in initial position facilitated production; function words in medial position were not omitted; and when stress fell on an initial functor (WH-interrogatives), it was not omitted (Goodglass, Gleason, Bernholtz, & Hyde, 1972).

Goodglass (1962, 1968, 1976) has proposed a hypothesis that links these observations to the characteristic dysprosodic speech of Broca's aphasics and to their methods of compensating for their disability. He argues that the greatest difficulty is in the initial mobilization of speech output. Once speech has been mobilized, it may continue with less difficulty for a few words until a pause is reached. The initiation of an utterance requires a "salient" element but its continuation may not. Because the patient cannot begin an utterance with unstressed words, he will omit them in favor of the first salient word to occur in the sentence. Once speech has been initiated, even unstressed elements may be carried along in the rhythm of speaking. "Saliency" is defined as the psychological result of a word's stress, phonological prominence, information load, and affective value.

The "stress/saliency" hypothesis successfully explains a large proportion of the omissions made by Broca's aphasics. Nonetheless, it leaves some data unexplained. The sentence completion task was administered to a group of agrammatic patients, who produced the hypothesized tendency to omit initial unstressed function words (Gleason, Goodglass, Green, Ackerman, & Hyde, 1975). There were some cases, however, in which stress and position were overshadowed by other factors. The auxiliary verb "will", occurring noninitially, was consistently omitted. In fact, it was omitted even more often than the auxiliary "do" when it occurred in initial position. Similarly, omission of the copula was independent of its position in the sentence. There was some evidence that more omissions occurred when the overall sentence frame was more difficult for the patient (other things being equal). Imperative constructions were by far the easiest to produce, and their medial articles or possessive pronouns were never omitted.

The stress/saliency hypothesis provides no basis on which to predict what appears to be a selective omission of noninitial unstressed function words. After the utterance has been initiated (by whatever means), the patient still omits some functors more than others and finds some constructions harder than others.

The factors influencing which items will be omitted and which will be retained are still unknown. It is clear that the items that are usually omitted—the grammatical morphemes—are just those syntactic elements that function to signal the organization of the surface structure of the sentence. It is equally true that as a class of items they tend to have little phonological prominence and usually do not take stress. Their tendency to be omitted could reflect a phonological reduction to stressed elements or a loss of units that may be syntactically important but are relatively "empty" semantically. Neither explanation accounts entirely for the description of agrammatic speech that is now available, that is, for the items that tend to be *included* as well as for those that are omitted.

In keeping with the arguments advanced here, we would expect that if the Broca syndrome is actually the result of a disruption of language structure or process at the syntactic level of organization, then elements of this deficit should be manifested in other aspects of language behavior. Specifically, any aspect of language performance that demands syntactic processing should be affected in some way. Recent research on nonproductive aspects of language in Broca's aphasia has provided information on this question and at the same time has considerably broadened the definition of the syndrome.

One of the defining characteristics of Broca's aphasia in the clinical literature has been relatively intact comprehension (Goodglass & Kaplan, 1972). Broca patients seem to understand quite well when they are spoken to, and their performance on the comprehension sections of most standard aphasia batteries is typically good. Recently, tests devised to probe subtle defects of comprehension that might escape clinical notice have detected comprehension problems among Broca's aphasics (DeRenzi & Vignolo, 1962; Poeck, Kerschensteiner, & Hartje, 1972).

Discussion of results of comprehension studies has emphasized that the pattern of performance across patient types is generally quite similar. Parisi and Pizzamiglio (1970) developed a test of syntactic comprehension using a sentence/picture matching task. The patients tested (of whom almost half were classified as Broca's) exhibited a very consistent pattern of performance on the syntactic constructions that were tested. The authors concluded that syntactic competence was not selectively impaired in different classes of patients. A similar conclusion was reached by Shewan and Canter (1971) and Shewan (1976), who report a consistent hierarchy of difficulty across patient types on a test of auditory comprehension.

These (and other) results have been cited to support the long-standing view that comprehension of speech is a relatively "unitary" process that is not subject to selective impairment of its components (Boller, Kim, & Mack, 1977). We have previously offered arguments against this "unitary" view of comprehension and have argued that lexical and syntactic components of comprehension are indeed selectively impaired by brain damage (Caramazza & Berndt, 1978). The reason that this selective disruption was not uncovered by the studies cited previously is that they were not designed to separate syntactic abilities from lexical factors and other information that the patient has about the conversational setting, the context, the examiner's expectations, and so forth. Unless the situation is very carefully constructed, it is impossible to assess the relative contribution of these independent components in a highly redundant system. The assessment of syntactic comprehension is particularly vexing because syntax cannot be meaningfully separated from other components (as lexical comprehension might be, for example) but must be evaluated by carefully controlling the contribution of other factors.

Parisi and Pizzamiglio (1970) correctly included items that could not be interpreted through lexical understanding alone (e.g., reversible passives such as "the cat is chased by the dog") but failed to provide a means for assessing the underlying cause of the patient's error. Thus, all patients who failed to understand a sentence (either for syntactic or semantic reasons) could choose either the correct picture or a distractor portraying a syntactic reversal. Shewan and Canter (1971) did not include any items that *required* syntactic analysis; that is, all sentences could be interpreted on the basis of individual lexical items and knowledge of the world (e.g., "the letter was mailed by the man"), and all distractors probed lexical understanding. It is, therefore, not surprising that the pattern of performance was similar across diagnostic groups: Homogeneity of performance was induced by the task, which did not measure syntactic comprehension.

When the experimental task is designed so that syntactic processing is *required* for a successful interpretation of a sentence, and when alternatives are provided to the patient that probe the nature of his errors, clear differences emerge between the comprehension of Broca's and other types of aphasics. Heilman and Scholes (1976) designed a sentence/picture matching task to test auditory comprehension in several groups of patients. The task utilized the fact that certain ambiguous sentences with indirect object constructions (e.g., "he showed her bird seed") can be disambiguated syntactically by inserting a definite article to parse the indirect object and direct object constitutents. The different meanings of "he showed her bird the seed" and "he showed her the bird seed" are signaled syntactically by the placement of the definite article. The pictured alternatives included a syntactic distractor (a picture of the incorrectly parsed indirect/direct objects) and two lexical distractors. The nine Broca patients tested made very few lexical errors but chose the syntactic distractor in close to half the trials. A group of posterior (Wernicke's) aphasics performed at chance, choosing lexical or syntactic distractors randomly.

This study has demonstrated that patients with apparently good comprehension have difficulty using the definite article to parse a sentence into constituents. The article is usually regarded as one of the "expendable" elements of a sentence, and any explanation of agrammatic speech that stresses economy of effort would relegate articles to the category of nonessential elements that the patient chooses to delete. In the task used by Heilman and Scholes, however, the article was not utilized by the Broca patients despite its important syntactic function. In a very different type of experiment, Goodenough, Zurif, and Weintraub (1977) demonstrated that Broca's aphasics are similarly insensitive to the semantic information supplied by the article.

Studies such as these, in which the Broca patient's comprehension difficulty clearly involves a faulty processing of function words, appear to provide an obvious analog to agrammatic production. When patients have difficulty with syntactic elements in spontaneous speech, they will most likely have difficulty with them in comprehension as well (Zurif & Blumstein, 1978).

Additional information regarding the Broca patient's "receptive" problem with function words was obtained in a task that probed the patient's memory for the structural organization of sentences (Caramazza, Zurif, & Gardner, 1978). Memory for function words was significantly impaired relative to content words, even though sentences were heard immediately prior to the probe.

One implication of this work is that the syntactic comprehension deficit suffered by Broca's aphasics is a result of a defective ability to process the function words, which are assumed to be importantly involved in the assignment of syntactic roles in sentence comprehension. For example, as just shown, there are many situations in which the parsing of a sentence into its constituents hinges on the placement of a function word. Syntactic processing clearly involves more than processing function words, however. It is important to determine whether the Broca patient has syntactic difficulties that cannot be attributed to faulty processing of functors but that involve other syntactic cues such as word order. Several studies are relevant to this issue.

Caramazza and Zurif (1976) presented patients with center-embedded, object-relative constructions in a sentence–picture matching task. Experimental sentences included sentences with strong semantic constraints ("the apple that the boy is eating is red"); semantically reversible sentences ("the horse that the bear is kicking is brown"); and semantically improbable sentences ("the man that the horse is riding is fat"). A set of active declarative sentences with two underlying propositions was included as a control ("the girl is kicking a green ball"). The pictures from which the patient was required to choose portrayed a correct alternative, a lexical, or a syntactic distractor.

The performance of five Broca's aphasics differed markedly from that of five Wernicke patients and five normal controls. The agrammatic patients performed well on control sentences and on the center-embedded constructions with strong semantic constraints, but their performance declined substantially on the two sentence types without or with misleading semantic information. When performance was analyzed across all sentence types as a function of the distractor chosen, these same patients had difficulty only with distractors that portrayed a syntactically based alternative. Performance on reversible or implausible sentences was at chance level when the patients were presented with a choice of pictures that included a syntactic distractor.

Correct comprehension of these center-embedded constructions requires syntactic processing that goes beyond a single function word marker. Although the pronoun *that* was included in the test sentences to signal the relative clause, these constructions can be understood by normal speakers even without the pronoun marker (Fodor & Garrett, 1967). The pronoun is only one among several surface cues that signal the relations among clauses in a sentence. Thus, syntactic comprehension in this case depends on the patient's ability to assign agent and object roles to the two noun phrases on the basis of surface structure cues that may or may not include function words. A similar result was recently reported by Goodglass, Blumstein, Gleason, Hyde, Green, and Statlender (1979), who used a subject-relative center-embedded sentence without a relative pronoun to mark the clause (e.g., "the man greeted by his wife was smoking a pipe").

These studies demonstrate further that Broca's aphasics have a deficit in comprehension that impairs their ability to use syntactic structure to interpret sentences. In addition, they suggest that the syntactic deficit is not a simple by-product of a failure to process function words (phonologically based or otherwise). Another very striking finding is that the ability of the Broca patients to interpret lengthy and complex sentences is very well preserved when they are given lexical items that provide a unique interpretation and/or when the alternative pictures can be rejected on the basis of lexical information alone.

A set of studies completed recently supplements these comments. Schwartz, Saffran, and Marin (1980) have reported several experiments probing the agrammatic aphasic's ability to use word-order cues to interpret sentences. In this study (unlike the reports of Caramazza & Zurif, 1976, and Goodglass et al., 1979), the sentence materials presented to the patient were very simple, even though they could not be interpreted by lexical knowledge alone. These tasks required syntactic processing of word-order information.

Agrammatic patients were tested on their ability to understand reversible phrases using locative prepositions ("the circle is above the square"). Three picture types were presented: the correct alternative, a syntactic distractor (square above circle), and a lexical distractor (circle inside square). Patients had a great deal of difficulty with this task, choosing the syntactic distractor in close to half the trials. In contrast, few errors were made to the lexical distractors. In another experiment, the same patients were presented with reversible active ("the dog chases the cat") and passive sentences ("the cat is chased by the dog"). Their task was to choose the correct depiction of the sentence from two alternatives that portrayed the correct agent/action/object sequence and its reversal. Two of the five patients performed well on the active sentences and much more poorly on the passives. The remaining three patients performed at chance on both types of sentences. This finding indicates that Broca's aphasics have great difficulty identifying the semantic relations among elements when they are forced to rely on syntactic cues, even in simple sentences. If lexical strategies can be utilized to arrive at a correct interpretation, however, comprehension appears to be quite good.

Several other methods are available for determining the extent of the aphasic patient's appreciation of syntactic structure. Techniques have been developed that require the patient to shift attention from the meaning of a sentence and focus instead on its structure. These methods offer a powerful means of investigating syntactic abilities without requiring verbal output. In addition, they allow tests of constructions that cannot be included in comprehension tasks, such as sentences that cannot be pictured. Most important, they remove the performance demands of "real-time" processing, such as the necessity of short-term memory storage. One such task involves metalinguistic judgments. Nonetheless, patients' performance on metalinguistic tasks must be carefully interpreted, because it is not known how the ability to perform in metalinguistic tasks is related to the patient's actual use of language. Luria (1975) reports that some patient types have difficulty "objectifying" language that is disproportionate to the severity of their other symptoms.

The most direct metalinguistic technique is to require the patient to evaluate the grammatical correctness of an utterance. Luria (1976, 1977) found that agrammatic speakers had much more difficulty detecting syntactic (mainly inflectional) errors than semantic anomalies. Gardner, Denes, and Zurif (1975) found that all patients had more trouble detecting syntactic than semantic errors but that agrammatic patients had the most difficulty with number agreement and word-order violations.

Von Stockert and Bader (1976) measured detection of grammatical anomalies less directly. These authors presented German-speaking aphasic patients with printed sentences that had been cut into parts to be rearranged into sentences. Thirty declarative sentences were cut into three parts so that the two noun phrases were isolated. Ten sentences were described as "normal" declarative sentences ("the children/ are playing in/ the garden"). Ten more sentences placed syntactic structure in opposition to semantic plausibility by exploiting the fact that in German subject nouns are differentiated from object nouns by a morphological variation in the accompanying article (e.g., "the rabbit [marked as subject] / shoots/ the hunter" [marked as object]). Ten additional sentences were grammatically structured nonsense, which again utilized the case-marking function of the article in German (e.g., "the womp/ yolls/ the clopper" [marked as object]).

Both Broca's and Wernicke's aphasics performed quite well with the "normal" sentences despite the fact that the Wernicke patients exhibited a serious comprehension deficit for written material. The Wernicke group continued to perform well on the other sentence types, but the Broca group had great difficulty ordering the elements using only the morphological cues. When the syntactically correct order was highly implausible, the Broca patients were correct on only 11% of the sentences. Most of the incorrect orderings produced by the Broca group reversed the position of the two noun phrases, which produced sentences that were plausible but syntactically deviant. These findings supplement comprehension studies showing that Broca patients have difficulty utilizing specifically syntactic information but perform well when lexical cues are available.

A metalinguistic task that was originally designed to obtain intuitions about sentence structure from normal subjects has been used extensively to test aphasic patients (Zurif, Caramazza, & Myerson, 1972). The patient is shown a printed sentence (which remains in view) and is presented with successive triads of all possible combinations of the words from the sentence. For each triad, the patient is asked to indicate the two words that "go best together" in the stimulus sentence. These successive judgments are organized into a word relatedness matrix that serves as input to a hierarchical clustering algorithm (Johnson, 1967). Applications of this method to the relatedness judgments of normal speakers have yielded hierarchically organized solutions that map closely onto the theoretical pattern of nested sentence constituents (Levelt, 1970).

Zurif et al. (1972) replicated for their control group the pattern usually found with normal subjects; that is, articles and nouns were judged as closely related within noun phrases (NPs), and subjects were distinguished from predicates. A group of Broca's aphasics, in contrast, tended to link content words together, producing clear violations of normal surface structure organization. The function words were not completely ignored, but were often grouped inappropriately together. The aphasic patients were more successful in producing a tight NP when it was marked by a function word that conveyed more meaning than an article. For example, a tightly organized object NP was produced by the Broca patients for the sentence "where are *my shoes?*", suggesting that these patients may be differentially sensitive to the semantic value of function words.

In order to investigate this possibility more fully, the triadic comparison procedure was administered in several subsequent studies that systematically varied the information content of the sentence functors (Zurif & Caramazza, 1976; Zurif, Green, Caramazza, & Goodenough, 1976). Sentence frames were included that allowed an evaluation of patients' differential sensitivity to articles and possessive pronouns. It was found that as the information load of the sentence was increased, the advantage of the pronoun over the article as an NP marker was attenuated; that is, when there was little other semantically important information in the sentence, the importance of the pronoun relative to its noun was enhanced. When sentences contained important lexical information in competition with the pronoun and its noun, the pronoun was no longer grouped appropriately. Similar results are reported by Kolk (1978b), who found that agrammatic patients were largely unable to form tight NP clusters, regardless of whether the modifiers were articles or adjectives, in semantically complex sentences.

There were other indications that the information value of the functor in relation to the other words of the sentence was an important factor in determining whether the aphasic patients would produce normal constituent structures. Sentences were included in which a preposition served as the single cue to the underlying semantic relations. In "stories were read $\{^{to}_{by}\}$ John," for example, the preposition is critically important to signaling the role of "John" as agent or as recipient of the action. Broca's aphasics were successful in creating preposition/noun clusters in sentences such as these but did not produce normal groupings when the same word did not serve this crucial function ("she likes *to* eat candy").

The syntactic basis of the agrammatic patients' performance on these triadic comparison tasks has been questioned by Kellar (1978), who again raises the importance of stress for Broca patients. Kellar's hypothesis is that the stressed words of a sentence are inordinately "salient" for the aphasic patient. The patient's increased sensitivity to the prosodic aspects of sentence structure "masks" his "weakened" syntactic knowledge. The abnormal relatedness judgments that have been obtained in metalinguistic tasks are thus attributed to the fact that content words are stressed and function words are unstressed.

To investigate the role of stress more fully, Kellar constructed two sets of sentences that systematically varied stress assignment. One set of sentences utilized unstressed articles as NP markers in interrogative ("where are the shoes?") and truncated passive sentences ("the cows were milked"). A second set was similar in structure but substituted a stressed pronoun or adjective for the article ("where are my shoes?"; "red cows were milked"). For the first set of sentences (with articles marking the NPs) the pattern of results obtained by Zurif and co-workers was replicated. In the second set of sentences, the finding of interest does not involve an increased number of groupings for the adjective or pronoun and the noun it modifies (e.g., "red cows"). As noted previously, a tightening of NP constituents would be expected when these semantically important items were substituted for the articles. The interesting finding was that patients more often grouped semantically and structurally unrelated elements in the sentence if both were stressed; that is, "red" and "milked" were grouped more often than "the" and "milked."

This study has shown that it is possible to mainpulate sentence stress so that the aphasic patient loses all sense of proper sentence organization. Because the disproportionate importance of stress for these patients is related to their impaired ability to rely on syntactic information, these results do not support a stress-based argument as the cause of the deficit found in agrammatic patients. Instead, the patient's reliance on stress appears to be a compensatory mechanism that results from his inability to use other information.

These results have demonstrated rather convincingly that the syndrome of Broca's aphasia is not limited to a productive ("expressive") deficit. Furthermore, the results dealing with comprehension and with metalinguistic abilities have suggested that it is the syntactic elements of language that are disturbed in this syndrome.

Another symptom that is not generally associated with Broca's aphasia has recently been demonstrated in at least some Broca patients, and again the suggestions has been made that a syntactic impairment is involved. Reading disturbances in adults that occur as a result of brain damage are associated with lesions in the posterior portion of the dominant hemisphere (Benson & Geschwind, 1969). The occurence of reading difficulties in patients with damage limited to the frontal lobe would not be predicted by most models of the localization of function. Benson (1977) reports that occurrence of such patients—Broca's aphasics with "alexia"—have been recorded in the literature since the late nineteenth century and have been particularly vexing cases for proponents of localizationist theories of brain function.

Benson (1977) investigated the frequency of occurrence of reading impairments in Broca's aphasia. Sixty-one patients exhibiting the symptoms of Broca's aphasia, but no sign of posterior pathology, were tested on comprehension of single words and of sentences. Over half of the group exhibited a "severe alexia," defined as frequent errors on a word/picture matching task and failure to comprehend most sentences. Another 17 patients (classified as "mildly alexic") could carry out some written commands and understand parts of a written paragraph. Only 10 patients appeared to have normal reading ability. Based on these data, Benson argues that an impaired ability to read is "the rule rather than the exception" in Broca's aphasia.

There is some evidence that the comprehension disturbance for written material that Benson demonstrated among Broca's aphasics is a result of the syntactic disorder that also undermines their auditory comprehension; that is, the reading comprehension of Broca patients is especially impaired when the test materials require syntactic analysis. Samuels and Benson (1979) found that Broca's aphasics had particular difficulty understanding sentences in which syntactic processing was especially important for the assignment of a correct interpretation. Patients' performance was impaired regardless of whether sentences were presented aurally or visually (Caramazza, Berndt, Basili, & Koller, in press).

Several studies have been reported on the oral reading abilities of Broca patients, even though Benson has argued that oral reading is not an appropriate test of reading performance (Benson, 1977; Benson & Geschwind, 1969). Gardner and Zurif (1975) tested the oral reading of several categories of patients and found that picturable nouns were the easiest category for almost all patients to read. Broca's aphasics had the greatest difficulty reading abstract nouns and long nonnouns, followed by grammatical particles and short nonnouns. These results demonstrate that the oral reading performance of agrammatic patients is not based on their articulatory difficulties—picturable nouns were easier to read even when long and somewhat difficult to pronounce (e.g., hydrant) compared to the short and easily articulated grammatical particles (at, on). It should be noted that the easiest category of word for the Broca patients to read aloud contained precisely the words that occur most often in their agrammatic output: concrete nouns. Although their ability to read function words was impaired relative to nouns, it was not more deficient than their performance with other nonconcrete categories in this study. The "agrammatic" pattern that characterizes the speech of these patients was not particularly noted in their oral reading.

Marin, Saffran, and Schwartz (1976) have stated that "agrammatic reading" is "not uncommon" among aphasics who are agrammatic in their spontaneous speech, and several cases of agrammatic oral reading among Broca patients have been reported (Andreewsky & Seron, 1975; Friederici & Schoenle, 1980; Schwartz, Saffran, & Marin, 1977). Nonetheless, the results obtained by Gardner and Zurif discussed previously cast doubt on the hypothesis that agrammatic oral reading is a general symptom of Broca's aphasia. We have recently suggested that the cases of agrammatic reading that have been reported reflect the occasional overlap of another symptom complex with the Broca syndrome (Caramazza, Berndt, & Hart, 1981). Specifically, the inability to read function words aloud is one of the characteristics of a reading disorder that has been termed "deep" or "phonemic" dyslexia (Marshall & Newcombe, 1966, 1973; Shallice & Warrington, 1975). Deep dyslexics cannot read function words orally and have difficulty in general reading abstract words. They have trouble identifying visually dissimilar rhyming words (rough/cuff), recognizing homophones (through/threw), and producing real words from homophonic spellings (trane) (Saffran & Marin, 1977). An important characteristic of the oral reading of the deep dyslexic is frequent production of semantic paralexias—reading errors that are semantically but not phonologically related to the target (Marshall & Newcombe, 1973).

The dominant explanation for the syndrome of deep dyslexia is that the patient cannot perform a grapheme-to-phoneme translation but can access the lexicon directly from the grapheme (without phonological recoding) for some words but not for others. The lexical items that can be most easily accessed by this direct route are "concrete" or "imageable," whereas more abstract words (including the grammatical function words) presumably cannot be accessed directly. The cases of "agrammatic reading" that have been reported (Andreewsky & Seron, 1975; Friederici & Schoenle, 1980) may in fact have been cases of deep dyslexia—the other symptoms of the reading disorder were not uncovered by the testing that was reported.

It should be noted that the hypothesis that Broca's aphasia reflects a deficit of the syntactic component does not predict agrammatic oral reading of lists of words as a characteristic of the syndrome. Even if a patient were completely unable to process the grammatical function words, he should still be able to produce verbal approximations of those words when reading aloud by using the grapheme-to-phoneme conversion rules that normal speakers use to read regular non-words (Coltheart, 1978). We have reported data on the oral reading performance of four Broca patients that support this argument (Caramazza, Berndt, & Hart, 1981). Although the four patients produced agrammatic speech and asyntactic visual and auditory comprehension, one patient had no particular difficulty reading function words aloud. Despite his clear syntactic difficulties, he was able to read function words and abstract nouns about as well as he could read substantives. We believe that his grapheme-to-phoneme conversion system was operating efficiently. Two other patients, who appeared to be agrammatic readers, also had trouble reading abstract nouns and nonwords and produced occasional semantic paralexias. We have argued that, in addition to being Broca's aphasics, these patients are deep dyslexics. It is difficult to estimate the incidence of overlap of these two syndromes, and there is no theoretical reason to predict their co-occurrence. At this time, it must be assumed that "agrammatic" oral reading among Broca's aphasics is not a by-product of their (syntactically based) difficulty with function words but reflects instead a reading disorder that is not necessarily part of the Broca syndrome.

The picture of Broca's aphasia that has emerged from this review, though still sketchy, differs somewhat from the original description. The agrammatic speech of these patients has not yet been adequately characterized in linguistic terms, but an apparently useful compensatory mechanism has been isolated; that is, the Broca patients appear to rely on stress as an aid in the initiation of utterances. Very little is known about the speech produced by patients within this group other than the general facts summarized concerning their characteristic omission of particular items. The structure of utterances that are produced, except in the most severely impaired patients, has been virtually unexplored.

The ability of the Broca patient to comprehend language has been shown to be deficient under particular circumstances—specifically, when syntactic processing is required for intepretation and contextual cues are not available. The ability of these patients to make judgments about syntactic relations among words in sentences is similarly impaired. Reading comprehension is now believed to be affected in the Broca syndrome, and this deficit seems also to reflect the impairment of a syntactic processing mechanism.

We have offered a tentative explanation for this redefined syndrome of Broca's aphasia based on the theoretical assumption that the symptoms as described are manifestations of an impaired component or components of language processing (Berndt, & Caramazza, 1980a). Our specific neuropsychological claim is that Broca's area (and immediately adjacent regions) subserve the processing of syntactic information; when this area is destroyed, the syntactic parser is disrupted.

The pattern of impaired comprehension that has been demonstrated among Broca patients is most easily explained as a syntactically based deficit. If the syntactic parser is indeed impaired in Broca's aphasia, comprehension would still be possible to the extent that it can be based solely on semantic information; that is, a semantic interpretation can be assigned to the available lexical information without adequate syntactic input. Patients' responses in comprehension tasks would then reflect strategies based on intact lexical understanding and contextual information. For example, one such strategy might be to scan the major lexical items and assign an interpretation based on the most likely relationship among those items (Caramazza & Zurif, 1976).

All the syntactic parsing models that have been proposed to date assign an important role to the grammatical morphemes that determine logical relations (deep grammatical roles) among the major lexical items (see Clark & Clark, 1977; Frazier, 1979, for review). For example, the grammatical morphemes provide cues about sentences structure that can be used while the input is being processed so that tentative interpretations can be assigned immediately. The introduction of a noun phrase or an embedded clause, the formulation of a question, distinctions between active and passive sentences and between subordinate and main clauses are all signaled by grammatical morphemes (Kimball, 1973; 1975). Without an effective syntactic parsing system that makes use of the grammatical morphemes, correct syntactic analysis cannot be performed and comprehension will be asyntactic.

As we have seen, the comprehension deficits in Broca's aphasia are not simply the result of poor parsing due to the failure to process function words, although this explanation does account for some interesting features that have been observed. There are other deficits that should result from syntactic parsing failure that are not associated strictly with function-word processing failure. In fact, comprehension problems should be evident for *any* sentence that cannot be unambiguously interpreted using semantic strategies alone. Thus, this account provides a motivated explanation for all the results in which asyntactic comprehension has been demonstrated, as well as for the residual comprehension abilities of Broca patients.

A disruption of the syntactic parsing mechanism would also have a predictable effect on patients' verbal output. Lexical items with a purely syntactic function would not be selected correctly, and speech would consist entirely of major lexical items; that is, patients' utterances would be expected to be agrammatic. In addition, without adequately selected syntactic structures, there should be other output problems such as word-order disturbances (Saffran, Schwartz, & Marin, 1980).

We have argued that the pattern of speech production that is characteristic of Broca's aphasia results from a combination of two primary deficits and the operation of compensatory mechanisms that are employed in an attempt to establish communication. The two primary deficits involve the syntactic parsing system with resulting agrammatism, as set forth. Other features of the speech that is characteristic of Broca's aphasia cannot be attributed to a syntactic deficit but seem to result instead from an often severe impairment of the physiological mechanisms responsible for the articulation of speech. This articulatory deficit is theoretically and practically separable from the syntactic deficit that results in asyntactic comprehension and agrammatic speech. In principle, it should be possible to find pure cases of aphasia in which only the syntactic component, or only the articulatory component, is impaired (Lecours & Lhermitte, 1976). The pattern of agrammatic speech found in the Broca syndrome is thus viewed as a reflection of patients' efforts to convey a message in the face of disturbed articulatory abilities (resulting in distorted, effortful, dysprosodic speech) and an impaired syntactic parser (interfering with the selection of grammatical morphemes).

Our theoretical view of the Broca syndrome is that it represents an example of a situation in which an isolable component of language processing (syntax) is actually disrupted as a result of brain damage. The deficit resulting in such a case should be manifested in all tasks that require the participation of the affected component. The syndrome of Conduction aphasia presents a different set of circumstances: syntactic deficits that are demonstrated in some types of tasks but not in others.

Conduction Aphasia

Several reports have indicated that conduction aphasics perform very much like Broca patients in comprehension tasks that require syntactic processing (Caramazza & Zurif, 1976; Heilman & Scholes, 1976; Saffran & Marin, 1975). Despite their asyntactic comprehension, and unlike the Broca patients, conduction aphasics demonstrate no sign of a syntactic disorder in their speech production. This result might mean that the analysis of language organization in the brain in terms of processing components is incorrect (i.e., destruction of the syntactic component does not result in impairment at all levels). Alternatively, a more selective demonstration of syntactic deficits might indicate that under some conditions the patient is unable to utilize a processing component that is essentially intact.

We have recently completed an investigation of the patterns of symptoms that co-occur with asyntactic comprehension (Caramazza, Berndt, Basili, & Koller, in press). Four patients were tested: a conduction aphasic, two Broca patients (of different severity levels), and a mildly impaired Wernicke's aphasic. Each patient received a battery of tests including a sentence comprehension task (presented both visually and aurally), an oral reading task (with function words, nouns, verbs, and adjectives), a sentence anagram task, and a story completion task. Performance in all tests was compared to determine each patient's ability to make effective use of syntactic information under the various conditions. The two Broca patients exhibited the total syntactic involvement described in the previous section: agrammatic speech, asyntactic comprehension of written and spoken sentences, and asyntactic sentence construction. The conduction aphasic produced relatively normal speech in the story completion, read the lists of words in the oral reading task with very few errors, and constructed sentences with little difficulty in the anagram task. However, his comprehension was asyntactic in both the visual and auditory modalities. The mildly impaired Wernicke patient demonstrated no sign of a syntactic deficit.

We believe that the best explanation for this dissociation among symptoms is that the syntactic processing mechanism is intact in Conduction aphasia but inaccessible in the course of comprehension (Caramazza, Basili, Koller, & Berndt, in press). This explanation is based on the assumption that the Conduction aphasic we tested suffers from an auditory-verbal short-term memory (STM) disorder (Warrington & Shallice, 1969). This limitation in working memory prevents the elaboration of the syntactic relations among lexical items, resulting in an overreliance on the more easily processed and better-represented semantic information in the major lexical items; that is, a limitation in STM prevents the (intact) syntactic parser from functioning successfully because it interferes with the temporary storage of the output of its syntactic analysis during processing. The result is the construction of inadequate syntactic representations for sentences.

An important implication of this dissociation among symptoms is that it strengthens the claim for the representation of a syntactic parsing mechanism that operates independently of lexical, phonological, and semantic integrative processes. If this analysis is correct, the syndrome of Conduction aphasia provides the basis for a detailed study of the relationship between the functioning of the syntactic parser and the other processing components in the various tasks.

For present purposes, however, the most relevant aspect of the results of this study is the co-occurrence of symptoms in the two agrammatic patients. All language functions assessed clearly indicated a disruption of syntactic processing; that is, no matter what language tasks the patients were required to perform, their behavior revealed an impairment that was proportional to the amount of syntactic processing required to perform the task adequately. This highly selective impairment of a processing component strongly supports the view that language processes are isolable under conditions of focal brain damage. In addition, it provides neurolinguistic evidence tor the psychological reality of an independent syntactic processing device.

STUDIES OF THE LEXICON IN APHASIA

All types of aphasic patients have some difficulty processing individual words: They may have trouble "finding" the right word to express what they have in mind; they may inadvertently produce an unintended word; they may misunderstand a word that is spoken to them. "Word-finding" difficulties of some description are pervasive in aphasia (Goodglass & Geschwind, 1976). As a corollary, the type of aphasia that is most clearly characterized by a difficulty finding the names for things (anomic aphasia) is the hardest syndrome to localize neuroanatomically. In fact, the clearest demonstrations of systematic lexical breakdown in aphasia have been made in cases of diffuse cortical involvement (Schwartz, Marin, & Saffran, 1979; Warrington, 1975). Thus, although it is generally believed that lexical semantic problems are most prevalent among patients with posterior damage, it may be difficult to be more precise about the localization of the lexical component. This situation might result from the fact that lexical information is fairly diffusely represented in the brain; alternatively, it may reflect nothing more than our ignorance about how lexical knowledge is structured and a concomitant inability to design tasks that can selectively tap processing components that might be more discretely localized.

In that regard, it is useful to consider what it is that a person "knows" when he knows the meaning of a word. The simplest case involves the concrete referential situation—the use of a particular word to refer to a specific object. Recent thinking on the relationship between a word and the object that it represents has rejected the notion that a simple association exists between word and object. The word is matched not to a particular object but to a class of objects that must be represented conceptually by some configuration of perceptual attributes, functional information, etc. (Miller & Johnson-Laird, 1976). The precise characterization of this conceptual information (e.g., as sets of features, as a mental image, or as exemplars around a prototype) is not important here; it is necessary only to note that what is known about a word's meaning—even in the concrete referential situation—constitutes a complex and abstract lexical concept.

There are other important aspects to knowing what a word means, although these are somewhat less investigated in aphasia research. Part of what must be stored in the organization of the lexicon is information about relations among words and their related concepts. Recognizing superordinate/subordinate and coordinate relations among lexical items and appreciating synonymy, antonymy, and homonymy are important aspects of knowing the meanings of those items. This knowledge requires that information in the lexicon is stored in such a way that these relations are accessible.

By far the most investigated lexical capacity in aphasia is the ability to name objects on confrontation. It has been pointed out that this is not an activity that is typical of normal language use (Lesser, 1978), and it is probably not a very good index of a patient's overall lexical knowledge. Nonetheless, it is an ability that is often impaired in aphasia; as such, it has received a great deal of attention.

There are two aspects of naming performance that have been particularly interesting to researchers. First, patients' inability to name objects is rarely total, and some items appear to be easier to name than others. Factors with some value as predictors of whether the correct name will be produced include word frequency (Wepman, Bock, Jones, & Van Pelt, 1956), picturability (Goodglass, Hyde, & Blumstein, 1969) and "operativity" (Gardner, 1973). Second, when an incorrect item is produced, it is often a word that is related in meaning to the target (Schuell & Jenkins, 1961). In some respects, these semantically related substitutions are similar to the word associations produced by normal speakers (Rinnert & Whitaker, 1973), suggesting an orderly breakdown in the lexical system.

Two hypotheses have been advanced to explain patients' naming difficulties.[2] The dominant view until very recently is that the structure of the lexicon is undisturbed but that the patient is unable to "arouse" or to "retrieve" the intact lexical item. Put differently, the threshold for evoking a particular word is raised, such that more information than usual may be necessary before the word can be retrieved. Within this view, providing multiple inputs through several modalities should increase the chances that an object will be named (North, 1971). This "retrieval" hypothesis is supported by the fact that objects that cannot be named on some occasions may be named easily under different conditions, suggesting that the patient has difficulty accessing an intact lexical representation.

An alternative view is that naming disorders result from an actual disruption of some aspect of the lexicon (Caramazza & Berndt, 1978). It is argued that the patient's failure to name an object correctly and his frequent production of an incorrect but related word reflects a central disorganization of lexical information. One implication of this view is that the comprehension of lexical items should be affected in patients with naming disorders, a requirement that is usually not assumed to be the case in anomic aphasia (Geschwind, 1967). It has been pointed out, however, that lexical comprehension tasks are typically designed so

---

[2]We are limiting our discussion to naming disturbances that are part of a more widespread aphasic condition; modality-specific anomias that result from callosal disconnection (Geschwind, 1967) are not included here.

that performance will be good even if the patient has retained only partial knowledge of a word's meaning (Lesser, 1978). For example, Gainotti (1976) has argued that there is a correlation between production difficulties at the semantic level (e.g., difficulty naming or frequent production of semantic paraphasias) and what he calls "semantic discrimination" problems when the comprehension task is designed with semantically related distractor items.

Several studies have been reported recently that attempt to assess the status of lexical knowledge in aphasia. All of these employ techniques for assessing lexical knowledge that go beyond simple confrontation naming tasks, although several studies explicitly compare their results with patients' ability to name objects.

Goodglass and Baker (1976) attempted to chart the associational structure among groups of words and to link that structure to patients' naming ability. Stimulus words were eight high-frequency and eight low-frequency picturable nouns depicted on cards and presented visually for naming to groups of "high comprehension" and "low comprehension" aphasics and to several control groups. After the naming data had been obtained, the pictures were shown a second time while a series of 14 words was read. Of these, 7 words were unrealted distractors and 7 words were in some associational relationship with the target. These were the name of the item, the superordinate category to which the item belonged, the name of an attribute typically characterizing the item, the name of another (coordinate) member of the same category, the name of an action associated with the item (functional associate), and the name of a situation or context in which the item would be found (functional context). Patients were instructed to squeeze a response bulb whenever one of the words "reminded" them of the pictured target.

All patients recognized the name of the pictured objects, although many patients had been unable to produce it. The control subjects and those patients with good comprehension exhibited a similar pattern of associations: The clearest associates were the superordinate category name, the descriptive attribute, and the functional context. The responses of these patients to the other associates, though correct, were markedly slower than responses to these three strongest associates. Patients with poor comprehension (presumed to have posterior damage) differed from the other patients in that they had difficulty recognizing both functional contexts and functional associates. Goodglass and Baker argue that the failure to recognize this type of association among words reflects a qualitative change in the semantic organization of these patients. Furthermore, they suggest that the inability to retrieve words in a naming task may be in part a function of a breakdown of the semantic structure. Although all patients could recognize the name of the depicted object, many patients had not previously been able to produce that name. All patients responded most quickly to associates of words they had been able to produce, and the patients with poor comprehension were much less likely to respond to associates of words they had failed to produce. The ability to produce a name for an item seems to depend on the convergence of concurrently activated associations that trigger the appropriate naming response. To the extent that a picture of an object arouses an incomplete set of associations (i.e., to the extent that lexical structure is disrupted), naming ability will be impaired.

Another study that looked at the breakdown of the associational network of words was reported for French-speaking aphasic patients (Lhermitte, Dérouesné, & Lecours, 1971). Again, patients were asked to say whether (and how closely) words were related to each other in two types of tasks. Errors were classified as indicating a breakdown in hierarchical structure or as a "widening" or "narrowing" of the semantic field. All types of patients produced some errors in all three categories, but the posterior-damaged patients produced the most serious semantic structural violations by tending to broaden a semantic category to include unrelated associates.

These two studies, although they indicate some disruption of the relationship among lexical items in a semantic field, do not make any assumptions about how the items within the field are related; that is, we have no information concerning the features that are shared by several related words (e.g., a target noun and a functional associate). Two studies have been reported that constrain severely the features that characterize the target items, so that data might be obtained on the types of information that the patient has difficulty utilizing in the selection of a name.

Whitehouse, Caramazza, & Zurif (1978) adapted a study that had been designed to investigate normal speakers' construction of conceptual category boundaries among closely related items (Labov, 1973). The task used 24 line drawings of container-type objects that varied continuously on the ratio of width-to-height, and discretely in presence or absence of a handle. Some stimuli are consistently labeled "cup" by normal speakers; others are called "bowl" or "glass" depending on the width/height ratio, and still others are "borderline" objects that normal speakers name inconsistently. In some trials this perceptual information was supplemented by a functional context that depicted something being poured into the container; coffee, cereal, or ice water for "cup," "bowl," and "glass" contexts, respectively.

For normal speakers, functional information is especially useful in the "borderline" cases in which the perceptual features of the object yield a picture that is neither a clear-cut bowl nor cup, for example. In these cases, functional information is used to decide between the two possible names. Thus, the task requires a sensitivity to category boundaries—that is, to whether an item is a good example or a borderline instance of some category. It also demands an ability to integrate perceptual and functional information in determining category membership.

Whitehouse et al. (1978) presented this task to 10 aphasic patients (five Broca's and five Anomics). The Broca's aphasics named items inconsistently, primarily at the boundary between two caregories; the "clear-cut" instances were named reliably. In addition, the anterior-damaged patients used the functional information effectively, shifting the fuzzy category boundary with shifts in context. In contrast, the anomic patients anmed the objects inconsistently without regard to their typicality of a particular category and appeared largely unable to use functional information to name objects.

We have interpreted this result as an indication that the anomic patients are suffering from a disorganization of the lexical representations of the relevant items (Caramazza & Berndt, 1978). A retrieval-based argument of naming impairment would necessarily predict that patients would have less difficulty naming a highly prototypical item when pictured in an appropriate context. Yet the anomic patients named as inconsistently in this situation as they did when they were presented with conflicting information.

We have recently used another approach to determine the level at which naming breakdown occurs (Caramazza, Berndt, & Brownell, in press). Twenty unclassified aphasic patients and 10 controls were tested in two tasks using a subset of the stimuli employed by Whitehouse and co-workers. The 14 stimuli depicted seven variations in width with a constant height, both with and without a handle. The appropriate labels, therefore, were "cup" and "bowl." In the first task, patients were asked to judge the perceptual similarity between all possible pairs of stimuli, and they were trained to respond using a 7-point similarity scale. In the second task, patients were asked to identify each object as a "cup" or a "bowl," both when the picture was presented alone and with "coffee" and "cereal" context pictures.

The similarity judgments were analyzed using a multidimensional scaling procedure to determine whether the patients had used both dimensions of variation (width and handle) in making their judgments. Before this analysis was done, the aphasic patients were divided into homogeneous subgroupings using an Inverse Principal Components Analysis. Two groups emerged (of 14 and 6 patients each), and the scaling analysis was carried out separately for each group. The solution for the group of 14 subjects yielded two interpretable dimensions corresponding to the dimensions of variation in the stimulus set. This same subset of aphasic patients produced essentially normal naming data for the stimulus objects. These patients were obviously aware that some stimuli were clear examples of each category although others were not; in addition, this group used the context information, when it was provided, to shift the category boundary in the appropriate direction.

In contrast, the scaling solution for the subgroup of six patients yielded only one interpretable dimension that appeared to correspond to the handle/no handle feature. These patients apparently were not sensitive to the important dimension of width variation in making their judgments of similarity. In the naming task, this group had great difficulty producing consistent labels for the items in this severely constrained stimulus set. Thus, in this study an impairment of the ability to name objects is accompanied by a parallel inability to integrate two dimensions of perceptual variation in a nonlanguage task. We believe that these results provide additional evidence that a disruption of the conceptual structure of the lexicon is at the root of naming deficits in many types of aphasic patients.

The performance of patients in these last two studies was based on their ability to perform a perceptual analysis of the items to recover the carefully controlled features of variation in the stimulus set. Much lexical knowledge involves an appreciation of features of meaning that are considerably more abstract than these and that are therefore not as easily manipulated in experiments.

Recent attempts to describe the organization of the lexicon in normal speakers have assumed that semantic information is internally stored as sets of abstract features of meaning that are represented as single components in a binary (contrastive) organization (Bierwisch, 1970; Miller, 1972). Some of these components (e.g., ± animate) are basic conceptual features of many items in the lexicon and are relatively systematic in the language (Katz & Fodor, 1963). Other features (e.g., ± ferocious) separate individual word meanings from each other beyond the more general information provided by the basic features. Other distinctions have been made between types of semantic features (Miller, 1969; Smith, Shoben, & Rips, 1974), all of which capture the basic difference between the formal, hierarchically organized components that "define" lexical items as classes and the more idiosyncratic features that distinguish between individual lexical items. These latter "characteristic" features may result more from an individual's personal associations with a particular word (e.g., "+ can fly" as a feature of the word "bird") than from its dictionary definition.

Zurif, Caramazza, Myerson, and Galvin (1974) constructed a set of 12 stimulus words that overlapped on both types of features. The most basic defining feature was (± human), which divided the set into two parts; human (mother, wife, cook, partner, knight, husband) and nonhuman (shark, trout, dog, tiger, turtle, crocodile). Ten aphasic patients (five anterior- and five posterior-damaged) and five control subjects were presented with three of these items at a time and asked to indicate which two were the most similar in meaning. Patients' judgments of similarity for all possible combinations of the 12 words were analyzed using hierarchical clustering and multidimensional scaling to extract the structural organization that the patients had imposed on the items.

Both anterior-damaged and control patients essentially separated the human from the animal items. The posterior-damaged patients, despite the fact that they had been able to recognize a definition of the words on a pretest, failed to separate the human from the animal terms. This very basic feature, which is part of the meaning of many words, was not used effectively by the posterior patients in performing this task.

After making the basic human/animal distinction, the anterior aphasics did not cluster the animal items as did the controls but had difficulty using the defining feature of species membership. These patients generated two clusters of animals that violated the species boundary and seemed to be based on a characteristic feature that divided the animals into "dangerous" (shark, crocodile, tiger) and "harmless" (trout, turtle).

An important implication of this study is that disorganization of lexical knowledge may not be evident in tasks requiring simple identification of word meanings. Even when the semantic disruption involves very basic and general meaning components, as it did for the posterior patients in this study, the patient may be able to perform quite well in some identification tasks. A more subtle disruption of lexical knowledge has been demonstrated among the anterior patients, such that their organization of the stimuli reflected a reliance on somewhat accidental, possibly affective features of meaning rather than on the defining feature of species membership. It is important to note that such use of characteristic features would not affect the ability of anterior patients to identify pictures or definitions of the target items; nonetheless, it demonstrates a definite restriction of their semantic organization.

Another aspect of lexical representation that has been widely investigated among normal speakers and is now being probed in aphasia is the organization of semantic memory into a superordinate/subordinate hierarchy. Extensive information is available concerning normal speakers' categorization abilities, and several models have been offered to explain the structural and processing components of this system. One influential argument is that semantic categories are organized around prototypical instances ("good members" of a category), with other instances related through a series of "family resemblances" to the most typical instances (Rosch & Mervis, 1975).

Although there is considerable disagreement about the adequacy of this particular model (Martin & Caramazza, 1980), including whether its predictions are different from those made on the basis of a feature model such as sketched previously (Caramazza, Hersh, & Torgerson, 1976; Smith et al., 1974), it is an empirical fact that typical instances of a category are verified more quickly than atypical instances; that is, a normal adult can affirm that a "robin" is a "bird" considerably faster than he can say that a "penguin" is a "bird." Regardless of the processes that might be involved, it appears that typicality (or whatever set of circumstances yields typicality) is an important aspect of the organization of semantic categories. It is interesting to consider, therefore, whether aphasic patients are sensitive typicality.

Grossman (1978) asked four anterior- and three posterior-damaged aphasic patients to name as many items as possible from two superordinate categories. Patients' responses were evaluated on the basis of established typicality norms, and both groups were found to have produced both typical and atypical members of each category. In addition, posterior patients tended to produce highly typical items initially, gradually moving to the category boundary and ultimately naming items that were not members of the category. Anterior patients did not follow an orderly pattern with regard to typicality and rarely produced out-of-category responses. This finding suggests not only that posterior aphasics are sensitive to typicality but that they rely on this feature of semantic organization to structure their responses.

Further evidence concerning the importance of typicality to posterior patients' performance with superordinate categories is reported (Grober, Perecman, Kellar, & Brown, 1980). Six nonfluent and eight fluent aphasic patients and two controls were tested in two speeded categorization tasks. Patients were asked to say whether a picture (task 1) or a printed word (task 2) was or was not an instance of a particular superordinate category. Both groups of patients performed somewhat better with typical instances, but the posterior group was much more seriously affected by an item's typicality; that is, they performed reasonably well with highly typical instances and significantly worse with atypical instances. The authors interpret this result in terms of the distinction between defining and characteristic features, described previously. This argument rests on the assertion that typical instances are good members of a category because they involve both defining and characteristic features, whereas atypical instances involve primarily defining features. Within this analysis, then, it may be that posterior aphasics rely on characteristic features and consequently do best with typical category members. Alternative explanations are possible, and all would presumably require some disruption of the normal structure of semantic categories for the posterior, but not the anterior, patients tested in this study.

The research papers reviewed here demonstrate some new approaches to the study of lexical knowledge in aphasia. Although we cannot conclude anything specific about the precise form that lexical breakdown takes in aphasia, several general statements can be made on the basis of this work. First, the type of tasks typically used to assess patients' understanding of word meanings (confrontation naming and picture/word matching) do not by themselves provide an adequate assessment of lexical knowledge. New techniques are required to probe the full range of patients' knowledge of a word's meaning, including its relationship to other lexical items. Second, many aphasic patients, particularly those with posterior cortical involvement, appear to have experienced a partial disruption of the semantic representation of word meanings, and this involvement may or may not extend to an inability to name objects or to identify the referents of words.

SEMANTIC OPERATIONS IN APHASIA

Understanding the meaning of a sentence requires an understanding of the lexical and syntactic information contained in the sentence and the combination and integration of that information into a unified semantic representation. Unlike lexical meanings, sentence meanings are novel, complex representations that are uniquely constructed for each sentence in a given context. The processes involved in constructing sentence meanings have not been the subject of much psycholinguistic research, although the topic has received considerable theoretical attention (Katz, 1972; Lakoff, 1971). Although it is generally agreed that some sort of combinatorial operation is involved in sentential semantics, there is little information available concerning the nature of that set of operations.

There has been a corresponding neglect of semantic operations in aphasia research. Luria's (1970) discussion of the syndrome that he calls "semantic aphasia" may be the only systematic attempt to characterize a selective deficit of these combinatorial abilities. Luria argues that the semantic aphasic is unable to understand complex sentences, despite good understanding of individual lexical items, because of an inability to "unify individual stimulations into a single, simultaneous pattern [p. 226]."

We have recently reported a study that lends some support to Luria's assertion that semantic operations can be selectively impaired by brain damage (Berndt & Caramazza, 1980b). Seventeen aphasic patients (unclassified prior to testing) were presented with sentences describing some contrastive feature of two named individuals (e.g., "John is tall; Bill is short"). The attributes described by the sentence adjectives were portrayed in pairs of pictures that accompanied each problem (e.g., a tall and a short man). Patients listened to the orally presented problem and pointed to one of the two pictures in response to a question (e.g., "Who is John?"). Four types of problems were constructed that combined the two linguistic operations of negation and comparison (see Table 10.2), so that a measure was obtained of patients' ability to comprehend these operations alone (problems 2 and 3) and in combination (problem 4). A total of 70 problems, using four adjective contrasts, was administered to each patient.

The result with the most significance for the present discussion is that some of the aphasic patients had a great deal of difficulty with the problem types that required the combination of the operations of comparison and negation. In order to investigate whether patients who have difficulty combining semantic information also have difficulty integrating visual/spatial information (as Luria suggested), we analyzed performance separately for the two subgroups of patients that had emerged on the perceptual integration task described in the previous section (Caramazza, Berndt, & Brownell, in press). Recall that one subgroup of patients was able to integrate two dimensions of perceptual variation, and another group of patients had been unable to utilize both dimensions. When the

TABLE 10.2
Problem Types—Semantic Operations Study

	Uncompared	*Comparative*
Affirmative	1. John is old. Bill is young. Who is John?	2. Sue is older than Jean. Who is Sue?
Negative	3. Sam is old. Joe is not old. Who is Sam?	4. Pat is not younger than Meg. Who is Pat?

sentence comprehension data for these two subgroups was analyzed separately, it was found that the group that performed well on the perceptual integration task did not have significantly greater difficulty with the problem types that combined two operations. The second group, in contrast, performed at chance with the negative/comparative problems, despite relatively good performance with these operations when encountered one at a time. This one group of patients, then, appears to be particularly impaired in their ability to combine and integrate information to produce a unified perceptual or semantic representation.

These subgroups were not based on a classification system or assumptions about locus of lesion but were constructed on the basis of the patients' similarity ratings of the "cups/bowls" stimuli. Using the normal procedures for classifying patients, these six would not have emerged as a particularly homogeneous group, but all of them had some signs of posterior involvement (fluent, paraphasic speech and/or relatively poor comprehension). However, there were several other patients with symptoms of posterior pathology who did well on the integration tasks. Clearly, more information is needed to describe the symptoms that co-occur with the disruption of semantic operations. It may be that the current taxonomy of syndromes obscures the selective involvement of this aspect of language.

CONCLUSION: THE IMPORTANCE OF APHASIA RESEARCH

The study of aphasic patients is motivated primarily by clincal considerations. The goal is to understand the nature of language breakdown so that well-motivated programs for the retraining of aphasic patients can be designed. The clinical assessment of language disturbances depends critically on theoretical views, either explicit or implicit, about the nature of aphasic syndromes. A better understanding of the processing mechanisms that are impaired in various aphasic syndromes will contribute importantly to the refinement of clinical diagnostic procedures. These developments will also have implications for therapeutic programs to the extent that we can separate the processing operations that are spared from the mechanisms that are impaired in a particular aphasic syndrome. Based on the assumption that the most successful therapuetic programs entail training the patient to develop alternative strategies to make maximal use of spared language capacities, it is important to have a clear understanding of which language components are impaired and which are spared in various patient types.

Relevance for Psycholinguistic Theories

In addition to its clinical value, research on aphasia has implications for normal language processing—both for the development of psycholinguistic and neurolinguistic theories. To date, the contribution of aphasia research to the understanding of psycholinguistic processes has been meager. One factor contributing to this situation is certainly the fact that the dominant issues in this area of research were primarily clinical or neurological in nature—interests somewhat removed from the concerns of the psycholinguist. Another critical factor has been psycholinguistic theory itself; the vague and poorly articulated psycholinguistic theories that have been proposed over the years have not provided sufficient structure to permit their ready extension to the analysis of aphasic language. This situation has not been remedied to any great extent in the recent past. Despite voluminous sets of data on many important aspects of language processing, there exists no integrated processing theory of language comprehension or production. Given the state of the art in psycholinguistics, therefore, it seems presumptuous to single out research on aphasia for having failed to contribute significantly to normal psycholinguistic theory (Fodor, Bever, & Garrett, 1974). The goal should be to articulate empirically testable hypotheses of language processing in the areas of both normal and pathological language.

In such a cooperative enterprise, the study of aphasia has much to offer in that it can provide a natural untangling of processing components that in the normal spekaer/hearer may be inaccessible to direct experimental investigation. Two examples can readily illustrate the perhaps indispensible role of aphasia research.

One issue of considerable interest in psycholinguistic theory concerns the pattern of interaction between syntactic and semantic processes in sentence parsing and comprehension (Frazier, 1979). Undoubtedly, both types of processes are engaged in some interactive fashion in normal sentence comprehension. Indeed, it is difficult to imagine an experimental procedure that could be designed to reveal the types of sentential-semantic processes normally engaged in comprehension. It is impossible to consider such semantic information outside the context of syntactic structure. This question can be approached by studying aphasic patients in whom the ability to process syntactic information has been disrupted. In this context, Broca's aphasia offers a unique opportunity because of the apparently selective disturbance of syntactic processes in that syndrome. The Broca patient's inability to use syntactic information and his intact ability to process semantic information allows an investigation of the semantic operations and strategies that can be recruited in the process of comprehension with minimal interference from syntactic processing (Caramazza & Zurif, 1976).

An analogous situation exists in the case of those Conduction aphasics who may have an auditory-verbal short-term memory disorder (Shallice & Warrington, 1977). Here the components of processing that are untangled provide the opportunity to address the issue of the role of working memory in sentence comprehension (Caramazza, Basili, Koller, & Berndt, in press) or the functioning of long-term memory independently of short-term memory (Saffran & Marin, 1975). Focusing briefly on the first of these two dissociations, we have shown that such patients can make effective use of syntactic information in various language tasks in which short-term memory limitations can be circumvented. However, when working memory *must* function normally for adequate sentence processing, as in sentence comprehension, Conduction aphasics are impaired in a very specific way. Clearly, the study of such patients could provide invaluable data on the interaction of memory and language processes.

In this discussion we may have inadvertently led the reader to infer that brain damage provides discrete dissociations of processing components such that when a particular component is impaired, all remaining psychological functions continue to work as they did in the intact brain. We must emphasize again that actual cases do not always present the clear situations we have described. Nonetheless, the study of the types of pathological cases discussed here may offer the best means available for investigating the functioning of the components of language and other cognitive processes.

Relevance for Neurolinguistic Theory

Aphasia research makes an extremely valuable contribution to the construction of neurolinguistic theory (i.e., to theories about how language is represented in the brain). The goal of neurolinguistic theory is to account for the psychological processes that constitute language in terms of the neuroanatomical and neurophysiological machinery capable of implementing those processes. Currently, there are no theoretical formulations that consider the full richness of language processing within a neuroanatomical and neurophysiological framework. In fact, we are not even in a position to spell out the range of facts that must be accounted for by a minimally adequate neurolinguistic theory. One problem is that the levels of analysis in the relevant domains (psycholinguistics and neurophysiology, for example) are grossly incommensurate: There is no theoretical vocabulary available that can relate these two domains. Despite these problems, data are accumulating, primarily from aphasia research, on which neurolinguistic theory can be built.

The evidence from aphasia has established unequivocally that there is a far-from-random pattern to the language dissolution that occurs in adults after focal brain damage. On the basis of the established pattern of correlations between aphasic symptoms and the geographical distribution of damage to the brain, an attempt can be made to construct a topographical characterization of the cortical representation of language. An adequate characterization at this level would constitute an important first step toward the ultimate goal of specifying the neurophysiological processes subserving language functions. Of course, there are difficulties even at the level of correlating function with brain structures: specifically, with regard to the precise nature of the processing deficits assumed to underlie a clinical syndrome and the relationship of impaired processing components to the locus of brain damage (see Berndt & Caramazza, 1980a, for discussion). However assuming that we can determine which language-processing components are impaired in various syndromes (and our review indicates that considerable progress has been made in this regard), the remaining issue of the relationship of brain structures to psychological functions is not beyond the scope of our current methods of analysis.

This is not to say that there is general agreement on the question of whether psychological functions are localized in discrete regions of the brain. Although there are conflicting viewpoints on this issue, they cannot be resolved empirically. The two major explanations of the brain/function correlations found in aphasia make similar predictions concerning a patient's behavior consequent to damage in a particular area. The "strict localizationist" hypothesis maintains that discrete parts of the brain are specialized for particular functions. The claim is that the lesioned area is the actual repository of the component of processing assumed to be impaired in the resulting syndrome. Thus, for example, Broca's aphasia is assumed to result from a lesion to a brain structure that carries out syntactic processing of language. An alternative view (Luria, 1970) makes the weaker claim that the lesioned area is not itself the repository of a discrete component of processing but that this brain structure is *necessary* for the normal execution of the process in question. Thus, continuing with the example of Broca's aphasia, syntactic processing is not carried out in Broca's area; syntactic deficits result because the language processes that remain intact cannot carry out syntactic processes without the normal functioning of the affected area.

It should be obvious that the two hypotheses are formally equivalent; clearly, there are no situations in which the two would make contrasting behavioral predictions. This is a theoretical issue that is not resolvable at the level of aphasia research. The point that should not be overlooked is that proponents of both views admit to the importance of particular brain structures for the normal execution of some specified function. It is at this level that major progress is now possible through detailed analyses of aphasic syndromes.

Finally, it should be noted that our review of psycholinguistic deficits in aphasia has revealed an intriguing pattern in the extent to which components of language processing can be selectively impaired. There are two aspects to this pattern. The first concerns the occurrence of aphasic impairments readily describalbe in terms of a disorder of a major language-processing component. The second concerns the localizability of the lesion responsible for the observed aphasic symptoms. Our impression is that it is relatively easy to characterize syntactic impairments and that such impairments are closely associated with lesions in the anterior zones of the language area. In contrast, phonological and semantic deficits appear to take many different forms and can result from insult to widely varying sites. There are probably several explanations for this observed pattern, and the most interesting is that syntactic processing enjoys some special biological status that is not shared by the other components.

There is some evidence in support of this hypothesis. Studies of the language capacities of the right hemipshere in split-brain patients have consistently demonstrated that the right hemisphere can carry out considerable language processing (Gazzaniga & Sperry, 1967; Zaidel, 1978). However, these capacities are limited to phonological and semantic processes; the disconnected right hemisphere appears to be totally incapable of carrying out syntactic analysis. Even more compelling evidence on the inability of the right hemisphere to perform syntactic operations has been obtained in the hemidecortication studies (Dennis & Kohn, 1975). Hemidecorticated patients have had the entire cortex of one of the hemispheres removed at a very early age, usually as a treatment for intractable epilepsy. Patients without a right-hemisphere cortex develop normal language capacities. Patients without a left-hemisphere cortex develop considerable language skills, including speech. However, careful analysis of the language capacities of these latter patients reveals marked syntactic-processing deficits (Dennis & Whitaker, 1976). In other words, the right hemisphere can assume phonological and semantic processes but cannot take over syntactic processes. The hemidecortication studies suggest that the brain is organized with considerable plasticity in which (probably homologous) regions of one hemisphere can take over the functions normally carried out by the dominant hemisphere. The striking exception is syntactic processing, which appears to be a specialized and unique skill of the left hemisphere. The data from aphasia restrict even further the brain regions that subserve syntactic processing to Broca's area and perhaps portions of the precentral gyrus (Mohr, 1976). Analogously, the data from aphasia support the contention that phonological and semantic processes may be only weakly localized in the left hemisphere. The question of why there should be such asymmetries is an intriguing issue worthy of close scrutiny.

The study of aphasia offers an important source of information about the functioning of the components of language and about the relationship between language and the brain. Considerable progress has been made since Wernicke proposed his theory of language/brain organization, although the basic structure of the classical theory continues to provide a framework for current investigations of aphasia. The primary advances that have been made since Wernicke's time have involved elaboration of the psychological processes that function in the normal language system. Knowledge in this area has been developed through the cooperative efforts of linguistics, psychologists, and psycholinguists who have formulated theories of language and developed the research methods to test those theories. Future developments in the field of aphasia research, which will ultimately contribute importantly to our understanding of language and of the brain, are dependent on continuing interdisciplinary cooperation and to theoretical and methodological advances in the fields of neurophysiology, linguistics, and psycholinguistics.

ACKNOWLEDGMENTS

The preparation of this chapter was supported by NIH Research Grant 14099 to The Johns Hopkins University. The original research reported here was performed at the Fort Howard Veterans Administration Medical Center. We would like to thank Dr. Annamaria Basili, Chief, and the staff of the Department of Audiology and Speech Pathology for their continuing cooperation in this research.

REFERENCES

Alajouanine, T., Ombredane, A., & Durand, M. *Le Syndrome de la Désintégration Phonetique dans l'Aphasie*. Paris: Mason, 1939.
Andreewsky, E., & Seron, X. Implicit processing of grammatical rules in a classical case of agrammatism. *Cortex*, 1975, *11*, 379-390.
Benson, D. F. Fluency in aphasia: Correlation with radioactive scan localization. *Cortex*, 1967, *3*, 373-394.
Benson, D. F. The third alexia. *Archives of Neurology*, 1977, *34*, 327-331.
Benson, D. F., & Geschwind, N. The alexias. In P. J. Vinken & G. W. Bryun (Eds.), *Handbook of clinical neurology* (Vol. 4). Amsterdam: North Holland, 1969.
Benson, D. F., & Geschwind, N. The aphasias and related disturbances. In A. B. Baker & L. H. Baker (Eds.), *Clincal neurology* (Vol. 1). Hagerstown: Harper & Row, 1977.
Benson, D. F., Sheremata, W. A., Bouchard, R., Segarra, J. M., Price, E., & Geschwind, N. Conduction aphasia: A clinicopathological study. *Archives of Neurology*, 1973, *28*, 339-346.
Benton, A. L., & Joynt, R. J. Early descriptions of aphasia. *Archives of Neurology*, 1960, *3*, 109-126.
Berndt, R., & Caramazza, A. A redefinition of the syndrome of Broca's aphasia: Implications for a neuropsychological model of language. *Applied Psycholinguistics*, 1980, *1*, 225-278. (a)
Berndt, R., & Caramazza, A. Semantic operations deficits in sentence comprehension. *Psychological Research*, 1980, *41*, 169-177. (b)
Bierwisch, M. Semantics. In J. Lyons, (Ed.), *New horizons in linguistics*. Middlesex, England: Penguin Books, 1970.
Blumstein, S. E. *A phonological investigation of aphasic speech*. The Hague: Mouton, 1973.
Blumstein, S. E. Neurolinguistics: Language-brain relationships. In S. B. Filskov & T. J. Boll (Eds.), *Handbook of clinical neuropsychology*. New York: Wiley, 1980.
Blumstein, S. E., Baker, E., & Goodglass, H. Phonological factors in auditory comprehension in aphasia. *Neuropsychologia*, 1977, *15*, 19-30.
Blumstein, S. E., Cooper, W. E., Zurif, E. B., & Caramazza, A. The perception and production of voice-onset time in aphasia. *Neurpsychologia*, 1977, *15*, 371-383.
Blumstein, S. E., & Goodglass, H. The perception of stress as a semantic cue in aphasia. *JSHR*, 1972, *15*, 800-806.
Boller, F., & Green, E. Comprehension in severe aphasics. *Cortex*, 1972, *8*, 382-394.
Boller, F., Kim, Y., & Mack, J. Auditory comprehension in aphasia. In H. Whitaker & H. A. Whitaker (Eds.), *Studies in neurolinguistics* (Vol. 3). New York: Academic Press, 1977.
Brown, J. W. *Aphasia, apraxia, and agnosia*. Springfield, Ill.: Charles C Thomas, 1972.
Brown, J. W. *Mind, brain, and consciousness*. New York: Academic Press, 1977.
Caramazza, A. Basili, A. G., Koller, J. J., & Berndt, R. S. *An investigation of repetition and language processing in a case of conduction aphasia*. Brain and Language, in press.
Caramazza, A., & Berndt, R. S. Semantic and syntactic processes in aphasia: A review of the literature. *Psychological Bulletin*, 1978, *85*, 898-918.
Caramazza, A., Berndt, R. S., Basili, A. G., & Koller, J. J. Syntactic processing deficits in aphasia. *Cortex*, in press.
Caramazza, A., Berndt, R. S., & Brownell, H. H. The semantic deficit hypothesis: Perceptual parsing and object classification by aphasic patients. *Brain and Language*, in press.
Caramazza, A., Berndt, R. S., & Hart, J. "Agrammatic" reading. In F. J. Pirozzolo & M. C. Wittrock (Eds.) *Neuropsychological and cognitive processes in reading*. New York: Academic Press, 1981.
Caramazza, A., Hersh, H., & Torgerson, W. S. Subjective structures and operations in semantic memory. *Journal of Verbal Learning and Verbal Behavior*, 1976, *15*, 103-117.

Caramazza, A., & Zurif, E. B. Dissociation of algorithmic and heuristic processes in language comprehension: Evidence from aphasia. *Brain and Language,* 1976 *3,* 572-582.
Caramazza, A., Zurif, E. B., & Gardner, H. Sentence memory in aphasia. *Neuropsychologia,* 1978, *16,* 661-669.
Chomsky, N. *Aspects of the theory of syntax.* Cambridge, Mass.: MIT Press, 1965.
Clark, H. H., & Clark, E. V. *Psychology and language.* New York: Harcourt Brace Jovanovich, 1977.
Coltheart, M. Lexical access in simple reading tasks. In Geoffrey Underwood (Ed.), *Strategies of information processing.* London: Academic Press, 1978.
Dennis, M., & Kohn, B. Comprehension of syntax in infantile hemiplegics after cerebral hemidecortication: Left-hemisphere superiortiy. *Brain and Language,* 1975, *2,* 472-482.
Dennis, M., & Whitaker, H. H. Language acquisition following hemidecortication. *Brain and Language,* 1976, *3,* 404 433.
DeRenzi, E., & Vignolo, L. A. The token test: A sensitive test to detect receptive disturbances in aphasics. *Brain,* 1962, *85,* 665-678.
Eggert, G. H. *Wernicke's works on aphasia.* The Hague: Mouton, 1977.
Fodor, J. A., Bever, T., & Garrett, M. F. *The psychology of language: An introduction to psycholinguistics and generative grammar.* New York: McGraw-Hill, 1974.
Fodor, J. A., & Garrett, M. F. Some syntactic determinants of sentential complexity. *Perception and Psychophysics,* 1967, *2,* 289-296.
Foss, D. J., & Hakes, D. T. *Psycholinguistics: An introduction to the psychology of language.* Englewood Cliffs, N.J.: Prentice-Hall, 1978.
Frazier, L. *On comprehending sentences: Syntactic parsing strategies.* Bloomington, Ind.: Indiana University Linguistics Club, 1979.
Freud, S. *On aphasia* (E. Stendle, Translator). London: Imago, 1953.
Friederici, A. D., & Schoenle, P. W. Computational dissociation of two vocabulary types: Evidence from aphasia. *Neuropsychologia,* 1980, *18,* 11-20.
Gainotti, G. The relationship between semantic impairment in comprehension and naming in aphasic patients. *British Journal Disorders of Communication,* 1976, *11,* 57-61.
Gardner, H. The contribution of operativity to naming capacity in aphasic patients. *Neuropsychologia,* 1973, *11,* 213-220.
Gardner, H., Denes, G., & Zurif, E. Critical reading at the sentence level in aphasia. *Cortex,* 1975, *11,* 60-72.
Gardner, H., & Zurif, E. 'Bee' but not 'be': Oral reading of single words in aphasia and alexia. *Neuropsychologia,* 1975, *13,* 181-190.
Gazzaniga, M. S., & Sperry, R. W. Language after section of the cerebral commissures. *Brain,* 1967, *90,* 131-148.
Geschwind, N. Disconnection syndromes in animals and man. *Brain,* 1965, *88,* 237-294, 585-644.
Geschwind, N. The varieties of naming errors. *Cortex,* 1967, *3,* 97-112.
Gleason, J. B., Goodglass, H., Green, E., Ackerman, N., & Hyde, M. R. The retrieval of syntax in Broca's aphasia. *Brain and Language,* 1975, *2,* 451-471.
Goldstein, K. *Language and language disturbances.* New York: Grune & Stratton, 1948.
Goodenough, C., Zurif, E., & Weintraub, S. Aphasics' attention to grammatical morphemes. *Language and Speech,* 1977, *20,* 11-19.
Goodglass, H. Redefining the concept of agrammatism in aphasia. In L. Croatto & C. Croatto-Martinolli (Eds.), *Proceedings of the XIIth international speech and voice therapy conference.* Padua, Italy, 1962.
Goodglass, H. Studies on the grammar of aphasics. In S. Rosenberg & K. Joplin (Eds.), *Developments in applied psycholinguistics research.* New York: Macmillan, 1968.
Goodglass, H. Agrammatism. In H. Whitaker & H. A. Whitaker (Eds.), *Studies in neurolinguistics* (Vol. 1). New York: Academic Press, 1976.

Goodglass, H., & Baker, E. Semantic field, naming and auditory comprehension in aphasia. *Brain and Language*, 1976, *3*, 359-374.
Goodglass, H., Blumstein, S. E., Gleason, J. B., Hyde, M. R., Green, E., & Statlender, S. The effect of syntactic encoding on sentence comprehension in aphasia. *Brain and Language*, 1979, *7*, 201-209.
Goodglass, H., Fodor, I. G., & Schulhoff, C. Prosodic factors in grammar-evidence from aphasia. *Journal of Speech and Hearing Research*, 1967, 10(1), 5-20.
Goodglass, H., & Geschwind, N. Language disorders (aphasia). In E. C. Carterette & M. P. Friedman (Eds.), *Handbook of perception* (Vol. 7), *Speech and Language*. New York: Academic Press, 1976.
Goodglass, H., Gleason, J. B., Bernholtz, N. A., & Hyde, M. R. Some linguistic structures in the speech of a Broca's aphasic. *Cortex*, 1972, *8*, 191-212.
Goodglass, H., Hyde, M. R., & Blumstein, S. Frequency, picturability, and the availability of nouns in aphasia. *Cortex*, 1969, *5*, 104-119.
Goodglass, H., & Kaplan, E. *The assessment of aphasia and related disorders*. Philadelphia: Lea and Febiger, 1972.
Goodglass, H., Quadfasel, F. A., & Timberlake, W. H. Phrase length and the type and severity of aphasia. *Cortex*, 1964, *1*, 133-153.
Green, E., & Howes, D. The nature of conduction aphasia: A study of anatomic and clinical features and of underlying mechanisms. In H. Whitaker & H. A. Whitaker (Eds.) *Studies in neurolinguistics* (Vol. 3). New York: Academic Press, 1977.
Grober, E., Perecman, E., Kellar, L., & Brown, J. Lexical knowledge in anterior and posterior aphasics. *Brain and Language*, 1980, *10*, 318-330.
Grossman, M. The game of the name: An examination of linguistic reference after brain damage. *Brain and Language*, 1978, *6*, 112-119.
Head, H. *Aphasia and kindred disorders of speech* (Vols. 1 and 2). London: Cambridge University Press, 1926.
Hécaen, H., & Angelergues, R. *Pathologie du Langage*. Paris: Larousse, 1965.
Heilman, K. M., & Scholes, R. T. The nature of comprehension errors in Broca's, conduction, and Wernicke's aphasics. *Cortex*, 1976, *12*(3), 258-265.
Howes, D. Some experimental investigations of language in aphasia. In K. Salzinger & S. Salzinger (Eds.), *Research in verbal behavior and some neurophysiological implications*. New York: Academic Press, 1967.
Isserlin, M. Uber Agrammatismus. *Zeitschrift fur die Gesamte Neurologie and Psychiatrie*, 1922, *75*, 332-416.
Jackson, J. H. Affections of speech from disease of the brain. *Brain*, 1878, *1*, 304-330.
Jakobson, R. Two aspects of language and two types of aphasic disturbances. In R. Jakobson & M. Halle (Eds.), *Fundamentals of language*. The Hague: Mouton, 1956.
Jakobson, R. Towards a linguistic typology of aphasic impairments. In A. V. S. deReuck & M. O'Connor (Eds.), *Disorders of language*. Boston: Little, Brown, & Co., 1964.
Johnson, S. C. Hierarchical clustering schemes. *Psychometrika*, 1967, *32*, 241-254.
Katz, J. *Semantic theory*. New York: Harper & Row, 1972.
Katz, J., & Fodor, J. A. The structure of a semantic theory. *Language*, 1963, *39*, 170-210.
Kean, M. L. The linguistic interpretation of aphasic syndromes: Agrammatism in Broca's aphasia, an example. *Cognition*, 1977, *5*, 9-46.
Kean, M. L. The linguistic interpretation of aphasic syndromes. In E. Walker (Ed.), *Explorations in the biology of language*. Montgomery, Vt.: Bradford Books, 1978.
Kellar, L. *Stress and syntax in aphasia*. Paper presented at the meeting of the Academy of Aphasia, Chicago, 1978.
Kertesz, A., Harlock, W., & Coates, R. Computer tomographic localization, lesion size, and prognosis in aphasia and nonverbal impairment. *Brain and Language*, 1979, *8*, 34-50.

Kertesz, A., Lesk, D., & McCabe, P. Isotope localization of infarcts in aphasia. *Archives of Neurology,* 1977, *34,* 590-601.
Kimball, J. Seven principles of surface structure parsing in natural language. *Cognition,* 1973, *2,* 15-47.
Kimball, J. Predictive analysis and over-the-top parsing. In J. Kimball (Ed.), *Syntax and Semantics* (Vol. IV). New York: Academic Press, 1975.
Kolk, H. H. J. The linguistic interpretation of Broca's aphasia: A reply to M. L. Kean. *Cognition,* 1978, *6,* 353-361. (a)
Kolk, H. H. J. Judgments of sentence structure in Broca's aphasia. *Neuropsychologia,* 1978, *16,* 617-625. (b)
Labov, W. The boundaries of words and their meanings. In C.-J. N. Bailey & R. W. Shuy (Eds.), *New Ways of analyzing variation in English,* Washington, D.C.: Georgetown University Press, 1973.
Lakoff, G. On generative semantics. In D. Steinberg & L. Jakobovits (Eds.), *Semantics: An interdisciplinary reader in philosophy, linguistics and psychology.* Cambridge: Cambridge University Press, 1971.
Lecours, A. R., & Caplan, D. Review of "A phonological investigation of aphasic speech" by S. E. Blumstein. *Brain and Language,* 1975, *2,* 237-254.
Lecours, A. R., & Lhermitte, F. The pure form of phonetic disintegration syndrome (pure anarthria): Anatomo-clinical report of a historical case. *Brain and Language,* 1976, *3,* 88-113.
Lenneberg, E. H. The neurology of language. *Daedalus,* 1973, *102,* 115-133.
Lesser, R. *Linguistic investigations of aphasia.* New York: North-Holland, 1978.
Levelt, W. J. M. A scaling approach to the study of syntactic relations. In G. B. Flores d'Arcais & W. J. M. Levelt (Eds.), *Advances in psycholinguistics.* Amsterdam: North Holland, 1970.
Lhermitte, F., Derouesné, J., & Lecours, A. R. Contribution a l'etude des troubles semantique dans l'aphasie. *Revue Neurologique,* 1971, *125,* 81-101.
Liberman, A. M., Cooper, F., Shankweiler, D., & Studdert-Kennedy, M. Perception of the speech code. *Psychological Review,* 1967, *74,* 431-459.
Lichtheim, L. On aphasia. *Brain,* 1885, *7,* 433-484.
Lisker, L., & Abramson, A. S. A cross-language study of voicing in initial stops: Acoustical measurements. *Word,* 1964, *20,* 384-422.
Locke, S., Caplan, D., & Keller, L. *A study in neurolinguistics.* Springfield, Ill.: Charles C Thomas, 1973.
Luria, A. R. Factors and forms of aphasia. In A. V. S. deReuck & M. O'Connor (Eds.), *Disorders of language.* London: Churchill, 1964.
Luria, A. R. *Human brain and psychological processes.* New York: Harper & Row, 1966.
Luria, A. R. *[Traumatic Aphasia]* (English translation) The Hague: Mouton, 1970. (Originally published 1947.)
Luria, A. R. Two kinds of disorders in the comprehension of grammatical constructions. *Linguistics,* 1975, *154/155,* 47-56.
Luria, A. R. *Basic problems of neurolinguistics.* The Hague: Mouton, 1976.
Luria, A. R. Disturbances of grammatical operations in semantic aphasia. *Neurolingustics,* 1977, *6,* 169-176.
Marie, P. The third frontal convolution plays no special role in the function of language. In M. F. Cole & M. Cole (Eds.), *Pierre Marie's papers on speech disorders.* New York: Hafner, 1960.
Marin, O. S. M., Saffran, E. M., & Schwartz, M. F. Dissociations of language in aphasia: Implications for normal functions. *Annals of the New York Academy of Sciences,* 1976, *280,* 868-884.
Marshall, J. C., & Newcombe, F. Syntactic and semantic errors in paralexia. *Neuropsychologia,* 1966, *4,* 169-176.
Marshall, J. C., & Newcombe, F. Patterns of paralexia: A psycholinguistic approach. *Journal of Psycholinguistic Research,* 1973, *2,* 175-199.

Martin, R., & Caramazza, A. Classification in well-defined and ill-defined categories: Evidence for common processing strategies. *Journal of Experimental Psychology: General*, 1980, *109*, 320-353.

McGlone, J. Sex differences in functional brain asymmetry. *Cortex*, 1978, *14*, 122-128.

Miller, G. A. A psychological method to investigate verbal concepts. *Journal of Mathematical Psychology*, 1969, *6*, 169-191.

Miller, G. A. English verbs of motion: A case study in semantics and lexical memory. In A. W. Melton & E. Martin (Eds.), *Coding processes in human memory*, Washington, D.C.: Winston, 1972.

Miller, G. A., & Johnson-Laird, P. N. *Language and perception*. Cambridge, Mass.: Belknap Press of Harvard University Press, 1976.

Mohr, J. R. Broca's area and Broca's aphasia. In H. Whitaker & H. A. Whitaker (Eds.), *Studies in neurolinguistics* (Vol. 1). New York: Academic Press, 1976.

Naeser, M. A., & Hayward, R. W. Lesion localization in aphasia with cranial computed tomography and the Boston diagnostic aphasia exam. *Neurology*, 1978, *28*, 545-551.

North, B. *Effects of stimulus redundancy on naming disorders in aphasia*. Unpublished doctoral dissertation, Boston University, 1971.

Ojemann, G. A., & Whitaker, H. A. Language localization and variability. *Brain and Language*, 1978, *6*, 239-260.

Parisi, D., & Pizzamiglio, L. Syntactic comprehension in aphasia. *Cortex*, 1970, *6*, 204-215.

Poeck, K., Kerschensteiner, M., & Hartje, W. A quantitative study on language understanding in fluent and nonfluent aphasia. *Cortex*, 1972, *8*, 299-304.

Rinnert, C., & Whitaker, H. A. Semantic confusions by aphasic patients, *Cortex*, 1973, *9*, 56-81.

Rosch, E., & Mervis, C. B. Family resemblances: Studies in the internal structure of categories. *Cognitive Psychology*, 1975, *7*, 573-605.

Saffran, E. M., & Marin, O. S. M. Immediate memory for word lists and sentences in a patient with deficient auditory short term memory. *Brain and Language*, 1975, *2*, 420-433.

Saffran, E. M., & Marin, O. S. M. Reading without phonology: Evidence from aphasia. *Quarterly Journal of Experimental Psychology*, 1977, *29*, 515-525.

Saffran, E. M., Schwartz, M. F., & Marin, O. S. M. The word order problem in agrammatism: II. Production. *Brain and Language*, 1980, *10*, 263-280.

Samuels, J. A., & Benson, D. F. Some aspects of language comprehension in anterior aphasia. *Brain and Language*, 1979, *8*, 275-286.

Schuell, H., & Jenkins, J. The nature of language deficit in aphasia. *Psychological Review*, 1959, *66*, 45-67.

Schuell, H., & Jenkins, J. Reduction of vocabulary in aphasia. *Brain*, 1961, *84*, 243-261.

Schwartz, M. F., Marin, O. S. M., & Saffran, E. M. Dissociations of language function in dementia: A case study. *Brain and Language*, 1979, *7*, 277-306.

Schwartz, M. F., Saffran, E. M., & Marin, O. S. M. *An analysis of agrammatic reading in aphasia*. Paper presented at the meeting of the International Neuropsychological Society, Santa Fe, New Mexico, Feb. 1977.

Schwartz, M. F., Saffran, E. M., & Marin, O. S. M. The word order problem in agrammatism: I. Comprehension. *Brain and Language*, 1980, Vol. *10*, 249-262.

Shallice, T., & Warrington, E. K. Auditory-verbal short-term memory impairment and conduction aphasia. *Brain and Language*, 1977, *4*, 479-491.

Shewan, C. M. Error pattern in auditory comprehension of adult aphasics. *Cortex*, 1976, *12*, 325-336.

Shewan, C. M., & Canter, C. J. Effects of vocabulary, syntax, and sentence length on auditory comprehension in aphasic patients. *Cortex*, 1971, *7*, 209-226.

Smith, E. E., Shoben, E. J., & Rips, L. J. Structure and process in semantic memory: A featural model for semantic decisions. *Psychological Review*, 1974, *81*, 214-241.

von Stockert, T. R., & Bader, L. Some relations of grammar and lexicon in aphasia. *Cortex,* 1976, *12,* 49-60.
Warrington, E. K. The selective impairment of semantic memory. *Quarterly Journal of Experimental Psychology,* 1975, *27,* 635-657.
Warrington, E. K., & Shallice, T. The selective impairment of auditory verbal short-term memory. *Brain,* 1969, *92,* 885-896.
Weigl, E., & Bierwisch, M. Neuropsychology and linguistics: Topics of common research. *Foundations of Language,* 1970, *6,* 1-30.
Weisenberg, T., & McBride, K. *Aphasia.* New York: Commonwealth Fund, 1935.
Wepman, J. M., Bock, R. D., Jones, L. V., & Van Pelt, D. Psycholinguistic study of aphasia: Revision of the question of anomia. *Journal of Speech and Hearing Disorders,* 1956, *21,* 468-477.
Whitaker, H. A. Linguistic competence: Evidence from aphasia. *Glossa,* 1970, *4*(1), 46-54.
Whitaker, H. A., & Selnes, O. A. Anatomic variations in the cortex: Individual differences and the problem of the localization of language functions. In S. Harnad, H. Steklis, & J. Lancaster (Eds.), *Origin and evolution of language and speech.* New York: New York Academy of Sciences, 1976.
Whitehouse, P., Caramazza, A., & Zurif, E. Naming in aphasia: Interacting effects of form and function. *Brain and Language,* 1978, *6,* 63-74.
Zaidel, E. Auditory language comprehension in the right hemisphere: A comparison with child language and aphasia. In A. Caramazza & E. B. Zurif (Eds.), *The acquisition and breakdown of language: Parallels and divergencies.* Baltimore: Johns Hopkins University Press, 1978.
Zurif, E., & Blumstein, S. Language and the brain. In M. Halle, J. Bresnan, & G. Miller (Eds.), *Linguistic theory and psychological reality.* Cambridge, Mass.: MIT Press, 1978.
Zurif, E., & Caramazza, A. Psycholinguistic structures in aphasia: Studies in syntax and semantics. In H. Whitaker & H. A. Whitaker (Eds.) *Studies in neurolinguistics* (Vol. 1). New York: Academic Press, 1976.
Zurif, E., & Caramazza, A. Comprehension, memory and levels of representation: A perspective from aphasia. In J. Kavanaugh & W. Strange (Eds.), *Speech and language in the laboratory, school and clinic.* Cambridge, Mass.: MIT Press, 1978.
Zurif, E. B., Caramazza, A., & Myerson, R. Grammatical judgments of agrammatic aphasics. *Neuropsychologia,* 1972, *10,* 405-417.
Zurif, E. B., Caramazza, A., Myerson, R., & Galvin, J. Semantic feature representations for normal and aphasic language. *Brain and Language,* 1974, *1,* 167-187.
Zurif, E. B., Green, E., Caramazza, A., & Goodenough, C. Grammatical intuitions of aphasic patients: Sensitivity to functors. *Cortex,* 1976, *12,* 183-186.

11 Adult Schizophrenic Language

Sheldon Rosenberg
Leonard Abbeduto
Department of Psychology
University of Illinois at Chicago Circle

ANTICIPATORY REMARKS

As the present review shows, what has come to be known as *schizophrenic language* (SL) is not found in all individuals who are diagnosed as schizophrenic. Moreover, in those patients who do display SL, the syndrome occurs intermittently and, except in some severe cases, infrequently. Furthermore, when we talk about SL, we are talking about characteristics of spontaneous speech production; we do not know whether the syndrome has a counterpart in speech comprehension. From these observations alone, particularly the first two, one tends to conclude that SL is not a disorder of language competence (i.e., of underlying syntactic, semantic, phonological, lexical–morphological, pragmatic knowledge) but of language performance.

The fact that we do not as yet know whether or not SL has a counterpart in language comprehension is due mainly to the intermittent nature of SL. Among other things, we need to be able to examine speech comprehension in schizophrenics during episodes of SL in speech production (Rochester & Martin, 1979).

It is interesting to note here that other (nonlinguistic) symptoms (delusional thinking, hallucinations, bizarre behavior and associations, social withdrawal, high anxiety, paranoid tendencies, ambivalence, attentional hyperactivity and hypoactivity, and fixation) that are thought to characterize schizophrenia do not occur in all individuals so diagnosed (with the exceptions, possibly, of delusional thinking, high anxiety, and attentional deficit). Also, those that do occur appear to occur intermittently and with varying frequencies.

In addition to these observations regarding SL, in the literature we found evidence that what appears to characterize SL is not unique to schizophrenia but is found sometimes in normal individuals, in mania, and in some aphasics. This is not surprising, however, because a biological system as structured as language is likely to be disrupted in limited ways regardless of the etiology of the disruption.

INTRODUCTION

There was no attempt in the present chapter to review all the available literature on language and schizophrenia. Rather, in keeping with the main objective of the present book, we limited ourselves chiefly to the work that has reflected developments in basic psycholinguistics and related areas of cognitive psychology since Chomsky (1957) appeared on the scene. Reviews that reflect earlier orientations can be found in, for example, Broen (1968), Kasanin (1954), Laffal (1979), Maher (1966), and Vetter (1968a). Language, however, has always been a central concern of researchers and clinicans working on schizophrenia (Bleuler, 1950), as have related cognitive disorders (Arieti, 1974; Schwartz, 1978a).

Arieti's (1974) clinical account of cognitive disorders in schizophrenia is frequently cited. He alludes to the attentional deficits in schizophrenia but points out that such deficits are not unique to this disorder; they also occur in cases of brain damage. One of the most common cognitive characteristics of schizophrenia, according to Arieti, is delusions, which he attributes in many instances to *paleologic* thinking. The schizophrenic engages in paleologic thought "in order to escape anxiety that would be disastrous to his inner self and to his conception of himself. As long as he interprets reality with Aristotelian logic, he is aware of the unbearable truth, and the state of panic persists [p. 229]." Paleologic occurs in varying degrees among schizophrenics and involves a confusion of the physical and psychological worlds. In this regard, Arieti cites the phenomenon of *teleologic causality,* that is, the belief that things happen because someone willed them to happen. Another characteristic of schizophrenic thinking that Arieti discusses in this context is the tendency for inferences to dominate descriptions, as, for example, in the case of a patient with paranoic tendencies who believes he is being poisoned and concludes, therefore, that a glass of water someone has given him contains poison.

Some of the clinical features of schizophrenic thinking are to be found in normal individuals as well, as Arieti points out, but this is more easily corrected in the latter population.

Temporal orientation is another aspect of cognition that is affected in schizophrenia; specifically, what happens is that, in order to reduce anxiety, the schizophrenic comes gradually to be dominated by the present, no longer anticipating the future.

Arieti's (1974) view of language (i.e., speech) in schizophrenia is that SL is so affected by schizophrenic thought processes as to produce, typically, "a prompt diagnosis [p. 249]." In the most striking cases, the speech of schizophrenics is incoherent. Moreover, Arieti sees in the speech of schizophrenic patients a tendency to emphasize the denotative (specific reference making) and verbal (nonsemantic–phonological) attributes of words at the expense of their connotative (general catgorical) attributes, as, for example, in the case in which, in response to a request for a definition of the word *book,* a patient responded "It depends what book you are refering to [p. 250]." In addition, Arieti disagrees with the claim that metaphorical usage abounds in SL (Forrest, 1968) and proposes rather that schizophrenics display just the opposite tendency as regards metaphorical language. Finally, Arieti finds, in his analysis of schizophrenic cognition, a lack of purpose in the discourse of schizophrenics.

This is by no means all there is to Arieti's fascinating account of the language and thinking behavior of schizophrenic patients, but we need not attempt to describe it in any greater detail in the present chapter.

One of the most critical reviews of the concept of schizophrenia to appear in recent years is that of Cromwell (1975). Cromwell points out that a continuing problem in the field of schizophrenia concerns the status of the subclassifications of the disorder. Do they represent separate disorders or "separate personalities or cognitive styles onto which a single disorder has been afflicted [p. 595]." Progress in research has been made, however, by classifying schizophrenics in terms of: (1) premorbid adjustment (whether the disorder appeared suddenly or after years of adjustment problems); (2) the presence or absence of paranoid symptoms; and (3) length of hospitalization or chronicity. Prognosis in schizophrenia is particularly tied to premorbid adjustment, but the classifications, generally, tend to reduce within-group variability in performance in a variety of situations.

As Cromwell's (1975) review indicates, much attention has been directed in the laboratory in recent years toward the task of identifying the underlying cognitive and other dynamics of this three-way classification system, the result of which has been to make investigators question the significance of the clinical symptoms of schizophrenia for understanding the underlying mental disorder (see, also, the critical discussion on pp. 187–189 in Space & Cromwell, 1978, concerning the symptoms and etiology of schizophrenia). Unfortunately, as the reader will soon see, the recent research on SL has been little affected by the important research on the three-way classification system discussed by Cromwell.

SCHIZOPHRENIC SPEECH PRODUCTION

Our story begins with the claims of Cromwell and Dokecki (1968) concerning adult schizophrenic language that were based on informal clinical observations that antedated psycholinguistic accounts. These investigators noted, first of all, that the language produced by schizophrenics is largely "coherent and indistinguishable from [p. 212]" that of normals. Thus the observation that SL is intermittent and infrequent, on the average, is not new. Second, from the standpoint of the listener, SL is incoherent. Thus it becomes important to identify the source of the incoherence. Third, according to Cromwell and Dokecki's observations, the source in most instances is not the grammatical structure of SL but disruptions in the underlying thought process that produce "peculiar semantic behavior [p. 212]." Fourth, they found evidence of a disruption in semantic continuity from one sentence to another and from one paragraph to another. Fifth, although rare, there are instances in which within-sentence syntax is disrupted to produce what is referred to as word salad, although the specific example presented by Cromwell and Dokecki (p. 221) does not, from a linguistic standpoint, appear to be ungrammatical. Sixth, these authors noted the occurrence of neologisms (new word coinage) in SL. Finally, schizophrenics seem less likely to notice disruptions in their speech than are normals when their speech is disrupted.

In a more specific vein, these investigators proposed that the peculiar semanic behavior that characterizes SL manifests itself in idiosyncratic associations, peculiar (uncommon) semantic reactions, loose—inclusive and exclusive—conceptualization, perseverative sets, word blocking or repression, fragmented sequences of ideas, word salads, neologisms, hallucinations, delusions, and bizarre ideas. Moreover, they went on to propose that what characterizes SL can be accounted for in many instances by an intermittent inability to disattend from stimuli once they have been attended to (see, also, Cromwell's discussion of stimulus redundancy in his 1975 review).

In several of the examples of SL that Cromwell and Dokecki (1968) present, it does seem to be the case that at one level the patients do not appear to be able to stay with the topic of discourse but rather are disrupted, and unpredictably so, by immediately preceding contextual (linguistic and nonlinguistic) stimuli. However, as intriguing as this account of SL is, it clearly needs to be fleshed out with a more systematic representation of the linguistic structure of schizophrenic speech samples. Moreover, from a reliability standpoint, no systematic procedure or procedures for sampling SL were specified. (But this is a problem that plagues most studies of the speech of schizophrenics.) In addition, the disattention account does not explain the particular form of the speech disruptions in SL. Furthermore, it is not based upon a consideration of the likely components of the speech planning and execution processes, although to be completely fair it must be pointed out that the theory of speech production was in its infancy in the

1960s. Finally, and the authors were aware of this, there are alternatives to the disattention account that result from the confounding of information-processing components and operations. Thus it is possible, for example, that the source or sources of the disruptions in SL lie at a deeper or earlier level of information processing than the immediately preceding stimuli. It is interesting to note, however, that distractibility continues to occupy an important place in attempts to account for the incoherence of SL (Oltmanns & Neale, 1978; Salzinger, Portnoy, & Feldman, 1978). But still not ruled out are the deeper analyses of the cognitive deficit in schizophrenia (Arieti, 1974), and in addition those that emphasize the anxiety, stress, and general arousal levels that schizophrenics tend to operate under (Shimkunas, 1978, pp. 226-227).

Possibly the earliest review to reflect developments in psycholinguistics brought about by the Chomskian revolution in linguistics is that of Pavy (1968), who was highly critical of studies of adult schizophrenic language that emphasized the word to the exclusion of more complex levels of linguistic structure. Moreover, Pavy pointed out, and rightly so, that available research did not begin with characterizations of mature linguistic knowledge and performance in normal individuals against which to assess the language of schizophrenic patients. Indeed, it was clear to the present writers very early that students of SL were slow to recognize the potential of contemporary linguistics and psycholinguistics for characterizing mature linguistic knowlege and performance.

Serious examination of the language performance of adult schizoprehnics in a linguistic and psycholinguistic vein is exemplified in the observations of Brown (1973). This investigator had "private conversations with a wide variety of schizophrenic patients . . . [p. 396]," all of whom were receiving medication. They were also those patients who were willing to talk to him. Initially, he could detect no communality but "however normal the patient was in talking about most subjects, eventually we came upon an area of delusion (p. 396)." In regard to the linguistic characteristics of the speech of the schizophrenic patients he observed, Brown found no evidence of linguistic rule violation at any level of linguistic structure. He did, however, report finding, intermittently, much evidence of disordered thought.

Chaika's Observations. Chaika (1974) took issue with Brown's (1973) conclusions regarding the speech of schizophrenics when she claimed that there are hospitalized patients diagnosed as schizophrenics, a portion of whom intermittently display speech containing linguistically deviant features. She proposes, moreover, that the occurrence of SL may not be something the patient has any control over, that what characterizes SL is not necessarily a reflection of an underlying thought disorder but might possibly be the result of a disorder in the language production areas of the brain.

Chaika's (1974) examination of taped data from an adult female on thorazine who was diagnosed as schizophrenic and data from the literature led her to identify six features in SL which, "especially in combination, differ from other kinds of linguistic deviance [p. 257]," for example, deviance that can be found in poetry or in the speech of aphasic patients. The first involves a problem in matching the semantic features of intended meanings with real-word phonological strings, as evidenced in the occurrence of gibberish and neologisms. The strings produced, however, do not violate the phonological rules of the language. Second, there is a tendency for more of the semantic features of words than are relevant to a discourse segment to attract the patient's attention, as in "My mother's name was Bill... and coo? St. Valentine's Day is the offical startin' of the breeding season of the birds. All buzzards can coo (p. 260)." Third, SL displays a tendency to be distracted, inappropriately, by a word's phonological attributes, as in "I had a little goldfish too. Like a clown. Happy Hallowe'en down [p. 271]." Fourth, Chaika notes a difficulty in maintaining a topic in discourse. Fifth, she proposes that schizophrenics producing SL suffer from a "disruption in the ability to apply [p. 275]" syntactic and discourse rules. Sixth, she finds, finally, evidence for a disruption of speech monitoring, that is, a failure to detect errors.

It is interesting to note how little Chaika's (1974) account differs from that of Cromwell and Dokecki (1968) at a descriptive level. Indeed, their accounts even suffer from a number of the same limitations. Chaika, however, made no reference to Cromwell and Dokecki's article. Where they differ, of course, is mainly in their proposals regarding the origin of the peculiar features of SL. For Cromwell and Dokecki, these features can be traced generally to disruptions in underlying thought processes and more specifically to a cognitive attentional deficit rather than to a language disturbance that is independent of nonlinguistic cognitive disruptions.

With few exceptions, the disturbances that appear to characterize the schizophrenic speech samples Chaika (1974) cites appear to us to be semantic in origin. Syntactic-rule violations were rare and phonological violations nonexistent. Moreover, the intermittent nature of SL and the low frequency of occurrence of linguistic-rule violations does not suggest that schizophrenics who produce SL might be suffering from a disorder in the language production areas of the brain. Finally, it is not at all clear why the features she identifies, with the exception of the agrammatisms, should be considered to be *linguistic* in origin.

A claim that Chaika (1974) made, and one that we have not mentioned thus far, was that the errors she found in SL were not the same as those that are made normally, at least as far as the degree of disruption is concerned. This proposal has been challenged by Fromkin (1975), a student of speech errors. According to this observer, Chaika's six characteristics of SL are not unique but are found among the speech errors normal individuals make. In addition, Fromkin points out that normals frequently fail to correct their slips of the tongue. Moreover, Fromkin insists that what Chaika treats as being linguistic disruptions in discourse are really social and psychological in origin.

Thus, according to Fromkin (1975), what is disrupted in SL is not linguistic in origin nor unique to schizophrenics.

The question of the uniqueness of the types of disruptions found in SL has also been addressed by Lecours and Vanier-Clément (1976), who proposed, on the basis of their observations, that the disruptions in question are found in varying degrees in the speech of jargonaphasics, normals, and schizophrenics. Moreover, these investigators suggested among other things that the origin of the characteristics of SL is not linguistic but to be found in the thinking of schizophrenic speakers.

The results of a study of speech in mania are also relevant to the question of the uniqueness of SL. Although the report of their study is incomplete, Durbin and Martin's (1977) observations of the speech of six acute manic patients suggest that some overlap exists between aspects of SL and speech disruptions in mania.

DiSimoni, Darley, and Aronson (1977) examined the response patterns of chronic, neurologically intact schizophrenics on a battery of tests involving reading, writing, speaking, and listening. The subjects were 9 males and 18 females; all but one male was paranoid, whereas the females were more heterogeneous. Most of the subjects had received shock therapy; IQs ranged from 69 to 130 among 20 subjects on whom they had test data. The means for CA and years of education were, respectively, 36.3 and 11.3.

DiSimoni et al. (1977) mentioned that some of their subjects demonstrated obvious comprehension difficulties at the time of testing. Such subjects, however, were not excluded from the analysis. Moreover, according to these investigators, many of the subjects were anxious about the testing and expressed a constant desire for the session to end. Thus optimal performance may not have been obtained from these subjects.

The tests employed were based upon the aphasia battery of Halpern, Darley, and Brown (1973). Various dimensions of intellectual and language functioning were assessed via 30 subtests; these included auditory retention span, auditory comprehension, reading comprehension, writing, and expression of ideas. Most of the subtests were scored according to percentage errors. Expression of ideas (oral) was scored along four dimensions: syntactic correctness, adequacy (errors of substitution, deletion, and addition and degree of response elaboration), relevance (to the topic), and fluency (i.e., vocal hesitations). Although rescoring reliabilities were high, the scorer was evidently aware of the subjects' diagnoses and the same observer scored the protocols each time.

Among the findings in this investigation were the following: (1) the greatest percentage of errors occurred on the relevance dimension, whereas syntactic errors were infrequent and responses for the most part were adequate; (2) reading comprehension was also a problem area for these schizophrenics; (3) as far as rank is concerned, auditory comprehension performance fell midway between relevance and syntax. The range of individual differences on relevance and auditory comprehension, however, complicates the interpretation of these findings.

DiSimoni et al. (1977) also compared their subjects' performance with that of Halpern et al.'s (1973) subjects (aphasic, general intellectual impairment, apraxia of speech, and confused language). There are two major problems with their comparisons, however. First, no statistical analyses of the data were performed and, second, it was not possible to match the subject groups on any relevant variables (e.g., CA, IQ, duration of illness). As a result, group differences in test performance are impossible to interpret.

There appeared to be no dimension that uniquely distinguished schizophrenics from all other groups. There were overall differences between schizophrenics and aphasics, however. Unlike the former, the latter performed well on relevance but did have problems with adequacy, syntactic correctness, and auditory retention span.

Although we are unable to interpret DiSimoni et al.'s (1977) group comparisons, it does appear that the finding that, as a group, their schizophrenics encountered the greatest difficulty producing relevant responses is consistent with the observations others have made in the area of spontaneous speech. The reader will recall, however, our comments regarding subject selection, scoring reliability, and individual differences.

It would be of interest to determine how *subgroups* of schizophrenics perform on an aphasia test battery in comparison with appropriately matched *subgroups* of aphasic patients. We must hope, therefore, that other investigators will attempt to replicate DiSimoni et al.'s study with appropriate controls, data analyses, and reliability checks.

To return to our discussion of Chaika's (1974) proposals, Chaika attempted to respond to Fromkin (1975) and to Lecours and Vanier-Clément (1976) in a subsequent article (1977), although we do not say anything here regarding her comments concerning the latter. With respect to Fromkin's claim that the anomalies of SL do not differ from normal speech errors, Chaika points out that although the speech errors of normals can usually be understood with reference to available context, the deviant utterances of schizophrenics usually cannot, "although [they] can often be understood by reference to the rules of the language itself [p. 465]." Unfortunately, in the absence of a statistical rendition of "usually," it is impossible to evaluate Chaika's observation. In addition, the situation is further complicated by the absence of statistical estimates of the frequencies of occurrence of the various types of schizophrenic and normal errors. Moreover, no procedure is described for reliably determining when an utterance is not consistent with available context.

In a more specific vein, Chaika (1977) states, among other things, that: (1) the neologisms produced by schizophrenics are often not easily related to intended meanings; (2) schizophrenic word salads contain syntactic disruptions that are more severe than those we typically find in everyday speech errors; (3) some of the disruptions that characterize SL, although they may also occur in the speech of normals, are more severe, more persistent over discourse, and less subject to control by the speaker; (4) unlike normal slips of the tongue, the various disruptions in SL occur in combination; (5) rules of discourse use should be considered to be linguistic rather than social or psychological in origin; and (6) deviant thinking is not a necessary concomitant to linguistic deviance. Chaika (1977) concludes, finally: "I would revise my original analysis in that I now assume less difference between schizophasia [SL] and jargonaphasia than before. However, my assumption remains of a true break in normal language competence of schizophrenics [p. 474]."

Three ideas emerge from this second article of Chaika. First, the differences one observes between schizophrenics and normals as regards speech disruption are a matter of degree rather than of kind; second, there is a degree of contextual inappropriateness (although intermittent) in the content and structure of discourse that is to be considered as being symptomatic of a disorder that affects speech behavior; and, third, the disorder in question is one of linguistic competence or knowledge rather than of linguistic performance.

We cannot argue with the first two conclusions, because we feel that even the literature on SL prior to the appearance of Chaika's original article (1974) justifies (at least tentatively) these conclusions (or working hypotheses). It is still questionable, however, whether that literature plus Chaika's observations require the third conclusion. The predominantly semantic nature of the disruptions in SL and their intermittence and infrequency in the population of schizophrenics who display SL (based, of course, on our tentative informal estimates) are more indicative of a disorder that is nonlinguistic rather than linguistic in orgin.

Herbert and Waltensperger (1980) have recently reported on a case of a chronic paranoid schizophrenic who displayed some frequent agrammatic errors in speech and writing that are not typical of SL but are found in certain aphasic and other neurological conditions. They raised, however, the possibility that the patient in question was suffering from a secondary neurological disorder.

Rochester's Observations. Possibly the most systematic examination of discourse processes in schizophrenics, from a contemporary psycholinguistic standpoint, is to be found in the work of Rochester and her associates (Martin & Rochester, 1975; Rochester & Martin, 1977, 1979; Rochester, Martin, & Thurston, 1977; Rochester, Thurston, & Rupp, 1977). Our discussion, however, is limited to the recent book-length monograph by Rochester & Martin (1979), which is important not only because it presents new data but because it contains the most comprehensive critical review of the literature on SL that has appeared to date.

The subjects for their study were two groups of patients ($N = 10$ each) diagnosed as schizophrenic who did not display alcoholism or organic impairment and 10 normal control subjects. The two groups of schizophrenics, however, were the most closely matched of the three. Two groups of schizophrenic patients, thought-disordered (TD) and nonthought-disordered (NTD) were identified on the basis of independent evaluation by two psychiatrists of videotaped interviews and evaluation by lay judges. The psychiatrists applied criteria having to do with classical linguistic symptoms of "thought-disorder" (i.e., aberrant flow or coherence of speech rather than aberrant content or topic) and the lay judges then checked the protocols for incoherence. The resulting match between the lay judges and the clinical assessments was close. Incoherence in 7% or more of a schizophrenic's sentences resulted in a diagnosis of thought-process-disorder, or thought-disorder for short.

The schizophrenic subjects were relatively young, in their mid 20s on the average, and had similar vocabulary scores and educational backgrounds. Almost all the schizophrenic subjects were on medication. The speech samples analyzed by Rochester and Martin (1979) were derived from three contexts: interviews, a task in which subjects were asked to describe and then explain cartoons and one that involved retelling a narrative.

In brief, the chief question these investigators asked was what is the basis for the incoherence in the speech of TD schizophrenics? The answer they achieved was made possible in large measure by the application of Halliday and Hasan's (1976) linguistic analysis of cohesion in English discourse.

It will not be possible for us to summarize all the interesting observations made by Rochester and Martin. We have to limit ourselves to the highlights. In one set of analyses, context (i.e., task) contributed more to discourse cohesion than did group differences. Thus both the normals and the schizophrenics were sensitive to differential task demands. The narratives produced by the schizophrenics as a group were less cohesive than those the normal subjects produced, however. The investigators were unable to explain the TD schizophrenics' lowered cohesion here, but lower productivity was invoked as a possible explanation of the NTD speakers' performance. Another finding of interest is that during interviews, the TD subjects exceeded their NTD counterparts in their use of lexical cohesion (i.e., cohesion through interclause word repetition, root repetition, synonymity, or superordinate–subordinate relatedness), although there were individual differences noted. Moreover, as Rochester and Martin (1979) note, high degrees of lexical cohesion in the TD group *did not appear to serve to maintain the topic of conversation* (because of the production of context-irrelevant phonological and/or semantic associations; i.e., constrained or limited lexical usage), a not unexpected finding, given the earlier literature on SL, as Rochester and Martin indicate. Also, because this tendency was only found in the unstructured interviews, we have further confirmation of the intermittent nature of schizophrenic speech disruptions.

It should be emphasized at this juncture that, according to Rochester and Martin's analysis, excluded from SL or schizophasic language in the case of TD schizophrenics, is discourse that is coherent but contains bizarre or strange content. It is also interesting to note that Rochester and Martin's TD features are included among Chaika's (1974) features of SL and that Chaika also excludes coherent but bizarre content from her formulation. Moreover, for Chaika also, schizophrenic speech disruptions are intermittent. Where these investigators appear to differ is in regard to the features of agrammatisms, gibberish, neologisms, and self-monitoring.

The Cromwell and Dokecki (1968) analysis, it is recalled, also tends to include only intermittently incoherent speech segments, as well as gibberish, neologisms, agrammatisms, and self-monitoring deficit as aspects of SL.

In subsequent analyses, Rochester and Martin (1979) turned their attention, for example, to the reference system of nominal groups in discourse that is used to talk about the participants. This system is one of several "phoricity" systems in English that serve to "structure utterances on the basis of what speakers assume their listeners know [p. 103]." Their interest, furthermore, was in the "referring which occurs within language [p. 103]" rather than with reference to the nonlinguistic environment and, in particular, in how much a speaker helps a listener identify referenced participants.

As in the previous analysis, Rochester and Martin (1979) found evidence of task effects and both similarities and differences among their groups. We summarize their findings only briefly.

On the basis of a summary discriminant function analysis, they indicate that their TD subjects differed from the other groups in that they displayed "problems with systems which present and presume information [p. 174]" and a dependence on lexical features for discourse linkage. The disruptions, however, were clearly intermittent rather than continuous and appeared in a tendency to depend on situational context (both nonlinguistic and earlier linguistic) rather than on their own immediate verbal resources.

Thus, according to these investigators, the problems that TD speakers have are not the kinds that produce word salads, neologisms, or word-finding failures but are organized at the level of discourse encoding. They point out, however, subsequently, that their findings regarding grammatical and morphological deviance need to be checked using controlled assessment procedures. The discourse disruption was described, finally, as an occasional failure "to use sufficiently elaborate verbal encoding strategies [p. 203]" to meet the needs of the listener.

In their attempt to explain their findings, Rochester and Martin (1979) make a number of observations. Among them are the following: (1) because the appropriate data are not available, we cannot determine whether the discourse failures of TD schizophrenics are related, or reduceable, to any impairments in general information-processing capabilities; (2) although there is little to suggest that TD speakers are suffering from a form of intermittent aphasia from the observations made thus far regarding syntax, morphology, lexicon, phonology, and intonation, inasmuch as the structures of discourse cohesion they analyzed are also linguistic (or chiefly so) and there is some evidence of left-hemisphere brain dysfunctioning in schizophrenia (but see our later discussion of the relevant literature), we must keep an open mind on the issue of whether TD speakers are suffering from some form of language disorder, although, given the results of the research on mania, the problem may be one associated with certain psychoses rather than one that occurs only in certain schizophrenics; (3) although there is evidence of left-hemisphere involvement (and possibly some right-hemisphere involvement as well) in TD schizophrenics, associated with a condition of high emotional arousal, we must not forget that their speech is, for the most part, mature and free of disruptions; (4) there is reason to hypothesize that increased responsivity to phenothiazine played a role in the results for NTD schizophrenics.

One limitation of Rochester and Martin's (1979) investigation is that there was no attempt to ascertain the incidence of coherent semantically bizarre or strange utterances in their TD and NTD subjects and to submit samples of such utterances to analyses for discourse cohesion. But, then, this is not a problem unique to their study. Second, it will be necessary to replicate their study using a wider variety of schizophrenic subjects so as to be able to relate the linguistic findings to the three-way classification (i.e., premorbid adjustment, and so on) discussed by Cromwell (1975) and others.

Other limitations of this study are discussed by the authors themselves and, therefore, are not discussed here.

Other studies. Levy (1968) examined changes in the spontaneous speech of four schizophrenics due to chlorphromazine as measured by proportion of subordinate clauses. Speech was elicited in four conditions: psychiatric interview, description of pictures, proverb interpretation, and expressing opinions on abstract topics. All subjects were tested: (1) on admission, at which time they were off medication; (2) approximately a week later and 2 days after starting to receive a standard dosage of chlorpromazine; and (3) at recovery, with no attempt to control for medication dosage between testings 2 and 3. It is clear, however, that drug condition was seriously confounded with the "natural course" of the disorder as well as with repeated testing, making Levy's results ambiguous.

Levy (1968) found that: (1) in the abstract topics and proverb interpretation conditions, there was a drop in the proportion of subordinate clauses from admission to on-drug; (2) there were significant increases in that proportion from admission to recovery phase in the proverb and interview conditions; and (3) there were no drug-associated changes in the description condition, which exhibited the lowest proportion of subordinate clauses of all four speech-eliciting conditions. Levy concluded that chlorpromazine at first decreases the structural complexity of spontaneous speech, with subsequent recovery of complexity, this effect being evident only in situations eliciting structurally complex speech. The confounding noted here, however, makes this conclusion speculative.

Smith (1970) studied schizophrenics' communication abilities within the framework of the Rosenberg and Cohen (1966) model. In the task employed by Rosenberg and Cohen, one word of a pair (e.g., *robber–thief*) is designated as referent and the speaker's task is to provide a one-word clue that will allow a listener to select the referent over the nonreferent of the pair. Rosenberg and

Cohen hypothesized that the mature speaker first covertly produces a free associate to the referent. The speaker then edits the potential clue by comparing its relative associative strengths to the referent and nonreferent (i.e., by determining its potential communicative effectiveness).

Smith (1970) hypothesized that the purported communication deficit of schizophrenics is localized at the second, comparison, stage and reported results he felt were consistent with this expectation. The speakers in this investigation were a group of normal and a group of thought-disordered schizophrenics matched on age and education. The subjects as a group were of normal or above verbal IQ. Most of the schizophrenic subjects were receiving medication. The listeners were normal undergraduates.

We are fortunate to have available a detailed review by Cohen (1978) of the research he has carried out with his associates on referential communication processes in schizophrenics, mainly acute patients. On the basis of his examination of the literature on SL, Cohen proposes that the speech of schizophrenics displays "a disturbance of communication rather than of language per se; its most dependable feature is that listeners find the patient's referents too elusive to grasp [p. 1]." Of particular interest to the present review is Cohen's discussion of a study of referential communication in which the task involved the description of colored discs varying in number and degree of similarity. The subjects were acute, first-admission, nonparanoid schizophrenics who were not on medication during the experiment and normal hospital employees. Among other things, Cohen noted that task complexity tended to decrease communicability of the schizophrenics' descriptions to a greater extent than it did the normals'. Moreover, the schizophrenics' descriptions of the referents tended, on the average, to be longer than those of the normals and, in a number of instances, to stray from the requirements of the task, as, for example, in the following excerpts from the Appendix of Cohen's (1978) article.

-It's blue. Makes me sick.
-A blue only matched by Hilda's eye. Rip it out! Fast!
-Oy vehs mir! This is what a color is? This is what I have to talk about? This here? Such a color? Like a can of salmon. Maybe some vinegar. Eat. [pp. 27, 29]

According to Cohen (1978), "Perhaps the single most distinctive feature of the schizophrenics' lengthy utterances was this tendency for responses to lose their connection with the referent [p. 18]."

In the remainder of his review article, Cohen addresses himself to such matters as the extension of the research with acute schizophrenics to chronic patients and an essentially information-processing explanation of the disruptions in schizophrenics' referent communication capabilities.

A number of recent studies have attempted to distinguish the spontaneous speech of schizophrenics from that of various nonschizophrenic controls on the basis of the ease with which typed transcripts of the speech are comprehended by normal adults. The most popular variant of this approach has employed the cloze procedure (Taylor, 1953). In this procedure, transcripts of samples of schizophrenic connected discourse, with words deleted (typically every fourth or fifth word), are presented to normal adults for completion. The cloze score for each passage is the number of words filled in correctly (i.e., verbatim). This score is supposed to be a measure of the extent to which the person completing the passage can use the surrounding verbal context to guess the missing words. Presumably, linguistic (e.g., semantic, syntactic, pragmatic) deviancies within the passage will make the context less useful and result in a lower cloze score. The cloze scores for schizophrenic passages are compared to those of various controls (e.g., normals). Such studies typically hypothesize that schizophrenic passages will have lower cloze scores than those of normals.

Studies that rely on the comprehension performance of normals as a means of distinguishing schizophrenic and nonschizophrenic speech display some methodological flaws. For example, in these studies the exact topics of discussion are not always identical for the schizophrenic and control groups, and therefore group differences in cloze scores or other measures of comprehensibility are difficult to interpret. A more appropriate method of eliciting speech would rely on, for example, a standard set of pictures to be described. Second, as stated previously, the subjects whose comprehension serves as the measure of deviant speech are typically normals. Presumably, such subjects will be more familiar with the life experiences and knowledge of other normals than with those of schizophrenics. This alone might lead to better comprehension of the former's than the latter's speech.

Manschreck, Maher, Rucklos, and White (1979) employed the cloze method in order to compare the predictability of schizophrenic and normal speech. The schizophrenics, however, were also older ($\bar{X}$ CA = 29) and less educated ($\bar{X}$ = 12.6 years) than the normals ($\bar{X}$ CA = 24, $\bar{X}$ education = 15.6 years), although these researchers did not test these differences statistically. Additionally, two of the eight "normal" controls, in fact, had psychiatric problems. Moreover, no IQ data were presented. Most of the schizophrenics were receiving medication. These initial differences, of course, make it difficult to determine the source of any normal–schizophrenic differences in cloze scores. The schizophrenics were identified and subcategorized as TD or NTD on the basis of interview ratings on the Schedule for Affective Disorders and Schizophrenia (Spitzer & Endicott, 1975) and the Research Diagnostic Criteria (Spitzer, Endicott, & Robbins, 1975). TD and NTD subjects did not differ in age, education, chronicity, presence of hallucinatory or delusional symptoms, severity of illness, or medication. The subjects described a painting and their descriptions were transcribed into fourth- and fifth-word deletion versions. In transcribing, vocal hesitations were excluded.

Manschreck et al. (1979) found that although there were no significant differences in the groups' mean cloze scores for the fourth-word deletions, on the fifth-word deletions, TD schizophrenics' cloze scores were significantly lower than those of the other two groups who did not differ. These researchers concluded that the predictability of TD schizophrenic speech only is deficient relative to normals' speech.

Unfortunately, there are a number of methodological (including statistical) problems with the Manschreck et al. (1979) study, in addition to those already mentioned, that make their results ambiguous.

In contrast to Manschreck et al.'s findings, Rutter, Draffan, and Davies (1977) had earlier found no relation between spontaneous speech, as measured by cloze scores, and the presence of thought disorder in acute schizophrenics ($\bar{X}$ CA = 34.5). Thought disorder was assessed on the "intensity" and "consistency" scales of Bannister and Fransella (1966). Four normal undergraduates completed fourth- and fifth-word deletion versions of each schizophrenic's spontaneously produced passage.[1]

Silverman (1973), still earlier, had hypothesized that schizophrenic speech is characterized by frequent, inappropriate repetitions; therefore, both the Type Token Ratio (TTR; a measure of vocabulary diversity) and the cloze scores for such speech will be lower than for normal speech. Subjects' monologues were transcribed into fourth- and fifth-word deletion versions and submitted to three normals and one psychiatric patient for completion. TTRs were calculated for the same passages. It is important to note that a standard set of speech-eliciting topics was not employed. The subject groups consisted of eight "active" schizophrenics judged to be TD and seven subjects who showed no signs of active schizophrenia; the latter included normals, remitted schizophrenics, and other psychiatric patients. Given the mixed nature of the control group, the meaning of group comparisons on the dependent measures is not at all clear. Moreover, although the two groups did not differ significantly in age, no other relevant subject characteristics were presented (e.g., IQ, education).

Before considering Silverman's (1973) results, it should be noted that the statistical analyses were questionable. For example, although most subjects contributed only one speech passage, others contributed two, but the correlation between passages of the same subject was not considered. Silverman found that the schizophrenic passages had significantly lower cloze scores than those of the controls. It was also observed that cloze and TTR scores were significantly positively correlated. This result is meaningless, however, because the correlation holds only for a biased subset of the sample. Specifically, Silverman excluded two schizophrenics from the correlational analysis who differed from other group members *on the dependent measures,* on the basis of a reanalysis of their clinical records. Obviously this maneuver biased the data in favor of the initial expectations.

---

[1]Manschreck et al. (1979) suggested that Rutter et al. (1977) had actually misclassified their schizophrenics. Thus their TD group probably included some NTD patients.

Hart and Payne (1973); Moroz and Fosmire (1966); Rutter, Wishner, Kopytynska, and Button (1978); Salzinger, Portnoy, and Feldman (1964); and Silverman (1972) have also utilized the cloze procedure to assess the predictability of schizophrenic speech, but we mention these studies only in passing.

Although they did not employ the cloze procedure, Gerver, Lawson, and Gerver (1976) did rely on normal adults' comprehension of schizophrenics' and normals' speech as the basis for differentiating the two. Gerver et al. elicited language samples on standard topics (i.e., responses to two questions of the WAIS comprehension subtest) from schizophrenics ($\bar{X}$ CA = 30; $\bar{X}$ IQ = 101.2), other psychiatric patients ($\bar{X}$ CA = 35; $\bar{X}$ IQ = 102.9), and normals ($\bar{X}$ CA = 31.7; $\bar{X}$ IQ = 106.7). The schizophrenic group, unlike the other groups, was predominantly male. This confounding of sex ratio and diagnosis, of course, complicates interpretation of the results. Typed transcripts of the speech samples were rated by first-year clinical psychology students on a set of adjectives derived from those commonly used to describe schizophrenic speech (e.g., *abnormal, schizophrenic, confused, tangential, metaphorical*) and from those of Danks and Glucksberg (1970: "meaningful," "ungrammatical," and "familiar").

Gerver et al. (1976) found that the groups were discriminated on only the adjective "inappropriate" on one question and the adjective "metaphorical" on another. Because these were the only significant differences out of 30 separate univariate analyses of variance, it is clear that the speech of the groups was not differentiated by the raters.

Rutter (1979) also relied on normals' comprehension to discriminate schizophrenic from normal speech, although he did not employ the cloze method. Rutter obtained uninterrupted speech samples from nonparanoid schizophrenics and normal medical patients. The conversational topic was the "reason for hospitalization." Transcripts of the passages were divided into sentences and the divisions were then compared with those of five normals. (Unfortunately, contrary to Rutter's claim, interrater agreement was low.) The sentences, as determined by the original transcriber, were each typed on separate cards. The cards for a passage were presented in random order (with the exception that the lead sentence was identified) to undergraduates whose task was to order them correctly. The dependent variable was the number of correct transitions between the sentences in the orderings of the undergraduates. It should be noted that vocal hesitations were not excluded from the transcripts.

Rutter (1979) found that overall the reconstruction scores did not differ for the normal and schizophrenic passages. However, there were more correct orderings of three or more sentences than of two sentences for the normal passages but not for the schizophrenic passages. Rutter concluded that there is "a detectable abnormality in schizophrenic speech which affects its comprehensibility but that it stems from the relationships *between* sentences rather than the content of individual sentences [p. 359]."

Recently, some investigators have compared the pattern of silent (unfilled) pauses and vocal hesitations in the spontaneous speech of schizophrenics and normals. Most psycholinguists studying dysfluencies in normal speech (Boomer, 1965; Butterworth & Goldman-Eisler, 1979; Goldman-Eisler, 1968) have assumed that hesitations index forward speech planning. Researchers studying schizophrenic speech have taken a similar position. (See Rosenberg, 1977, however, for a critique of this assumption.)

In the study discussed previously, Silverman (1973) also hypothesized that the inappropriate speech of schizophrenics is the result of a failure to plan and, consequently, to pause and, therefore: (1) their pause-time/speech-time ratio should be less than that of normals; and (2) cloze scores, TTRs, and pause/speech ratios should be positively correlated. These hypotheses received no support, however.

As pointed out earlier, Rochester and Martin (1979) have shown that TD speakers sometimes have difficulty generating coherent sequences of clauses. It is interesting to note that they also display a tendency to produce *longer* silent hesitations at clause boundaries than do other subjects, accompanied by *fewer* voiced hesitations at clause boundaries during interviews (Rochester, Thurston, & Rupp, 1977). The source of this pattern of vocal and silent hesitations is still to be determined, however.

Clemmer (1980) compared the patterns of speech dysfluencies of schizophrenics and normals within the paradigm of O'Connell and his colleagues (O'Connell & Kowal, 1972; O'Connell, Kowal, & Hörmann, 1969; Sabin, Clemmer, O'Connell, & Kowal, 1979). Subjects read aloud and then retold stories; one version contained a contradiction in a target sentence (the "unusual" version), another did not (the "ordinary" version). Interpretation of the results, however, is complicated by the fact that the ordinary story was always presented prior to the unusual one. There were two subject groups, one schizophrenic and the other normal. Pairs of subjects were matched (across groups) on race, sex, educational level, and age. The schizophrenics varied in terms of subtype, length of hospitalization, and chronicity, and two of the 20 had received partial lobotomies. All schizophrenics were receiving medication.

Before considering Clemmer's results, it should be noted that in one phase of data analysis four separate univariate analyses of variance were performed for each of 24 dysfluency variables, many of which could be expected to be significant by chance alone. Clemmer does not consider this possibility in discussing his findings, however. Moreover, failure to include a psychiatric control raises questions as to whether any observed difference in the hesitation behavior of schizophrenics relative to normals is unique to that disorder or characterizes some larger set of mental patients. But this is a common control failure in studies of SL.

Clemmer (1980) observed that in reading aloud the schizophrenics were less fluent than the normals on various measures (e.g., more frequent pauses, longer reading times, more frequent vocal hestiations, and slower speech rates). Most of these differences were found for only one or the other of the story contents employed. Clemmer concluded that schizophrenics are less fluent readers than normals. Four points regarding this conclusion need to be made, however. First, although the groups were equated on education, there was no attempt to match them on the basis of a *current* assessment of their reading skills; perhaps Clemmer's findings indicate only that poor readers are less fluent than average readers regardless of diagnosis. Second, Clemmer's finding concerning reading was that both groups were affected similarly by the version manipulation; both were less fluent on the unusual than on the ordinary stories. Thus even if schizophrenics are less fluent readers than normals, they do not differ qualitatively from normals. Third, a number of diagnosis × sex interactions qualified the conclusion that schizophrenics are less fluent readers than normals: (1) for one story content, the difference between speech and articulation (speech minus pause) rates was greater for schizophrenic than for normal women, but the reverse was true for males; and (2) for one story content, mean silent pause duration was greater in the unusual than in the ordinary version for normal men and schizophrenic women but not for the schizophrenic males and normal females. Finally, discriminant analyses (a more appropriate statistical analysis than separate univariate analyses of variance) indicated that diagnosis could not be reliably discriminated on the basis of the reading fluency measures. Thus Clemmer's conclusions regarding reading fluency appear unwarranted.

For the retellings, all significant group differences were limited to one of the two story contents. Schizophrenics produced vocal hesitations more frequently than normals and, although both subject groups produced more vocal hestiations in retelling unusual than ordinary stories, the difference was greater for normals due to the fact that normals produced few hesitations on the ordinary stories. For this same story content, discriminant analyses distinguished between diagnostic groups for the ordinary but not for the unusual versions. Clemmer (1980) interprets these results as consistent with studies of sentence memory (Truscott, 1970), indicating a schizophrenic deficit in the ability to use increased contextual constraint to guide memorial processes.

Andreasen (1979a) has developed the Scale for the Assessment of Thought, Language, and Communication, a set of 18 dimensions or categories for describing aspects of spontaneous speech. Moreover, it is claimed (Andreasen, 1979b) that schizophrenics can be distinguished from other disordered populations along these dimensions. Most of the dimensions, Andreasen claims, describe those aspects of language usually taken to be indicative of thought disorder rather than any specifically linguistic deficit.

Andreasen (1979a) attempted to assess the reliabilities of the separate dimensions of the scale. Associated with each dimension is a rating scale. Interrater reliabilities were computed for two scorers' ratings of the live or taped interview behavior of groups of manics, depressives, and schizophrenics. The interview questions ranged from personal to impersonal and from concrete to abstract. Andreasen found that, of the dimensions that were applied by the scorers frequently enough to be assessed, most demonstrated moderate, acceptable levels of reliability.

Two points need to be made concerning Andreasen's assessment of reliabilities and the scale in general. First, the dimensions are not mutually exclusive, and raters employed as many dimensions as they felt were needed to describe the language performance of any given subject. This makes it difficult to assess the reliabilities computed for the separate dimensions. Specifically, if the raters could not distinguish between two or more dimensions because they were conceptually similar or their boundaries were vague, they may have treated these dimensions as forming a single superordinate category and applied the dimensions together. In this regard, Andreasen (1979b) did find positive correlations between many of the categories; this might indicate these characteristics are distinct but tend to occur together in subjects' speech or simply that the raters could not discriminate between them so that if one was applied to a subject the related ones were as well. Second, a more general problem with the scale is that ratings (in both Andreasen 1979a and 1979b) were carried out at the end of the interview. The scale is not designed to include actual, ongoing behavior frequency counts as the basis for dimension decisions; the ratings, therefore, are dependent on the raters' general impressions, memory, and skill in detecting sometimes subtle evidence of the presence in subjects' speech of the various dimensions. Because of the subjective nature of the ratings, additional methodological problems arise.

Andreasen (1979b) used the Scale for the Assessment of Thought, Language, and Communication to rate the language of CA- and education-matched groups of schizophrenics, manics, and depressives. The subjects met the appropriate criteria according to Spitzer et al. (1975). Most subjects were receiving medication and most were tested within the first week of hospitalization, while they still showed severe symptoms. The diagnostic groups differed somewhat in number of prior hospitalizations and on their sex ratios. Two raters judged the subjects at the end of either live or taped interviews.

Among Andreasen's results were the following: (1) many dimensions occurred rarely, even some thought to be important indicators of schizophrenic language and thought disorder, such as neologisms (Vetter, 1968b), incoherence, or word salad and clanging (i.e., rhyming); (2) most manics and schizophrenics received global ratings of thought disorder but few depressives did; however (3) schizophrenics were characterized as having a "negative" thought disorder as expressed by poverty of speech (i.e., not very talkative, speak primarily when required to, answer questions with brief utterances) and poverty of content (i.e., adequate in amount but conveys little information; rambling), although manics had a positive thought disorder characterized primarily by pressure of speech (i.e., extremely fast rate of speaking) and distractability (i.e., stopping in the middle of a sentence to talk about something in the immediate environment); and (4) not all the schizophrenic subjects exhibited negative thought disorder. Needless to say, in the main, Andreasen's findings overlap those of Rochester and Martin (1979) and others.

Harrow and Prosen (1979) have claimed that a significant aspect of schizophrenics' disordered language is an "intermingling" of irrelevant material (from past or current experiences) with their current language topic; that is, the schizophrenic is unable to inhibit the verbal expression of inappropriate (to the current conversational context) associations. The subjects, all of whom were in the acute stage of their disorders, were schizophrenics (paranoid and nonparanoid as determined by the New Haven Schizophrenia Index) and psychiatric patients matched on mean CA, education, and WAIS IQ. There were three stages of data collection: (I) language samples were elicited via a standard set of questions; (II) a week later, a standard set of questions was employed to seek the subjects' reasons for their responses in the previous phase; and (III) the reasons were rated for the source of bizarre responses (e.g., concrete thought, faculty logic, intermingling).

Harrow and Prosen (1979) claim that, in Stage III, interrater reliabilities were satisfactory; however, this claim is difficult to evaluate because no data were provided. Additionally, it is not clear whether the raters were blind to the subjects' diagnoses. Finally, one must raise the question as to whether a rater can ever be blind to diagnosis. Specifically, some aspect of a subject's verbal and/or nonverbal behavior may indicate the presence of a form of schizophrenia. Clearly, this might bias the raters' subjsequent judgments, especially if the raters were knowledgeable as to the specific hypotheses or the purported general features of schizophrenic language.

Not surprisingly, Harrow and Prosen (1979) found, on the basis of the ratings, evidence of intermingling in most of the schizophrenics and many of the psychiatric patients. Moreover, for both subject populations, the intermingled material appeared to be from a number of areas of their personal past experiences rather than from one central concern. These researchers concluded that "these strange verbalizations are based on rationales which make sense in terms of patients' own experiences when looked at from their points of view [p. 295]." The patients deficit, according to Harrow and Prosen, involves an inability and/or unwillingness to monitor language to inhibit this intermingling. (See also Andreasen & Pfohl, 1976; Harrow & Prosen, 1978; Rosenberg & Tucker, 1979; Siegel, Harrow, Reilly, & Tucker, 1976).

Methodological issues aside, intermingling, it should be pointed out, is what appears to characterize the subject protocols reproduced in Cohen's (1978) article (pp. 26-33), inasmuch as the schizophrenic subjects appear to have departed from the requirements of the task to interject personal matter that is not known to the listener. The referential communication task used by Cohen and others appears to be particularly useful for generating samples of SL and it has the advantages, moreover, of standard stimulus and task conditions, nonnoxious stimuli, and an objectively defined domain of reference. A possible disadvantage, however, is that it is artificial.

Rutter (1977a, 1977b) has recently examined the verbal and visual conversational behavior of schizophrenics; only results concerning verbal communication are considered here, however. Rutter (1977a) compared the conversational behavior of groups of schizophrenics, depressives, neurotics and personality disorders, and normal medical patients. Group comparisons are complicated, however, because no data were provided on IQ, CA, education, medication, or other relevant variables. Dyadic conversations were obtained from each subject in each of two conditions: with a normal person and with a person of the same diagnostic category. It should be noted that in the latter condition the members of the dyad were matched only on diagnosis; therefore, the members of medical-patient dyads were also more likely to be matched on other relevant variables such as IQ than any of the psychiatric dyads because the former were presumably in the normal IQ range, whereas the latter may not have been. Similarly, within the psychiatric dyads the severity of the disorder may have differed in the two members, thus introducing an additional source of variance not present in the normal medical patients. Thus, interpretation of group differences is further complicated.

Among the 15 speech measures examined were the following: percentage of conversational time spent speaking; total number of spoken words; mean length of utterance (in words); percentage of conversational time spent in parallel speech (i.e., both participants speaking at the same time); percentage of conversational time spent in silence; percentage of utterances terminating as questions; speech disturbance ratio (filled pauses, stutters, etc.); and the frequency of acknowledgments (e.g., *mm–hmm*). It should be noted before discussing the results that the statistical analyses employed were inappropriate. First, separate univariate analyses of variance were carried out for each of the dependent measures; multivariate analysis of variance would have been more appropriate. Second, in some cases *t*-tests on selected comparisons were performed after analyses of variance had yielded no significant effects.

In general, there were few significant differences between the groups, but given the numerous separate analyses performed a few significant effects could be expected by chance. First, medical patients spent a greater percentage of time in parallel speech and used more acknowledgments than the other groups. Second, in the normal partner condition, schizophrenics tended to use shorter utterances and produced fewer speech disturbances than the other groups, although in the same partner condition they produced questions more frequently and acknowledgments less frequently. Finally, all groups behaved similarly in the two conversational situations. This last finding is difficult to interpret, because the normal medical patients were, in essence, conversing with members of the same diagnostic group in both conditions, whereas psychiatric subjects were not. It might be expected, then, that if the psychiatric patients were capable of adjusting their messages to their listeners' levels, their behavior might differ across different listeners; that it did not might indicate a deficit rather than conversational skill. It should also be mentioned that only 5 minutes of conversation were obtained from each subject in each condition. Such a small sample may not be sufficient to capture the conversational skills and/or deficits of the groups.

In a second study, Rutter (1977a) found no differences between chronic (hospitalized continuously for 2 years or more) and recently admitted schizophrenics on any of the speech measures in their conversations with normals. However, here again, although the groups were of (roughly) the same CAs, there was no indication that they were matched on IQ, medication, or other relevant variables.

Rutter (1977b) examined the conversations of remitted and acute schizophrenics and normal medical patients. Although the subjects of all groups ranged in age from 18 to 60, it appears that there was no attempt to match the groups on CA or other relevant variables. Each subject discussed personal/emotional and neutral topics with a female nurse in a dyadic situation. The speech measures employed were the same as those of Rutter (1977a). There were no group differences on any of the speech measures and all groups spoke more and had more parallel speech on the emotional than on the neutral topics.

Rausch, Prescott, and De Wolfe (1980) compared sentence production in recently admitted (2 to 6 months current hospitalization) schizophrenics (process and reactive), left-hemisphere-damaged aphasics, and normals via a task in which subjects ordered sentences whose words had been scrambled. Kolers, Park, and Dell (1979) have studied normals' performance in a similar task and argued that sentence production abilities are being assessed, but this is open to question. Rausch et al.'s groups were matched on CA and educational level. In the "cards" task, each word of a sentence appeared on a separate card and subjects were to place them in the proper sequence. In the "graphics" task, the entire scrambled sentence was presented on a single card and subjects were to write the correctly ordered sentence. Various syntactic structures were employed. Aphasics took longer to complete both tasks and correctly ordered fewer sentences in both tasks than did normals and schizophrenics, who did not differ significantly. The only significant difference between schizophrenics and normals was on sentences that contained both direct and indirect objects; the former made more reordering errors than the latter, but both made fewer errors than aphasics. Process and reactive schizophrenics were not significantly different on any measure.

Watson (1974) tested the hypothesis that schizophrenics are deficient in monitoring auditory feedback, which might, presumably, be one of the causes of their supposedly disordered speech. Subjects read prose passages under conditions of delayed auditory feedback (DAF) and natural feedback. Subjects were normal hearing process schizophrenics, reactive schizophrenics, and normal medical patients matched on CA (29.0, 32.8, and 33.6, respectively) and education (11.6, 11.6, and 11.7 years, respectively). The schizophrenic groups were also matched on length of hospitalization and all were receiving phenothiazenes or similar drugs. The schizophrenic subtypes were distinguished on the basis of their scores on the Ullmann-Giovannoni Process-Reactive Scale (Ullmann & Giovannoni, 1964).

Watson (1974) found that the time needed to read the passage was longer in the DAF than in the natural feedback condition and that the disruptive effects of DAF were attenuated only if a narrow range of feedback frequencies were transmitted in the delay conditions. Although the groups differed in mean reading time in all conditions, with process schizophrenics being the slowest, all were similarly affected by DAF; that is, neither process nor reactive schizophrenics differed from normals in their ability to monitor auditory feedback. Moreover, as Watson suggests, group differences in mean reading times might have been due to differences in drug dosages.

The majority of the studies reviewed in this section on *other studies* display serious methodological and/or statistical flaws and, as a result, we are unable to feel confident with their findings. Methodological and statistical problems abound in the cloze studies, and there have been some conflicting findings, but the trend appears to be for speech samples of schizophrenics to generate lower cloze scores. Needless to say, it would be interesting to determine cloze performance for the passages examined by Rochester and Martin (1979) and the referential communication protocols in Cohen (1978). Given these investigators' observations concerning discourse cohesion and topic maintenance, one would expect that the cloze scores for the SL portions of their protocols would be lower than those for the nondisrupted portions.

The reader interested in schizophrenic speech comprehensibility will want to examine the review by Salzinger et al. (1978), which we mention in passing. Although interpreted differently, the findings they discuss are not inconsistent with those of Rochester and Martin (1979).

With the exception of Rochester, Thurston, and Rupp (1977), the research on vocal and silent hesitations is not without its methodological and statistical problems. What appear to be needed here, in addition to obvious methodological and statistical improvements, are, among other things, comparisons among incoherent, coherent but bizarre, and nondisrupted speech samples of TD and NTD speakers (with appropriate controls) as to silent and vocal hesitations. However, even if reliable data on speech dysfluencies in schizophrenia become available, we still face the important task of identifying, unambiguously, the psycholinguistic, information-processing, and other (e.g., affective) functions of such disruptions in both normal speakers and subgroups of schizophrenics (Rosenberg, 1977).

Although confounded, the findings of the research by Andreasen (1979a, 1979b) and the work on intermingling overlap with other findings in the literature regarding the features of SL. Finally, the most productive program of research on SL we encountered in the present series of studies was that on referential communication processes, for reasons cited previously.

SCHIZOPHRENIC COMPREHENSION

Because of the episodic nature of SL and schizophrenic symptomatology generally, standard short-term laboratory studies of language comprehension in schizophrenics need to be interpreted with care.[2] We have no counterpart to the technique used by Rochester and Martin (1979) and others that first identifies samples of spontaneous incoherent speech and then attempts to determine the reasons for the incoherence. Moreover, the task of deciding upon the language materials to be used in a study of comprehension is not without its problems. Do we use materials that display features of SL or do we use normal materials?

We could, of course, attempt to measure comprehension performance repeatedly in previously identified TD speakers, but we would have to deal, then, not only with the problem of the episodic nature of SL and the materials problem but with the problem of repeated testing as well.

Included in the present section are studies that used standard language comprehension tasks from the basic experimental psycholinguistic laboratory as well as studies of sentence and discourse memory, the latter for the reason that input comprehension can be expected to play an important role in determining the level and organization of memorial performance (Bransford & McCarrell, 1974). In addition, language comprehension and memorial tasks are frequently difficult to distinguish, because they both involve input encoding and memorial processes. Where they differ is in the fact that in memorial tasks subjects are typically presented with more input than can be reproduced in a single pass, which introduces the problem of determining whether forgetting reflects original encoding, memory maintenance activities (rehearsal), or retrieval processes, or some combination of these variables.

Deckner and Blanton (1969) exployed the cloze method to examine schizophrenics' ability to use contextual constraints. The subjects completed tenth-, eighth-, and fifth-word deletion versions of a standard set of prose passages. These authors reasoned that if schizophrenics simply ignore context when responding (i.e., are overexclusive) they will be unaffected by the rate of deletion; however, if they are overinclusive, their performance should deteriorate as the amount of context increases. The performance of normal subjects should, on the other hand, improve from the fifth- to the tenth-word deletion versions. Deckner and Blanton's schizophrenics were divided into good and poor premorbid groups on the basis of their scores on Phillips' Scale of Premorbid Adjustment (Phillips,

---

[2]This concern also applies to studies such as that of Watson (1974).

1953). The former also had a shorter duration of illness as measured by years since first hospitalization (7.09 and 9.93, respectively). A normal control was also included. The groups were matched on age, and PPVT IQ, and all the subjects had completed at least the sixth grade, were able to read at a fifth-grade or better level, and all were male. There was no mention of whether the schizophrenics were on medication, however.

Deckner and Blanton found that although schizophrenics did poorer overall (a finding that could be due to any number of variables), all three groups were equally affected by the deletion variable (i.e., performance was best on the tenth-word and worst on the fifth-word deletion versions). Evidently, the schizophrenics based their responses on contextual constraints just as did the normals.

deSilva and Hemsley (1977) also employed the cloze procedure to investigate acute and chronic schizophrenics' and normals' comprehension. These investigators reasoned that if Broen (1968) was correct, and acutes are overinclusive and chronics are overexclusive, then the performance of the former group should deteriorate as the amount of available contextual information increases, whereas the latter should be unaffected by rate of deletion. deSilva and Hemsley employed fourth-, seventh-, and tenth-word deletion versions of standard prose passages. Although the normals and the combined schizophrenic group did not differ in CA or WAIS vocabulary levels, the chronics were significantly older than the acutes ($\bar{X}$ CA = 42.3 and 27.0, respectively. Most of the schizophrenics were on medication.

deSilva and Hemsley found that the schizophrenics' cloze performance was worse than that of the normals on all deletion versions and, whereas the normals improved from the fourth- to the tenth-word deletion versions, the schizophrenics deteriorated. Moreover, consistent with Broen's hypothesis, the performance of the acutes deteriorated with increased context, whereas that of the chronics remained the same.

Rochester (1973) examined CA- and education-matched schizophrenics' and normals' subjective location of clicks presented in meaningful sentences and randomly ordered digit strings. Rochester hypothesized that schizophrenics are deficient in the processing of all auditory information, whether structured or not; that is, she assumed (for reasons that are not clear) that the schizophrenic deficit involves low-level, general sensory-processing skills rather than an inability to use linguistic structure. Most of her schizophrenics were on phenothiazines and thus, as Rochester points out, diagnostic group was confounded with medication.

Rochester (1973) found that when the two types of stimuli were presented on alternating trials, there was no significant difference in correct localization between the subject groups, although when the stimuli were blocked by types, the performance of the normals was significantly better than that of the schizophrenics. For both groups, localization was better in the digit sequences than in the sentences. This might be interpreted as indicating that schizophrenics, like normals, were influenced by the presence of linguistic structure, although Rochester makes no such claim. Further, there was a statistically significant association between the two stimulus types; however, prediction from one stimulus type to the other was better for schizophrenics than for normals.

Rochester, Harris, and Seeman (1973) also used the click paradigm to study schizophrenic comprehension. They presented two versions of each sentence of a set (adopted from Garrett, Bever, & Fodor, 1966) to different groups. The versions shared a common sequence of words. The shared portions of the two versions differed in their linguistic structure but not acoustically or in their click placements. Subjects either located the clicks on written versions of each sentence after its auditory presentation (the "given" condition) or recalled the sentences themselves before locating the clicks (the "recall" condition). The study was designed to determine whether schizophrenics' click location, like normals', was differentially affected by differences in the linguistic structure of the two sentence versions and whether both groups tended to displace the clicks toward major constituent boundaries (Fodor, Bever, & Garrett, 1974).

Rochester et al.'s (1973) subjects were native English schizophrenic and normal speakers matched on age, education, and sex ratio but not on IQ, and although most of the schizophrenics were receiving medication, Rochester et al. presented evidence that performance in this task is not influenced by medication.

Among Rochester et al.'s results were the following. Although normals and schizophrenics did not differ in their correct recall of click locations in the recall condition, the former were significantly superior in the given condition. In the given condition, normals incorrectly located the clicks in the major constituent boundary for one sentence version. Schizophrenics' performance was influenced to an even greater extent by linguistic structure; they tended to incorrectly locate the clicks in the major constituent boundary in both sentence versions in the given condition and in one version in the recall condition. Moreover, the groups did not differ in the tendency for their click location errors to be toward the major constituent boundary.

Carpenter (1976) examined schizophrenics' use of linguistic structure in comprehension. It should be mentioned here, however, that although Carpenter interprets her results in terms of subjects' reliance on syntax, she is aware that syntactic and semantic structure were confounded in her materials. Therefore, the neutral term *linguistic structure* is used in describing her study.

This criticism, we should add, applies to the study of Rochester et al. (1973) as well.

Schizophrenics were assigned to either a good or a poor premorbid group on the basis of social adjustment ratings. The groups were matched on age, years of education, sex ratio, and mean medication dosage. Moreover, none had received electroconvulsive therapy or had signs of organic brain damage, and all were acute. Normal undergraduates and normal 11-year-old controls were included as well. All subjects were monolingual English speakers, but no IQ data were provided. Subjects were tested in three tasks. All were first tested in the recall of randomly ordered word strings. They were also tested in a modified version of Jarvella's (1971) task. In this task, subjects heard passages of text that were stopped at various points. At each stop, subjects recalled as much of the preceding two clauses as possible. The clauses belonged to either the same or different sentences. In the third task, subjects heard sentences in which clicks were heard superimposed in either the major clause boundary or in the monosyllabic words on either side of the boundary. Subjects were then asked to locate the clicks on their recalled version of a sentence.

Among other things, Carpenter (1976) observed that: (1) normals' recall of the random strings was significantly better than that of good premorbids and children, who did not differ, with poor premorbids' recall being significantly below that of the other groups; (2) in the Jarvella task, all groups recalled more from clauses immediately preceding the stops than from the next to last clauses, and all groups' recall of the next to last clause was better when both clauses were from the same sentence than when they were from different sentences; and (3) in the click task, although there were group differences in overall recall, all groups correctly recalled a larger percentage of the clicks in clause boundaries than those on either side, and only poor premorbids did not demonstrate the often reported tendency (Fodor et al., 1974) to prepose clicks in recall. Carpenter found no consistent correlations between medication or premorbid ratings and performance in any of the tasks. In general, then, her results indicated that both good and poor premorbids make use of linguistic structure to comprehend and recall verbal material, as do normal adults and children.

Neufeld (1977, 1978) employed a sentence-verification task in order to assess schizophrenic comprehension. Neufeld worked within the framework of an information-processing model based on those of Carpenter and Just (1975, 1976) and Sternberg (1969). On this view, there are four processing stages involved in sentence verification: (a) sentential and pictorial stimuli are encoded in terms of their abstract constituents; (b) sequential, constituent-by-constituent comparison of the two representations takes place; (c) the results of the comparison are translated into a response; and (d) response execution. When mean verification latencies are plotted by the number of required constituent comparisons for normal adults, the slope of the function is the time required for each constituent comparison, whereas the remaining stages determine the intercept's value.

In a varification task in which picture and sentence were simultaneously presented, Neufeld (1977) found that the intercept of the latency function was greater for the schizophrenics than for the normals but that there were no group differences in the slopes of the functions. This was taken to indicate that the observed schizophrenic quantitative comprehension deficit was specific to Stage a, c, and/or d.

Neufeld (1978) attempted to determine if the schizophrenic deficit was at Stage a. Schizophrenics were assigned to paranoid and nonparanoid groups on the basis of the criteria of Gordon and Gregson (1970). A normal control was also included. The groups did not differ in social position, occupational level, sex ratio, age, years of education, or WAIS-Clarke IQ, and the schizophrenic groups did not differ in cumulative hospitalization or mean drug dosage.

Neufeld reasoned that if the schizophrenic deficit was specific to Stage a, the groups' latency functions should not differ when the time required for encoding the sentence (i.e., Stage a) is excluded from the measured latency interval. Neufeld attempted to accomplish this by allowing sufficient time for encoding the sentence *prior* to the presentation of the picture (and, thus, prior to the start of the measured latency). It is clear, however, that although this manipulation may exclude sentential encoding from the latencies, it introduces other important factors (e.g., memory for and retrieval of the representations) that might differentially affect the groups' latencies. The sentences differed in the number of comparison operations required (i.e., in the number of constituents they were composed of).

Among other things, Neufeld (1978) observed that: (1) intercepts of the latency functions did not differ significantly for the groups; (2) the slope of the normals' function was significantly lower than that of the schizophrenic groups who did not differ, indicating that the schizophrenics took more time per comparison than the normals; and (3) each group's mean latency increased linearly with the number of required comparison operations, as predicted by Carpenter and Just's model. Moreover, the group differences were unrelated to medication dosage.

Taken together the results of Neufeld's studies suggest that schizophrenics do not differ qualitatively from normals in their verification task performance but that they are slower in making sentence-picture comparisons when they must retrieve the sentences from memory. When memory is of lesser importance (i.e., when simultaneous picture and sentence presentation is used), however, the schizophrenics appear to exhibit a quantitative deficit located at Neufeld's Stage a.

Pogue-Geile and Oltmanns (1980) employed a speech shadowing task in order to investigate the comprehension processes of schizophrenic, depressed, and manic patients and normals. The subjects in each psychiatric group were recent hospital admissions diagnosed according to the criteria of Spitzer et al. (1977). It should be noted that although the groups were matched on education, the schizophrenics had more prior hospitalizations than the other clinical groups and had a lower occupational status than the normals; there were psychiatric group differences in type of medication received; IQ data were not reported; and the groups were not matched on CA, although the schizophrenics and normals did not differ significantly. Moreover, the normal group was all-male, whereas the patient groups were heterogenous as regards sex. These initial group differences make interpretation of the results difficult. In one condition of the experimental task, subjects shadowed a monotically presented passage of text; in the other, they shadowed a passage presented to one ear, while a distractor passage was presented to the other. However, the no-distraction condition always preceded the distraction condition; differences between these conditions, therefore, are difficult to evaluate. Subjects' subsequent recall of the shadowed passages was also tested, but we do not discuss this aspect of the study.

Pogue-Geile and Oltmanns (1980) found that there were no differences between the diagnostic groups in the overall percentage of correctly shadowed words, and no group was affected by the distraction variable in the shadowing task. Moreover, the only difference between the schizophrenics and the other groups was in the frequency of various types of errors of commission; the schizophrenics tended to insert semantically irrelevant words and phrases more frequently than the other groups. However, like the other groups, when incorrect in shadowing, schizophrenics typically inserted paraphrases or semantically related material and made few syntactic errors. In general, then, these results indicate similar comprehension processes for schizophrenics and normals: Both rely on linguistic structure to anticipate forthcoming words. Pogue-Geile and Oltmanns suggested that schizophrenics' "irrelevant" errors resulted from a short-term memory deficit (i.e., on occasion they fail to retrieve prior contextual information and thus, rather than anticipate subsequent words, they "guess" at them).

Truscott (1970) employed a version of Marks and Miller's (1964) paradigm to study schizophrenic recall. The stimulus types presented were: (1) meaningful sentences; (2) anomalous but grammatical sentences; (3) semantically related word strings (with semantic relatedness being based on experimenter intuition); and (4) random word strings (i.e., neither meaningful, grammatical, nor semantically related). All instances of each stimulus type were presented together in one block with recall tested after each block.

The subjects were chronic, hospitalized schizophrenics (on medication) and normal medical patients matched on mean CA (33.1 and 34.5, respectively), years of education (11.9 and 12, respectively), verbal IQ (WAIS-scaled score equivalents of 10.7 and 11.7, respectively), and socioeconomic status. The schizophrenics had been diagnosed as such by three or more hospital staff members and were tested 3 to 4 weeks after their current admission.

Truscott (1970) found that the normals recalled more words correctly than the schizophrenics for each type of stimulus, with the differences being greatest on the meaningful sentences. For both subject groups, however, the number of correctly recalled words decreased in the following order: meaningful sentences, semantically related strings, random strings, and anomalous sentences. Why anomalous sentences were recalled more poorly than random strings is not clear. However, the difference between anomalous and random strings was quite small.

A number of problems make interpretation of Truscott's (1970) findings difficult, however. First, low imageability rather than linguistic structure may have been responsible for the poor performance on random strings and anomalous sentences. Second, the design of the study (and this is a common problem in studies of sentence and discourse recall) does not make it possible to determine whether the findings were due to stimulus encoding (i.e., comprehension) differences, rehearsal factors, or memory retrieval factors, or some combination of these variables. Combining recall (free and prompted) with recognition measures would help differentiate between these different explanations. The interested reader should consult the basic research literature in the area of memory for information regarding this matter. Third, examination of individual subjects' recall performance might have indicated performance patterns different from the overall group trends in some of the subjects. But this problem is not limited to Truscott's study. Fourth, Truscott treated a word as having been correctly recalled only if it was recalled in the exact position it had occupied in the original stimulus. The measure recall-regardless-of-position would have provided an estimate of total output. Further, it is not clear how Truscott's recall criterion handled partial recall; for example, in the case in which only one word of a stimulus was recalled.

It should be pointed out here that Gerver (1967) had found earlier that although chronic schizophrenics' (TD) overall immediate recall performance on normal sentences, anomalous sentences, and random strings was lower than that of controls (normals and psychiatric patients), their performance improved from random strings to anomalous sentences to normal sentences. Their schizophrenic subjects, it is interesting to note, had significantly lower WAIS vocabulary scores than their controls.

Straube, Barth, and König (1979) employed the Marks and Miller (1964) paradigm to examine the recall performance of German-speaking normals, psychiatric patients (alcoholics), and acute and chronic schizophrenics matched on CA and digit recall ability. The stimuli were word strings, anomalous sentences, and meaningful sentences, each recorded under various levels of masking noise.

Straube et al. (1979) observed that, for all groups, performance was best on meaningful sentences and worst on word strings. All groups, then, made use of linguistic structure to facilitate performance. Only high levels of masking noise adversely affected performance, and then only on random word strings; this was true for all groups. Finally, only the chronics performed at a significantly lower level than the normals, with the deficit *decreasing* as linguistic constraint increased such that the groups did not differ on meaningful sentences.

Koh, Marusarz, and Rosen (1980) studied sentence memory in schizophrenics, psychiatric patients, and normals matched on education, WAIS vocabulary scores, and socioeconomic status. The former two were also matched on median length of hospitalization. Although the mean age of psychiatric patients was greater than that of normals (26 and 22, respectively), neither differed from the schizophrenics ($\bar{X}$ CA = 24). In Session 1, subjects were visually presented sets of declarative sentences (in two structural versions). Sentence memory was tested in free recall after each set and at the end of the session and in cued recall at the session's end. In Session 2, subjects unscrambled declaratives with their words scrambled and rated the difficulty of doing so. This was followed by tests of incidental and then cued recall.

Koh et al. (1980) obtained the same pattern of results whether recall was scored in terms of number of words or complete sentences (verbatim and paraphrases) correctly remembered. These researchers found that in Session 1 the schizophrenics recalled significantly less material than the other groups in the total recall task and less than the normals in cued recall. In Session 2 there were no significant group differences on either recall task. Koh et al. also applied a clustering procedure to the Session 1 recall data. For both sentence types, the schizophrenics imposed the same hierarchical structures as did the normals. The psychiatric controls differed slightly from the other groups on one of the sentence types.

The results of this study suggested that schizophrenics represent sentences (structurally) the same as do normals but that the former do not spontaneously employ strategies that make efficient use of this structure to facilitate recall. However, when encouraged by the task to use these strategies (as in the unscrambling task), they do so as efficiently as normals. (See also Koh, 1978, for a discussion of encoding and memorial processes in schizophrenics.)

A number of studies have employed the Miller and Selfridge (1950) paradigm to investigate schizophrenics' use of linguistic structure in recall. In this procedure, subjects are given word lists varying in their statistical approximation to English, from randomly ordered words to grammatical and meaningful sentences. The standard finding regarding the performance of normals in this task is that recall improves with increasing order of approximation to English, indicating that normals use linguistic structure (and very likely increased imageability as well) in memorial performance.

Maher, Manschreck, and Rucklos (1980) examined the relationship between throught disorder and schizophrenic verbal recall using the Miller and Selfridge paradigm. Subjects were assigned to a schizophrenic, a mixed psychiatric, or a normal group on the basis of the Research Diagnostic Criteria of Spitzer et al. (1975). All were free of medical illness and matched on years of education. However, no intellectual assessments were made. Moreover, no information regarding medication was provided. The schizophrenic group was further divided into TD and NTD subjects; however, no data were provided regarding age or education or other subject variables and, consequently, any performance differences between the subtypes are uninterpretable. The materials to be recalled ranged from zero-order approximations to English (randomly ordered words) to text.

Maher et al. (1980) found that when initial differences in recall ability were controlled for, the TD schizophrenics' recall was significantly below that of the normals on a number of the orders of approximation, whereas NTD schizophrenics, psychiatric, and normal controls were not significantly different on any of the orders. Further, a number of measures demonstrated that the NTD schizophrenics benefited more from increased contextual constraints than did the TD subjects. However, multiple t-tests were used to make these comparisons (the probability levels of the tests were not adjusted for multiple tests), and thus these differences must be viewed cautiously.

In earlier investigations in this area, Lewinsohn and Elwood (1961) found no evidence that matched schizophrenics are less sensitive than controls to increasing amounts of contextual constraint, but other researchers (Lawson, McGhie, & Chapman, 1964; Levy & Maxwell, 1968; Raeburn & Tong, 1968) have reported finding evidence of impairment in the use of contextual constraint in at least some schizophrenics. Needless to say, contradictory findings in this area are not surprising, given the intermittent nature of schizophrenic symptomatology.

Knight and Sims-Knight (1979) examined schizophrenic recall performance on a modified version of Bransford and Franks' (1971) paradigm. In a question-answering task, subjects were presented sentences containing the component ideas of a complex idea or prototype. Following this acquisition phase, the subjects were tested for their incidental recognition of sentences containing the prototypes' components (cases), both those seen during acquisition (''old'') and those not seen previously (''new''; i.e., sentences coding new combinations of the components) and sentences not derived from the prototypes (noncases). Subjects also rated their confidence in their recognition responses. In both acquisition and recognition the number of component ideas encoded in a single sentence was varied.

In this study, the schizophrenic subjects were assigned to the following groups: good premorbid acute, poor premorbid cute, and poor premorbid chronic on the basis of ratings. Acutes were defined as having 2 years or less total hospitalization, chronics as having 3 years or more. A nonpsychotic psychiatric and a normal control group were also included. The four patient groups were matched on their Shipley vocabulary scores and although the chronics were significantly older than the other groups, age did not correlate with task performance. It should be noted, however, that the characteristics of the normals were not provided.

All groups performed well in acquisition, indicating that all had adequately encoded the sentences presented, and thus initial differences in acquisition cannot account for group performance differences in recognition. Among other things, Knight and Sims-Knight (1979) observed the following: (1) the recognition ratings of all groups discriminated cases from noncases, although chronics were less sure they had not previously seen noncases than were all other groups except the good premorbid acutes; (2) chronics and nonpsychotics were more confident than normals that they had previously seen new cases; (3) for the normals, nonpsychotics, and good premorbids only, as the number of component ideas encoded by the new cases increased (from one to four), so did the subjects' confidence that the sentence was old. These researchers concluded on the basis of these and other findings that although the schizophrenics stored the acquisition sentences as efficiently as normals, only the good premorbids organized and integrated these components into unified representations of the complex ideas as did normals and nonpsychotics.

This is as much of the literature on language comprehension (and memory) that we need to discuss in the context of the present review. (The reader who is interested in a broader approach to verbal processes in schizophrenia, however, will want to examine the articles by, for example, Chapman, 1979; Chapman & Chapman, 1973, 1978; Chapman, Chapman, & Daut, 1976; Chapman, Chapman, & Miller, 1964; Neuringer, Fiske, Schmidt, & Goldstein, 1972; and Williams, Hemsley, & Denning-Duke, 1976).

Taking into account methodological and other shortcomings of the studies reviewed here, it is reasonable to conclude that no consistent pattern of disruptions in comprehension (and/or memorial) performance emerges when schizophrenics (as a group and by subgroups) are compared with normals. Rather, we find that schizophrenics are, in the main, sensitive to the linguistic structure of the artificial language input of the laboratory (see, also, the conclusions of Miller & Phelan, 1980, and Rothbaum, Routh, Feagans, Kinney, & Vasu, 1979), although they may occasionally fail to utilize (for unknown reasons) their knowledge fully. However, although the overall findings are consistent with the occasional (both within and between subjects) nature of schizophrenic symptomatology, it is also possible that the materials and tasks utilized in the studies reviewed here may not have engaged, in most instances, the symptomatology of the schizophrenic subjects. Obviously, much more work needs to be done on language comprehension and related memorial processes in schizophrenics.

CORTICAL FUNCTIONING AND LANGUAGE IN SCHIZOPHRENIA

There are a number of suggestions in the literature of an association between cortical functioning deficits and schizophrenia that relate to schizophrenic language and other disruptions. A number of the relevant articles are discussed now under the headings "Left-Hemisphere Dysfunction," "Defective Interhemispheric Transmission," and "Lateralization."

Left-Hemisphere Dysfunction. Flor-Henry (1969) found that temporal lobe epileptics with schizophrenic-like symptomatology had cortical damage localized in the left temporal lobe or bilaterally, whereas those with manic–depressive characteristics appeared to have right-hemisphere lesions.

Gruzelier and Venables (1974) examined laterality and anxiety level in schizophrenics by measuring skin conductance-orienting responses (on both hands) to repeated auditory stimuli (tones). Their subjects were institutionalized and noninstitutionalized schizophrenics, depressives, and patients with personality disorders, most of whom were on medication. It should be noted that the institutionalized schizophrenics were, on the average, older than the other groups, although this difference was not tested statistically. Moreover, no attempt was made to match the groups on important variables such as education or IQ, and no data were presented on handedness. Thus, group differences must be interpreted cautiously.

Gruzelier and Venables (1974) classified the schizophrenics as either "responders" or "nonresponders." Subjects of the first type showed extremely slow habituation (relative to normals; Gruzelier & Venables, 1972) or a failure to habituate to the tone sequence (as measured by their electrodermal-orienting responses), whereas the latter showed almost a complete lack of orienting responses. Schizophrenic responders also exhibited higher skin-conductance levels and more frequent spontaneous fluctuations in those levels than schizophrenic nonresponders. Gruzelier and Venables (1974) found normals (Gruzelier & Venables, 1972) to fall between these two extremes, and therefore it was concluded that responders and nonresponders were a high- and a low-arousal group, respectively. Moreover, the responder–nonresponder distinction was unrelated to age, length of institutionalization, medication, or traditional schizophrenic diagnostic subtypes. Although a few responders and nonresponders were found in the nonschizophrenic groups, the majority of these subjects, like normals, exhibited rapid habituation to the tone series.

Among other things, Gruzelier and Venables (1974) also found that for bilateral schizophrenic responders, response amplitudes were significantly higher on the right than on the left hand, with the same trend being exhibited by the personality disorders. Normals showed similar bilateral asymmetry (Gruzelier & Venables, 1972). It was also observed that schizophrenic responders exhibited labile bilateral differences in skin-conductance levels, with the direction of the difference moving toward higher right-hand than left-hand levels as arousal level increased. Moreover, the observed bilateral differences were greater than those found previously for normals (Gruzelier & Venables, 1972). However, this abnormal lateralization pattern was not unique to schizophrenics; it also characterized the personality disorder subjects. Finally, Gruzelier and Venables (1974) observed that the number of subjects who exhibited unilateral nonresponding in the left hand was greater in the schizophrenic than the nonschizophrenic groups. This was suggestive of left-hemisphere underactivation because they assumed that the electrodermal response is mediated ipsilaterally. It should be noted, however, that only a few of the schizophrenics were unilateral nonresponders.

It should be pointed out here that Shimkunas (1978) has convincingly argued that Gruzelier and Venables (1974; Gruzelier, 1973; Gruzelier & Venables, 1973) "mistakenly assumed ipsilateral, not contralateral, hemispheric mediation of electrodermal activity [p. 210]." Thus, their data are more consistent with left-hemispheric overactivation in at least some schizophrenics, but more about Shimkunas' article later.

Gruzelier and Hammond (1980) employed a dichotic listening task to assess laterilization of function in right-handed CA-matched male chronic schizophrenics and normals. However, mean IQ might have differed for the groups; the mean for the schizophrenics was 88, but no data were reported for the normals. Group performance differences, therefore, might not be due solely to diagnostic differences. Schizophrenic performance was assessed in the following phases (in the order given): on medication, off medication (on placebo), and return to original medication levels. The influence of drug phase on performance is not discussed here, however, because: (1) it was confounded with amount of practice in the task; and (2) it had only limited effects on dichotic task performance. In the dichotic task, different digit sequences were simultaneously presented to the ears and the subjects were to recall the sequences immediately after presentation. The sequences to the ears were either equl or unequal in intensity and recall was either "free" or "directed" (i.e., digit report was either not constrained or one of the ears was designated, prior to stimulus presentation, as having to be reported first).

Among other things, Gruzelier and Hammond (1980) found that there was no difference between the schizophrenics and normals in the percentage of correctly recalled digits, and both demonstrated an overall right-ear superiority in recall. However, when schizophrenic responders and nonresponders were compared, it was found that the former had poorer recall and a greater right-ear advantage than the latter. Moreover, the responders had difficulty when the right-ear input was louder than the attention-directed left-ear input, whereas the nonresponders had bilateral difficulty in inhibiting the processing of the louder input and the controls showed reduced accuracy only when the left-ear input was louder than the attention-directed right-ear input. Gruzelier and Hammond took this as evidence that schizophrenic responders suffer from a deficit in inhibiting left-hemisphere processing.

Gruzelier and Hammond (1980) also found that the serial position recall curves of the normals exhibited both primacy and recency effects, whereas those of the schizophrenics—apparently primarily responders—evidenced only recency. The lack of a primacy effect was most apparent for the louder of the ears or, when the intensities were equal, for the left ear. It also appeared that there was a tradeoff between recency and primacy (i.e., the stronger, one effect; the weaker, the other). Gruzelier and Hammond, on the basis of Craik and Lockhart's (1972) interpretation of primacy and recency, speculated that the schizophrenics, especially the responders, engaged in primarily phonetic processing of the stimuli, whereas the normals relied more on semantic encoding.

Lerner, Nachshon, and Carmon (1977) examined right-handed paranoid schizophrenics', nonparanoid schizophrenics', and normals' processing of digit sequences simultaneously presented to the two ears, a different string per ear. Identification was tested after each sequence and order was not constrained. All the schizophrenics were on medication; no other subject data were reported, however.

Among other things, these researchers found that: (1) the highest percentage of "shifts" (i.e., switching one ear to the other in digit report) occurred for normals and the lowest for paranoids, with nonparanoids being intermediates; (2) normals reported more digits correctly than the other groups who did not differ; and (3) the relative right-ear advantage decreased in the order paranoids, nonparanoids, normals. It is important to note that the greater relative ear difference of schizophrenics was not interpreted as indicating differences in lateralization of function. Instead it was taken to be the result of the schizophrenics' greater reliance on a "successive" (i.e., report first the right ear then the left ear) than on a "shift" processing strategy; reporting the right-ear input first results in a decay of the stored left-ear input.[3]

Gur (1978) has provided evidence regarding both left-hemisphere dysfunction and overactivation. In one study, she employed modified versions of Levy and Reid's (1976) Dot Location and Syllable Tests. In the former, subjects are required to indicate the spatial position of a dot presented tachistoscopically to either the right or the left visual field. In the Syllable Test, CVC syllables are tachistoscopically presented to the right or left field and the subject's task is to pronounce the syllables. In both tasks, optimum presentation thresholds were determined for each subject individually.

All subjects were right-handed and were free of neurological deficits. The schizophrenic and normal groups were matched on age, education, socioeconomic background, and sex ratio. Most of the schizophrenics had been hospitalized previously and all were on phenothiazines, but Gur presents evidence that she interprets as indicating that laterality is not influenced by medication in these tasks. Subjects whose visual sensitivity differed greatly for the left and right fields were excluded.

Gur (1978) found, for the Dot Location Test, that although the schizophrenics performed poorer than the normals in both visual fields, both groups performed better on items presented to the left (and thus projected to the right hemisphere) than to the right. Both the schizophrenics and the normals, then, processed spatial information better in the right than in the left hemisphere. On the verbal test (Syllable Test), whereas the normals demonstrated the expected right field (left hemisphere) advantage, the schizophrenics performed better on items presented to the left visual field (right hemisphere), with no differences between paranoids and nonparanoids. Gur presented evidence to indicate that the subjects did not move their eyes toward the stimuli presented and engage, therefore, both hemispheres in the processing.

These results, together with Gur's claim that the right hemisphere is incapable of phonetic analysis (Levy & Trevarthen, 1977), were interpreted as suggesting

---

[3]It should be noted, however, that the adoption of the successive strategy by the schizophrenics may be the direct result of their inability to inhibit left-hemisphere processing.

that schizophrenics suffer from a left-hemisphere-processing dysfunction. This deficit is attenuated only when the right hemisphere first performs some preliminary analyses on the input prior to callosal transfer to the poorly functioning left hemisphere.

Although Gur is unclear as to the specific nature of the right- and left-hemisphere processes involved in the Syllable Test performance of the schizophrenics, Pic'l, Magaro and Wade (1979) have offered some interesting suggestions. Specifically, they hypothesized that the left-hemisphere linguistic processing of the schizophrenics proceeds at such a slow pace that the representation of the input has faded before processing is complete. The deficit is attenuated when the input is to the right hemisphere first because the right is responsible for forming the iconic representation of the stimuli, a representation lasting long enough to accommodate the slow left hemisphere.

In a second study, Gur (1978) examined differences in hemispheric activation by measuring initial lateral eye movements (LEMs) during the processing of verbal and spatial questions of an emotional or nonemotional nature. Previous research (Schwartz, Davidson, & Maer, 1975) had indicated that, in normal adults, verbal material, which involves primarily left-hemisphere processing, produces right LEMs, whereas spatial and emotional material, which activates primarily the right hemisphere, produces left LEMs. Eye movements were scored from videotapes by two scorers who achieved a high percentage of agreement. There were two experimental conditions; in one, the experimenter faced the subject; in the other, the experimenter was located behind the subject, in order to assess the effect of experimenter location on LEM.

The subjects in Gur's second study were paranoid schizophrenics, nonparanoid schizophrenics, and normals matched on age, education, and socioeconomic status. All were right-handed and free of neurological damage. All of these (multiple admission) schizophrenics were on medication.

The dependent variable was the percentage of all LEMs that were right LEMs (indicating left-hemisphere activation). The schizophrenic groups, which did not differ, showed more right LEMs than did the normals, although all groups exhibited a higher percentage of right LEMs on verbal than on spatial items.

Gur (1978) considered two possible interpretations of the results of her two studies. First, unlike in brain-damaged patients, where there is compensation for the deficit, the combination of left-hemisphere (verbal) dysfunction and overactivation together cause the purported schizophrenic cognitive deficit. Second, the schizophrenic's left-hemisphere dysfunction is the result of the overactivation.

One other interesting result of Gur's lateral-eye-movement study should be considered. She observed that the schizophrenic males and normal females showed similar patterns of right-LEM responses to the various stimulus types, whereas normal males demonstrated patterns like those of schizophrenic females. It should be recalled that Clemmer (1980) found some evidence of a similar type of diagnosis by sex interaction on measures of speech hesitation.

It should be noted that a major limitation of Gur's (1978) studies is the failure to include a nonschizophrenic, psychiatric group. The deficits (relative to normals) she observed might not be unique to schizophrenics; they may be characteristic of other diagnostic groups or of all hospitalized patients.

Schweitzer, Becker, and Welsh (1978) have also suggested that schizophrenics evidence abnormal hemispheric lateralization. These researchers examined LEMs following questions about verbal–emotional, verbal–nonemotional, spatial–emotional, and spatial–nonemotional material. Schweitzer et al. found that: (1) right-handed schizophrenics had a higher percentage of right-LEMs than CA- and education-matched right-handed normals for all question types except the spatial–nonemotional items on which there was no difference; and (2) although normals exhibited higher percentages of right LEMs on both verbal-emotional and nonemotional questions than on spatial–emotional items, schizophrenics had a higher percentage on spatial–emotional than on spatial–nonemotional questions. Schweitzer et al. concluded that the schizophrenics tended to process spatial and emotional as well as verbal material in the left hemisphere.

There are some serious problems with the Schweitzer et al. (1978) study, however. First, regarding (2), multiple t-tests were performed and, therefore, the probability levels of the comparisons may not have reached significance if family test levels had been adopted. Second, the experimenter who asked the questions scored LEM during the test session. Consequently, the scorer was not blind to either subject diagnosis or question content; moreover, there were no LEM scoring reliability checks. Third, no psychiatric control group was tested.

Schweitzer (1979), in another study, examined lateralization of function in schizophrenics as indexed by LEM. The subjects (right-handed) were schizophrenics ($\bar{X}$ CA = 36.1) and psychotic unipolar depressives ($\bar{X}$ CA = 33.7); the former were being treated on phenothiazines, the latter with tricyclic antidepressants. No other relevant subject data (e.g., duration of illness, IQ) were provided and, therefore, Schweitzer's conclusions are tentative at best. The material, procedures, and scoring were mainly those of Schweitzer et al. (1978) and thus similar methodological criticisms apply here as well.

Schweitzer (1979) found that the schizophrenics had a higher percentage of right LEMs than depressives on almost all types of materials, but the difference was greatest on spatial and emotional items. Schweitzer's schizophrenics did not differ from those of Schweitzer et al. (1978), so the combined sample was compared to both the normals of Schweitzer et al. and the depressed patients, and again it appeared that schizophrenics engaged in more left-hemisphere processing of all material than the other groups, and this was especially true for spatial and emotional material, which is supposedly processed in the right hemisphere by normals. Normals and depressives showed the same pattern of lateralization.

Torrey (1980) examined the occurrence of signs of neurological abnormalities in subjects identified by Spitzer et al.'s (1977) Research Diagnostic Criteria as being schizophrenic, with the following subtypes included: acute, subacute, chronic, and subchronic. The sample had a mean CA of 33.4, was two-thirds male, composed primarily of blacks, the time since first referral for treatment ranged from 1 month to 44 years ($\overline{X} = 11.3$), and almost all were on fluphenazine. No data on handedness were presented, however. The primary neurological tests were for graphthesia and the Face–Hand Test. In the former, on each trial a number is drawn on the subject's hand and if it cannot be identified by touch alone, the subject is positive for graphthesia. In the latter, a subject must indicate when his or her hand and face are simultaneously touched; abnormalities are said to be present if only one of the locations is identified.

Torrey (1980) found that few of the subacutes or acutes were positive on one or both of the tests, whereas almost half of the chronic and subchronic groups combined were. Torrey points out that this finding may have resulted from duration of illness or duration of medication, because the two are impossible to separate in practice. (This is a major problem for studies that examine the effects of chronicity, however.) More important, for present purposes, Torrey observed that most of the subjects who were positive for a test in only one hand were usually positive on the right, indicating left-hemisphere dysfunction. Torrey then retested between 2 and 19 months later as many of the chronics and subchronics who were positive or equivocal on the first test as possible. Of the 12 who exhibited lateralization of the abnormalities, 10 were positive on the right hand. Those with abnormalities did not differ from those without on CA, CAT scans, EEG, or (as determined by family interviews) age of first psychiatric referral, family history of schizophrenia, history of childhood CNS trauma or infection, and premorbid adjustment; however, the former group had a longer duration of illness and included more subjects who were first referred for treatment before CA 17. Thus, Torrey's results provide some evidence of a left-hemisphere deficit. However, as Torrey points out, these neurological signs are not unique to schizophrenics.

Bull and Venables (1974) did not find any evidence of abnormal lateralization or defective interhemispheric transfer in schizophrenics. Their subjects were right-handed paranoid schizophrenics, nonparanoid schizophrenics, and a mixed group of depressives and normals. The groups were matched on CA and vocabulary level. The stimuli were lists of monotically presented word lists.

Bull and Venables (1974) found, among other things, that neither the schizophrenics nor nonschizophrenics exhibited any difference in number of stimulus words reported due to ear of presentation. Further, the schizophrenics' recall was significantly poorer than that of the controls for both ears at high and low frequencies, regardless of whether the stimuli were unfiltered or filtered. The schizophrenic recall deficit, however, was not due to auditory insensitivity.

Clooney and Murray (1977) analyzed paranoid and nonparanoid schizophrenics' and normals' reaction times in making same–different judgments of tachistoscopically presented letter clusters. Subjects were all right-handed. For no group was there any difference in performance on left- and right-visual field items; that is, there was no schizophrenic left-hemisphere-processing deficit.

Pic'l et al. (1979), however, have pointed out that the presentation exposure times employed by Clooney and Murray were of sufficient duration to allow eye movements and thus stimulus processing by both hemispheres.

Pic'l et al. (1979) examined lateralization in the following subject groups: paranoid schizophrenics, nonparanoid schizophrenics, psychiatric patients, and normals. All subjects were right-handed, and the groups were matched on socioeconomic status. Although there were group differences in chronological age, medication level, and premorbid adjustment ratings, these variables were not significantly correlated with task performance. However, the psychiatirc controls and nonparanoids were less educated than the normals and paranoids, who did not differ, and this variable was significantly correlated with performance on the letter identification task. Not surprisingly, the groups differed in rated severity of pathology, which was also significantly correlated with letter identification performance. Unfortunately, no IQ data were reported by these researchers.

Two tasks from Kimura (1966) were employed to assess lateralization of function. One task involved judgments of the numerosity of arrays of dots presented tachistoscopically to one or the other visual field. The right hemisphere is more efficient on this task than the left (Kimura, 1966). The second task required subjects to identify sequences of four letters tachistoscopically presented to the right or the left visual field; performance on right-visual-field items is superior to that on left-visual-field items for normals (Kimura, 1966). Pic'l et al. (1979) presented the stimuli of both tasks at a duration that did not allow eye movements to occur. The dot task preceded letter identification for all subjects.

Pic'l et al. (1979) found that, in the dot task, nonparanoids performed significantly poorer than the other groups, who did not differ. Moreover, the nonparanoids were the only subjects to be unaffected by differences in the size of the arrays. However, for no group were there hemisphere differences in performance. It should be noted that the dependent variable in this task was not the number of incorrect trials; it was, instead, the difference between actual and judged numerosity. It would have been useful if the data had been reported in terms of the frequency of incorrect items as well.

A hemisphere difference was observed in the letter identification task; right-visual-field (left-hemisphere) presentation resulted in significantly better performance than left-field presentation for all groups except psychiatric controls. Group performance differences were due to the education variable. In this task too, the dependent variable was the number of letters missed. Taken together, Pic'l et al.'s results show no evidence of differences in lateralization of function between schizophrenics and normals nor a schizophrenic left-hemisphere dysfunction.

Pic'l et al. (1979) also interpret a nonsignificant tendency in the dot task for nonparanoids to perform better on right- than left-hemisphere items, whereas the reverse was true for the other groups, as indicating that the former preferred right-hemisphere holistic processing and the latter relied more on left-hemisphere serial processing. The fact that nonparanoids were unaffected by numerosity in the dot task is also consistent with this hypothesis. Thus, the poorer overall performance of the nonparanoids indicated that their preferred strategy was not the most efficient one or that they were unable to transfer the information to the left for serial processing due to defective interhemispheric transmission.

Defective Interhemispheric Transmission. Beaumont and Dimond (1973) tachistoscopically presented letters, digits, and abstract shapes to the right, to the left, or to both visual fields of schizophrenics and normals. The subjects' task was to match stimulus pairs, either across or within visual fields. It was found that the schizophrenic group performed poorly when matching either letters or shapes across the visual fields. Beaumont and Dimond concluded that the schizophrenics suffered from an inability to efficiently transfer information across the hemispheres. However, as Gur (1978) has pointed out, the schizophrenics also performed poorly relative to normals when matching letters in the left hemisphere (right visual field); consequently, their results might indicate a deficit in the left hemisphere rather than defective callosal transfer.

Green (1978) employed a tactile, object-sorting task in order to assess interhemispheric transfer in schizophrenics, neurotics, and normals. However, initial group differences in mean age and type of medication and the fact that no data concerning IQ, duration of illness, or length of hospitalization were reported complicates interpretation of Green's results.

Green observed, among other things, that schizophrenics required more learning trials to criterion when the task involved coordinating tactual information from both hands than when the same information was available to only one hand and required significantly more relearning trials to criterion to reproduce an object ordering previously learned on one hand with the opposite hand than with the same hand. The control groups, however, did not show differences on either measure. Green, therefore, concluded that the schizophrenics demonstrated a deficit of interhemispheric callosal transfer similar to that observed in split-brain monkeys.

Dimond, Scammell, Pryce, Huws, and Gray (1979) examined the incidence of left-hand anomia in right-handed chronic schizophrenics, psychiatric patients and normals. Left-hand anomia, an inability to name objects placed in the left hand, has been assumed to be indicative of inadequate callosal transfer as found in patients with servered corpus callosums. Dimond et al. found that although no naming errors were made by the mixed psychiatric patients and normals, the schizophrenics made significantly more errors in left- than right-hand naming. However, only one-third of the schizoprhenics made errors, and even they made relatively few. Dimond et al., therefore, concluded that schizophrenia is not always associated with a callosal transfer deficit, and when it is, it does not involve a complete lack of transfer but rather what could be characterized as "noisy" communication between the hemispheres.

It should be noted, however, that Dimond et al. (1979) did not determine whether the subjects who made errors, in fact, could discriminate perceptually the objects they could not name, that is, whether the deficit was a perceptual or a naming one. Thus, it is not clear whether their results indicate problems of interhemispheric transfer or of right-hemisphere functioning.

Green and Kotenko (1980) presented stories to their subjects either monaurally or binaurally and then tested their comprehension via content questions. Their groups were male schizophrenics ($\bar{X}$ CA = 39, $\bar{X}$ verbal IQ = 100, $\bar{X}$ time since first hospitalization = 5.7 years), female schizophrenics ($\bar{X}$ CA = 53.2, $\bar{X}$ verbal IQ = 91.4, $\bar{X}$ time since first hospitalization = 13.6 years), psychiatric patients ($\bar{X}$ CA = 43, $\bar{X}$ verbal IQ = 104, $\bar{X}$ time since first hospitalization = 2.6 years) and normals ($\bar{X}$ CA = 32, $\bar{X}$ verbal IQ = 101.2). The schizophrenic subjects, in addition to being diagnosed as such by their institutional staff, were judged to have one or more of Schneider's first-rank symptoms (1959) and had a history of hallucinations. Most of the schizophrenics were receiving medication; however, many of the psychiatric controls were not. All subjects were right-handed and none suffered from hearing difficulties.

Among other things, Green and Kotenko (1980) observed that: (1) both schizophrenic groups demonstrated a left-ear disadvantage, whereas neither control group did (and this result was not attributable to initial differences in sex, age, or verbal IQ); (2) the left-ear deficit was greater in schizophrenic females than males; (3) schizophrenics performed worse in the binaural presentation condition than in the right-ear-only condition, whereas the reverse was true for both control groups; (d) for schizophrenics, the greater the binaural deficit, the greater the left-ear disadvantage and the lower the overall comprehension performance, whereas for normals and psychiatric controls the higher the overall comprehension performance, the lower the binaural advantage. Some evidence was presented that suggested that the results were not due to medication differences.

Green and Kotenko (1980) argued that the left-ear deficit in schizophrenics indicates that they suffer from deficient interhemispheric transmission, whereas the binaural deficit suggests that the interhemispheric transmission deficit results in distortion of left-ear inputs and thus such inputs act as distracting "noise." One practical implication of these results is that the schizophrenic quantitative comprehension deficit is exaggerated under binaural conditions.

Lateralization. Gur (1977) found that in a sample of 200 schizophrenics there was a higher incidence of left-sidedness (assessed via laterality scales of hand, foot, and eye dominance) than in a sample of 200 normal controls.

Boklage (1977) reexamined Gottesman and Shields' (1972) twin data in an attempt to investigate the relationship between schizophrenia and abnormal lateralization. Boklage observed, among other things, that: (1) there was a significantly higher concordance for schizophrenia among monozygotic (MZ) twinships in which both members were right-handed than in those that included at least one left-hander; (2) the incidence of non-right-handedness was higher in monozygotic than in dizygotic (DZ) twinships with at least one schizophrenic member; and (3) the incidence of non-right-handedness was greater in schizophrenic than in normal MZ twinships. These and other findings led Boklage to conclude that schizophrenia, abnormal lateralization, and MZ twinning itself result from a genetically determined asymmetry of embryonic development.

Luchins, Pollin, and Wyatt (1980) examined handedness in 14 MZ twinships in which at least one twin was schizophrenic. Contrary to Boklage's (1977) findings, there was no difference in concordance rate between twinships with two right-handed members (2RH) and those in which at least one member was left-handed (1-2LH). However, 2RH schizophrenics were observed to have more severe "nuclear" forms of the disorder than 1-2LH schizophrenics. Moreover, in the combined sample of discordant twinships of Boklage and Luchins et al., left-handed members of 1-2LH twinships were schizophrenic more often and were heavier at birth than right-handed members; in 2RH twinships, the schizophrenic twin tended to be lighter at birth than the nonschizophrenic twin.

Luchins et al. (1980) interpret these results as indicating the existence of different subtypes of schizophrenia each with a unique etiology. Specifically, the schizophrenia of concordant 2RH twinships is primarily the result of (unidentified) genetic factors, whereas that of discordant 2RH twinships is caused by (unidentified) intrauterine factors associated with low birth weight. As regards the "milder" schizophrenia of 1-2LH twins, some factor predisposes the twinship to abnormal lateralization (left-handedness) and also leads to the development of the disorder. It should be noted that: (1) the responsible factor in 1-2LH MZ twinships might also operate in dizygotic twinships and singletons as well; and (2) there must be a set of interacting factors causing the milder disorder because, contrary to Boklage's results, Luchins et al. found that the incidence of left-handedness in schizophrenic MZ twinships was no greater than in nonschizophrenic MZ twinships; that is, abnormal lateralization (left-handedness) is only rarely accompanied by schizophrenia.

Luchins, Weinberger, and Wyatt (1979) examined laterality and its relation to the severity of the schizophrenic disorder. Diagnosis was made on the basis of the Research Diagnostic Criteria of Spitzer et al. (1977) and chronics (the severe form of the disorder) were defined as subjects whose current psychotic episode lasted for at least a year or who had not completely recovered from prior episodes. Luchins et al. (1979) employed the laterality test of Zamura and Kaelbling (1965); subjects who used their right hand, foot, or eye on most items were classified as right-handed, all others as demonstrating abnormal laterlization (i.e., non-right-handedness). They also tested for the presence of torque, which is associated with non-right-handedness.

Luchins et al. (1979) found that although right- and non-right handed subjects did not differ in age, age at onset of illness, or duration of illness, a significantly greater percentage of the former than the latter were also chronics, and the former spent a greater percentage of their years of illness in hospitals. Although subjects with torque did not differ in chronological age or age of illness onset from those without it, the former had a significantly shorter duration of illness and less hospitalization than the latter. Moreover, all subjects with torque were acute; all those without were chronic. These results suggest that non-right-handedness is associated with a mild form of schizophrenia.

Discussion. Thus, Flor-Henry's (1969) observations suggested that schizophrenics may be suffering from some kind of left-hemisphere malfunction. Gruzelier and Venables' (1974) and Gruzelier and Hammond's (1980) observations, moreover, suggested that in schizophrenics one finds a pattern of left-hemisphere overactivation associated with high anxiety (see Gruzelier, 1973, and Gruzelier and Venables, 1973, for some purported evidence of differences between acute and chronic schizophrenics in hemispheric activation). There were some confounding variables operating in these studies, however. In Gruzelier & Venables, 1974, for example, in addition to the subject confounds noted here, and the fact that there was no indication of whether subjects were right- or left-handed, their institutionalized schizophrenics were very likely all chronics. In the case of Gruzelier and Hammond (1980), in addition to the problems noted previously, their schizophrenic subjects were evidently only chronics. Additionally, Gruzelier and Venables (1974) noted that the pattern of abnormal lateralization that characterized the performance of the schizophrenics was also present in personality-disordered patients.

The findings of Gur's (1978) studies, taken together, seemed to indicate a combination of left-hemisphere dysfunction and overactivation that may lead to some right-hemispheric processing of verbal input. However, although the subjects in these studies were right-handed, it is not possible to determine chronicity from the information given on the schizophrenic subjects or whether some of the results might be true of nonschizophrenic psychiatric controls.

The findings of Schweitzer et al. (1978) suggested that the left hemisphere in schizophrenics processes both verbal and spatial–emotional material, but problems of data scoring and analysis, as well as an absence of information on chronicity, leave us with questions regarding these findings.

So it goes with the majority of the remaining studies we reviewed: methodological problems (including a problem we have not mentioned thus far, namely, that of determining premorbid adjustment), inconsistent findings, and the like. Thus, as interesting as the topic of schizophrenic cortical functioning is, the literature in this area must be interpreted with care.

A substantial portion of the then available literature on hemispheric asymmetry and its relationship to schizophrenic thought disorder was examined and integrated in a seminal article by Shimkunas (1978). Shimkunas begins his article with a review of the basic literature on the lateralization of functions in the cortex and points out that "emotionally, as well as spatially oriented cognitive activity reliably shows right-hemisphere advantage, while the left hemisphere appears to be engaged by verbal and nonemotional conceptual processes [p. 207]." Moreover, he indicates, among other things, that "When a hemisphere attempts to process in a manner inconsistent with its capabilities, deviant responses may be expected [p. 207]."

As regards the question of the nature or mode of interaction between the left and right hemispheres, Shimkunas' (1978) review indicates that, although much work remains to be done on this issue, one particular theoretical view has received considerable attention, namely, the view that the mode of interaction between the hemispheres "is that of competition [p. 207]." According to Shimkunas, the idea is "that the hemispheres may operate in alternation, with situational demands determining the excitation of one over the other [p. 207]." However, although competition may characterize initial excitation, with the hemisphere that is activated being determined by whether the input being attended to is temporal–verbal or spatial–emotional, as Shimkunas points out, "neither hemisphere is probably ever fully inactive [p. 209]."

In the course of his review, Shimkunas (1978) examined not only literature on cortical functioning in schizophrenics but literature on emotional arousal and cognitive functioning as well. His conclusions regarding all this literature (which he appears to share, in the main, with some other theorists) are stated in the following excerpts from his article.

A basic assumption underlying the present conceptualization of schizophrenia is that intensified emotional arousal serves as a catalyst for thought disorder. Overexcitation of the left hemisphere appears to initiate disturbed verbal conceptualizations by means of altering the cortical interpretation of perceptual input. Levels of excitation of both the left hemisphere in acute schizophrenics and the right hemisphere in chronics are assumed to reach maximal ergotrophic proportions . . . , hence, exceeding the normal limits of the inverted U performance function [p. 226].

Schizophrenia is conceptualized to be an asymmetrical dysfunction in corticohemispheric integration. Overexcitation of the left hemisphere during the acute stage disrupts effective verbal–conceptual reasoning and focal attentional information processing. Right-hemisphere overexcitation during chronicity intensifies perceptual–emotional mediation, potentiating narrowed attention to subcortically stimulated imagery in the context of behavioral withdrawal. During acute stages of schizophrenic disorganization, left-hemisphere verbal–temporal information-processing strategies break down, seeking compensation in right-hemisphere perceptual–emotional mediation. The right hemisphere's orientation toward simultaneous processing potentiates increased attention to temporally immediate environmental cues. Failures in hemispheric integration and left-hemisphere discrimination of conceptual similarity and generalization lead to over-inclusive autistic verbal behaviors. With chronicity, asymmetrical shifts in cortically mediated arousal may leave the schizophrenic with vestigial remains of disorganized thinking learned during acute stages and maintained by high left-hemisphere reactivity.

Intensified right-hemisphere-mediated internal imagery and hallucination further distort thinking and potentiate withdrawal behaviors. In both cases, an integrated organismic response to the external environment is further handicapped by the malfunctioning of interhemispheric nerve fibers. This serves to disconnect conceptual from perceptual and emotional mediation, resulting in the discontinuity between thought and emotion that has been observed in schizophrenia [pp. 227–228]. (Quotations from Shimkunas, 1978, reproduced with permission of the publisher.)

Although Shimkunas' claims that "intensified emotional arousal serves as a catalyst for thought disorder" (including verbal dysfunction), and that attentional deficits figure in both the verbal and nonverbal cognitive functioning of schizophrenics, appear to be consistent with a wide variety of observations and plausible speculations in the literature, the claims regarding the cortical hemispheric organization of the schizophrenic dysfunction must be treated for the time being as working hypotheses. For one thing, it is not yet clear whether the intensified arousal is the sole cause of the characteristics of hemispheric activity in schizophrenia. One could speculate, given, for example, the results of the research on handedness (lateralization), that the characteristics in question are the result of intensified arousal acting upon an already disordered corticohemispheric system or that they indicate right-hemisphere dominance (Rochester & Martin, 1979). Second, the research in this area has not been without its methodological problems and negative findings and, moreover, needs to be expanded on the topic of interhemispheric transfer. Third, the model appears to predict more disruption in language behavior in schizophrenics than is evident from the available research on language production and comprehension (as does, of course, the view that schizophrenics suffer from a disordered left hemisphere). Schizophrenic language disruptions, it needs to be emphasized, are occasional, both within and between subjects. And related to this concern is the possibility of individual differences in corticohemispheric functioning within subgroups of schizophrenics, as well as the possibility that some of the patterns of corticohemispheric functioning that have been observed are not entirely limited to schizophrenic psychiatric patients. Fourth, the lateralization of psycholinguistic and nonlinguistic functions in schizophrenics has not by any means been fully examined experimentally in the investigations that have appeared in the literature to date. Finally, there exist in the literature psychodynamic accounts of some of the symptomatology of schizophrenia (in particular, delusions and illogical thinking generally; see our earlier discussion of Arieti's, 1974, proposals regarding schizophrenic cognitive dysfunctions) that do not appear to require assumptions concerning underlying cortical hemispheric functioning.

Obviously, much more research is required before we have a clear picture of cortical functioning and its implications for schizophrenic symptomatology. In the area of language behavior, we look in particular for research on hemispheric functions and interactions in TD and NTD subgroups of schizophrenics of the sort studied by Rochester and Martin (1979), in research designs that also include, however, patients whose speech disruptions are characterized by bizarre but not incoherent utterances, along with appropriate differentiations regarding premorbid adjustment, chronicity, paranoid symptomatology, and drug usage.

CONCLUDING REMARKS

A substantial segment of the literature we have attempted to review here displays a myriad of methodological and other problems (see, also, the critical comments of Schwartz, 1978b). Confoundings abound, making even working generalizations difficult to come by. One reason for this state of affairs, of course, is that the disorder itself suffers from periodic definitional upheavals. Another is that it is difficult to come by subjects who have been diagnosed as schizophrenic who are not on medication. Moreover, because of this, chronicity and certain independent variables in experiments tend to be confounded with time on drugs.

However, although there appear to be some built-in problems that have proved difficult to deal with, there is no reason for the many failures one still finds in the published literature to have appropriate control groups that are matched on the relevant variables (e.g., IQ, hospitalization). In addition, the experimental approach to studying schizophrenia must come to grips with the phenomena of intermittent symptomatology and individual differences, or investigators will continue to waste time, energy, and money on studies whose results are doomed ahead of time to be uninterpretable.

Last, but not least, one finds even very recent investigations in the published literature that do not articulate fully with relevant basic research and theory in psycholinguistics and related areas of cognitive psychology.

Given the state of our knowledge concerning language comprehension and cortical functioning in schizophrenia, there is no need for us to say anything more here about these topics. Despite problems, however, some progress has been made in describing schizophrenic disruptions in speech production.

Most of the methodological and other problems that the literature on SL suffers from were discussed earlier. It is sufficient for us to attempt only some summary statements (or, rather, working hypotheses) here regarding the findings of the more promising studies in this area.

In the main, the speech of schizophrenics, both within and between subjects and across contexts, is coherent and free of linguistic disruptions. Thus there is no evidence that would compel us to propose that schizophrenics suffer from a disorder of linguistic competence or knowledge. However, when disruptions do occur, they tend to display a tendency to interject contextually (linguistically and nonlinguistically) irrelevant material into ongoing discourse that may range all the way from a whole theme down to an irrelevant semantic or phonological lexical association. When the irrelevant material departs substantially from the immediate situation or is unknown to the listener or fails to display linguistic and other obligations of discourse cohesion, it becomes incoherent to the listener and, as a result, tends to prompt him or her to assume (rightly or wrongly) the existence of underlying thought disorder. When the irrelevant material is coherent, it may contain, nonetheless, bizarre content, one common feature of which is delusions. Rare among all samples of SL, however, are agrammatical utterances, neologisms, and gibberish.

The occasional existence of irrelevant material in the speech of some schizophrenics suggests that these patients may sometimes fail to monitor their speech planning and execution processes so as to take into account the needs of the listener, but it is also possible that for them, during these episodes, the needs of the listener are not relevant. What is relevant is a grim, ever-present anxiety that sometimes distorts attention and perception (including temporal orientation; Arieti, 1974) and compels them to seek relief in self-serving linguistic expression. Why the resulting linguistic expression takes the form it does, however, remains a mystery.

What we have claimed here regarding SL has also been claimed sometimes of the speech of some normals, aphasics, and manics, so there is nothing unique to schizophrenia in these features. Some of these features, however, may occur more frequently in the speech of schizophrenics than in that of members of the other groups mentioned, particularly delusional utterances.

It should be emphasized here, as a final cautionary note, that the present review has been a selective one. The interested reader, therefore, will want to consult other recent reviews (in particular, those of Rochester & Martin, 1979, and Schwartz, 1978b), for discussions of matters not dealt with in the present chapter.

REFERENCES

Andreasen, N. C. Thought, language and communication disorders: I. Clinical assessment, definition of terms, and evaluation of their reliability. *Archives of General Psychiatry,* 1979, *36,* 1315-1321. (a)

Andreasen, N. C. Thought, language, and communication disorders: II. Diagnostic significance. *Archives of General Psychiatry,* 1979, *36,* 1325-1330. (b)

Andreasen, N. C., & Pfohl, B. Linguistic analysis of speech in affective disorders. *Archives of General Psychiatry,* 1976, *33,* 1361-1367.

Arieti, S. *Interpretation of schizophrenia* (2nd ed.). New York: Basic Books, 1974.

Bannister, D., & Fransella, F. A grid test of schizophrenic thought disorder. *British Journal of Social and Clinical Psychology,* 1966, *5,* 95-102.

Beaumont, J. G., & Dimond, S. J. Brain disconnection and schizophrenia. *British Journal of Psychiatry,* 1973, *123,* 661-662.

Bleuler, E. *Dementia praecox: Or the group of schizophrenias.* New York: International Universities Press, 1950. (Originally published 1911.)

Boklage, C. E. Schizophrenia, brain asymmetry, and twinning: Cellular relationship with etiological and possible prognostic implications. *Biological Psychiatry,* 1977, *12,* 19-35.

Boomer, D. S. Hesitation and grammatical encoding. *Language and Speech,* 1965, *8,* 148-158.

Bransford, J. D., & Franks, J. J. The abstraction of linguistic ideas. *Cognitive Psychology,* 1971, *2,* 331-350.

Bransford, J. D., & McCarrell, N. S. A sketch of a cognitive approach to comprehension. In W. Weimer & D. Palermo (Eds.), *Cognition and the symbolic processes.* Hillsdale, N.J.: Lawrence Erlbaum Associates, 1974.

Broen, W. E., Jr. *Schizophrenia research and theory.* New York: Academic Press, 1968.

Brown, R. Schizophrenia, language and reality. *American Psychologist,* 1973, *28,* 395-403.

Bull, H. C., & Venables, P. H. Speech perception in schizophrenia. *British Journal of Psychiatry,* 1974, *125,* 350-354.

Butterworth, B., & Goldman-Eisler, F. Recent studies on cognitive rhythm. In A. W. Siegman & S. Feldstein (Eds.), *Of speech and time: Temporal speech patterns in interpersonal contexts.* Hillsdale, N.J.: Lawrence Erlbaum Associates, 1979.

Carpenter, M. D. Sensitivity to syntactic structure: Good versus poor premorbid schizophrenics. *Journal of Abnormal Psychology,* 1976, *85,* 41-50.

Carpenter, P. A., & Just, M. A. Sentence comprehension: A psycholinguistic processing model of verification. *Psychological Review,* 1975, *82,* 45-73.

Carpenter, P. A. & Just, M. A. Models of sentence verification and linguistic comprehension. *Psychological Review,* 1976, *83,* 318-322.

Chaika, E. A linguist looks at "schizophrenic" language. *Brain and Language,* 1974, *1,* 257-276.

Chaika, E. Schizophrenic speech, slips of the tongue, and jargonaphasia: A reply to Fromkin and Lecours and Vanier-Clément. *Brain and Language,* 1977, *4,* 464-475.

Chapman, L. J. Recent advances in the study of schizophrenic cognition. *Schizophrenia Bulletin,* 1979, *5,* 568-580.

Chapman, L. J., & Chapman, J. P. *Disordered thought in schizophrenia.* New York: Appleton-Century-Crofts, 1973.

Chapman, L. J., & Chapman, J. P. The measurement of differential deficit. *Journal of Psychiatric Research,* 1978, *14,* 303-311.

Chapman, L. J., Chapman, J. P., & Daut, R. L. Schizophrenic inability to disattend from strong aspects of meaning. *Journal of Abnormal Psychology,* 1976, *85,* 35-40.

Chapman, L. J., Chapman, J. P., & Miller, G. A. A theory of verbal behavior in schizophrenia. In B. A. Maher (Ed.), *Progress in experimental personality research* (Vol. 1). New York: Academic Press, 1964.

Chomsky, N. *Syntactic structures.* The Hauge: Mouton, 1957.

Clemmer, E. J. Psycholinguistic aspects of pauses and temporal patterns in schizophrenic speech. *Journal of Psycholinguistic Research,* 1980, *9,* 161-186.

Clooney, J. L., & Murray, D. J. Same-different judgments in paranoid and schizophrenic patients: A laterality study. *Journal of Abnormal Psychology,* 1977, *86,* 655-658.

Cohen, B. D. Referent communication disturbances in schizophrenia. In S. Schwartz (Ed.), *Language and Cognition in schizophrenia.* Hillsdale, N.J.: Lawrence Erlbaum Associates, 1978.

Craik, F. I. M., & Lockhart, R. S. Levels of processing: A framework for memory research. *Journal of Verbal Learning and Verbal Behavior,* 1972, *11,* 671-684.

Cromwell, R. L. Assessment of schizophrenia. *Annual Review of Psychology,* 1975, *76,* 593-620.

Cromwell, R. L., & Dokecki, P. R. Schizophrenic language: A disattention interpretation. In S. Rosenberg & J. Koplin (Eds.), *Developments in applied psycholinguistics research.* New York: MacMillan, 1968.

Danks, J. H., & Glucksberg, S. Psychological scaling of linguistic properties. *Language and Speech,* 1970, *13,* 118-138.

Deckner, C. W., & Blanton, R. L. Effect of context and strength of association on schizophrenic verbal behavior. *Journal of Abnormal Psychology,* 1969, *74,* 348-351.

deSilva, W. P., & Hemsley, D. R. The influence of context on language perception in schizophrenia. *British Journal of Social and Clinical Psychology,* 1977, *16,* 337-345.

Dimond, S. J., Scammell, R. E., Pryce, I. G., Dafydd, H., & Gray, C. Callosal transfer and left-hand anomia in schizophrenia. *Biological Psychiatry,* 1979, *14,* 735-740.

DiSimoni, F. G., Darley, F. L., & Aronson, A. E. Patterns of dysfunction in schizophrenic patients on an aphasia test battery. *Journal of Speech & Hearing Disorders,* 1977, *42,* 498-513.

Durbin, M., & Martin, R. L. Speech in mania: Syntactic aspects. *Brain and Language,* 1977, *4,* 208-218.

Flor-Henry, P. Psychosis and temporal lobe epilepsy. A controlled investigation. *Epilepsia,* 1969, *10,* 363-395.

Fodor, J. A., Bever, T. G., & Garrett, M. F. *The psychology of language: An introduction to psycholinguistics and generative grammar.* New York: McGraw-Hill, 1974.

Forrest, D. V. Poiesis and the language of schizophrenia. In H. J. Vetter (Ed.), *Language behavior in schizophrenia.* Springfield, Ill.: Thomas, 1968.

Fromkin, V. A. A linguist looks at "A linguist looks at 'Schizophrenic language.'" *Brain and Language,* 1975, *2,* 495-500.

Garrett, M. F., Bever, T. G., & Fodor, J. A. The active use of grammar in speech perception. *Perception and Psychophysics,* 1966, *1,* 30-32.

Gerver, D. Linguistic rules and the perception and recall of speech by schizophrenic patients. *British Journal of Social and Clinical Psychology,* 1967, *6,* 204-211.

Gerver, D., Lawson, J. S., & Gerver, M. E. Schizophrenic speech: A factor-analytic approach. *Language & Speech,* 1976, *19,* 46-56.

Goldman-Eisler, F. *Psycholinguistics: Experiments in spontaneous speech.* New York: Academic Press, 1968.

Gordon, A. V., & Gregson, R. A. M. The symptom-sign inventory and diagnostic differentia for paranoid and nonparanoid schizophrenics. *British Journal of Social and Clinical Psychology,* 1970, *9,* 347-356.

Gottesman, I. I., & Shields, J. *Schizophrenia and genetics: A twin study vantage point.* New York: Academic Press, 1972.

Green, P. Defective interhemispheric transfer in schizophrenia. *Journal of Abnormal Psychology,* 1978, *87,* 472-480.

Green, P., & Kotenko, V. Superior speech comprehension in schizophrenics under monaural versus binaural listening conditions. *Journal of Abnormal Psychology,* 1980, *89,* 399-408.

Gruzelier, J. H. Bilateral asymmetry of skin conductance orienting activity and levels in schizophrenics. *Biological Psychiatry,* 1973, *1,* 21-41.

Gruzelier, J. H., & Hammond, N. V. Lateralized deficits and drug influences on the dichotic listening of schizophrenic patients. *Biological Psychiatry,* 1980, *15,* 759-780.

Gruzelier, J. H., & Venables, P. H. Skin conductance orienting activity in a heterogeneous sample of schizophrenics: Possible evidence of limbic dysfunction. *Journal of Nervous and Mental Disease,* 1972, *155,* 277-287.

Gruzelier, J. H., & Venables, P. H. Skin conductance responses to tones with and without attentional significance in schizophrenic and nonschizophrenic psychiatric patients. *Neuropsychologia,* 1973, *11,* 221-230.

Gruzelier, J. H., & Venables, P. H. Bimodality and lateral asymmetry of skin conductance orienting activity in schizophrenics: Replication and evidence of lateral asymmetry in patients with depression and disorder of personality. *Biological Psychiatry,* 1974, *8,* 55-73.

Gur, R. E. Motoric laterality imbalance in schizophrenia: A possible concomitant of left-hemisphere dysfunction. *Archives of General Psychiatry,* 1977, *34,* 33-37.

Gur, R. E. Left hemisphere dysfunction and left hemisphere overactivation in schizophrenia. *Journal of Abnormal Psychology,* 1978, *87,* 226-238.

Halliday, M. A. K., & Hasan, R. *Cohesion in English.* London: Longman, 1976.

Halpern, H., Darley, F. L., & Brown, J. R. Differential language and neurologic characteristics in cerebral involvement. *Journal of Speech and Hearing Disorders,* 1973, *38,* 162-173.

Harrow, M., & Prosen, M. Intermingling and disordered logic as influences on schizophrenic "thought disorders." *Archives of General Psychiatry,* 1978, *35,* 1213-1221.

Harrow, M., & Prosen, M. Schizophrenic thought disorders: Bizarre associations and intermingling. *American Journal of Psychiatry,* 1979, *136,* 293-296.

Hart, D. S., & Payne, R. W. Language structure and predictability in overinclusive patients. *British Journal of Psychiatry,* 1973, *123,* 643-652.

Herbert, R. K., & Waltensperger, K. Z. Schizophrasia: Case study of a paranoid schizophrenic's language. *Applied Psycholinguistics,* 1980, *1,* 81-93.

Jarvella, R. J. Syntactic processing of connected speech. *Journal of Verbal Learning and Verbal Behavior,* 1971, *10,* 409-416.

Kasanin, J. S. (Ed.). *Language and thought in schizophrenia.* Berkeley, Calif.: University of California Press, 1954.

Kimura, D. Dual functional asymmetry of the brain in visual perception. *Neuropsychologia,* 1966, *4,* 275-285.

Knight, R. A., & Sims-Knight, J. E. Integration of linguistic ideas in schizophrenics. *Journal of Abnormal Psychology,* 1979, *88,* 191-202.

Koh, S. D. Remembering of verbal materials by schizophrenic young adults. In S. Schwartz (Ed.), *Language and cognition in schizophrenia.* Hillsdale, N.J.: Lawrence Erlbaum Associates, 1978.

Koh, S. D., Marusarz, T. Z., & Rosen, A. J. Remembering of sentences by schizophrenic young adults. *Journal of Abnormal Psychology,* 1980, *89,* 291-294.

Kolers, P. A., Park, N. W., & Dell, G. S. On sentential anagrams: Making sentences out of words. *Journal of Psycholinguistic Research,* 1979, *8,* 165-192.

Laffal, J. *A source document in schizophrenia.* Hope Valley, R.I.: Gallery Press, 1979.

Lawson, J. S., McGhie, A., & Chapman, J. Perception of speech in schizophrenia. *British Journal of Psychology,* 1964, *110,* 375-380.

Lecours, A. R., & Vanier-Clément, M. Schizophasia and jargonaphasia: A comparative description with comments on Chaika's and Fromkin's respective looks at "schizophrenic" language. *Brain and Language,* 1976, *3,* 516-565.

Lerner, J., Nachshon, I., & Carmon, A. Responses of paranoid and nonparanoid schizophrenics in a dichotic listening task. *Journal of Nervous and Mental Disease,* 1977, *164,* 247-252.

Levy, J., & Reid, M. Variations in writing posture and cerebral organization. *Science,* 1976, *194,* 337-339.

Levy, J., & Trevarthen, C. Perceptual semantics and phonetic aspects' of elementary language processes in split-brain patients. *Brain,* 1977, *100,* 105-118.

Levy, R. The effect of chlorpromazine on sentence structure of schizophrenic patients. *Psychopharmacologia,* 1968, *13,* 426-432.

Levy, R., & Maxwell, A. E. The effect of verbal context on the recall of schizophrenics and other psychiatric patients. *British Journal of Psychology,* 1968, *114,* 311-316.

Lewinsohn, P. M., & Elwood, D. L. The role of contextual constraint on the learning of language samples in schizophrenia. *Journal of Nervous and Mental Disease,* 1961, *133,* 79-81.

Luchins, D., Pollin, W., & Wyatt, R. J. Laterality in monozygotic schizophrenic twins: An alternative hypothesis. *Biological Psychiatry,* 1980, *15,* 87-95.

Luchins, D. J., Weinberger, D. R., & Wyatt, R. J. Anomalous laterlization associated with a milder form of schizophrenia. *American Journal of Psychiatry,* 1979, *136,* 1598-1599.

Maher, B. A. Schizophrenia: Language and thought. In B. A. Maher (Ed.), *Principles of psychopathology.* New York: McGraw-Hill, 1966.

Maher, B. A., Manschreck, T. C., & Rucklos, M. E. Contextual constraint and the recall of verbal material in schizophrenia: The effect of thought disorder. *British Journal of Psychiatry,* 1980, *137,* 69-73.

Manschreck, T. C., Maher, B. A., Rucklos, M., & White, M. The predictability of thought disordered speech in schizophrenic patients. *British Journal of Psychiatry,* 1979, *134,* 595-601.
Marks, L. E., & Miller, G. A. The role of semantic and syntactic constrains in memorization of English sentences. *Journal of Verbal Learning and Verbal Behavior,* 1964, *3,* 1-5.
Martin, J. R., & Rochester, S. R. Cohesion and reference in schizophrenic speech. In A. Makkai & V. B. Makkai (Eds.), *The first Lacus forum, 1974.* Columbia, S.C.: Hornblum Press, 1975.
Miller, G., & Selfridge, J. Verbal context and the recall of meaningful material. *American Journal of Psychology,* 1950, *63,* 176-185.
Miller, W. K., & Phelan, J. G. Comparison of adult schizophrenics with matched normal native speakers of English as to acceptability of English sentences. *Journal of Psycholinguistic Research,* 1980, *9,* 579-593.
Moroz, M. O., & Fosmire, R. F. Application of cloze procedure to schizophrenic language. *Diseases of the Nervous System,* 1966, *27,* 408-410.
Neufeld, R. W. J. Components of processing deficit among paranoid and nonparanoid schizophrenics. *Journal of Abnormal Psychology,* 1977, *86,* 60-64.
Neufeld, R. W. J. The nature of deficit among paranoid and nonparanoid schizophrenics in the interpretation of sentences: An information processing approach. *Journal of Clinical Psychology,* 1978, *34,* 333-339.
Neuringer, C., Fiske, P. J., Schmidt, M. W., & Goldstein, G. Adherence to strong verbal meaning definitions in schizophrenics. *Journal of Genetic Psychology,* 1972, *121,* 315-323.
O'Connell, D. C., & Kowal, S. Cross-linguistic pause and rate phenomena in adults and adolescents. *Journal of Psycholinguistic Research,* 1972, *1,* 155-164.
O'Connell, D. C., Kowal, S., & Hörmann, H. Semantic determinants of pauses. *Psychologische Forschung,* 1969, *33,* 50-67.
Oltmanns, T. F., & Neale, J. M. Distractibility in relation to other aspects of schizophrenic disorder. In S. Schwartz (Ed.), *Language and cognition in schizophrenia.* Hillsdale, N.J.: Lawrence Erlbaum Associates, 1978.
Pavy, D. Verbal behavior in schizophrenia: A review of recent studies. *Psychological Bulletin,* 1968, *70,* 164-178.
Phillips, L. Case history data and prognosis in schizophrenia. *Journal of Nervous and Mental Disease,* 1953, *117,* 515-525.
Pic'l, A. K., Magaro, P. A., & Wade, E. A. Hemispheric functioning in paranoid and nonparanoid schizophrenia. *Biological Psychiatry,* 1979, *14,* 891-904.
Pogue-Geile, M. F., & Oltmanns, T. F. Sentence perception and distractability in schizophrenic, manic and depressed patients. *Journal of Abnormal Psychology,* 1980, *89,* 115-124.
Raeburn, K. M., & Tong, J. E. Experiments on contextual constraint in schizophrenia. *British Journal of Psychiatry,* 1968, *114,* 43-52.
Rausch, M. A., Prescott, T. E., & DeWolfe, A. A. Schizophrenic and aphasic language: Discriminable or not? *Journal of Consulting and Clinical Psychology,* 1980, *48,* 63-70.
Rochester, S. R. The role of information processing in the sentence decoding of schizophrenic listeners. *Journal of Nervous and Mental Disease,* 1973, *164,* 247-252.
Rochester, S. R., Harris, J., & Seeman, M. V. Sentence processing in schizophrenic listeners. *Journal of Abnormal Psychology,* 1973, *82,* 350-356.
Rochester, S. R., & Martin, J. R. The art of referring: The speaker's use of noun phrases to instruct the listener. In R. O. Freedle (Ed.), *Discourse production and comprehension* (Vol. 1). Norwood, N.J.: Ablex, 1977.
Rochester, S. R., & Martin, J. *Crazy talk.* New York: Plenum, 1979.
Rochester, S. R., Martin, J. R., & Thurston, S. Thought process disorder in schizophrenia: The listener's task. *Brain and Language,* 1977, *4,* 95-114.
Rochester, S. R., Thurston, S., & Rupp, J. Hesitations as clues to failures in coherence: Studies of the thought-disordered speaker. In S. Rosenberg (Ed.), *Sentence production.* Hillsdale, N.J.: Lawrence Erlbaum Associates, 1977.

Rosenberg, S. Semantic constraints on sentence production: An experimental approach. In S. Rosenberg (Ed.), *Sentence production: Developments in research and theory.* Hillsdale, N.J.: Lawrence Erlbaum Associates, 1977.

Rosenberg, S. D., & Cohen, B. D. Referential processes of speakers and listeners. *Psychological Review,* 1966, *73,* 208-231.

Rosenberg, S. D., & Tucker, G. J. Verbal behavior and schizophrenia: The semantic dimension. *Archives of General Psychiatry,* 1979, *36,* 1331-1340.

Rothbaum, P. A., Routh, D. K., Feagans, D. L., Kinney, L., & Vasu, E. Schizophrenics' difficulties in understanding ambiguous sentences. *Bulletin of the Psychonomic Society,* 1979, *13,* 199-202.

Rutter, D. R. Speech patterning in recently admitted and chronic long-stay schizophrenic patients. *British Journal of Social & Clinical Psychology,* 1977, *16,* 47-55. (a)

Rutter, D. R. Visual interaction and speech patterning in remitted and acute schizophrenic patients. *British Journal of Social & Clinical Psychology,* 1977, *16,* 357-361. (b)

Rutter, D. R. The reconstruction of schizophrenic speech. *British Journal of Psychiatry,* 1979, *134,* 356-359.

Rutter, D. R., Draffan, J., & Davies, J. Thought disorder and the predictability of schizophrenic speech. *British Journal of Psychiatry,* 1977, *131,* 67-68.

Rutter, D. R., Wishner, J., Kopytynska, H., & Button, M. The predictability of speech in schizophrenic patients. *British Journal of Psychiatry,* 1978, *132,* 228-232.

Sabin, E. J., Clemmer, E. J., O'Connell, D. C., & Kowal, S. A pausalogical approach to speech development. In A. W. Siegman & S. Feldstein (Eds.), *Of speech and time: Temporal speech patterns in interpersonal contexts.* Hillsdale, N.J.: Lawrence Erlbaum Associates, 1979.

Salzinger, K., Portnoy, S., & Feldman, R. S. Verbal behavior of schizophrenic and normal subjects. *Annals of the New York Academy of Sciences,* 1964, *105,* 845-860.

Salzinger, K., Portnoy, S., & Feldman, R. S. Communicability deficit in schizophrenics resulting from a more general deficit. In S. Schwartz (Ed.), *Language and cognition in schizophrenia.* Hillsdale, N.J.: Lawrence Erlbaum Associates, 1978.

Schneider, K. *Clinical psychopathology.* New York: Grune & Stratton, 1959.

Schwartz, G. E., Davidson, R. J., & Maer, F. Right hemisphere lateralization for emotion in the human brain: Interactions with cognition. *Science,* 1975, *190,* 286-288.

Schwartz, S. (Ed.). *Language and cognition in schizophrenia.* Hillsdale, N.J.: Lawrence Erlbaum Associates, 1978. (a)

Schwartz, S. Language and cognition in schizophrenia: A review and synthesis. In S. Schwartz (Ed.), *Language and cognition in schizophrenia.* Hillsdale, N.J.: Lawrence Erlbaum Associates, 1978. (b)

Schweitzer, L Differences of cerebral lateralization among schizophrenic and depressed patients. *Biological Psychiatry,* 1979, *14,* 721-734.

Schweitzer, L., Becker, E., & Welsh, H. Abnormalities of cerebral lateralization in schizophrenia patients. *Archives of General Psychiatry,* 1978, *35,* 982-989.

Shimkunas, A. Hemispheric asymmetry and schizophrenic thought disorder. In S. Schwartz, (Ed.), *Language and cognition in schizophrenia.* Hillsdale, N.J.: Lawrence Erlbaum Associates, 1978.

Siegel, A., Harrow, M., Reilly, F. E., & Tucker, G. J. Loose associations and disordered speech patterns in chronic schizophrenia. *Journal of Nervous & Mental Disease,* 1976, *162,* 105-112.

Silverman, G. Psycholinguistics of schizophrenic language. *Psychological Medicine,* 1972, *2,* 254-259.

Silverman, G. Redundancy, repetition and pausing in schizophrenic speech. *British Journal of Psychiatry,* 1973, *122,* 407-413.

Smith, E. E. Associative and editing processes in schizophrenic communication. *Journal of Abnormal Psychology,* 1970, *2,* 182-186.

Space, L. G., & Cromwell, R. L. Personal constructs among schizophrenic patients. In S. Schwartz

(Ed.), *Language and cognition in schizophrenia*. Hillsdale, N.J.: Lawrence Erlbaum Associates, 1978.

Spitzer, R., & Endicott, J. *Schedule for affective disorders and schizophrenia (SADS)* (2nd ed.). New York: Biometrics Research. New York State Psychiatric Institute, 1975.

Spitzer, R. L., Endicott, J., & Robbins, E. *Research diagnostic criteria (RDC) for a selected group of functional disorders* (2nd ed.). New York: Biometrics Research, New York State Psychiatric Institute, 1975.

Spitzer, R. L., Endicott, J., & Robbins, E. *Research diagnostic criteria (RDC) for a selected group of functional disorders* (3rd ed.). New York: Biometrics Research, New York State Psychiatric Institute, 1977.

Sternberg, S. The discovery of processing stages: Extension of Donders' method. *Acta Psychologica,* 1969, *30,* 276-315.

Straube, E., Barth, V., & König, B. Do schizophrenics use linguistic rules in speech recall? *British Journal of Social and Abnormal Psychology,* 1979, *18,* 407-415.

Taylor, W. L. "Cloze procedure": A new tool for measuring readability. *Journalism Quarterly,* 1953, *30,* 415-433.

Torrey, E. F. Neurological abnormalities in schizophrenic patients. *Biological Psychiatry,* 1980, *15,* 381-388.

Truscott, I. P. Contextual constraint and schizophrenic language. *Journal of Consulting and Clinical Psychology,* 1970, *35,* 189-194.

Ullmann, L. P., & Giovannoni, J. M. The development of a self-report measure of the process-reactive continuum. *Journal of Nervous and Mental Disease,* 1964, *138,* 38-42.

Vetter, H. J. (Ed.). *Language behavior in schizophrenia*. Springfield, Ill.: Thomas, 1968. (a)

Vetter, H. J. New word coinage in the psychopathological context. *Psychiatry Quarterly,* 1968, *42,* 298-312. (b)

Watson, S. J. Effect of delayed auditory feedback on process and reactive schizophrenic subjects. *Journal of Abnormal Psychology,* 1974, *83,* 609-615.

Williams, R. M., Hemsley, D. R., & Denning-Duke, C. Language behavior in acute and chronic schizophrenia. *British Journal of Social and Clinical Psychology,* 1976, *15,* 73-83.

Zamura, E. N., & Kaelbling, R. Memory and electroconvulsive therapy. *American Journal of Psychiatry,* 1965, *122,* 546-554.

Author Index

Numbers appearing in italic refer to bibliographic information.

A

Aaronson, D., 4, *20*
Abbeduto, L., 16, *21*
Abelson, R. P., 10, *29,* 211, *216,* 258, *294*
Abrahamsen, A. A., 3, *21*
Abramson, A. S., 497, *533*
Ackerman, N., 503, *531*
Adams, M. J., 272, *290*
Aderman, D., 102, 103, 104, 105, 115, *186*
Adis, Castro, G., 116, *194*
Adjemian, C., 229, 230, *251*
Agar, M., 276, 278, 282, *290*
Ahlgren, I., 461, *469*
Aitchison, J., 5, *21*
Alajouanine, T., 495, *530*
Albert, M. L., 4, 12, *21, 28,* 247, *251*
Albertini, J., 309, 322
Alford, J. A., 93, *190*
Allen, D. V., 344, 348, *386*
Allmeyer, D. H., 84, 121, *189*
Altschuler, K., 454, *474*
Andersen, R., 225, 228, 250, *251*
Andersen, R. W., *21,* 217, 221, *251*
Anderson, D., 316, *325*
Anderson, J. R., 4, 6, *21,* 72, 81, *186,* 268, *294*
Anderson, E., 288, *290*
Anderson, R. C., 4, 14, *21,* 258, 263, 269, *290, 293*
Anderson, V., 209, *214*
Anderson, W. G., 54, 67, *191*
Andreasen, N. C., 554, 555, 559, *584*
Andreasen, N. J., 556, *584*
Andreewsky, E., 511, 512, *530*
Angelergues, R., 495, *532*
Anglin, J. M., 3, *21,* 353, 354, *386*
Anthony, D. A., 435, *469*
Antinucci, F., 310, *322*
Appelman, I. B., 90, *186*
Applegate, J., 315, *322*
Apolloni, T., 380, 383, *387, 390*
Aram, D., 295, 296, *322*
Arieti, S., 538, 539, 541, 582, 584, *584*
Arlman, Rupp, A., 5, *30*
Arnold, D., 89, *187*
Arnow, M. S., 437, *475*
Aronson, A. E., 543, 544, *586*
Ashbrook, E., 462, 463, *473*
Astor-Stetson, E. C., 89, *187*
Atkinson, R. C., 36, 40, *186*
Atlas, M., 209, 213, *214*
Augustine, L., 316, *325*
Aurnhammer-Frith, U., 398, 400, *424*
Austin, G. A., 286, *291*

B

Babb, R., 457, 468, *469*
Babbini, B. E., 445, *470*

AUTHOR INDEX

Bader, L., 508, *535*
Baer, D. M., 380, *386*
Bailey, N., 221, *251*
Baker, D., 454, *472*
Baker, E., 499, 518, *530, 532*
Baker, L., 261, *290,* 401, 404, 405, 406, 409, 410, *424, 425*
Bakker, D., 5, *31*
Bakker, D. J., 5, *29,* 157, *186*
Balkan, L., 245, *251*
Ball, J., 312, *322*
Baltaxe, C., 400, 403, 404, 406, *424*
Balthazar, E. E., 8, *28*
Bannister, D., 551, *584*
Barclay, C. R., 330, *386*
Bard, B., 12, 17, *29*
Barnitz, J., 260, 270, *293*
Baron, J., 49, 55, 56, 60, 70, 90, 107, 111, 115, 127, 128, 129, 131, 132, 135, 136, 141, 143, 145, 164, 165, 172, 178, 179, *186*
Barritt, L. S., 354, 370, *391*
Barron, R. W., 115, 135, *186*
Barry, R. J., 411, *425*
Bartak, L., 395, 396, 401, 404, 409, 410, 420, *424, 425, 427*
Bartel, N. R., 343, 348, *386*
Barth, V., 566, *590*
Bartlett, S., 307, *325*
Bartolucci, G., 361, 363, *386,* 397, 401, *425, 427*
Basili, A. G., 511, 515, 526, *530*
Bass, K., 301, *322*
Basser, L., 297, *322*
Bates, E., 3, *21,* 364, *386,* 404, *425,* 459, *470*
Bates, M., 469, *470*
Baumal, R., 92, 93, 94, 135, 171, *196*
Beaulieu, M., 409, *427*
Beaumont, J. G., 577, *584*
Beck, B., 410, 411, *427*
Becker, C. A., 54, *186*
Becker, E., 574, 580, *589*
Bedrosian, J. L., 336, 367, *386, 389*
Begg, I., 137, *186, 187*
Begy, G., 161, *194*
Beilin, H., 6, *21*
Beit-Hallahmi, B., 231, *253*
Bell, M. S., 268, *292*
Bellugi, U., 4, *26,* 399, *425,* 434, 448, 456, 461, 462, 463, 464, *470, 471, 472*
Belmont, J. M., 373, *387*
Benaroya, S., 421, 422, *425*

Bender, J., 311, *322*
Bender, L. A., 146, *187*
Bender, N. L., 355, *386*
Benedict, H., 5, *21, 25*
Bennett, S. W., 354, 370, *391*
Benson, D. F., 483, 484, 487, 488, 489, 510, 511, *530, 534*
Benson, J. D., 265, *290*
Benton, A. L., 297, 303, *322,* 477, *530*
Ben-Zeev, S., 246, *251*
Berberich, J. P., 418, *427*
Bereiter, C., 209, 210, 213, *214, 216*
Berger, M., 11, *31*
Berko, J., 345, 346, *386*
Berlin, B., 286, *290*
Berlin, C. I., 5, *27*
Berndt, R. S., 493, 500, 501, 504, 511, 512, 513, 515, 517, 520, 524, 526, 527, *530*
Bernero, R., 432, *470*
Bernhardt, B., 316, 318, *323*
Bernholtz, N. A., 502, *532*
Bernstein, D., 307, *326*
Berrian, R. W., 54, 67, *191*
Berry, G. W., 365, 377, *389*
Berry, P., 4, *21,* 349, 375, *386*
Besner, D., 53, 54, 55, 56, 70, 127, 178, *188*
Bettelheim, B., 413, 414, *425*
Bever, T. G., 5, *21,* 526, *531,* 562, 563, *586*
Beveridge, M. C., 365, 366, *386*
Bialer, I., 8, *31*
Biemiller, A., 64, 125, 136, *187*
Bierwisch, M., 502, 521, *530, 535*
Birch, H., 157, *187*
Birch, J., 466, *474*
Bishop, C. H., 135, *189*
Bjork, E. L., 60, 83, 85, 88, *187, 189*
Black, J. B., 211, *214,* 260, *290*
Blank, M., 5, 8, 17, *21,* 337, 351, *386*
Blanton, R. L., 448, 449, *473,* 560, *586*
Bleuler, E., *585*
Bliss, D., 416, *428*
Bliss, L. S., 344, 348, *386*
Block, E. M., 4, *21*
Bloom, L., 4, 8, 11, *21, 26,* 235, 239, *251,* 304, *322,* 433, 462, *470*
Blott, J. P., 11, *27,* 382, *389*
Blount, B. G., 5, *21*
Blue, M., 344, *391*
Blumstein, S. E., 4, *21,* 495, 496, 497, 498, 499, 500, 505, 506, 507, 517, *530, 532, 535*
Bobrow, D. B., 272, *290*

AUTHOR INDEX

Bock, R. D., 517, *535*
Boder, E., 143, 144, 145, 146, 147, 164, *187*
Boies, S. L., 203, 204, 210, *215*
Boklage, C. E., 578, 579, *585*
Bolders, J. G., 6, *27,* 310, 318, 319, 325
Boller, F., 488, 504, *530*
Bonnycastle, D., 455, *471*
Bonvillian, J. D., 5, *21, 23,* 420, 421, *425*
Boomer, D. S., 553, *585*
Born, B., 417, *428*
Bornstein, H., 435, 436, *470*
Bothwell, H., 432, *470*
Bouchard, R., 487, *530*
Boucher, J., 397, 398, 411, *425*
Bouma, H., 109, 110, *187*
Bower, G., 264, *290*
Bower, G. H., 211, *214,* 260, *290*
Bowerman, M. F., 5, 11, *21,* 311, *322,* 337, 340, 351, *386,* 462, *470*
Boyes-Braem, P., 459, 460, *470*
Bradbury, B., 345, 347, *389*
Bradley, D., 395, *425*
Bradshaw, J. L., 54, *187*
Brady, D. O., 421, *425*
Bragg, B., 434, 436, *470*
Braine, M., 462, *470*
Brand, J., 6, *30*
Brannon, R. C. L., 231, *253*
Bransford, J. D., 6, *21,* 375, *386,* 560, 568, *585*
Branston, M. B., 337, *389*
Brantley, J. C., 5, *26*
Brasel, K., 457, 467, 468, *470*
Bremer, C., 160, 167, *194*
Bressman, B., 124, *194*
Bressnan, J., 3, *25*
Brewer, L., 459, 466, *470*
Brewer, W. F., 51, 52, *187*
Bridges, A., 5, *21*
Brimer, A., 438, *470*
Brittain, M. M., 156, *187*
Britton, J. L., 204, 206, *214*
Broadbent, D. E., 41, 47, 112, 113, *187*
Broen, P., 8, *22*
Broen, W. E., Jr., 538, 561, *585*
Brooks, C., 206, *214*
Brooks, L., 116, 129, 130, 179, *187*
Brophy, J. E., 283, *290*
Brown, A. C., 259, *290*
Brown, A. L., 330, *386*
Brown, C. H., 286, *291, 294*

Brown, C. R., 113, *187*
Brown, H., 317, *325*
Brown, I., Jr., 11, *21*
Brown, J. R., 543, *587*
Brown, J., 301, *322,* 523, *532*
Brown, J. W., 484, 485, *530*
Brown, R., 3, 4, *22,* 221, 222, *251,* 308, 309, 314, *322,* 336, 339, 340, 341, 346, 348, 351, 353, 362, 377, *386,* 399, *425,* 456, 462, *470, 471,* 541, *585*
Brown, W. S., Jr., 359, *390*
Brownell, H. H., 520, 524, *530*
Bruce, B., 201, *214*
Bruck, M., 246, *251*
Bruner, J. S., 6, *28, 29,* 40, 41, 46, 59, 68, 71, 80, 101, 121, 187, *193,* 286, *291*
Bruno, K. J., 14, *22*
Bryant, P. E., 376, *386, 387*
Bryen, D., 343, 348, *386*
Brzoska, M. A., 354, 357, *392*
Buckholt, J. A., 376, 377, 379, *387, 390*
Budoff, M., 354, *388*
Buium, N., 378, 379, *387*
Bull, H. C., 575, *585*
Bullowa, M., 6, *22*
Burgess, T., 204, 206, *214*
Burke, D., 6, *26*
Burling, R., 226, *251*
Burns, M., 375, *389*
Buros, O. K., 8, *22*
Burt, M., 4, *22,* 217, *251*
Burt, M. K., 220, 221, 222, 227, *252*
Burton, J. K., 5, *31*
Butler, B., 156, 166, *187*
Butterfield, E. C., 373, *387*
Butterworth, B., 553, *585*
Button, M., 552, *589*
Byers, H., 278, *291*
Byers, P., 278, *291*

C

Caccamise, F., 459, 466, *470, 472*
Cairns, H. S., 6, *22*
Calfee, R. C., 37, 118, 149, *187, 197*
Calnan, M., 8, *29*
Camaioni, L., 404, *425*
Cameron, A. C., 14, *25*
Camp, B. W., 144, 145, 164, *187*
Campbell, B., 406, *425*
Campbell, D. T., 250, *252*

Campbell, R., 304, *325*
Cancino, H., 217, 220, 221, 222, 225, 227, *252, 253*
Canter, C. J., 504, *534*
Canter, S. M., 8, *26*, 307, *325*
Cantwell, D. P., 8, *22*, 396, 401, 404, 405, 406, 409, 410, *424, 425*
Caplan, D., 5, *22*, 499, 502, *533*
Caramazza, A., 4, *22*, 493, 497, 498, 499, 500, 501, 502, 504, 505, 506, 507, 508, 509, 511, 512, 513, 514, 515, 517, 519, 520, 521, 522, 524, 526, 527, *530, 531, 534, 535*
Carlson, C. F., 413, 414, *426*
Carmon, A., 571, *587*
Carpenter, P. A., 563, *585*
Carpenter, R., 300, 310, 318, *323, 327*
Carr, D. B., 6, *22*
Carr, T. C., 89, *187*
Carroll, J. B., 4, 14, *22, 24*, 167, *187*, 330, *387*
Carrow, E., 8, *22*, 226, *252*, 453, *470*
Carrow, M. A., 343, *387*
Carrow, M. W., 8, *22*
Carter, B., 151, *192*
Carter, J. F., 263, *293*
Casey, L. D., 422, *425*
Cattell, J. McK., 33, 40, 41, 71, 80, 116, *187*
Cazden, C. B., 4, *22*, 279, *291*, 462, *470*
Celce-Murcia, M., 221, 235, *255*
Cervantes, R., 242, *252*
Chafe, W. L., 258, 278, *291*, 352, *387*
Chaika, E., 541, 542, 544, 545, 546, *585*
Chalfant, J., 304, *323*
Chall, J., 129, 141, 145, *187*, 439, *470*
Chambers, S. M., 55, 62, 70, 112, 121, *189*
Chapman, L. J., 569, *585*
Chapman, J., 568, *587*
Chapman, J. P., 569, *585*
Chapman, R. S., 5, 8, *22*, 149, *187, 197*, 302, *323*, 336, 337, *389*
Charrow, V., 466, *470*
Chen, C. C., 161, *194*
Cherry, R., 199, *214*
Cheseldine, S., 382, *387*
Chi, M. T. H., 6, *22*
Chiesi, H. L., 268, *294*
Chomsky, C., 128, 138, *187*
Chomsky, N., 1, 3, *22*, 51, *188*, 307, *323, 377, 387*, 398, 401, *425*, 443, 468, *470*, 493, 502, *531*, 538, *585*

Churchill, D., 419, *426*
Churchill, D. W., 421, *425*
Ciciarelli, A., 8, *22*
Clark, E. V., 3, 4, 5, 6, 7, 11, 14, *22, 23*, 354, 364, 369, *387*, 460, *470*, 492, 494, 513, *531*
Clark, H. H., 3, 4, 5, 6, 7, 11, 14, *22, 23*, 354, 364, 369, *387*, 492, 494, 513, *531*
Clark, J. M., 137, *186*
Clark, R., 341, *387*
Clarke, M. A., 231, *252*
Clement, R., 231, *253*
Clements, P., 263, *291*
Clemmer, E. J., 553, 554, 573, *585, 589*
Clooney, J. L., 575, *585*
Coates, R., 490, *532*
Coggins, T. E., 353, 362, *387*
Cogniat, R., 266, *291*
Cohen, B. D., 548, 549, 556, 559, *585, 589*
Cohen, M., 5, *24*
Cohen, R. L., 6, *23*, 373, *387*
Colby, K. M., 411, *425*
Cole, B., 358, *389*
Cole, M., 287, *291, 292*
Cole, R. A., 5, *23*
Collins, A., 99, *188*, 201, *214*, 272, *290*
Collins, A. M., 99, *188*
Collins, Algren, M., 459, 461, 463, 464, 465, *470*
Collins, W. A., 3, 5, *23*
Coltheart, M., 53, 54, 55, 56, 70, 127, 178, *188*, 512, *531*
Comer, P., 116, *193*
Compton, A., 315, 316, 317, 318, *323*
Condon, W. S., 277, *291*
Connally, J. E., 11, *28*
Conrad, R., 4, *23*, 54, *188*, 432, 438, 446, 448, 450, 451, *471*
Cook, V. J., 217, 224, 240, *252*
Cooke, S., 380, *387*
Cooke, T. P., 380, 383, *387, 390*
Cooper, C., 199, 203, 204, 206, 213, *214, 215*
Cooper, D. E., 5, *23*
Cooper, F. S., 66, *192*, 497, *533*
Cooper, R. L., 443, *471*
Cooper, W. E., 14, *23*, 497, 498, 499, *530*
Copley, B., 199, *214*
Corcoran, D. W. J., 54, 95, 98, 126, *188*
Corder, S. P., 220, 229, 234, *252*
Corkin, S., 157, *188*
Cornett, O., 435, *471*

Cornwell, A. C., 354, *387*
Corrigan, R., 4, 6, 11, *23*, 337, *387*
Corson, H., 467, 468, *471*
Cosca, C., 282, *292*
Cosky, M. J., 52, 111, 116, 123, *188, 190*
Court, D., 311, *325*
Cousins, A., 309, *323*
Cox, A., 395, 396, 401, 404, 410, 420, *425*
Craig, E., 463, *471*
Craig, H. K., 4, 8, *23*
Craik, F. I. M., 571, *585*
Cramblit, N. S., 298, 299, *323*, 378, *387*
Crist, W. B., 110, *192*
Crockett, D. J., 8, *23, 25*
Cromer, R. F., 4, 6, *23*, 297, 303, *323*, 329, 350, 385, *387*, 395, *426*
Cromer, W., 156, 160, 161, *188, 195*
Cromwell, R. L., 539, 540, 542, 547, 548, *585, 589*
Cronbach, L. J., 250, *252*
Cronnell, B., 44, 46, 116, 122, 172, *195*
Cross, T., 312, *322*
Crothers, E. J., 263, *291*
Crouse, M. B., 156, *197*
Crystal, D., 3, 8, 11, *23*, 463, *471*
Cummins, J., 247, *252*
Cundari, L., 357, *392*
Cunitz, A. R., 37, *190*
Cunningham, C., 299, *326*
Curcio, F., *427*
Curtis, B., 305, 306, *327*
Curtis, R. A., 6, *27*
Curtiss, S., 4, 12, *23*

D

Dalby, M., 297, *323*
Dafydd, H., 577, *586*
Dale, P. S., 3, 7, 8, 11, *23*, 415, *426*, 461, 462, *471*
Danks, J. H., 552, *585*
Darley, F. L., 543, 544, *586, 587*
Darnton, B., 314, *324*
Dato, D. P., 227, *252*
Daut, R. L., 569, *585*
Davelaar, E., 53, 54, 55, 56, 70, 127, 178, *188*
Davidson, H. P., 108, *188*
Davidson, R. J., 573, *589*
Davies, J., 551, *589*
Davis, A., 283, *291*

Davis, H., 430, 431, *471*
Dawis, R. V., 285, *291*
DeAjuriaguerra, J., 12, *23*, 295, 301, 303, *323*
deBeaugrande, R., 4, *23*, 263, *291*
Deckner, C. W., 560, *586*
deJong, W., 5, *31*
Delattre, P. C., 66, *192*
Dell, G. S., 558, *587*
DeLong, G. R., 411, *426*
Denes, G., 508, *531*
deHirsch, K., 155, *188, 191*
Denckla, M. B., 155, *188*
Denning-Duke, C., 569, *590*
Dennis, M., 5, *23*, 529, *531*
DePaulo, B. M., 5, *23*
DeRenzi, E., 504, *531*
Derouesné, J., 519, *533*
DeSetto, L., 147, 150, 157, 158, 159, 179, *196*
deSilva, W. P., 561, *586*
DesLauriers, A. M., 413, 414, *426*
Despert, J. L., 406, *426*
Deutsch, W., 5, *24*
Dever, R., 347, 348, *387*
Dever, R. B., 344, 369, *390*
deVilliers, J. G., 3, 4, 5, 6, 8, *24*, 461, 462, *471*
deVilliers, P. A., 3, 4, 6, 8, *24*, 461, 462, *471*
Devin, J., 313, *326*
Dewart, M. H., 372, *387*
DeWolfe, A. A., 558, *588*
DiFrancesca, S., 438, *471*
Dihoff, R., 302, *323*
Diller, K., 4, *24*, 217, *252*
Dimond, S. J., 577, *584, 586*
Dingwall, W. O., 5, *24*
DiSimoni, F. G., 543, 544, *586*
Dockecki, P. R., 540, 542, 547, *585*
Dodd, B., 359, 360, 361, 362, 363, *387*
Dodge, R., 33, 40, *188*
Doehring, D. G., 125, *188*, 455, *471*
Dolcourt, J. L., 144, 145, 164, *187*
Dollard, J., 283, *291*
Dolley, D. G., 349, *391*
Dominic, J. F., 199, *214*
Donaldson, M., 6, 7, 13, *24*, 337, *387*
Dooley, J. F., 339, 340, 348, 351, 353, 382, *388*
Dore, J., 6, *24*
Douglass, A., 5, *28*
Dowley, G., 287, *292*

AUTHOR INDEX

Dowling, K., 5, *29*
Draffan, J., 551, *589*
Dressler, W., 263, *291*
Drewnowski, A., 95, 97, 98, 116, 135, 162, 163, 177, 185, *188*
Duchan, J. F., 351, *388*
Dugas, J. L., 373, *388*
Dulay, H. C., 4, *22*, 217, 220, 221, 222, 227, *251, 252*
Dull, C. Y., 231, *253*
Dumas, G., 228, 229, 235, *256*
Dunn-Rankin, P., 108, 109, *188*
Durand, M., 495, *530*
Durbin, M., 12, *24*, 543, *586*
Durr, W. K., 440, *473*

E

Edwards, J. R., 4, 12, *24*
Edwards, M., 316, 318, *323*
Eggert, G. H., 478, *531*
Ehri, L., 125, 131, *188*
Eichelman, W. H., 113, *188*
Eilers, R. E., 5, *24*
Eisenberg, L., 397, *426*
Eisenson, J., 297, 305, *323, 326*
Elardo, R., 11, *24*
Elwood, D. L., 568, *587*
Embry, M., 409, *427*
Endicott, J., 550, 555, 564, 567, 574, 579, *590*
Eppel, P., 397, *425*
Erdige, S., 8, *30*
Erdmann, B., 33, 40, *188*
Erickson, J. G., 351, *388*
Ericsson, K. A., 203, *214*
Eriksen, C. W., 67, *188,* 448, *471*
Erikson, F., 277, *291*
Erreich, A., 4, *24*
Ervin-Tripp, S., 237, *252*
Essen, J., 8, *29*
Estes, W. K., 38, 60, 79, 80, 81, 82, 83, 84, 85, 86, 87, 88, 90, 92, 94, 95, 101, 103, 104, 105, 106, 108, 120, 121, 171, 172, 176, 181, 187, *188, 189*
Evans, D., 335, 348, *388*
Evans, M. A., 420, 421, *428*

F

Fant, C. G. M., 109, *191*
Farwell, C., 315, *323*

Fathman, A., 227, 237, *252*
Fay, D., 403, *426*
Feagans, D. L., 569, *589*
Feigenbaum, E. A., 44, 90, *189*
Feldman, C., 245, *252*
Feldman, H., 19, *25,* 459, *471, 472*
Feldman, R. S., 541, 552, 559, *589*
Feldstein, S., 14, *30*
Felix, S. W., 223, *252*
Felker, D. B., 12, 14, *24*
Ferguson, C. A., 5, *30,* 239, *256,* 377, *391*
Ferneti, C. I., 376, *389*
Fey, M., 313, *323*
Fey, S., 313, *323*
Fillmore, C. J., 3, 4, *24,* 205, *214,* 310, *323*
Fillmore, L. W., 235, 236, *252*
Fine, J., 290, *291*
Finocchiaro, M., 4, *22,* 217, *251*
Fischer, F. W., 151, *192*
Fischer, S., 463, 465, *471*
Fish, B., 406, *428*
Fisher, L., 66, *192*
Fishman, J., 289, *291*
Fiske, P. J., 569, *588*
Fleisher, S., 199, *214*
Fletcher, D., 466, *470*
Fletcher, J., 469, *471*
Fletcher, P., 3, 8, 11, *23, 25*
Flor-Henry, P., 569, 580, *586*
Flower, L. S., 200, 202, 203, 205, 206, 210, 213, *214, 215*
Flowers, D. M., 371, *388*
Fluharty, N. B., 8, *24*
Fodor, I. G., 502, *532*
Fodor, J. A., 506, 521, 526, *531, 532,* 562, 563, *586*
Folger, M. K., 6, *24,* 302, 317, *323, 326,* 337, *388*
Forrest, D. V., 539, *586*
Forrest, T., 305, *326*
Forster, K. I., 55, 56, 62, 70, 112, 121, 124, 127, 139, 178, 183, *189, 195*
Fosmire, R. F., 552, *588*
Foss, D. J., 3, 5, 6, 7, 14, *24,* 369, *388,* 492, *531*
Fouts, R. S., 420, *426*
Foxen, T., 349, *386*
Fowler, C., 151, *192*
Frake, C. O., 275, *291*
Francis, W. N., 166, *191*
Franklin, E., 8, *21*

Franks, J. J., 568, *585*
Fransella, F., 551, *584*
Fraser, C., 5, *24*, 456, *471*
Frazier, L., 513, 526, *531*
Frederiksen, C. H., 199, *214*, 263, 270, 271, *291*
Frederiksen, J. F., 53, 55, 70, 112, 121, *189*
Freed, B., 240, *253*
Freedle, R. O., 4, 14, *22, 24*, 258, 261, 262, 267, 268, 271, 273, 285, 287, 288, *291, 292, 293*
Freedman, P., 310, 318, *323*
Freeman, R. B., 219, *255*
Fremgen, A., 403, *426*
Freud, S., 479, *531*
Friederici, A. D., 511, 512, *531*
Friedlander, B. Z., 5, 8, *31*
Friedman, K. A., 11, *24*
Friedman, L., 434, 463, *471*
Friedman, P., 8, 11, *24, 26*
Frisina, D. R., 466, *474*
Frith, U., 144, 164, *189*
Fromkin, V. A., 12, *23, 24*, 203, *215*, 542, 544, *586*
Fulwiler, R. L., 420, *426*
Furrow, D., 5, *25*
Furth, H., 437, 447, 454, *471*
Fry, M. A., 155, 156, *189*

G

Gaddes, W. H., 8, *25*
Gagne, E. D., 268, *292*
Gainotti, G., 518, *531*
Gall, F., 297, *323*
Gallagher, T., 314, *323, 324*
Gallagher, T. M., 4, 8, *23, 28*
Galvin, J., 521, *535*
Gardner, G. T., 44, 171, 182, *195*
Gardner, H., 505, 508, 511, 517, *531*
Gardner, R. C., 231, *253*
Gardner, W. I., 347, *387*
Garman, M., 3, 8, 11, *23, 25*
Garrett, M. F., 506, 526, *531*, 562, 563, *586*
Garside, R., 311, *325*
Gazzaniga, M. S., 528, *531*
Geers, A., 453, 454, *471*
Gelman, R., 313, *326*
Genesse, F., 13, *25*
Gentner, D., 201, *214*
George, H. V., 220, *253*

Gerber, R., 199, *214*
Gerver, D., 552, 566, *586*
Gerver, M. E., 552, *586*
Geschwind, N., 297, *324*, 408, *426*, 480, 484, 487, 488, 489, 490, 510, 511, 516, 517, 530, *531, 532*
Giannelli, W., 4, *28*, 350, *390*
Gibson, E. J., 4, *25*, 37, 41, 46, 63, 64, 65, 68, 69, 79, 91, 95, 102, 103, 106, 109, 118, 120, 121, 124, 125, 128, 134, 135, 136, 138, 157, 175, 176, 178, 180, 185, *189, 190*
Gibson, J. J., 63, 109, 121, *189*
Giddan, J., 418, *428*
Giovannoni, J. M., 559, *590*
Glanzer, M., 37, *190*
Gleason, J. B., 502, 503, 506, 507, *531, 532*
Gleitman, H., 377, *390*
Gleitman, L. R., 66, *194*, 377, *390*
Glenn, C. G., 258, 260, 271, *294*
Glicksman, L., 231, *253*
Glidden, L. M., 356, 369, *388*
Glucksberg, S., 552, *585*
Glushko, R. J., 172, *190*
Goebel, R., 5, *29*
Gold, C., 91, 93, 135, 171, *196*
Goldberg, K. E., 379, *387*
Goldin-Meadow, S., 5, 19, *25*, 459, *472*
Goldfarb, N., 409, *426*
Goldfarb, W., 409, 410, *426, 427*
Goldiamond, I., 112, *190*
Goldman, S. R., 127, 154, 161, *193*
Goldman-Eisler, F., 203, *215*, 553, 585, *586*
Goldstein, G., 569, *588*
Goldstein, K., 480, 485, *531*
Goldstein, R., 297, *324*
Golinkoff, R. M., 6, *25*, 124, 153, *190*
Gomez, L. M., 54, *186*
Good, T. L., 283, *290*
Goodenough, C., 505, 509, *531, 535*
Goodglass, H., 4, *25*, 297, *324*, 483, 484, 485, 488, 489, 490, 499, 500, 501, 502, 503, 504, 506, 507, 516, 517, 518, *530, 531, 532*
Goodman, K. S., 98, 167, *190*
Goodnow, J. J., 286, *291*
Gordon, A. V., 564, *586*
Gordon, K., 382, *389*
Gottesman, I. I., 578, *584*
Gouch, P. E., 51, 52, *195*
Gough, J., 240, *253*
Gough, P. B., 39, 51, 52, 55, 65, 92, 93, 111, 116, 123, 126, 174, *190, 194*

Gould, J. D., 202, 203, 204, 210, 213, *215*
Gowie, C. J., 6, *25*
Graesser, A. C., 271, *292*
Graham, J. T., 345, *388*
Graham, L. W., 345, *388*
Graham, N. C., 374, *388*
Grandstaff, N., 297, *325*
Gray, C., 577, *586*
Gray, V. A., 14, *25*
Greaves, W. S., 265, *290*
Green, E., 487, 488, 503, 506, 507, 509, *530, 531, 532, 535*
Green, P., 577, 578, *586*
Greenbaum, S., 3, *28*
Greenberg, G., 354, *388*
Greenberg, J. H., 3, 5, *25*
Greenberg, S. N., 89, *190*
Greene, E., 271, *293*
Greenfield, D., 397, *428*
Greenfield, P., 6, *25*, 311, 312, *324, 326*
Greenough, D., 349, *388*
Gregg, L., 199, *215*
Gregory, M. J., 265, *292*
Gregson, R. A. M., 564, *586*
Grieve, R., 406, *425*
Grimes, J. E., 263, 264, 279, *292*
Grober, E., 523, *532*
Groher, M., 316, *325*
Grossman, H. J., 329, *388*
Grossman, M., 522, *532*
Gruzelier, J. H., 569, 570, 571, 580, *586*
Guess, D., 380, *386*
Guignard, F., 295, 301, 303, *323*
Guillaume, P., 311, *324*
Guinet, L., 138, *189*
Guiora, A. Z., 231, *253*
Gumperz, J., 273, 274, *292*
Gur, R. E., 572, 573, 574, 577, 578, 580, *586*
Guralnick, M. J., 379, *388*
Gustafson, L., 12, *25*
Gustason, G., 436, 452, 457, *472*
Guthrie, J. T., 156, *190*
Gutmann, A. J., 379, *388*
Guttman, L., 225, *253*

H

Haas, W., 315, 318, 321, *324*
Haber, L., 321, *324*
Hains, S., 156, 166, *187*
Hakes, D. T., 3, 5, 6, 7, 14, *24*, 369, *388*, 492, *531*

Hakuta, K., 5, *24*, 217, 220, 221, 222, 225, 227, 228, 235, *253*
Hale, G., 261, 262, 271, *292*
Hall, W. S., 285, 287, 288, *292*
Halle, M., 3, *25*, 51, 109, *188, 191*, 398, *425*
Halliday, M. A. K., 3, *25*, 290, *292*, 546, *587*
Halpern, H., 543, *587*
Hamayan, E., 13, *25*
Hamilton, M. L., 4, 12, *31*
Hammermeister, F., 438, *472*
Hammond, M., 41, 46, 68, 102, 103, 118, *190*
Hammond, N. V., 571, 580, *586*
Handscombe, R.J., 265, *292*
Hansen, D., 66, *190*
Hardyck, C. D., 54, 126, *190*, 448, *472*
Harlock, W., 490, *532*
Harris, J., 562, *588*
Harris, R. J., 14, *22*
Harrison, M. I., 440, *473*
Harrison, R. H., 354, *388*
Harrow, M., 556, *587, 589*
Hart, B., 8, *25*
Hart, D. S., 552, *587*
Hart, J., 511, 512, *530*
Hartje, W., 504, *534*
Hartley, R. N., 131, *190*
Hartmann, M., 382, *389*
Hartung, J., 418, *426*
Hasan, R., 3, *25*, 290, *292*, 546, *587*
Hass, W., 341, 369, *389*
Hassing, Y., 5, *30*
Hatch, E., 4, *25*, 217, 222, 225, 235, 236, 240, 248, *253, 256*
Hatfield, N., 459, 466, *470, 472*
Hauser, S. L., 411, *426*
Haviland, S. E., 44, 45, 67, 88, *195*
Hawkins, W. F., 112, *190*
Hayes, J. R., 200, 202, 203, 205, 206, 210, 213, *214, 215*
Haynes, J., 285, *291*
Hayward, R. W., 486, 488, 489, *534*
Head, H., 481, *532*
Healy, A. F., 95, 97, 98, 116, 135, 162, 163, 171, 185, *188, 190*
Hebert, R. K., 545, *587*
Hécaen, H., 5, *25*, 495, *532*
Hedge, M. N., 5, *25*
Hedrick, D., 8, *25*, 316, *325*
Heider, F., 443, *472*
Heider, G., 443, *472*
Heilman, K. M., 410, *426*, 505, 514, *532*
Helfgott, J., 151, *190*

Heller, M. S., 283, *292*
Hemsley, D. R., 561, 569, *586, 590*
Henderson, L., 75, 80, *190*
Henik, A., 71, 80, *191*
Henzl, V. W., 240, *253*
Herman, L. M., 45, 171, *190*
Hermann, K., 146, 147, *191*
Hermelin, B., 402, 403, *426, 427*
Hernandez-Chavez, E., 4, *22,* 222, *252*
Herrmann, D. J., 36, 40, *186*
Hersh, H., 522, *530*
Hier, D. B., 411, *426*
Higginbotham, M. W., 271, *292*
Hinckley, A., 297, 311, 316, *324*
Hingtgen, J., 419, *428*
Hiscock, M., 5, *25*
Hoar, N., 314, *324*
Hoefnagel-Höhle, M., 5, 14, *30,* 237, *256*
Hogaboam, T. W., 113, 154, 161, *193*
Hogberg, B., 12, *25*
Holder, R., 316, *325*
Holley-Wilcox, P., 93, *190*
Hollien, H., 359, *390*
Holvoet, J. F., 376, *389*
Hood, L., 235, 239, *251*
Horan, E. A., 5, *21*
Hörmann, H., 553, *588*
Horn, J. L., 10, *25,* 330, *388*
Hornby, P. A., 4, *25,* 218, *253*
Howes, D. H., 112, *191, 195,* 483, 487, 501, *532*
Howlin, P., 8, 11, *22, 31,* 404, 406, *425*
Hoy, E. A., 366, *388*
Hoyle, H., 297, 301, *325*
Hsu, J. R., 6, *22*
Huang, J., 235, *253*
Huber, W., 295, *324*
Huebner, T., 222, *253*
Huey, E. B., 33, 116, *191*
Hughes, L. F., 5, *27*
Hunt, J. McV., 302, 303, *327,* 338, *391*
Hunt, K. W., 211, *215*
Huntley, R. M. C., 8, *29*
Huttenlocher, J., 5, 6, 8, *25, 26*
Huxley, R., 3, 5, 6, *26*
Hyde, M. R., 502, 503, 506, 507, 517, *531, 532*
Hymes, D., 4, *22,* 273, 279, *291, 292*

I

Ianco-Worral, A. D., 245, *253*
Imedadze, N. V., 218, 226, 235, *253*

Inglis, S., 298, 299, *327*
Ingnar, D. H., 12, *25*
Ingram, D., 4, 7, 13, *26,* 302, 308, 316, 318, 321, *324, 325,* 359, *388,* 401, *427*
Ingram, E., 3, 5, 6, *26*
Ingram, F., 66, *192*
Ingram, T., 296, *324*
Ingram, T. T. S., 8, *26*
Inhelder, B., 6, *26,* 301, *324*
Irvin, D., 8, *26*
Isserlin, M., 501, *532*

J

Jackson, G., 283, *292*
Jackson, J. H., 479, *532*
Jackson, M. D., 167, *191*
Jacobs, R. A., 3, *26*
Jaeggi, A., 295, 301, 303, *323*
Jakobovits, L. A., 240, *253*
Jakobson, R., 109, *191,* 481, 502, *532*
James, A. L., 411, *425*
James, C., 51, 52, *195*
Jansky, J., 155, *188, 191*
Jarvella, R. J., 3, 6, 7, *30,* 374, *390,* 563, *587*
Jay, S. M., 5, *26*
Jeffree, D., 381, *388*
Jenkins, J., 483, 517, *534*
Jensema, C., 433, 445, 446, 452, 455, *472, 474*
Jobse, J., *30*
John, V. P., 4, *22,* 279, *291*
Johnson, C. S., 155, 156, *189*
Johnson, D., 143, 145, 149, *191, 197*
Johnson, D. L., 8, *26*
Johnson, M. L., 12, 17, *29*
Johnson, N. F., 38, 42, 61, 71, 72, 73, 74, 75, 76, 78, 80, 105, 107, 115, 122, 173, *191*
Johnson, N. S., 258, 259, 270, 271, *293,* 355, *386*
Johnson, S. C., 508, *532*
Johnson-Laird, P. N., 350, *388,* 516, *534*
Johnston, J., 301, 303, 306, 308, 309, 310, *324*
Johnston, J. C., 42, 87, 88, *191*
Jonasson, J., 53, 54, 55, 56, 70, 127, 178, *188*
Jones, B., 4, *28,* 432, 439, *474*
Jones, H., 6, *28*
Jones, L. V., 517, *535*
Jones, M., 459, *472*
Joosten, J., 5, *30*
Jordon, I. K., 452, *472*
Joynt, R. J., 477, *530*
Just, M. A., 563, *585*

K

Kaelbling, R., 579, *590*
Kagan, D. M., 13, *26,* 202, *215*
Kahn, J. V., 337, 338, *388*
Kahneman, D., 71, 80, *191*
Kaiser, J. S., 161, *194*
Kallingas, G., 420, *428*
Kallmann, F., 454, *474*
Kaman, M., 146, 147, 171, 179, *196*
Kamhi, A., 301, 308, 310, *324*
Kandel, G., 146, *196*
Kannapell, B. M., 466, *472*
Kanner, L., 393, 395, 397, *426*
Kantowitz, B. H., 45, 171, *190*
Kaplan, E., 4, *25,* 484, 485, 490, 499, 504, *532*
Karchmer, M., 433, 438, 445, *472, 475*
Karlan, G. R., 382, *391*
Karlin, J. E., 98, *194*
Kasanin, J. S., 538, *587*
Katz, J., 521, 524, *532*
Katz, L., 76, *193*
Kavanagh, J. F., 4, *26,* 53, *191,* 448, *472*
Kay, P., 286, *290*
Kazminsky, E., 260, *293*
Kean, M. L., 500, 501, *532*
Keehn, S., 343, 348, *386*
Keen, R. H., 122, *191*
Keeton, A., 5, *26*
Keil, F., 5, *26*
Keilitz, I., 376, *389*
Kellar, L., 500, 509, 523, *532*
Kellas, G., 373, *388*
Keller, L., 502, *533*
Kelly, R. R., 5, *31*
Kempler, D., 4, *24*
Kempton, W., *292*
Kerr, J. L., 6, *25*
Kerschensteiner, M., 295, *324,* 504, *534*
Kertesz, A., 486, 488, 490, *532, 533*
Kessel, F. S., 4, *21*
Kessler, C., 226, *253,* 308, *324*
Kiernan, C., 376, *390*
Kim, Y., 504, *530*
Kimball, J., 513, *533*
Kimura, D., 576, *587*
King, C. M., 8, 18, *28*
King-Sun Fu, 265, *294*
Kinneavy, J., 204, *215*
Kinney, L., 569, *589*
Kinsbourne, M., 5, *25, 26,* 143, 145, *191,* 411, *426*

Kintsch, W., 207, 210, 213, *215,* 258, 260, 263, 271, *293*
Kirk, S. A., 8, *26,* 453, *472*
Kirk, W. D., 8, *26,* 453, *472*
Klapp, S. T., 54, 67, *191,* 449, *472*
Klatt, D., 398, *428*
Kleffner, F., 297, *324*
Kleiman, G. M., 97, 127, *191*
Klein, D., 409, *426*
Klein, L. S., 421, 422, *425*
Klein, N. K., 331, *388*
Klima, E. S., 4, *26,* 349, *388,* 434, 448, 461, 462, 463, 464, 470, *472*
Klitzke, D., 60, 61, 75, 76, 77, 107, 121, 171, *192*
Knight, R. A., 568, *587*
Kocher, F., 295, 301, 303, *323*
Koegel, R. L., 418, 419, 422, *427*
Koenigsknecht, R. A., 8, *26*
Koh, D. S., 566, 567, *587*
Koh, S., 467, *475*
Kohler, W., 40, *191*
Kohn, B., 529, *531*
Kohn, L. L., 5, 8, *22*
Kolers, P. A., 52, 161, *191, 558, 587*
Kolk, H. H. J., 500, 509, *533*
Koller, J. J., 511, 515, 526, *530*
Kolvin, I., 396, *427*
König, B., 566, *590*
Koplin, J. H., 3, *29*
Kopytynska, H., 552, *589*
Kotenko, V., 578, *586*
Kottas, B., 89, *187*
Kowal, S., 553, *588, 589*
Kracke, I., 297, *324*
Krashen, S. D., 5, 12, *23, 26,* 219, 221, 232, 235, 237, 238, 240, *251, 253, 254*
Kriegsmann, E., 298, 299, *327*
Kroll, J. F., 53, 55, 70, 112, 121, *189*
Krueger, L. E., 54, 76, 89, 97, 122, *190, 191*
Kucera, H., 166, *191*
Kuchar, E., 420, 421, *428*
Kuczaj, S. A., II, 6, *26*
Kushner, S. L., 247, *254*

L

LaBerge, D., 56, 80, 95, 103, 105, 106, 107, 110, 127, 160, 167, 171, 181, 184, *191, 192, 194, 195*
Labov, W., 519, *533*
Lackner, J. R., 344, *389,* 395, *427*

Lacy, O. L., 116, *193*
Laffal, J., 538, *587*
Lahey, M., 4, 8, 11, *21, 26,* 304, *322,* 433, *470*
Lakoff, G., 524, *533*
Lamb, M. J., 375, *391*
Lambert, L., 8, *29*
Lambert, W., 231, *253*
Lambert, W. E., 231, 245, 246, *251, 254, 255*
Lamberts, F., 349, 351, 375, 383, *389, 391*
Lamendella, J., 218, 230, *254, 256*
Lance, D., 220, *254*
Landau, W., 297, *324*
Landry, R. G., 245, *254*
Lane, H., 454, *472*
Langford, W., 155, *188*
Laosa, L., 282, 283, *293*
Larsen, D. N., 231, *254*
Larsen-Freeman, D., 217, 222, *254*
Larson, G. W., 8, *26*
Lawson, J. S., 552, 568, *586, 587*
Layton, T. L., 352, *389*
Lecours, A. R., 490, 499, 514, 519, *533,* 543, 544, *587*
Lee, L. L., 4, 8, *26,* 307, 318, *324, 325,* 361, *389,* 401, *427,* 453, *472*
Lehmukuhle, S. W., 89, *187*
Lehr, E., 440, *473*
LeMay, M., 411, *426*
Lenneberg, E., 3, 4, 5, 6, *27,* 411, *427*
Lenneberg, E. H., 3, 4, 5, 6, *27,* 237, *254,* 333, *389,* 502, *533*
Lennard, H., 409, *427*
Lent, J. R., 376, *389*
Leonard, L. B., 5, 6, 11, 12, *24, 27, 31,* 297, 302, 303, 306, 307, 309, 310, 313, 317, 318, 319, 321, *323, 325, 326,* 337, 358, 382, *388, 389*
Leopold, W. F., 225, 226, 248, *254*
Lerner, J., 571, *587*
Lesgold, A. M., 127, 154, *193*
Lesk, D., 486, 488, *533*
Lesser, R., 4, *27,* 484, 517, 518, *533*
Levelt, W. J. M., 3, 5, 6, 7, *27, 30,* 508, *533*
Levin, H., 4, *25,* 64, 65, 128, *189, 192*
Levin, S. R., 3, *27*
Levinson, P., 316, *325*
Levitt, H., 469, *472*
Levy, B. A., 127, *192*
Levy, D., 409, 410, *426*
Levy, J., 410, 411, *427,* 572, *587*
Levy, R., 548, 568, *587*

Lewinsohn, P. M., 568, *587*
Lewis, S. S., 53, 54, 55, *194*
Lhermitte, F., 490, 514, 519, *533*
Liberman, A. M., 66, 150, 151, *192, 195,* 497, *533*
Liberman, I. Y., 151, *192, 195*
Lichtheim, L., 485, *533*
Lieber, C. W., 371, *389*
Liebergott, J., 301, *322*
Lightbown, P., 235, 239, *251*
Liles, B., 307, *325*
Limber, J., 8, *27*
Ling, A., 455, *471*
Ling, D., 432, 446, *472*
Lisker, L., 497, *533*
Lloyd, L. L., 4, 11, *29,* 380, *390*
Locke, J., 449, *473*
Locke, S., 502, *533*
Locke, V., 449, *473*
Lockhart, R. S., 571, *585*
Lockhead, G. R., 110, *192*
Lockyer, L., 397, *428*
Loftus, E., 99, *188*
Long, M., 237, *254*
Longhurst, T. M., 8, *27,* 364, 365, *389*
Lorentz, J., 316, 318, *325*
Lorge, I., 112, *196*
Lorsch, N., 419, *427*
Lott, D., 44, 46, 116, 122, 172, *195*
Lovaas, O. I., 414, 415, 416, 417, 418, 419, 422, *427*
Lovell, K., 297, 301, *325,* 345, 347, *389*
Lovitt, T. C., 380, *391*
Lowe, A., 304, *325*
Lozar, B., 341, 369, *389*
Luchins, D., 579, *587*
Lundberg, J., 124, *192*
Luria, A. R., 481, 484, 485, 499, 502, 507, 524, 528, *533*
Luszcz, M. A., 373, *390*
Luterman, D., 453, *473*
Lyle, J. G., 331, 332, 333, *389*

M

MacDonald, J. D., 11, *27,* 382, *389*
Mack, J., 504, *530*
MacKay, D. G., 67, *192*
Mackworth, N., 297, *325*
Macnamara, J., 6, *27,* 224, 240, 247, *254*
MacVean, M., 295, *326*

MacWhinney, B., 4, *27*
Maehr, M., 282, *293*
Madden, C., 221, *251*
Maer, F., 573, *589*
Magaro, P. A., 573, 576, *588*
Magner, M. E., 454, *473*
Maher, B. A., 538, 550, 551, 567, *587, 588*
Mahler, M. S., 413, *427*
Mahoney, G. J., 11, *27*, 376, 377, *390*
Mandel, T. S., 260, *293*
Mandler, G., 92, 93, 94, 135, 171, *196*
Mandler, J., 258, 259, 269, 270, 271, 287, *293*
Manelis, L., 90, 112, 115, 135, 172, 173, 182, *192*
Manschreck, T. C., 550, 551, 567, *587, 588*
Maguard, M., 295, 301, 303, *323*
Mar, H. H., 356, 369, *388*
Marcel, A. J., 168, *193*
Marchbanks, G., 128, *192*
Marge, M., 8, *26*
Marie, P., 480, *533*
Marin, O. S. M., 507, 511, 512, 514, 516, 526, *533, 534*
Marks, C., 81, *31*
Marks, C. H., 443, *475*
Marks, L. E., 565, 566, *588*
Marmurek, H. H. C., 78, 173, *192*
Marquardt, T., 316, *325*
Marshall, J. C., 118, 167, 178, *192*, 511, 512, *533*
Marshall, W., 443, *473*
Marslen-Wilson, W., 5, *31*
Martin, J., 298, *325*
Martin, J. R., 4, *29*, 290, 293, 537, 545, 546, 547, 548, 553, 556, 559, 560, 582, 583, 584, *588*
Martin, N., 204, 206, *214*
Martin, R., 522, *534*
Martin, R. L., 12, *24, 543, *586*
Marusanz, T. Z., 566, 567, *587*
Mason, J., 260, 270, *293*
Mason, M., 149, 164, 166, 172, *192*
Massaro, D. W., 38, 42, 45, 49, 51, 52, 53, 56, 57, 58, 59, 60, 61, 70, 71, 75, 76, 77, 80, 83, 84, 85, 88, 89, 92, 105, 107, 120, 121, 171, 174, 175, 181, *192, 196*
Matsuhashi, A., 204, 206, 213, *215*
Matthews, J., 6, *30*
Mattingly, I. G., 4, *26, 53, 191*, 448, *472*
Maxwell, A. E., 568, *587*
May, M., 297, *326*

May, W. H., 286, *293*
Mayzner, M. S., 60, 149, 166, *192*
McBride, K., 483, 485, *535*
McCabe, A. E., 6, *30*
McCabe, P., 486, 488, *533*
McCarrell, N. S., 375, *386, 560, 585*
McCarthy, J., 453, *472*
McCauley, C., 355, 356, 357, *389, 391, 392*
McClelland, J. L., 42, 87, 88, 167, *191*
McClosky, M., 262, *293*
McClure, E., 260, 270, *293*
McConkey, R., 382, *387*
McConkie, G., 268, *293*
McCormick, C., 160, 167, *193*
McCowen, A., 440, *473*
McDonald, J. D., 210, *216*
McDowell, P., 420, *428*
McGarrigle, J., 6, *24*
McGhie, A., 568, *587*
McGinnies, E., 116, *193*
McGlone, J., 491, *534*
McGuigan, F. J., 448, *473*
McIntire, M., 459, 460, 461, 462, *473*
McIntyre, C. K., 448, 449, *473*
McKee, P., 440, *473*
McKnight, J. R., 366, *388*
McLaughlin, B., 4, *27*, 217, 218, 221, 226, 232, 237, 238, 240, 245, 247, 248, 249, *254, 256*
McLean, J. E., 4, 11, *30*
Mcleod, A., 204, 206, *214*
McPherson, H., 420, 421, *428*
Meadow, K., 456, 459, 460, 461, 462, 466, *473, 474*
Meaney, M., 421, 422, *425*
Meehan, J. R., 211, 212, 213, *215*
Mehan, H., 243, *255*
Mein, R., 342, *389*
Meline, T., 313, *325*
Mellon, J. C., 209, *215*
Menyuk, P., 3, *27, 297, 307, 318, *325, 400, 427*
Mersel, J., 418, *428*
Mervis, C. B., 522, *534*
Mesalam, L., 5, *27*
Meshoulam, U., 147, *196*
Messer, D. J., 5, *27*
Meyer, D. E., 54, 98, 99, 100, 101, 112, 126, 127, 135, 161, *193*
Meyer, B. J. F., 262, 263, 264, 268, *293*
Meyers, D., 409, 410, *426, 427*

AUTHOR INDEX 603

Mezrich, J. J., 90, *193*
Mikeš, M., 226, 235, *255*
Milewski, J., 17, *21*
Miller, G., 567, *588*
Miller, G. A., 3, 5, *25, 27,* 40, 41, 46, 59, 68, 71, 80, 121, *193,* 516, 521, *534,* 565, 566, 569, *585, 588*
Miller, H., 311, *325*
Miller, J., 310, 317, 318, 319, *325*
Miller, J. F., 5, 8, 11, *22, 27,* 329, 336, 337, 385, *389, 392*
Miller, L., 11, *27*
Miller, N., 419, *427*
Miller, W. K., 569, *588*
Mills, B., 298, 299, *327*
Miner, L., 8, *30*
Milon, J. P., 227, *255*
Milone, M., 433, *472*
Mirabile, P. J., 5, *27*
Miron, M. S., 286, *293*
Mittler, P., 366, 372, 381, *386, 388, 392*
Moerk, E. L., 4, 6, 12, *27, 28*
Moffett, J., 204, 206, *215*
Mohr, J. R., 485, 529, *534*
Molfese, D. L., 3, *28,* 219, *255*
Monroe, M., 155, *193*
Montague, J. C., Jr., 359, *390*
Montague, W. E., 4, 14, *21,* 67, *188,* 258, 263, *290, 293,* 448, *471*
Montanelli, D., 439, 440, 441, 442, 443, *474, 475*
Moog, J., 453, 454, *471*
Moore, J. M., 5, *24*
Moores, D., 438, *473*
Morehead, A. E., 3, 4, *28*
Morehead, D. M., 3, 4, *28,* 308, *325,* 401, *427*
Morkovin, B. V., 456, *473*
Morley, M., 295, 311, *325*
Moroz, M. O., 552, *588*
Morton, J., 5, *28,* 46, 47, 62, 70, 93, 94, 101, 113, 124, 126, 127, 135, 138, 139, 171, *193, 196*
Moskowitz, B., 463, *473*
Moskowitz, S., 437, *475*
Muehl, S., 155, 156, *189*
Muise, J. G., 71, 80, *196*
Muma, J. R., 8, 11, *28*
Munsinger, H., 5, *28*
Murphy, M. D., 259, *290*
Murray, D. J., 575, *585*
Murrell, G. A., 124, 138, *193*
Murrel, M., 226, *255*
Musil, A., 420, *428*
Myerson, R., 508, 521, *535*
Myklebust, H., 143, 145, *191*
Myklebust, H. R., 443, *473*

N

Nachshon, I., 571, *587*
Naeser, M. A., 486, 488, 489, *534*
Namir, L., 4, *29,* 434, 463, *474*
Naor, E. M., 8, *28*
Naremore, R. C., 5, *31,* 344, 369, *390*
Natalicio, D. S., 220, 227, *255*
Natalicio, L. F. S., 220, 227, *255*
Nation, J., 295, 296, *322, 327*
Naus, M., 258, *292*
Neale, J. M., 541, *588*
Neisser, A., 41, 45, 47, 101, 102, 112, *193*
Nelson, K., 5, *25, 28,* 459, *473*
Nelson, K. E., 3, *28,* 420, 421, *425*
Nemser, W., 229, 234, *255*
Neufeld, R. W. J., 563, 564, *588*
Neuringer, C., 569, *588*
Newbigging, P. L., 45, *193*
Newcomb, W., 469, *472*
Newcombe, F., 118, 167, *192,* 511, 512, *533*
Newell, A., 200, *215*
Newfield, M. U., 346, *390*
Newhoff, M., 5, *27*
Newman, L., 460, *473*
Newport, E. L., 377, *390* 462, 463, *473*
Nice, M., 311, *325*
Nichols, I. A., 333, *389*
Nickerson, N., 7, 13, *28*
Ninio, A., 6, *28*
Nisbett, R. E., 203, *215*
Nix, D., 275, *293*
Norman, D. A., 272, *290*
Norris, J. A., 8, *31*
North, B., 517, *534*
Novak, G., 299, *327*
Novik, N., 76, *193*
Nystrand, M., 210, *215*

O

Obler, L. K., 4, 12, *21, 28,* 274, *251*
O'Connell, D. C., 553, *588, 589*
O'Connor, C., 313, *323*

O'Connor, N., 4, 28, 330, 342, 389, 390, 402, 403, 426
Odell, L., 199, 203, 214
Odom, P. B., 448, 449, 473
Ogden, P., 455, 473
Ogilvie, H., 421, 422, 425
O'Hare, F., 209, 215
Ojemann, G. A., 491, 534
Oller, D., 316, 325
Oller, J., 231, 255
Oller, J. W., 230, 256
Olson, D. R., 7, 13, 28
Oltmanns, T. F., 541, 564, 565, 588
Ombredane, A., 495, 530
O'Neill, M. A., 439, 473
Ornitz, E. M., 409, 427
Orton, S. T., 146, 147, 193
Osgood, C., 286, 293
Osser, H., 41, 46, 63, 68, 102, 103, 109, 118, 121, 124, 128, 134, 135, 189, 190

P

Paccia-Cooper, J., 14, 23, 406, 407, 427
Padgug, E. J., 5, 21
Paivio, A., 263, 294
Palermo, D. S., 3, 28, 219, 255
Palyo, W. J., 383, 390
Papania, N., 353, 390
Paris, S. G., 376, 377, 390
Parisi, D., 4, 28, 310, 322, 350, 390, 504, 534
Park, N. W., 558, 587
Parker, L. L., 241, 255
Parkison, C., 411, 425
Patterson, D., 437, 473
Patterson, K., 168, 193
Patti, S., 299, 325
Paul-Brown, D., 379, 388
Pavy, D., 541, 588
Payne, R. W., 552, 587
Pea, R. D., 390
Peal, E. 245, 255
Pearson, P. D., 113, 193
Pedersen, J., 309, 327
Pennington, F. M., 373, 390
Perecman, E., 523, 532
Perez, E., 242, 243, 244, 256
Perfetti, C. A., 5, 23, 98, 113, 127, 154, 161, 162, 171, 193, 194, 354, 391
Perloff, B. F., 418, 427
Perry, F. L., Jr., 5, 8, 28

Petersen, R. J., 103, 105, 194
Peterson, C., 316, 325
Peterson, M. K., 8, 30
Petrie, I., 295, 326
Petrinovich, L. F., 54, 126, 190, 448, 472
Pfetzing, D., 436, 457, 472
Pfohl, B., 556, 584
Phelan, J. G., 569, 588
Phillips, L., 560, 588
Philips, S. U., 280, 293
Piaget, J., 300, 326
Piattelli-Palmarini, M., 5, 6, 28
Pichert, J. W., 263, 269, 290, 293
Pick, A. D., 41, 46, 63, 68, 102, 103, 109, 118, 121, 124, 128, 134, 135, 189, 190
Pic'l, A. K., 573, 576, 588
Pierce, J. R., 98, 194
Pierce, S. J., 361, 363, 386, 397, 401, 425, 427
Piercy, M., 304, 305, 326, 327
Pillsbury, W. B., 33, 44, 116, 117, 194
Pinter, R., 437, 473
Pittenger, J. B., 115, 135, 136, 186
Pizzamiglio, L., 504, 534
Poeck, K., 504, 534
Pogue-Geile, M. F., 564, 565, 588
Pollack, D., 436, 473
Pollack, E., 316, 326
Pollack, M., 409, 426
Pollack, M. D., 67, 188, 448, 471
Pollard-Gott, L., 262, 293
Pollatsek, A., 114, 115, 116, 125, 135, 136, 172, 173, 182, 194, 197
Pollin, W., 579, 587
Polloway, E., 329, 391
Poppen, R., 297, 305, 326
Porter, J., 222, 255
Porter, R. J., Jr., 5, 27
Portnoy, S., 541, 552, 559, 589
Postman, L., 40, 41, 46, 59, 68, 71, 80, 116, 121, 193, 194
Power, D., 4, 28, 432, 439, 440, 441, 442, 443, 469, 473, 474
Powers, J. E., 6, 25
Prather, E., 8, 25, 316, 325
Prawat, R. W., 6, 28
Prescott, T. E., 558, 588
Presnell, L., 453, 454, 473
Pribram, K., 297, 325
Price, E., 487, 530
Price-Williams, D., 368, 390
Prinz, P., 312, 326

Prosen, M., 556, *587*
Prutting, C. A., 8, 11, *28*, 367, *386*
Pruzek, R. M., 147, 157, 158, 159, *196*
Pryce, I. G., 577, *586*
Pugh, G. A., 437, *474*
Purcell, D. G., 89, 123, *194*, *195*

Q

Quadfasel, F. A., 408, *426*, 483, *532*
Quigley, S. P., 4, 8, 18, *28*, 432, 435, 439, 440, 441, 442, 443, 444, 445, 457, 459, 466, 467, 468, 469, *470*, *472*, *473*, *474*, *475*
Quillian, M. R., 99, *188*
Quirk, R., 3, *28*

R

Raeburn, K. M., 568, *588*
Raeburn, V. P., 5, *21*
Ragain, R. D., 355, *391*
Rainer, J., 454, *474*
Ramstad, V., 301, 303, *324*
Rapin, I., 295, 296, 297, *326*
Rasbury, W. C., 5, *29*
Rasmussen, M., 416, *428*
Ratner, N., 6, *29*
Ratusnik, D. L., 8, *29*
Raulin, A. E., 155, *194*
Rausch, M. A., 558, *588*
Ravem, R., 227, *255*
Ravenette, A. T., 155, *194*
Rawlings, B., 433, *474*
Rayner, K., 161, *194*
Razel, M., 5, *29*
Reber, A. S., 4, *29*
Reder, S., 84, 121, *189*, 287, *292*
Redmond, A., 301, *322*
Rees, N. S., 8, 11, *29*, 297, 304, 316, *326*, 364, *390*
Reicher, G., 42, 45, 52, 59, 60, 69, 71, 80, 86, 87, 88, 102, *194*
Reichle, J., 337, *389*
Reid, B., 376, *390*
Reid, M., 572, *587*
Reilly, F. E., 556, *589*
Reynell, J., 8, *29*, 401, *427*
Richards, J. C., 4, *29*, 217, 220, *255*
Richardson, K., 8, *29*
Richman, N., 295, *326*
Riding, R. J., 376, *390*

Rieber, R., 4, *20*
Rigler, D., 12, *23*
Rigler, M., 12, *23*
Rinnert, C., 517, *534*
Rips, L. J., 521, 522, *534*
Risley, T., 418, *427*
Ritchie, W. C., 4, *29*, 217, *255*
Ritvo, E. R., 409, *427*
Rivers, W., 240, *255*, 287, *294*
Roaden, S. K., 357, *389*
Robbins, E., 550, 555, 564, 567, 574, 579, *590*
Roberts, A., 406, *428*
Roberts, K. T., 131, *188*
Roberts, N., 5, *24*
Robertson, S. P., 271, *292*
Rochester, S., 4, *29*, 290, *293*
Rochester, S. R., 537, 545, 546, 547, 548, 553, 556, 559, 560, 561, 562, 582, 583, 584, *588*
Rocissano, L., 239, *251*
Rodgon, M. M., 6, *29*
Rogers, T. S., 66, *190*
Rohrman, N. L., 51, *194*
Rondal, J. A., 379, *388*, *390*
Roodin, P. A., 375, *391*
Rosansky, E. J., 222, 225, 227, *252*, *255*
Rosch, E., 522, *534*
Rosemont, H., Jr., 5, *29*
Rosen, A. J., 566, 567, *587*
Rosen, H., 204, 206, *214*
Rosen, R., 452, *472*
Rosenbaum, P. S., 3, *26*
Rosenberg, S., 3, 13, 14, 16, *21*, *29*, 205, 206, *215*, 329, 342, 369, 374, 385, *390*, 553, 559, *589*
Rosenberg, S. D., 548, 556, *589*
Rosenberger, E. F., 333, *389*
Rosenberger, P. B., 411, *426*
Rosenstein, J., 443, *471*
Rosinski, R. R., 124, 153, *190*, *194*
Rosman, N. P., 411, *426*
Ross, R. T., 108, 171, *194*
Roth, S., 98, 162, *194*, 295, 301, 303, *323*
Rothbaum, P. A., 569, *589*
Routh, D. K., 5, *26*, 569, *589*
Rozin, P., 66, 124, *194*
Rubenstein, H., 53, 54, 55, 113, *187*, *194*
Rubenstein, M. A., 53, 54, 55, *194*
Rubin, A. D., 201, *214*
Rublevich, B., 122, *191*
Rubovits, P., 282, *293*
Rucklos, M. E., 550, 551, 567, *587*, *588*

Ruddell, R. B., 288, *293*
Ruddy, M. G., 54, 98, 99, 100, 101, 112, 126, 127, 135, 161, *193*
Rudel, R., 155, *188*
Ruder, K., 8, *31*
Rūke-Dravina, V., 226, *255*
Rumelhart, D. E., 37, 42, 44, 46, 47, 63, 78, 105, 126, 181, 183, *194*, 258, 263, *293*
Rupp, J., 545, 553, 559, *588*
Russel, K., 469, *474*
Rutherford, R. B., 379, *387*
Rutter, D. R., 551, 552, 557, 558, *589*
Rutter, M., 8, *22*, 395, 396, 397, 399, 401, 404, 405, 406, 409, 410, 420, *424, 425, 427, 428*
Ryan, J., 334, 335, *390*
Rynders, J., 378, 379, *387*

S

Sabsay, S., 368, *390*
Sachs, J., 12, 17, *29*, 313, *326*
Safford, P. L., 331, *388*
Saffran, E. M., 507, 511, 512, 514, 516, 526, *533, 534*
Salzinger, K., 541, 552, 559, *589*
Samuels, J. A., 511, *534*
Samuels, S. J., 56, 80, 95, 105, 106, 107, 110, 127, 160, 161, 167, 171, 181, 184, *192, 193, 194, 195*
Sandberg, T., 6, *23*, 373, *387*
Sander, L. W., 277, *291*
Sartinsky, M., 199, *214*
Sattler, J. M., 8, *29*
Satz, P., 5, *29*, 411, *428*
Scammell, R. E., 577, *586*
Scanlon, D. M., 151, 155, 157, 158, 159, *196*
Scarborough, D. L., 4, *29*
Scarcella, R. C., 235, 237, *254*
Scardamalia, M., 207, 209, 210, 213, *214, 215, 216*
Schachter, J., 221, 235, *255*
Schaeffer, B., 418, 420, *427*
Schank, R. C., 10, *29*, 205, 211, *216*, 258, *294*
Scharf, D. J., 8, *29*
Scheffelin, M., 304, *323*
Schery, T., 306, 309, *324*
Schiefelbusch, R. L., 3, 4, 11, *29*, 329, 380, 385, *391*
Schiff, W., 109, 135, *189*

Schindler, R. M., 114, 115, 116, 125, 135, 136, 172, 173, 182, *194, 197*
Schlanger, B. B., 346, 358, 362, *390, 391*
Schlesinger, H., 456, 459, 460, 461, 462, 465, *474*
Schlesinger, I. M., 4, *29*, 434, 463, *474*
Schmid, E., 295, 301, 303, *323*
Schmidt, M. W., 569, *588*
Schmitt, P., 439, *474*
Schneider, K., 578, *589*
Schoenle, P. W., 511, 512, *531*
Scholes, I. B., 5, *29*
Scholes, R. J., 5, *29*, 505, 514, *532*
Scholl, M., 409, *426*
Schrandt, T. A., M., 8, *27*
Schreibman, L., 418, 422, *427*
Schubert, G., 316, *325*
Schuell, H., 483, 517, *534*
Schuler, A. L., 383, *390*
Schulhoff, C., 502, *532*
Schultz, R. W., 84, *196*
Schumann, J. H., 227, 230, 236, *252, 255*
Schustack, M. W., 268, *294*
Schvaneveldt, R. W., 54, 98, 99, 100, 101, 112, 126, 135, 161, *186, 193*
Schwartz, G. E., 573, *589*
Schwartz, J., 416, *428*
Schwartz, L., 258, *292*
Schwartz, M. F., 507, 511, 514, 516, *533, 534*
Schwartz, R., 310, 317, 321, *325, 326*
Schwartz, S., 538, 583, 584, *589*
Schwarz, M., 275, *293*
Schweitzer, L., 574, 580, *589*
Scott, C., 295, *326*
Scovel, T., 231, 238, *253, 255*
Scribner, S., 287, *291*
Searle, J. R., 3, *29, 30*
Searleman, A., 411, *428*
Seaver, W. B., 284, *294*
Seely, P. B., 11, *27*
Seeman, M. V., 562, *588*
Segalowitz, N., 247, *255*
Segarra, J. M., 408, *426, 487, 530*
Selfridge, J., 567, *588*
Seliger, H. W., 219, 238, *256*
Selinker, L., 228, 229, 230, 234, 235, *256*
Selnes, O. A., 491, *535*
Semel, M. S., 156, *197*
Semmel, M. I., 349, 354, 370, *391*
Sengul, C. J., 4, *23*

Seron, X., 511, 512, *530*
Shallice, T., 167, *194*, 511, 515, 526, *534, 535*
Shankweiler, D., 150, 151, *192, 195*, 497, *533*
Shannon, C. E., 41, *195*
Shapira, R., 240, *253*
Shapiro, T., 406, *428*
Sharifi, H., 352, *389*
Shattuck-Hufnagel, S., 398, *428*
Shatz, M., 5, 8, *30,* 307, 313, *326*
Shen, M., 245, *252*
Sheremata, W. A., 487, *530*
Shewan, C. M., 504, *534*
Shields, J., 578, *586*
Shiffrin, R. M., 44, 171, 182, *195*
Shimkunas, A., 541, 570, 580, 581, 582, *589*
Shoben, E. J., 521, 522, *534*
Shore, J. M., 376, *390*
Shotick, A., 344, *391*
Shriner, T. H., 8, *30*
Shulman, M., 8, *29, 307, 325, 326*
Shurcliff, A., 41, 63, 64, 121, *190*
Shuy, R. W., 244, *256*
Shwedel, A., 5, 8, *28*
Siddall, H., 297, 301, *325*
Siegel, A., 556, *589*
Siegel, G. M., 8, *22,* 298, 299, 378, *387*
Siegel, L., 299, *326*
Siegel, L. S., 6, *30*
Siegman, A. W., 14, *30*
Silverman, G., 551, 552, 553, *589*
Silverman, S. R., 430, 452, *471, 474*
Simmons, A., 443, *474*
Simmons, J., 400, 403, 404, 406, *424*
Simmons, J. Q., 418, *427*
Simon, H., 203, *214*
Simon, H. A., 200, *215*
Simouse, A. D., 421, *425*
Sims-Knight, J. E., 568, *587*
Sinclair, A., 3, 6, 7, *30*
Sinclair, H., 6, *30,* 403, *428*
Sinclair-deZwart, H., 6, *30*
Siojo, L. R., 285, *291*
Siple, P., 42, 46, 47, 63, 78, 105, 126, 183, *194,* 434, 448, 463, 466, *470 472, 474*
Skaar, E., 60, 83, 85, 88, *189*
Skarakis, E., 312, *326*
Slobin, D. I., 4, 14, *30,* 235, 251, *256*
Sloboda, J. A., 70, 74, 75, 76, 77, 78, 80, 107, 173, *195*
Sloman, L., 420, 421, *428*

Smalley, W. A., 231, *254*
Smart, B., 209, *214*
Smart, D., 209, *214*
Smeets, P. M., 381, *391*
Smith, E. E., 39, 43, 44, 45, 48, 50, 63, 65, 66, 67, 68, 69, 70, 71, 88, 102, 103, 104, 105, 115, 117, 123, 134, 176, 178, *186, 195,* 521, 522, *534,* 548, 549, *589*
Smith, F., 4, *30,* 42, 44, 45, 46, 50, 61, 63, 78, 98, 105, 114, 116, 120, 122, 126, 168, 172, *195*
Smith, H., 146, *196*
Smith, J., 109, 135, *189*
Smith, J. D., 329, *391*
Smith, J. O., 380, *391*
Smith, N. V., 3, *30,* 359, 360, 361, *391,* 439, *474*
Smith, W. R., 271, *292*
Smythe, P. C., 231, *253*
Snow, C. E., 5, 14, *30,* 237, 239, *256,* 377, *391*
Snow, R. E., 250, *252*
Snowling, M. J., 152, *195*
Snyder-McLean, L. K., 4, 11, *30,* 302, 303, 312, 326, 380, *391*
Solomon, R. L., 112, *191, 195*
Sommers, R. K., 8, *30,* 371, 377, *391*
Soriano, L. V., 285, *291*
Space, L. G., 539, *589*
Spector, A., 89, 123, *194, 195*
Sperber, R. D., 355, 356, 357, *389, 391, 392*
Sperling, G. A., 37, 51, 52, *195*
Sperry, R. W., 528, *531*
Spiegel, B., 382, *389*
Spilich, G. J., 268, *294*
Spiro, R. T., 4, 14, *21,* 258, *290*
Spitz, H. H., 371, *389*
Spitzer, R., 550, 555, 564, 567, 574, 579, *590*
Spoehr, K. T., 39, 43, 44, 45, 48, 50, 63, 65, 66, 67, 68, 69, 70, 71, 103, 115, 117, 123, 126, 134, 176, 178, *195*
Staikoff, J., 410, 411, *427*
Stanley, J. C., 250, *252*
Stanovich, K. E., 89, 123, *194*
Stark, J., 297, 303, 305, *326,* 415, 418, *428*
Stark, R., 296, 305, 306, *327*
Starkey, K. L., 371, 377, *391*
Starr, S., 5, *31*
Statlender, S., 506, 507, *532*
Steckol, K. F., 309, 310, 321, *325,* 358, *389*

Steger, J. A., 146, 147, 150, 171, 179, *196*
Stein, N. L., 258, 260, 271, *294*
Steinberg, E. R., 199, *215, 216*
Steiner, R., 156, 160, 161, *195*
Steinkamp, M., 4, *28,* 432, 439, 440, 441, 442, 443, *474*
Stengel, E., 406, 407, *428*
Stern, C., 234, *256*
Stern, W., 234, *256*
Sternberg, S., 563, *590*
Stevens-Long, J., 416, 418, *427, 428*
Stevenson, J., 295, *326*
Stewart, D. M., 4, 12, *31*
Stewart, M., 51, 52, *195*
Stewart, W., 51, *190*
Stewart, W. A., 288, *294*
Stick, S. L., 8, *31*
Stoel-Gammon, C., 362, 363, *391*
Stokoe, W. C., Jr., 434, 459, 466, 468, *474*
Straker, D., 289, *294*
Strange, W., 4, *26*
Straube, E., 566, *590*
Strawson, C., 70, 131, 132, 164, 165, 172, 179 *186*
Streeter, M., 316, *323*
Streiner, D., 397, *425*
Striefel, S., 381, 382, *391*
Stuckless, E. R., 443, 466, *474, 475*
Studdert-Kennedy, M., 497, *533*
Studt, A., 113, *193*
Stumpf, C., 311, *326*
Sulzer, B., 416, 417, *428*
Summers, P. A., 8, *26*
Suppes, P., 469, *471*
Swain, M., 228, 229, 231, 233, 235, *256*
Swann, W., 372, *392*
Swisher, L., 452, *475*
Swope, S., 301, *322*

T

Taeschner, T., 218, 226, *256*
Taft, M., 124, 139, *194, 195*
Tager, Flusberg, H. B., 5, *24,* 307, *326*
Tallal, P., 296, 303, 304, 305, 306, *326, 327*
Tannen, D., 257, 278, *294*
Tanz, C., 6, *31*
Tatham, A., 365, *386*
Tatham, S. M., 288, *294*
Taylor, A. M., 382, *391*
Taylor, B. P., 221, 235, *256*

Taylor, G. A., 60, 61, 121, *192*
Taylor, I., 247, *256*
Taylor, J., 375, 377, *386*
Taylor, L., 443, 444, *475*
Taylor, W. L., 550, *590*
Terry, P., 160, 167, *195*
Teunssen, J., 5, *29*
Theios, J., 71, 80, *196*
Thompson, M. C., 42, 59, 60, 83, 88, 89, 107, *196*
Thorndike, E. L., 112, *196*
Thorndyke, P., 259, 270, *294*
Thurlow, M. L., 382, *391*
Thurston, I., 49, 90, 135, *186*
Thurston, S., 545, 553, 559, *588*
Timberlake, W. H., 483, *532*
Tissot, R., 12, *23*
Todres, A. K., 262, *293*
Tomlinson-Keasy, C., 5, *31*
Tong, J. E., 568, *588*
Torgerson, W. S., 522, *530*
Torneus, M., 124, *192*
Torrey, E. F., 574, 575, *590*
Trantham, C., 309, *327*
Travers, J. R., 52, *196*
Treiman, R. A., 151, *196*
Treisman, A. M., 247, *256*, 374, *391*
Trembath, A. A., 4, *31*
Tresselt, M. E., 60, 149, 166, *192*
Trevarthen, C., 572, *587*
Troike, R. C., 242, 243, 244, *256*
Truscott, I. P., 554, 565, *590*
Trybus, R., 438, 445, 446, 452, 455, *472, 475*
Tucker, D. J., 376, *389*
Tucker, G. J., 556, *589*
Tucker, G. R., 245, 246, *251, 254*
Tucker, R., 231, *256*
Tulving, E., 91, 93, 94, 135, 171, *196*
Turner, T. J., 211, *214,* 260, *290*
Turnure, J., 378, 379, *387*
Turnure, J. E., 382, *391*
Tuxworth, J., 374, *391*
Tyler, L. K., 5, *31*

U

Ullmann, L. P., 559, *590*
Underwood, B. J., 84, *196*
Upfold, D., 137, *187*
Uzgiris, I. C., 302, 303, *327* 338, *391*

V

Vaisse, L., 297, *327*
Valian, V., 4, *24*
van der Molen, H., 124, 139, *196*
van der Spuy, H., 299, *326*
Van der Vlugt, H., 5, *29*
van Dijk, T. A., 207, 213, *215*, 290, *294*
Van Duyne, J. J., 5, *31*
Vanier-Clément, M., 543, 544, *587*
Van Kleeck, A., 300, 313, *327*
Van Pelt, D., 517, *535*
Varni, J. W., 419, *427*
Vasta, R., 12, *31*
Vasu, E., 569, *589*
Vellutino, F. R., 4, *31*, 37, 146, 147, 149, 150, 151, 152, 153, 154, 155, 156, 157, 158, 159, 171, 179, *196*
Venables, P. H., 569, 570, 575, 580, *585*, *586*
Venezky, R. L., 51, 60, 61, 121, 149, *187*, *192*, *196*, *197*
Vernon, M., 430, 467, *475*
Vesonder, G. T., 268, *294*
Vetter, H. J., 538, 555, *590*
Vigil, N. A., 230, *256*
Vignolo, L. A., 504, *531*
Vihman, M. M., 226, *256*
Voeltz, L., 400, *428*
Vogel, S. A., 156, *197*
Volterra, V., 218, 226, *256*, 404, *425*
von Stockert, T. R., 535, *535*
Vorster, J., 5, *30*
Voss, J. F., 268, *294*

W

Wade, E. A., 573, 576, *588*
Wagner, Gough, J., 222, 240, *256*
Walker, E., 5, *31*
Walker, E. C. T., 14, *23*
Walker, G., 344, 348, *386*
Walker, H. J., 375, *391*
Waller, T. G., 153, *197*
Walsh, B. F., 383, *391*
Waltensperger, K. Z., 545, *587*
Wang, W. S.-Y., 4, *24*
Warren, R. P., 206, *214*
Warrington, E. G., 516, *535*
Warrington, E. K., 143, 145, 167, *191*, *194*, 511, 515, 526, *534*, *535*

Waryas, C. L., 8, 11, *31*
Washington, D. S., 5, *31*
Wasterman, M. A., 6, *25*
Watson, L., 313, *327*
Watson, R. T., 410, *426*
Watson, S. J., 558, 559, 560, *590*
Weber, J., 315, *327*
Weber, R. M., 64, 125, 136, *197*
Webster, D. D., 420, 421, *428*
Weeks, T. E., 280, *294*, 311, *327*
Weener, P. D., 349, 351, *389*
Weening, D. L., 54, 126, *188*
Weigl, E., 502, *535*
Weil, C., 356, 357, *392*
Weinberger, D. R., 579, *587*
Weiner, P., 295, 298, 303, *327*
Weintraub, S., 505, *531*
Weir, R., 400, 404, *428*
Weisenberg, T., 483, 485, *535*
Weiss, H., 417, *428*
Weiss, M. E., 122, *191*
Well, A. D., 114, 115, 116, 125, 135, 136, 172, 173, 182, *194*, *197*
Wells, G., 6, *31*
Welsh, H., 574, 580, *589*
Wepman, J. M., 150, *197*, 341, 369, *389*, 517, *535*
Werner, L., 311, *327*
Wertheim, G., 305, *326*
Wertheimer, M., 40, *197*
Wescourt, K. T., 36, 40, *186*
Wesley, S., 421, 422, *425*
Wetherby, B., 382, *391*
Wetstone, H. S., 5, 8, *31*
Wheeler, A., 416, 417, *428*
Wheeler, D. D., 42, 44, 45, 52, 59, 61, 69, 71, 80, 86, 87, 88, 90, 115, *197*
Wheeler, K. E., 124, *194*
Wheldall, K., 343, 348, 372, 381, *388*, *392*
Whitaker, H. A., 5, *23*, 406, 407, *428*, 491, 502, 517, 529, 531, *534*, *535*
White, G., 286, *294*
White, M., 550, 551, *588*
White, M. A., 283, *292*
White, M. N., 167, *187*
Whitehouse, P., 519, *535*
Whitehurst, G., 299, *327*
Whitehurst, G. J., 4, 12, *31*
Whiteman, M. F., 199, *214*
Wiener, M., 156, 160, 161, *188*, *195*
Wiig, E. H., 12, *31*, 156, *197*

Wilbur, R. B., 434, 439, 440, 441, 442, 443, 463, *474, 475*
Wilce, L. S., 131, *188*
Wilcox, M. J., 12, *31,* 317, *326*
Wilde, W., 297, *327*
Willbrand, M. L., 11, *31*
Williams, A. M., 8, *31*
Williams, R., 287, *294,* 301, *327*
Williams, R. M., 569, *590*
Wilson, B., 295, 296, 297, *326*
Wilson, D., 3, *30*
Wilson, K., 469, *470*
Wilson, T. D., 137, *187,* 203, *215*
Wilson, W. R., 5, *24*
Winstead, L., 316, *325*
Winters, J. J., 354, 357, *392*
Winters, J. J., Jr., 357, *392*
Winzemer, J., 4, *24*
Wishner, J., 552, *589*
Witelson, S., 411, *428*
Witkowski, S. R., 286, *294*
Wode, H., 221, 224, 227, 235, *256*
Wolf, M., 155, *197,* 418, *427*
Wolk, S., 433, *472*
Wolpaw, T., 295, *327*
Woodle, A., 316, *325*
Wrightstone, J. W., 437, *475*
Wulbert, M., 298, 299, *327*
Wyatt, R. L., 579, *587*
Wyke, M. A., 4, *31*

XYZ

Yarbrough, D. B., 268, *292*
Yoder, D. E., 8, *31,* 329, 385, *392*
Yonas, A., 41, 63, 64, 121, *190*
Youniss, J., 447, *471*
Yuille, J. C., 263, *294*
Yule, W., 11, *31*
Zadeh, L. A., 265, *294*
Zaidel, E., 528, *535*
Zaumura, E. N., 579, *590*
Zawolkow, E., 436, 457, *472*
Zifcak, M., 151, *197*
Zorn, G., 299, *327*
Zurif, E., 495, 505, 508, 511, 519, *531, 535*
Zurif, E. B., 4, *22,* 495, 497, 498, 499, 502, 505, 506, 507, 508, 509, 513, 514, 521, 526, *530, 531, 535*

Subject Index

A

Aphasia, adult, 19-20, 477-529
  agrammatism, 501
  alexia with agraphia, 489
  anomic aphasia, 487-488
  aphemia, 490
  Broca's aphasia, 484-486, 496-500, 501-514
    comprehension deficits in, 504-514
  classification and localization in, 490-492
  conduction aphasia, 487, 514-516
  deep dyslexia in, 512-513
  expressive vs receptive disorders in, 483
  fluent vs nonfluent, 483
  global aphasia, 488
  introduction to, 477-483
    Broca's area, 477
    classical theory, 479-481
    Goodglass's contribution, 482-483
    Jakobson's views, 481-482
    Wernicke's area, 478-480
  lexical disorders in, 516-523
  model of normal language organization and, 492-494
  neurolinguistic theory and, 527-529
  overview of, 19-20
  paragrammatism, 501
  phonological disorders in, 495-500
  psycholinguistic theory and, 525-527
  pure alexia, 489
  pure word deafness, 489
  semantic disorders in, 523-525
  stress/saliency hypothesis in, 503
  syntactic disorders in, 501-516
  transcortical motor aphasia, 488-489
  transcortical sensory aphasia, 489
  Wernicke's aphasia, 486-487, 496-500, 506, 508
Applied psycholinguistics, 1-20
  defined, 1-2
  major questions in, 3-7
  overview of, 12-20
    aphasia, adult, 19-20
    deafness, language in, 17-19
    discourse processes, 14-15
    infantile autism, language in, 17
    language impairment, 15-16
    mental retardation, language in, 16-17
    reading, 13
    schizophrenic language, adult, 20
    second-language learning, 14
    writing, 13-14
  publications in, 1-3, 4
Autism (*see* Infantile autism, language in)

B, C, D

Bilingualism (*see* Second-language learning)
Cognition-language relationships, 300-303, 337-338, 402-403, 447-451

611

Cognition-language relationships (*cont.*)
  deafness and, 447–451
  infantile autism and, 402–403
  language impairment and, 300–303
  mental retardation and, 337–338
Deafness, language in, 17–19, 429–469
  cognition and, 447–451
    inner language, 448–450
    internal speech, 450–451
  communication patterns and, 452
  conclusions, 468–469
  deafness, defined, 429–433
  development of, 433–434, 452–466
    American Sign Language, 458–466
    manual English, 456–458
    oral English, 452–456
  educational needs and, 431–433
  intervention systems and, 434–437, 466–468
    American Sign Language, 434, 466–468
    manual English, 434–436
    oral English, 436–437
  language performance, 437–447, 454
    reading, 437–439, 454
    speech intelligibility, 445–446
    summary, 446–447
    syntax, 439–443
    writing, 443–445, 454
  overview of, 17–19
Developmental dysphasia (*see* Language impairment)
Discourse processes, 14–15, 257–290
  communication and, 272–290
    bilingual classroom interaction, 282–285
    breakdown of, 273–290
    linguistic differences, 285–289
    patterns of, among Native Americans, 279–282
    social context of, 272–273
  expository processing and, 261–262
  final remarks, 290
  hierarchical structure and, 272
  overview of, 14–15
  prose, basic structures in, 263–264
  rhetorical labels and, 265–267
  schema theory and, 258–261
  text, levels in, 264
  transformation of information in, 262–271
    priming effects, 267–269
    reordering, 269–270
    simplification and/or destruction of text, 271

Dyslexia (*see* Word recognition, reading disability)

H, I

Hearing impairment (*see* Deafness, language in)
Infantile autism, language in, 17, 393–424
  characteristics of, 408
  childhood schizophrenia and, 396
  cognitive deficit and, 402–403
  comprehension vs production, 394–395
  conclusions, 422–424
  delay vs deviancy, 395
  development of, 397, 412
  developmental dysphasia and, 396
  diagnostic criteria and, 397
  echolalia and, 405–408
  etiology of, 409–412
    hemispheric (cerebral) dysfunction theory, 410–412
    psychological hypothesis, 409–410
  Kanner's description, 393–394
  language knowledge vs language use, 394
  language levels, 395
  mental retardation and, 395–396
  methodological issues, 395
  overview of, 17
  phonology of, 397–399
  pragmatics of, 403–405
  semantics of, 403
  syntax of, 399–403
  treatment of, 412–422
    behavior modification, 414–420
    psychotherapeutic approach, 412–414
    sign language therapy, 420–422
Intelligence, 330
  crystallized, 330
  fluid, 330

L

Language development, 307–321, 332–335, 339–341, 345–353, 357–359, 362–363, 384–385, 397–412, 433–434, 452–466
  deafness and, 433–434, 452–466
  infantile autism and, 397–412
  language impairment and, 307–321
  mental retardation and, 332–335, 339–341, 345–353, 357–359, 362–363, 384–385
Language impairment, 15–16, 295–322
  criteria of, 296

SUBJECT INDEX   613

delay vs difference in, 318-321
etiology and correlates of, 297-306
   auditory and speech perception, 304-306
   cognitive factors, 300-303
   environmental factors, 298-300
individual differences in, 295-296
language development and, 307-321
long-term effects of, 295
overview of, 15-16
phonology in, 315-318
pragmatics in, 312-314
semantics in, 310-312
   lexicon, 310 311
   semantic relations, 310
summary of, 321-322
syntax in, 307-309
   grammatical morpheme usage, 308-309
terminology in, 297
Language intervention, 11-12, 380-384, 412-422, 434-437, 466-468
   deafness and, 434-437, 466-468
   infantile autism and, 412-422
   introduction to, 11-12
   mental retardation and, 380-384
Lexicon, 310-311, 353-358, 516-523
   adult aphasia and, 516-523
   language impairment and, 310-311
   mental retardation and, 353-358
Linguistic maturity, measurement of, 7-11

M

Mental retardation, language in, 16-17, 329-385
   chronological age (CA) and, 332-333, 336-337, 347, 349, 353, 355-356, 371, 375-376, 379
   cognitive development and, 337-338
   development of, 332-335, 339-341, 345-353, 357-359, 362-363, 384-385
   discussion of, 384-385
   Down's syndrome and, 332-336, 339-341, 352-354, 359-363, 371-372, 378-382
   etiology and, 336-337
   institutionalization and, 333, 336-337, 341-342, 344-347, 356-360, 364-366, 368, 370
   IQ and, 333, 346, 358-359, 364-365, 371
   linguistic environment and, 377-380
   linguistic performance and, 330, 368-377
      memory for linguistic input, 373-376
      passivity, 330, 369
      speech comprehension, 370-373
      speech production, 369-370
   mental age (MA) and, 332, 343-345, 347-350, 353-356, 362, 371, 373, 375, 379
   MLU and, 334-335, 339-340, 352-353, 362-363, 379, 384
   multidimensional studies of, 331-341
   overview of, 16-17
   phonology of, 358-363
   pragmatics of, 364-368
      communicative effectiveness, 366-367
      conversation, 367 368
      referential communication, 364-366
   preliminaries to, 329-331
      cognitive development, 331
      intelligence, 329-330
   semantics of, 351-358
      informativeness, 358
      lexicon, 353-358
      semantic relations, 351-353
   syntax of, 331-351
      grammatical morpheme usage, 345-349
      sentence behavior, 349
   training of, 380-384
Mothers' speech to children, 298-300, 377-380, 409-410
   infantile autism and, 409-410
   language impairment and, 298-300
   mental retardation and, 377-380

P

Phonology, 315-318, 358-363, 397-399, 495-500
   adult aphasia and, 495-500
   infantile autism and, 397-399
   language impairment and, 315-318
   mental retardation and, 358-363
Pragmatics, 312-314, 364-368, 403-405
   infantile autism and, 403-405
   language impairment and, 312-314
   mental retardation and, 364-368

R, S

Reading (*see* Word recognition)
Reading disability (*see* Word recognition, reading disability)
Schizophrenic language, adult, 19-20, 537-584
   aphasia and, 543-544

SUBJECT INDEX

Schizophrenic language, adult (cont.)
  assessment scale for, 554-556
  Chaika's view of, 541-545
    Fromkin's critique of, 542
  cognitive disorders and, 538-539
  conclusions, 583-584
  cortical functioning and, 569-583
    defective interhemispheric transmission, 577-578
    discussion, 580-583
    lateralization, 578-580
    left-hemispheric dysfunction, 569-577
  disattention view of, 540-541
  hesitations in speech and, 553-554
  intermingling in, 556-557
  mania and, 543
  normals' comprehension of, 550-552
  overview of, 19-20, 537-538
  recall performance and, 565-569
  referential communication processes in, 548-549
  Rochester's view of, 545-548
  speech comprehension aspects of, 560-569
  speech production aspects of, 540-560
  subclassifications of schizophrenia and, 539
  thought-disordered vs nonthought-disordered aspects of, 545-548
Second-language learning, 14, 217-251
  Bilingual Education Act, 217
  bilingualism, 217, 219, 226, 241-248
    assessment of, 244
    cognition and, 245-248
    competence in, 243-248
    definitional problems and education in, 241-242
    programs, evaluation of, 242
    programs, future of, 242-243
  conclusion, 248-251
  definitions, 218-219
  development, 224-236
    acquisition heuristics in, 234-236
    adult studies of, 230-236
    child studies of, 226-230
    fossilization in, 230
    interlanguage in, 228-230
    monitor model of, 232-234
  English as a second language (ESL), 219-220
    bilingual education and, 219
    TESOL, 219
  overview of, 14
  processes in, 220-224
    error analysis of, 220-221
    first-language acquisition and, 220-224
    morphene acquisition studies and, 221-222
  teaching in, 236-243
    communication model and, 240-241
    input and conversational interactions and, 238-240
    learner's age and, 237-238
Semantics, 310-312, 351-358, 403, 523-525
  adult aphasia and, 523-525
  infantile autism and, 403
  language impairment and, 310-312
  mental retardation and, 351-358
Syntax, 307-309, 331-351, 399-403, 439-443, 501-516
  adult aphasia and, 501-516
  deafness and, 439-443
  infantile autism and, 399-403
  language impairment and, 307-309
  mental retardation and, 331-351

W

Word recognition, 13, 33-186
  context effects in, 79-106
    expectancies, 102-104
    lexical priming, 98-101
    sentence contexts, 91-94
    summary of, 104-106
    thematic material, 95-98
    word priority effect, 80-81
    word superiority effect, 44, 80-91
  development of, 64-65, 108-111, 136-141, 157-167
  Estes' model, 80-87
  F. Smith's theory, 45-47
  Gibson's cluster theory, 63-65
  Gough's serial processing model, 51-56
  logogen, 94
  Massaro's parallel processing model, 56-62
  overview of, 13
  reading disability, 141-170
    phonologic processing, 150-153
    semantic and syntactic processing, 153-157
    summary, 168-170
    visual processing, 146-150
    word-processing differences, 141-146
    word-processing strategies, 157-168
  redundancy, 120-126
  Rumelhart and Siple's theory, 47-50
  Spoehr and Smith's theory, 65-71

synthesis, 170-186
three-stage memory model, 36-38
types of information in, 38-40
unit of perception in, 40-79
   component letter theories, 50-62
   feature theories, 44-50
   Johnson's pattern-unit theory, 71-78
   letter group theories, 62-71
   whole word view, 40-43
word familiarity, 111-117
word frequency (*see* word familiarity)
word length and, 116-117
word recognition vs word identification, 117-120
word stimulus effects in, 106-140
   graphic, 107-111
   orthographic, 111-126
   phonologic, 126-134
   semantic-syntactic, 134-139
   summary, 139-140
Writing, 13-14, 199-213
   ability, levels of, 206-208
   computer use in, 211-213
   conclusions, 213
   crisis in, 199-200
   facilitation of, 208-211
   overview of, 13-14
   pauses during, 204-206
      critique of, 205
      experimental approach to, 205-206
   protocol analysis of, 200-204
      critique of, 202-204
   text comprehension and production model and, 207-208